MITSUI

MITSUI

THREE CENTURIES OF JAPANESE BUSINESS

by JOHN G. ROBERTS
foreword by CHITOSHI YANAGA

New York · WEATHERHILL · Tokyo

The design used on the binding and chapter-opening pages is a modern version of the emblem used by Echigoya. This crest, consisting of the ideograph for "three" (mitsu) enclosed in a stylized form of the ideograph for "well" (i), is read "Mitsui." The proprietors of this crest, Mitsui & Co., Ltd., have generously extended permission for its use in this book. Reproduced on the endpapers is a woodblock print from the series Toto Meisho (Famous Places in Edo) by Ando Hiroshige (1797–1858). This print is titled "Surugacho" and shows Mitsui's Echigoya, with Mount Fuji in the background.

First edition, 1973
Second printing, 1974

Published by John Weatherhill, Inc., 149 Madison Avenue, New York, New York 10016, with editorial offices at 7-6-13 Roppongi, Minato-ku, Tokyo 106, Japan. Protected by copyright under terms of the International Copyright Union; all rights reserved. Printed and first published in Japan.

Library of Congress Cataloging in Publication Data: Roberts, John G. / Mitsui: three centuries of Japanese business. / Bibliography: p.   / 1. Mitsui zaibatsu. 2. Business and politics—Japan. I. Title. / HD2907. R62 / 332.1'0952 / 73-9856 / ISBN 0-8348-0080-2

Contents

Foreword

AT THE END OF WORLD WAR II in 1945 Japan was a shambles. Her industrial production had dropped to a mere forty percent of what it had been at its peak. The whole nation seemed to be in a state of stupor induced by the defeat, as well as by the loss of old beliefs, loved ones, homes, and livelihoods. People were dying of starvation on the streets. It was generally thought that Japan had been reduced to a fourth-rate power. Even the Japanese themselves believed that the chances of regaining their former status as a major world power were nil. Yet once they accepted defeat and its inevitable consequences, they applied themselves singlemindedly to the task of rebuilding their war-devastated land.

No time was lost on self-pity, regret over the mistake of waging a hopeless war, or hatred of the conquerors. With resilience, determination, and accommodation, the nation quickly lifted itself from the ashes of defeat. In the space of a mere dozen years, it achieved the position of leading shipbuilder in the world. In a span of less than a generation, Japan's economic recovery was complete. She became the world's third great industrial power, surpassing the dreams of her most rabid ultranationalists during the heyday of militarism in the 1930s.

Needless to say, the tense and fluid international situation immediately following the war, which was highlighted by the struggle between the Communist and Free Worlds, played an important part in Japan's rapid economic resurgence. However, no economic miracle would have been possible without the deeply-rooted traditions, historical experiences, or technical and organizational skills of the Japanese people.

From an economic point of view, Japan is no longer considered a non-Western nation. Technologically advanced far beyond the confines of Asian capabilities and potential, she is invariably grouped with Western, rather than Asian, nations. Despite her industrially advanced status, she is decidedly more traditional and Asian in the nonmaterial aspects of life, such as thought, behavior, and values, all of which profoundly influence her economic and industrial activities at home and abroad.

Mitsui: Three Centuries of Japanese Business is an impressive study of how the House of Mitsui began and developed into a huge economic empire. More than any other corporate entity, Mitsui symbolizes continuity and change and represents the economic growth and development of Japan during the past three hundred years. Furthermore, it is the prototype of the powerful combines, or zaibatsu, which emerged in the late nineteenth century and served as instruments of national policy in the building of a modern industrial Japan. As such they were the handmaidens in the government's program of modernization and industrialization along the lines of Western capitalism.

The founder of the House of Mitsui showed rare foresight in voluntarily abandoning the family's samurai status to become a merchant, or *chonin*. Starting out as a small brewery for making sakè and soy, then expanding into a modest draper's shop and money exchange, Mitsui eventually became a huge conglomerate encompassing practically every type of business and industrial enterprise: banking, insurance, shipping, foreign trade, retail merchandising, construction, engineering, mining, brewing, textiles, chemicals, paper, glass, electronics, optics, and real estate.

In addition to its various enterprises, Mitsui became the fiscal agent in Osaka of the Tokugawa government near the end of the seventeenth century, continuing in this capacity for more than a century and a half. But toward the end of the feudal regime, it found itself in serious difficulties brought on by mismanagement. To rectify the situation, it recruited Minomura Rizaemon, a manager of uncommon ability, who not only injected new vigor into its operations but turned them around, and laid solid foundations for a great economic empire. Through an efficient information network, Minomura learned of the sharply declining fortunes of the bakufu, well before the crucial battle of Toba-Fushimi in 1868. Whereupon he began cultivating intimate relations with the future leaders of the anti-bakufu forces, notably Ito, Inoue, and Yamagata of Choshu. After the Meiji Restoration, Mitsui severed its relations with the Tokugawa forces and helped to raise war funds needed by the Meiji government to put down the resistance of the die-hard bakufu supporters.

Following the demise of the feudal regime in 1868, the House of Mitsui provided valuable expertise and resources toward the building of the new Japan. It responded to the urgent call of the Meiji government and furnished desperately needed funds for its operations. As the government's fiscal agent, it received deposits, disbursed funds, handled trade, and even issued its own paper currency, since its credit was better than the government's. It was no accident, therefore, that Mitsui was regarded as the de facto Ministry of Finance of the Meiji government until the establishment of the Bank of Japan in 1882. By helping to put the nation's finances on a sound basis, Mitsui not only won recognition, but actually worked itself into the financial structure of the government. The intimate relationship which was assiduously developed between Mitsui and the government provided a model for other enterprises.

Mitsui's success was based not only on its policy of recruiting talent, which included the adoption of promising young men into the family, but also on its ability to obtain valuable advance intelligence regarding the government's moves, as well as to maintain close ties with the government. Among the innovations which have been attributed to Mitsui are sales on a strictly cash basis, emphasis on small profit per unit and large sales volume, which still is characteristic of Japanese business operations, a unique concept of the trading company, and the founding of the first Japanese chamber of commerce.

Mitsui's various roles in war and peace are well-known to historians of Japanese business. It has participated in the development of Manchuria, Korea, and China and in the expansion of Japan's trade and influence, both economic and political, in various parts of the world. Its far-flung activities have enabled it to gather all kinds of valuable information, not only for its own business operations, but also for the government in its formulation of policies and conduct of diplomacy.

In the phenomenal economic recovery following the war, Mitsui worked closely with other combines to ameliorate the harsh, if not vindictive, occupation policy which could have resulted in the complete dissolution of the zaibatsu. Thus, representatives of the zaibatsu effectively functioned as a moderating influence to restrain overzealous occupation officials from totally dismantling Japan's economic structure. These same representatives convinced John Foster Dulles, the personal envoy of the president, that a generous peace treaty would insure Japan's role as a reliable ally of the United States in the Far East. It was no surprise, therefore, that Dulles met with the Japanese representatives as well as the Supreme Commander for the Allied Powers, General Douglas MacArthur, in the Mitsui Building in downtown Tokyo, the citadel of zaibatsu prestige and power.

In explaining the postwar resurgence of Japan as a first-rate economic power, the author reveals the close collaboration between the government and the big-business establishment. He also shows how decisions were reached and policies formulated in informal social gatherings of small, intimate cliques at teahouses as well as in the executive suites of big business and high government officials. A detailed account of the Miike coal miners' strike provides insight into the modus operandi of big business in dealing with labor troubles. The author also follows closely the events which generated the strong anti-Kishi sentiments in the nation, resulting in the cancellation of President Eisenhower's projected visit in 1960.

This outstanding work on the history of the House of Mitsui is valuable reading for those interested in the development of Japanese business as well as the postwar rise of Japan as the world's third industrial power of the twentieth century.

CHITOSHI YANAGA
Professor Emeritus of Political Science
Yale University

Author's Preface

WHEN I WAS A LITTLE BOY, I was bundled off to Sunday school regularly, clutching a small pink envelope containing a few nickels and dimes. Since there was a candy store lurking between home and the Presbyterian church of my parents' choice, the envelope did not always arrive unopened. But since the contribution was intended for the succor of pitiable Japanese heathens, conscience overcame craving as often as not, and I assume that some of the money was eventually used for this purpose by "our man in Tokyo," the Reverend August Reischauer.

After that initial exposure, my attitude toward Japan passed through the stages of indifference, disapproval, hatred, and again to pity and indifference until, in 1959—several decades and two wars later—I landed in Japan as a tourist. Observing the feverish reconstruction of the cities and the signs of economic expansion on all sides, I found myself intellectually and emotionally unprepared to assess the results of my boyhood's small investment. What was one to think of all this vigorous, determined activity, in which great masses of people seemed to act as one? Pity would have been impertinent, indifference inconceivable, and hatred absurd. Only astonishment and wonder would do. I realized for the first time that a unique kind of ferment beyond my comprehension was in progress, and that I had better set about repairing my ignorance.

The least answerable of my questions related to the nature of the forces at work and the means by which they were being directed. What kind of a show was this, and who was running it? At the time, a great confrontation between the right and the left in Japan was shaping up, and it was easy to become confused by political superficialities. But it was soon apparent to me that the propulsion came from an essentially united people, and that despite talk of social upheaval, guidance of the nation remained firmly in the hands of a small elite called *zaikai* in Japan and "big business" elsewhere. As a step toward understanding the processes involved, I began to study and write about the economy, finance, and industry for publications in Japan and abroad.

In the late 1960s Mitsui Bussan Kaisha invited me to write a history of the venerable Mitsui concern. Rashly, I accepted because I thought it would be a good chance to learn something about Japanese economic history. The result, born from sore travail, was a series of fifteen articles called "The Mitsui Story" that appeared in *Mitsui Trade News* between 1969 and 1972. On the basis of research conducted for that project (in which Mitsui Bussan cooperated fully) I began an independent work, the outcome of which is *Mitsui*.

I should like to emphasize that this is not an "authorized history." Although officials of several Mitsui companies have been most helpful in providing information and references, the selection of material and the opinions presented here are my own. No member of any Mitsui company has seen any part of the manuscript, and therefore no one but myself can be held responsible for any errors, omissions, or other faults that may be found in these pages. And although Mitsui Bussan has kindly permitted its familiar emblem to be used as a decoration in the book, it must not be construed as being an endorsement of this history or of anything in it.

In Japan, the family name precedes the given name, and that custom has been observed in this book. The spelling of names is always a problem because they must be transliterated from ideographs that may have many readings. Furthermore, Japanese are accustomed to changing their names for various reasons. In rendering names I have tried to use the reading and spelling preferred by the person concerned and have also used the name under which that person is or was best known. Honorifics, used invariably in Japan, have been omitted here.

In assembling and evaluating historical material, I had to cope as best I could with an overabundance of opinions and a dearth of hard facts. Even in ascertaining the number of deaths resulting from the Great Kanto Earthquake of 1923, one finds several "authoritative" figures, all different. Until 1945 Japan was a closed society, in which freedom of inquiry and expression were severely limited, and credence was based upon authority rather than veracity. Yet to hedge each fact with disclaimers would be unduly cumbersome in a book of this kind, so in most cases I have given the data or versions of events that I considered to be the most valid, without qualification. I entreat the reader to view cautiously the portions dealing with prewar history. Some small parts of the book have appeared, in different forms, in the *Far Eastern Economic Review, Burroughs Clearing House, Corporate Financing,* and the *Meanjin Quarterly*.

In preparing to write this book I have talked with scores of persons connected in some way with the eleven Mitsui families or with the Mitsui group of enterprises bearing their name. I shall cite only a few individuals who are representative of their particular organizations, while extending heartfelt thanks to others who have been no less helpful.

Particular thanks are due to Mitsui Hachiroemon Takakimi, present head of the main family; Mitsui Takasumi, chairman of the Mitsui Foundation, and Mrs. Mitsui; Mitsui Reiko, who is compiling a history of the House; Mitsui Takamitsu, heir of Hachiroemon; Mitsui Takanaru, head of a branch family, and Mrs. Mitsui.

Of those connected with the Mitsui families, I wish to thank Shirane Matsusuke, a former vice-minister handling the Imperial Household's finances; Minomura Seiichiro, a descendant of a famous manager of the Mitsui concern; and Minomura Tomoyuki, also a descendant. Of special help has been the historian Yamaguchi Eizo, custodian of the Mitsui family archives. For general information about Japan and its history I am beholden to Nishi Haruhiko, former Vice-minister of Foreign Affairs; his son Teruhiko, Honorary Consul of Ireland in Japan; Shirai Kuni, proprietor of the Yamaguchi teahouse, at which the leaders of modern Japan have congregated since the Meiji era; and Sakamoto Moriaki, an expert on the history of the Satsuma clan.

Former high officials (now elder statesmen) of Mitsui enterprises whom I have interviewed with interest and benefit are Sato Kiichiro of Mitsui Bank; former finance minister Mukai Tadaharu; Tashiro Shigeki of Toray Industries; and Niizeki Yasutaro, Mizukami Tatsuzo, and Tanabe Shunsuke of Mitsui Bussan. At Mitsui Real Estate Development I learned much from president Edo Hideo; and at Mitsukoshi, from president Okada Shigeru. President Omoto Shimpei and chairman Kurata Okito, of Mitsui Mining and of Mitsui Mining & Smelting, respectively, were especially generous with their time. At Mitsui Bussan I had very enlightening conversations with president Wakasugi Sueyuki; Sakurauchi Takeshi, then adviser to the board; and Ogino Sachu, general manager of the finance department. In addition, I talked with numerous directors, managers, and superintendents of Mitsui Mining, Mining & Smelting, Aluminum, Petrochemical, Shipbuilding & Engineering, Bussan, Bank, and other companies of the group, whose courtesy and helpfulness are deeply appreciated.

Among those unconnected with Mitsui but deserving of special thanks are Takahata Seiichi, former chairman of the Nissho trading company, and Eleanor Hadley, a noted authority on Japanese oligopolies. For early guidance in the arcana of Japanese politics I wish to thank sociologist Shibata Tokue, Director of the General Planning and Coordination Bureau, Tokyo Metropolitan Government; theorist Muto Ichiyo; historian David Condè; and editor Uyeno Kazuma. For patient assistance in research, I express my thanks to Kurotaki Mitsugu, Furuyama Eiji, and the library staffs of the Foreign Correspondents Club and International House of Japan. Constructive editorial help has been given by Martin Davidson and Rebecca Davis. And finally, I offer my deepest gratitude to Yamakawa Midori for her able and energetic research, translation, and general help, without which this book could never been completed.

MITSUI

1 · From Sword to Soroban

MITSUI IS THE WORLD'S OLDEST large-scale business enterprise. The Mitsui family opened its first shop five years before the Pilgrims landed in New England, and established a bank—still operating in the same location—in 1683, a decade before the Bank of England was founded. Late in the 1860s, soon after the Civil War in the United States, the House of Mitsui gave indispensable help to the revolutionaries who toppled the ancient military regime in Japan and loosened the shackles of feudalism. From then on Mitsui was in the forefront of Japan's economic modernization, and by the early twentieth century it was a dominant political force in the fast-rising nation.

The power and reputation of the concern reached full maturity after the First World War, and in the nineteen twenties and thirties the name Mitsui inspired respect and awe, or hatred and fear, throughout the Japanese empire. The skies above Japan's cities darkened with the smoke from Mitsui's mills and factories. The rivers grew turbid with the outpourings from their mines, metal refineries, and pulp mills. The earth shook from the vibrations of their hydraulic presses, pile drivers, and blastings. Mighty ships glided down the ramps of Mitsui dockyards to join the fleet of Mitsui vessels plowing through remote seas, bringing raw materials for Mitsui industries, or carrying away the goods they produced in quantities that at first astonished and then appalled the world.

From the northern frontiers in Hokkaido to Kyushu in the south Japanese men, women, and children toiled in Mitsui's forests, fisheries, and plantations. They labored ceaselessly in the stifling labyrinths of Mitsui mines and in small workshops, wholesale houses, docks, warehouses, lumberyards, and quarries owned or controlled by Mitsui. University graduates competed fiercely for employment in the offices of Mitsui banks and insurance and commercial houses, the most puissant and prestigious in the nation.

Although the people may have been unaware of it, a large share of the necessities and luxuries they purchased were produced or distributed by Mitsui, and perhaps one out of every ten Japanese was dependent upon a Mitsui enterprise or subsidiary for the wages with which to buy them. In Japan's colonies—Formosa, Korea, and South Sakhalin—as well as in Manchuria and parts of China proper Mitsui operated the most productive concessions, and imported their products to Japan or exported them to other countries. Mitsui was the main backer and beneficiary of the South Manchurian Railway, the largest single private enterprise in the Japanese empire, and sponsored armies of mercenaries for the penetration and pacification of China. Mitsui supplied arms and money first in 1912 for Sun Yat-sen's revolution to overthrow the Manchu dynasty and then in 1932 to restore the same dynasty in Manchuria— which Mitsui had once nearly succeeded in buying outright from corrupt Chinese politicians.

Mitsui Bussan Kaisha, known abroad as Mitsui and Company, spanned the globe with its trading and shipping network, through which it handled about forty percent of Japan's exports and imports. More extensive and better organized than the Japanese foreign office, it conducted diplomacy for the government and gathered not only commercial information but political and military intelligence that was often of decisive importance to the nation.

In 1905, during the Russo-Japanese War, managers of Bussan's branch office in Shanghai followed the movements of the czar's Baltic Fleet, flashed accurate information to the Japanese high command, and enabled the imperial navy to win one of the greatest sea battles of modern times. During the First World War Mitsui Bussan obtained advanced military aviation technology by purchasing a large American aircraft manufacturing plant and virtually monopolized sales of aircraft in Japan for a long time thereafter. Two decades later coded messages planted in Bussan's trade reports from Honolulu helped Japanese intelligence to keep abreast of the disposition and movements of the United States Navy's warships at Pearl Harbor up to the morning of December 7, 1941. Throughout the Second World War Mitsui men, secretly commissioned as intelligence officers (and other officers disguised as Mitsui employees), worked for the fatherland wherever the company was permitted to operate. Bussan's branches served as virtual appendages of the military government in the vast but short-lived "Greater East Asia Co-Prosperity Sphere."

Mitsui was Japan's largest private contributor to charitable institutions, hospitals, schools, and patriotic organizations. Its paternalistic manufacturing and mining enterprises adopted some of the most advanced labor practices of the West, and their employees enjoyed the best wages and working conditions in the country. Yet the Mitsuis were hated as exploiters and profiteers. In the 1930s their highest executives were advised to wear bulletproof vests, and two who ignored this counsel were assassinated—by members of secret societies that were subsidized by other Mitsui executives. It was Mitsui that provided both precious radium for cancer research in Japan and opium for the pacification of occupied regions in Asia. Mitsui factories made the dyestuffs for the colorful Japanese fabrics that gained worldwide favor; but, when national policy dictated, the same plants were converted to the production of military explosives and chemical weapons for wars of aggression. Mitsui's leaders were the most effective opponents of communism in Japan, and a Mitsui subsidiary supplied a major share of the weapons used by the czarist regime in its futile effort to crush the Russian revolution. The same weapons, ironically, were instrumental in assuring the victory of Lenin's Bolsheviks and establishing the Soviet Union.

Controlling as it did one of the major prewar political parties in Japan, Mitsui could influence legislation, arrange the appointment of friendly cabinets, and make its imprint upon foreign policy. Independently or in collaboration with other *zaibatsu,* or family-controlled financial cliques, it could often thwart power-hungry bureaucrats and militarists, promote necessary administrative reforms, and oust incompetent governments. Its officials, using economic leverage, also had the power to suppress reform movements, smash unions, imprison or liquidate agitators, and secure immunity for miscreants within their own ranks. Their hatchet men included cabinet ministers, military officers, police chiefs, newspaper editors, and bosses of terrorist societies, who would stop at nothing in supporting the interests of their protectors.

Mitsui's trade and overseas investment programs boosted the nation's power and prestige, smoothing the way for its expansion in foreign markets and giving it access to vitally needed raw materials. Among the zaibatsu Mitsui stood out as an advocate of peaceful trade and international good will, yet its decisions sometimes fueled the flames of war and determined the rise or fall of foreign governments.

The four largest zaibatsu owned about twenty-five percent of Japan's corporate assets, and just two of them were responsible for three-fourths of Japan's overseas investments during the height of Japanese imperialism. Standing head and shoulders above the others was Mitsui, whose sprawling empire embraced every significant sector of industry, finance, and commerce, and employed as many as three million people domestically and overseas.

At the head of this empire was the Mitsui holding company, which under a succession of names ruled its vassal businesses in much the same way as the Tokugawa shoguns had exacted obedience from the feudal lords of Japan. And, like those shoguns, who governed in the name of the imperial court, the main company was subject to a higher authority. In this case the "emperor" heading the main family was Baron Mitsui Hachiroemon, a direct descendant of the Mitsui who had founded the House three hundred years before. The princes in this sovereign House were the heads of the ten branch families, who were bound together by a formal constitution dating from the establishment's second generation. This unusual document prescribed explicit responsibilities, duties, policies, and behavior expected of each individual, as well as the unalterable hierarchy of the families, their shares in the proceeds of the business, and the nature of official and personal relationships to be maintained among them.

The perpetuation of a family's fortune and position by a written code is not unusual in the world, or even in Japan. What distinguished the House of Mitsui from other wealthy and influential families was its rapid development into a national institution and its tenure of quasi-official status through the tumultuous events of modern history until its enforced collapse in 1945. In this respect there is a strong similarity between Mitsui and the European houses of Rothschild and Krupp, whose activities also were closely bound up with the fortunes of empire. But the Mitsui influence emerged much earlier, and seems to have been more pervasive than was that of any European or American financial house. Without the support of Mitsui the momentous Meiji revolution of 1868 could scarcely have succeeded, and in the subsequent decades of the nation's metamorphosis Mitsui was the foundation upon which the modern Japanese economy was built. The role that individual Mitsuis played in those developments is uncertain, but their participation was considered to be so essential that collectively they became virtual hostages of the state.

The parallel between the House of Mitsui and the imperial family of Japan is striking. Its origins were shrouded in the same kind of official mythology, and its structure and regulations were elaborated by the same legal authorities who rationalized the juridical basis of imperial rule. In times of peril its continuation was assured by government intervention; its matrimonial alliances (eventually with some of the emperor's relatives) were arranged with equally fine discrimination; and the personal activities of its members usually were immune from scrutiny and criticism. At the height of its power its leaders—whose positions were hereditary—were supervised by the same elder statesmen who surrounded the emperor, and the decisions of its administrators were subject to their veto. Like personages of the imperial house, the Mitsuis' chiefs were seldom seen by anyone except peers of the realm, high executives, or members of their households. Their faces were known to the public only through official portraits, and their activities only from carefully censored news reports. But the features of two

Mitsuis, like those of Emperor Meiji, were known to every literate Japanese and revered by many: the founder of the House as a major enterprise, Mitsui Hachirobei Takatoshi, was portrayed in the primary-school readers issued to every boy in the country; and the likeness of his remarkable mother, Shuho, appeared in similar books for girls. Accompanying the pictures were homilies extolling the thrift, enterprise, diligence, and foresight of those worthies, presented as examples to be followed by every upright youth.

The first Mitsui shop was established not by Hachirobei but by his father, Sokubei Takatoshi, whose claim to fame lay in his foresight and courage in renouncing his rank as a samurai, or warrior-aristocrat, to become a lowly tradesman. Sokubei's forebears had been provincial lords of minor importance but of substantial estate. It is difficult to trace their pedigree for more than a few centuries, because class-conscious Japanese have always tended to cherish flattering legends about their origins. The Mitsuis are no exception: in prewar days, when history was their handmaiden, their obliging genealogists tried seriously to trace the clan's ancestry back to the Fujiwaras, who, like the emperors, were legendary descendants of Amaterasu Omikami, the Sun Goddess.

According to one legend, a member of the Fujiwara family who was named Umanosuke Nobunari left Kyoto about A.D. 1100 (during the period of the first crusades in Europe) to take up his abode in nearby Omi Province. The new settler, while looking over his property, extending along the shore of Lake Biwa, discovered that it had three wells. In one of them he found a treasure in gold coins. To commemorate this good fortune he changed his name to Mitsui, which means "three wells."

The Mitsuis' history, as distinguished from their mythology, seems to begin late in the Muromachi period, at about the time when, on the other side of the world, Christopher Columbus was asking the rulers of Portugal and Spain to finance his visionary projects. At that time the Mitsuis were retainers, with samurai rank, of the Rokkaku branch of the Sasaki clan in Omi province. Those Sasakis, famous as warriors, belonged to the Omi Genji, descendants of Minamoto Yoritomo (1148–99). That military genius, having defeated the dominant Taira clan with the help of Sasaki's samurai, had been appointed by the emperor in 1192 as the first *seii-tai-shogun,* or "barbarian-quelling generalissimo," and had introduced the *bakufu,* the system of government by shoguns, which thereafter would control Japan. Three hundred years later the Sasakis were still firmly ensconced in their Omi stronghold.

Amid the anarchy that prevailed during most years from 1300 to

1600, every samurai home had to be an armed camp, and the family unit took on tactical as well as social importance. Kannonji castle, fortress of the Sasaki lords, was besieged repeatedly, and neighbors less stoutly defended were in constant jeopardy. The Mitsuis, small in stature and delicate in build, owed their survival to the power of the Sasaki daimyo, whom they apparently served as administrators rather than fighters. Even so, the Mitsuis must have been of rather high rank, for late in the fifteenth century they were able to marry one of their daughters to Takahisa, a younger son of Lord Sasaki.

Because of the need for continuity and solidarity in the family, it had become customary for a father to bequeath his entire estate to his oldest or most capable son, or, if he lacked a natural heir, to adopt as a son the husband of one of his daughters. Such an adopted heir, or *yoshi,* was Sasaki Takahisa, who became head and protector of the Mitsui house.

Takahisa built a castle at Namazue, east of Lake Biwa, where the Mitsuis lived as a petty daimyo clan under the aegis of the Sasaki warlords. Little is known of Takahisa's descendants during their occupancy of Namazue castle, but as samurai they must have followed the code of knighthood known today as *bushido.* This inflexible and ungentle brand of chivalry, introduced by Takahisa's ancestors, the Minamoto shoguns, emphasized courage in battle and loyalty to one's liege lord even at the sacrifice of one's fortune and family, with death by *seppuku,* or ritual disembowelment, as the compulsory alternative to dishonor. The true warrior had to show indifference in the face of danger, hardship, love, and death. Unlike European knights, a samurai was forbidden to display sentiment, and in his austerity he was contemptuous of material gain. His rewards for enduring a spartan and dangerous life were the prestige of being near the top level in a rigidly stratified society, and the privilege of wearing two swords, the temper of which he was free to test upon the unresisting flesh of peasants, craftsmen, merchants, or outcasts whenever he saw fit.

Provincial life in those dark ages was neither comfortable nor secure, for one never knew when a band of samurai, bellowing defiance, with swords flashing and torches alight, might swagger into a village or manor, to leave it a blazing shambles. For those thick-skinned gentry bloodshed was the badge of manliness, and individual mayhem or indiscriminate massacre the very meat and marrow of life.

The most bloodthirsty warlord of the sixteenth century was Oda Nobunaga, a minor daimyo who nursed the high ambition of bringing all of Japan under his sway. In his rampage through central Japan he trampled over anyone or anything that lay in his path. To curb the influence of the Buddhist warrior-priests, who then held great secular power, he set thousands of temples ablaze and slaughtered every one of their defenders.

Among those who impeded Nobunaga's advance through Omi on his march toward Kyoto were the Sasakis and their vassals, whose martial skills, valor, and fortified castles availed them nothing against the savagery of the invaders. During Nobunaga's onslaught sixteen castles, including those of the Sasakis and the Mitsuis, were razed or captured. The few survivors of the Sasaki clan were subjugated, and thereafter the Rokkaku House of Sasaki vanished from the annals of Japan's history.

The Mitsuis, meanwhile, were demonstrating the prudence for which later they were to become renowned. The head of the House, Takayasu, Lord of Echigo, sensing the approaching danger, told his servants to pack whatever valuables were portable, and fled with them, his family, and a few retainers. With phenomenal luck (another characteristic of the Mitsuis), they made their way across central Honshu to Ise Bay, and at length found refuge near the peaceful town of Matsusaka, where as an unemployed samurai Takayasu had plenty of time to think upon this lesson in the disadvantages of bushido.

Within a decade after the defeat of the Sasakis in 1568 Oda Nobunaga had subdued most of Japan, and after his death the task of unification was pursued successively by his ablest generals, Toyotomi Hideyoshi and Tokugawa Ieyasu. But rivalry between Hideyoshi's followers and Ieyasu once again divided the country into two warring camps. The showdown came in 1600, when two mighty armies—about 160,000 men in all—joined in battle at Sekigahara, near Nagoya. Ieyasu won the day, took forty thousand heads as trophies, and emerged as undisputed ruler of Japan. By redistributing the fiefs in such a way that his most loyal vassals could keep watch over those whose reliability was questionable, he prevented any effective challenge to his rule. In consultation with Japan's wisest scholars he established the Tokugawa shogunate, the government that endured from 1603 until 1868.

A detached but interested observer of Ieyasu's victories and reforms was Mitsui Sokubei Takatoshi, eldest son of the Takayasu who had been Lord of Echigo. Apparently a gentleman of leisure if not of afflu- ence, Sokubei had taken root in Matsusaka, a market center for the fertile and relatively prosperous Ise Province, now a part of Mie Pre- fecture. But he had not become a rustic, for Matsusaka was near a busy port for coastal trade and was also a stopping point for pilgrims jour- neying to the Grand Shrines of Ise, then as now the most sacred place of worship for believers in Shinto. Sailors, pilgrims, and traveling mer- chants brought news quickly to Matsusaka, and from them Sokubei was

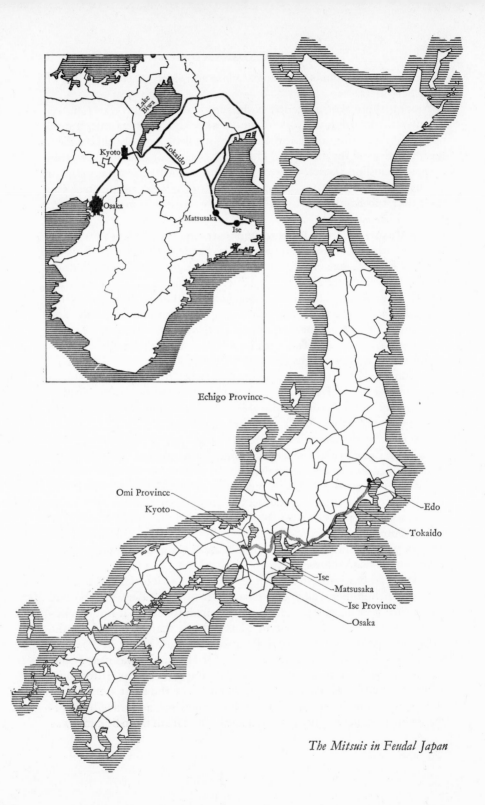

Echigo Province

Omi Province

Kyoto

Edo

Tokaido

Ise

Matsusaka

Ise Province

Osaka

The Mitsuis in Feudal Japan

able to judge the trend of the times. He also took occasional trips to Edo (now called Tokyo), where Ieyasu had built an enormous castle as headquarters for his tightly organized bakufu government. What astonished Sokubei most was the rapid growth of the town lying outside the walls of Ieyasu's fortress, which was some two miles in diameter, and the ever more important role that trade was playing in the life of the bakufu's populous capital.

Officially, commerce was considered a parasitic occupation, and the *chonin,* the merchants or townsmen, occupied a social rank just one step above the *eta,* the outcasts, who were not classified as human beings. Sumptuary laws prohibited the chonin from wearing fine clothing, using certain forms of speech, or living in districts of the city that were inhabited by samurai.

But during the sixteenth century, despite almost constant warfare and political chaos nationally, workers in agriculture, industry, and trade had shown considerable improvement in the amounts and quality of their goods. As local warlords brought weaker neighbors under their sway, feudal unity was strengthened and internal commerce was fostered. Concurrently, the traditional system of bartering rice for handicrafts and other commodities was being gradually supplanted by the use of money. Burdened by the costs of warfare, daimyo borrowed to meet expenses, and prosperous commoners, not only merchants but landholders and priests as well, became moneylenders.

As the money economy developed, the merchant class grew in numbers and, despite formal kinds of discrimination, was tolerated and even on occasion given official status. The best appointments fell to those who had helped Tokugawa Ieyasu before the Battle of Sekigahara by providing his troops with supplies on credit. In Edo as well as in Osaka —the commercial center of western Japan—they even took part in city administration. Those long-sleeved quartermasters to the bakufu enjoyed a status far above other members of their class, and their positions had the advantage of being hereditary.

From such observations, and the unfortunate experiences of his own family, Sokubei formulated an original vision of Japan's future and the Mitsuis' place in it. He could see that, in a country thoroughly pacified by a central government, the role of the warrior class inevitably would wane. The likelihood of wars with other countries was remote, since Ieyasu, alarmed both by the susceptibility of his countrymen to the Christian religion and by the power of European ships, had begun tightening the exclusion laws directed against foreign traders and missionaries. Sokubei could also see that under the orderly rule of the bakufu agriculture, industry, and domestic trade would thrive and that despite any rules to the contrary those people who were qualified to engage in business would rise in power and affluence. Reputed to be the shrewdest and most ubiquitous merchants in Japan were the men of Omi, his ancestral home, and of Ise, his adopted one. It was not unreasonable to believe that, in such a setting and with a modest amount of capital, a Mitsui could also succeed in business. At some point in his cogitations upon these matters he made the secret resolution, breathtaking but perfectly logical, to exchange his samurai's swords for the *soroban*—the abacus of a Japanese tradesmen.

His choice of a time for reaching that decision was most appropriate, if not prophetic. In 1616, the final year of his life, Tokugawa Ieyasu eliminated the last contender for supremacy and left his worthy son Hidetada, who had succeeded him as nominal shogun eleven years earlier, securely in command of the unified empire. In the same year all ports except Nagasaki and Hirado were closed to European ships, as a measure for regulating foreign trade and preventing the conquest of Japan by those aggressive Europeans. At this significant time in history Sokubei made a trip to Edo. Upon his return, perhaps with his imagination inflamed by the prosperity he had seen there, he assembled his household—his wife Shuho, several children, retainers, and servants—to inform them of their impending descent to plebeian status. His task was not made easier by the mutely accusing presence of an exceptionally large suit of armor, once worn by his more courageous ancestors and brought from Omi during Nobunaga's onslaught. But now there was no daimyo to whom the Mitsuis owed fealty, and as head of the House, Sokubei's first duty to his ancestors was to repair its fortunes. Bowing to the family shrine and clapping his hands smartly, he explained his intention to sacrifice the Mitsuis' hallowed but empty privileges for the sake of their material welfare: "A great peace is at hand," he declared solemnly. "The shogun rules firmly and with justice at Edo. No more shall we have to live by the sword. I have seen that great profit can be made honorably. I shall brew sakè and soy sauce, and we shall prosper."[1]

This simple speech, made in 1616, and recorded in the family chronicles more than three hundred years ago, marked the beginning of the Mitsuis' financial empire.

2 · Echigoya
the Shunned

IN FEUDAL JAPAN political and military activity centered upon the strongholds of the shogun and his vassals, who lived as sumptuously as the rice yields of their fiefs permitted. At their castle-courts, surrounded by mazes of walls and moats, they assembled retainers, soldiers, craftsmen, concubines, and servants, whose needs and fancies engendered trade. Markets grew up outside the castle walls and developed into populous settlements. In just that way the ancient Chinese ideograph for "market" had come to represent "town" or "city," as well. The castle town of Matsusaka was fortunate in being under the protection of a daimyo who headed the Kii branch of the Tokugawa family and enjoyed the bakufu's favor. Lord Kii's courtiers and retainers received ample stipends, and local business was further enhanced by the steady stream of pilgrims traveling to and from Ise's shrines. Mitsui Sokubei could not have chosen a better starting point for his career as a chonin.

The brewing of sakè and of soy sauce are relatively simple processes, requiring only a small amount of capital and a few workers who know the traditional skills. Sokubei's brewery was different from others only in being run by a former samurai. People began calling it *Echigo-dono-no-sakaya*, Lord Echigo's sakè shop, because his father had borne that title. The appellation suggests that Sokubei was respected, but that commoners were somewhat in awe of this aristocratic brewer. At any rate they were slow to patronize his shop, and business was poor at first. What little of it there was Echigo-dono managed badly. Although he was adept at light verse and calligraphy, he was clumsy with figures and even worse at drumming up trade.

It was his wife Shuho, the daughter of a successful merchant, who stood between Sokubei and failure. Although she had married him when she was only thirteen years old, and began to bear children soon afterward, she found time to participate in business affairs and showed remarkable aptitude as she matured. Unencumbered with social pretensions, she could talk to customers in their own dialect and gained favor with their servants by offering them tea or tobacco when they came on errands. On market days farmers from the countryside were in a festive mood, and pilgrims and other wayfarers were always thirsty when they arrived in Matsusaka. Under Shuho's cajoling, customers at the shop often spent more than they should have and had to borrow money for the journey home, leaving their valuables as security. From this practice it was only a short step to pawnbroking, a business she established as a sideline. Interest on loans and income from selling unredeemed pledges turned out to be more profitable than brewing, and Echigo-dono's shop began to prosper.

Taking warning from the prodigality of others, Shuho cultivated the trait for which she is best remembered—thrift. As a young mother with four sons and four daughters to provide for, she served very frugal meals, and no one was allowed to leave until his rice bowl was empty. Even when she could afford silk she and her children wore cotton, which was grown, spun, and woven in the Ise region. Every youngster was required to contribute to the welfare of all by doing useful tasks, which formed the most important part of his meager education.

When Sokubei died prematurely in 1633 his widow found consolation in religion and work. Rising at daybreak, she would bathe in cold water and pray to the Buddha and to Shinto deities before starting her day's labors, which extended well into the night. Despite her professional conviviality in the shop she led an increasingly austere life privately, and her frugality earned her a reputation for miserliness.

Shuho worshiped frequently at the temples, but to avoid wasting time she and her maids would do a bit of scavenging on the way home. They would collect discarded sandals and horseshoes, which were woven from straw, to be used as fuel or compost. Paper strings, with which men and women tied their hair, were picked up, spliced, and wound into big balls for use in the shop.

In Shuho's household nothing was wasted. The lees from the sakè and soy vats were converted into edible byproducts, ordure was saved for fertilizer, clothing was handed down until it was threadbare, and even broken utensils were put to some unexpected use. Thus a bottomless vat was converted into a cistern, and a leaky wooden dipper became a flowerpot stand. In such an eccentric matriarchy, Sokubei's children, the first generation of Mitsui commoners, acquired the values that were to bring fortune to his descendants.

The most flourishing market in Japan was Edo, whose inhabitants— called Edokko—were renowned as spendthrifts. Many merchants of Omi and Ise joined the rush to the shogun's capital on the sound theory that a fool and his money are soon parted. When Shuho's eldest son, Saburozaemon Toshitsugu, was thoroughly trained at Matsusaka she sent him to Edo with capital to open a draper's shop called Echigoya. Assisted by the third son, Saburobei Shigetoshi, he was not long in establishing his own business house, which in time was known as the "nail-puller," or *kuginuki,* Mitsui from the shape of his emblem. The second son, Seibei Hiroshige, was adopted into another family, leaving the youngest, Hachirobei Takatoshi, at home to assist Shuho.

Hachirobei, born in 1622, showed conspicuous talent from childhood, and it would have been natural for him eventually to inherit the business of Echigo-dono in Matsusaka. But Shuho, sensing that he could become a great merchant, sent him to Saburozaemon in Edo as an apprentice when he was only fourteen years old. Hachirobei proved to be so able that the brothers soon opened a second shop, also called Echigoya. The less talented Shigetoshi returned to Matsusaka to help Shuho, and Saburozaemon went to Kyoto to organize a cloth-purchasing system. This left young Hachirobei in charge of the Edo shops, which he managed with gratifying success.

On the national scene the new bakufu regime was effecting dramatic changes, many of them unintentionally favorable to the merchant class. The third Tokugawa shogun, Iemitsu (who ruled from 1623 to 1651), took extreme measures to curtail all foreign influences. Having closed the country to foreign trade, he forbade Japanese to leave the country, upon pain of death. To ensure isolation he made it a crime to build ships large enough for overseas voyages, and he established monopolies to handle the tightly controlled foreign commerce conducted through the last open port, Nagasaki. Foreign missionaries landing in Japan were put to the sword, and at least twenty thousand Japanese Christians who staged a revolt in Kyushu were massacred. When an embassy of Portuguese came to ask for a restoration of trade privileges their ship was burned and fifty-seven of the intruders were decapitated. Such fanatical isolationism, although costly to the economy, protected domestic producers and traders against competition from foreigners and the nation from conquest.

Iemitsu was suspicious even of his own vassals and, beginning in 1634, enforced the system of *sankin kotai,* under which they were required to spend several months of each year in Edo. When a daimyo returned to his own domain he had to leave his wife and children behind as hostages. This system made it necessary for each daimyo to build a residence in Edo and maintain a full-time staff there as well as on his fief. On his travels to and from the shogun's court he had to be accompanied by a retinue of a size and degree of elegance befitting his rank. All this was ruinously expensive, as Iemitsu intended it to be, and the daimyo had no recourse but to borrow money from the merchants. Such business usually was profitable, but risky, because a chonin had no legal way to compel a daimyo to pay his debts.

As the years passed, Hachirobei observed the business world cannily and developed his own ideas. He saw, for example, that the people who flocked in from all over Japan to become townsmen were coalescing into a new and prosperous class. Yet tradition-minded merchants like Saburozaemon concentrated their sales efforts upon the aristocrats, to whom they were forced to extend liberal credit. Hachirobei longed to be independent and to try new ideas, but *enryo*—restraint or reserve— kept him from competing with his elder brother. Then, when he was twenty-eight, his hopes were dashed by the death of Shigetoshi, which obliged him to return to Matsusaka and help the aging Shuho run the family business.

Echigo-dono's brewery and pawnshop were too humdrum to hold the interest of an Edo chonin, so Hachirobei set up a side business as a moneylender. This he was well able to do, for during his fourteen years in Edo he had saved about fifteen hundred *ryo,* equivalent to nearly seven hundred and fifty pounds sterling in silver. (At certain times during the Tokugawa period a ryo was equivalent to about one pound sterling, but the discrepancy must be noted because, by international standards, silver was grossly overvalued in Japan.) For the modest sum of sixty ryo he bought the estate of another merchant. Then he took a wife, Jusan, who had been picked for him by Shuho. His fifteen-year-old bride, a merchant's daughter like her mother-in-law, was energetic and levelheaded. Having established his own house, into which sons and daughters were born in quick succession, Hachirobei was well launched as a provincial banker with a reasonably promising, if not exciting, future.

Shrewd operators such as Hachirobei learned to spread their risks in various ways, forming syndicates with their relatives and fellow merchants, or borrowing short-term capital from temples and shrines and relending it to daimyo. Hachirobei also learned the tricks of rice trading. The daimyo usually repaid their loans in rice, but later would find it necessary to borrow rice with which to pay the stipends of their samurai. By various manipulations familiar to experienced commodities speculators, the merchants caused the market to fluctuate widely and, with foreknowledge of price changes, managed to turn neat profits both ways, in addition to the high rates of interest they charged. Another phase of Hachirobei's business was lending money to farming villages, with mortgages as collateral, for developing virgin land, handicraft workshops, or new agricultural products. In this sense he was a pioneer industrial capitalist.

As the "great peace" foreseen by Sokubei settled over the land in the mid-seventeenth century, the Matsusaka Mitsuis' fortune grew substantially. Jusan raised six sons, all of whom listened dutifully to Hachirobei's lecturing and heeded his counsel. One of them wrote in later years: "Soju [Hachirobei's posthumous name] said that if one loaned ten [units] of silver at 1.2 percent a month, it would be doubled in five years, and in fifty years would become ten thousand [units]. Therefore, one should make the most of even small amounts, for even a petty clerk could become a millionaire in time."[1]

Hachirobei did not always follow his own advice, however. He had often warned his elder brother Saburozaemon against lending to daimyo, and the latter had come to the brink of bankruptcy by ignoring the admonition. Yet Hachirobei continued to lend money to the lord Kii—perhaps because a refusal would have been more hazardous than the loan itself. That preeminent daimyo, as head of one of the three Tokugawa families from which a shogun could be selected, was a relatively good risk, of course, but Hachirobei was still worried. Although the Tokugawa domains produced almost one-third of the nation's rice, the extravagance of the shogun's court and the folly or knavery of his ministers were leading the nation to ruin. Merchants knew that some officials were embezzling vast sums; in fact, one of them, after a life of flagrant profligacy, had provided himself with a coffin of solid gold. Iemitsu set down severe regulations to curb the extravagances of others, but when he died his own lavish way of life was revealed. At Edo Castle there were so many retainers that Iemitsu's successor found it necessary to dismiss three thousand of them—mostly females.

In 1673, when Hachirobei was fifty-one years of age, he reached a decision no less bold and prophetic than that of his father: from now on he would not risk his modest fortune upon the whim of any daimyo. Like Sokubei, he would dare to follow the trend of the times and devote himself to business with commoners. Having his mother's blessing, he moved to Kyoto with his family and opened a business devoted initially to the procurement of fabrics. Leaving his eldest son, Takahira, in charge, he took his second son to Edo in the same year and opened a small shop in a good location adjacent to the mismanaged "nailpuller" establishment of his late brother. Here he began to sell the fashionable Nishijin brocades and other silks purchased in Kyoto or elsewhere. When the shops were running smoothly, he left the everyday management to his six sons and spent most of his time traveling and studying business conditions in general. (Today we would call that market research.)

His Edo shop, called Echigoya after its defunct precursors, fronted on Honcho-dori, where the most stylish drapers' shops were clustered. Those merchants sold goods mainly to daimyo or upper-class samurai families by showing samples or actual bolts of cloth at the customers' mansions. However, Hachirobei had neither the opportunity nor the

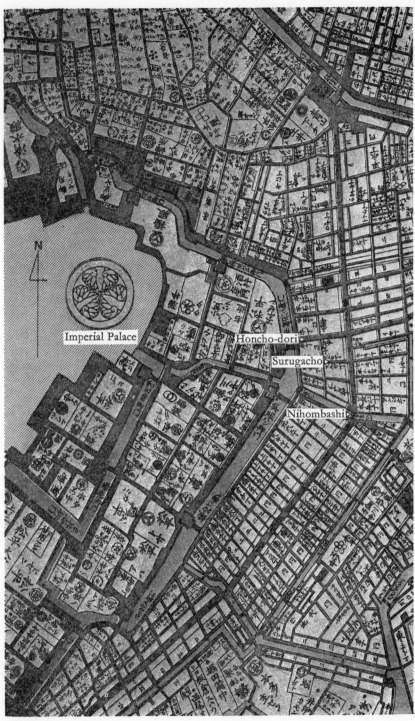

The Mitsuis in Edo

incentive to cater to such aristocrats, who settled their accounts only twice a year at best. To compensate for this deficiency, Hachirobei laid in large stocks at Kyoto and sold them at wholesale prices to smaller merchants in the provinces. The profit margin was small, but rapid turnover and prompt payment made such a system worthwhile.

The costly fabrics handled by the merchants of Honcho-dori were sold only by the whole piece, sufficient to make a kimono, and this practice limited their sales. Hachirobei, aware that there was quite a lot of cash jingling in the coin pouches of the common people, was seeking new ways to expand the market. A precious clue came from one of his clerks, who patronized the public baths and enjoyed listening to the chatter of the female bathers. A favorite topic of conversation, he told Hachirobei, was cloth: women were especially eager to find small pieces that could be used for making pouches, personal ornaments, or covers for treasured objects. Since no merchant was foolish enough to cut into a bolt for such a trifling sale, women had to be satisfied with exchanging remnants left over from kimono-making.

When Hachirobei had mulled over this bit of information, he conceived a daring experiment: he would sell cloth in any length desired. For this privilege, he soon discovered, customers were willing to pay a much higher unit price. And since his wholesale business enabled him to maintain an exceptionally attractive variety of stock, customers flocked to his establishment. Encouraged by their enthusiastic response, he again flouted tradition by selling his materials—not only pieces but whole lengths as well—for spot cash only.

The latter innovation was resented by aristocrats, but it reduced his credit risks significantly, and had other advantages as well. By purchasing on credit and selling for cash, Hachirobei was able to employ his capital more briskly than his competitors. Since he knew where he stood at all times, he was able to calculate costs more precisely, reduce his markup, and sell at fixed prices. This eliminated haggling, a time-honored but time-wasting custom, and gave the purchaser assurance that he was not being cheated. The efficacy of Hachirobei's new methods was soon apparent. Within a year after his arrival in Edo he had prospered so immensely that he opened a new shop in the same street, having six times the frontage of the old one, and employed some fifteen clerks, five apprentices, and several servants at both stores.

Predictably, Echigoya's unorthodox methods first irritated and then infuriated competitors. Their rage reached the boiling point when Hachirobei snatched a big order for crepe from his rival, Matsuya. Having violated a gentlemen's agreement against underselling, the Mitsuis were ostracized by the merchants' guild and before long Echigoya was known as "the shunned." Some envious rivals tried to incite the clerks to revolt against Hachirobei, but his staff remained loyal. Then those adversaries bought a house next door to Echigoya, built a toilet close to the Mitsui kitchen, and let their sewage overflow into it. Hachirobei tried to change the location, which he already had outgrown, but whenever he found a suitable building his tormentors managed to prevent his leasing it.

Finally Hachirobei discovered a house for sale in Surugacho, near Nihombashi, and bought it secretly. When the remodeling of that new shop was nearly completed, there was a disastrous fire, one of the frequent conflagrations known as "the flowers of Edo." All of Honcho's high-class shops, along with Echigoya, were burned down; but Hachirobei was able to open his new establishment in Surugacho almost immediately and enjoyed a tremendous advantage thereby. Soon after the fire Hachirobei first put up his famous signboard, still preserved in the Mitsui museum, announcing *Genkin, Kakene nashi*—cash only, fixed prices.

The historian Arai Hakuseki, a contemporary of Hachirobei, wrote in his book *Shinsho,* a collection of essays: "Echigoya of Surugacho has two stores in Edo and an authorized exchange house for the shogunate. One of the stores deals in dry goods [presumably silks] and the other sells cotton. It is said that the two stores have combined daily sales amounting to 1,000 ryo, or 360,000 ryo a year, on a cash basis."[2]

By that time at least seven merchants had begun to imitate Echigoya's methods. Some adopted its emblem and even its name, which was becoming almost a generic term for the cash-payment, one-price style of merchandising. After the move to Nihombashi, Mitsui stopped using the "nailpuller" crest and designed a new one, which has survived with slight modification to the present. An additional motive for the change was the fact that the founder of Edo's famous Yoshiwara brothel district, Shoji Jin'emon, used a family crest almost identical with that of the Mitsuis, which in its turn was appropriated by another notorious whoremaster. This must have been humiliating to the Mitsuis, who were reputed for their sobriety and rectitude. But there really was no escape from imitators: a later brothel keeper in Yoshiwara used to lure the cheapskate trade by distributing a handbill bearing a picture quite similar to Echigoya's sign, advertising ladies of the night for "spot cash, at fixed prices."

The Surugacho site was considered the most attractive commercial location in Edo. It was so named because on clear days the view of Mount Fuji resembled that seen from Suruga Province (now called Shizuoka Prefecture). As business swelled, Hachirobei added lines of merchandise, especially cheaper cottons and pongee, appealing to families of lower-ranking samurai and to commoners of slender means.

As the premises expanded, Echigoya became one of the sightseeing features of the city, whose population had reached half a million by 1700. The shop was a favorite subject for painters, and inspired a seemingly endless series of colored woodblock prints. Original impressions of such prints can still be found in Tokyo's curio shops, which indicates that the editions were quite large.

Long before the concept of advertising had made its impact upon the West, Hachirobei and his sons were masters of indirect persuasion. The weather in Edo being unpredictable, Echigoya's customers not infrequently were surprised by rainstorms. This gave Hachirobei the idea of lending his customers oiled-paper umbrellas. On rainy days the streets of central Edo blossomed with them, each one conspicuously emblazoned with the Mitsui mark. Hachirobei also befriended playwrights, authors, and poets, who showed their gratitude by further enhancing Mitsui's public image in both speech and writing.

Before the end of the seventeenth century, Mitsui's staff of several hundred employees enjoyed a good many fringe benefits then scarcely known in Japan or elsewhere. It is recorded that employees were required to work for only a specified number of hours, and were given regular rest periods during the course of each day. Some thought was given to health and sanitation, and decent dormitories were provided. Echigoya gave clerks on-the-job training in manners, speech, and personal appearance; and for those with seniority a rudimentary profit-sharing system was established. To keep track of such a large volume of business, Hachirobei originated a form of double-entry bookkeeping similar to that used in Europe.

As Echigoya flourished Hachirobei set up branch establishments in Kyoto and Osaka, anticipating the chain store system popularized in America about 1860 by the Atlantic & Pacific Tea Company. However, a competitor, Iseya (which also originated in Matsusaka), seems to have anticipated Echigoya by setting up a chain of textile outlets in all the wards of Edo even before the Mitsuis began branching in earnest.

Echigoya was situated almost exactly where its direct descendant, the main Mitsukoshi Department Store, stands today, in Tokyo's central Nihombashi district. Antedating John Wanamaker's emporium in Philadelphia by almost two hundred years, Echigoya may have been the world's first department store. In 1700 it was Japan's largest store, just as Mitsukoshi is today. But Echigoya would be quite unfamiliar to modern shoppers, who expect quick service. The customers, ducking in under the *noren,* the short curtains hung in doorways, found themselves in a great hall. A raised platform covered with sweet-smelling tatami was its only fixture. Greeted politely by one of the chief clerks, customers would remove their wooden clogs or their sandals and take seats on the matting or upon silk cushions. The clerk would engage them in light conversation as tea was served. According to the status or interests of the customer, the chatter would turn to art, literature, poetry, some titillating scandal involving a popular geisha, or a new play at the Kabuki-za. Only after such niceties had been observed would the customer be expected to turn his attention to bolts of material brought from the warehouse by apprentices.

Echigoya attained great fame during the Genroku era (1688–1704), when the culture of the new urban bourgeoisie reached full flower. The wealth of the chonin had evoked the so-called floating world— *ukiyo*—of refined but evanescent pleasures that inspired artists, poets, playwrights, and novelists. This was also the high point of Kabuki, the theater of chonin, in which the glories and tragedies of samurai life were presented. One of the most talented novelists of the period was Ihara Saikaku, son of an Osaka merchant and author of *Nihon Eitai-gura* (Japan's Eternal Treasure House). This true-to-life book describes leading merchants of the day and relates wittily the ways in which they made their fortunes.

Of Echigoya, Saikaku wrote: "At Surugacho, a man named Mitsui Kuroemon [Hachirobei] opened a shop of 9 ken by 40 ken [roughly 54 feet by 239 feet], adopting the cash-payment, fixed-price system. There are forty-odd clerks, each engaged in a different category of business. For example, one is handling brocade, two men are selling silks from Hino and Gunnai, one is in *habutae* [a smooth silk], one in *saya* [a textured silk]. One sells *hakama* [a skirtlike garment for men] and another woolens. Thus divided, they sell velvet by one-inch squares, brocade large enough to make a tweezer case, or red satin enough to cover a spear insignia. When ceremonial costumes are required in a hurry, the shop lets the servants wait and has the regalia made up immediately by several dozens of their own tailors. . . . To look at the shop owner, he appears no different from others, with his eyes, nose, and limbs in the usual arrangement; but he is clever at his business. This is an example of a really big merchant."[3]

3 · The Source of Happiness Is Prudence

SEVENTEENTH-CENTURY JAPAN, disdainfully aloof from the outside world and socially constrained in the web of feudalism, is mistakenly believed to have been a backward country. Actually it was relatively advanced, comparing favorably with Elizabethan England economically and with the Celestial Empire culturally. There were innumerable laws and regulations to prevent change, yet a new economic system was stirring within the body of the old; and a new bourgeois class, with its matching culture, was asserting itself with brash disregard for social barriers.

At the time Hachirobei appeared upon the business scene the groundwork for industry had already been laid. Handicrafts were well developed, and each province produced its own specialties in amounts exceeding local requirements. The level of technical competence was high, and division of labor in the workshops made production reasonably efficient. Transportation by land and sea was slow but adequate. The sankin-kotai system instituted by Shogun Iemitsu in 1634 had improved the highroads leading to Edo from different parts of the country. And a well-organized distribution system made it easy to exchange agricultural and industrial products for money.

There had been a steady advance in the yields of farms, and rice was more plentiful than it had ever been. But the daimyo, to meet mounting expenses, exacted larger and larger shares of the peasants' crops—usually fifty percent or more—and reduced the rice stipends allotted to their samurai. The crushing poverty of the countryfolk drove more and more young men to the cities to seek employment, and the wives and daughters of impecunious samurai, like those of peasants, eked out a living in domestic industries. Under these circumstances merchants were able to accumulate capital that was not laggard in mating with the emerging proletariat to beget more enterprises.

Thus Hachirobei's world, although feudal in concept and structure, showed many resemblances to the precapitalistic economies of Europe. From his phenomenal success in business, one can assume that Hachirobei had a basic understanding of this paradoxical economy and the

23

rich opportunities it offered for the future. But being a realist, he recognized that the big sums of money needed for increasing trade and industry were still locked in the coffers of the bakufu. He also knew that merchants were still at the mercy of aristocrats and that without official patronage he could lose his fortune overnight.

The shortest road to security was to become an official purveyor to the government. In those days the bakufu procured its fabrics and apparel from six houses of *gofuku-shi* (something like "kimono masters"), whose appointment was hereditary. Breaking into this monopoly was next to impossible, but the sagacious Hachirobei found a way to do so. One of his relatives from Matsusaka, a *go* champion named Doetsu, was being employed to play exhibition matches and teach the game to bakufu officials. Doetsu's work brought him into contact with Lord Makino Narisada of Bingo, an influential adviser to the Edo court. Hachirobei persuaded Doetsu to put in a good word for Echigoya, and this made it possible for him to become acquainted with Makino. He hewed to his purpose so diligently that at last, in 1687, "the shunned" Echigoya was appointed a supplier of cloth to the bakufu.

At this time Hachirobei's residence was in Kyoto, so he delegated his eldest son, Hachiroemon Takahira, to manage the business with the bakufu in Edo. Takahira must have done his work well, for two years later, in 1689, the Mitsuis were made purveyors of apparel, ornaments, and personal accessories to Shogun Tsunayoshi. In this position they held the highest rank attainable by townsmen and were given a suitable dwelling with a frontage of thirty-six feet.

The honor was great, of course, and kimono masters usually basked complacently in their privileged status. But the elder Hachirobei ridiculed them as not being real businessmen. "Don't forget that we are merchants," he used to tell his sons. "Our trade is the most important thing; official business is just an ornament." This warning reflected the fact that purveying to the shogun was troublesome, and sometimes unprofitable, because of long delays in payment. Nevertheless, Hachirobei accepted every preferment, profitable or otherwise, with a show of gratitude, and his motives are easily guessed: merchants, importuning clients to pay their debts, made powerful enemies and needed powerful protectors; such ambitious schemes as those of Hachirobei could not be realized without influential connections; and the timely information necessary for survival in those uncertain days could best be picked up in court circles.

The intelligence of most interest to Hachirobei was that concerning the circulation of money, the medium so essential to trade. Even before moving to Surugacho he had managed a small exchange house adjacent to Echigoya, and in 1683, after combating the guild for ten years, he was permitted to establish his own. Since the money-changers of Edo were concentrated around Surugacho, he was continually in touch with fluctuations in the relative values of gold, silver, copper, and iron monies, as well as with the dubious sorts of scrip issued by daimyo. Within eight years he had established similar exchange brokerages, called *ryogaeya,* in Kyoto, the imperial capital, and in Osaka, where the bakufu's treasury was located. With this network of ryogaeya, Hachirobei was able to eliminate the high commissions he had been charged for settling his accounts with suppliers and to collect such fees from fellow merchants who lacked similar exchange facilities.

Even in those days the ryogaeya were performing the basic operations of modern banks, accepting deposits, granting loans against collateral, discounting notes, and issuing trade vouchers that also served as banknotes. Such vouchers had only local circulation until Hachirobei expanded the business into a nationwide bill-of-exchange system. He was scrupulous in his operations, and to insure probity he placed each of the three ryogaeya under the management of one of his sons, with the stipulation that the position was to be hereditary. The Mitsuis' reputation was so unblemished that their "wrapped money," bearing the seal and signature of the respective manager, usually was accepted at its face value without being counted.

Most significant for the fortunes of the House was Hachirobei's idea of reforming the bakufu's money-transfer system. In 1691, when his Osaka exchange shop was opened, the House of Mitsui became an official money-changer for the bakufu's treasury. From then on banking was Hachirobei's main business, and although the Echigoya shops continued to grow apace, his plans were devoted to high finance rather than to merchandising.

He had long observed that, while Edo's merchants bought foodstuffs and merchandise in Osaka and sent money there in return, the government was collecting taxes from the same region and sending the coins to Edo. Such transfers of currency were made by way of the Tokaido, the highroad from Edo to Kyoto, and trains of horses laden with *senryobako,* the boxes containing one thousand ryo of gold or silver, could be seen passing each other—going in opposite directions. This cumbersome and redundant method was also dangerous, inasmuch as highway robbery was not uncommon.

Hachirobei's reputation was so good that he was able to persuade the treasury officials to adopt his system, already perfected, of sending remittances by money order instead of by cash. Thereafter, as money accumulated in the treasury it was loaned to Osaka's money-changers. They in turn loaned it to merchants, who used the funds to purchase commodities for shipment to Edo. When delivery was completed the wholesalers in Edo would pay the local representative of the respective ryogaeya, who would then repay the original loan to the bakufu in Edo. At first the treasury allowed 60 days for repayment, but later extended the period to as long as 150 days, without interest. Thus the exchange brokers were able to relend the money at high interest rates and to make a generous profit from this simple operation.

Naturally, all the big ryogaeya were anxious to get a share of this business, but only twelve were appointed as *o-kawase,* or honorable money-exchangers, in 1691. Ten of them formed a partnership called *junin-gumi,* the ten-man company; and the eldest Mitsui son, Hachiroemon Takahira of Kyoto, and his brother Jiroemon Takatomi, representing the Edo headquarters, constituted the *ninin-gumi,* or two-man company. Later this was expanded into the *sannin-gumi,* or three-man company, when their brother Gennosuke of Osaka was appointed to the group.

Those thirteen money-changers, actually bankers by then, were elevated to a special status with the bakufu's accounting agency, being listed in official gazettes and privileged to greet the shogun's family at the ceremonies of the New Year. This was the greatest honor ever accorded members of the despised merchant class; but more important to the aging Hachirobei was the fact that his sons were firmly entrenched near the source of political power.

Not that Hachirobei sought any share of that power for his descendants. The proud Sasakis had crumbled before the might of Oda Nobunaga, just as in their turn the families of Oda Nobunaga and Toyotomi Hideyoshi had been eclipsed or exterminated by the Tokugawas. Other chonin may have dreamed of equality with the samurai, in order to seek political careers, but not Hachirobei. What he wanted was wealth, and more wealth. Yet his esteem for money was not evidence of mere megalomania or greed for possessions. Luxury and ostentation were as distasteful to him as dissipation and lechery; positions of honor were as mere baubles; and even economic power was only a means to an end. The elusive treasure he sought, as had Tokugawa Ieyasu before him, was permanence—the perpetuation of his line, unchallenged for ages to come. In the political realm the imperial family and the Tokugawa shoguns held a monopoly upon permanence, but why could not a merchant found a financial dynasty no less enduring?

As the seventeenth century drew toward its close, Hachirobei was able to view the results of his efforts with considerable satisfaction. From his headquarters at Kyoto he supervised prosperous shops and exchange houses in Japan's three major cities, as well as the original establishment in Matsusaka. But by then his guiding hand was unnecessary, for among the eleven sons (not to mention the five daughters) produced by Jusan there were six whom he considered qualified to carry on the business. They were capable and well schooled in the patriarch's methods and principles. But there was no guarantee that they would not become competitive among themselves, and in his twilight years he pondered over the composing of a last will and testament that would preserve the integrity and solidarity of the house.

Before his death in 1694 he read the document to his sons and daughters, explaining how his estate was to be shared. Rather than leaving it all to the eldest son, as would have been customary, he designated each of five younger sons as the head of a new *hon-ke,* or main house, who would inherit a fixed share of the fortune. Two other sons and an adopted son-in-law were to be endowed also, and he ordered them to set up branch or associate families. But none was to be fully independent, for all nine houses owed fealty to the head of the senior house.

This innovation gave rise to a system of nomenclature that is complex even for Japan, where family names are exceptionally baffling. In feudal times the clan we call Mitsui was known publicly as Echigoya. As was the case with most of the world's commoners, the chonin were not entitled to bear surnames that might be confused with those of superior classes. The Mitsuis, like other merchants, used the trade name of their shop as a kind of surname. But since they were of samurai lineage they were entitled to retain their old surname of Mitsui. This was used privately by all except three of the associate families, which bore instead the names Onoda, Nagai, and Iehara until the Meiji era.

The given names of male Mitsuis usually begin with the character *taka* (high or tall), after Sasaki Takahisa, the most famous of their presumed ancestors, and this custom has prevailed to the present generation. Thus Hachirobei's favorite sons were named, in order of arrival, Takahira, Takatomi, Takaharu, Takatomo, another Takaharu,* and Takahisa. Takahira (also called Sochiku Echigoya Hachirobei) bore the name Hachiroemon because he was the eldest son of Hachirobei, who was number eight (*hachi*) among Shuho's progeny. Hachiroemon be-

---

* One may well ask why there were two Takaharus. The "haru" of the elder Takaharu's name was written with a different character from that of the younger one. For most characters used in writing Japanese names several varied readings are possible, and the "correct" one depends upon the whim of the parents or of the bearer. The correct reading of some names cannot be determined unless one has heard them pronounced or seen them written in phonetic characters. Therefore, there is wild confusion in the transliteration of historical names, complicated by the fact that the Japanese commonly changed their given names or even their surnames at crucial points in their lives, and always received a new one after death.

came the usual hereditary title of the head of the senior house. Other Mitsui family heads also had titular names indicating their business positions. Saburosuke ran the Kyoto exchange shop, and Jiroemon and Gennosuke had the same function in Edo and Osaka, respectively. The suffix -*suke* originally meant vice-manager, and -*emon,* helper.

In addition, each family had a name indicating the location of its residence and its rank in the hierarchy. For example, the senior house was called *Kita-ke* (North family), the first main family *Isarago-ke,* and the second *Shimmachi-ke.* Thus the name Mitsui Saburosuke Takaharu of Shimmachi-ke meant "Takaharu, heir of the Mitsuis' Shimmachi family, heading the exchange shop in Kyoto." The positional titles (Hachiroemon, Jiroemon, and so on) were not rigidly hereditary, being passed from one family to another as occasion required, but such changes were not common.

Fortunately for Hachirobei's plans, his eldest son Hachiroemon Takahira proved to be a worthy heir. Recognizing that, without the guidance of his father, the nine houses would need some controlling organ, he established the Mitsui *Omotokata,* or great main headquarters, to regulate the affairs of the group of houses that came to be known as Mitsui-gumi. The word *gumi* may be translated as "company" or "association." Before Japanese corporate law was codified, gumi was the usual designation for a family enterprise.

The descendants of Hachirobei have been referred to rather generally as a family, household, house, clan, tribe, or gumi, but for an understanding of the Mitsui structure and its significance some more precise definitions are necessary. In old Japan the family, not the individual, was the social unit. It was also the economic unit, and theoretically, only its head could own property, transact business, or make decisions affecting the family and its members. The household, however, included unrelated persons, not only the wives of sons but also those people who were economically dependent upon the family, such as clerks, servants, workers, and their respective families. Such a unit was called an *ie,* or house. All members of the house were dependent upon the head, who was usually the eldest son of his predecessor or the adopted husband of the eldest daughter. When younger sons married they established their own houses (unless they were adopted into another family), and daughters became members of their husbands' houses. The house, then, was a group of persons bound together by obedience to the head, whose authority derived from the founder. The relationship between the head and the members, based upon the code of ancestor veneration and filial piety, was similar to if not identical with that between the emperor and his subjects.

Ordinarily, the official ties between the head of a house and his married sons and daughters, other than his heir, were weak. Consanguinity did not mean mutual responsibility among related houses; once a son had left the house he was independent (and usually self-supporting as well), except that filial piety required him to be attentive to his parents and to assist them in time of need. Otherwise, the economic relationship implicit in the house concept was no longer obligatory. Naturally, the ties of affection were not subject to any such prescription.

The unique feature of the House of Mitsui was the fact that Hachirobei combined the houses of his sons into a more comprehensive economic unit, making all of them obedient to one head, representing the founder. What he did, in effect, was to form a superhouse, composed not of individuals but of houses whose unifying element was a common ancestry. By doing so, he made possible the formation of a corporate body, or gumi, capable of engaging in capitalistic enterprise within a feudal economy. Mitsui-gumi was, to some extent, a joint-stock corporation of limited liability. That is to say, the houses composing it could unite part of their assets for long-range endeavors of considerable scale yet still survive the bankruptcy of joint businesses, since one house was not legally responsible for the debts of another.

In the feudal period such house-laws applied only to the samurai class, for whose perpetuation they were codified. But because Hachirobei's forebears had been members of the noble Sasaki house, he was familiar with its rules of organization and adapted them to his merchant-class family with spectacular results, both for the Mitsuis and for the future economic structure of Japan.

Mitsui-gumi, this house of houses, was structurally a partnership built upon mutual trust and cooperation. The shops and exchange houses were managed independently and were shared according to rule. Employees of one establishment were considered to be employees of all. The income of each family was fixed, and none was allowed to exceed it. Instead of accumulating capital separately the six brothers pooled it in Omotokata, which they owned jointly and from which they could borrow operating funds at seven- to ten-percent annual interest, depending on the amount. And to Omotokata they turned in fixed dividends ranging from seventeen to twenty percent of the annual net income of all the businesses comprising Mitsui-gumi.

Because the Mitsuis were meticulous bookkeepers and kept important documents ever since the end of the Genroku era, or the beginning of the eighteenth century, the details of their operations can be learned by studying the huge parchment-bound ledgers of hand-laid paper still perfectly preserved in the Mitsui Bunko, a modern fireproof library and museum maintained by the family in Tokyo. Scholars, including members of the family, frequently consult these tomes to discover or verify facts concerning Japan's political and economic development. Mitsui's records presumably are representative of methods employed by leading merchants of their times, but they must have been better kept than were those of the average merchant, because Mitsui-gumi had been appointed in 1707 to handle the government's accounting.

From the company's records, written clearly by many different hands, one discovers that business in Tokugawa days was systematically and rationally organized. The Mitsuis, employing their own double-entry system, kept official books of at least two kinds: one for half-yearly settlements of short-term loans, interest, dividends, and such items; and another for the "grand settlement" that was made every three years. The latter was the occasion for balancing accounts with Omotokata. An interesting feature of this settlement was the payment of a bonus to employees amounting to one percent of the profit that had been retained during the period. Whether or not this was the origin of Japan's present-day bonus system, it indicates that incentive pay was already a part of Mitsui's business style.

Of immeasurable importance to the durability of Mitsui-gumi was its system of reserves, which kept it afloat when other companies foundered. The terms they used to describe their reserves are unfamiliar today, but one can imagine the contingencies for which they were devised. At the top was the "shop's foundation" reserve for working capital. There were also a reserve to cover payments of principal and interest upon borrowings; a "lay-aside" fund (perhaps for defraying unanticipated expenses); and finally, the "cellar silver," a hoard of coins and bullion to be dug up only when every other resource had been exhausted.

For almost eighteen years the o-kawase, as the official money-changers were called—the competitors' junin-gumi and the Mitsuis' sannin-gumi —monopolized the government's currency-transfer business, using its interest-free money for terms of five months before having to repay it. In addition, they were entrusted with exchanging new currency for old and with receiving proceeds from the sale of government-owned rice for transfer to Edo (also without paying interest).

But the disclosure of huge peculations by treasury officials aroused the suspicions of the bakufu's authorities. In 1709 they issued a peremptory order to the thirteen o-kawase to pay back at once all the money they had borrowed. Those who had not prepared for such a senseless and merciless move were unable to comply, of course, and a number of them were ruined. Mitsui's sannin-gumi, however, drawing upon the resources of Omotokata, and perhaps even digging into the "cellar silver," came through that crisis nicely.

It is doubtful that the Mitsuis were taken by surprise. Since their appointment as o-kawase they had improved their standing with Lord Makino, one of Shogun Tsunayoshi's ministers. It was perhaps through his intervention that Mitsui Jiroemon had been elected chief of the fiscal agents in Edo in 1702. This position, and his connection with the shogun's court, must have provided Jiroemon with some hint that the bakufu's loans would be called. At any rate, such experiences fortified Mitsui-gumi's policy of taking every precaution against surprise attacks.

The vicissitudes of the post-Genroku period demonstrated to the chonin that despite their rising prosperity and power they were still at the mercy of a corrupt, irrational, and often vengeful government. One of the wealthiest merchant families was that founded by Yodoya Keian, a war contractor for Hideyoshi. In the Genroku era the Yodoya heir Saburoemon (also known as Tatsugoro) cut a fine figure in the "floating world" of Osaka, spending freely his profits from trading in lumber and rice and making loans to daimyo. Flouting the sumptuary laws requiring chonin to dress modestly, he frequented the pleasure quarters wearing white silk kimono into which his family crest was worked ostentatiously. In 1709, when the treasury loans were called in, the bakufu confiscated Yodoya's entire fortune and the house was banished from Osaka, Kyoto, and Edo. This downfall, probably engineered by daimyo who were deeply in his debt, served as a warning to other chonin to be ever on guard against vanity and complacency.

The wealth of the leading merchants of the day may be gauged by a partial accounting of the property confiscated from Yodoya. According to one modern historian, it included 50 pairs of gold screens, 3 jeweled toy ships, 373 carpets, 13,266 pounds of "liquid gold," 273 large precious stones and innumerable small stones, 2 chests of gold, 3,000 *oban* (large gold coins each worth about 9 ryo), 120,000 ryo worth of other gold coins, 7 million pounds of silver, 150 boats, 730 warehouses, 17 treasurehouses, 160 granaries, 92 houses and shops, 367 acres of cypress forest, and an annual rice stipend of 55 tons.[1]

During this period the bakufu's worsening financial plight was aggravated by a series of natural disasters. In the Kanto earthquake of 1703 some 150,000 people in Edo died, and in 1707–8 Mount Fuji erupted, devastating hundreds of square miles of rich farmland. Later a large part of Kyoto burned, a tidal wave swept over the southern coast of Kii Province (in present-day Wakayama Prefecture), and floods ruined crops in the fertile provinces around Kyoto, Nara, and Osaka. Rehabilitation costs were enormous, and to replenish the treasury, already depleted by embezzlement, the bakufu resorted to the debasement of money.

Frequent recoinages over a long period had caused confusion and public loss of confidence in the currency. In one new issue alone the value of gold one-ryo coins was reduced by half, and of silver coins by three-fourths. Since gold was the main currency of Edo and silver that of Osaka, there was monetary confusion in addition to inflation. By 1720 many merchants were failing under such difficulties, and the Mitsuis also suffered serious reversals. Fortunately, the sharing of losses through Omotokata enabled them to weather the storm, which lasted four years.

Hachirobei's sons, who might be called the originators of scientific management in Japan, tried seriously to analyze the successes and failures of the chonin, and to draw guiding principles from them. Such inquiries led to the writing of *Chonin Kokenroku* (Merchants' Observations), the oldest surviving literary work of a Mitsui. Written by Takafusa, a grandson of Hachirobei, it is a collection of anecdotes about wealthy men who went bankrupt. The lugubrious tales, told to the author by his father Takahira and by several shop managers and clerks, cited examples of merchants who had lost their fortunes through religious fanaticism, personal extravagance, lending to daimyo, overweening ambition, and similar departures from sensible stewardship. One of the stories is about Hachirobei's elder brother Saburozaemon, with whom he had served his apprenticeship. Saburozaemon, head of the short-lived "nailpuller" Mitsui, owed his failure to having brought up his sons as gentlemen instead of as merchants, encouraging artistic endeavors such as the Noh drama, and associating with frivolous wastrels.

The original *Kokenroku* probably was completed in 1719. It is no longer in the possession of the family, but the date is known because one ledger shows that on a certain day a quantity of paper was purchased to make hand-written copies for the clan. It was not published then, but was borrowed by other merchants who had their own copies made, and it became quite famous. More than twenty such manuscript versions are preserved in the Mitsui Bunko. In the Meiji era it finally was published, with numerous errors, and widely distributed.

Absorbing the lessons taught by hard times, Takahira, the heir of old Hachirobei, found the wisdom of his father fully vindicated. In order to establish that wisdom as the foundation of Mitsui-gumi and of its growing enterprises, he decided to draft a constitution codifying the precepts and principles that had brought the House safely through its first and second generations.

Takahira worked on the document, purportedly a redraft of his father's will, in his spare time for a decade, and promulgated it as his own will in 1722, the centenary of Hachirobei's birth. According to family legend, Takahira, then in his seventieth year, assembled the heads of the five main branch families, showed them a quiver of arrows, and broke one of the shafts in two. Then he bound six arrows together and invited his brothers in turn to break the sheaf. None could, and the truth of the ancient parable was demonstrated once again, as a prelude to the first reading of the Mitsui *kaken,* or house constitution.

The general clauses repeat homilies that might have been applied beneficially by anyone. For example, clan members were admonished to promote the mutual welfare with one accord, to be considerate in their relations with one another, to respect those in authority and show kindness to subordinates. "Thrift is the basis of prosperity," they were told, "but luxury ruins a man." They were emphatically and repeatedly warned against religious excesses. "It is one's duty to believe in the gods and Buddha and follow the laws of Confucianism," the kaken advised, but not to donate excessive sums. "Instead of wasting gold and silver on temples and shrines, you should make appropriate contributions to the poor and suffering, and you will be rewarded ten-thousandfold."

There were also some simple but pithy business precepts, stating essentially:

Be diligent and watchful, or your business will be taken away by others.

Farsightedness is essential: do not miss great opportunities by pursuing trivial ones close at hand.

Avoid speculation of all kinds, and do not touch upon unfamiliar lines of business.

Calling for very special emphasis were the selection and treatment of the chief clerks or shop managers—whose designated role was to guard the business of the House, give appropriate advice when necessary, and correct blunders made by their masters. Clan members were adjured to keep an eye on younger clerks and train worthy candidates for responsible positions, being careful not to overlook any men of talent. The number of hired managers was to be limited to six or seven—three from Kyoto, two from Edo, and one (or perhaps two) from Osaka—presumably to prevent any local clique from gaining too much influence. The Mitsuis' concern for their retainers was shown in the clause providing that "a considerable amount of silver shall be set aside as a reserve fund for the benefit of elderly employees of the house" suffering from misfortune or calamities.

The main body of the constitution, however, was devoted to regulations preserving solidarity, harmony, and rectitude, as well as assuring fair dealing among family members. The most important of these can be summarized as follows:

Descendants of the House shall forever obey these rules without fail.

The head of the senior main family, Hachiroemon, shall be regarded as head of the House and obeyed as if he were a parent.

When there is no competent heir to succeed Hachiroemon, a son may be adopted from among other members of the House, or a female may succeed as head.

Boys of the families are to be apprenticed at the age of twelve or thirteen, serving at Kyoto, Edo, and Osaka and learn the rudiments of the business until the age of twenty-five. By the age of thirty they are expected to be capable of managing a shop.

The shares of house assets shall be allotted to member families as specified (see Appendix A), but 10 of the 220 shares shall be set aside for deserving offspring other than the heirs. Daughters of the families are to be married to sons of Mitsui clan members whenever possible, but are to be given suitable dowries otherwise.

Second and younger sons shall be allowed to establish families at about thirty years of age, if they are considered sufficiently capable; in such cases they may use the business name Echigoya, but not the surname Mitsui without special permission. It will not be necessary to establish any more branch or associate families.

Three capable older members are to be appointed as chief directors of the House to oversee all the branch shops. Monthly meetings with the managers of all shops are to be held for discussion of important business.

House members are not encouraged to enter government service because it might cause them to neglect family affairs. "Do not forget that we are merchants. You must regard your dealings with the government as a sideline of your business."

To prevent rivalry among the families, Takahira established the hierarchy of the six main branches and three associate families for all time. Although the number of families was later expanded from nine to eleven, and the title "Hachiroemon" passed to other main families on several occasions, this hierarchy was observed until the mid-twentieth century and undoubtedly saved the clan many times over from deadly feuds or dissolution. Provision also was made to punish miscreants by expelling them from the family and sending them into the priesthood, along with profligates incapable of caring for their families.

Fortunately, Hachiroemon Takahira lived for fifteen years after reading his "will," and was able to set an example for his brothers as elucidated in one of the clauses: "During the remainder of my life . . . I shall save as much as I can . . . and such savings will be deposited with the chief accountant. The exact sum of such savings shall be submitted to me for my perusal once a year. The amount deposited during the year shall be handed to me at the earliest possible date after the third of January every year."

While instructing his kinsmen in the organization and auditing of their finances, he warned them about overexpansion, dispersion of resources, and rash lending. "When lending money, one needs a solid mortgage," he warned. "If the borrower cannot repay in due time, recognize his limitations. One may lose some money, but that is better than to incur a bigger loss later on." But as for lending to daimyo, he was dead set against it, for even the great Lord Kii of the Tokugawa line eventually had defaulted on a debt to Hachirobei.

"Do not lend to daimyo," Takahira warned. "The lender develops an obsequious attitude, and recovery of the money is difficult. If one forms an unsound relationship with a daimyo and gets too deeply involved, one's ship will sink from the heavy load."

Many of Takahira's precepts were ignored or violated at one time or another, but one of them was observed without any known exceptions:

"Never forget the kindness of *tenka-sama* [the honorable men in power], for when society is peaceful, business can be carried on safely. Those of the same blood should never forget *ho-on* [repayment of kindness] and gratitude toward the state. Tenka-sama's decrees should be carried out faithfully, even by the lowest employees."

To this last admonition a profound sagacity may be imputed. At the time it was written, tenka-sama (an epithet which can also be translated as "the sovereign of all things under heaven") was the ruling shogun. But Takahira said nothing about the shogun or the Tokugawa family that monopolized the supreme position. Perhaps he was disillusioned by the defaulting of Lord Kii, or by the corruption of the bakufu, or by the aberrations of the successive shoguns and their sycophants. Or possibly, being of the literati, he had acquired enough awareness of history to realize that the *tenno,* or emperor, in Kyoto, although virtually an almsman of the Tokugawas, was also a potential tenka-sama.

Whatever Takahira may have been thinking when he codified the House law, its two dominant themes—permanence and flexibility—come through most clearly. His homely philosophy was further refined in the years remaining to him, and when he died in 1737 he left to his heir a hanging scroll upon which he had inscribed the essence of his experience: "The source of happiness is prudence."

4 · "Remember We Are Merchants"

A GAME POPULAR AMONG JAPANESE CHILDREN and known the world over is *jankenpon*, in which two or more players extend their hands simultaneously to symbolize rock, scissors, or paper. Rock can break scissors, scissors can cut paper, and paper can wrap rock, and at each turn the losers are eliminated. This game suggests the class system of feudal Japan, with rock representing the peasants, scissors the two-sworded men, and paper the merchants. In fact, samurai used the term "paper people" in referring to the chonin, although they were learning to their discomfiture that paper could wrap steel blades as well as rocks.

The three classes, all victims of the social system in which they were trapped by law, became mutually embittered because the struggles of each to solve its problems separately aggravated the plight of the others. Ieyasu's "great peace" had deprived the samurai of opportunities to perform glorious deeds, and the money system that was being awkwardly superimposed upon the country's agricultural economy put them at the mercy of the merchants. But both samurai and chonin classes were parasitic upon the peasants, who were plunged into ever deeper misery and often resorted to violence against the merchants, to be cut down in turn by the samurai. The peasants' only alternative was to join the urban chonin and become merchants themselves if they could save up a little capital. But with so few channels for enterprise left open to them by the bakufu, the increasingly numerous chonin competed intensely within the narrow market, and few escaped ruin.

Of the survivors, those who migrated from Ise Province were most ubiquitous—or at least the most noticeable. In the early eighteenth century there was a saying: "The commonest things in Edo are Ise merchants, Inari shrines, and dog turds." This juxtaposition indicates the low esteem in which people like the Mitsuis were held.

The merchants, subject to persecution or the confiscation of their property by the bakufu and often cheated by daimyo or samurai debtors, also suffered pillage and arson at the hands of outraged peasants or mobs of hungry townsmen. To prosper in such a world they had to be cringingly obsequious toward their superiors, ruthlessly competitive with their equals, and pitilessly grasping in their dealings with people more helpless than they. In short, the accusations heaped upon the Jews of Europe applied equally to the merchants of Japan—and for the same reasons.

The Mitsuis, being the most successful, were probably among the least loved. Unlike so many of their colleagues, who shared the foibles and weaknesses of the chonin in general, they seem to have been puritanical and almost obsessively diligent. Considering the exigencies of the age, one could scarcely expect them to have thrived otherwise. What is surprising is the evidence that, despite the lowliness of their calling and their relentless pursuit of profit, they made some very respectable contributions to the cultural life of the nation and, indirectly, to its political metamorphosis.

The Mitsuis were enjoined by their House's regulations to avoid extravagant contributions to temples and shrines, but there is no reason to suspect that they were less pious than their contemporaries. While living in Matsusaka, Hachirobei had frequently visited the Grand Shrines of Ise. After moving to Kyoto he joined the *Ise-ko,* the Ise pilgrims' association, and made a visit to the holy places every year. As privileged purveyors to the bakufu he and his sons had access also to the outer precincts of the hallowed imperial court, contributed toward its upkeep, and served as bearers of the *o-mikoshi,* the portable shrines, that were paraded through Kyoto's streets during Shinto festivals. After their brush with bankruptcy in the 1720s they donated funds for enlarging the compound of Mimeguri Jinja in Edo and building an annex in which their tutelary gods Ebisu and Daikoku were enshrined. These were two of the traditional "Seven Gods of Luck" worshiped by townsmen, along with the fox-messenger of the Inari shrines.

Since the good will of the townspeople had been the basis of the Mitsuis' fortune, which fluctuated with the general prosperity, their patronage of folk shrines and the gods of luck may have been a form of insurance, or at the least a sound business policy. For their personal worship, however, they favored the more dignified Tendai sect of pantheistic Buddhism, introduced from China in the ninth century. Hachirobei and his descendants worshiped at Shinnyo-do, a Tendai temple upon a hilltop in Kyoto, and were entombed there. In the lofty main hall, built in the seventeenth century, are several splendidly carved altars encrusted with gold. In a secluded corner behind the main altar are the ancestral shrines of the Mitsuis, behind whose portals stand row upon row of gold-lacquered wooden tablets bearing the names of all the deceased heirs from Hachirobei onward. These are ranked strictly according to the precedence of the branches: the head family, Kita-ke, in the center, is flanked by the hon-ke, or main branches, while the collateral branches are placed in a separate compartment.

A similar hierarchy is observed in the adjacent graveyard, overlooked by a stately pagoda and shaded by huge cryptomeria trees. The head-stones of the first and second generations stand on a slightly elevated terrace, with those of Hachirobei and Jusan at the center.

In this timeless place, to which the din of modern Kyoto's traffic scarcely penetrates, some twelve generations of Mitsuis sleep in ordered ranks, each in his proper station in death as in life. Among them are no statesmen, soldiers, or professional men. One, long ago, became a Buddhist priest after retirement from business, and others earned respect for their accomplishments in several avocations. But all of them, true to Hachirobei's teachings, were merchants first, and indulged other aspirations only after having discharged their obligations to the family, the clan, and the state. In that way they found the permanence for which the founder had yearned and striven.

As they prospered, the chonin donated generously to their favorite temples and shrines, thereby paying most of the costs of a renaissance in religious art and architecture. They also invigorated traditional art forms, such as Noh, while developing new ones—notably Kabuki, which reached its peak of creativeness about two hundred years ago. Before that time Mitsui Jiroemon Takanari emerged as a recognized writer of *joruri,* or ballad dramas for the theater. Under the pen name Ki no Jotaro (taken from his master Ki no Kaion, a composer of comic *tanka,* or verses of thirty-one syllables), he collaborated in writing a historical play that is still in the Kabuki repertoire. Another coauthor was the famous Utei Emba, a carpenter who had become a popular reciter of the comic stories called *rakugo.*

In the Tokugawa period people associated with the theater were ostracized by the "better classes." It is true that joruri and rakugo were considered more respectable than Kabuki, but still it was unusual for the scion of a prominent merchant family to consort with stage folk. The explanation is that Takanari took up the theater only after abandon-ing his business career. He could do so because a conflict had developed among the Mitsui families over a questionable business transaction. Threatened by the bakufu, they had had to find a scapegoat. So Taka-nari, a younger son and thus "expendable," assumed responsibility for the unpleasant situation and resigned his position as chief of the ryo-gaeya in Edo. Only then, when he no longer represented Mitsui-gumi, did he feel free to indulge his interest in the theater.

While cherishing the prestige they enjoyed within their own class, the Mitsuis still heeded the founder's reminder—"we are merchants"

—and made no pretense of being anything else. During the times when many chonin were eager to marry their sons and daughters into samurai families (a feat that could be accomplished by financial means) Mitsuis married only chonin, preferably other Mitsuis, as recommended by their constitution, until the class system was abolished officially in 1870.

Their tastes, however, became increasingly aristocratic. Several poets of Mitsui blood won recognition in their lifetimes. In the plastic arts the Mitsuis were patrons of many of the leading painters, including Hiroshige and Utamaro. One of the greatest among those artists was Maruyama Okyo, later a painter for the imperial court, who introduced new and lasting styles derived from Chinese and European examples. Some of his creations are still prized possessions of the head family. The renowned ceramist Eiraku Hozen, whose pottery made for the tea ceremony is now priceless, was another Mitsui protégé.

The Mitsuis' interest in scholarship began by accident rather than through inclination. In the late eighteenth century it so happened that Mitsui Takakage, heading one of the two branch families that remained in Matsusaka, lived next door to a scholar named Motoori Norinaga. The heir of an Ise merchant house that had recently become bankrupt in Edo, Motoori practiced medicine for a livelihood, but devoted most of his time to study, and to writing and lecturing upon the Japanese classics that after centuries of neglect were being discovered again by scholars. One of his special interests was *Genji Monogatari,* the great novel written in the eleventh century by Murasaki Shikibu, a lady-in-waiting at the imperial court.

Indifferent as a physician, Motoori proved to be one of Japan's most important thinkers, and Takakage was among his early disciples. When he was in his mid-thirties Motoori, at the urging of the outstanding classicist Kamo no Mabuchi, undertook a prodigious task. This was the writing of the *Kojiki Den,* which eventually became a forty-eight-volume commentary upon the *Kojiki,* an eighth-century compilation of Japanese "history," folk wisdom, and mythology. The *Kojiki Den,* which took thirty-five years to complete, is regarded as one of Japan's outstanding historical and literary works, and the Mitsuis take considerable pride in the fact that Takakage's financial support of Motoori Norinaga helped to make it possible. One of their dearest possessions is a *wagon,* an older type of koto, presented to Takakage by Motoori, with a message of commendation attached.

Using the most advanced methods of philology and linguistics then known, Motoori sought to establish the original meaning of the *Kojiki,* which he accepted as the holy writ of Shinto. Beginning with events that happened before the dawn of Japanese history, the *Kojiki* recounts the creation and the founding of the imperial house upon orders of the Sun Goddess, Amaterasu. Such studies were gratifying to the people of Ise and Kii provinces because of their strong interest in the Grand Shrines at Ise, which were dedicated to Amaterasu herself and to the spirits of others of the imperial ancestors.

Motoori's exhaustive study, although conducted more or less "scientifically," was essentially a revival of half-forgotten myths and superstitions. Yet ultimately the *Kojiki Den* and other writings of its kind had an extremely significant impact upon Japan's political development and history.

Since the triumph of Ieyasu in 1600 his bakufu government had sedulously fostered the myth that the Tokugawas ruled by divine right. The imperial house presumably had delegated full authority to the Tokugawa shoguns for all time. The emperor, although formally revered as the chief deity of Shinto, actually lived upon the parsimonious charity of the shogunate. Surrounded by hereditary nobles, he played the role of high priest in hollow rituals symbolizing the continuity of the dynasty and hence the legitimacy of Tokugawa rule.

The bakufu paid little heed to Shinto itself. The official ideology was a mixture of imported Buddhist and neo-Confucian precepts superimposed upon a native culture that in itself was viewed disdainfully by conservative scholars, who found their inspiration in the Chinese classics. The Tokugawas were interested only in the permanence of their rule and discouraged any objective study or creative thought concerning historical or social matters.

Indifferent to the public weal, the bakufu did little to relieve suffering from successive disasters and pestilences. In Motoori's time the great famine of Temmei, which lasted from 1783 to 1787, is estimated to have reduced the population by a million. It is said that in the castle town of Hirosaki in northern Honshu eighty thousand people starved to death, after having eaten all the dogs and cats in the vicinity. In many villages there was not a single survivor to bury the dead, whose corpses were consumed by birds and beasts.

Such hardships, aggravated by official corruption and speculation, provoked numerous and violent revolts. During the Temmei famine, when the price of rice tripled, there were more than one hundred and fifty uprisings among peasants and townsmen.

Concurrently, intellectuals were beginning to question not only the virtue and administrative competence of the Tokugawas but also their interpretations of history and the legitimacy of their reign. Almost forgotten classics of Japanese history, mythology, and literature—the *Nihon Shoki,* Japan's oldest official chronicles, and the *Man'yoshu* anthology of poetry, as well as the *Kojiki*—were studied to rediscover the spiritual essence of Japanese life and the precepts for benevolent rule that had been lost under the Tokugawa despots. This led gradually to a revival of ancient Japanese ideals and ethics, especially those related to the supremacy of the imperial house. Independent studies along these lines coalesced into a movement known as *kokugaku,* or national learning, of which Motoori Norinaga was the brightest exponent. Implicit in kokugaku was the suspicion that the Tokugawas were usurpers and that their violation of eternal laws laid down by the gods had caused Japan's decay.

The Tokugawas were not oblivious to the situation, and some of them were trying to discover what had gone wrong with their formula. In 1787, when the Temmei crisis was at its peak, Tokugawa Harusada, daimyo of Kii, summoned Motoori Norinaga to ask his opinions and advice upon problems racking the nation. This inspired Motoori to write *The Secret Book of the Jeweled Comb Box,* dedicated to Harusada, in which he developed his views on social unrest, the economic problems of the several classes, and the nature of commerce. This was perhaps the first time that a Tokugawa had deigned to consult a nationalist scholar, and the event was doubly significant because Motoori was a member of a chonin class by birth and training. In his youth he had been adopted by and apprenticed to a paper merchant. Finding business distasteful, he had turned to religious scholarship, while applying the practical knowledge and empiricism of commerce to his intellectual tasks.

Motoori's teachings must have seemed shockingly radical to the daimyo, as well as to the numerous chonin and priests who attended his lectures. He not only attacked their traditional beliefs in Buddhism and Confucianism but was strongly critical of the principles and methods upon which their prosperity rested. Concerning private property he asserted that, although Amaterasu Omikami and the imperial household had entrusted the affairs of state to the Tokugawas and administration of the provinces to the daimyo, "no people in a fief are private people, and no land is private land," since everything and everyone belonged to the emperor.

He saw great injustices in commerce, and chided rich merchants and aristocrats for living in idleness while "lower people" did all the work. Particularly reprehensible in Motoori's view was the alliance between business and government that was the cornerstone of Mitsui policy from beginning to end. The donation of money to the government for business advantage "will enable the rich further to increase their wealth and will do great harm to the poor," he said. "Even something that would help the rulers' finances should be wholly prohibited if it is harmful to the lower people."[1]

The immediate effect of Motoori's teaching upon the Mitsuis, several of whom were included among his five hundred disciples, is not recorded. The diaries of Takakage, no scholar himself, give only such information as "Today I attended Motoori's lecture," or record the master's visit, in his role as physician, to an ailing Mitsui. There can be little doubt that exposure to the ideas of Japan's pioneer "economic adviser" had some impact upon their thinking, even though they applied his precepts in reverse. (A modern parallel is found in most of present-day Japan's capitalist leaders, who were influenced in their university courses by Marxist professors.) More significant, however, was the early awareness, inculcated in their disciples by Motoori and other national scholars, that the Tokugawas were usurpers and that the imperial family could offer to the oppressed people of Japan a morally acceptable alternative to the tyranny of the bakufu.

5 · Legacy of
the Barbarians

AFTER ITS FIRST CENTURY, one of unprecedented grandeur and prosperity, the Tokugawa shogunate went into decline, its vitality sapped by a futile struggle against change. In the feudal structure each class and every individual in it was part of a monolith held together by presumably indissoluble relationships. Yet the burgeoning mercantile economy, in obedience to its own inexorable laws, had already altered the nature of those relationships. The bakufu, organically incapable of adjusting the social structure to changing conditions, met successive crises with stronger doses of the same old medicine—tyranny and isolation.

At the beginning of the Tokugawa period, which lasted from 1603 to 1868, Japan had been a relatively advanced, outward-looking country, ready to claim a respected place among the world's nations. But seclusion, made all the more possible by her geographical remoteness, paralyzed Japan's social creativity and intellectual growth at a time when the industrial revolution was transforming the Western world and preparing its countries for global expansion. Then, as Japan stagnated, European navies opened up most of Southeast Asia to trade and colonization. In the first half of the nineteenth century the British established a solid position in China, while the Russians began reaching across the Siberian wilderness to develop new territories at the mouth of the Amur River, little more than five hundred miles from the shores of Japan.

For commercial or political reasons all the European naval powers were trying to establish amicable relations with Japan, and exploratory visits by foreign ships became frequent. The Russian empire, intent upon dominating Korea and Manchuria, needed a friendly Japan on its eastern flank. The British, apprehensive of a Russian advance into China, hoped to forestall it by wooing the Japanese. The United States, as a newcomer, was at a great disadvantage in regions preempted by Europeans and saw virginal Japan as its last chance to stake a claim in Asia. As America's closest neighbor across the Pacific, Japan could be a naval outpost of great value; but under control of hostile powers it could also be a threat. Japan's ports were needed as supply bases for American merchantmen and whalers; trade prospects, though unevaluated, were enticing; and for zealous Christian missionaries there were those millions of heathens known to be susceptible to conversion.

Japan ,was doubly inviting because of its suspected vulnerability. As E. H. Norman has pointed out: "In the middle of the 19th Century Japan was as weak as contemporary Burma or Siam, facing the modern world without allies, without a fleet or modern army, with no monies in its treasury, its industry still handicraft, its trade negligible, its poverty profound."[1]

The armies charged with defending Japan were vitiated by a peace that had lasted two hundred and fifty years. When Commodore Perry's men landed in 1853 they encountered warriors clad in armor made of silk, leather, and thin plates of metal, very similar to that worn by Sasaki Takahisa in the fifteenth century. Guns were in common use, but most of them were relics of past European wars, muzzleloading flintlocks, muskets, and such, while other troops were armed with swords, spears, and bows. This was the same year in which Samuel Colt started the mass production of small arms at Hartford, Connecticut. From the viewpoint of the "Dutch Scholars," which coincided in this respect with that of the exponents of nationalism, the bakufu had betrayed sacred Nippon by making it impotent to repel the onslaught of the barbarians.

Perry assumed that the reluctance of the shogun's representatives to accept his reasonable terms was due to ignorance or to encrusted tradition, not realizing that he was forcing them to make a choice between two forms of committing suicide—a dagger in the belly, or slow poison. They knew that refusal of Perry's terms would lead to eventual attack either by the United States or by European powers. Yet acceptance of those terms would be used by the bakufu's enemies to inflame malcontents of all classes.

The daimyo were almost equally divided over the course to be taken, so with characteristic Japanese ambivalence the bakufu "harmonized" the opposing views. By going through the motions of signing a treaty, they would gain time for rebuilding their defenses along modern lines; concurrently, they would use their new contacts with the West to learn its military science and then drive out the interlopers once and for all. By such reasoning they tried to reconcile a breach in tradition, represented by a treaty, with their responsibility for expelling the barbarians.

Under these inauspicious circumstances Japan and the United States concluded the Treaty of Kanagawa, Japan's first diplomatic recognition of a Western power, on March 31, 1854. This so-called wood and water treaty gave Americans ships access to two minor ports, Shimoda and Hakodate, and the right of refuge and supply. It also authorized the installation of a United States consul, if and when such an official was needed. Using this excuse (and much to the anguish of the bakufu), Townsend Harris arrived in Shimoda two years later, demanding a residence, an audience with the shogun, the conclusion of a commercial treaty, and the opening of more ports.

Eventually, in December 1857, he was received at Edo Castle with full ceremony; and after having to endure more than another year of bureaucratic obstruction and infuriating evasions, in 1858 he won a Treaty of Amity and Commerce that provided for freedom of trade, the opening of Kobe and Yokohama (both seaports adjacent to Japan's largest cities), and the right of residence for Americans in the open ports, as well as in Edo itself.

The Japanese had been assured that trade would bring the nation great benefits and strengthen the government, but its immediate effects after the opening of Yokohama in 1859 were worse than even the pessimists had imagined. At first fewer than fifty Caucasians lived in the new international settlement, built and maintained at government expense. But as word of the singular opportunities for profit circulated abroad, the number of fortune seekers multiplied. Conspicuous among them were drifters, sots, and brawling sailors, who quickly confirmed Japan's worst suspicions about the barbarians.

Hardly more agreeable to the Japanese were foreign merchants, who sniffed out the weaknesses in the country's economy and exploited them without mercy. They found the most serious flaw in its currency system. The bakufu, having been out of touch with world finance for centuries, had manipulated coinage values arbitrarily (and naively), with the result that the exchange rate between gold and silver was one to five, or one to six, whereas in foreign money markets it was about one to fifteen. The standard international currency in East Asia was the Mexican dollar, a silver coin minted in Hong Kong and the United States, as well as in Mexico. Under treaty provisions the exchange rate in Japan was set at three silver *bu* for one Mexican dollar. The Japanese gold *koban* coin (worth one ryo) cost four bu. Shrewd barbarians immediately saw that with an outlay of 100 dollars a man could buy 300 bu and exchange them for 75 koban. Then, when exported, those 75 koban would fetch at least 150 dollars, and as much as 270 dollars, depending upon their gold content.

This dollar-bu-koban trick became an obsession among the foreigners; and even diplomats, including Harris and members of his staff, played it to amplify their salaries. The bakufu tried clumsily to read-just the coinage in order to stop such plunder, but succeeded only in stopping trade entirely and antagonizing the foreign powers, who in-sisted upon their treaty rights. Before the currency matter was settled such a drainage of gold had occurred that Japan's monetary system was disrupted. Sporadic demand for export commodities, and excessive supplies of imported goods, caused wild fluctuations in prices. Sudden changes in the price of rice affected the whole economy, imposing severe hardships upon peasants and poorer townsmen. Such fluctua-tions were manipulated by merchants to the disadvantage of daimyo and samurai, whose incomes were measured in rice and seemed always to shrink when converted into money.

Since trade in the open ports was monopolized by the foreigners and conducted through official channels, it brought little profit to native merchants and none to the bakufu, saddled as it was with astronomical expenses related to the foreign incursion. Income from duties was minimal because Harris had included in his treaty a clause allowing for-eigners to set the tariff rates, which of course they kept extremely low. This provision made it impossible to protect domestic industry and invited a flood of cheap factory-made foreign goods that ruined in-numerable handicraft enterprises upon which the families of peasants and impoverished samurai had depended for their cash income.

These economic woes were no less distressing to the Mitsuis, with whom business had been going badly for a long time. Ordinarily, the misfortunes of the upper classes brought advantages to the merchants, but lately there had been too much misfortune. In the 1840s debts of the daimyo had risen so alarmingly that fully three-fourths of the rice crop sent to Osaka was owed in advance as interest to moneylenders. Bad debts had mounted commensurately, and among the exchange houses it was estimated that twenty percent of their capital stagnated in the form of uncollected loans.

For the two previous decades calamities had been striking in relent-less succession. During the Tempo era (1830–44) crop failures had brought repeated famines, some so severe that the streets of many towns were littered with unburied corpses. When the bakufu did noth-ing to alleviate the people's sufferings, a scholarly police official named Oshio Heihachiro was spurred into action. Realizing the futility of persuasion, he conceived the desperate scheme of staging a revolt in Osaka, seizing the wealth of the merchants, and using it to finance a peasant militia strong enough to challenge the bakufu. In order to begin the rebellion and feed his followers—among whom were samurai and *ronin,* or lordless samurai, as well as townsmen and farmers—he sold his beloved books and manuscripts.

Being a man of conscience, Oshio first petitioned the bakufu and leading merchants, such as Mitsui and Konoike, to distribute some of the rice from their bulging granaries. When these pleas were ignored he secretly distributed swords to his few hundred cohorts and, on February 19, 1837, assembled his little band for an assault upon Osaka's mercantile district. "First we must kill all the officials who have made the poor suffer," he commanded, "and then we must go on to slaughter all the rich men."

The bakufu was fully informed of the plot, but the police were so incompetent and cowardly in the face of an armed mob that the rioters were able to run wild through the streets for hours. The revolt centered upon the warehouses of the merchants, which yielded such enormous amounts of treasure that the rebels were unable to carry all of it away. As the looters struggled with bales of rice and boxes of silver, the shops and warehouses were set afire, and soon flames were raging across the city. The rebels, immobilized by their greed, were easily dispersed by soldiers from the local garrison and, as he knew he must, Oshio killed himself. The Mitsuis and their property seem to have been almost unscathed. But the losses of merchants and householders in general were tremendous, for in the conflagration, which lasted three days, about eighteen thousand shops and homes were destroyed.

The revolt, which spread to other areas, aroused the stupefied bakufu to action, unfortunately of a counterproductive kind. In the so-called Tempo reforms that followed, hunger in the overpopulated cities was relieved by ordering surplus townsmen to go back to the farms. Luxurious living was prohibited by stricter sumptuary laws. And since monopolistic commerce stifled production and caused scarcities, the centuries-old *tonya*—trading corporations or wholesalers' guilds—were abolished, with the result that the commodity-distribution system was crippled.

Business stagnated. After the barbarians landed it got worse, even for Mitsui. With financial distress and uneasiness on every side, people just weren't buying piece goods, and Echigoya's retail trade declined dangerously. Inflation had raised personnel costs, but feudal custom forbade discharging anyone. During these trials a Mitsui-gumi executive wrote in the company's logbook: "No business paying, only expenditures swelling."

The bakufu became insatiably hungry for money and levied forced loans of fearsome size upon the merchants. Mitsui-gumi, tapped for 200,000 ryo early in 1859, put up a stronger protest than usual, explaining: "Before and since the arrival of the Black Ships, Mitsui's business had been declining, and expenses are increasing because of earthquake and fire." The amount demanded was greater than the entire capital of the House's dry-goods shops and amounted to more than twenty-five percent of the total assets entered in Mitsui's books.

The levy could not be refused outright because Mitsui-gumi was still doing a good deal of official business for the bakufu. Furthermore, the House stood to gain considerable benefits by cooperating. For example, after the signing of the Treaty of Amity and Commerce the Edo Mitsuis had applied secretly for permission to open a branch exchange shop in Yokohama. When they proved themselves compliant about the loan, the accounting magistrate responded to their petition in these reassuring terms: "As foreign powers are coming to Japan in May, 1859, and only the Mitsuis could deal with foreign countries who are eager to trade, the shogun graciously allows the opening of a shop there."[2]

Japanese merchants still were forbidden to engage in foreign trade directly, but the bakufu was anxious to conduct business efficiently at Yokohama as a demonstration of the shogun's sincerity in enforcing the treaties. The Mitsuis seem to have been willing to assist in this endeavor because familiarity with trade in the open ports (until then a monopoly of the bakufu) would put them in a favorable position if and when private trade became permissible.

The project seems to have been reasonable in concept, but the way in which it was carried out indicates that in the centuries since Hachirobei's death the unity of the clan had suffered. In the Edo shops there were two influential but competing *banto*, or clerks, Saito Junzo and Sakurai Yohei. The former favored the new venture, but Sakurai opposed it because it contravened the provision in the Mitsuis' constitution against being involved in unfamiliar business. Out of deference to Sakurai, Saito agreed to establish a dry-goods shop instead of a foreign exchange house. But then he used it as a front for exchange operations, thus achieving his purpose. The Edo Mitsuis must have known what Saito was doing and acquiesced in his plan, but apparently he proceeded without consulting Omotokata in Kyoto, a surprising omission, and one that caused serious trouble later on.

The Yokohama branch was indeed a legitimate retail shop, as attested by a ledger entry describing its first sales to foreigners. On June 2, 1859, the day the port opened, a Russian and an American stopped in and bought some brocades. They must have found the prices right and passed the word around, for on the following day two Americans ordered so much material that it had to be brought up from Kyoto. Eventually, however, the branch's main business was the custody of treasury funds in Yokohama and Kanagawa, acting as official money-changer in far-off Hakodate, and handling receipts, payments, and taxes in nearby Yokosuka, where an iron works had been built. Such business should have been conducted by a regular money-exchange shop, of course. The confusion resulting from the hybrid establishment was described by Saito's stepson: "We had to go back and forth between Yokohama and Edo, and were quite busy. Because the port was newly opened, a large amount of money came in and out, and most of it was kept at the Yokohama branch. Clerks from the Echigoya *gofukuten* [draper's shop] took care of the business, and on the side they also loaned money like an exchange house. But we made mistakes in moneylending and as things went on like this it was quite unsatisfactory because it looked as if a merchant was handling official business."

The persistence of such a dangerous anomaly indicates that Omotokata was either ignorant of the real state of affairs or no longer able to exercise control. The precise reason for this failure of leadership is not apparent, but there is no reason to believe that the Mitsuis were immune to the general disarray and desperation that convulsed Japan as the shogunate struggled against its impending doom.

6 · Trade of Blood and Guile

TOWNSEND HARRIS, HAVING OPENED Japan's doors to trade, was eager to open its mind to the inestimable advantages of commerce. He knew that the Japanese people, after their long seclusion, would be indelibly impressed with the manifestations of the Western world, and he hoped that his own country would be the model for Japan's renaissance. Through the good offices of the shogun's *tairo,* or chief minister, Lord Ii Naosuke, who had been instrumental in concluding the Treaty of Amity and Commerce, Harris arranged that a Grand Embassy be sent to Washington in 1860 to exchange ratifications.

A mission of nearly eighty daimyo and samurai was transported across the Pacific to San Francisco aboard an American side-wheeler, crossed the Isthmus of Panama by railway, and proceeded by ship to the United States. In Washington its members met President James Buchanan and his cabinet, got a good look at some of the achievements of a Western society, and incidentally made a sensational impression upon the American public. Beneath the windows of their rooms at Willard's Hotel, near the White House, as newspapers reported, hundreds of women and girls, "handsome and prettily dressed, have been . . . throwing up bouquets, candy and all sorts of nick-nacks, calling out 'Japonee, Japonee! give me a fan, won't you?' "[1]

New York was enraptured by the exotic visitors in their elegant apparel, and their ceremonial procession attracted huge throngs. One spectator, Walt Whitman, was inspired to write the poem "A Broadway Pageant," part of which declared:

> Over the Western sea hither from Niphon come,
> Courteous, the swarth-cheek'd two-sworded envoys,
> Leaning back in their open barouches, bare-headed, impassive,
> Ride to-day through Manhattan.

Thoughtful efforts were made to arouse the envoys' interest in American science, technology, government, and the naval and military arts. The noble guests were unexpectedly responsive, asking many questions, taking notes, and keeping detailed diaries. One of the most studious was

Oguri Tadamasa, Lord of Bungo, who was allowed to observe the operation of the United States Mint at Philadelphia in preparation for reorganizing Japan's antiquated currency system and, by so doing, unwittingly reviving the ebbing fortunes of the Mitsuis.

When the embassy returned to Japan, however, there was no rejoicing. The increase of Yokohama's foreign population had generated a groundswell of xenophobia, and anyone associating with the barbarians was regarded suspiciously. The outlanders who had flocked to the treaty port were not a prepossessing breed on the whole, and even at best they grated upon Japanese sensibilities. As Sir Ernest Satow, then a young interpreter for the British diplomatic mission, observed: "They affronted the feelings of samurai by their independent demeanour, so different from the cringing subservience to which the rules of Japanese etiquette condemned the Japanese merchant."[2]

Their lust for gold and grog, and their intolerable assumption of superiority (seemingly confirmed by the results of business dealings with Japanese, in which foreigners usually won), goaded patriotic samurai into fury. Those who were not stirred by feelings of nationalism were still forced to recognize the economic disadvantages of foreign trade, as domestic industries succumbed to the assault of cheaper products. It was also widely believed that forcible conquest of Japan by one or another of the barbarian nations was only a matter of time.

For evils real or anticipated, patriots blamed the shogun, who had admitted the foreigners against the wishes of the emperor. Soon after the departure of the embassy to Washington, the tairo, Lord Ii, was assassinated by nationalists, whose slogan *"Sonno! Joi!"*—Revere the Emperor! Expel the Barbarians!—was on the lips of discontented samurai and ronin throughout Japan.

In 1859, the year that Yokohama was opened to foreign trade, three foreigners and a Japanese interpreter were murdered in cold blood. A conflagration destroyed a large part of the settlement, and soon afterward the French Legation in Edo was burned. In January 1861, Townsend Harris' secretary, the amiable Henry Heusken, was ambushed by ronin and slashed to death in Edo, and in July the British Legation repulsed an attack by a band of ronin in which two Englishmen were killed and two wounded.

Rumor and panic ignited the tinder of public discontent. Inflation and crop failure provoked more peasant uprisings in the country and rice riots in the cities. Smuggling and highway robbery were widespread and, as police power disintegrated, propertied people entrusted their safety to bosses who controlled gangs of armed outlaws. The occasional violence against foreigners was as nothing compared with the

subversive plotting, assassinations, and internecine fighting that paralyzed the bakufu.

Much of the disorder that shattered the long peace of the Tokugawa
period was contrived and executed by radical intellectuals of the sonno-
joi persuasion. Some of them were motivated by a sincere loathing of
foreigners, but the more sensible among them, entertaining a wholesome respect for the West and its achievements, used antiforeignism as
a club with which to batter the bakufu, the principal target of their
hatred.

The most formidable opponents of the shogunate were the Satsuma
and Choshu *han,* or clans, in southern and western Japan. Because the
daimyo of those fiefs had not rallied to the banner of Tokugawa Ieyasu
before the Battle of Sekigahara in 1600, their descendants had been regarded as unreliable elements ever since. Without repudiating their
vows of fealty to the shogun, those resentful *tozama,* or "outside han,"
nevertheless conducted their affairs with insolent disregard for his authority.

Satsuma, with its capital in Kagoshima at the southeastern tip of
Kyushu, held suzerainty over the Ryukyu Islands, which served as a
bridge for trade with China. Remote from Edo and the interference of
the bakufu, Satsuma had evaded the full effect of the seclusion laws, and
through foreign contacts had adopted relatively advanced industrial
methods, improved its naval and military arms, and amassed some commercial capital. Choshu, strategically located along the Straits of Shimonoseki, the gateway for shipping between the Inland Sea and Nagasaki,
had also prospered from trade based upon a well-organized agricultural
and handicraft economy and had developed its martial capacities beyond
those countenanced by the bakufu.

These two han, and a few others in the western region—notably Tosa
on the island of Shikoku and Hizen near Nagasaki—had much in common. The daimyo themselves and their hereditary ministers in most
cases had succumbed to the inanition of languorous Tokugawa court
life, and their practical affairs were handled by younger samurai of
vigor and ability. Many of the latter were adherents of the national
learning taught by Motoori Norinaga and his successors, and supported
the principles of sonno joi. Wanting to reform and modernize their
provinces, they chafed under the restrictions and interferences of the
bakufu. In their commercial and financial dealings they kept in close
contact with the provincial merchants and those of the big cities as well.
The merchants, a mundane lot, probably were skeptical of the nationalist ideologies, but having suffered grievous losses from the foreign incursion, and despairing of any benefits from foreign trade under the

bakufu, they listened sympathetically to the samurai who advocated sonno joi.

The tozama samurai, many of whom were stationed in Kyoto to share the defense of the imperial court with men from the other han, found kindred spirits among the *kuge*, the nobles at the court. Embittered by the shabby treatment they had received from the Tokugawa usurpers, the kuge also responded to the nationalist teachings. Thus, there was forming a vague coalition of the most militant samurai of the western han, merchants, and court nobles—all calling for expulsion of the foreigners, curbing of the bakufu, and a corresponding increase in the power of the imperial court.

Among and within the tozama han there were schisms reflecting those of national scope. The radicals were moving toward a position of *tobaku,* overthrow of the bakufu, while conservatives favored a more moderate course of *kobu gattai,* or union of the shogunate and the imperial court. Satsuma and Choshu, long rivals for the favor of Kyoto, were divided over this issue. In Choshu the tobaku contingent was ascendant, while the kobu-gattai adherents dominated Satsuma. Variations of this ideological split caused factional struggles within the han and armed clashes between them as they vied for physical control over the court and the person of the emperor, whose importance as a talisman of power was rising.

Most injurious to the shogunate were the depredations of radical samurai and ronin against the foreigners, whose envoys were losing patience with the bakufu's vacillation as well as its weaknesses. In 1862, when Anglo-Japanese relations were thus strained, a fresh outrage brought matters to a head.

On a fine September afternoon an English merchant named Richardson went riding out of Yokohama with two colleagues and a lady friend. Heading toward Edo on the broad Tokaido, they encountered the vanguard of a daimyo's procession moving in the opposite direction. Richardson, a newcomer, was unfamiliar with road etiquette and failed to dismount or leave the highway as was obligatory when a personage of higher rank was passing. The personage in question happened to be Shimazu Hisamitsu, the actual leader of Satsuma, whose samurai were notorious for their belligerence. When Richardson, ignoring all warnings, persisted in riding against the oncoming procession, he and his party were attacked by Satsuma's swordsmen. Richardson was slashed mortally and the two men with him were severely wounded.

The angry foreign settlers and their troops in Yokohama clamored for immediate retaliation, and Satsuma's warriors were equally ready for battle with the barbarians. The outbreak of war then and there was prevented by the leaders of both sides, who managed to restrain the hotheads. The British chargé d'affaires decided prudently that the issue was a diplomatic one to be handled by Great Britain's Foreign Office, and confined himself to lodging a stern protest with the Japanese government.

But while the foreign envoys still fumed, the bakufu's impotence was demonstrated again when unidentified arsonists destroyed the British Legation, newly built and just ready for occupancy. In the following March London's terms for settling the Richardson affair reached Yokohama. To the consternation of the bakufu in Edo the British demanded, in addition to a formal apology, the payment of 100,000 pounds sterling as a penalty. Satsuma was to execute those samurai who had committed the offense and to pay an additional 25,000 pounds compensation. The Foreign Office made it clear that the only alternative was war.

The bakufu procrastinated in replying to these demands and used the time gained to prepare for hostilities. Concurrently, the sonno-joi extremists maneuvered the imperial court into issuing a futile order for the expulsion of foreigners. The bakufu, unable to refuse an imperial command, reluctantly set the expulsion date for June 25 of the same year and, while still negotiating with Britain's envoys, made secret preparations to enforce it. These moves became known to the British, who responded by strengthening their fleet and issuing an ultimatum that the shogunate pay, within twenty days, the 100,000-pound indemnity together with 10,000 pounds already due for compensating the families of victims of earlier attacks. As tensions mounted seventeen foreign warships and six merchantmen were assembled for the defense of residents in the treaty ports.

This display of power had the desired effect. At the last minute the bakufu capitulated and delivered to the British chargé d'affaires the sum of 440,000 Mexican dollars—most of it practically confiscated from the merchants of Osaka.

The foreign envoys were assured, unofficially, that the bakufu had abandoned its plans to carry out the order for expulsion, and the indemnity was regarded as a token of their sincerity. But officially the order was still in effect, and on the appointed day the incorrigible samurai of Choshu took independent action to enforce it. Two Choshu vessels fired upon the American merchantman *Pembroke* passing through the Straits of Shimonoseki, and in succeeding weeks other foreign ships were attacked there.

The Western diplomats, realizing at last that the bakufu was unable to control the outside han, now adopted a policy of conciliating the shogunate while chastising its internal enemies. In July American and French merchantmen destroyed two Choshu gunboats and some forts at Shimonoseki, but the straits remained closed. Then, early in August, the British sent a naval squadron to Satsuma to exact payment of the additional indemnity and the punishment of Richardson's murderers.

The demand was rejected rather insolently, so the Britons righteously bombarded Kagoshima, Satsuma's castle town, setting a considerable part of it ablaze, and then burned several ships for good measure. It was not a clear-cut victory, since the British suffered many casualties and, battered by a wild typhoon, decided to withdraw. But the demonstration forced Satsuma to recognize the superiority of Western naval power and to meet Britain's terms.

Shimazu Hisamitsu of Satsuma, already neck-deep in debt to the Osaka chonin, had no such sum as 25,000 pounds. But he did have a resourceful helper in the person of Okubo Toshimichi, an opportunistic young samurai who alternated between radicalism and moderation. Having swung back to a moderate position at the time, he was on speaking terms with the bakufu's officials. He went to visit one of the higher councilors, Itakura Katsukiyo, Lord of Iga, and argued that the bakufu, being responsible for having admitted the foreigners, should pay Satsuma's indemnity.

Itakura, aware of the impoverished bakufu's finances (at one time it had little more than 20,000 ryo in its treasury), was stubborn in his refusal, but Okubo was adamant. Taking his cue from the bakufu's extortionist tactics, he sent two swordsmen to Itakura's residence with the information that, unless the "loan" was forthcoming, the British chargé d'affaires would be assassinated immediately. Itakura wavered. Such a deed would not merely humiliate the bakufu but could mean war against the foreign powers. Yet to arrest Okubo and his bullies would antagonize Satsuma and inflame the han's radicals. He gave in, and promised Okubo that he would "borrow" the money from the Mitsuis —who had provided a sizable share of the 110,000-pound indemnity the bakufu already had paid to the British.

Caught in the squeeze between invasion and insurrection, the bakufu yielded to its critics and instituted a number of reforms. For one, the sankin kotai was reduced to a token hundred-day sojourn in Edo every three years, and the families of daimyo were no longer held in Edo as hostages. This relieved the daimyo of a heavy financial burden, but it also gave the dissidents among them more time and resources for their machinations against the shogun.

In 1861, to further the kobu-gattai policy of uniting Japan's embattled factions through a reconciliation between the imperial court and the shogunate, the fifteen-year-old Shogun Iemochi had been wedded to the emperor's sister. But perversely, the Kyoto loyalists saw this as an attempt by the bakufu to secure imperial sanction of the treaties, so far stubbornly withheld. The kobu-gattai strategy failed and the shogunate, bereft of a policy, drifted helplessly.

Through the intervention of the radicals the youthful shogun was forced to accept a "guardian" (in effect, a regent) amenable to the guidance of the imperial factions. This was Tokugawa Hitotsubashi Keiki (also known as Yoshinobu), son of the ultranationalist Lord of Mito. An able and reasonably enlightened young man, Keiki was responsive to advisers working toward domestic harmony and conciliation of the Western powers. But paradoxically, the shogun himself, under coercion from imperialists in Kyoto, just then was setting a new date for the final expulsion of Westerners. The extremists, pressing their advantage, obtained an imperial order that Shogun Iemochi should visit Kyoto, presumably to reach an understanding with the emperor concerning the treaties. This was the crowning humiliation, for no shogun had deigned to visit the sovereign during the past two hundred and thirty years.

In March 1863, the "barbarian-quelling generalissimo" started his journey down the Tokaido, escorted by three thousand brilliantly caparisoned retainers and troops. The Edo merchants were tapped for contributions as a matter of course, and the Mitsuis recorded in their ledger an item of ten thousand ryo "for sending off the shogun." There was some consolation, however. Echigoya was still the leading purveyor of cloth to the bakufu, and the making of uniforms and ceremonial attire for the journey kept the shop profitably occupied for weeks. But soon after this respite from business doldrums a deeper depression set in. The shogun had intended to stay in Kyoto for only ten days, but his opponents found it useful to keep him there under their control and his advisers in a state of confusion. So there Iemochi remained, languishing amid the refurbished splendors of Nijo Castle, month after month. Kyoto had become the arena of action, leaving Edo a political vacuum. The foreign envoys, who were not permitted to visit Kyoto, had to deal with powerless underlings left behind in Edo and could learn little about the fateful decisions being made in the remote imperial city. Antiforeign samurai and ronin now swarmed into the capital, shattering its tranquillity by their murderous assaults upon moderates and even fellow radicals who had admitted the inevitability of intercourse with foreigners. To curb the zealots the bakufu organized mercenary units of *soshi*, political bullies, recruited from among the flotsam of ronin, gamblers, thugs, and desperadoes who roamed the troubled land. Their influx brought a certain prosperity to the city, but as the police cowered before the swashbucklers, robbery, looting, and arson became the order of the day.

The more important chonin, being in touch with stewards of the tozama daimyo and also under the bakufu's protection as suppliers and fiscal agents, were spared these depredations. But the Mitsuis, from their vantage in Kyoto—one of their mansions was adjacent to Nijo Castle—sensed the calamitous events that were about to happen and tried to find the political connections that would bring them through safely.

In the early part of 1863 the loyalists from Choshu were still securely entrenched at court. Working through certain kuge secretly allied with their cause, they could gain imperial backing for their undertakings, however rash. It was they who had coerced the court into ordering the bakufu to expel the barbarians. Even more quixotic was their program for mobilizing an imperial expedition, with the emperor riding at its head, to sweep the interlopers out of Japan. Such a move was tantamount to having the emperor take over the official functions of the shogun, while leaving Choshu supreme.

The emperor, well indoctrinated by sonno-joi nobles, gave his blessing even to this devious scheme. But after Choshu's virtual declaration of war at Shimonoseki, and the debacle of Satsuma at Kagoshima, his majesty grew more cautious. Realizing that the country had been saddled with an untenable foreign policy, he cooled toward the nobles being manipulated by Choshu's hotheads and showed increasing favor to those of moderate inclination. Satsuma, chastened by the British, had taken leadership of the kobu-gattai moderates and began to gain the imperial favor that Choshu was losing.

Choshu's continued plots and provocations outraged Satsuma and its temporary ally Aizu, a pro-Tokugawa han in northern Honshu, whose daimyo was then military governor of Kyoto. Suspecting (or inventing) a Choshu conspiracy to recover its position by treachery, Satsuma and Aizu leaders informed the emperor—indirectly, of course, for not even daimyo could approach that godly being in person—and won his permission to take forcible countermeasures. Accordingly, on September 30, 1863, they staged a coup d'état and sequestered the palace. Civil war was avoided when Satsuma produced an imperial edict forbidding violence, and Choshu, whose protestations of reverence for the emperor were unsurpassed, was persuaded to withdraw its soldiers. But the Satsuma-Aizu coup, though bloodless, ended the long Tokugawa peace. For two and a half centuries political change in Japan had been effected gradually by means of sycophancy, intrigue, and subtle treachery. But after this confrontation the key to supremacy was to be naked military power. Ominously, Choshu's men took with them, in defiance of the court, seven nobles sympathetic to sonno joi, with the clear indication that they would return to reinstate them at court by force of arms.

The wellspring of sonno-joi nationalism in Choshu was a school established by a young military instructor named Yoshida Shoin. An intellectual prodigy, he had quickly absorbed the Chinese classics that were still the stock in trade of orthodox scholarship; but he was more attracted to the national learning, notably the works of the Mituis' erstwhile teacher Motoori Norinaga, which convinced him that Japan was truly the land of the gods and that the emperor was its rightful sovereign. Yoshida believed that the Tokugawas, having betrayed his majesty's trust, had neglected the country's defenses and exposed it to the depredations of inferior breeds of men. Moreover, the bakufu, cravenly shirking its duty, had stooped to parley with the aliens, and soon those intruders would try to subjugate the Japanese race. It was the duty of every loyal Japanese, he insisted, to reimplant the ancient virtues, purge the country of foreigners and their influences, and restore the emperor to the supremacy ordained by the gods for ages eternal. Only then could sacred Nippon attain its destiny and assert its leadership in the world. (Prophetically, Yoshida also advocated subduing Korea and annexing Manchuria, Formosa, and the Philippines.) Such were the teachings of this provincial messiah, who had a profound impact upon his contemporaries, inspired the twentieth-century militarists, and is a hallowed figure still in Japan's nationalist pantheon.

Yoshida was fanatically antiforeign, but not ignorantly so. Having delved into foreign books, he had learned much about the new military technology and the way it was used. Being informed about foreign affairs, he knew how the British had first gone to China to trade, then introduced opium as a means of saving their gold and silver, and finally subjugated the government that had tried to abolish the baneful traffic. Hoping to save his country from the fate of China, Yoshida roamed Japan as a ronin, spreading the sonno-joi gospel and hatching plots to realize its aims.

He knew that without science and technology Japan would be helpless before the Western offensive, so he decided to go abroad and study them. In 1854, with elaborate but transparent secrecy reminiscent of Tom Sawyer's, he boarded one of Commodore Perry's ships in the dead of night and pleaded to be taken to America. Rebuffed, he was set ashore and arrested by the bakufu for the crime of having attempted to leave the country. After being released from prison through the leniency of his daimyo, he was allowed to start a school, at which he taught the sonno-joi philosophy along with his own brand of the martial arts admixed with Confucianism. The most spirited of the younger samurai attended his classes, and were conquered by his fervent patriotism, devotion to the emperor, and belief in Japan's future greatness. From his school in Hagi, a castle town north of Shimonoseki in Choshu, came a group of men with a new understanding of Japanese history, social conditions, and political processes. Despite their unrealistic program of excluding all foreigners, they had a generally accurate view of the world —and especially of Japan's alarming insecurity as a target of imperialism. Above all, they espoused a coherent national polity and were sustained by an unshakeable conviction that it would eventually prevail.

Yoshida, one of the first major exponents of tobaku, the overthrow of the shogunate, was executed in 1859 for his part in an assassination plot against a bakufu official. But his former students intensified their efforts, in concert with loyalist samurai and ronin of other han, to topple the Tokugawa dynasty. They were ringleaders in the assaults upon foreigners and the destruction of their legations, in goading their hans' governments into defying the shogun, and inflaming antiforeign feeling within the imperial court. It was those prophets of modern militarism who established in Japan the principle, not yet disproved, that political power grows from the barrel of a gun.

Among the brightest alumni of Yoshida's school were Ito Hirobumi and Inoue Kaoru—to use the names by which they were known in later years. In May 1863, thirteen months before the events at Shimonoseki and Kagoshima, they and three other young samurai of Choshu received their daimyo's permission to leave Japan secretly in order to study in England. Their purpose in going was to acquire the knowledge necessary for carrying out their subversive plans and for strengthening the military and economic potential of Japan.

Arrangements for their passage from Yokohama were made by an English merchant, Thomas Glover, and cleared with his consulate there. The five adventurers, all in their early twenties, embarked under cover of darkness aboard a ship owned by Jardine, Matheson and Company, the most powerful trading firm in the Orient. At Shanghai they were met by Jardine's agent William Keswick (one of whose descendants is today chairman of the same company) and put aboard two London-bound sailing ships. Their intention was to learn something about navigation while enjoying the comforts of being passengers, but because they could not express themselves in English the five landlubbers were put to work as apprentice seamen aboard their respective ships.

Ito and Inoue were mortified by their demotion to coolie status and found the incessant toil and coarse food an almost unbearable hardship. Yet even in the unremitting adversity that came with sailing before the mast they never stopped thinking about the plight of Japan and, in passionate discussions, refining their plans for its salvation. Mutual support pulled them through the four-month voyage and strengthened the bonds of friendship that enabled them to weather political storms in later years, when Ito was Japan's most illustrious and longest-serving prime minister, and Inoue, statesman extraordinary, managed the nation's finances and foreign affairs while also guiding the destinies of the House of Mitsui.

A sojourn of several months in London, with visits to shipyards, arsenals, and factories, convinced the five samurai students that Japan faced a long period of development before it could compete with Western powers in either war or peace. They were aghast when news of Choshu's attacks upon foreign vessels, and of Kagoshima's ordeal, reached London. Early in 1864, as the situation in Japan worsened, they learned that an allied fleet was being assembled to attack Shimonoseki, and that Choshu's leaders were eager to accept the challenge. Ito and Inoue, hoping that they might be able to divert Choshu from such a foolhardy course, sailed for Japan without delay.

When they arrived at Yokohama they found an imposing armada of seventeen foreign warships and some seven thousand troops. Received by the British Minister, Sir Rutherford Alcock, they urged him to postpone the attack long enough for them to attempt a peace mission to Choshu. Had he known that those eloquent youths were members of the band that had burned his country's new legation less than two years previously, he would have turned them out, but their gentlemanly behavior aroused no suspicion. Because he was anxious to avoid unnecessary carnage (which would have provoked criticism from the liberals at home in Britain), Alcock decided to give them time to try their luck.

With British help Ito and Inoue landed on the shore of their native province and proceeded overland in disguise. Reaching the headquarters of Lord Mori Motonari, then in Yamaguchi, northeast of Shimonoseki, they were given an audience and spent many hours, talking over a map of the world, explaining Japan's vulnerability and the folly of Choshu's making armed resistance to overwhelmingly superior forces. The daimyo was impressed with their learning and sympathized with the appeal, but other leaders of the han remained obdurate, and even suggested that the would-be peacemakers had sold out to the enemy. At the risk of being assassinated they persisted in their arguments for several days, but to no avail. After reporting their failure to British representatives waiting aboard a warship near the Straits of Shimonoseki, they returned to Yamaguchi, heavy-hearted but fully prepared to die for Choshu.

It seemed to them that their fellow disciples of Yoshida, who were then in charge of the han's military forces and influenced the policies of its government, were caught in the grip of a suicidal mania. Not content with having twisted the lion's tail, thereby provoking certain retaliation by sea, they had decided—even as the enemy was preparing its attack—to seize the Imperial Palace by force and "liberate the emperor from his evil counselors" so that he could lead a grand offensive against the barbarians.

Buoying up the confidence of the zealots was their army, which they had revolutionized. Instead of leaving all the fighting to aristocratic swordsmen and subordinate troops armed with bows and spears, Yoshida's pupils—several of whom were to be future leaders of the nation—had recruited commoners, trained them to use rifles, and organized them into militia units, in some of which peasants marched beside samurai. The new units, called *shotai,* were led by the most radical samurai and indoctrinated with the sonno-joi philosophy of Yoshida, as well as with *Yamato damashii,* the fighting spirit of old Nippon. Shouting down the objections of wiser men, the ultraradicals won permission to send their troops to Kyoto. In August 1864 several crack units sailed up the Inland Sea to Osaka, and from there marched in full battle regalia to the outskirts of Kyoto. They took positions so close to the city that the flickering of their campfires could be seen from the watchtowers of Nijo Castle. This advance in itself indicated the impotence of the bakufu and the irresolution of the court.

Choshu's final appeal for the emperor's pardon for its earlier offenses was rejected, and its troops were ordered to withdraw. Although they were hopelessly outnumbered, the "loyalist" shotai remained defiant, remembering Yoshida's precept, "It is unworthy of a samurai to be overly concerned with the consequences when the action itself is virtuous."

They attacked fearlessly, fought with superhuman ferocity, and managed to reach the Hamaguri-mon, the "Forbidden Gate" of the palace, which only the emperor was allowed to use. There the battle raged for hours as the inhabitants of neighboring quarters fled with their portable treasures to the surrounding hills. Most of the Mitsuis' homes were in the central part of the city, just south of the Imperial Palace. Warned in advance, their households had been evacuated to safer precincts, leaving servants and guards to watch over the tightly shuttered dwellings, offices, and shops.

The Mitsui elders, informed of developments by courier, assumed that after the shooting was over the situation would settle down to what passed as normal in those chaotic days. But in the battle Choshu's guns set fire to a building within the palace compound. The imperial fire brigade was unable to function in the battle zone, and a brisk wind spread the flames, which swept southward through the heart of Kyoto.

In the conflagration some 38,000 dwellings were destroyed. Five of the six mansions of the main Mitsui families were burned to the ground, together with their business buildings. Other merchant families were similarly stricken. The disaster was not total only because persons of property kept their valuables, art objects, and documents—as they still do today—in fireproof *kura,* storehouses with thick earthen or stone walls fitted with iron doors and shutters. Thus the Mitsuis saved their account books dating back to the seventeenth century, Motoori's gifts to Takakage, and priceless paintings and scrolls that are still in their possession. There was also the cellar silver, buried deep underground. But there was no insurance on the buildings, and the financial blow was stunning.

Choshu's zealots were defeated, of course, and, after burying many of their comrades, the survivors straggled home in utter disgrace. Before they had time to recover, news came that the allied fleet had sailed from Yokohama, amid great rejoicing of its foreign inhabitants, to give Choshu a thrashing.

The blunder at Kyoto had brought the Choshu leaders to their senses, and they sent Ito Hirobumi posthaste to the allied fleet's anchorage near the entrance to the Straits of Shimonoseki to make a truce. But he arrived too late, and by midday the fleet of fifteen British, French, Dutch, and American vessels was under way. At Shimonoseki, Inoue Kaoru saw the approaching enemy warships with dismay. Choshu's artillerymen had not been informed that a truce was being sought, and they intended to start shooting as soon as the vessels came within range. It took Inoue two hours to persuade the artillery commanders to hold their fire. Then he set out in a small boat, but when he reached the allied flagship and announced that his government was ready to negotiate, he was told that the ships were already moving into battle positions and that the issue would be settled now with guns, not words.

At ten minutes past four in the afternoon of September 5, 1864, an exchange of cannonfire began the Battle of Shimonoseki. It proved to be devastating to the Choshu forts, but scarcely touched the attacking vessels. Although the straits were only a mile wide at most, the fleet was able to keep out of range and most of the defenders' shots fell short of their marks. On the third day of the battle, which wiped out Choshu's coastal defenses but cost the attackers only eight men dead and thirty wounded, Ito and Inoue came alongside the flagship to make arrangements for the daimyo's formal surrender. A week later these inseparables, whose stock had risen greatly since their abortive peace mission, assisted their superiors in negotiating the Convention of Shimonoseki, under which Choshu agreed to meet very stiff terms, including the payment of an unspecified sum as indemnity.

The Battle of Shimonoseki, which was highly instructive for Japanese patriots, had other important consequences. Choshu, by signing a pact with foreigners, had lost its claim to moral superiority over the shogunate, and its favorite cry, "expel the barbarians," became meaningless. Having entered into direct relations with foreigners, Satsuma and Choshu hastened to use their new connections as a means of intensifying pressure upon the shogun. The allies helped matters by demanding a preposterous indemnity of three million dollars, which Choshu, with its small revenues, was unable to pay. The shogunate, already sinking under the expenses of military preparations, diplomatic missions abroad, maintenance and supervision of treaty ports, and indemnities for repeated attacks on foreigners, had to assume responsibility for Choshu's debt, too.

This series of shocks, precipitated by the well-meaning Americans and aggravated by European diplomats and traders, brought despair to the chonin, whose enforced loans to the bakufu had increased beyond all reason. How the Mitsuis read those ominous signs can only be conjectured. It is improbable that they recognized the long-range benefits eventually to be gained from all this tumult. The fact that their principal role in the momentous events of the early 1860s was to keep on pouring precious gold into a bottomless bag may be sufficient to explain their ebbing loyalty to the bakufu and their eventual alliance with its most implacable enemies, the nationalists of Choshu.

 7 · The Man
from Nowhere

THE TWILIGHT OF THE SHOGUNATE, known in Japan as the *bakumatsu,* fascinates historians because it released the forces that were to modernize Japan. But for the Mitsuis it was the most harrowing time they were ever to experience. Heading the House then and for many years thereafter was Mitsui Hachiroemon Takayoshi,* eighth consecutive heir of founder Hachirobei. During his lifetime Takayoshi was called Kofuku, which means "fortunate," and he was indeed the luckiest Mitsui of all, threading his way among the pitfalls and ambushes of the bakumatsu as though personally guided by the fox deity of the Inari shrines.

An urbane and sensitive man, he was a devotee of *chanoyu,* the tea ceremony, a perceptive collector of art, and a creator of tapestrylike *sensai,* collages made from swatches of silk (an accomplishment for which later he won national recognition). His cultivation and sociability made him a welcome guest at the courts of local daimyo and a popular figure in chonin society, but the personal qualities that enabled him to emerge unscathed from the rough-and-tumble episodes of the bakumatsu upheaval are more difficult to detect.

His descendant, Mitsui Reiko, who has done intensive research in the family's history, provides one clue to his success. "Our grandfather Kofuku," she told the author, "was a broad-minded man: he had good foresight and an eye for selecting people."

It is a fact that Kofuku won a reputation for making bold and correct decisions that influenced the destiny of Japan, as well as that of the House of Mitsui. How much of the praise he may deserve is a matter of opinion, but there is no doubt that his "eye for selecting people" saved the clan in a time of confusion and panic. For without the services of Minomura Rizaemon, his personally-appointed *obanto* (literally, "great clerk," but actually chief manager), the Mitsui name would have passed into oblivion a century ago.

* The name Hachiroemon was always given by Omotokata to the Mitsui in each generation who was selected to lead the entire house. Usually Hachiroemon was the eldest son of the Kita-ke (north family), which was supreme among the hon-ke, or main families.

The astonishing changes in Minomura's fortunes and station illustrate the play of social forces that loosened feudal class ties and doomed the shogunate. If we can believe his own colorful account, Minomura was born of samurai stock yet served as a common laborer, fish-dealer's apprentice, lackey, peddler, and money-changer, before emerging in his thirties as a banker and, eventually, the most eminent business executive of his day.

In his memoirs, dictated during his later years (it is believed that he was illiterate, or nearly so), he said that his father was a samurai from northern Honshu who, having incurred the wrath of his fellow warriors, became a ronin. His only son, the future Minomura, was left an orphan at the age of seven.

After a poverty-stricken boyhood in Kyushu and Kyoto, the young man, whose original given name is unknown, but who at that time called himself Kimura, became an itinerant laborer in early adolescence. In his nineteenth year the road-weary Kimura turned up in Edo, where he found a steady job as live-in apprentice to a dealer in dried sardines. Or so he said, later in life, although a more widely accepted version stated that his employer was a money-changer. Possibly neither is true, for "the man from nowhere," as he has been called, invented many details of his past, perhaps to conceal a lowly origin or other matters he preferred to have forgotten.

Whatever his adventures may have been, he was a conscientious worker. Upon completing his apprenticeship he was recommended by his master for the position of footman at the mansion of Oguri Tadataka, a lordly retainer of the shogun. In this humble position Kimura was frequently in the company of Oguri's heir, Tadamasa,* and the two formed an affectionate and enduring relationship.

A confectioner named Minogawa Rihachi, owner of a shop called Kinokuniya, was impressed by the personality and cleverness of the young footman and offered him his daughter in marriage. Kimura accepted and thus became the yoshi, or adopted son-in-law and heir, of Minogawa. It was a step downward socially from the Oguri mansion to the confectioner's shop, but the move earned him the respectable name Minogawa no Rihachi, the first of several appellations he was to take during his climb from obscurity. Just as the Mitsuis were called Echigoya, a cognomen derived from the name of their shop in Edo, so were Rihachi and his adoptive family commonly called Kinokuniya. His job was to peddle the confections made by the family and, as he called on customers, carrying his baskets of sweets and the steelyard for weigh-

* As Lord of Bungo, Tadamasa visited the United States in 1860, a member of Japan's first diplomatic mission to the West. He also held the title of Lord of Kozuke and was commonly known as Kozukenosuke in his later years.

ing them out, he learned the rudiments of business and cultivated friendships with tradesmen. Within ten years he had accumulated enough capital and experience to go into business for himself.

In the early 1850s, at the time when Perry was organizing his first expedition to Japan, Rihachi, then thirty-two years old, bought an interest in a tiny money-exchange shop. Later in the decade he attracted the attention of Mitsui's managers by his shrewdness during the time of confusion and anxiety in the money market, as the bakufu manipulated the coinage to cope with the gold drain the foreigners were causing at Yokohama.

Rihachi suddenly showed an unaccountable interest in buying a certain type of koban (an elongated gold coin) minted in the Tempo era, a dozen years previously. When he ran out of cash he pawned his hoard to borrow funds with which he bought more Tempo koban, repeating the process as often as his capital permitted. Within a short time the bakufu, having secretly debased the currency, announced a change in rates that nearly tripled the value of Rihachi's coins.

Rihachi then got an introduction to the Mitsui ryogaeya, which, despite having the best private intelligence system in Japan, remained ignorant of the impending value change until the day it was declared. When Rihachi came in with his heavy bags of gold, a ripple of astonishment spread among the members of the ryogaeya. In a very short time his coup became known to obanto Saito Junzo, the most influential employee of the Mitsuis' Edo shop.

From then on Rihachi was a familiar figure around the Mitsui ryogaeya and was given the nickname Kinori (made from the initial sounds of Kinokuniya no Rihachi). It didn't take Saito very long to learn that Kinori was acquainted with Oguri Tadamasa, who, having succeeded his father as Lord of Bungo, was now an important official in the bakufu's accounting department. It was probably during one of Kinori's frequent visits to Oguri's home in the Kanda district of Edo, near Kinokuniya, that he had picked up the tip about the imminent revaluation of the koban.

Rihachi-Kinori's relationship with the Mitsuis during the next few years is obscure. They had no reason to trust him, because undoubtedly he was an informant for Oguri. However, their operations were predicated upon exploiting talent, gleaning advance information, and currying favor in high places. So they patronized Kinori, perhaps in the hope that he might render them a significant service some day. In this they were not mistaken, although they had to wait several years before the opportunity arrived.

While upstart Rihachi prospered in mysterious ways, the fortunes of long-established chonin continued to sag under the increasing weight of forced loans. The heaviest of those burdens fell upon the Mitsuis. At the same time, the foundations of the house were being eaten away by the termites of mismanagement. The weakest point in the structure was the Yokohama gofukuten, whose anomalous fiscal operations, instituted by Saito in 1859, have been described. Not only were the shop's dry-goods clerks playing fast and loose with public funds, but the executives too were speculating in silver and had overextended their loans to silk merchants.

Silk was the main export commodity, as the demand for both raw fiber and silkworm eggs boomed after a silkworm blight that swept through Europe in the early 1860s. The Japanese silk merchants were good risks because their guild had been granted a monopoly by the bakufu. But taking advantage of the general confusion, some silk-producing han began selling directly to foreign merchants, an arrangement that was advantageous to both parties. The bakufu, seeing its revenue threatened, imposed stricter controls, banned the export of silkworm eggs, and taxed the raw-silk traffic so heavily that producers could no longer make a profit. As a result the native silk merchants were unable to repay their debts to Echigoya.

Since the money being loaned by Echigoya at Yokohama came from customs revenues, it had to be remitted to the shogunate's treasury at regular intervals. Because of misfeasance and bad luck the shop found its shortages mounting. Officials of the bakufu treasury, aware of the unsavory situation, seem to have been using it as grounds for blackmail. When Echigoya pleaded for a reduction in the forced loans being levied upon the chonin, treasury officials hinted that unless Mitsui complied the government would demand immediate repayment of all public funds or, if necessary, would confiscate the House's assets.

Omotokata's long neglect of this dangerous condition defies understanding, unless it is assumed that Hachiroemon Kofuku was too preoccupied with the turmoil in Kyoto to supervise the operations in Edo and Yokohama. Or had he and the other Mitsui family heads composing Omotokata become too effete to cope with it? Whatever the reason, they had allowed their reserves, carefully accumulated during the centuries, to dwindle to perilously low levels.

A principal cause of the bakufu's plight, and hence that of the chonin, was the intransigence of the Choshu han, which had caused the Mitsuis such grievous losses in the Kyoto conflagration. Now at last, exhausted by three successive defeats, Choshu was easily subdued by the bakufu's forces. Yet the victorious commander, Saigo Takamori of Satsuma, was himself an ardent nationalist. In his sympathy with the loyalist cause he laid down such mild surrender terms that Choshu recovered strength rapidly. After some elaborate maneuverings by which Yoshida Shoin's disciples gained leadership in the civil affairs of the han, the formidable shotai units were again being trained for a comeback.

One of the most powerful men in the bakufu's government was Oguri Tadamasa, who, having used the knowledge gained in Philadelphia to improve Japan's coinage system, was promoted to the position of foreign affairs commissioner. Profoundly loyal to the shogun, he had been dissatisfied when Choshu was chastised so lightly after having occasioned so much distress, and he had been outraged when the han refused to accept even the mild punishment imposed upon it by Saigo. Moreover, it was no longer a secret that the new British Minister, Sir Harry Parkes, had been cultivating the friendship of Satsuma and Choshu, who were receiving contraband military equipment of advanced design from English merchants. If neglected, this smuggling could make the two han invincible.

Oguri, who was also commissioner of the army and navy, decided that no time should be lost in dealing Choshu a blow from which it would never recover. The French Minister concurred. Having improved relations with the shogunate, France had promised financial assistance and even military support against the rebellious han if they were wanted. With French help the army was being modernized, a strong fleet was being built, and a naval dockyard and foundry had been established at Yokosuka. To bring other recalcitrant daimyo back into line, the shogunate attempted to reimpose the sankin-kotai system; and as an assertion of the bakufu's authority, the shogun himself went to Osaka at the head of a large army and established his headquarters there.

In anticipation of his departure there was a flurry of business at Mitsui's Echigoya, followed by a dead calm as the bakufu's activity shifted to the Osaka region. Western diplomats were pressing relentlessly for both the opening of the port at Hyogo (now called Kobe) and the right of residence in nearby Osaka. In fact, they had offered to cancel the indemnity demanded from Choshu if those concessions were made. But the bakufu, fearing reprisals from han opposed to the opening, strained every resource and paid the first installment of 500,000 dollars at a time when preparations for the punitive expedition against Choshu were depleting the government's revenue.

Early in 1864 the Mitsuis had been squeezed for more than a million ryo. Later that spring they had to hand over more than 40,000 pounds of silver, worth 150,000 ryo. From the end of 1863 to the middle of 1866 the House was forced to "lend" the bakufu at least 3.5 million ryo. Reeling from these successive raids, Omotokata called for an emergency accounting, which revealed an appalling situation. At Yokohama

Echigoya's public-funds account showed shortages of 110,000 ryo and of 10,000 dollars in foreign silver. But forced loans to the bakufu had so depleted the central reserves that even this relatively modest sum could not be advanced by Omotokata, and the other shops could offer little assistance.

As a last recourse, Hachiroemon Kofuku instructed the Osaka gofukuten to borrow as much as possible from former clerks who had established businesses of their own. It was the common practice then, as it still is, to reward an employee for long and faithful service with the privilege and even the means of setting himself up independently in business. Naturally such assistance incurred a lasting obligation of gratitude to the original house. By an appeal to conscience, Omotokata gleaned 50,000 ryo, to be held as an emergency fund to stave off the bakufu momentarily in case it should demand immediate settlement of accounts. But the once-mighty House of Mitsui was close to ruin, for the collapse of the Edo Echigoya would undoubtedly bring down all of the affiliated shops and Omotokata as well.

Such was Mitsui's situation when in mid-August the shogun's long-awaited punitive expedition reached Choshu and launched its offensive. The enormous expense of the campaign was laid upon the backs of the merchants, of course, and the commissioner of finance—the versatile Oguri wearing yet another of his official hats—informed the Osaka exchange shop that the Mitsuis were expected to provide a loan of 500,000 ryo. This was ten times the amount held in their emergency reserve, and would mean their liquidation unless some way could be found to evade it. One possibility was to make a direct appeal to the bakufu for a remission of the levy. But this would have required Echigoya to disclose its irregularities at Yokohama, a course that might have been worse than bankruptcy.

Omotokata had a number of very sound excuses for a delay and used them successfully. While the matter was still under deliberation, Oguri hit upon a plan for mitigating the financial panic brought on by the Choshu campaign. His solution was to lend Edo's merchants the revenues from the customs office at Yokohama, accepting their inventories as collateral. The Mitsuis (who had made such a mess of government business in the foreign settlement) were ordered to handle the disbursements. This assignment terrified Omotokata. Already close to insolvency from too much government business, the House wanted no further entanglement with the unpredictable bakufu.

It is true that they had prospered from their government commissions in good times, but now, in bad times, the hazards were too great. Of the junin-gumi, the ten fiscal agents appointed in the 1690s, all but a few had gone bankrupt. Bankers who survived the bad times—and of those Mitsui, Ono, Shimada, and Konoike were the most conspicuous—had become so cautious about loans and credits that lesser merchants were starved for operating funds. Therefore the fulfillment of Oguri's plan to advance loans against merchandise was imperative if the total collapse of Edo's economy was to be prevented. Furthermore, the Mitsuis' peculiar situation made it suicidal for them to antagonize Oguri by refusing to cooperate.

Only a miracle could extricate them from the tightening jaws of the trap in which they were caught, and it was obanto Saito Junzo of Echigoya who achieved it when he enlisted the services of "Kinori-san." Doing so took no great imagination, since Kinokuniya Rihachi was a regular client of the Edo exchange shop and personally acquainted with its director, Mitsui Jiroemon Takaakira, whom he sometimes accompanied on jaunts to the countryside or to house parties at the estates of minor daimyo.

It was not in keeping with Mitsui's dignity to ask favors of an upstart like Rihachi. But his influence with the commissioner of finance meant much more than dignity, so Saito swallowed his pride and paid a visit to Rihachi. The details of their conversation are unrecorded, but there is little doubt that he sought Rihachi's advice, as well as his intervention with Oguri. According to one story, Rihachi was deeply touched by the plight of his colleagues and by Saito's trust in him. It is probable, however, that the ambitious banker set a very high price upon his services, for what he got from them was far beyond any offer the Mitsuis had ever dreamed of making.

Until then Rihachi had been a stranger to most of the family, so it was decided in Edo that he be taken to Kyoto by two high-ranking banto to present his plan, or at least the part of it that could be discussed. In the presence of Hachiroemon Kofuku and five other family heads, Rihachi modestly explained his precedent-shattering scheme. In order to prevent a repetition of past errors, he maintained, the exchange business, and private lending as well, should be separated from the Echigoya gofukuten. Furthermore, all government commissions should be handled by a separate *goyodokoro,* or official business establishment, placed directly under the supervision of Omotokata. In other words, the monolithic house was to be divided, so that if a failure occurred in one line of business, as seemed more than possible, the other branches need not be dragged down with it.

Rihachi made a favorable impression, and the merit of his idea was generally recognized. But the condition proposed by Saito through his envoys—that Rihachi be appointed manager of the goyodokoro—seemed impossible to accept. A Japanese business house rarely employed "outsiders" for such important jobs, which were entrusted only to men who had entered the firm in youth and worked their way up the ladder under the scrutiny of their elders. This tradition is so deeply ingrained that it persists today.

Yet none of the Mitsuis wanted to handle the risky government business at such a time, and who but Rihachi would be both able enough and acceptable to the commissioner of finance? Then, too, they must have thought, this new man might somehow work upon Oguri's sympathies to reduce the amounts of the loans he had levied.

The decision rested with Hachiroemon, who had been meditating upon the House's vicissitudes and probably had refreshed his memory concerning its constitution. According to one article of that respected document, the essential role of a manager was to guard the business of the House, give appropriate advice if the master erred, and correct blunders already made. But his obanto had become careless, given unsound advice, and compounded their masters' errors. Perhaps this bold Rihachi, who had improved his fortune while all about him others were losing theirs, would be able to set matters aright.

Hachiroemon realized, too, that he had been remiss in observing the article which instructed the masters to keep an eye upon talented younger men, "without any oversights," and to train the most promising of them as managers. Because of his carelessness the House had no obanto of sufficient mettle to save it now in time of trial. Could Rihachi prevent the ultimate disaster? It was the obvious intention of the founder that younger men of talent be drawn from the regular staff, but the employment of an outsider, even one in middle age, was not definitely prohibited. After considering the unknown perils that still lay ahead, Hachiroemon decided that Rihachi was indispensable and appointed him, at the age of forty-five, as manager of the proposed goyodokoro.

The minutes of the Omotokata meeting at which this decision was made are prosaic enough. Dated November 2, 1866, the entry states that two banto of the Edo exchange house "accompanied a man named Minogawa Rihachi, who was appointed in charge of this matter," after having been duly evaluated. But a letter dispatched to Edo by special messenger indicates that the conference touched upon some points too delicate to be put into writing. Announcing the departure of Rihachi and his companions from Kyoto, the writer confided: "It will take twelve days on the Tokaido. If they arrive [in Edo] safely, they will tell you the secret details of the matters we have discussed, so please be alert."[1]

Through this chain of circumstances Kinokuniya Minogawa Rihachi, born Kimura, and also known as Minogawa Kinori, won his unprecedented appointment, as well as a permanent name. For his exalted position among merchants and his association with the men in power, the "man from nowhere" needed a new name that would conceal his plebeian past. Perhaps as an encouragement to loyalty, he was permitted to take *mi,* the first character of Mitsui. To that he added *no* from Minogawa (the name of his adoptive father), and *mura* from Kimura (the name of his real father). And he changed his given name to Rizaemon, which he felt was more dignified than Rihachi. So equipped, and with the prayerful backing of his new employers, Minomura Rizaemon proceeded to shore up the decrepit House of Mitsui against the rising typhoon of the bakumatsu.

8 · Picking the Winner

OFTEN, AFTER A WAR, those who failed to support the winning side openly claim to have done so secretly and spare no pains to prove that they had preferred the victors even before the war began. In the wake of the Meiji revolution Japan's leading merchants and their claques made a case that, although their houses had been formally allied with the shogunate and favored by it, their true sympathies of course had always been with the imperial court.

The Mitsuis' protestations of prior loyalty to the emperor were perhaps the most convincing. Since the days of Hachirobei they had been Kyoto people at heart, registering the births of their children and burying their dead there. They contributed regularly and in seemly amounts to the festivals for which the capital was famous. They financed the imperial court's modest projects for construction and improvement whenever the bakufu's dole was inadequate; and when the great Imperial Palace burned in 1855 they supplied a large part of the funds for rebuilding it. They also made much of the fact that they had been patrons of Motoori Norinaga, greatest of the national scholars. "Motoori and his followers breathed into large numbers of their countrymen the spirit of devotion to the Imperial Family and the exaltation of the Japanese genius,"[1] as E. H. Norman wrote, and are given much of the credit for the eventual overthrow of the shogunate and the abolition of feudalism.

Of more immediate significance were the cash contributions the Mitsuis and other chonin made to the emperor's cause. Most historians agree that those were voluntary, but a noted Japanese economic scholar, Honjo Eijiro, while admitting that the wars of the restoration were fought and won with funds supplied by the chonin, insisted that they were obtained by coercion.[2] There is evidence to support both opinions, but common sense leads to the conclusion that the chonin (like their counterparts in Europe, the Fuggers and Rothschilds, and like the Rockefellers and Morgans in the United States) made a practice of establishing themselves in the favor of more than one contender for power. The record shows clearly that the Mitsuis, whatever their sentiments may have been, kept their main stake upon the bakufu's number until the very end of the Tokugawa regime, although they were hedging with substantial side bets laid upon the opposition.

Unfortunately for the facts of Japanese history, the prudence of the people involved and the high incidence of natural disasters in Japan have removed all but a few traces of the Mitsuis' collaboration in the intrigues attending the collapse of the bakufu. Records were kept; and some of them must have been dangerously revealing, because a number of those relating to the gestation and birth of Japan's capitalist economy were secretly entrusted by the Mitsuis to Minomura Rizaemon. They remained under seal, presumably unread, in the Minomura family's storehouse in Tokyo until 1923, when it was destroyed by the Kanto earthquake.

It is probable that no man outside the government knew more about the clandestine transactions during the bakumatsu and the Meiji upheaval than did Minomura. As the brain behind Japan's most influential private enterprise and the commander of its resources, he extended his investigations into the highest circles of both the court and the shogunate and was also privy to the machinations of those who, in truth, managed to usurp the power of both. Undoubtedly the documents in his possession would have helped to interpret the reasons for some of the almost incredible events that took place in those crucial years. But because the exposure of certain state or private secrets would have unraveled the fabric of the carefully woven Meiji mythology and incurred the wrath of the personages whose power and wealth were supported by it, the evidence had to be suppressed.

In partial compensation for that loss, the Mitsuis' passion for compiling business information, and their orderliness and exactitude in recording it, have left a voluminous collection of ledgers, letters, instructions, agreements, and chronicles that miraculously have escaped both natural and man-made disasters. From these sources it is known that the Mitsuis had established business relations of long standing with the antishogunate Satsuma and Choshu han and were acquainted with a number of their agents or stewards. In 1866, for example, two prominent Satsuma loyalists—Saigo Takamori and Komatsu Takewaki— called at the Mitsui's main shop in Kyoto. As a pretext they asked to examine a rare piece of Chinese calligraphy known to be in Hachiroemon's possession. Saburosuke's chief clerk, recalling the incident, wrote that the two samurai were extremely polite to Hachiroemon, as if talking with their master. Thereafter relations between Mitsui and the Satsuma loyalists deepened. Other names appearing in the Mitsui's visitors' books of those years, without comment as to the nature of their business, were those of Goto Shojiro, a retainer of the Kochi han and later a cabinet minister; Mutsu Munemitsu, a samurai of the Kii han who was to serve with distinction as foreign minister; that redoubtable pair, Inoue Kaoru and Ito Hirobumi of Choshu; and court noble Prince Iwakura Tomomi. All these men performed indispensable services in overthrowing the bakufu, and their visits to the Mitsuis became more frequent as the crisis approached.

Of greatest importance was Iwakura, the ringleader of loyalist plotters in Kyoto. Having served the emperor as a page, he had risen to influence in court circles. Then, for his role in arranging the marriage of the emperor's sister to the shogun, he had incurred the wrath of the radicals at court. Accused of being a bakufu sycophant, he had been ordered into seclusion for five years. Like most of the kuge, he had a very small income. To supplement it, he turned his residence into a gambling den, taking advantage of the fact that the kuge were not subject to search by the bakufu. This sideline brought him into contact with wandering gamblers, many of whom were loyalist ronin, who may have converted him to radicalism. At any event, he became an eager conspirator, and with such a clientele he was able to conduct espionage and possibly guerrilla-type operations all over Japan.

The banished prince still had lines of communication extending into the imperial court—indeed, into the emperor's bedchamber—for working closely with him was the kuge Nakayama Tadayasu, whose daughter Yoshiko was his majesty's favorite concubine and the mother of his son Mutsuhito. Iwakura was linked most strongly with the han of Choshu, but he also maintained close contact with Satsuma through Okubo Toshimichi, who, with his boyhood friend Saigo Takamori, was rapidly gaining control over that han's affairs. It was recognized that those two han had enough power to overthrow the bakufu if only they would work together. Unfortunately, Choshu's radicals hated their Satsuma rivals, and the feud seemed irreconcilable. Iwakura, helped by ronin friendly to both sides (and independently by the British diplomats and merchants), worked tirelessly to effect a reconciliation. In 1866 the two contending han reached an agreement—the so-called Sat-Cho alliance—that meant doom for the Tokugawas.

This alliance was concluded by Okubo, Saigo, Komatsu, and Kido Koin. These men, with their Satsuma-Choshu comrades and a few others from the han of Aki, Tosa, and Hizen, were the ones who organized and executed the coup that overthrew the shogunate, and who monopolized the top positions in the new government for several decades afterward. Whatever the significance of the fact may be, nearly all of them are known to have been in consultation with the Mitsuis or their banto during the three years preceding the Meiji revolution, which is misleadingly called a "restoration."

It was the policy of the Mitsuis not to skimp when the stakes were high. Having appraised these patriots and their chances of success, the House treated them generously. One chronicler, writing in the 1930s, stated: "When we look at swordplay on the stage and screen, we often forget where the money came from. But even loyalists of the Meiji Restoration could not live without eating, so expenses for their livelihoods alone must have been great. Besides, expenses for their punishing the bakufu and paying geisha . . . were enormous. Of course Satsuma and Choshu had funds, but wealthy merchants, including the Mitsuis were behind them."[3]

Minomura's relationships with those dissident samurai and nobles before he joined Mitsui are not clear, but it is significant that their connection with the house became conspicuous in the year he was appointed obanto. One of his descendants said that Minomura was quite close to those statesmen-to-be and that when they visited Mitsui he was the one with whom they usually conferred. To preserve secrecy, Minomura would take his visitors for a walk in the garden, where they could converse without fear of eavesdroppers, for spies lurked everywhere and most of the matters being discussed would have been extremely compromising.

Minomura's connections with the loyalist samurai and nobles kept the Mitsuis well informed about their activities and plans. At the same time Minomura himself was a valuable source of information about the bakufu, inasmuch as his position as chief of Mitsui's new office for handling official funds brought him into frequent contact with Lord Oguri in Edo.

Another source of useful intelligence was Mutsu Munemitsu, a retainer of Lord Kii, who was a member of the Tokugawa family. While completing his studies in Kyoto, Mutsu had been living as a *shosei*—a combination houseboy and protégé—in the household of Mitsui Saburosuke Takaaki, heir of Hachiroemon Kofuku. Mutsu also had an entree at nearby Nijo Castle, the shogun's headquarters in Kyoto.

Commanding as he did these and other important sources of intelligence, Minomura may have been as well informed about the developing situation as were the conspirators themselves; and he surely knew more than the bakufu did, despite its elaborate espionage network. There is nothing in all this to prove that Mitsui-gumi was an active party to the loyalist conspiracy, but this is precisely the kind of information that would have been most carefully concealed by the Mitsuis and their friends, for obvious reasons. Furthermore, the rewards that Mitsui ultimately received from the successful plotters were far out of proportion to their recorded contributions. These facts and probabilities lead to speculation that the Mitsuis may have been more deeply involved in the revolution than is commonly supposed.

The Mitsuis' motives can be guessed from an appraisal of the situation in which they were caught. It will be recalled that Minomura's friend Oguri, minister of the armed forces, had risked everything upon sending a second punitive expedition against Choshu. But the campaign went badly from the start because the men of Choshu had been armed with modern weapons and ships by the British and because Satsuma (presumably the mainstay of the bakufu) was in secret alliance with Choshu. In 1866 the bakufu's forces, which had been sent to chastise Choshu, were being defeated ignominiously on all fronts. The death of Shogun Tokugawa Iemochi in September gave the bakufu a pretext for suspending hostilities without admitting defeat. But the shogunate's government was left in perilous condition, having to load the costs of demobilizing the punitive expedition upon an already prostrate economy. (It was soon after Iemochi's death that Lord Oguri imposed upon Mitsui the forced loan of 500,000 ryo, and designated the House to administer the relief loans in Edo.)

Meanwhile, a shortage of food and consequent price increases attributed to speculation provoked riots in Edo. Led by priests, angry mobs attacked money-changers and merchants of rice and sakè. In November, immediately after Minomura Rizaemon returned to Edo from Kyoto with his new name and position, a terrible conflagration razed the greater part of Yokohama, including the customs house from which he was to draw funds for those relief loans to distressed merchants. Less than three weeks later another fire gutted the Nihombashi district in Edo, destroying so many structures that, someone calculated, if they had been placed side by side they would have extended more than thirty miles.

The losses to Mitsui must have been severe. But the confusion resulting from those events, compounded by a reorganization in the bakufu accompanying the accession of a new shogun, gave the Mitsuis a good excuse for further delay in paying the money demanded by Lord Oguri. Then, early in 1867, while the populace was observing the New Year holidays, the death of Emperor Komei again plunged the nation into official mourning, during which time business was suspended.

The cause of Komei's death is still a moot point among historians. A most knowledgeable British diplomat, Sir Ernest Satow, recalled in his memoirs, published in 1921: "Rumour attributed the decease to small-pox, but several years later I was assured by a Japanese well acquainted with what went on behind the scenes that he had been poisoned. He was by conviction utterly opposed to any concessions to foreigners, and had therefore been removed out of the way by those who foresaw that the coming downfall of the *Baku-fu* would force the court into direct relations with foreign powers."[4] Another possible motive for assassination lay in the fact that Emperor Komei was favorably disposed toward the new shogun, Tokugawa Hitotsubashi Keiki, and therefore would not approve the extreme antibakufu policy of the loyalists.

Japanese historians today generally believe that the "smallpox" responsible for the emperor's untimely death at the age of thirty-seven was actually a poison administered at the behest of Prince Iwakura.* The evidence to support this belief is scanty, but the motives that make it probable are compelling: for example, the replacement of Komei by the pliable fourteen-year-old Prince Mutsuhito, who could be dominated by radicals opposed to the bakufu, enabled the Sat-Cho allies to obtain the "imperial edicts" they needed for legitimizing their subsequent coup d'état.

In any event, although no one would accuse the Mitsuis of having taken a part in the regicide, the death of Emperor Komei marked the turning point in their declining fortunes.

It might appear from all this that the Mitsuis were committed to the imperial cause. Yet the fact remains that even while they were intensifying their collusion with the loyalists they were also keeping in the good graces of the bakufu. When the fifty-day period of mourning for the dead emperor was over, Minomura paid a visit to his benefactor Oguri and presented a letter of proxy from Hachiroemon Kofuku. There is no record of his arguments for the bakufu's leniency toward his employers in the matter of that enforced loan of 500,000 ryo, but as one of Mitsui's clerks noted cryptically, "not a small amount of money was spent on the project." Regardless of pecuniary inducements, however, Oguri stood to gain more from a viable and grateful House of Mitsui than from an embittered bankrupt one, especially since he needed its help in a new financial maneuver. So he graciously reduced the amount of the levy from half a million ryo to a mere 180,000 ryo, payable in easy installments. He also led Minomura to understand that no further loans would be demanded for the time being. No issue was made, apparently, of the missing customs-house revenues at the Yokohama office of Echigoya, and the name of Mitsui remained immaculate.

Correspondence pursuant to this transaction indicates that it was

---

* *The Japan Biographical Encyclopedia, 1964–65* (pp. 2011–12) states that Prince Iwakura "is said to have engineered the murder by poisoning of Emperor Komei, whose antiforeign stand was the only great obstacle to the ultimate opening of the country to foreign intercourse."

unorthodox, to say the least. A letter, addressed to "the Honorable Commissioner" (presumably intended for Oguri's underlings) and endorsed by Minomura Rizaemon, warned: "We hereby acknowledge the submission of the written authorization, which was duly forwarded to [o]motokata-sama.

"However, we were secretly ordered that if the above mentioned matter of a pardon should leak out to the general public, those involved with the use of the seal will be affected, so that each one of you should keep it in mind never to let it be known outside; it should only be known among us."[5]

After this triumph Minomura enjoyed the full confidence of the Mitsuis, and because he was usually at hand when important matters were discussed people called him "Hachiroemon's shadow." By his masterful organization and management, the goyodokoro—which he eventually developed into Mitsui Bank—soon showed enough profit to salvage other branches of the business. The worst of the storm had been weathered, but the trickiest sailing lay ahead.

The new shogun's progressive reforms, especially his modernization of the bakufu's military forces, dismayed the rebels. Prince Iwakura wrote: "The actions of the present Shogun Keiki are resolute, courageous and of great aspiration; he is a strong enemy not to be despised."[6] And Kido Koin warned: "If the opportunity to restore court government is now lost, and the lead is taken by the bakufu, then it will truly be as if one were seeing the rebirth of Ieyasu."[7] The British, who had done so much to strengthen Keiki's enemies, now reconsidered their strategy. If the shogun proved able to meet their requests, there would be no point in fomenting rebellion against him. Also they feared losing ground to the French, who were endeavoring to make Keiki's regime a success.

Minomura Rizaemon, too, was fully aware of these possibilities. And like the British minister, he had not become so deeply involved with the loyalists that retreat was impossible. Furthermore, the Mitsuis were more heavily obligated than ever to the bakufu and carefully avoided any show of ingratitude. Rizaemon, objectively studying his intelligence reports, saw that the shogunate was by no means to be counted out, and he was prepared to greet a victory by either side.

Lord Oguri did not hesitate to take advantage of the Mitsuis' indebtedness to him. In great need of funds, he ended the centuries-old ban on paper money and ordered the issue of notes convertible to gold, for local circulation. But with public confidence in the bakufu at a low ebb, he needed the good name of Mitsui to ensure acceptance of the gold notes. Thus redemption of the bakufu's first paper money was guaranteed by Mitsui-gumi, which in effect served as a national bank for the Tokugawa regime while at the same time financing arrangements for its overthrow. It was through such opportunism that the House earned the nickname "double-dealing Mitsui," applied for decades afterward whenever a Mitsui-controlled company was caught in equivocal business dealings.

Despite the favorable impression he had made on the foreigners, the new shogun was unable to establish his influence over the daimyo, without whose troops he could not hope to remain in power. And after the accession of Prince Mutsuhito to the imperial throne, with the style and title of Emperor Meiji, the court radicals, under the guidance of Iwakura, accelerated their machinations to seize control of the nation.

Only then did the Mitsuis show any overt sign of dissidence. In preparing for the opening of Hyogo port, Lord Oguri organized the Hyogo Shosha, Japan's first joint-stock company after the European pattern. Its function was to conduct foreign trade and to issue more paper money to finance the port's operations. Leading merchants were invited to participate, and the most prominent, Mitsui Hachiroemon, was appointed president of the company. Mitsui goyodokoro had no alternative but to handle the currency issue, but upon Minomura's advice Hachiroemon declined the honor of heading the trading firm or of investing in it. As a result, subscriptions by other merchants were so paltry that the company was stillborn. Mitsui's refusal to take the lead was in perfect accord with the position of Prince Iwakura and his Sat-Cho cohorts, who privately favored opening Osaka and Hyogo to foreign trade but fought to prevent that from happening as long as the bakufu remained in power.

Since the founding of their House it had been the standing policy of the Mitsuis to show special respect to the lords of Kii, whose patronage at one time had been of great value. For centuries they had observed the custom of greeting ceremoniously the incumbent daimyo of Kii whenever he visited Kyoto. But Lord Kii was a Tokugawa, and as the Mitsuis veered toward an openly neutral position they abandoned the ancient formality. When Hachiroemon Kofuku was accused of disrespect for doing so, he pleaded ill-health and begged Lord Kii's forgiveness, but with that unmistakable neglect of duty the alienation of the House of Mitsui from the Tokugawas was declared, most subtly.

In the autumn of 1867 the richly variegated foliage in the gardens of Nijo Castle brought no joy to the young shogun. He knew that despite his earnest efforts he had failed, and it came as no surprise to him when, late in October, he was presented with a thoughtfully worded memorial. Composed by some of the more moderate imperialists of the Tosa han, it recommended that he resign his position for the sake of peace. "There is endless merit in a man's knowing when to have done," Carlyle had written, and Keiki showed this merit to a creditable degree. In November he announced his decision to yield the reins of government to his sovereign. Assuming responsibility for the unhappy situation which had developed since the foreigners had entered the country, he said, ". . . if authority is restored to the Emperor, and matters of high policy are decided by His Majesty after national deliberations, then by unity of thought and effort the country can hold its own with all the nations of the world."[8]

The change was not to be made in such a gentlemanly way, however. The men about to take charge, although most of them were still in their youth, were seasoned soldiers bearing the scars of battles and skirmishes in which they had lost many of their comrades. They were not content with a resignation that left the bakufu in charge of the nation's administration, even temporarily, and the Tokugawa family in possession of vast domains from the wealth of which they could rebuild their power. The Sat-Cho loyalists were determined to smash the Tokugawa's bakufu system from top to bottom, and had made elaborate plans to do just that. Their campaign to seize control was already under way, and gaining irresistible momentum.

In July of 1867 the Sat-Cho leaders had met at Prince Iwakura's residence, signed a pact to carry out a coup d'état, and begun to train their armed forces intensively for this purpose. Early in November, when they learned of Keiki's impending resignation, they sent Okubo posthaste to Iwakura with a petition asking the emperor for authorization to overthrow the bakufu. Through Prince Nakayama, the emperor's grandfather and tutor, Iwakura received written orders to this effect and passed them secretly to the Satsuma and Choshu leaders. By the time Keiki announced his resignation as shogun, crack troops of both clans were on their way to Kyoto, where units of several sympathetic daimyo were stationed to "protect" the court. Thus already there was in existence an "imperial army," and serving it discreetly as quartermaster was the House of Mitsui—which was still official purveyor and banker to the dying bakufu.

Since the bakufu still held the nation's purse strings, as well as its administrative offices, the court could do nothing with its hypothetical power. As the first anniversary of the late Emperor Komei's death approached, Prince Iwakura requested funds from Shogun Keiki, who was still in residence at Nijo Castle in Kyoto, ostensibly for the purpose of conducting appropriate memorial services. But all he could get from the shogun's treasurer, Lord Oguri, was a pittance of one thousand ryo, so he hit upon another stratagem. On December 23, as the Choshu forces were approaching Kyoto, he organized a "donation-accepting office," or *kinkoku suitosho*. Its real purpose became apparent three days later, when an imperial messenger came to the imposing new residence of Mitsui Saburosuke, head of the exchange house in Kyoto, with a notice that read: "As the shogunate returned the reins of government to the emperor . . . the imperial court is taking over national administration. Since the shogunate has yet to hand over the state treasury, however, the imperial court is without savings, so a procurement office is being set up. . . . There is every indication that fighting may break out at any time between the imperial and shogunate forces, and a shortage of money for general expenses and military funds is feared. Your organization has long been providing exchange service for the imperial court. You are requested to take charge of the procurement office. You must make every effort in the imperial cause."[9]

This blunt demand, unsigned but presumably sent by Iwakura's order, made it necessary at last for the House of Mitsui to declare full and open allegiance to one side or the other, and a family conference was convened immediately. Since Minomura already had acquainted his employers with the situation and declared his intention to part from Lord Oguri once and for all, there was little need for discussion. The time for dissimulation was over, and it was agreed that Mitsui would back the imperial side exclusively.

Saburosuke was ready when a representative of the "imperial treasury" (which did not exist) called at his mansion late that evening with a summons to appear at the palace. He was wearing his formal kimono embellished with the "four eyes" of the Sasaki crest, and as he stepped into the palanquin provided for him he carried a heavy parcel wrapped, as is the custom, in a heavy silk cloth. Escorted by lantern bearers and swordsmen clad in armor, he was borne to the appointed place and was received almost obsequiously by court officials. They offered him, as head of the Kyoto Mitsui-gumi, the position of exchange agent for the imperial government. They also requested him to take charge of the organization for soliciting donations for the court. Showing the humility proper to his status as a chonin, Saburosuke accepted the appointments gracefully. Then he unwrapped the lacquered box he had brought. It contained one thousand gold ryo—quite probably the first private gift offered to the new imperial government.

Saburosuke's assigned task was to solicit funds from Ono-gumi and Shimada-gumi, who were still reluctant to provoke the bakufu by aiding its enemies. Meanwhile the "donation-accepting office" had been set up at one gate of the Imperial Palace, and other wealthy people were contributing to it. Kumagaya Kyuemon, a merchant friend of Prince Iwakura, gave one thousand ryo and one hundred and fifty pairs of *futon,* or padded sleeping quilts, for the soldiers then swarming into the city. A temple in Nara sent one thousand bales of rice, and the powerful Buddhist temple Nishi Hongan-ji in Kyoto donated three thousand ryo. The general public also helped, supplying ten thousand pairs of straw sandals, several thousand rice bowls, and quantities of foodstuffs, raw cotton, and charcoal. These voluntary gifts amounted to nearly forty thousand ryo in cash, in addition to contributions in kind; in contrast, Ono and Shimada, merchants whose prestige was overshadowed only by Mitsui's, made a "poor mouth" and produced only one thousand ryo between them. Their parsimony then was to become a cause for intense regret later.

Since 1864 the Choshu army had been banished from Kyoto, and obediently, it remained encamped outside the city. But on the second day of 1868, by the old calendar, the government of the Choshu han was pardoned by imperial decree, and Kido Koin led its troops triumphantly into Kyoto on the following day. Meanwhile Iwakura summoned several fence-straddling daimyo to a conference at which he revealed the existence of the emperor's orders to overthrow the bakufu, thereby gaining their support. According to prearranged plan, the loyalist units surrounded the palace as Saigo and Kido displayed their authorization to relieve the shogun's forces then on guard. Inside the palace Iwakura, in the presence of the bewildered boy-emperor, proclaimed the "Imperial Restoration," together with the decision that Hitotsubashi Keiki, the fifteenth and the last of the Tokugawa shoguns, was to relinquish all his positions and titles and that the Tokugawa family, except for those few of its members who had sided with the loyalists, was to surrender its vast domains to the imperial court.

Incredibly, this decree was accepted by the shogun, who withdrew from Nijo Castle with his disgruntled followers a few days later and headed for Osaka. Nijo Castle was promptly occupied by troops of the imperial government, now under the control of princes Iwakura and Sanjo Sanetomi, a few hereditary retainers of the rebel clans, and a dozen "country samurai" from Satsuma, Choshu, and neighboring provinces.

This was very convenient for the newly appointed court bankers, the Mitsuis, who established their headquarters at Saburosuke's mansion just across the moat from Nijo Castle. The fact that the Mitsuis and their hired manager-general, Minomura, were personally acquainted with most if not all of the "honorable men in power" was even more gratifying.

There was one serious weakness in their position, however: with a war of unknown dimensions looming, the honorable men in power needed enormous sums of money, immediately. And the Mitsuis, who had been trying so hard for so long to be relieved of all official business, now found themselves saddled with the obligation to refill the new government's nearly empty treasury.

9 · By Appointment to the Emperor

ON THE FIRST DAY OF YEAR ONE of the Meiji era,* the Mitsui households, having suspended all business activities for the long New Year holidays, gathered at their respective mansions for quiet celebration, rest, and communion with the spirits of their ancestors. But the customary silence of Kyoto was broken by the tread of marching feet, the pounding of hooves, and the rumbling of wheels over cobblestones, as the emperor's soldiers rushed to defend Kyoto from approaching enemies. The shogun, yielding to the protestations of his retainers and loyal daimyo who were determined to fight for the wealth and power to which they were accustomed, had mobilized an army at Osaka. His forces, which outnumbered the emperor's troops by five to one, were marching on Kyoto, and a long siege was expected.

The imperial army lacked almost everything except zeal, but such was the strength of custom that Yuri Kimimasa, Iwakura's financial assistant in charge of "accepting donations," had locked his office and taken his customary five-day New Year's furlough. In consequence, the feasting at Mitsui Saburosuke's home was interrupted by the arrival of a messenger from the court, who presented an urgent request for money. The Mitsui men withdrew reluctantly to the countinghouse, where, late into the night, the jingle of coins and the clicking of soroban could be heard—perhaps punctuated by an occasional sigh as Saburosuke watched the firm's "cellar silver" depleted once again to protect a risky investment. Before dawn of the second day a squad of soldiers commanded by a young artillery captain arrived with a handcart and hauled the treasure—about two thousand ryo—to imperial army headquarters.

This, and presumably similar contributions from other merchants, enabled the imperial troops—aided by superior organization and tactics—to rout the bakufu's army in the brief but decisive battle fought at Toba and Fushimi, just south of Kyoto. Victory gave them a breathing spell to consolidate their forces and enough prestige to command

---

* According to the lunar calendar, but late in January of 1868 by the Western style of reckoning.

support in western Japan while gathering strength for conquering Edo and the north. But the war was just beginning, and the need for money was crucial. To rely upon public generosity at that juncture would have been fatuous, and the "donation-accepting office" regressed to the bakufu's favorite expedient of extracting forced loans. Announcing this detested policy as tactfully as possibly, Yuri Kimimasa ordered the following proclamation to be posted:

"Concerning the Restoration, various preparations have been made but financial difficulties remain. In case of necessity, the government will conduct an investigation, so everyone is requested to keep money on hand. Therefore, you are advised to refrain from transferring large sums of cash.

January, 1868, The Imperial Donation-Accepting Office"[1]

This was actually the declaration of a moratorium on financial transactions, intended to freeze the funds of merchants so they could be commandeered by the emperor's government. It was aimed directly at the Mitsuis, who were most active in the money-order business. For if Mitsui-gumi were to cash all notes presented for payment it would be short of funds needed for the financial operations of the imperial court. The Mitsuis had the unhappy task of trying to convince other cynical merchants that the new forced loans, unlike those of the bakufu, would be paid back sometime, somehow. Whether or not anyone believed them, they managed to collect more than four hundred thousand ryo, enough to meet emergency needs. In appreciation, the accounting magistrate treated Mitsui Saburosuke to a repast at which mutual loyalty was pledged in sakè. Grateful at having survived yet another financial ordeal and having saved face once again, the Mitsuis, together with the Shimadas and the Onos, donated an additional ten thousand ryo on the following day.

But the moratorium was only a stopgap measure. Immediately after the Battle of Toba and Fushimi, Prince Iwakura called a business meeting attended by Okubo, Yuri Kimimasa, and other ministers to establish a real treasury. Most of them, unaccustomed to handling money, were thinking in very small terms. But Yuri, who had been entrusted with managing the new government's finances, entertained grander ideas. He reasoned that since there were three million households in Japan the nation should be able to raise three million ryo without difficulty. This hypothesis being agreed upon, they worked out a plan to extract that sum—not from the people as a whole but from wealthy merchants. After thinking about the criteria of wealth, they decided: "In foreign countries, those who possess two steamships and fifty boats are considered merchants of ordinary scale."[2]

To reassure the chonin, they promised: "In the Meiji Restoration, those houses who remain loyal will surely prosper." But since disloyalty would be a national disgrace, the names of the leading mercantile houses were to be placed upon the rolls of possible donors, just as a precaution. Three books listing the rich chonin of Kyoto, Omi, and Osaka were prepared by Mitsui, serving as the government's informant. On this basis Yuri summoned one hundred merchants who were considered best able to contribute and apprised them of their duty.

Mitsui-gumi was offered the privilege of collecting the money from the other houses but was not very confident of success. After some preliminary inquiries Saburosuke submitted the following letter to the imperial court:

"Be it known, with due reverence:

"We hereby accept your honorable order. We shall do our best, although three million ryo is a great sum. As ordered, we shall try to collect from both the upper and lower categories. But among the famous Osaka merchants there are many whose shops are closed, or their businesses suspended. So please consider this to avoid unpopularity. Since we are officially appointed money-changers, we have often lent money [to the court]. We shall try to persuade those who are not willing."[3]

There seems to be no authentic record of the results of this squeeze, but according to one account it was oversubscribed in less than a year. The creation of such a large national "loan" in the face of widespread distrust of the new government was an impressive demonstration of Mitsui's influence. Although the claim has never been made, the name of Mitsui seems to have been as potent a symbol in the financial world as was that of the imperial house in the political realm. This may explain why, time after time, tottering Mitsui enterprises were rescued from collapse by the bakufu, as well as by its successor regime.

These high-handed maneuvers of the imperial government caused much anguish and not infrequent ruin among the merchant class, but for some chonin the benefits far outweighed the losses. For example, early in 1868 the leading houses of Mitsui, Ono, and Shimada were appointed to manage the collection and disbursement of tax revenues, a privilege that enabled them to extend their business activities and, no less important, to use tax funds on hand for supporting current operations. Thus even when their own liquid capital declined to the vanishing point, they were able to recoup swiftly by deft manipulation of public money.

To the people outside Kyoto the existence of an imperial government was no more than a rumor because it had not yet shown its face in the provinces and the countryside. Hoping to project an image of power, Iwakura organized a *chimbu,* or pacification expedition, not to use force against the people but just to let them know that the government had the means of doing so whenever it might be necessary. Five thousand troops marched off in splendid array from Kyoto, but ran out of funds almost immediately. Iwakura could not requisition money or supplies from the people along the route without losing face, so he appealed to the Mitsuis. They supplied several thousand ryo, but took the precaution of assigning to the chimbu two accountants as quartermasters. As the expedition moved eastward by fits and starts those unhappy banto spent most of their time traveling back to Kyoto with empty strongboxes and rejoining the hungry troops with full ones.

Zigzagging through central Honshu, the chimbu crossed the mountains and approached Edo, the stronghold of pro-Tokugawa sentiment, where Iwakura hoped to make the greatest impression. Encamped on the Musashi plains, his men were only a day's march from Edo, ready to occupy it when the circumstances permitted. But again, to his discomfiture, supplies ran short, and the imperial troops could not very well have entered the city as beggars. Lacking any alternative, he issued an order to the Mitsui clerks for a thousand bales of polished rice to be stored in Edo in readiness for the arrival of his chimbu. The money for purchasing it was of course to be advanced by Mitsui-gumi. When the clerks accepted this order without hesitation he was so delighted that he summoned them into his presence and commended them personally for their spirit.

It was not an easy assignment to purchase food for five thousand enemy troops in the very shadow of the bakufu's citadel, but Mitsui-gumi managed to do it and stored the rice in one of the firm's warehouses at Fukagawa along the Sumida River. When they reported back to chimbu headquarters, Iwakura showed his gratitude by inviting the House of Mitsui to provide an additional one hundred thousand ryo for the campaign, which was approaching a climax as the main body of imperial troops approached from the direction of Kyoto.

Iwakura's request put the Mitsuis in a tight spot. The situation in Edo was becoming chaotic and the exchange business was paralyzed. Unable to borrow from established ryogaeya, the Mitsuis sent out clerks to borrow cash from small shopkeepers, and amassed 35,000 ryo, all in silver *ichibu* pieces worth a bit more than a shilling each. If raising this much money on short notice was difficult, delivering it to Iwakura's headquarters was even more so. Edo was surrounded by the bakufu's troops in defensive positions and ambushes, and wayfarers were being harassed by irregulars and marauders. Any cargo not confiscated by the bakufu would probably have fallen prey to robbers. Mitsui's resourceful clerks were not to be thwarted so easily, however. On the Sumida River, especially where it passed between Mukojima and Yoshiwara's brothel quarters, there were many pleasure craft for rent. Those small, roofed boats, some fitted with sliding screens for the sake of privacy, were used in fine weather for outings, bathing parties, or discreet dalliance, often with geisha or courtesans. But in the month of March there was little demand for them, and one of the boatmen was easily persuaded to take a party of respectably dressed merchants on a long cruise.

On the eve of departure Mitsui's employees wrapped the bags of silver in straw matting and hid them under the flooring of the boat. Three clerks were aboard when the floating treasury, laden with approximately a ton and a half of silver, headed upstream in the morning. But they didn't look like clerks, and much less like conspirators. To the casual observer they seemed to be carefree gentlemen on a holiday, and when other boats came within hailing distance the trio strengthened the illusion by pouring sakè for each other and singing tipsily. Nevertheless, the boat was stopped by a bakufu patrol, and the boatman was asked why such a craft with only a few passengers rode so low in the water. The amateur smugglers thought that their game was ended, and one of them reported later that his "liver was chilled" with fear. But, somehow, they talked their way out of the trap, and at last arrived safely at their destination, near Iwakura's headquarters, with their precious cargo.[4]

Despite these financial difficulties, within two months after seizing power the Sat-Cho group had organized a powerful army and the bakufu's position had become hopeless. But in Edo some diehards, in defiance of the deposed shogun's wishes, were determined to resist the imperialists. Leading the irreconcilables were Lord Oguri, then minister of the bakufu's armed forces, and Enomoto Takeaki, commander of its navy. Enomoto refused to surrender the fleet and withdrew it to Hokkaido, continuing from there the war at sea. Oguri, equally obstinate, gathered remnants of the bakufu's army and formed a three thousand-man militia unit called the *shogitai*. By then the Mitsuis presumably had severed their business connections with the bakufu. But in Japan the acceptance of favors incurs a lifelong obligation, called *giri,* the fulfillment of which is as binding as is duty to one's ancestors. Minomura's sense of obligation toward his benefactor Oguri was particularly strong. Thus, even after the formal surrender of Edo to the imperial forces, Mitsui-gumi gave financial support to Oguri's shogitai, although their fortune was staked upon the victory of its enemies.

This support was unavailing, however. Entrenched upon Ueno hill (now included in Tokyo's Ueno Park) the shogitai fought a memorable but losing battle, in which most of Kan'ei temple, enshrining the guardian deities of the Tokugawa dynasty, was consumed by fire. Oguri, Lord of Bungo, would still not admit defeat. Escaping from Edo with some of his men, he made his way northward to join other holdouts, but was captured and beheaded.

This exceptional instance of drumhead justice was tragic and also unfair, for the no less intransigent Enomoto and other bakufu stalwarts were pardoned and became prominent statesmen of the Meiji era. It was also shortsighted, because Oguri alone knew the answers to many questions that puzzled the bakufu's successors. One mystery, still unsolved, was the disappearance of the shogun's rumored treasure, accumulated since the days of Tokugawa Ieyasu. It is generally believed that Oguri had taken the precaution of hiding it in the mountains during the bakumatsu period and hoped to use it for supporting a countercoup in the name of the Tokugawas. Since his death talk about the shogun's hoard of gold coins, believed to be worth hundreds of millions of dollars, has lured innumerable treasure hunters, who have literally riddled the lower slopes of Mount Akagi, in Gumma Prefecture, where Oguri was slain and where the gold is supposed to lie buried.*

After Edo was pacified it was renamed Tokyo, meaning "eastern capital," on December 3, 1868, and the shogun's spacious castle was renovated for occupancy by the young emperor and his court. In November 1868, when military operations in the northern provinces had been completed, Emperor Meiji emerged from seclusion in Kyoto and made the four-hundred-mile journey to his new capital. His grand procession to Tokyo was actually a proclamation of the imperial government's legitimacy, and no expense was spared to make the triumph impressive. His Majesty's palanquin, borne by sixteen robust men, was escorted along the Tokaido by one thousand nobles, lords, samurai, and foot soldiers, all wearing their most splendid attire.

One of those said to have accompanied the emperor was his treasurer, Mitsui Saburosuke Takaaki, son and heir of Hachiroemon Kofuku. The privilege was costly, inasmuch as the house had been tapped for fifty thousand ryo to defray expenses of the journey. But it was as bread cast upon the waters, for the transfer of the court to Tokyo started a veri-

---

* Most persistent of the treasure hunters are members of the Mizuno family, descended from hereditary retainers of the Tokugawas, who have been digging trenches and tunnels on Mount Akagi for three generations, according to Tanaka Yoshihiro, writing in the *Mainichi Daily News*, January 3, 1973.

table boom in the new capital. Although the sophisticated Edokko in general were unenthusiastic about being governed by "country samurai," they wanted to look their best for the occasion and spent their money freely at Tokyo's stores, including Echigoya, on clothes, ornaments, and other extravagances for the welcoming on November 26.

The military campaign of the civil war and the emperor's journey cost the Mitsuis at least 250,000 ryo in addition to all the contributions they had made before the Restoration. Yet the imperial treasury remained empty, and the merchants, disillusioned by the new government's abuse of the old system of levying loans, were unresponsive to pleas for more funds. Because their distrust was paralyzing the economy, the government decided to issue paper money as a means of repaying funds already borrowed and of priming the rusty pump of business. This paper currency, called *dajokansatsu,* or finance-ministry notes, was made by a woodblock printer who lived in one of the Mitsui compounds. The reputable companies of Mitsui, Ono, and Shimada were delegated to distribute the notes in accordance with a plan devised by Yuri Kimimasa: each of the three hundred lords of the country was allowed to borrow one ryo for each koku of rice produced upon his land, without interest if repaid within five years.

Those finance-ministry notes were not convertible, and their only guarantee was the imperial chrysanthemum crest they bore. They were accepted fairly well in the Kyoto area and in Osaka, where merchants were accustomed to handling paper currency, but were spurned by people in Tokyo and the north, who trusted only hard cash. When the decision was made to move the imperial capital to Tokyo, it became imperative to establish a sound monetary system there, and this could not be done without the help of Tokyo's merchants. Apparently it was Minomura who saw the only way to win their cooperation. In a letter to Kido, a leading member of the governing junta, Okubo wrote: "We have discussed raising money and forced loans. Concerning the proposition by Mitsui and others about circulating the money, Mitsui, Kashima, etc. will soon study it among themselves. A Minomura Rizaemon, proxy of Mitsui, has guaranteed circulation of paper money, and the like-minded merchants will do their best."[5]

Minomura proposed that the government organize the rich chonin of Tokyo and, by promising appropriate benefits, persuade them to undertake circulation of the unpopular dajokansatsu. Naturally, his employers were to be at the center of the operation. Four leading merchants, advised by Minomura, agreed that in order to inspire public confidence in the paper money it should be distributed together with the familiar gold and silver currency when it was put into circulation. As an incentive, those merchants who handled the new money were to receive a commission for every note passed. Accordingly, an official bureau was established with Mitsui Saburosuke and two of his assistants in charge. Tokyo's merchants were persuaded to accept this plan, and within eighteen months forty-eight million ryo in paper money were put into circulation. Such was the precarious beginning of Japan's modern currency system.

Nevertheless, the government lacked the coin and bullion needed both for paying its debts abroad and especially for backing its dubious currency at home. Consequently, several big merchants were summoned to a meeting where they were given a shocking ultimatum: they were to supply 860,000 ryo in gold or silver at once, in exchange for paper. The largest quota fell to the Mitsuis, who were instructed to provide a total of 300,000 ryo. They also were delegated to collect the quotas from a dozen other merchants being held responsible for the remainder of the sum. Minomura convinced the treasury that the Mitsuis could not produce so much money on demand, but agreed to advance fifty thousand ryo. How they did it is a mystery, but on the appointed day they paid the fifty thousand ryo, together with ten thousand more from Ono and Shimada, and some tens of thousands that ostensibly were "donated" by the people of Tokyo but actually were advanced by Mitsui without interest.

For this signal service to the government four Mitsui family heads—Hachiroemon, Jiroemon, Gennosuke, and Saburosuke—were awarded five hundred bales of rice each, appointed official accountants to the government, and granted the samurais' privilege of bearing two swords —an honor that their ancestor Sokubei had forsworn happily two and a half centuries earlier.

The Meiji leaders, most of whom were still in their early thirties, were driven by the ambition to modernize Japan's institutions so the nation could become strong, remain independent, and command respect in the world. Blandly ignoring the fact that not long ago they had been in the vanguard of the movement to expel the barbarians, they exhorted their countrymen to imitate those same barbarians as a patriotic duty. More or less united in fealty to their juvenile god-monarch, they plunged impatiently ahead with a host of reforms affecting every aspect of public life.

Their most critical problems were economic. Japan's people subsisted mainly upon the products of agriculture, in which some eighty percent of them were engaged. Since the income per person was only about sixty-five dollars a year, the accumulation of capital even for agricultural development was painfully slow. Industry was still almost entirely in the handicraft stage, transportation was rudimentary, and communications were primitive. Because the division of the country into approximately three hundred semiautonomous han precluded the effective application of any uniform program of development, feudalism and everything it entailed had to be abolished. The daimyo of Choshu was the first to return his fief to the emperor. Other daimyo whose clansmen had been most active in the restoration agreed to do the same and signed a memorial, composed by Kido, which stated in part: "The place where we live is the Emperor's land, and the food which we eat is grown by the Emperor's men. How can we make it our own? We now reverently offer up the list of our possessions and men, with the prayer that the Emperor will take good measures for rewarding those to whom reward is due, and for taking from them to whom punishment is due. . . . Let all the affairs of the empire great and small be referred to him."[6]

This declaration, like many of those made in the name of the restoration, seems to have been taken almost verbatim from works by the Mitsuis' old teacher Motoori, or by the Choshu prophet Yoshida Shoin, who in turn had based their thoughts and writings upon Japan's earliest classics. In this way reforms that otherwise might have been regarded as extremely radical were given the aura of unimpeachable authority and were accepted dutifully, if not with enthusiasm.

In 1869 all the daimyo offered their fiefs to the emperor. Within a period of two years the prefectural system was established, replacing the hundreds of han, and the feudal order crumbled, clearing the way for the creation of new and centralized national institutions.

Most significant were the legal abolition of class distinctions and the liberation of the people to follow occupations of their choice, travel freely, marry as they wished, and buy or sell land. Many obstructions to commerce and industry were removed. Japanese were encouraged to go abroad for study, foreigners were invited to come to Japan and were paid well to teach or practice their specialties, and the government took an active role in importing foreign goods, apparatus, and manufacturing plants to familiarize the people with modern industry and its products.

The burden of financing those innovations, together with the costs of armaments, paying interest on foreign debts, and compensating about 400,000 jobless samurai, was almost unbearable. In 1868, the first year of the Meiji era, the government spent twenty-five million yen, although ordinary revenue was only 3.5 million yen. (The yen, at that time approximately equivalent in value to the United States dollar, replaced the old ryo denomination in that inaugural year.) Forced loans and other borrowings from Japanese and foreign merchants amounted to 5.4 million yen, leaving a deficit of about sixteen million, which increased by another ten million in 1869. Partly in order to meet this

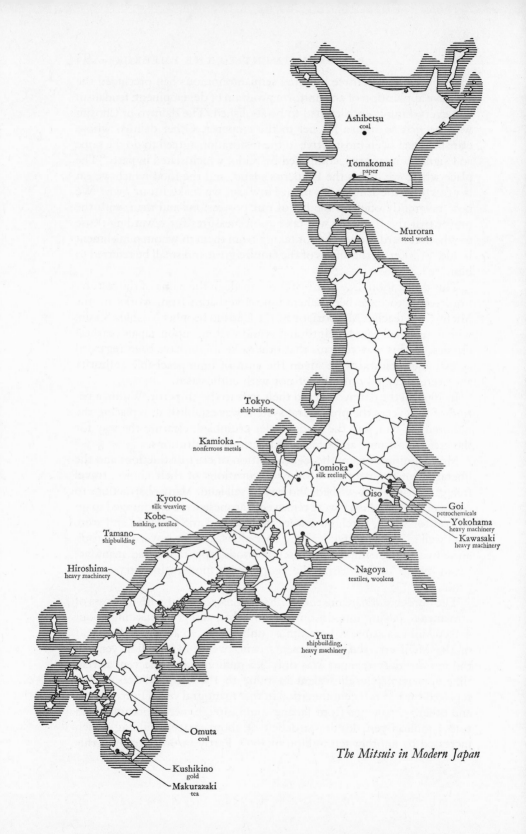

Ashibetsu
coal

Tomakomai
paper

Muroran
steel works

Tokyo
shipbuilding

Kamioka
nonferrous metals

Tomioka
silk reeling

Oiso

Goi
petrochemicals

Yokohama
heavy machinery

Kawasaki
heavy machinery

Kyoto
silk weaving

Kobe
banking, textiles

Tamano
shipbuilding

Hiroshima
heavy machinery

Nagoya
textiles, woolens

Yura
shipbuilding,
heavy machinery

Omuta
coal

Kushikino
gold

Makurazaki
tea

The Mitsuis in Modern Japan

emergency the government had started issuing those nonconvertible banknotes that the Mitsuis helped to promote. But because their exchange value against specie quickly dropped by nearly one-half, the financial situation remained very delicate indeed, and the economy was floundering.

At the center of power in Japan was the so-called Sat-Cho oligarchy, consisting of Okubo, Saigo, Matsukata Masayoshi, and Kuroda Kiyotaka from Satsuma, and Kido, Ito, Inoue Kaoru, Yamagata Aritomo, and Katsura Taro from Choshu. These daring men, together with Okuma Shigenobu of Hizen, Itagaki Taisuke of Tosa, and, later, the nobleman from Kyoto, Saionji Kimmochi, dominated Japan's successive governments from 1868 until after the Meiji era ended in 1912.

Most intimately associated with the Mitsuis was Inoue Kaoru, who served the government under various titles as an all-around administrator. Inoue, like so many of the other new leaders, had taken his apprenticeship as *yonin,* or business manager, for his han in Choshu. It was quite natural that the yonin should have close relations with the merchants, and it has been said with some reason that basically the Meiji Restoration was a consequence of the coalition between yonin and chonin. It may be assumed that the Mitsuis' house rule of cultivating the "honorable men in power" first drew them to Inoue, just as they had been drawn to Oguri, his recent predecessor in the bakufu. But in this later time the attraction between Inoue and the Mitsuis was mutual, because the financial situation which confronted Inoue was unimaginably complex, and none but the big merchants and their banto could understand how to deal with it. In addition to sustaining the rising flood of its own depreciating banknotes, the government undertook to redeem the different kinds of scrip that had been issued by many of the former han, all of which brought the amount of paper money in circulation to almost one hundred million yen. Thus Inoue and his staff recruited for the new Ministry of Finance practically wallowed in more than sixteen hundred different kinds of paper notes, as well as in debased gold and silver coins from assorted periods, and copper, brass, and iron coins of the most diverse shapes, sizes, and provenance—not to mention innumerable counterfeits in all categories.

The currency problem was ameliorated somewhat after Ito Hirobumi, also serving as a vice-minister of finance, returned in 1871 from a visit to the United States, where he had studied the American money system. He persuaded his government to adopt the decimal system (the yen being valued at one hundred sen) and supervised the establishment of a modern mint in Osaka.

The Mitsuis were appointed agents for the mint, under Inoue's supervision, to exchange new coins or bullion for old money. For the purpose Mitsui-gumi set up official money-exchange offices called *goyo kawase-za* in Yokohama, Kyoto, Osaka, Kobe (the new name for Hyogo), and Hakodate. Such close collaboration between the treasury and Mitsui-gumi brought complaints from rivals to the effect that the Ministry of Finance was actually located in the Mitsui headquarters at Surugacho. The barb was not unjustified for, in 1872, soon after the mint opened, the Mitsuis were authorized to issue about ten million yen worth of convertible notes, naturally at an attractive profit. Mitsui-gumi's goyo kawase-za further extended its activities to handle money exchanging for about seventy-five local governments in the new prefectures.

Such a friendly relationship between the government and the Mitsuis was blamed on Inoue, who had extended his influence into every department of the central administration, although he was only a vice-minister. His self-aggrandizement, financial as well as political, was especially repugnant to Saigo Takamori of Satsuma, an idealist who despised political chicanery and personal covetousness. When he was invited to a party given by Inoue for Prince Iwakura and other statesmen, Saigo expressed his feelings with his usual bluntness. Pouring a cup of sakè, he offered it to his host, saying loudly: "This is for you, Inoue, the banto of Mitsui." Inoue seemed not to be offended, but the remark alarmed others who sensed growing cleavages in the Sat-Cho ranks.

Tensions were relieved somewhat by the departure of a mission to the United States and to Europe with the double purpose of trying to gain revisions of the unequal treaties that had been thrust upon Japan by the Western powers in the 1850s and of observing Western society in order to improve Japanese institutions. The mission, which departed late in 1871, was headed by Prince Iwakura and included forty-six high officials, among whom were Okubo, Ito, and Kido. Accompanying them were more than fifty students of both sexes who intended to study abroad. Among the students were Dan Takuma, a future obanto of Mitsui, and his friend Kaneko Kentaro, who later helped Ito to write the Meiji constitution, promulgated in 1889.

Most of those students were offspring of nobles or prominent samurai families; the children of helpful merchants seem to have been overlooked. Inoue, who had more than a casual interest in the future of the Mitsuis, realized that if they were to keep pace with the times they would have to broaden the experiences of their sons. Until then no Mitsui had ever traveled abroad, so none had more than a secondhand knowledge of modern methods of business and finance. In consultation with Minomura, Inoue prevailed upon Omotokata to send five of the Mitsui youths, ranging in age from seventeen to twenty-two years, to the United States for study and training. They sailed from Japan in February 1872. At first they attended a preparatory school in New Jersey, but then, instead of going on to college, they took their higher education in the textile mills of Lowell, Massachusetts. One died in the United States, but the others spent two years abroad and later served their family's House with distinction.

This wise move indicated Inoue's concern over the fact that few of the old-line merchants, including the Mitsuis, had shown enough imagination or flexibility to become leaders in the changing economy. While Mitsui-gumi, as usual, had aligned itself with the men in power and secured the lion's share of official business, it had made no adjustment to the tremendous social changes that were occurring. The economic upheaval had brought ruin to many merchants, who accordingly were unable to repay their debts to Mitsui. The clothing and textile business, upon which the prosperity of the house had long rested, had gone to pieces. And especially since the recent shift of the center of political action from Kyoto to Tokyo, the old structure of Omotokata had become obsolete. But the Mitsuis, as though mesmerized by their venerable traditions, were unable to cope with these new developments and the problems they created. Instead, they depended upon the genius of Minomura for everything. In the six years since he had attained his new name and position "the man from nowhere" had made his influence so pervasive that he seemed to have become the Mitsui's master rather than their servant.

In the early 1870s, at the insistence of Minomura, the Mitsuis' textile branches were separated from their money exchanges, and the authority of the Tokyo office, in which he was the power, took precedence over Omotokata. Control over holdings of specie, government funds, loans, and securities was transferred to the exchange offices, and Omotokata (in other words, the family heads) no longer was entrusted with direct management of the business. Instead of continuing to enjoy their fixed shares of Mitsui-gumi's profits, the several branches of the concern were put on a self-supporting basis and made responsible for their respective losses. The three-year accounting period was reduced to six months, and each branch office was entitled to keep twenty percent of the profits it produced during that period. Bonuses were to be paid to the company's officers according to the quality of their performance; and members of the family were enjoined to "devote themselves to the promotion of business without objection." Clerks were given higher salaries, but also they were to be held strictly responsible for shortages in their accounts.

This downgrading of the families was resented, naturally, but even more outrageous was Minomura's decision to uproot them from their luxurious homes in Kyoto and transplant them to Tokyo, Osaka, Kobe, and Yokohama. Not only were their social habits to be disrupted: they were given blunt orders to get to work. The article of reorganization concerning their exile from Kyoto stated: "The heads of the families will go to the offices of which the respective family is in charge. The eldest son of each will be free to select live-out or live-in status, [but] the second son and younger sons will live in and work the same as clerks. Omotokata will increase payment for board, but will no longer pay for incidental expenditures."[7]

Behind Minomura's strategy was his cherished hope to convert Mitsui-gumi from a general merchant house and money-changer into a great banking concern. An opportunity to do so appeared in 1871, when Inoue gave him to understand that the finance ministry would favor Mitsui's establishing a full-fledged bank after the American or European pattern, with branches in Japan's major cities and the privilege of issuing its own notes as legal tender. A petition to that effect was submitted by Mitsui-gumi and approved by the cabinet within a month. Confident of success, Minomura hired a master carpenter named Shimizu Kisuke, who drew up plans and started to construct an imposing five-story building. Shimizu, whose descendants now build skyscrapers and atomic energy plants, had never seen a bank, but his imagination was uninhibited, and soon Tokyoites watched with wonder and admiration as Japan's largest foreign-style building took shape. As one non-Japanese observer commented, it was called "foreign-style" because it was foreign to any style of architecture on earth. But before the splendid edifice was finished the government canceled its approval of a Mitsui bank in favor of a plan to establish national banks like those in the United States. This reversal seems to have been the work of Inoue's assistant, Shibusawa Eiichi, who convinced his superiors that a bank capable of supporting the nation's currency system and fostering its industries would have to be more broadly based than a family bank could be. Inoue agreed that the best course for the country was to form a coalition of big financiers for the joint establishment of a national bank, with shares open to public subscription.

The biggest exchange houses were those of Mitsui and Ono, then competing fiercely to expand their shares of government business. The first problem was to persuade them to work together. As a preliminary step, Inoue and Shibusawa summoned representatives of the two houses to a meeting at Inoue's mansion. Shibusawa opened it with this admonition: "There is a rumor that the Mitsui and Ono companies are not on good terms. If the rumor be true, it is regrettable indeed, as both companies are doing the same business for the government. They should not be prey to the spirit of rivalry and jealousy."

The competing financiers managed to suppress their hostility, and the Mitsui-Ono Ginko was set up immediately as exclusive agent for the government's exchange business, in anticipation of the National Bank Act then being drafted by Ito. The act was promulgated in 1872, and a year afterward the Mitsui-Ono partnership became the Dai-Ichi Kokuritsu Ginko, or First National Bank. Thirty thousand shares, each with a face value of one yen, were issued. Twenty thousand were taken up by Mitsui and Ono, and the other ten thousand were offered to the public.

The equal division of shares between Mitsui and Ono raised the problem of who would be boss of the bank. The neat but impracticable solution was to have two presidents, Mitsui Hachiroemon and Ono Zensuke, serving terms in alternate months. There were alternate vice-presidents and alternate managing directors as well. To avert the confusion sure to arise from this dichotomy, Shibusawa promised Minomura secretly that he would serve in the position of general superintendent. However, Minomura also entered the group picture as deputy president, in place of Hachiroemon, who excused himself from taking an active role because of age and infirmity.

The Mitsuis' chagrin at having been denied an exclusive franchise was aggravated by the government's insistence that they surrender their new building to Dai-Ichi Kokuritsu Ginko. Mitsui-gumi House, as it was called, had become the showplace of Tokyo and no less popular as a subject for painters and printmakers than Echigoya had been in an earlier time. Minomura shrugged off this disappointment and called in Shimizu to design a new bank building, having no doubt that his petition would be accepted eventually, as the organic weaknesses in Dai-Ichi Kokuritsu Ginko showed their effects.

Gripped by the fever to modernize, the Meiji reformers raided the treasury without restraint, incurring bigger and bigger deficits. Roads, railways, and telegraph lines were spreading across the country. Harbor works, lighthouses, warehouses, and public buildings were provided to assist foreign trade and shipping, which were burgeoning. Prefectural governments, compulsory universal education, a postal system, and mandatory military service for all able males were inaugurated in quick succession. Okuma Shigenobu returned from Europe excited with the idea of industrialization; but the men in charge of finances, knowing that revenues still brought in little more than half the amount of money being spent, foresaw only disaster rather than Okuma's vision.

Partly to avoid being blamed for the nation's financial difficulties, Inoue and Shibusawa (already under sharp attack for their favoritism toward certain businessmen) resigned together, but not without releasing a joint statement in which they criticized the management of private business as well as of public finance. Thereupon Shibusawa took the supervisory job at Dai-Ichi Kokuritsu Ginko. And Inoue had time at last to take stock of the ungainly Mitsui enterprises and to analyze their operations.

What Inoue found was deplorable. The House of Mitsui, once a model of progressive business organization, had become, like the shogunate upon which it was modeled, a loose agglomeration of semi-independent operations, each encrusted with the barnacles of tradition. The Tokyo office and Omotokata in Kyoto worked at cross-purposes, as resentful family heads and jealous banto either ignored or sabotaged the innovations of the upstart Minomura. He knew how to win the affection and cooperation of his underlings, but his blunt plebeian manner repelled some Mitsuis, and his appearance may have embarrassed them. Although in his own luxurious home (a gift from Hachiroemon) he wore the finest of silks, on the job he wore cheap cotton kimono and dirty straw sandals. He also had a habit of laughing loudly, thereby exposing the gaps left by several missing front teeth.

The family heads living in Kyoto had resisted his order to move to new posts, so upon Inoue's advice a second general headquarters, Tokyo Omotokata, was set up. Minomura was put in charge of liaison and planning, under nominal supervision of Mitsui Saburosuke and Mitsui Jiroemon, who appeared at the office on alternate days. Very soon it became clear that with no more authority than that conferred upon him by Hachiroemon (who had little of it himself) Minomura could not enforce his reforms. In 1875, when another great national crisis loomed, Inoue intervened directly to shake the clan out of its complacency. Summoning eighteen family heads and senior banto to his palatial residence in Tokyo, he told them how matters stood. His unsparing assessment must have frightened them, for afterward Minomura was presented with a power of attorney bearing the seals of the heads of five main families. This amazing document gave him a virtual dictatorship over the affairs of the clan and its business organ, Mitsui-gumi.

The families' members were given three days to express their "frank opinions" concerning this dispensation. However, it was made perfectly clear to them that the only alternative to approval was to part company with the clan. There was no audible objection, and Minomura became superintendent of Omotokata as the proxy of Hachiroemon Kofuku, who now was free to devote himself to his silk collages, the tea ceremony, and what remained of a cultivated social life in those materialistic Meiji times.

Under the influence of Inoue and Minomura, Tokyo Omotokata's charter was revised in a manner foreshadowing the modern concept of corporate management as distinct from simple ownership of assets: "Omotokata is the solid base of the Mitsui clan, whose duty is to protect the property and other assets bequeathed by its ancestors. . . . The family assets of Mitsui-gumi belong to Mitsui-gumi and not to the Messrs. Mitsui. All those concerned should recognize the distinction, and none should regard those assets as his private property."[8] The charter also stated that any family member who might be found unworthy of his position because of extravagance, disobedience, or unauthorized indebtedness was to be punished with confinement at home, or, if he proved to be incorrigible, with expulsion from the clan.

Minomura must have exercised his power judiciously, for he won the respect of his employers and colleagues and the affection of his subordinates. Indeed, the Mitsuis had a tendency to depend upon him too much. Once, when he sought their help in improving the business, he pleaded: "I cannot overcome this difficulty alone. . . . I am not confident of success unless all Mitsui family members cooperate and work as one person. . . . As I have told you repeatedly, I am just an employee, and if you rely on me you cannot expect the clan to survive very long."[9]

Perhaps worried about what would happen to the house in the event of his death, he tried to recruit Shibusawa Eiichi, an extremely talented financier who had entered the business world under his auspices. In his old age Shibusawa recalled Minomura's efforts in this direction: "Mr. Minomura of the Mitsui, wishing to make me his successor, one day called on me and gave me a suit of clothes with the family crest of the Mitsui. But I told him that I would be pleased to serve the Mitsui as an adviser, but not as its employee. I felt that I could be of some help to the firm. This incident was the origin of the friendship between the Mitsui and myself."[10]

By alternate entreaties and browbeating Minomura managed to reinvigorate the enterprise, giving the viable units some coherence and lopping off much deadwood. The Tokyo Echigoya, then in perilous condition, was set up as a separate company called Mitsui Clothing Store, under the management of a related family bearing the name Mitsukoshi. ("Koshi" is an alternate reading of the character meaning "echi" in Echigoya. It will be remembered that the former hereditary title of the Mitsui family head was Lord of Echigo, and that the name had been associated with the clan ever since.) With the retail lines permanently divorced from the money-exchange business, Minomura consolidated the financial offices to form a new organization called Exchange Bank Mitsui-Gumi. In 1874 the new edifice was completed and topped with a huge dolphin cast in bronze. According to folklore, the green dolphin would protect it from fire; but the bank needed a more potent talisman against the holocaust that, as Inoue had predicted, would soon threaten the financial structure of Japan.

After the establishment of Dai-Ichi Kokuritsu Ginko, the private exchange houses, like Mitsui's, no longer issued paper money for the government, although they still performed exchequer services for prefectures and collected taxes for the central government. Mitsui also retained its appointment as agent for the mint. Ono-gumi, lacking this perquisite, concentrated its efforts on tax collecting, far outstripping Mitsui. However, Mitsui was also holding funds for the army, five ministries, and other government agencies. Deposits of official money, without interest, provided the three houses with ample funds. Ono-gumi, trying to overtake Mitsui, was investing adventurously in mining, speculating in rice, and otherwise expanding its business. Mitsui and Shimada also were operating quite freely with tax funds, because the government required no collateral.

In 1874, when again the finance ministry was in trouble with its paper money, it demanded that private holders of official funds post sound collateral amounting to as much as one-third of the value of such deposits. Despite this warning signal the three houses continued their profitable games until late in 1875, when the ministry suddenly announced that they would have to post collateral equal in value to the amounts of the deposits. At that time Ono-gumi, which had extended its tax-collecting network to forty prefectures, had debts of more than seven million yen and assets of only 170,000 yen. Unable either to put up enough collateral or to repay the official deposits, the firm collapsed. At the same time Shimada-gumi also went bankrupt.

Mitsui was in poor condition too, with government deposits of some four million yen, and only two million yen worth of acceptable securities. The House, including the bank, held general deposits and silver amounting to about eight million yen, but with a financial panic in full cry the Mitsuis could not risk using that money to pay the government.

How, then, did they escape bankruptcy? The answer to that question may have been lost forever when the Minomura storehouse was destroyed by the earthquake in 1923. But by maneuvers that appeared to be miraculous, Minomura presented the finance ministry with government bonds, land certificates, and other gilt-edged securities sufficient to save the House of Mitsui.

It is known that he was not taken by surprise. Some time before the ministry's ultimatum Inoue, by his own account, had warned Minomura that Ono-gumi was on the verge of bankruptcy, and advised Mitsui to disentangle its finances from those of Ono. Since Inoue was in close contact with the Minister of Finance, Okuma Shigenobu, it seems likely that he knew of the minister's intention to demand higher collateral. In fact, there is reason to believe that the ministry's move was part of a plan to eliminate the two rival houses of Ono and Shimada (who had been tardy in their support of the Restoration's regime) and to make Mitsui supreme. This hypothesis is supported by Rizaemon's great-grandson, Minomura Seiichiro, who wrote recently: "It is true that the collateral-increase decree brought on a crisis for Mitsui [as well as for Ono and Shimada]. But it was so arranged that Mitsui alone would survive, taking advantage of official protection."[11]

Another possible motive for this plot, if such existed, was the need to shake Ono-gumi out of the management of Dai-Ichi Kokuritsu Ginko, whose affairs had fallen into disorder under its schizophrenic management. After Ono-gumi's collapse, Shibusawa had the bank's books examined by Allan Shand, a young English banker employed by the finance ministry to teach Western bookkeeping to Japan's budding bureaucrats. His competence and thoroughness impressed Shibusawa, who relied upon him heavily during his incumbency and for many years afterward. The mare's-nest that Shand uncovered is clearly described by a modern historian: "This, the first governmental inspection of a bank in Japan, revealed complete lack of uniformity and confusion in bookkeeping practices of the first years of the national banks. Violations of the Bank Law had occurred, such as: the granting of large loans (¥1,300,000) to Onogumi and lesser amounts to some individuals without security. The currency reserve was not sufficient to meet a sudden demand by depositors for their money. The influence of Onogumi was too great, the evaluation of the bank's holdings of lands was too high, and the main building itself was not suitable for Western banking procedures."[12]

When these "extraordinary events" had ended, the Mitsuis bore no ill will toward their erstwhile rival and magnanimously interceded with minister Okuma to give the vanquished house enough time for liquidating its indebtedness. The Onos did so punctiliously, and their obanto turned over even his personal fortune to creditors, ending up with only the kimono on his back. The Onos and Shimadas remained in business, but on so diminished a scale that Mitsui stood alone as the great financial house in Japan and the major shareholder in the national bank.

The Mitsuis gave full credit for their salvation to Minomura, extolling him in a letter of commendation: "You have forgotten to sleep or eat in your intense efforts to support and promote the interests of the Mitsui house. When the extraordinary events concerning the mortgages occurred, you took unutterable pains and experienced agonies that would have wrung the bowels of an ordinary man. But thanks to your effort, peace has been restored to Mitsui."[13]

For this achievement Minomura received, along with more substantial emoluments, a treasured kakemono handed down through the generations from the Mitsuis' ancestors. And, perhaps because of his unending worries, he acquired at that time a stomach disorder from which he never recovered.

10 · Foundations in Banking and Commerce

THROUGHOUT THE REMAINDER of the Meiji era the imperial party's oligarchs went to extraordinary lengths to nurture and protect a few favored commercial houses. It is easy to imagine that their solicitude for those merchants, whom they rescued from bankruptcy again and again, was inspired by acquisitiveness. But although most of the statesmen eventually were enriched by their relationship with the entrepreneurs and lived as lavishly as had many a daimyo before them, they were no mere henchmen of big business. In Western societies capitalists habitually suborned complaisant politicians into serving their purposes; but in Meiji Japan the politicians had to create the capitalists first.

Being in charge of the nation's finances at a time when the accounting system was in chaos, the statesmen needed no personal assistance from the merchants in the making of fortunes. Politicians were in a position to dispose of public assets and to dispense concessions as they pleased. Rewards for loyal service were unstinting, and the men in power usually looked the other way when their colleagues passed out those rewards to deserving friends or even to themselves. (It is written that one minister of finance, having prepared the issue of some new paper money, arranged to have a cartload of "samples" delivered privately to his home.[1]) But in general the new statesmen used the country's scant wealth judiciously, and their pampering of certain merchants, which bore a superficial resemblance to Tammany Hall graft, actually was a part of their peculiar strategy for building a strong, rich country.

In the political realm the new oligarchs held control over the imperial family, the unassailable bulwark of tradition and symbol of the national faith. In military matters the qualifications of their associates were recognized: Choshu's men took charge of the army, while Satsuma's dominated the navy. But in questions of finance, which could also determine the success or failure of the imperial government, they most certainly needed outside help. Their citadel on the economic front was Mitsui, whose good name they used as a mark of respectability for untried and often risky projects. The skill and experience of the Mitsuis themselves were valuable, of course. But in the kaleidoscopic shifts and changes of the early restoration period the Mitsuis' already outmoded knowledge was less relevant than was their usefulness as an impressive façade behind which to hide a makeshift financial structure.

The paternalistic role of the government was a decisive factor in the rise of Mitsui as a modern bank. The recently organized Exchange Bank Mitsui-Gumi, a joint-stock company, was already operating under its own regulations, but Minomura was anxious to obtain financial sanction as well as permission to use the title "ginko," as a national bank did, and to adopt a limited-liability system that would protect the house from meeting the same fate as had befallen Ono-gumi.

In 1875 the Mitsuis submitted a petition to this effect, pointing out that there were no officially recognized rules concerning general banks, and pleaded: "Though we are ignorant and uninformed and not confident that we ourselves can formulate perfect rules, yet we dare to present for your esteemed consideration . . . our drafts of bank rules and other documents in the hope that you will instruct and enlighten us." The form of organization chosen and the reasons for its choice were stated in the prospectus: "Companies are of various kinds, but the best is the Société Anonyme, in which the names of members do not appear. Its policy and system are decided by majority votes and are carried out openly, thus insuring justice and fairness. Moreover, the articles of association and regulations are all subject to the approval of the Government and must be strictly observed. The new organization terminates the relationship of master and servant. We all become, equally, friends as members of the new society and hope to share the benefits it may bring by making our hearts as one and working together."[2]

Finance minister Okuma ignored the petition at first, but a national crisis was developing over an expected rebellion, and Dai-Ichi National Bank was still weak from the collapse of Ono-gumi. Mitsui's request was granted finally, with the exception that the stockholders were required to assume unlimited liability. That is, in the event of the bank's failure each stockholder was responsible not only for his own share of the debts but also for that of others unable to repay theirs. Otherwise the newly chartered bank was allowed to follow its previously established rules and was given the privilege of handling the government accounts that had been entrusted to its predecessor. These terms were accepted.

Mitsui Bank, with offices in Japan's four biggest cities and twenty-four major towns, was inaugurated on July 1, 1876. At the ceremony Minomura's message revealed his concern over the weakness of the clan and the exasperation he must have felt at having to push its members up the hill of success: "It must not be forgotten that in undertaking a deed one tends to pay great attention to it in the beginning but gets tired as the work proceeds. . . . This is the general habit of humanity. So even if the purpose is beautiful and there is a good system, laziness makes one's efforts useless. That is why I hope that you, dear partners, will resist this tendency . . . continuing to do your best so that this bank will develop gloriously and make profits to be shared by all of you."[3]

Unfortunately, Minomura could not deliver his admonition in person because he was seriously ill. But he was still worried about the bank's excessive dependence upon official business and its vulnerability to the whims of politicians. Therefore, he dictated another petition to the finance ministry: "If the government should change its current practice and withdraw the money deposited with us, we shall find it very difficult to keep going. . . . If such a situation should arise, our company's distress aside, the flow of private capital would be obstructed and financial operations paralyzed. Considering this, we urge you to continue to allow us, for the coming few years at least, to handle official money of government ministries and agencies and not to change that policy."[4] To this plea Okuma replied: "Your request will be granted and you will be entrusted with official money without fail."[5] So despite the existence of the state-sponsored Dai-Ichi National Bank, Mitsui continued to handle a major share of the government's finances until the Bank of Japan was founded in 1882.

Mitsui Bank (known as Mitsui Ginko in Japan), with headquarters in Tokyo's Surugacho, started with a capital of two million yen divided into twenty thousand shares, of which ten thousand were subscribed by Omotokata, five thousand by nine Mitsui families, and the remainder by employees. There were 383 shareholders, most of whom held only one or two shares. This formal participation of the staff in the profits of the enterprise was one of the fruits of Minomura's democratic policy, under which the principal managers, including vice-directors, were elected by the shareholders, and all the employees down to the junior clerks were called "officers."

The economic thinkers in government—especially Inoue, Shibusawa, and Okuma—were under constant harassment in their efforts to stabilize finance. But meanwhile they never lost sight of the fact that Japan's survival as an independent country lay in foreign trade. Even after the opening of the treaty ports, virtually all overseas commerce had remained in the hands of foreign merchants. And since treaty provisions had set customs duties at the low rate of five percent, the government earned very little revenue from this source. Although overseas trade was increasing rapidly, imports greatly exceeded exports; and to pay for imports the government had to expend abroad approximately seventy million dollars in gold and silver during the 1870s—a ruinous sum considering the nation's poverty. Indeed, with such an adverse trade balance Japan could ill afford the imported machinery, transportation equipment, steel,.and other materials necessary for starting its industrial revolution.

Soon after coming to power, the government organized the Tokyo Commerce and Trade Company, a joint enterprise of which Mitsui Hachiroemon was president. At the same time the House of Mitsui sought to expand domestic and foreign trade through its retail shops in Tokyo, Yokohama, Osaka, and the old branch in Nagasaki. Those efforts met with little success; and in 1875 Minomura, at Inoue's urging, decided to use the prefectural branches of Mitsui's reorganized bank for handling merchandise as well as money. As part of this program various trading activities were consolidated to form a new company, Mitsui-gumi Kokusan-kata (National Products Company). One section of it consisted of an old, rather humdrum venture conducting trade with the Izu Islands, south of Tokyo. A second section supplied silk and grain to foreign traders and imported blankets for the army ministry. A third transported cargo between Niigata and Yokohama. There was also a section supplying Mitsui-brand tea for export.

Kokusan-kata's first big business came when the government began to emphasize the exportation of rice in order to sustain prices and earn foreign currency. With a loan of half a million yen from the treasury, the company bought up rice from the provinces and shipped it to Europe. Having no branches abroad, Mitsui-gumi worked through Japanese government officials stationed in London, who acted as Kokusan-kata's agents. In this way Kokusan-kata became the first Japanese company to conduct foreign trade abroad.

While helping the Mitsuis to organize Kokusan-kata, Inoue used his government connections to start his own trading enterprise. Known as Senshu Kaisha, or First Profit Company, the firm handled rice exports through foreign merchants, marketed the output of lead, silver, and coal mines owned by the government, and obtained a monopoly for the importing of steel. The manager Inoue recruited was Masuda Takashi, once a cavalry officer for the bakufu, who had shown talent as one of his subordinates in the mint. As a lad Masuda had been an office boy at the United States Legation in Edo, where he learned English and stood ready to defend Minister Townsend Harris against threatened attacks by antiforeign ronin. Because his father was a bakufu official, Masuda had been educated in the Chinese classics; and he had seen something of the world as a member of a government mission to the United States and France. After the Meiji upheaval his father was employed by philosopher-educator Fukuzawa Yukichi and, as his assistant, took part in the Westernization of many Japanese intellectuals.

Masuda's background, especially in foreign languages and Western thinking, was to prove very useful in surmounting the communications barrier, which had long obstructed trade. Since Japanese and foreign merchants were equally ignorant of one another's language, they employed Chinese clerks, known by the Portuguese name of compradors, to conduct the actual business. The compradors could read Japanese (it being written mainly in Chinese ideographs) and spoke a little of the language, as well as the pidgin English current in Asia's seaports. Many foreigners considered the compradors to be more honest than their Japanese employers, but the latter despised and distrusted them.

Masuda's aversion to the compradors was strong and did not mellow with the years. In 1910 he wrote: "They aimed only at obtaining commissions . . . never troubling themselves about the real interests of trade. The relations between Japanese and foreign merchants were thus greatly estranged, and the intimacy and confidence so necessary to the smooth working of business relations . . . were entirely lacking. Great inconvenience was experienced by Japanese merchants, who could neither obtain goods without cash payments, nor receive their own dues without actual delivery of the goods. The compradors invariably took the profits, and it was not an uncommon occurrence to see a foreign merchant, who had failed in business, working in the employment of his old comprador."[6]

Masuda had been trained in practical mathematics by his father, who was famous for his rapid calculations by ancient Chinese formulas and for his ability to use three soroban simultaneously. Thus Senshu Kaisha's young manager was more than a match for any comprador. His talent, however, was outweighed by the defects of Inoue's other partners, who either withdrew their capital abruptly or embarrassed the firm by speculation, bribery, or counterfeiting. Inoue himself was in trouble because of his (and Shibusawa's) conspicuous liberality in selling the government-owned Ashio copper mines to Furukawa Ichibei, son-in-law of Ono-gumi's obanto, at a suspiciously low price. In consequence, while Senshu Kaisha was still only a few weeks old, the Ministry of Justice brought Inoue to trial and he was found guilty on charges that could have incurred a prison term of two years. Such was his prestige, however, that he got off with a fine of thirty yen and soon was appointed to the newly formed national senate. Immediately thereafter he was sent to Korea as Japan's ambassador plenipotentiary. Even before he returned from this mission in 1877 he was too deeply engrossed in political problems to keep his mind on anything so mundane as trading. Although the very able Masuda had earned a profit of 150,000 yen for the firm, Inoue decided to go out of business.

The need for developing Japanese trade independent of foreign control was as urgent as ever, but Mitsui's Kokusan-kata, with its haphazard structure, was obviously inadequate for the purpose. Minister of Finance Okuma, concerned over Inoue's intended withdrawal from trade, called in Minomura Rizaemon and proposed that Mitsui absorb Senshu Kaisha and build a stronger firm. Minomura, knowing that Okuma was closely connected with Tosa and Satsuma merchants in competition with Mitsui, was incredulous. But upon consulting Inoue and deputy finance minister Matsukata Masayoshi, he was assured that Okuma meant what he said. With this encouragement, Mitsui in 1876—after the establishment of Mitsui Bank—merged Senshu Kaisha with Kokusan-kata to form Mitsui Bussan Kaisha, known abroad ever since as Mitsui and Company.

Masuda described the creation of the company in his autobiography: "Minomura proposed to Inoue that a trading firm be organized as part of the Mitsui business and that people from Senshu Kaisha be invited to take charge of it. Inoue agreed and asked me to be president of the new company. Minomura also came to me to make the same request. At last I agreed. A salary was to be paid me under contract, but I had to assume full responsibility for the company. Even if it should fail, Mitsui would be absolved of all responsibility. My assets were small, but I poured them all into the new company.

"I told Minomura that business must be commission-based. I meant that the company should not undertake business that would compel it to assume all the risk. I also said that speculation should be avoided. Minomura agreed, and Inoue of course was of the same opinion. Once we agreed on this point I said that everything should be left to me, with no interference. They said 'all right,' and entrusted me with everything. But they said they would not provide any capital. All I could get was permission to overdraw my account at Mitsui Bank by fifty thousand yen."[7]

The new company's rather flowery prospectus expressed the promoters' intention "to export overseas surplus products of the Imperial Land, to import . . . products needed at home, and thereby to engage in intercourse with the ten thousand countries of the Universe."[8] Upon this grand design and slender capital Masuda developed the prototype of the *sogo shosha,* or general trading company, that played such a significant role in modernizing the Japanese economy.

In founding the company the Mitsuis took no initiative whatever, and even Minomura's approach was extremely hesitant. Instead of assigning family heads or their first-born sons to its management, he ap-

pointed Takenosuke, seventh son of Hachiroemon Kofuku, and Yonosuke, third son of another of Kofuku's sons, both of whom had gone to
the United States for study five years previously. Otherwise, the clan
took a strictly hands-off attitude for reasons apparent in the contract
signed by the heads of the main and the branch families (which by now
had increased to eleven). The contract began optimistically: "We have
carried out extraordinary reforms in Mitsui, abolished Mitsui-gumi and
established Mitsui Exchange Bank on the great fortress of Omotokata.
We ourselves are stockholders of the bank, so that our business will
prosper forever and be enjoyed by us equally."

But after that preamble the promoters' anxiety asserted itself: "As
stated already, the purpose of founding the new company is to ensure
our livelihood in case Mitsui Bank is closed down. That is why we
picked Takenosuke and Yonosuke as initiators of the new company.
Having entrusted these two persons with the management of the new
company as distinct from Mitsui Bank, the rest of us will be absolved of
responsibility even if the new company should suffer fatal losses or be
forced out of business by natural disaster. Then the rest of us would
have no duty to repay debts run up by the new company."[9] This odd
disavowal seems to have been intended to convince the Mitsuis that the
new firm, which they called simply "Bussan" (literally, "product company"), would protect their future. But it is evident that the writers had
little confidence in the undertaking and actually were protecting themselves against criticism and indebtedness in the event of its failure.

The manager of Bussan's foreign trade section was Magoshi Kyohei,
whose only previous business experience had been the managing of an
inn. A riddle making the rounds in Mitsui's parent firm revealed their
opinion of Bussan: "What is the cheapest thing in Tokyo nowadays?"
The answer: "Magoshi's salary." The bright young man, who later put
Bussan into the brewing business and became a beer tycoon in his own
right, was earning thirteen yen a month.

Other promising talents who joined Bussan's small staff in the early
years were Fujise Seijiro, whose heir married into Masuda's family;
Yamamoto Jotaro, later a great political boss and president of the South
Manchurian Railway; and Fukui Kikusaburo, who did much to broaden
and internationalize Mitsui's business. These three in turn served as
obanto of Bussan under the guidance of Masuda, who watched over the
firm for more than seventy years.

At the time of its founding in 1876 Bussan's main exports were coal
from the state-owned colliery at Miike in Kyushu and surplus rice. The
firm also imported blankets and woolens for the army. Most valuable
was the agency for coal, which Masuda took on at the request of Ito
Hirobumi, then Minister of Industry. Later, in relating the circum-

stances, Masuda quoted Ito as saying: "Masuda, since you are establishing Mitsui Bussan to engage in foreign trade, it would be good if you
handled the coal from Miike colliery. If you are willing to undertake
this, we will not be tight. You can acquire the coal at cost price and get
started on it directly."[10]

Masuda didn't know much about coal, but he had been familiar with
mining administration since childhood. His father had served as magistrate in charge of convict labor at the gold mines on Sado Island and
later was assigned to developing mining in Hokkaido. Masuda knew
that Bussan could not compete in copper, dominated as that was by
Sumitomo, under the patronage of Prince Iwakura, and by Furukawa
Ichibei, who had bought the Ashio mines. Wanting to establish a foothold in mining, Masuda accepted Ito's offer with alacrity, and Bussan
became sole purchasing agent for the government's mining bureau.
This gave it a monopoly over exports of coal. In due course Bussan
came into possession of the nation's richest coal, lead, and zinc mines,
as well as important deposits of gold, silver, and sulfur.

Through a branch in Shanghai, Bussan began exporting coal just as
the Europeans were establishing modern factories and mills there; and
eventually it secured a lion's share of the China market, as well as a ship
bunkering business in Hong Kong, Singapore, and other Oriental
ports. At the beginning of its history Bussan's annual coal-export
volume was a mere 27,000 tons. During the next nine years Masuda and
Magoshi boosted it to 1,837,000 tons, an increase of 6,800 percent.
They had discovered the magic formula for making profits without
taking risks.

Whether by design or otherwise, Bank and Bussan formed a most felici-
tous combination, the advantages of which soon became apparent.
The first successful innovation made possible by Bank-Bussan teamwork was the issuance of exchange bills for commodities. After the internal revenue system had been modernized, the farmers were required
to pay their land taxes in cash instead of grain. But it seemed that whenever there was a bumper crop prices sagged and producers were hard
pressed to meet their obligations to the government. Seeing opportunity in this situation, Minomura obtained permission from the finance
ministry to undertake the purchase of rice with bills that could be used
to pay taxes. Until then merchants handling official money were prohibited from offering loans, but under the new plan Bussan's branches
were thus able, in effect, to lend money. The inauguration of Mitsui
Bank and Bussan in 1876 happened to coincide with another bumper
crop of rice, but with Bussan conducting a widespread purchasing

operation with Bank's money, the House of Mitsui supported the price of rice and saved many farmers from ruin while substantially increasing the government's revenue, as well as its own profits.

By such integration of finance and commerce Mitsui in fact laid the groundwork for a rationally organized capitalist system to supplant the economy of feudalism. Because of his foresight and persistence in assisting that change, Minomura Rizaemon has been called, with some justice, the "father of Japanese capitalism." The role of Mitsui in Japan's economic development—as a public institution rather than a private enterprise—was confirmed six months after Bank's founding, when the heads of seven Mitsui families were summoned to the Ministry of Finance.

There minister Okuma informed them very bluntly that the privileges they had been granted by the government were predicated not upon their personal worthiness but upon expectations of their future services to the state: "The times are changing," the finance minister's lecture began. "The daimyo have returned their fiefs to the emperor, and the system of hereditary stipends for the nobility and samurai has been revised. Rich families like Shimada and Ono have gone bankrupt, and have been dispersed; only the Mitsuis maintain their traditional prestige. . . . The government, on its part, has been deeply concerned with protecting the Mitsui clan. As to the foundation of Mitsui Bank, it must be remembered that Minomura Rizaemon, foreseeing the trend of the times, petitioned the government to that effect. Believing that the preservation of a traditional wealthy house would contribute to the general interests of the nation, the government decided . . . to permit the establishment of Mitsui Bank solely to perpetuate the prosperity of the family.

"Therefore, the Mitsuis have no cause for complaint. If any should be dissatisfied with the new system and cling to traditional ways, the government's intention of favoring Mitsui with special privileges will not be binding. These matters concern not only the private affairs of your family but also the development of the state treasury, since Mitsui's financial condition involves that of the state. All who share the family title of Mitsui assume an inescapable responsibility."[11]

Possibly this warning was inspired by the fact that the guiding hand of Minomura had slipped from the helm, and by the discovery that the family heads had been laggard in obeying his earlier instructions. While Minomura Rizaemon lay upon his deathbed, Minister of Finance Okuma ordered Omotokata to make Hachiroemon Kofuku move permanently from Kyoto to Tokyo. Other members of the family who had been assigned to local branches of the bank were instructed to report immediately to their respective offices and to settle their households nearby. Furthermore, all members of the Mitsui family were to "refrain from misconduct."

The timing of Okuma's admonition is significant, for the Meiji government had just survived its worst political test and anticipated an economic crisis in consequence. The problem centered upon the displaced samurai. In general they had adjusted quite well to the new order by taking up careers in the military services, police force, assorted businesses, or the professions. But among the less adaptable individuals discontent smoldered. This was increased in 1876 when, in its perennial attempts to balance the budget, the government commuted the pensions it had been paying samurai since 1872 to disappointingly small terminal payments in bonds. Aggravating the injury, a law was passed depriving the proud warriors of the privilege of wearing their two swords. The indignation of disaffected samurai was exploited by patriots and politicians who chose to be critical of the oligarchy's arbitrary rule, corruption, and disregard for tradition.

The most eloquent critic of the oligarchy was Marshal Saigo Takamori, who had won the people's affection by his openheartedness and incandescent patriotism. A self-righteous defender of the national purity and an advocate of a vague kind of populism, Saigo was outraged by Okubo Toshimichi's opportunism and imperious political style. He was disgusted by backsliders, such as Okubo, Ito, and Inoue, who having seized power in the name of the emperor, now consorted with moneylenders and lived in suspect opulence, attended by scores of servants. Uncomfortable in his command of the nation's new peasant army and thwarted in his hopes for an expedition to subdue Korea, Saigo stalked out of the government and withdrew to his native Kagoshima. There, surrounded by men of similar sentiments, he incited opposition against Okubo's dictatorial management of the government. He did not advocate armed revolt, but by 1877 his followers had mobilized an army of about forty thousand men, mostly implacable samurai; and their officers persuaded him to lead them in a rebellion that again plunged the nation into civil war.

Minister of Home Affairs Okubo, backed by the imperial court and most of the Meiji oligarchs, was equal to the challenge. With a considerably larger conscript army—organized by General Yamagata Aritomo, transported by Mitsubishi's ships, supplied by Mitsui Bussan, and paid by Mitsui Bank—the central government executed a successful counteroffensive in Kyushu, the center of disaffection, and demonstrated once and for all its ability to rule the nation.

The Satsuma Revolt of 1877 was far more costly than the restoration skirmishes had been, taking a toll of some thirty thousand lives, includ-

1. *Mitsui Hachirobei Takatoshi (1622–94), founder of the Mitsui business empire, and his wife, Jusan, as portrayed on a scroll painted in the late seventeenth century.*

2. Mitsui Hachirobei's elder brother established this draper's shop at Edo in the 1630s. Known as the "nailpuller Mitsui," it lasted only a few decades.

3. Mitsui Hachirobei's money exchange (at left in picture) was established at Edo in 1683, ten years before the Bank of England was founded.

4. *Echigoya, founded in Edo by Mitsui Hachirobei in the 1670s, revolutionized merchandising in Japan. Mitsukoshi Department Store in Tokyo is Echigoya's direct successor.*

6. *Mitsui-gumi's second venture in foreign-style edifices was built for Mitsui Bank, founded in 1876. The Mitsui main office building today stands in almost the same location, near Nihombashi, Tokyo.*

5. *Mitsui-gumi House in Tokyo, built for the firm in the early 1870s, was soon requisitioned by the government to accommodate Japan's first national bank, Dai-Ichi Kokuritsu Ginko.*

7 (below). *Oji Paper Company, founded by Shibusawa Eiichi in 1873, used imported modern machinery to make Western-style paper. The company was acquired by Mitsui in the 1890s and has dominated the industry ever since.*

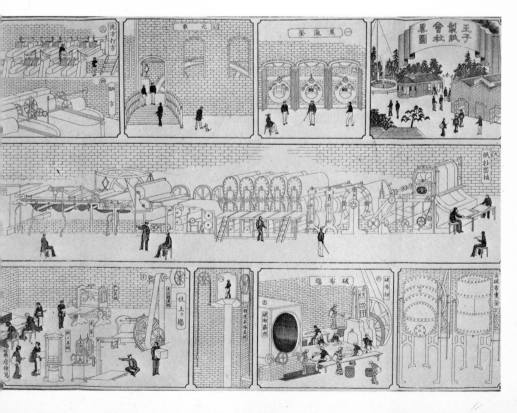

8. *Mitsui-gumi's administrators in the 1870s.* Seated, left to right: *Saito Junzo, a manager; Mitsui Hachiroemon Kofuku, then head of the House; Shibusawa Eiichi, a business associate; and Minomura Rizaemon, chief manager. Standing: Nagata Jinshichi; Kofuku's son Saburosuke Takaaki (the Meiji government's first treasurer); and their kinsman, Mitsui Takayoshi.*

9. *Masuda Takashi (1848–1938), as he appeared in 1865. Earlier, he had worked for Townsend Harris, first United States Minister to Japan. Eleven years later Masuda helped to organize Mitsui Bussan.*

10. In 1872, five young Mitsui sons were sent to the United States for study and to observe American business practices. Among the five were, left, Takenosuke Takahisa (1855–1914), a younger son of Hachiroemon Kofuku, and, right, Yonosuke Takaaki (1856–1921), one of Kofuku's grandsons. Both men became managers of Mitsui Bussan when it was founded; and in time, both established new branch families.

11. *Minomura Rizaemon (1821–77), "the man from nowhere," joined Mitsui-gumi's administrative staff just before the Meiji Restoration and guided the House brilliantly during the new government's first stormy decade.*

12. *Mitsui Hachiroemon Takayoshi (Kofuku; 1808–85), eighth heir of the senior family, was one of the very few merchants who successfully made the transition from Tokugawa feudalism to modern capitalism.*

13. *Minomura Rizaemon, sometimes* ▷ *called "the father of Japanese capitalism," served as loyal deputy and alter ego to Mitsui Hachiroemon Kofuku.*

14. Seated, *Marquis Ito Hirobumi (1841–1909), Japan's first prime minister under its new cabinet system, with Hibi Osuke, chief manager of Mitsukoshi Department Store, in the 1890s.*

15. Nakamigawa Hikojiro (1854–1901) *was one of Mitsui's great leaders. As chief manager of the House during the 1890s, he transformed it into a modern enterprise. Many of its most distinguished executives during the twentieth century were his protégés.*

16. One of Nakamigawa's bright young men was Fujihara Ginjiro (1869–1960). Put in charge of the ailing Oji Paper Company in the late 1890s, he built it into a mammoth enterprise.

17. Masuda Takashi developed Mitsui Bussan into Japan's largest trading company. In 1900, he succeeded Nakamigawa as chief manager of the whole Mitsui concern. After retiring in 1914, Masuda served as adviser to the House and to the nation for more than twenty years.

18. *Guided by Masuda Takashi, a group from Mitsui Gomei visited London in 1907 to study bank-ing practices. Only a few members of the party can be identified: (1) Fukuda Shugoro, (2) Hayashi Ken, (3) Masuda Takashi, (4) Toyama Tomozo, (5) daughter of Mitsui Saburosuke Takayoshi, (6) Mitsui Saburosuke Takayoshi, (7) his wife, (8) his kinsman, Mitsui Benzo.*

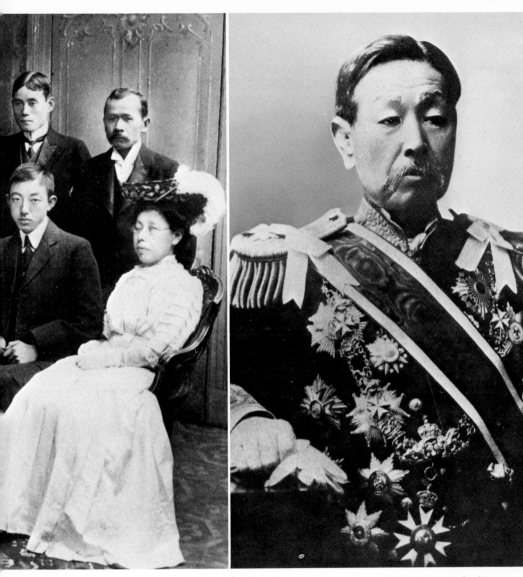

19. Marquis Inoue Kaoru (1835–1915) helped to shape Japan's economic and foreign policies. Because of his prompting, the House of Mitsui, too, was changed into a modern financial concern, created to serve the purposes of the Meiji government. This portrait was made in 1907.

Heibon-sha

21 (above). At Mitsui Mining Company's Miike colliery, miners worked nearly naked because of the heat. This photograph was taken about 1925.

Heibon-sha

22. Even late in the Meiji era coal mining in some places was primitive and brutalizing.

◁ *20. Advertisements from* The Russo-Japanese War Fully Illustrated, *an English-language periodical published from 1904 to 1905.*

23. Taken by Mitsui Takasumi in September 1923, soon after the Great Kanto Earthquake, this photograph records the visit of Prince Kuni Kunihiko and his family to the home of Baron Mitsui Hachiroemon Takamine in Tokyo, while inspecting the earthquake damage and relief measures in the neighborhood. (1) Toshiko, wife of Mitsui Hachiroemon Takakimi; (2) Baron Mitsui Hachiroemon Takamine; (3) Baroness Mitsui; (4) Princess Kuni Nobuko; (5) Princess Kuni Nagako, the present empress, then betrothed to Crown Prince Hirohito; (6) Princess Kuni, wife of the prince, and a descendant of the daimyo of Satsuma; (7) Prince Kuni, adviser to three emperors; and (8) his son, Prince Kuni Asaakira.

24. Mitsui Gomei building in Tokyo, after the Great Kanto Earthquake of September 1, 1923.

ing those of Saigo and many other able men. The financial drain was ruinous, and the treasury needed many years to recover from it. Yet, even though the conflict delayed the achievement of economic stability, it accelerated the development of a strong army that became a prime factor in stimulating industrial growth and a potent means both of expanding Japan's influence abroad and of solidifying its nationalistic philosophy at home.

This turn of events was immensely significant for the Mitsuis' future, but their immediate concern, as usual, was with the government's empty treasury. Their job, as they saw it, was to gather money, deliver it to the government in exchange for promises, and through enterprise in commerce and industry, to make those promises come true.

Balance sheets for the fiscal year 1877 showed that Minomura's initial estimate of Bank's profit—500,000 yen—was accurate within five percent, and that Bussan had also turned a neat profit. Nevertheless, he must have had misgivings about leaving the House of Mitsui in the hands of its heirs, none of whom displayed much talent for business. Like so many outstanding leaders, he had failed to groom a worthy successor. His adopted son Risuke was too young and impulsive, and obanto Saito Junzo had grown too old. Masuda Takashi was a great merchant, fine for Bussan, but no banker.

As for sources of official favor, Minomura knew that Mitsui had survived more by default than by merit and that competition would sharpen. Already Mitsubishi was thriving under Okuma's patronage and was favored by the Satsuma clique. Inevitably Mitsui's destiny seemed to be linked with that of the leaders from Choshu. In making his will Minomura emphasized his conviction that his employers should call upon Inoue Kaoru in time of need.

Such a time was not distant as Japan entered now upon the industrial phase of its development.

II · Capitalism,
Japanese Style

IN EUROPE THE SO-CALLED INDUSTRIAL REVOLUTION was actually a centuries-long evolution from feudalism through successive stages of mercantilism and laissez-faire enterprise to industrial capitalism. Yet Meiji Japan, by omitting the intermediate stages, made the vertiginous leap from feudalism to a recognizable form of capitalism in only one generation. Almost incredibly, the metamorphosis was achieved in a country lacking the resources necessary for modern industry, retarded in science and technology, and still in the dark ages politically. It is no cause for wonder, then, that the resulting system, despite superficial resemblances to those of Western capitalist societies, was mainly indigenous in its structure, methods, and goals.

Foreign businessmen, who had so easily snatched the lucrative overseas trade from the fumbling hands of the chonin, showed tolerant amusement toward the Japanese efforts to imitate the West. Typical of their patronizing attitude was an article that appeared in the *Japan Gazette* ninety years ago. The writer predicted that Japan would never realize its aim of becoming a rich country because "the advantages conferred by nature, with the exception of the climate, and the love of indolence and pleasure of the people themselves forbid it. The Japanese are a happy race, and being content with little are not likely to achieve much."

Some political and intellectual leaders were agitating for a representative government based upon Western liberalism; but Okubo, lacking confidence in his "unenlightened" people, stoutly opposed the introduction of all democratic processes. Backed by the increasingly conservative Prince Iwakura, he fought for a paternal despotism under which men of superior ability, acting upon orders from an all-powerful emperor, would make the Japanese people succeed in spite of themselves. Democracy, he said, "cannot be applied to a people who are accustomed to longstanding practices based on the old ways."[1]

Having studied the economies of the United States and European countries while visiting those enlightened places, Okubo concluded that the prosperity (and hence the strength) of any nation depends upon its productive capacity. But like most Japanese, he was unable to comprehend the roles of competition and a free market in stimulating economic activity. It was his firm belief that no country had succeeded in boosting its productive power without the patronage of its government. With this in mind he urged his fellow statesmen "to concentrate upon the encouragement of manufacturing industries and the increase of production generally" in order to establish the basis for wealth and power.

In 1877 the deaths of Saigo Takamori (who committed seppuku after the failure of his rebellion) and of Kido Koin (who died of tuberculosis) had left Okubo the undisputed chieftain of the Sat-Cho oligarchy, with Ito, Inoue, and Okuma supporting him energetically. Now the way was clear, Okubo said, for getting on with the main task, which was to "lay the foundations for a new social structure."

That task was made much more difficult by incorrigible folk who liked the old social structure and the values upon which they believed it to be based. The most vociferous opponents were former followers of Saigo, who preserved samurai traditions by reviving the martial arts, and not for purely sentimental reasons. Congregating in *dojo,* sports clubs or gymnasiums, to practice kendo, jujutsu, or judo, those "ronin" lamented the passing of the good old days while studying nationalist teachings, promoting militarism, and conspiring to punish the "evil counselors" whom they believed to be victimizing the emperor.

Since the battles during the restoration men of their beliefs had assassinated several political leaders in protest against their unorthodoxies and administrative reforms. Prince Iwakura was waylaid by assassins and badly wounded, and in May 1878 Okubo was stabbed to death. Thus the service of the greatest of the restoration's statesmen ended when he was only forty-seven years old. Displaying the intellectual confusion characteristic of their breed, the assassins, admirers of Saigo, insisted that they had killed Okubo because of his refusal to grant representative government. A more plausible motive, however, was their leaders' fanatical advocacy of military adventures overseas.

This issue had divided the oligarchy and frequently was used to arouse the people against the government. To interpret it as a struggle between the "hawks" and the "doves" of the time, however, would be to exaggerate the differences among various shades of nationalism. The militarists insisted upon demonstrating Japan's martial prowess immediately, while the economic modernizers wanted time to make Japan impregnable before inviting hostilities. Okubo, for example, had successfully thwarted Saigo's scheme for waging war against Korea, which would have aroused the restless Russian bear; but he had acquiesced in the invasion of Formosa because China, its dragon-protector, was sleeping soundly. Through that campaign he had wrested from China an indemnity worth nearly a million dollars, much of which was used to boost Japan's military strength.

In the interests of national defense Okubo and his cohorts had placed primary emphasis upon such heavy industries as munitions and ship-building. They were operating coal, sulfur, and metal mines and had greatly expanded transportation and communications networks with an eye to their military value. For such important facilities they did not wait for private initiative but proceeded with the same directness as did Germany's Bismarck, a statesman whom both Okubo and Ito had met and admired inordinately.

For Okubo's program, undertaken despite the financial havoc caused by the Saigo rebellion, the treasury had resorted to floating an issue of government bonds. Most people still associated them with the infamous forced loans of the bakufu, so public response was discouraging. But here, too, Inoue enlisted the support of the Mitsuis, who applied their energy and prestige to selling the bonds. By the closing date the entire issue of 12.5 million yen was subscribed—nearly all of it through Mitsui Bank. With this stake Japan embarked upon an unprecedented program of creating its own form of industrial capitalism.

By far the largest item in the government's budget was for building more railways, which had been started even before horse-drawn vehicles became common. Japan's first railway, connecting Tokyo and Yokohama, had been completed in 1872 at government expense, under the supervision of Inoue Masaru, one of the men from Choshu who as a youth had sailed to London with Ito and Inoue Kaoru. Most business-men, however, were reluctant to invest in such novel propositions. The Mitsuis tried to organize a railway company but failed, for once, to attract enough capital. When the Nippon Railway Company was set up under government auspices, investors had to be drawn in with incentives: the organizers were exempted from taxes and stockholders were guaranteed an eight-percent dividend. But the Mitsuis invested in it grudgingly, for with Masuda at the helm of Bussan they were able to make big profits from railroading without taking any direct risk.

Inasmuch as most of Japan's steel and rolling stock had to be imported, Masuda traveled to the industrial countries of the West making ground-floor deals. One was an exclusive contract with Andrew Carnegie's steel monopoly in America for selling its products in Japan. Thus Bussan was supplying the rails as well as the locomotives, cars, machinery, and coal for building and operating Japan's railways, which had laid about two thousand miles of track by the early 1890s. When the government needed something from abroad—be it artillery, steamships, medicines, engines, or patents for making them—Masuda knew where and how to get it, and usually Bussan was the middleman.

In its policy of hothouse capitalism the government seems to have favored Mitsui, but even then there was strong rivalry for the properties and privileges being dispensed. The most successful competitors were the other companies that later developed into powerful zaibatsu— Mitsubishi, Sumitomo, Yasuda, Asano, Furukawa, Kawasaki, Otani, and Okura. It is significant that of these still-active concerns only Mitsui and Sumitomo have a pre-Meiji merchant lineage. The others, almost without exception, were founded after the Meiji restoration by former samurai—imaginative, aggressive entrepreneurs whose boldness was due in part to the fact that they had so little to lose.

The most enterprising and perhaps the most merciless of those new-comers to business was Iwasaki Yataro, whose Mitsubishi concern was the only zaibatsu that seriously challenged Mitsui. The epic battle between the two giants has provided the most exciting episodes in modern Japanese business history, and it is still raging.

As a minor official of the Tosa han in Shikoku, Iwasaki gained prominence in his early twenties by successfully reorganizing the mismanaged Nagasaki branch of Tosa's trading company, which also operated ships between Shikoku and major seaport cities of Japan. In 1870, shortly before the daimiates were abolished, Iwasaki acquired the Tosa company's assets, including six steamships, and undertook responsibility for its liabilities, amounting to 300,000 yen on the books. For a samurai in modest circumstances to take over such a debt seemed foolhardy. But Iwasaki Yataro was as shrewd as he was bold: having been the company's accountant, presumably he was aware that the firm also had some 270,000 yen worth of assets, which had been hidden to fool the bakufu. Furthermore, with the abolition of the han, the imperial government took over the daimyo's debts, including those owed by Iwasaki's company. It would seem that he obtained free of charge a rather well capitalized establishment.

Even so, the competition from foreign shipping was so severe that his business languished until 1874, when the imperial government launched its punitive expedition against Formosa. Because the British and American governments took a neutral position, and accordingly could give no help to either combatant, the Japanese government needed ships to transport troops and supplies. Iwasaki, who was on intimate terms with Okubo and Minister of Finance Okuma (the trio used to make nocturnal excursions to the pleasure quarters of Yoshi-wara), was assigned to the task of conveying Japan's men and supplies to Formosa. The government supplemented his small fleet with additional ships purchased or chartered from foreign countries. Of the eleven million yen spent on this first of modern Japan's military adventures abroad, about eight million was expended for ships and other transportation costs. Iwasaki gained most of the financial benefit, for after the expeditionary force returned victorious from Formosa his company was given thirteen large steamships, worth 1.4 million yen.

In the following year, under a shipping-promotion program, Mitsubishi was awarded an annual subsidy of 250,000 yen, and the company was permitted to purchase eighteen government-owned ships on easy installments. When Saigo's rebellion broke out in Satsuma two years later, a dozen more ships were added (mostly at government expense) to Iwasaki's line, which handled the marine logistics for the campaign. This brought another ten million yen into Mitsubishi's coffers.

One reason for the government's generosity to Mitsubishi was Okubo's desire to break the foreigners' stranglehold on shipping in Japanese waters. The Pacific Mail Steamship Company of the United States had been monopolizing transportation on the Yokohama-Kobe-Nagasaki-Shanghai route but was driven out of business by Iwasaki, who then acquired its ships. The next contender was the British P. & O. line, the Peninsular and Oriental Steam Navigation Company, which had moved in to dominate the Yokohama–Shanghai route, but again Iwasaki was the victor. By the early 1880s he had received approximately ten million yen in subsidies, in addition to his huge profits, all of which enabled him to found an economic empire comprising banking, insurance, warehousing, trading, and shipbuilding. He also operated coal and copper mines that with the help of Okuma he had bought from the government for a pittance.

In time Iwasaki's autocratic style and unrelenting acquisitiveness antagonized the government and the public, as well as his injured competitors. Anti-Iwasaki sentiment came to the surface in 1878, after the assassination of Okubo Toshimichi and the exclusion of Okuma from the cabinet. Late that year a Tokyo newspaper charged Mitsubishi with neglect of its ships, irresponsibility in handling passengers and cargoes, profiteering on fares and freight costs, speculation in the stock market, and attempted monopolization of the financial world. The writer of those newspaper articles was a mouthpiece for Shibusawa Eiichi, whose business principles were diametrically opposed to those of Iwasaki.

Now that Mitsubishi had temporarily lost its influence with the government, other newspapermen joined the attack on both the shipping monopoly, popularly called "the Sea Goblin," and its protector Okuma. The characters of Okuma's surname mean "big bear," and at wrathful public demonstrations papier-mâché bears and goblins were burned in effigy. Under the influence of the ascendant Choshu clique

the government cancelled Mitsubishi's subsidy, imposed tough shipping regulations, and enacted a law forbidding shippers to engage in
other lines of business.

In retaliation Iwasaki started his own newspaper, using it and others
under Okuma's patronage to roll back the tide of public opinion.
Okuma too had his own political party, which was allied with that of
Itagaki Taisuke, a former Tosa samurai, and together they attacked the
government with such success that the Choshu clique found itself on
the defensive. In 1882 Inoue Kaoru, by then foreign minister, summoned Minomura's son Risuke and outlined his plan for splitting the
opposition. Itagaki was to be sent abroad on a contrived diplomatic
mission. His expenses were to be paid secretly by Mitsui, in return for
which the government would extend its exchequer business (then due
to terminate) for three years. Also Mitsui would be assisted in entering
the shipping business in order to break Iwasaki's monopoly. Minomura
Risuke, dreaming of a coup that would enable him to live up to his late
father's great name, agreed enthusiastically. That autumn Itagaki and
his ally Goto Shojiro, another mordant critic of the oligarchy, left
Yokohama for a leisurely trip to "observe European governments."
Apparently they had no suspicion that their travel fund of twenty thousand dollars had been provided by Mitsui to wreck their pro-Mitsubishi
party.[2]

Meanwhile Shibusawa and Masuda had organized a rival shipping
company with the assistance of Inoue and another Choshu loyalist,
Shinagawa Yajiro, then a vice-minister. The firm, called Kyodo Un'yu
Kaisha (United Transportation Company), was capitalized, jointly by
the government and private business, at six million yen—with Mitsui
as a major investor. The government's paradoxical campaign to destroy
a monopoly of its own creation started off bravely. In fact, competition
was so keen that the third-class fare between Yokohama and Kobe,
which had been set at 5.50 yen, dropped rapidly to 55 sen, one-tenth the
previous rate. The subjugation of the Sea Goblin and the reduction of
fares was welcomed by the public; but after Itagaki returned from
Europe and joined the stubborn Okuma in his campaign against Kyodo
Un'yu, the well-known fickleness of the Japanese people showed itself.
Their sympathy shifted toward Mitsubishi and against the government,
which was sustaining huge losses in the fare war while suppressing opposition by using police-state tactics. Kyodo Un'yu's shares dropped
to two-thirds of their face value, and the investors began to worry about
their money.

Iwasaki Yataro, pressing his advantage, proposed a merger of the
two shipping lines. To assure success, he solicited the intervention of
Minister of Agriculture and Commerce Saigo Tsugimichi (younger

brother of the late rebel Takamori), who had authority over transportation. According to one version, Iwasaki presented him with forty thousand yen for distribution among members of the Satsuma faction who supported Mitsubishi. Whatever the means used, the government agreed to the merger, from which Nippon Yusen Kabushiki Kaisha (Japan Mail Steamship Joint-Stock Company, or N.Y.K.) was born. The amalgamation, effected in 1885, was supposed to be arranged on an almost equal basis, with Mitsui getting seven million shares and Mitsubishi six million, and each side turning over twenty-nine ships to N.Y.K. To promote the sale of the remaining stock, the government guaranteed shareholders an eight-percent dividend each year for fifteen years.

Having escaped almost unscathed from the Kyodo Un'yu Kaisha fiasco, the Mitsuis felt doubly fortunate at having come out ahead of Mitsubishi in the new deal. But when the shareholders of N.Y.K. met to elect a board of directors, they learned to their dismay that Iwasaki had secretly bought up huge blocks of depreciated shares, which he now used to win control over the company. After hearing of that maneuver a newspaper commentator wrote: "Here a big monster called Nippon Yusen Kabushiki Kaisha, full of mystery, made a spectacular debut under the hue and cry of the majority of the people." Pointing out that Shibusawa, Masuda, and Shinagawa (the creators of Kyodo Un'yu) had been excluded from N.Y.K.'s board of directors, the writer went on to say that the outcome of the affair exposed two things: "The one is how hard the Satsuma clique in the Government, which had worked behind the scene in the union movement, endeavored to stamp out the Mitsui influence from the newly organized company. The other is that we can imagine how badly Messrs. Shibusawa and Masuda were mortified looking at the outcome."[3]

As the government struggled to build Japan's army, navy, and industry, production of consumer goods stagnated and the cost of imports remained high. It was obvious that in order to balance its trade Japan had to create industries capable of competing with those abroad. Since the old-line merchants were timorous, the government again intervened, bringing in machinery, technology, and instructors to set up model plants for producing paper, glass, cotton and wool textiles, soap, sugar, beer, and other exotic commodities. It has been said with authority that in the Meiji era before 1900 virtually all manufacturing of major foreign-style products in Japan was the result of government subsidy rather than of private initiative.

The Japanese commodity most in demand abroad was silk, export of which was indispensable to the economy. But most of it was produced in peasant households by antiquated and laborious methods, and the product was inferior to that of Europe. To improve it and yet reduce costs, the government subsidized the installation of power-driven filatures using foreign machinery. In 1872 a model silk-reeling mill was set up at Tomioka in Gumma Prefecture. The manager had been instructed to obtain the best machinery available regardless of cost, because eventually the filature would be sold to private owners.

When it was completed, with the help of French technicians, there was no dearth of applicants for jobs. Since at that time the samurai were scarcely able to survive the transition from feudalism, they were invited to send their daughters to the mill for training as machine operators. The young ladies welcomed the opportunity, and many reported for work with their servants and proper wardrobes. The filature, with the atmosphere of a finishing school rather than a factory, became a showcase for the modernizers, and in its first year of operation was visited by the emperor and empress.

The Mitsuis, with centuries of experience in marketing textiles, were also operating filatures and actively promoting sericulture. After Bussan came into being, the company imported superior silkworms and distributed them to cocoon raisers, who were trained by foreign instructors in Western methods of cultivation. In 1893, after the mill at Tomioka had served its purpose, the government turned it over to Mitsui at a nominal price; and it became one of their most profitable investments. By the end of the century Japan had about three thousand power-driven filatures, in addition to related spinning and weaving facilities, and output was so great that the country produced three-quarters of the world's raw silk.

Income from silk was the foundation for other light industries, the most important of which was cotton. In the 1870s Shibusawa Eiichi decided that Japan must produce good cotton yarn instead of importing it. With financial help from a group of merchants and twenty-one noblemen he established the Osaka Spinning Company in 1882 and imported machinery for it from England. The story is told that Shibusawa, wanting Japan's workingmen to learn about the newfangled machines from the West, had the steam-powered spinning frames assembled by his own crew of mechanics. At the first test run there was a deafening clatter and an astonishing disarray: all the machines were running in reverse. But the error was corrected without foreign help, and the mill became highly efficient under native supervision.

Businessmen had been skeptical because they couldn't imagine how Shibusawa expected to recover his money from so huge an investment in machinery. When the mill opened they had Shibusawa's very simple answer: at sundown its windows lighted up like giant fireflies and remained aglow throughout the night. Using hundreds of oil lamps, Shibusawa operated the mill twenty-four hours a day with no holidays. Soon afterward he installed electric lights, the first to be used in a Japanese mill. The Osaka Spinning Company—forerunner of today's Toyobo—was a success from the start, and visitors came from all over Japan to see Osaka's industrial miracle.

Won over by this feat, the Mitsuis decided to have a try at cotton themselves. With the help of Shibusawa and a group of textile wholesalers, they established the Tokyo Cotton Trading Company in 1886. Poorly managed, it failed in the following year and was reorganized in 1887 as the Kanegafuchi Spinning Company. Under full Mitsui control it was slow to gain momentum, but eventually became the largest textile company in Japan and still thrives under the name Kanebo.

Many other successful industries were established, at least in prototype, under the government's carrot-and-stick policy. Paper-making was one of them. While Shibusawa was still in the finance ministry he persuaded Mitsui-gumi and Shimada-gumi to invest some capital in a Western-style paper mill equipped with British machinery. The unfamiliar enterprise was slow to take hold. But Shibusawa, as its president, had confidence in the future of the paper industry and advised investors to be patient. In time the venture—known as the Oji Paper Company—became the largest enterprise of its kind in the Far East, a multinational empire in itself, and a phenomenal profit earner—for Mitsui, but not for Shibusawa, who was frozen out of both management and rewards.

Through the government's industrial-promotion policy, the Mitsuis acquired half a dozen of the country's biggest textile companies, which formed the basis of their industrial sector. At first nearly all the needed machinery was imported, but the government worried about such extravagance and started its own machine-making factory, bringing in many kinds of engines and other apparatus to be disassembled, analyzed, and imitated. The man in charge of this industrial school of sorts was an untutored mechanical genius named Tanaka Hisashige, inventor of the *mannen-tokei,* or "ten thousand year clock." Japanese engineers and machinists may not have been equal at first to the challenge of modern textile machinery, but they quickly mastered the steam engine. Tanaka's factory, which later became Shibaura Engineering Works, concentrated upon engines for sea-going vessels.

It was thus engaged, employing a staff of six hundred men, when taken over by the Mitsuis, and engines for factories were added to its line. As Kanegafuchi Spinning Company began expanding, the Shiba-ura Works was ordered to make a steam engine capable of generating thirteen hundred horsepower, far larger than any that had been built in Japan—or in many countries, for that matter. The job took three years to complete, and foreign observers doubted that the engine would ever run. But it worked perfectly, and after its installation at the Kanegafuchi mill in Kobe it operated without a halt until the mill was fully elec-trified thirty-two years later. Profiting from such experience, Shibaura refined its technology and in the mid-1890s entered the machine-tool field—the making of machines for making other machines—just as Japanese industry entered upon its first period of spectacular growth.

Thomas Edison's discovery of a practical incandescent lamp in 1879 (using a fiber of Japanese bamboo for a filament, incidentally) revolu-tionized the technology of illumination. Four years after Edison began manufacturing incandescent lamps an organization called Tokyo Elec-tric Light Company, financed by Mitsui, started its career. In that year electric lights were installed along Tokyo's Ginza, to the wonder of the populace. The caption on a popular print of the period gave this helpful explanation: "The lamp is not lighted by any flame but by some-thing called *ereki*. Bright light can be commanded from a place as much as a couple of miles away, and its luminosity can be compared to the sun and the moon."

Curiously, those primitive bulbs with their bamboo filaments lasted for as long as twelve hundred hours, perhaps double the lifetime of the "modern" product with metal filaments manufactured by today's Tokyo Shibaura Electric Company, or Toshiba, the successor to Tokyo Electric Light Company and the Shibaura Engineering Works, and by other such companies throughout the world.

As electrically lighted, around-the-clock spinning and weaving mills proliferated, raw cotton became a major import, monopolized by Bussan until Nippon Menka (today's Nichimen Trading Company) entered the field in 1892. Masuda had anticipated the textile boom by securing exclusive agencies for English cotton- and silk-processing machinery and thus involved Mitsui in all aspects of the textile business. Through integrated operations, Bussan eventually was able to import raw cotton, have it spun and woven, and then export the cloth to Eng-land at prices cheaper than those charged for cotton fabrics made in Manchester. In recognition, Osaka, the hub of the Japanese textile industry, became known as the "Manchester of the Orient."

Largely through Masuda's shrewdness, too, Japan wrested from foreigners a respectable share of Japan's overseas trade. In the early years of the Meiji era, Japanese companies handled only about one percent of their country's trade with foreign nations, but by 1900 the proportion had risen to thirty-one percent, with silk and other textiles far in the lead.

Although many blessings were showered upon the Mitsuis in the first decades of the Meiji era, somehow they failed to achieve the security they sought. Deficit financing in the wake of the Saigo rebellion of 1877 brought on a raging inflation, and finance minister Matsukata Masa-yoshi's efforts to control it provoked an economic crisis. While the Mitsuis were caught in that pinch a new misfortune was visited upon them: the operation of national tax funds, which had been Mitsui Bank's biggest business, was transferred to a government bureau, and then to Nippon Ginko, the Bank of Japan, when it was inaugurated in 1882. This central bank, owned jointly by the government and private financiers, was set up on the American plan, with Shibusawa, Ito, Inoue, and Okuma in supervisory positions. Mitsui Bank was represented on the board of directors by Minomura Risuke, but Mitsui's power was diluted when Yasuda Zenjiro, a self-made banker, and other rising financial tycoons were included as members of the board of Nippon Ginko.

Although Mitsui Bank was still handling tax revenues for many prefectural governments, the ending of its same service for the national treasury forced it to solicit new business. A shake-up in the bank's management replaced Mitsui Hachiroemon with Mitsui Saburosuke, but in sad truth no one seemed to be capable of making the important decisions. Like the Tokugawa shogunate after the arrival of Commodore Perry, Mitsui Bank's board of directors temporized by seeking the opinions of its "daimyo"—in this case some three hundred minor officers and lesser banto—and on the basis of their suggestions, all submitted confidentially, the Bank's commercial business rapidly expanded by appealing to small depositors and lending more money to outsiders.

But in 1890, before Mitsui Bank had time to solidify its position, another depression set in. Capital investments declined sharply, bankruptcies among its borrowers became epidemic, and early in 1891 rumors of approaching disaster were rife. One canard, published in a national newspaper, hinted that Mitsui Bank was about to fail, and fearful depositors started a run on the Kyoto branch. By the time it was brought under control, the Tokyo head office and its branches had been mobbed, and there wasn't enough cash to refund deposits because a major portion of the assets was tied up in slowly developing enterprises, the value of whose shares had fallen sharply.

The days of the family's hoard of "cellar silver" were long past, but the Mitsuis had not neglected to keep up friendly relations with the "honorable men in power," and once again they appealed to Inoue for help from the government. The outlook was bleak, since he and Ito were temporarily out of office. Minister of Finance Matsukata was a Satsuma man; and Kawada Koichiro, governor of the Bank of Japan, as well as a former partner of Iwasaki Yataro, was devoutly pro-Mitsubishi. Fortunately, the President of the Privy Council, General Yamagata Aritomo, Ito's classmate, was sympathetic to the plight of the Mitsuis, still the army's bankers and principal suppliers. With this leverage Kawada was prevailed upon to rescue the distressed Mitsui Bank with government funds loaned from Nippon Ginko.

This brush with bankruptcy convinced the Mitsuis that Inoue's services were indispensable, and in the same year, 1891, they invited him to become supreme adviser to the clan and its enterprises. Since Inoue continued to occupy cabinet positions after accepting Mitsui's offer, there was clear conflict of interest here, although in those days the drafting of a statesman in office to serve a business enterprise was not without precedent either in Japan or in other countries. Only twelve years earlier, in Germany, Alfred Krupp had appointed Hanns Jencke, a high official in the kaiser's treasury, as chief of his munitions company's general staff. Jencke's "arrival at the works marked the beginning of regular exchanges of personnel between the government and *die Firma;* henceforth Krupp proposals were far likelier to receive a sympathetic hearing in Berlin."[4]

From Inoue's point of view, what was good for Mitsui was good for Japan. As he explained to General Yamagata and Minister of Finance Matsukata: "The Mitsuis and our economy are very closely related; if failure were to overtake the Mitsuis, the repercussions . . . would not be small. Therefore, although their request to become top adviser is burdensome to me, I do not believe that I have any alternative but to accept. . . . If you endorse my views in this matter, I trust that I may in the future count on your strong support."[5]

Inoue attached stern conditions to his acceptance, insisting that he be empowered to make any reforms he deemed necessary to strengthen the defenses of the concern and to safeguard the family's fortune. As they had done with Minomura, the clan bowed to Inoue's wishes and even gave him complete freedom to rewrite the family's constitution.

How seriously he took this assignment may be judged by the fact that he hired the three most prominent legal talents in Japan to assist him. One was Gustave Boissonade, a Frenchman who had drafted Japan's civil and penal codes; his task was to study the constitutions of Europe's wealthiest families. The second was Hermann Roessler, an archconservative Prussian who had drafted Japan's commercial code and assisted Ito, Inoue, and others in writing the Meiji constitution, which took effect in 1890. But the actual drafting of the House of Mitsui's constitution was entrusted to Shibusawa's son-in-law, Hozumi Nobushige, a pioneer Japanese scholar of Western jurisprudence, dean of the Tokyo Imperial University Law School, and later a president of the emperor's privy council.

Hozumi Nobushige and his brother Yatsuka, also a law professor at the same university, were leading exponents of the "family-state" theory of national polity against those who were trying to abolish the legal basis for family headship. In Yatsuka's opinion the family system united the living with their ancestors. And since all Japanese are descended from a common ancestor, he argued, all of Japan's people are members of one great family. The head of a private family and the emperor, as branches of the same tree, thus derive their authority from the same source. The Hozumis, both of whom had been educated in Germany, are considered to have been responsible for introducing the concepts of emperor worship in the Meiji Constitution and those of the sanctity of the family head in the civil code.

Toward the end of the nineteenth century, scholars argued intensely over the assertions that the Japanese are one family, as well as one race, and that the emperor, as father of the nation, was the fountainhead of sovereignty. Official emphasis on this anachronistic concept presumably was directed against popular movements that were based upon democratic or socialistic ideology and was part of an effort to mobilize the people for the achievement of nationalistic aims. Since the House of Mitsui, like that of the emperor, had been clearly designated as an institution whose preeminence in the economy was essential to the nation's strength, it is plausible to believe that the appointment of Hozumi Nobushige to redraft the Mitsuis' constitution was intended to insure the permanence of their House as a keystone of national polity. The outcome of this undertaking indicates, in fact, that Hachiroemon Mitsui no longer exercised power in his own right and, like the emperor, had become another figurehead to be used by the oligarchs who ruled Japan.

12 · The Zaibatsu Builders

FOREIGNERS HAD GAINED ACCESS to Japan by force, and they remained there on their own terms, laid down in the discriminatory treaties they had imposed upon the dying shogunate. The men who governed Japan knew that neither they nor their countrymen could become masters in their own home until they had become sufficiently "civilized" to be accepted as equals. And that meant conforming to European and American standards of government, commerce, law, and social behavior. The reformers of Japan, therefore, undertook the enormous task of "Westernizing" the country culturally, as well as politically and economically. Their countrymen, a singularly adaptable people, took up the game with such enthusiasm that it became a veritable mania.

Leading the van in this cultural revolution, which reached its height during the early 1880s, was Minister of Foreign Affairs Inoue Kaoru, who demanded nothing less than the transformation of Japan into a "European-style empire." Everything that appeared to be quaint or anachronistic or shocking to outsiders—whether it was clothing, grooming, diet, behavior, art, or architecture—was subject to modification, more often for the worse than for the better. Nevertheless, Japan's imitation of the West, an inexhaustible source of amusement to foreigners, was not an admission of inferiority. Like hunting tribes who wear the skins of predatory animals in order to acquire their strength and cunning, the Japanese had a conscious purpose in adopting the trappings and mannerisms of the "barbarians."

That purpose, as Inoue and his friends saw it, was to satisfy the minimum standards set by the Western arbiters for admission to diplomatic equality, and then, at the very least, to revise the invidious treaties so that Japan could impose protective tariffs behind which a viable industrial structure could be established. In 1880 this goal was still distant, and domestic entrepreneurs were reluctant to take the field against foreign competitors whose superiority in almost every material respect was manifest. The makers of the Meiji government had three alternatives: to wait for the economic climate to become favorable, a process that would take several generations; to engage directly in business, despite the inexperience and ineptitude of the still feudalistic bureaucracy for such undertakings; or to give full support to those private businessmen who seemed to have the best chance of being successful. In 1868 the first alternative already had been rejected. The second was being followed out of grim necessity. But among the Sat-Cho oligarchs, the third had been decided upon as the organizing principle for the new economy.

In order to allow for continuity and growth in private business, it was necessary to establish enterprises that were solidly rooted in basic industries, versatile enough to undertake or to generate new ones, and strong enough financially to survive crises that might occur as they were growing. Many attempts had been made to organize merchants and other wealthy men into companies serving the state's economic policies, but the spirit of cooperation was slow to develop among them, and opportunism or clashes of personality led to failure and discouragement in most cases. Until a more liberal and enlightened business community could be developed, only centralized, dictatorial establishments could overcome those difficulties. It was on the basis of these stark necessities and limited options that the zaibatsu, those uniquely Japanese agglomerates that themselves became the massive building blocks of Japan's state capitalism, were erected.

The three men who transformed Mitsui's grab-bag of enterprises into a coherent and reasonably modern business organization were of a very different nature from their chonin predecessors. In contrast to the illiterate and insular Minomura, who had received only an apprentice's training, they were exceptionally well educated, widely traveled, highly cultivated professionals. More than most Japanese of their time, they had become Westernized in their habits and ways of thinking, especially with regard to matters of business. These great banto were Masuda Takashi, Japan's pioneer in world trade; Dan Takuma, who revolutionized mining through application of the techniques of modern engineering; and Nakamigawa Hikojiro, the financier who saved many an industry from failure by his unflinching and often ruthless rationality.

Until the 1880s the Mitsuis were essentially moneylenders and middlemen who also owned and operated numerous light industrial subsidiaries, most of which had been acquired by chance. Masuda was the one who built a foundation under this rickety structure by acquiring the basic resources to sustain it. Most of the mineral deposits that the Meiji government had inherited from the shogunate were still state owned and operated as strategic industries. But in the 1880s, following the third alternative of fostering private enterprise, the government began to sell those properties at nominal prices to the financial houses it favored. Richest of all those mineral resources were the Miike coal mines in Kyushu, and no one understood their value better than Masuda, who as the government-appointed agent for coal exports, once had tried to assess the extent of the deposits at Miike. They had not been systematically explored, but there was evidence that they were practically inexhaustible. Moreover, although the coal was not suitable for use in steelmaking, it served as an excellent fuel and was cheap to mine.

Yet when the government offered the Miike mines at auction in 1888 there were few bidders. The strongest and most favored contender was Mitsubishi, with its fuel-hungry steamship line and growing industries. Masuda was very eager to get the mines for Bussan; but the Mitsuis, with their usual caution about treading upon unfamiliar fields of business, were known to be opposed to acquiring them. Other interested parties were the reviving Ono-gumi and Asano Soichiro, an adventurous entrepreneur backed by Shibusawa, his relative by marriage. But it was a foregone conclusion that Mitsubishi, being so wealthy and in such good standing with the government, would win the mines.

To preserve anonymity the contenders' sealed bids were submitted by straw men. When the bids were opened, that of a certain Sasaki Hachiro, offering 4,555,000 yen, was the highest, followed closely by the bid of one Kawasaki Risaburo. To the surprise of almost everyone concerned, the Mitsuis' proxy, Sasaki, had won the prize from Mitsubishi's man by the slim margin of 2,300 yen. The bidding had been handled so discreetly that no great scandal over it could be contrived, even by enemies of the government, but experienced businessmen did believe that the closeness of the bids indicated a tip-off somewhere. Curiously, Masuda, the winner, was the one who denounced the bidding as a fraud: "The disposal of the Miike mine was an intrigue . . . among the followers of Okuma. When Mr. Okuma entered the Government he insisted that it was necessary to sell all the Government's property for reasons of financial adjustment. The disposal of the Miike Colliery was explained in these terms. But this was misrepresentation. Actually, it was because Mitsui was the Choshu safe [treasure box] and because Miike was the Mitsui safe that Okuma [patron of Mitsubishi] wanted to separate Miike from Mitsui."[1]

Okuma's plot, if such it was, seemed unbeatable, since he was foreign minister in a cabinet dominated by the generally pro-Mitsubishi Satsuma navy clique. However, the Minister of Justice was a Choshu man (and once a student in Yoshida Shoin's school); and just a few days before the bids were opened, his former classmate, Inoue Kaoru, replaced a navy man as Minister of Agriculture and Commerce, with jurisdiction over the transaction. Whatever means Inoue and Masuda may have used to win the mines, the Mitsuis were more than adequately compensated for their miserable defeat by Mitsubishi in the earlier battle of the steamship lines.

At the time of the purchase, which involved an initial payment of one million yen, acquiring the Miike mines was not considered a great stroke of good fortune. According to public opinion it was "an extraordinary venture," and prudent colleagues wondered how a trader, even one as talented as Masuda, would be able to operate a coal mine. But Masuda, although still unsure about the extent of Miike's subterranean riches, had already taken stock of a secret treasure that came with the premises—a young engineer named Dan Takuma.

Born the third son of a samurai in the coal country of Fukuoka, Dan joined Prince Iwakura's mission to foreign countries in 1871, when he was only thirteen years old. He and his friend Kaneko Kentaro were assigned to attend one of the mission's members, a lord from Fukuoka, and Dan recalled that during their travels he and Kaneko had had to share the same bed. Both boys completed their education in the United States, Kaneko at Harvard College, and Dan at Massachusetts Institute of Technology, where he earned a bachelor of science degree in mining engineering.

When Dan returned to Japan there were no jobs for mining engineers, so he taught English. Among his pupils were Hamaguchi Osachi and Shidehara Kijuro, both of whom later became prime ministers. But Dan, who was born near the Miike mines, had an unquenchable ambition, as he put it, "to enrich my country by bringing its resources to the surface." In 1881 he got his chance when the government hired him, at the munificent salary of four hundred dollars a year, to supervise operations at the Miike mines.

The most primitive mining methods were still being used, and there was little incentive for efficiency because most of the miners were either miserably paid *eta,* still treated as outcasts despite the edict of 1871, or convicts from local prisons, who cost nothing but their board and beds. But after Mitsui bought the mines Dan was able to demonstrate his mettle. The seams of coal were thick and broad but very soft, so that when a shaft was opened by the removal of coal cave-ins occurred frequently. Deep underground the temperature was well above 100°F, and hot water dripped from the walls and roofs of the shafts. A constant seepage of gas, and pervasive coal dust, caused explosions that sometimes took hundreds of lives. The health and safety of the men, women, and children digging or hauling coal were of no concern to the owners, since miners were considered to be expendable; but as the shafts they dug penetrated deeper, and extended farther under the bay, flooding forced them to abandon valuable seams.

Dan explained the situation and the remedy to Masuda and promised to cut mining costs sharply if Mitsui was willing to spend enough money on the equipment he needed. He seemed to know his business, so Masuda sent him abroad to observe drainage techniques and to procure machinery. He returned a year later with an enormous electrically driven turbine pump that cost Mitsui half a million yen, almost ten percent of the price of the mines.

A new kind of executive for Japan, Dan didn't mind getting dirty. He went into the shafts with the men, supervised the installation of the drainage system, and tinkered with the machinery until it functioned properly. With flooding brought under control, the most abundant deposits were made accessible again and production rose spectacularly.

But Dan's schooling had not prepared him for handling the labor problems and social disputes that bristled in the coal fields. The convicts were sullen or desperate men, and the free laborers in the Fukuoka region were the toughest, most intractable folk in Japan. For each crew of miners there were armed straw bosses who worked in pairs to keep them under constant surveillance and to protect each other if necessary. The foremen and company police, notorious ruffians and bullies, were a law unto themselves, and bloody brawls were an everyday occurrence. The situation was too much for the young engineer, a gentle and rather diffident man, and he needed someone who knew how to handle it.

Such a man soon appeared in the person of Noda Utaro, who had been born and bred in the coal country. Noda came unbidden to the Miike workings almost every day, helping out with odd jobs. He brought his own lunch box, wanted no salary, and asked only a jug of hot water for making his tea. He talked the miners' language and also had the kind of magnetic personality for which many Kyushu men—especially his hero, Saigo Takamori—are noted. He made his presence felt by unobtrusively taking control of personnel and community relations problems and eventually built up his own administrative machine among the workers of the company. When it was running smoothly, Dan, impressed with Noda's talent for managing people, persuaded him to stand for election to the prefectural assembly.

At that time only men of means were entitled to vote, but Noda had solid backing among the nationalists who controlled local and prefectural politics. The most powerful organization in that part of Kyushu was the Gen'yosha, or Black Ocean Society, organized by a lesser mining tycoon named Hiraoka Kotaro. It was guided by Toyama Mitsuru, an educated fanatic whose life work was to fulfill Saigo's dream of Japanese expansion upon the Asian continent and to curb, by terror if necessary, any domestic tendency toward obstructing it. While sending their agents into China, Manchuria, and Korea to serve as spies and to engage in clandestine political activity, those super-patriots also operated schools in Japan where they trained cadres. Exploiting feudalistic sentiments still strong in Japan, they recruited gangs of muscle men whom they used to inspire or subdue public unrest, intimidate political candidates or voters, suppress dissident laborers, and punish anyone of whom their bosses disapproved. The Black Ocean Society and comparable leagues were especially useful to mining and manufacturing companies, who supported them financially and through them could build or shatter the careers of would-be politicians.

With such dedicated backing, in addition to that of Mitsui, Noda was a remarkable success in politics. Within a decade after Mitsui took over the Miike mines Noda had graduated from the prefectural assembly to the National Diet, which met in Tokyo. Later he became a prominent figure in the powerful Rikken Seiyukai, the Friends of Constitutional Government Party, founded by Ito and others of the Choshu clique, which generally was considered to be at the service of the Mitsui and Sumitomo zaibatsu. (The Rikken Seiyukai, established in 1900, was eventually challenged by the Rikken Kaishinto, or Constitutional Progressive Party, bossed by Okuma and relatives of the Iwasaki family. Later called Minseito, or the Progressive Party, Rikken Kaishinto served the Mitsubishi zaibatsu in political affairs).

Amply financed by Mitsui and relieved of labor problems by the helpful Noda, the young technocrat Dan Takuma made the Miike mines immensely profitable. In fact, minerals were the bedrock upon which the towering structure of the Mitsui zaibatsu rose. Profiting further from the government's policy of turning over natural resources to businessmen, Masuda and Dan gained control over the long-worked but scarcely exploited Kamioka mines, literally mountains of lead and zinc ore liberally laced with silver, cadmium, and copper and showing even an occasional glint of gold. The mines at Kamioka, along with several other coal mines* and the best iron deposits in the country, fell easily into Mitsui's hands, with little more than a gentle push from Inoue and Ito. From private interests in Kagoshima, Masuda bought the Kushikino gold mine, once an important source of the Satsuma han's wealth but no longer profitable to the owners because the concentration of ore was too low to yield much by the old methods of processing. When worked by the newer cyanide process introduced by

* Richest of these collieries were the Yamano and Tagawa in Fukuoka Prefecture, and a coal mining and railway complex in Hokkaido, later called the Hokkaido Colliery and Steamship Company.

Dan, the Kushikino mine later became quite productive for Mitsui.

These diverse elements formed a splendidly balanced money machine that functioned well in war or peace, in boom or depression. Coal was needed at all times, and the cost of mining it at Miike was about twenty-five percent less than the national average. With Bussan vigorously selling the coal, output from half a dozen Mitsui mines accounted for more than a quarter of the nation's total production. Military expansion in preparation for wars against China and Russia created a seller's market for Mitsui's Kamioka lead (for bullets), Iwanobori sulfur (for gunpowder), and Kamaishi iron; and the rising chemical industry at Miike satisfied the demand for many byproducts of coal and of the several nonferrous minerals yielded by Mitsui's mines.

The greatest menace to the mining industry is an economic recession, for despite wild fluctuations in prices of minerals the exploitation of deposits should continue steadily. The price of gold changes but little, however, and by hoarding gold in boom times and selling it during recessions Mitsui was able not only to cover the costs of mining development without interruption but also to pick up choice pieces of property when less stable competitors faced bankruptcy. It is a significant fact that Mitsui, Mitsubishi, and Sumitomo all owned gold mines then and still do now. The value of the output of gold was insignificant compared with that of other products, yet the yellow metal (and to some extent silver) served as a kind of balance wheel to keep their mining enterprises running smoothly for decade after decade. Mining also supported their more risky manufacturing industries until they fared well enough to reach the break-even point.

It was Dan's coal that put Masuda's Bussan on the world's map. During the decade between 1891 and 1901 foreign trade became Bussan's main business, and its turnover rose fivefold. With branches in London, Paris, New York, Sydney, and all the main seaports of East and Southeast Asia, Bussan was by far the largest trading company in Japan and was beginning to overtake the great British houses. In the wake of the Sino-Japanese War of 1894–95 Bussan started its own steamship line to carry Miike's coal to Asian ports. Bussan was also getting into sugar, cotton, grain, lumber, and every other major commodity. It handled half the nation's machinery imports and supplied most of its steel.

And yet in the early 1890s, when Masuda and Dan were working together so successfully to build their respective enterprises, Mitsui Bank was falling sadly behind the times. The concern was like an army with two crack divisions but having no general staff worthy of the name. Since the death of Minomura Rizaemon the Bank had been headed successively by old Hachiroemon Kofuku and his heir, Saburosuke Taka-aki, the Meiji government's first treasurer. Business operations were directed by venerable banto, such as Saito Junzo, men of Minomura's generation who lacked the flexibility and imagination to cope with the uncertainties of constitutional government and the rigors of the new commercial and banking codes.

It was because of this deficiency in generalship that Inoue had accepted the position of supreme adviser in 1891 and begun renovating the House of Mitsui. But work on the House's new constitution had scarcely started; and having only barely escaped bankruptcy earlier that year, Mitsui Bank was at the mercy of any new storm that might arise. Inoue needed a man from outside who, as Minomura had done a generation before, could step in and, unhindered by old obligations, sensitivities, or taboos, slash away encumbrances and give the sound businesses a chance to grow.

The man of his choice was Nakamigawa Hikojiro, who more than satisfied Inoue's hopes and the Mitsuis' expectations. Like Minomura Rizaemon, Nakamigawa came to Mitsui late in his career and died young. But the exciting decade he spent with the house blazed a clear trail through the tangled forest of Japanese business. His achievement, in brief, was to wean Mitsui from its dependence upon government handouts, replace shortsighted opportunism with far-seeing economic logic, and, perhaps most important for Japan, to cultivate a new kind of businessman by bringing in university-educated managers capable of thinking, instead of merely promoting obedient apprentices plucked from the countinghouse.

Born in 1853 to a poor samurai family in the castle town of Nakatsu in Kyushu, Nakamigawa was most definitely an unusual child: he was quick to master the Chinese classics, and he developed an abnormal thirst for sakè at the age of six. Neither of these accomplishments would have taken him very far in Nakatsu, but his precocity attracted the interest of an uncle, who devoted considerable attention to his education. This was most fortunate for him, since the uncle happened to be Fukuzawa Yukichi, Japan's most influential Westernizer and, in 1868, the founder of Keio Gijuku, which later became Keio University. A biographer has said that Fukuzawa loved Nakamigawa Hikojiro more than his own children and had great ambitions for his future. As a student at Keio Gijuku, the young Hikojiro absorbed his uncle's teachings, which were quite liberal by Japanese standards of the time, and became an outspoken advocate of individualism, rationalism, and representative government.

Fukuzawa, whose first impressions of the outside world were formed during a trip to the United States in 1860 and to Europe in 1862, preached that "all men under the sun are equal." He was no visionary, however, and recognized that (as Orwell has said) "some men are more equal than others." In one of his many books about Occidental ways (in the 1870s all books in Japan about the West were popularly called "Fukuzawa books") he wrote: "At this time when our country is being opened we cannot talk about the unfortunate inequality between the rich and the poor. There is no one but the rich man that we can look to as we counter the opposition of the national trading wars. . . . Rich men are important for gathering capital in one place and making it work in some unified way. And where capital is already gathered in one place it gives free play to the inherent qualities of resources without any instruction from outsiders."[2] Acting on this conviction, Fukuzawa, a close associate of Iwasaki Yataro, supplied Mitsubishi with some of its most able managers.

Perhaps because of Fukuzawa's training, Nakamigawa, although penniless himself, gravitated to wealth. After his graduation from Keio Gijuku in 1871 he taught English for two years and then departed for study in England with a fellow alumnus, a mathematical genius named Koizumi Shinkichi, who later became president of Yokohama Specie Bank, and then in 1889 of Keio Gijuku. In London he became friends with the son of a former daimyo, Hachisuka Mochiaki, who in time headed Japan's House of Peers and the Ministry of Education. But the most valuable acquaintance Nakamigawa made in London was Inoue Kaoru, who marked him as a talent for exploitation in the future.

Nakamigawa returned to Japan a well-rounded cosmopolite, seemingly with all the qualifications and connections for becoming a successful bureaucrat. At that time a number of Fukuzawa's bright young men from Keio were being brought into the government's ministries by Okuma, in the hope that they would introduce a modicum of rationality and rectitude. Nakamigawa was given a job in the railway bureau, where for a couple of years he was able to observe the spoils system at its worst but was helpless to make any improvements. When Choshu again sat at the high end of the government seesaw, Inoue took the foreign affairs portfolio and chose Nakamigawa as his assistant. Nakamigawa seemed to have found a vocation in diplomacy, but his career soon foundered upon the rocks of political rivalry. When the other oligarchs turned upon Okuma and ousted him from office, the entire Keio contingent was purged with him, under suspicion of complicity in the improper disposal of government property.

Nakamigawa, the disillusioned idealist, then tried his hand at organizing a foreign-trade firm but failed for lack of capital and returned to Keio as a teacher. This happened in 1881, when pressure from Okuma and other liberals forced the government to announce, through an Imperial Rescript, that the people would be given a constitution and a parliament by 1890. From then on the nation was gripped in a craze of Western-style politicking, and partisan journalism throve. Fukuzawa, in league with Okuma's party and financed by Mitsubishi, started a daily newspaper called *Jiji Shimpo* (News of the Times) and made his nephew Nakamigawa its president. Staffed by Keio men and featuring the vigorous editorials of Fukuzawa, *Jiji Shimpo* won many readers by lambasting the established oligarchy and in consequence became quite profitable.

Now journalism became a shortcut to success, especially for poor samurai and sons of samurai who found the pen a good substitute for the sword. Nakamigawa, however, had little taste for demagoguery, and when Inoue Kaoru offered him a job as president of the new San'yo Railway Company he left the newspaper. The management of San'yo company was divided by rivalry between the dominant Mitsubishi faction of stockholders and a Choshu group that was in charge of construction. Nakamigawa was accepted as president because he was considered to be honest and neutral.

Such a man apparently was a rarity in the railway business, which through most of the Meiji era was dominated by the Choshu loyalist Inoue Masaru, head of the government's railroad bureau. A politician of the old school and boon companion of Ito and Inoue Kaoru since their London days, Inoue Masaru naturally favored fellow clansmen and their allies in business dealings. Most of the procurement for railways was still in the hands of Mitsui Bussan, while engineering contracts went to Fujita Denzaburo, a ruthless profiteer who had been a partner of Inoue Kaoru in Bussan's predecessor company, Senshu Kaisha. In this cozy situation cost was secondary to loyalty; and it is said that after Inoue Masaru left the bureau the expense of laying railway tracks dropped by half.

Customarily, materials and equipment were obtained through an arrangement with the railway bureau chief, who in turn worked through a foreign middleman. As president of San'yo company, Nakamigawa discovered that he was to be cut in on the profits. When the first "private commission" was presented to him discreetly, he accepted it. Then, to the consternation of his colleagues, he issued a formal receipt to the donor and turned the money over to the company.

He accomplished his purpose of healing the split in the management of San'yo, possibly by uniting both sides against him because of his priggish attitude toward graft and his insistence upon running a safe railroad. Besides wasting the stockholders' money on such frills as air brakes, he insisted upon buying enough land to lay a double track, anticipating the time when this trunk line, which extended along the Seto Inland Sea from Kobe to the Straits of Shimonoseki, would eventually become too congested for a single track. The board of directors capitulated, but he was made aware that he had outworn his welcome and resigned after serving less than four years. Then approaching the age of forty, the ex-bureaucrat, ex-businessman, ex-teacher, ex-journalist, and ex–company president looked like a failure.

The prospects for an executive with such a spotty record were dim at best, and during the financial crisis of 1890 opportunities of any sort were practically nonexistent. At this low point in Nakamigawa's career Inoue Kaoru offered him the job of rehabilitating Mitsui Bank. To Inoue's surprise the unemployed Nakamigawa refused. In his opinion the Mitsuis were too hidebound to make a successful transition to the twentieth century, and he doubted that they would give him enough authority to renovate their establishment. However, Inoue convinced the doubting Nakamigawa that he would have the freedom to make any reforms he wished. Thus for the second time in twenty-five years a middle-aged outsider, who had served several other masters and was scarcely acquainted with the Mitsuis, took command of their destinies.

In 1891, at the age of thirty-eight, Nakamigawa was appointed to the new post of managing director of Mitsui Bank, to serve under President Mitsui Takayasu, who was forty-two. The keynote of the new leadership was youth and, although the elders in the bank's employ were not uprooted, thereafter the important work was delegated to men in their twenties and thirties. Nakamigawa is remembered for having recruited more top-level managers for Mitsui than anyone before or since his time (and all without benefit of aptitude tests). His method, if immodest, was simple. He selected men whose background was the same as his own: sons of samurai families, university graduates, and journalists. Of twenty outstanding businessmen whom he employed, eighteen were graduates of Keio Gijuku, twelve were former newspapermen, and seven were from the staff of *Jiji Shimpo*. All became prominent industrialists or bankers, seven founded business empires of their own, and three rose to posts in the nation's cabinet.

After six months of intensive exploration, during which he dispassionately assessed the present and potential value of every Mitsui holding, Nakamigawa set to work upon a drastic program of elimination and consolidation. Old debts that had been allowed to drag on for various reasons were to be collected or the collateral was to be foreclosed. Stocks that did not give Mitsui management-control over the companies that had issued them were to be sold, so that capital could be concentrated effectively, especially in growing industries. (This meant, for example, selling Mitsui's holdings in Shibusawa's Dai-Ichi National Bank and in Mitsubishi's N.Y.K. steamship line.) In 1892 most of the mining enterprises were merged to form the Mitsui Mining Company, which, with Bussan and the Bank, became a third pillar of the concern. In the following year he inaugurated a reorganized corporate entity known as Gomei Kaisha Mitsui Ginko (Mitsui Partnership Bank), in which all the shares were held by Mitsui family heads. This move freed them from the unlimited liability feature of the Société Anonyme arrangement, which worried Nakamigawa.

Since Gomei Kaisha Mitsui Ginko was performing most of the functions of the old Omotokata, or great headquarters, the name of the latter body was changed to Motokata (dropping the prefix meaning "great"). Among the members of Motokata, in addition to family heads, were Nakamigawa and Masuda, with Shibusawa Eiichi as a consultant. Although only men bearing the Mitsui name were entitled to vote, the capacity of those votes to destroy the House by arbitrary decisions had been reduced. The general purpose of these changes was to get away from commercial banking and government service (because handling other people's money seemed to Nakamigawa a stupid occupation) and to move more aggressively into growing industrial fields.

In those few amazing years between 1895 and 1900, in order to attract and retain the best talents Nakamigawa adjusted salaries to offset the cost of living, introduced a merit-promotion plan to complement the seniority system, set up a pension fund, and originated the twice-yearly bonus. This bonus was so successful an incentive that before long it was adopted almost universally in Japan and is still a conspicuous feature of the economy.

In order to mobilize all the capital potentially available, Nakamigawa set up a special division for the collection of bad debts and made it clear that nothing and no one was to be sacred. The largest of the bad debts, amounting to about one million yen, or five percent of the bank's total of loans outstanding, was owed by Higashi Hongan-ji, the main temple for millions of Japanese members of the Jodo Shinshu Buddhist sect. Nakamigawa went to Kyoto personally, confronted the abbot, and told him to pay back the debt within a year or risk attachment of the temple, including the Amitabha (comparable in sacredness to the Holy Rood of Christianity). As a followup he delegated his most insistent collector, Fujiyama Raita (another Keio man), to prod Hongan-ji's priests into mounting a nationwide campaign for donations. To the abbot's surprise they raised over a million yen, enough not only to pay off the debt but to renovate the temple. Afterward, the iconoclastic Nakamigawa is reported to have said: "I feared I might descend into hell after my death, as an enemy of the Buddha. Instead, however, I may be admitted to Sukhavati [the Buddhist paradise] for a good deed."[3]

Not even the oligarchs were immune to Nakamigawa's devotion to Mitsui's capital. Ever since the swashbuckling days of the bakumatsu most of them had been spending far beyond their means upon travel, apparel, feasting, and geisha parties, and whenever they ran short of cash they turned to the merchants. Each clique had its own friendly banker, and Choshu's politicians knew that certain people at Mitsui were lenient toward them and their needs. If the amount required was not too large, one's seal or signature on an IOU was sufficient collateral. Such loans were not carried in the official books. Instead, the promissory notes were dropped into a locked container, known as the "hell box." Employees estimated that the promises it held were worth more than half a million yen, but no one ever knew for sure because it was never opened for an accounting.

Nakamigawa, either figuratively or literally, at last opened the "hell box." When General Katsura Taro, a Restoration hero from Choshu, balked at having to pay an overdue loan, Nakamigawa invoked the law and attached his mansion. On another occasion the prestigious Ito, who had dropped many an IOU into the "hell box," came to ask for a personal loan and was referred to Nakamigawa. The latter said he would gladly oblige the *genro,* the elder statesman, but what would he post as collateral? Ito said that his wife had a savings account at a branch of the bank. Instead of taking Ito's word for this, the managing director insisted upon making an inquiry. This breach of courtesy deeply offended Ito and earned Nakamigawa a reprimand from Inoue Kaoru. But the banker reminded Inoue that he had been entrusted with running things his own way, which for him meant that business came before friendship or politics.

Nakamigawa was equally unsentimental about foreclosures. When the Thirty-third Bank in Gumma Prefecture failed, a considerable amount of Mitsui money was involved. Fujiyama Raita, in charge of forfeited assets, seized three large silk mills upon which the defunct bank held mortgages. Still unsatisfied, he tried to take forcible possession of several farms that had been mortgaged without the owners' consent. Thwarted by the angry farmers, he confiscated the ruined banker's dwellings and personal property, including valuable heirlooms. Frequently the best items from such legal forays ended up in the storehouses of the Mitsuis, whose art collections, although oddly variegated, were becoming immensely valuable.

Nakamigawa's great passion, however, was the acquisition of production facilities, or of the capital for developing them, and he deployed his most talented assistants to help him fulfill this aim. An especially able man in this respect was his brother-in-law Asabuki Eiji, a fellow disciple of Fukuzawa, who took charge of those three repossessed silk mills and coordinated their activities with others, including the famous Tomioka filature, to form Japan's leading silk combine.

Sensing that textiles were soon to become the biggest profit-earner in Japan's foreign trade, Nakamigawa nursed along the cranky Kanegafuchi Spinning Mill at Kobe despite continuing losses. To set it aright he himself became president in 1893 and brought in Asabuki Eiji, a former Mitsubishi executive, to run it. Muto Sanji and Wada Toyoji, recent Keio graduates who had just returned from studying textile industries in foreign countries, were instructed to introduce the latest available technology and prepare the company to invade international markets. Kanegafuchi, called "Mitsui's prodigal mill," already had cost its owners a million yen without showing the slightest profit. Muto, after intensive studies of spinning technology, decided to make a yarn of finer count than any being produced in Japan. After buying up most of Kanegafuchi's stock still in the hands of "outsiders," Nakamigawa invested another half million yen or more of Mitsui's money to back Muto's hunch. It paid off so well that Kanegafuchi outstripped the other cotton spinners, launched an export business, and established a new mill in Shanghai as a beachhead for invading the vast China market.

Another losing proposition that Nakamigawa clung to tenaciously was the Shibaura Engineering Works, because he felt that inevitably production of heavy machinery must be the heart of Japanese industry. For Shibaura's rehabilitation he installed as president the hard-driving Fujiyama, who had shown a certain steadfastness by divorcing his first wife and marrying Nakamigawa's sister-in-law. Fujiyama was also delegated to salvage the Oji Paper Company, which was making little profit although it virtually monopolized the manufacture of Western-style paper in Japan.

Oji Paper was still controlled by Shibusawa Eiichi, who had lavished much wealth and energy upon making it a success. He had sent his nephew, Okawa Heizaburo, abroad to study the latest technology, and by 1890 an efficient production system had been worked out at Oji. All that was needed was more capital, so Shibusawa persuaded Mitsui Bank to increase its investment. Nakamigawa, taking advantage of Shibusawa's idealistic nature, used Mitsui's equity to maneuver him out of the management. Under Fujiyama's aggressive policy, Okawa, the most brilliant paper technologist in Japan, was replaced by a Mitsui engineer; and Fujihara Ginjiro, another of Nakamigawa's recruits from Keio, was put in charge of the organization. The new regime eventually built Oji Paper Company into one of Japan's largest enterprises.

While through these maneuvers Nakamigawa was roughing out the bold outlines of a zaibatsu, he discouraged the dispersion of capital into less meaningful fields, especially the retail clothing business and the wholesaling of handcrafted silks, which were the ancestral specialties of the Mitsuis. He also tried to bring Bussan under stronger control of Mitsui headquarters and to rationalize its operations by eliminating less profitable lines that were being handled by Masuda out of courtesy rather than for gain. These efforts were part of his grand design to sweep away the remnants of feudalism and to make Mitsui a clearly defined and articulated business enterprise, rather than a jumble of properties acquired more or less fortuitously, or an appendage of the government, or an instrument for advancing the fortunes of the men in the Meiji oligarchy.

But at the pinnacle of his success in revitalizing the concern he felt an increasing isolation and a sense of impending failure. Too young to have taken part in the struggles of the bakumatsu, that twilight of the Tokugawas, he was scornful of the long-winded, self-glorifying yarns told by older samurai about events still vivid in their memories. In his understanding of the principles and practices of capitalism he was far ahead of his time, but in absorbing the rationalism and puritan ethics of the West he had rejected prematurely the traditions of mutual loyalty, compromise, and decision by consensus that still ruled private and public life in Japan.

Through his single-mindedness and disregard for sentiment Naka-migawa had upset the more conservative of the Mitsuis. Masuda at Bussan strongly resented his impertinent meddling with the trading business. Shibusawa, who felt a paternal interest in the Mitsuis and a willingness to coexist with them, was alienated by Nakamigawa's harsh competitiveness. Discord in Motokata's advisory council, over which Nakamigawa presided and in which Shibusawa participated, caused Inoue Kaoru deep misgivings. Ito Hirobumi, who was to become prime minister once again, had been seriously affronted in his request for a loan, and all the oligarchs from Choshu were alarmed at Nakami-gawa's obvious efforts to sever the hidden ties that bound the Mitsuis to their political machine. Like a Nipponese Pandora, the impatient Nakamigawa was being pursued by the furies he had liberated when he opened that "hell box."

13 · Diplomacy by Other Means

IN 1897 FOREIGN MINISTER OKUMA SHIGENOBU said: "If we enquire what points are practically most important in the foreign policy of the Meiji Era, we find that to attain an equal footing with other Powers, as declared in the Imperial Edict at the Restoration, has been the impulse underlying all the national changes that have taken place."[1]

This policy was carried out in three successive stages: soft diplomacy, hard diplomacy, and war—which as Clausewitz taught, is only an extension of diplomacy by other means.

The leading exponents of the persuasive approach were Inoue, Ito, and Okuma. To create an atmosphere conducive to diplomacy as he had experienced it in Europe, Inoue, when he served as foreign minister, promoted the construction in Tokyo of a social center called Rokumeikan, or Hall of the Baying Stag, designed by an English architect in the style of an eighteenth-century German palace. Rokumeikan, completed in 1883, was the scene of balls, soirees, and charitable events at which ladies and gentlemen of international society could mingle with members of Japan's elite. One of its main functions was to give the studious Japanese a place to demonstrate their familiarity with European deportment, diversions, and cuisine.

The Japanese leaders, officially commoners, were at a disadvantage in relations with their titled European counterparts, but this deficiency was corrected in 1884 when a German-style peerage of five ranks—prince, marquis, count, viscount, and baron—was created. The former samurai loyalists, who had abolished social classes because they were "feudalistic," now emerged, in middle age, as self-appointed but nonetheless legitimate peers of the realm. Standing high among the new aristocrats were Ito, his protégé Saionji, General Yamagata, and Prime Minister Matsukata, all of whom eventually became princes, along with the former lords of Satsuma and Choshu and the last of the shoguns, Tokugawa Hitotsubashi Keiki.

Nearly all the Meiji era's political leaders, the former daimyo, the court nobles, and numerous statesmen in the shogunate's time received titles, but no merchants were so honored. This omission led Mitsui's forthright Masuda Takashi to complain: "If you consider how things really are in this country, you can see that it has not changed since pre-Restoration days. The men of commerce and industry . . . are not the equal of other classes in social prestige."[2]

The peerage was not merely a social ornament, however, nor even only a diplomatic device. Under the new constitution, still in preparation, there was to be a House of Peers whose important function was to prevent an elected House of Representatives from dominating the government. A seat in the House of Peers would bring the member into contact with most of the nation's distinguished personages, including members of the imperial family. It is not surprising, then, that the framers of the constitution had qualms about admitting tradesmen and moneylenders to that aristocratic conclave.

Soon after the creation of the peerage the luminaries of Japanese and foreign society were invited to a celebration. The following description in a Tokyo newspaper suggests the kind of international environment the oligarchy was trying to create:

"On the Emperor's birthday, as has become customary, Foreign Minister Inoue and Madame Inoue were hosts at a colorful soiree held at Rokumeikan.

"Among the guests who arrived at about 9 P.M. were members of the Imperial Family, Cabinet Ministers, Councillors, members of the diplomatic corps, directors and deputy members of government bureaus, officers of the Army and Navy, and members of the peerage, all accompanied by their wives. . . .

"The music in the garden seemed to blend with the surroundings, lights made the hall as bright as day. The guests enjoyed the dancing and the buffet supper, and seemed unmindful of the passage of time."[3]

Inoue, who pursued his goals with reptilian patience, apparently found the Rokumeikan ambiance ideal for developing his secret diplomacy for achieving the revision of those unequal treaties with the Western powers. Traditionalists, however, regarded the Hall of the Baying Stag as a sinkhole of debauchery and an affront to true Japanese culture. On one occasion a festive ball was invaded by a band of young patriots in samurai clothing, who herded the fashionably dressed guests off the waxed parquet and then performed a hair-raising sword dance as an example of the proper way to do things. Nationalistic editors and pamphleteers aimed their sharpest barbs at Rokumeikan, symbol of the diplomatic sellout to the barbarians.

In 1887, when the Rokumeikan period was at its height, Inoue was conducting what he thought were highly promising discussions with representatives of the foreign powers. In exchange for abolition of extraterritoriality, he agreed to allow foreigners unrestricted residence in Japan and, pending the Westernization of the legal system, to include foreign judges in Japanese courts of law when cases involving foreigners were being heard. When word of these "disgraceful" terms leaked out, there was a great outburst of public indignation. Amid mounting xenophobia inspired by nationalist reactionaries and anti-government liberals, Inoue resigned and Okuma took over the foreign affairs portfolio. Everyone was demanding prompt revision of the treaties, but few indeed were willing to endorse the compromises necessary to make that possible. Okuma continued to negotiate, supposedly in secrecy, but once again there was a leak revealing unpalatable details, which were used to stir up mob violence.

Okuma, like Inoue before him, was under severe pressure to resign. After an acrimonious imperial conference, he was returning to the foreign ministry when a young antiforeign zealot ran up to his carriage and hurled a bomb. The explosion injured Okuma's leg so badly that it had to be amputated. The assailant, investigation showed, was connected with the same terrorist band, the Black Ocean Society, whose activists had killed the brilliant Okubo Toshimichi and stabbed the liberal statesman Itagaki Taisuke. But public sentiment was such that Okuma's attacker, who committed seppuku on the spot, was praised for his patriotism, while the cabinet was obliged to resign.

This popular reaction against the conciliatory "Rokumeikan diplomacy" coincided with the inauguration of parliamentary government, the upsurge of political parties, a jingoist clamor for expansion on the continent, and successive economic crises that bred explosive discontent. The Sat-Cho oligarchs responded to these challenges by using calculated despotism in the guise of parliamentary rule. In preparation for worse things to come, the sanctity and authority of the emperor were reasserted in such proclamations as the Imperial Rescript on Education, which institutionalized Confucian ethics and Shinto myths. Issued in 1890, this doctrine, drummed into the heads of schoolchildren until the end of the Second World War, made it clear that education was not to be sought for personal fulfillment or knowledge for its own sake. Rather, it was absorbed as a duty to one's ancestors, parents, and the state; and part of that duty, in time of emergency, was to "guard and maintain the prosperity of Our Imperial Throne, coeval with heaven and earth."

The fact that such emergencies were expected is apparent from the government's persecution of its opponents. Before the general elections of 1892 Toyama Mitsuru's Black Ocean Society was agitating for an aggressive foreign policy and expansion of the military budget, and its leaders were privately assured that Prime Minister Matsukata Masayoshi would comply with their wishes. To assist friendly candidates, the home minister, a despot from Choshu, mobilized the police to harass their opponents. Toyama's men terrorized antigovernment candidates in the Fukuoka area, where Mitsui's ally Noda Utaro was campaigning. During the nationwide disturbances at least twenty-five people were killed and 380 were wounded, according to official reports; but even so, the opposition came out far ahead and continued to insist upon a tougher diplomacy.

Public uproar over those atrocities brought Ito Hirobumi back to the premiership. To strengthen his diplomacy, he appointed as foreign minister Mutsu Munemitsu, who in days of the bakumatsu had been Mitsui Saburosuke's protégé and Minomura's intelligence agent. In 1894, after two years of diligent negotiation, Mutsu won Britain's acceptance of a new treaty promising Japan diplomatic equality and tariff autonomy without any humiliating conditions attached. Although it was not to become effective for a few years, the knowledge that it had been won gave a great boost to Japanese self-esteem.

The oligarchs had been able, so far, to restrain the hotspurs who agitated for military conquests upon the mainland of Asia, but they had never rejected territorial expansion in principle. Without a foothold upon the continent, they believed, Japan could not hope to achieve either economic prosperity or military security. The most obvious steppingstone to Asia (or from Asia to Japan) was Korea. Japan had already gained special privileges there through the efforts of former ambassador Inoue. However, the Chinese claimed the "Hermit Kingdom" as a protectorate; and it was also coveted by the Russian empire, which had built up its forces in the Maritime Province, east of the Ussuri River, established a naval base in nearby Vladivostok (which means "Commanding the East"), and was preparing to move southward into Korea and Manchuria.

Korea's potential value as a colony was well understood by the Japanese, who had made it their best foreign market for cotton goods. Mitsui had already established textile and paper mills, light industrial ventures, and mining operations there, despite the instability of the Korean government. Agents of Japan's secret societies had been conducting intrigues and provoking subversion to win control of the country, but the Chinese were gaining political influence and their textiles were crowding out Japanese products. In 1894, during a Korean revolt inspired by Toyama's provocateurs, the Chinese sent troops to assist the Korean king. Japan seized this long-awaited opportunity and dispatched a much larger force to the Korean capital to "restore order."

Ito, a stickler for legality, wanted to settle the Korean question by diplomacy but was effectively opposed both by officers in Japan's army and navy, now confident of their readiness for a showdown with

China, and by civilian ultranationalists, who stirred up patriotic fervor. Setting a precedent followed in later conflicts, the imperial navy struck before war was declared, sinking a Chinese troopship, and the Sino-Japanese War began.

At the time Japan seemed to be absurdly weak, by European standards, and the government's financial resources were slim. Few foreign observers gave Japan more than a slight chance to defeat the incomparably larger country. Yet in the nine-month war that followed, Japan destroyed China's fleet, drove its ground forces out of Korea, and captured Port Arthur, as well as territories in Manchuria and Shantung.

In 1895, with the whole country at last united behind his government, Ito signed a peace treaty that gave Japan Formosa, the Pescadores islands, and, in China itself, Liaotung Peninsula, where the ports of Dairen and Port Arthur were situated. The treaty ended Chinese interference with Japan's ambitions in Korea and also won for Japan an indemnity equivalent to nearly 150 million dollars.

Having studied the behavior of other imperialist nations, the Japanese had started the war on the assumption that they could plunder a weaker nation without being chastised. Their assumption proved to be correct, but they soon realized that international custom provided no guarantee that their gains would be respected. Before popular rejoicing over the treaty had died down in Japan, Russia, France, and Germany virtually ordered the victor to return the Liaotung Peninsula to China, "to protect peace in the Far East." Their so-called Triple Intervention, which brought down the Ito cabinet, impressed Japan indelibly with the truth of Bismarck's dictum that "might makes right." It also exposed the hypocrisy of the intervening powers who, with Great Britain, proceeded to divide among themselves the territories that Japan had been forced to yield, thereby adding fuel for the flames of militant nationalism in Japan.

Nevertheless, Japan's material gains were substantial. Formosa, or Taiwan, was a valuable colony, and the indemnity from China, paid in bullion, enabled Japan to improve its financial system by adopting the gold standard, to strengthen its heavy industry, and build up military power for a later confrontation on the continent. Moreover, because of their unexpected triumph over China, the Japanese had risen in the esteem of the Western powers and were being evaluated as possible allies rather than as perennial victims of the white imperialists.

During the contest with China the Mitsuis, in their familiar role as purveyors to the government, got their first real taste of war business and found it to their liking. Japan had entered the war without sufficient preparation, and factories and mills that had been struggling under deficits suddenly were swamped with orders, accompanied by subsidies for expansion. Bussan's ships, docks, warehouses, and agencies for imported materials and machinery were essential to the war effort. Mitsui Mining, established as a separate company in 1892, supplied fuel, metals, and chemicals, while Bank marched in the forefront of the war-fund campaign.

All these activities, coordinated by Nakamigawa with cool precision, demonstrated beyond a doubt the capacity of the Mitsui zaibatsu to serve the national interest in war, as well as in peace. In recognition of the House's contributions, Mitsui Hachiroemon Takaaki, ninth heir of the senior Kita-ke family, was raised to the rank of baron. At last members of the Mitsui clan, who had led the merchants of Japan along the way from fourth-class citizenship to nominal equality with princes, could speak up boldly in the councils of state and could even arrange marriages for their children with those of the noblest families in the realm.

War profits and accelerated military expansion after the Triple Intervention seemed to vindicate Nakamigawa's industrial finance policy. Mitsui Bank's deposits and loans had increased significantly even without much business from the government, and ground had been broken for an imposing new headquarters building from which the concern could conduct its affairs in a more unified way. As Nakamigawa reached his mid-forties he was a living legend of success, with an unlimited future, a loving wife, and a houseful of healthy, promising children with whom to share that future.

But as the century drew to a close the burden of business problems began to weigh heavily upon him, and his personal relationships suffered in consequence. Other men of his class washed away their worries at exclusive teahouses or restaurants, where talented geisha coaxed them to drink, sing provincial songs, and make happy fools of themselves. In this Japanese way they engendered mutual trust and affection—the "belly-to-belly" friendships that are a vital part of Japanese business and political life.

Nakamigawa drank well, but he drank alone. When he came home from the office, frustrated by the mulishness of older colleagues or by bureaucratic interferences, he would call for a drink before he had his shoes off, and he drank continuously until he went to bed, with a big bottle of sakè, at once his addiction and his solace, beside him. This habit seems to have aggravated a chronic kidney ailment, which incapacitated him frequently.

At first Inoue had been tolerant of the headstrong obanto; but when he realized that his own subtle design for Mitsui's future was in jeopardy his disapproval of the younger man became unmistakable. Inasmuch as Inoue was a top adviser to the cabinet and became finance minister once again in 1898, his disfavor meant more than mere personal dislike. Because Nakamigawa frowned upon bribery as a way of obtaining favors, officials became less cooperative with Mitsui. Masuda Takashi, irked by Bank's controls over Bussan, was quietly building up an anti-Nakamigawa machine within the combine, and Dan Takuma was his firm ally. Meanwhile, a severe recession had burst many corporate bubbles inflated by the war, and some dark prophecies were uttered concerning Nakamigawa's loan and investment policies.

There was nothing very unusual about such business intrigues, which certainly were no novelty to the experienced Nakamigawa. But in the spring of 1900, as he lay ill with a bout of his old complaint, matters took a very sinister turn. In a sensational paper called *Ni-roku-Shimpo* (Twenty-six News), the headline "Immoral Conduct of the Mitsuis" introduced a series of articles concerning a long-past episode in which the House had acquired some choice properties by questionable means. Nakamigawa knew that the story was well founded, having been associated with the merchant who allegedly had been defrauded. He also knew that further revelations by the paper would damage not only the Mitsuis but several leading statesmen, as well.

Mitsui's managers had methods, usually effective, for influencing the venal press to deal gently with the firm. But the publisher of the offending paper, Akiyama Teisuke, was a nationalist agitator rather than a blackmailer, and not easily bought off. Furthermore, since he was an associate of terrorist chieftains, he could not be threatened. Through connections in the home ministry, Nakamigawa obtained a police injunction prohibiting further disclosures. But inexplicably, the newspaper paid little heed, softening a phrase here and there, perhaps, but continuing to spin out its sordid tale for week after week to a readership estimated at more than 150,000 subscribers.

The story began back in the early 1870s, when two merchant houses in Choshu, Yamashiroya and Mitaniya, were handling army finances for General Yamagata Aritomo. Yamashiro was charged with embezzlement and, when a nasty scandal loomed, he obligingly killed himself. Concurrently, a clerk of Mitaniya was misappropriating army funds for speculation. In 1873, having received an inside tip, he "borrowed" 810,000 yen from the government's treasure chest and tried to corner the market in lamp oil. To his horror, another speculator began selling short and the price went down precipitously. The short-seller happened to be Tokyo Shosha, a trading firm headed by Mitsui Hachiroemon (Kofuku) and run by Minomura Rizaemon. It may have been a coincidence, but Mitsui had a strong motive for such a maneuver: with Yamashiro already out of the way, all they had to do was to topple Mitani and they would have a monopoly over the army's business.

That is exactly what happened. The government, hearing somehow of the irregularities in Mitaniya, made an audit and found a shortage of 300,000 yen. General Yamagata was in charge but couldn't bring the matter into the open because he had been accepting favors—including the maintenance of a concubine—from the Mitanis, and the reputation of the army was at stake also. In consultation with Inoue and Shibusawa at the finance ministry, he and Mitani worked out a confidential deal. Mitani, still short fifty thousand yen, borrowed this amount from the Mitsuis, handing over fifty-three parcels of land in Tokyo as collateral. For this "favor" Mitsui-gumi was appointed to handle army finances in place of Mitaniya. In addition, the army and the finance ministries were to deposit 300,000 yen each with Mitsui for ten years, without interest. Thus Mitani was driven out of business, but Mitsui gave him a written pledge that the land, choice lots in the heart of the capital, would be returned to him after ten years.

When Mitani died, his heir Sankuro was still a minor, so the document was entrusted to an uncle. After the decade had elapsed, young Mitani tried to recover the pledge, but the uncle had also died and the document was never found. When the heir tried to approach the Mitsuis for redress, he was met by clerks who professed ignorance of the whole transaction. He then appealed to General Yamagata, who obviously was reluctant to reopen the matter. Shibusawa was more helpful and, knowing that the claim was legitimate, took it up with the Mitsuis but got only evasive answers. Nakamigawa was utterly unresponsive, and young Mitani seemed to have given up.

Nothing had been heard about the case for many years, but suddenly in 1900 the alleged secrets of the transaction—at least those most damaging to Mitsui—spilled forth upon the pages of *Twenty-six News*. One article declared: "All these fifty-three parcels of land are situated in the best part of the city. . . . At present value they would be worth several million yen. However, the Mitsuis stole the property from Mitani Sankuro on the excuse that he could not produce the pledge, and the Mitsui families are now living in luxury, extravagance, and immorality." The paper also alleged that in order to cheat Mitani, Mitsui's obanto, Saito Junzo, had bought the pledge covertly from Sankuro's uncle, a dissolute person who had died soon afterward under circumstances suggesting foul play.

These accusations were painful enough to the Mitsuis, to whom nothing was more precious than their good name. Their pain turned to agony when a fresh attack upon the House revealed alarming facts about losses the bank had suffered in the wake of the Sino-Japanese War and provoked a run on the main office and several branches. What threw them into a panic, however, was the information that behind the character assassin and presumably feeding him ammunition were their own trusted friends and protectors. Only then did they learn that Akiyama Teisuke, publisher of *Twenty-six News,* was acting in behalf of Prince Ito Hirobumi and that his paper was supported by the Mitsui's adviser, Count Inoue Kaoru, and by Prime Minister General Yamagata himself.

The motives behind their attack, and their reasons for conducting it through Akiyama, remain something of a mystery. However, it seems clear enough that Nakamigawa's policy of shaking Mitsui free of Choshu influence was at the heart of the incident. For ten years Inoue and Professor Hozumi Nobushige had been drafting a new constitution for the House of Mitsui. The lawyer, although guarded in his comments, admitted later that it was a very trying experience, indicating that the Mitsuis, or some of them at least, resented such interference in their affairs. It is also probable that Nakamigawa, seeking to build the concern into a Western-style enterprise, encouraged them to resist Inoue's stifling paternalism. But the conspiracy by the three genro and their journalist-henchman convinced the clan that further resistance could bring ruin, especially since the illness of Nakamigawa had left it leaderless.

Akiyama's agents had informed the Mitsuis privately about his terms for desisting. Of course Mitani Sankuro, as well as "other unfortunate old friends of the Mitsuis," was to be compensated. This intervention on behalf of the Mitanis was represented as a meritorious example of han loyalty, but since the young man finally settled for a paltry 10,000 yen it seems to have been only a pretext. Another term demanded that the exclusive Mitsui Club in central Tokyo be "purified." The club, a Japanese-style mansion built as a social center for the eleven Mitsui families and their guests, was viewed by some people as a second Roku-meikan, with all its invidious connotations. Receptions and parties at the club for Japanese and foreign dignitaries aroused envy among those who were not invited, and geisha parties or occasional ribaldry had given it a certain notoriety much exaggerated by those with a political ax to grind. Such criticisms were rather unfair, in view of the fact that there were very few places suitable for the entertainment of state guests and other important visitors in large groups in a cosmopolitan atmosphere with reasonable privacy. Furthermore, Ito himself was the most notorious womanizer among the oligarchs (it was said that during his several terms as prime minister he had consorted with more than a hundred women), while the Mitsuis and their obanto Nakamigawa were rather puritanical on this score. Sensibly, such charges were dropped and, in the end, the only significant demand made by Akiyama was that the Mitsuis accept and enforce Inoue's new constitution for the House.

In negotiations between Mitsui leaders and the publisher, mediated by Ito, the House capitulated abjectly. Only five days later, on July 1, 1900, all the family heads, together with their advisers and the chief banto of the principal Mitsui companies, convened at the Mitsui Club for the promulgation of the new constitution (see Appendix B). After the lengthy document was read aloud, all the family heads accepted it as the law of the clan and gave their sacred oath to uphold it.

In general, the revised House laws (kept secret for many years) perpetuated the same principles and precepts laid down in the founder's will. However, the revision was much better organized and more precise than older versions had been, specifying in detail the families' structure and interrelationships, ownership of property, maintenance of reserve funds, division of profits, settlement of disputes, hierarchy, and succession. Procedures were outlined for handling questions of marriage, adoption, divorce, retirement, establishment of separate families, and "such other matters which cause a significant change in the personal position or blood relationship of the members of the house." Conspicuously omitted were regulations concerning the conduct of business, presumably the responsibility of hired managers. However, there were very strict provisions concerning the occupations, public activities, and personal conduct of House members, as well as for the disciplining of those who violated those rules. The further isolation of clan members from business responsibility was implicit in the renaming of Motokata (general headquarters), which now became Mitsui-ke Dozokukai, or Mitsui Clan Council. This change could be interpreted as the Mitsuis' formal acknowledgment of the fact that their powers had been sharply circumscribed.

It is understandable that the family code drafted by Mitsui Hachiroemon Takahira in the seventeenth century would have been inadequate for the vastly larger, more complex operations of a twentieth-century zaibatsu. But why were such drastic means taken to impose the new constitution? And why, after taking almost ten years to prepare that constitution, were Inoue and his friends suddenly in such haste to make the Mitsuis accept it? There are no definite answers to these questions, but one can speculate that the Mitsui concern, which had been fostered so diligently by the Meiji leaders, had become indispensable to the fulfillment of their goals, and that the laissez-faire ideal pursued by Nakamigawa could have negated their efforts and their plans. Furthermore, just then Ito was organizing the Seiyukai Party as a power base for the Choshu clique. Through his protégé Saionji Kimmochi he had secured an alliance with the latter's brother, Baron Sumitomo Kichi-zaemon, one of Japan's wealthiest men. Inoue's job was to harness Mitsui to the new party, not only for the financial help it could give but also to keep the clan from supporting a rival clique or from becoming a political power in its own right.

In this connection it is revealing that under the provisions of the new constitution they adopted, members of the Mitsui families were forbidden to join any political party or associate themselves officially with any political activity. Also, they were to abstain from entering government service or participating in public organizations. These prohibitions, like those restricting the activities of the imperial family, presumably were designed to prevent the House from becoming too deeply involved in the fortunes of any particular regime or partisan movement. More to the point, the clan's acceptance of these limitations meant that they could not develop direct political influence commensurate with their economic strength. Nothing was said about financial contributions, however, and Mitsui is considered to have been a prime source of funds for the Seiyukai Party. Inaugurated only about two months after the Mitani controversy was settled, Seiyukai soon made the Choshu-Mitsui faction dominant over its Satsuma-Tosa-Mitsubishi rivals.

Another reason, and perhaps a more important one, for the oligarchs' impatience was the turbulent situation on the continent. In March the Russians tried to establish a naval base in Korea. Japan thwarted this move, but in June the Boxer insurgents precipitated an incident in China that called for Japan's immediate intervention and a frantic military buildup. This chronology may help to explain why the Mitsuis, although much richer and better organized than ever, found themselves as helplessly in thrall to the oligarchy as they had been at the dawn of the Meiji era.

The Boxer Rebellion gave Japan a perfect opportunity to show off the impressive military machine built up assiduously since the Sino-Japanese War. When Japanese troops joined the international forces to relieve the foreign legations besieged in Peking, they acquitted themselves creditably and won praise from many quarters for their impeccable discipline. The Russians got more substantial benefits from the incident, however: on the pretext of defense, they moved huge forces into Manchuria and ignored repeated requests to recall them. The presence of these troops intensified Japan's uneasiness over Russian encroachment in the region. Having completed the Trans-Siberian Railway, the Russians also had taken possession of Port Arthur and, not content with expanding into Manchuria, were strengthening their position in Korea.

Japan, in haste to preempt the peninsula, had overplayed its hand. Shortly after the Sino-Japanese War, agents of the Black Ocean Society, in connivance with the Japanese minister in Seoul (a Choshu general), had engineered the murder of the Korean queen. The king promptly took refuge in the Russian legation and his government came under the influence of czarist officials. Indignation over the brutal crime committed by Toyama's henchmen made necessary the trial of some of the culprits; and because of the exposure of Japan's terroristic "invisible government," the patient efforts of Ito and Inoue to take Korea peaceably came to naught.

Ito and Yamagata were still the strong men of the Choshu clique, which for the while had gained ascendancy over Satsuma. But they were sharply at odds over the continental issue. Yamagata wanted to accept London's overtures for an alliance and then deal with Russia by force of arms. Ito, who believed that Japan was unprepared for such a war and doubted Britain's willingness to form an alliance, preferred to reach an understanding with Russia and settle the Korean problem by diplomacy. But both hoped to preserve unity within the oligarchy and sought to reach a consensus.

Foreign Minister Komura Jutaro, an ardent nationalist, agreed with General Yamagata. He explained that Britain, then bogged down in the Boer War, could not continue alone in Asia against Russia and other European powers. Britain, like Japan, needed an ally in the Far East, he said, and was trying actively to enlist Japan's cooperation in penetrating the continent. Ito and Inoue, not convinced, at last sided with the other makers of Japan's policy, although they knew that alliance with Britain meant war with Russia.

The momentous Anglo-Japanese Alliance was signed in January 1902. It took notice of Japan's "special interests" in Korea and of Britain's in China. It also promised mutual support in case those interests were threatened. This represented a new dimension in world politics. Astonishingly, an Asian country had been accepted as a full ally by the world's greatest empire, and the legitimacy of Japan's ambition to stake its claim to parts of the Asian continent had been recognized tacitly.

Such an ambition was not at all reprehensible in the eyes of the Japanese and their new allies, nor even in those of their putative enemies. A Russian leader, for example, predicted that "the vast, dormant countries of the Far East" would be quickly divided up among powerful invaders, and that "the problem of each country concerned is to obtain as large a share as possible of the outlived Oriental states, especially of the Chinese Colossus."[1] The British, French, and Dutch had subjugated most of Southeast Asia and, with the Germans and Russians, were scrambling for concessions all along the China coast. The United States had extended its Pacific empire from Hawaii to Guam and the Philippines and now was promoting the "Open Door" policy to protect its own future position in China. If Japan was to get any share at all in the "vast, dormant" Orient, there was no time to be lost.

After treaty talks with Japan failed, the Russians became more aggressive. They insisted on exclusive control of Manchuria, and their posture in Korea became menacing. Negotiations with St. Petersburg were getting nowhere, and on February 6, 1904, Tokyo broke off relations with the czar's minister. Simultaneously, Russian troops crossed the Yalu River into Korea and the Japanese combined fleet sailed from Sasebo. Japanese torpedo boats attacked Russian ships at Port Arthur and, by the time war was declared on February 10, the Russian squadron stationed there was badly crippled. St. Petersburg protested Japan's breach of international law; but the British, although technically neutral, applauded "this act of daring which is destined to take a place of honor in naval annals," as the *Times* put it.

The Japanese now had their chance to avenge the losses suffered because of the Triple Intervention, and they set about doing so with immense enthusiasm. In peacetime Japanese public life had been disrupted by bickering, corruption, and cynicism, but once the war was begun the political mildew was neatly papered over with chauvinistic propaganda. The mediocre and unpopular Katsura Taro, put in by Yamagata as a stopgap premier, was able to tame the unruly politicians and remained in office longer than had any of his predecessors. The Japanese, digging their way out from under an avalanche of foreign ideas, seemed to have rediscovered their national identity and true vocation on the battlefield.

On the home front princes and poor men, police officials and condemned criminals, even hospital patients upon their deathbeds, contributed funds. The empress sold some of her jewelry and economized on food. Wealthy men, including the Mitsuis, sold works of art for the cause and stopped using their carriages so that more horses could be sent into battle. At the ornate mansion of Count Inoue the usual dried fish was omitted from the breakfast menu as a thrift measure, and twenty percent of the maids' wages was skimmed off for the army and navy. Youths indoctrinated with the Imperial Rescript on Education and Precepts to Soldiers and Sailors* responded by vying for assign-

---

* The Imperial Precepts to the soldiers and sailors, promulgated in 1882, stressed the divinity and eternal supremacy of the emperor and the duty of subjects to serve loyally, obediently, and courageously. Fighting men were informed that "duty is weightier than a mountain, while death is lighter than a feather."

ment to suicidal missions and died with praises of the emperor on their lips.

Bankers outdid themselves to raise funds for the war, upon which Japan spent 1.73 billion yen, more than seven times the cost of the war with China. Expenditures were defrayed with 1.3 billion yen from domestic bonds (every issue heavily oversubscribed) and 902 million yen in foreign loans, of which National City Bank and Kuhn, Loeb and Company of New York supplied 100 million.

The aristocracy and the business world lined up faithfully behind the imperial family, lending their names and presence to patriotic organizations, campaigns, and rallies. Their activities and contributions were chronicled exhaustively in an English-language periodical, the *Russo-Japanese War Fully Illustrated,* sponsored by Mitsui and carrying the advertising of its companies. The financial and social standing of the emerging zaibatsu in relation to the old aristocracy is indicated by the following news item: "*The Imperial Relief Association for Soldiers and Sailors* was established by nobles and prominent gentlemen in Tokyo. ... The president is H. I. H. Prince Arisugawa, the Vice-Presidents, Counts Matsukata and Inoue. ... Its originators have already contributed more than 1,000,000 yen. The subscription List is headed by munificent donations of yen 100,000 from Their Majesties, 10,000 from H. I. H. the Crown Prince, 5,000 from H. I. H. Prince Arisugawa, President of the Association, and 3,000 from all the other Imperial Princes."

A list appended to the article shows that the largest contributors, next to the emperor and empress, were barons Mitsui Hachiroemon and Iwasaki Hisaya (head of the Mitsubishi concern), who contributed fifty thousand yen each. Next, giving thirty thousand yen each, were Yasuda Zenjiro, Furukawa Junkichi, and Sumitomo Kichizaemon. The gifts of these zaibatsu heads were rather well matched by three Tokugawas, with a total of thirty thousand, and heirs of the Satsuma and Choshu daimyo, who gave thirty thousand yen each. Others contributing ten thousand yen or more were counts Inoue Kaoru and Matsukata Masayoshi, Baron Shibusawa Eiichi, four lesser zaibatsu leaders, and a few former court nobles and daimyo.

The two vice-presidents, both of them masterminds of the economy and former finance ministers, knew where the wealth of the nation lay and presumably tapped its owners according to their means. The result, a fairly comprehensive listing of Japan's great fortunes, shows the astonishing progress the merchants had made during the preceding decade. Most amazing is the fact that of the twenty-two leading donors (considering the imperial family as one unit) ten were related to the Mitsuis by marriage, or soon would be. Such a concentration of wealth, deliberately fostered by the government, was an important factor in attaining Japan's military mastery and in turn was accelerated by successive wars.

For five harrowing months the imperial army besieged the Russian forces at Port Arthur, losing sixty thousand men dead upon the field before the defenders withdrew. The Russians, having been virtually driven from the sea, were now completely dependent upon the single-track Trans-Siberian Railway for moving troops and supplies. The turning point was the epic Battle of Mukden, in which some 750,000 soldiers were locked in mortal combat for their emperors. The Japanese lost forty thousand men, but once again the Russians were forced back and Field Marshal Oyama Iwao, commanding Japan's expeditionary forces, made his triumphal entry into the ruined city. (Some of the older Mitsuis remembered Oyama as the artillery captain who had come to Saburosuke's mansion in Kyoto, early one morning in 1868, to fetch a cartload of silver for financing imperial troops during the first battle of the Meiji revolution.)

Serving less conspicuously but nonetheless effectively was Masuda Takashi, who had taken over as Mitsui's obanto after the death of Nakamigawa in 1901. Bussan had to supply almost everything the army needed and ship it to the war zone in Bussan's growing merchant fleet. As Japan's leading importer, the firm was receiving huge munitions shipments (obviously ordered well in advance) from Vickers in England, Krupp in Germany, and Carnegie in the United States, for whom it held agencies. And in the old Mitsui tradition, Bussan operated a crack intelligence network, now fed by dozens of overseas branches. Frequently Bussan was doing business in foreign cities before consulates had been established there, so Masuda's agents were requested to supply information to the government, as well as to Mitsui. Since the firm had offices in many Chinese and Manchurian ports, its intelligence was of great value in the campaign against Russia.

A classic tale about Mitsui Bussan concerns Yamamoto Jotaro, Masuda's most trusted lieutenant, who was chief of the Shanghai branch during the war. Yamamoto employed his singular talents to inspire a pro-Japanese atmosphere in China, buying up one daily newspaper and investing in others to influence editorial opinion. But his main task was that of a spymaster and saboteur. In collaboration with the Japanese military he expanded his operations to Hong Kong and Singapore, where imperial army and navy men posed as Bussan's employees. He gleaned information from Japanese shipping and business firms and paid foreign pilots and officers for reporting their observations. His agents kept constant watch over Russian procurement in Chinese ports. Whenever the enemy started ordering supplies Yamamoto contrived the disappearance of the desired items from the market.

When the Russians needed cargo vessels or lighters, Yamamoto forestalled them by chartering every bottom available.

Of crucial importance to the outcome of the war was Russia's Baltic Fleet, which had been dispatched to the Far East. Its progress toward the distant war zone was being watched with great interest by supporters of both sides. Because of Britain's alliance with Japan, the czar's warships were not allowed to pass through the Suez Canal and had to make the long voyage around Africa's Cape of Good Hope. In May 1905 the fleet finally appeared off the coast of Indochina and Yamamoto was instructed to keep it under surveillance.

His right-hand man, Mori Kaku, had already chartered a private yacht and now boarded it with several subordinates for a leisurely "pleasure cruise" that took them upon a zigzag course, touching Amoy, Hong Kong, Manila, and the Pescadores while they watched the Russian fleet. Its movements were reported to headquarters of the imperial navy through a secret wireless station Yamamoto had installed on an island near Shanghai. By May 20 Russian maneuvers convinced yachtsman Mori that the fleet would take the short passage through the Strait of Tsushima rather than a longer one through the Sea of Japan to the east of Tsushima. Mori flashed this message to Yamamoto, who relayed it to headquarters.

As a result of Yamamoto's thoroughness Admiral Togo Heihachiro, in command of the Japanese fleet, set a trap at the narrow passage between the island of Tsushima and the Korean coast. On May 27, 1905, the Russian admiral, ignoring the warnings of subordinates, sailed his fleet right into the ambush without taking even the elementary precaution of making a reconnaissance, although visibility was poor. Early in the afternoon Togo's battleships loomed out of the mist and opened fire, deliberately and with devastating effect.

In the two-day Battle of the Japan Sea, the Baltic Fleet, taken completely by surprise and unprepared for combat, was virtually destroyed and two-thirds of its eighteen thousand men were lost. For this superlative achievement Japan paid the modest price of three torpedo boats sunk and 116 men killed. "Even the Battle of Trafalgar could not match this," President Theodore Roosevelt declared, thus endorsing Togo's new nickname, "the Nelson of Japan."

Thanks to Bussan's intelligence work and the ineptitude of the Russian command, Togo's feat was somewhat like shooting fish in a rain barrel. But because of his smashing victory, the Russians had lost the war. All that remained was to find out how much they would pay for peace.

14 · The Best Laid Plans . . .

BEFORE OPENING HOSTILITIES against Russia the Japanese government wisely sent a representative to Washington with the mission of enlisting American support for its cause. The man chosen for the purpose was Baron Kaneko Kentaro, whose education at Harvard's Law School had made him a valuable assistant to Ito in framing the Meiji constitution and planning Japan's foreign policy. A paragon of discretion, Kaneko had long served as an adviser to the council of genro—the inner circle of oligarchs who made all the important decisions for the emperor—and more recently as Secretary of the Privy Council and a founding member of the Seiyukai Party. He was an expert in American affairs, knew the right people, and often assisted Mitsui's leaders, especially his brother-in-law Dan Takuma and Masuda Takashi, in making contacts or settling legal matters abroad.

Arriving in Washington at the beginning of the war, he found the American press generally hostile to Japan, but got a cordial reception at the White House from his former classmate at Harvard, Theodore Roosevelt. The Roughrider hero of the Spanish-American War was delighted to see little Japan wielding its own "big stick" so doughtily. He was ambitious also to advance America's neglected interests in China and was worried about the Russians, who already controlled one-sixth of the world's territory but hungered for more. Kaneko and Ambassador Takahira Kogoro unobtrusively provided Roosevelt with some reading material emphasizing the hypothesis that American capital, working in harmony with Japanese knowledge and experience in East Asian markets, would surely help both countries to prosper. Then, too, since the sportsman-president was interested in the martial arts, they found a jujutsu teacher for him. In such tactful ways Kaneko developed a cordial, almost an intimate, relationship with Roosevelt, who became an outspoken admirer of Japan as the war progressed favorably. He assured Kaneko of financial and moral support and confided to Secretary of State Hay that Japan should not be "robbed a second time of the fruits of victory."[1]

Kaneko, from his headquarters in New York, made good use of other

Harvard friends, among whom were some of America's leading financiers and publishers. With their help, and that of Mitsui Bussan, he won over influential sectors of American big business, and at the same time bombarded the public with articles, speeches, and indirect publicity that fully exploited the traditional American sympathy for the underdog and its dislike of czarist arrogance.

For more sophisticated audiences Kaneko played up the Russian menace and the advantages of a strong Japan. He insisted that Japan had won its special rights in Korea by sacrifices intended to prevent the "Russianization of Korea," and in an article in the November 1904 issue of the *North American Review,* entitled "The Yellow Peril is the Golden Opportunity for Japan," presented this enticing vision: "By reconciling and inter-assimilating the two civilizations, Japan hopes to introduce Western culture and science into the continent of Asia, and thus to open up for the benefit of the world, with equal privilege for every nation, and peace assured to all, the teeming wealth of the Chinese Empire."

Almost single-handedly, Kaneko transformed the popular image of the Japanese as lewd, shrewd, shifty heathens—or, at best, as clever imitators with a quaintly artistic bent—to that of clean-living, valorous defenders of justice. The Americans responded with impulsive generosity, contributing not only cash but also a corps of high-minded ladies eager to nurse the wounded heroes, warm clothing (several sizes too large), and (among other things) a superfluity of hominy grits.

The Japanese people, made supremely confident by military successes and the praise of foreigners, were willing to continue the war at any sacrifice necessary for total victory. But in eighteen months of fighting Japan had lost some 200,000 men, and the war minister had warned the council of genro: "We are at the end of our tether in ammunition, money, and military manpower." The government, whose foreign credit was stretched to the limit, recoiled from the bleak prospect of invading Siberia, and decided to end the war while there were still some advantages to be won. The czar's advisers felt the same way, for unrest among the proletariat and peasantry at home, aggravated by defeats at the front, had reached revolutionary proportions after the annihilation of the Baltic Fleet. Hoping to exploit Russia's desperation, Tokyo requested the mediation of President Roosevelt, who had expressed to Kaneko his willingness to accept the role.

Through the president's good offices a peace conference was held at Portsmouth, New Hampshire. Foreign Minister Komura Jutaro, negotiating for Japan, made exorbitant demands, believing he could bluff his adversary, Sergei Witte. The latter, however, knew that Japan's position was as difficult as Russia's and resisted stubbornly. During the conference Kaneko remained in New York, where he could hold press conferences explaining Japan's position and convey prudently phrased information to the president in frequent visits to his home at Oyster Bay.* Roosevelt was sympathetic but did not encourage Japan's more extreme terms. What he wanted from the conference was not an emasculated Russia but a more even balance of power that would prevent either adversary from overrunning China. When negotiations reached an impasse over an indemnity of seven billion dollars demanded by Japan, he stepped in nimbly with a compromise intended to curb Russian expansion without strengthening Japan's hand immoderately.

With the signing of the Portsmouth Treaty on September 5, 1905, the Japanese obtained no indemnity, but otherwise their gains were impressive and brought incalculable long-term benefits to the zaibatsu. In brief, the treaty called for Russia's recognition of Japan's paramount interests in Korea and cession of the lower half of Sakhalin Island; transfer to Japan of the lease on the strategic Liaotung Peninsula; as well as surrender to Japan of control over the southern section of the Manchurian Railway, extending northeast from Port Arthur to Changchun. Both Russia and Japan were to withdraw all troops from Manchuria, except railway guards, and to respect China's right to develop the region. But these restrictions allowed considerable leeway for expansion by both parties, and the peace terms were fair enough to allow a prompt reconciliation between the recently warring nations.

Objectively, Japan had been phenomenally lucky, and its rewards should have been considered adequate recompense for all losses suffered through the Triple Intervention. But the government, throughout the war, had both exaggerated victories and minimized losses. The people, unaware of Japan's difficult plight, had expected richer spoils. The ultranationalists, always ready to exploit discontent, denounced the Portsmouth Treaty as a sellout and demanded its rejection. The zaibatsu were accused of profiteering; and it was revealed that while patriotic people were going hungry for the cause of victory, Prime Minister

---

* The role of Kaneko in the Portsmouth conference has been variously evaluated, but there is a general belief that it was more important than his official position would signify. Witte's secretary, J. J. Korostovetz, wrote in his diary during the conference: "The counter balance to our influence is worked, I think, not so much by Komura as by Baron Kaneko, the Financial Agent of Japan in New York. He is in touch with bankers and statesmen, and to judge by what the newspapers say, he is often at President Roosevelt's house. . . . " After the terms of the treaty were settled, Korostovetz wrote: "It is said that Komura was forced to agree by an order from Tokyo, the chief mover being Baron Kaneko, and, in fact, all the members of the Japanese mission are supposed to have stood out for breaking off the negotiations." The secretary reported reading that Kaneko, at the last moment, had "applied through Prince Ito to the Mikado advising to forego the indemnity."[2]

Katsura Taro had given financier Yasuda Zenjiro a loan of six million yen at two-percent interest to bail out a sinking bank.

Opponents of the treaty were also giving wide circulation to a theory that Roosevelt had tricked Japan into fighting Russia in order to further American interests in Asia. This opinion was confirmed by the arrival of railroad magnate E. H. Harriman in Tokyo even before the treaty had been signed. Harriman was closely allied with Kuhn, Loeb and Company, which through Kaneko's influence with Roosevelt, had extended a large loan to Japan. Harriman was promoting a plan to form a globe-girdling transportation system by linking several railway and steamship lines. To fill one yawning gap he needed the South Manchurian Railway and had come to buy an interest in it. This was entirely in keeping with the idea of collaborating with American capitalists for opening Asian markets, which had been vigorously advocated by Inoue, Masuda, and Shibusawa, among others. Mitsui would naturally have been in the forefront of any such joint endeavor.

Prime Minister Katsura, having assured Roosevelt that Japan would honor the Open Door policy in Manchuria, was warmly favorable toward the joint-investment plan. The internationalists, however, had underestimated the fury of the chauvinists, who, upon Harriman's arrival, organized mass demonstrations aimed at abrogating the Portsmouth Treaty. On September fifth, the day the treaty was signed, some thirty thousand people congregated in Hibiya Park, adjacent to the Imperial Palace Plaza, to cheer the fire-breathing oratory of patriots. Afterward mobs led by skilled agitators ran through the streets, vandalizing a progovernment newspaper's office, as well as setting fire to scores of police boxes, streetcars, and several Christian churches. The tough old Prime Minister met force with force, and in two days of rioting more than five hundred people were wounded and seventeen killed, mostly by policemen's swords.

One suspected instigator of the anti-Portsmouth uprising was the Mitsuis' gadfly Akiyama Teisuke of the *Twenty-six News*. A more important one, however, was Uchida Ryohei, a disciple of Toyama Mitsuru and boss of the Kokuryukai (Black Dragon Society), a second-generation offshoot of the notorious Gen'yosha (Black Ocean Society). One purpose of the Black Dragon Society, established by Uchida in 1901, was to expel the Russians from all Manchurian territory south of the Amur River. (Kokuryu means Amur River, but the same characters stand for black dragon, hence the name Black Dragon Society by which the organization came to be known abroad.) Uchida and Toyama had been very active in promoting and supporting the war against Russia and of course were violently opposed to Japan's concessions at Portsmouth. Since their counsels had been ignored by the government, they helped to create this outburst of mayhem and arson to emphasize their opinions.

An unobstructed view of Hibiya Park could be had from the Mitsui Club, just across the avenue and close to the present location of the Imperial Hotel. It may be assumed that on the day the rioting began a number of Mitsui executives had assembled there for luncheon, as was their custom. It is also probable that they watched anxiously from upstairs windows as the official residence of the home minister, near the park, was surrounded by angry crowds that swelled to thirty thousand people before the residence was set afire.

Uchida, a political strategist rather than a rabble-rouser, was not among the rioters. He was close to the action, however. As a matter of fact, he too was in the Mitsui Club. An outstanding exponent of the martial arts, he had been requested to stage an exhibition of jujutsu at a party planned by Baron Mitsui Hachiroemon Takamine* in honor of the foreign guests and was rehearsing some of his pupils there. On the following day, while the sky was still murky from the smoke of conflagrations started by his activists, he was again at the club helping the baron and baroness Mitsui entertain Mr. Harriman and his daughter, American and other diplomats, and a representative selection of Japanese statesmen and financiers. Within the clubrooms, which displayed a combination of Japanese architecture and Victorian furnishings, the opulent draperies and carpets muted the clamor from outside. If Harriman and his entourage entertained any suspicion that the riots were anti-American or would jeopardize his plans, it was dispelled by his hosts and the muscular but dignified "guest artist" who sipped tea with them and, no doubt, showed a flattering interest in the American industrialist's comments.

As sporadic disturbances continued, Katsura, at the urging of Inoue and Ito, negotiated secretly with Harriman and reached an agreement to sell him a half interest in the South Manchurian Railway and mining rights, as well. It was one of those moments when history hung in the balance: the United States and Japan, joining hands for the development of Asia, might well have been able to change the course of world events.

Harriman left for home in October with such a belief. But a short time after his departure Japan's foreign minister Komura returned from the United States and scolded Katsura for his folly. The railway was a vital part of Japan's future on the continent. Moreover, the nation was still smoldering over the Portsmouth Treaty and its bloody aftermath,

---

* Takamine, who visited the United States in 1872 as a youth, was the youngest son of Hachiroemon Kofuku and succeeded his elder brother Hachiroemon Takaaki, who had adopted Takamine as his heir.

and signing away any part of Japan's precious rights in Manchuria could have had an explosive effect at home. The agreement was rescinded while Harriman was still in mid-Pacific, and Katsura, harassed by the nationalists, had no alternative but to resign.

The Portsmouth Treaty was ratified in spite of public opinion, but the terrorist bosses had demonstrated that even without official status or wealth they constituted a force that could be neither suppressed nor ignored. Their power, like that of the government and the zaibatsu, was deeply and broadly rooted, and they used it pitilessly. Yet the source of their power was not fear alone. They were respected by the masses because they created the illusions of expressing the people's will, which had all too few outlets, and of championing the oppressed by their direct, flamboyant actions. And they were tolerated by the elite because they made themselves useful in many ways, both at home and overseas.

Their most important function was to act as an unofficial vanguard, free of legal or moral restraints, in Japan's march westward. The spirit of "manifest destiny," thwarted for decades by Japan's semicolonial status and by foreign interference, at last had found full expression in the war against Russia. Toyama and his successors, practical men as well as visionaries, used it to whet the Japanese appetite for continental riches that seemed to be almost within reach. A sizeable minority of the nation's political and financial leaders, striving to earn the confidence of the West, hoped that their territorial ambitions could be satisfied by means condoned by their economic allies abroad. Yet even these men were susceptible to the blandishments as well as the threats of extremists, and thus were unable to make a clear-cut choice between internationalism and ultranationalism.

Unfortunately, the Western powers were equally ambiguous about Japan's role in Asia and the meaning of the Open Door policy. While negotiations at Portsmouth were still in progress, London secretly renewed the Anglo-Japanese Alliance, adding a clause recognizing Japan's right to exercise control over Korea. At about the same time America's Secretary of War, William Howard Taft, visited Tokyo and concluded an agreement with Katsura acknowledging that right, in exchange for Japan's pledge not to meddle with the Philippines. The French also gave approval to Japan's plans for expansion. With such support from Washington, London, and Paris, Ito Hirobumi persuaded the king of Korea to accept the status of a protectorate under which a Japanese resident-general—actually a proconsul—managed the smaller nation.

The resident-general was Ito himself, who hoped to bind Korea to Japan gradually by developing its resources and improving its economy. Drawing upon his experience in the early Meiji era he tried to institute widespread reforms. One of his schemes was an economic development venture, the Toyo Takushoku, or Oriental Colonization Company, in which the Japanese government shared ownership with Mitsui and other zaibatsu. Among the founders of the company was Noda Utaro, once the labor boss of the Miike mines, who had become vice-president of the Seiyukai.

Ito's policy was backed by Japan's newest prime minister, Saionji Kimmochi, his alter ego in the political world and the most liberal of the Choshu-line leaders. However, the Korean king did not want Japan's protection, benevolent or otherwise, so Ito forced him to abdicate in favor of his mentally retarded son. The Korean army was disbanded and Ito assumed dictatorial powers, which he was able to enforce only by brutal military suppression.

Before long the more belligerent General Katsura had become prime minister again, replacing Saionji, and with the army's connivance Uchida Ryohei's Black Dragon Society aggravated the disturbances in Korea to undermine Ito further. When the time was ripe, Toyama and some fellow extremists submitted a memorandum to the Japanese government, demanding annexation of the subordinate country, and Ito resigned. He realized that his approach had failed and that Japan's interests in Korea could be secured only by force. However, he felt that before making a drastic move Japan should reach an understanding with Russia, and for this purpose he journeyed to Manchuria to meet the Russian finance minister.

Known as the most garrulous of men, Ito for once accomplished his mission without saying a word: when he arrived at Harbin Station on October 26, 1909, bullets from the pistol of a young Korean nationalist silenced him forever. The assassination of Japan's most prominent statesman also quieted Inoue, Saionji, and other moderates at home and was the perfect pretext for bringing Korea under imperial rule in 1910. The death of Ito was ascribed to the fanaticism of one Korean, but it could not have been better arranged by Toyama and Uchida themselves. Nor by the Mitsuis, for their friend Noda, doubling as vice-president of the Oriental Colonization Company, also became governor-general of Korea.

The most valuable prize Japan had won from the Russo-Japanese War was the narrow railway zone that traversed southern Manchuria and served to open the whole region to Japanese penetration. The Russians still held rights to the Chinese Eastern Railway zone in northern Manchuria; thus the two countries were in a position to dominate a nominally Chinese territory four times as large as Japan and far richer in resources. Recognizing that their interests in the region were complementary rather than competitive, the two countries soon reached a private agreement defining their respective spheres of influence. American financiers, however, disappointed at having failed to acquire an interest in the Manchurian railways, worked out a counterplan to "neutralize" them and attempted to form an international consortium to develop Manchurian resources. These and other evidences of American ambitions in the region drew Japan and Russia into an alliance, concluded in 1907, by which they tried to establish their exclusive claim to exploit all of Manchuria, in disregard of the Open Door policy.

Development of Japan's sphere of influence was in the hands of the officials of the South Manchurian Railway Company (SMR), established in 1906 to complete and operate the line that joined the Chinese Eastern Railway at Harbin. Half the stock was owned by the government, and the largest private shareholders, other than the emperor, were Mitsui and Mitsubishi. Its business, in addition to transportation, included agriculture, mining, basic industry, light manufacturing, public utilities, and commerce, and it also took care of local government, taxation, policing, health, housing, and education. Thus its claim of being "the bearer of the light of civilization into Manchuria" was no idle boast.

The president and vice-president of SMR, the most powerful figures in the region, were appointed by the Japanese government, and naturally there was keen competition for those positions. The railway's future importance to the Japanese economy can be seen from the fact that by the 1930s there were a million Japanese subjects (mostly Koreans) living in southern Manchuria, which accounted for forty percent of Japan's trade. The first president, appointed by Saionji when he was prime minister, was Goto Shimpei, a physician-bureaucrat who had distinguished himself as civil administrator of Taiwan. Goto forged a powerful and effective organization to meet the challenges of Japan's Manchurian frontier. After that, however, the appointment usually was given to a representative of Mitsui or Mitsubishi, or of their respective political parties. This was a logical arrangement, since the two firms held the most extensive private concessions in the quasi colony and made by far the largest investments in it.

Manchuria's most valuable resources were coal and iron. The Fushun coal mine near Mukden was said to be the largest open-cut coal mine in the world and when fully developed resembled parts of the Grand Canyon of the Colorado. It was taken over by SMR, along with the abundant iron deposits at Anshan. The indemnity from China after the Sino-Japanese War had enabled the government to start constructing the Yawata Iron Works in Kyushu, and in 1901 Japan's first modern blast furnace had begun operating there. (Conforming with a Shinto ritual purportedly dating from the reign of Emperor Jimmu in the seventh century B.C., a priest kindled the fires with flint and steel.) Without reliable sources of cheap coking coal and iron ore, steelmaking had not been feasible economically, but the acquisition of Korean and Manchurian resources enabled the Yawata blast furnaces to work at full capacity. The zaibatsu had stayed aloof from iron and steel manufacturing, considering them too uncertain for private investment, but even so Mitsui had profited from them indirectly. For example, Mitsui Bussan brought in foreign machinery for the SMR's railway and mining activities, imported coal and iron ore in Bussan's ships for the Yawata furnaces, and distributed the products, taking a modest percentage on each transaction, while Bank made profits from financing the trade deals and from its investments in SMR and Yawata.

The decade following the Russo-Japanese War was one of vigorous economic expansion on all fronts and especially in Korea and Manchuria. The emperor now ruled an island empire more than a thousand miles long, a chain of archipelagoes extending from the Maritime Province of Siberia to the South China Sea. With a good foundation in basic industries at home, Japan was guaranteed not only access to the overseas resources necessary for nourishing them but also a foothold in the potentially vast markets of the Asian mainland.

The Japanese were no longer novices at colonization, having gained valuable experience in Taiwan since they had acquired it in 1895. On that fertile subtropical island, whose population was amenable to reform and responsive to economic incentives, development was rapid under an authoritarian civil administration backed by the military. It was a planned economy from the beginning, with the Japanese in supervisory roles while the subjugated Taiwanese did the heavy work. In the classic imperialist tradition, production was almost entirely agricultural, emphasizing rice, tea, sugar cane, and camphor. Most of the costs of colonization were met by the Japanese state, while private business reaped the benefits. The most profitable commodity was sugar, the largest producer of which was the Taiwan Sugar Company, established by Mitsui Bussan and managed under the strong personal control of Masuda. After the Russo-Japanese War Bussan's forestry department began large-scale cultivation of agricultural and forestry products on the island with considerable success. The best known of those was black tea, which enjoyed a near monopoly of the Japanese market.

Mitsui already had decades of experience in Korea, and when Japan's paramount interests in South Manchuria were recognized Bussan was well prepared to make a massive advance into the region. It set up offices in Mukden and other Manchurian cities, and the Dairen branch handled the export of Manchurian products. The most profitable of these proved to be soybeans, which were a staple foodstuff in Japan, as well as China. As early as 1895 Bussan had started an enterprise to market Manchurian soybeans; before 1900 it had become a million-dollar-a-year business. After the war with Russia, Masuda tried exporting the beans to Europe, where they were greeted as an economical source of edible oil. Within twenty years four-fifths of Manchuria's soybean production, which amounted to more than four million tons a year, was being shipped to Europe, mostly by Bussan. This was, of course, only one of hundreds of commodities handled by the firm, always alert to any opportunity for profit.

Bussan was agent not only for the various Mitsui enterprises but also for those of other zaibatsu, notably Sumitomo. It must be remembered that Japan had only recently begun to control its foreign trade; its businessmen were inexperienced in dealing directly with foreign countries and hampered by their ignorance of foreign languages, customs, laws, and commercial practices. Bussan, in contrast, was well versed in all these matters, had special contacts with foreign governments, was familiar with most of the commodities and products being bought and sold all over the world, had a network of branches through which to conduct transactions and gather market information, and was backed by a powerful bank. Therefore, most industrial companies entrusted their export-import business to Bussan, which easily assumed an organizing role, complementary to that of the South Manchurian Railway and the Oriental Colonization companies, in the nation's overseas expansion.

In 1907 Masuda, who had so stubbornly resisted Nakamigawa's encroachment, reorganized Bussan into a joint-stock company. Its capital, which had been less than a hundred thousand yen at the beginning, was increased to twenty million (and to one hundred million a decade later). The firm was departmentalized, so that each type of business was handled semi-independently, thereby giving the managers more opportunity to display initiative and more responsibility for producing a profit.

Mitsui Bank, housed since 1902 in the ornate steel and brick structure begun by Nakamigawa, was also conducting a considerable volume of international business. Correspondent arrangements had been made with Barclay & Co. of London, followed by tie-ups with other prestigious banking institutions abroad. In 1909 Mitsui Bank started tapping the European money-market by floating a bond issue of forty-four million francs in Paris for the municipal government at Kyoto.

Within Japan's growing overseas empire several "national policy" banks, set up under government auspices, were used to finance colonization. The Bank of Taiwan conducted business in south China and Singapore, as well as in Japan; the Bank of Chosen (replacing the Bank of Korea after 1911) served as that colony's central bank; the Industrial Bank of Japan extended loans for economic development in Korea and Manchuria; and the Yokohama Specie Bank, which had opened branch offices in Manchuria as early as 1900, conducted foreign-exchange operations and was actually issuing currency in the region, to the discomfiture of the Chinese. Yokohama Specie Bank was the principal agency for the financial penetration of China, lending Japanese treasury funds to the Chinese government, floating Chinese bonds in Japan, and assisting Japanese industrialists in their headlong advance into China proper. Yokohama Specie Bank was the main supplier of funds for Bussan's foreign trade, and Bussan in turn exerted a strong influence over the bank's management. As might be expected, the zaibatsu were large stockholders in these quasi-governmental banks and helped to determine their policies.

The annexation of new territories brought on a phenomenal boom in trade and manufacturing in Japan itself. Protective tariffs and increasing self-sufficiency in steel gave impetus to the shipbuilding, engineering, rolling stock, munitions, chemical, and machinery industries. Factories and railways were electrified, many city streets and homes were electrically illuminated, and thermal and hydroelectric power generation grew by leaps and bounds. The surge in trade with the mainland of Asia created strong demand for shipping, and the merchant marine grew rapidly. Japanese shipbuilding technology had progressed in step with the growth of the merchant marine, and by 1917 some sixty percent of the steam vessels in service were products of Japanese yards. In 1910 *Satsuma,* the world's largest warship at the time, was completed at the government's shipyard at Yokosuka.

Nevertheless, Japan still lagged far behind the West in technology, especially in heavy industries and manufactures requiring sophisticated techniques. The zaibatsu, knowing that they could not compete with foreign industrialists, had left most of the strategic industries—steel, naval shipbuilding, munitions, railway transportation, and communications—in the hands of the government. But they were eager to take advantage of the industrial opportunities offered by overseas expansion and were acquiring foreign processes, patents, and machinery essential for competitive production.

The leading private shipbuilders at the time were Mitsubishi and Kawasaki. (The latter firm, founded by a Satsuma samurai, was dominated by the Iwasaki and Matsukata families.) Both builders were producing marine engines under foreign patents, as was Shibaura Engineering Works. Masuda of Bussan, the most experienced importer of machinery, was a pioneer in technology as well. One of Mitsui's white elephants had been Tokyo Electric Light Co., which manufactured electrical equipment. Realizing that its methods were hopelessly outdated, in 1907 he made a deal with America's General Electric Corporation to buy an interest in Tokyo Electric Light Co. This arrangement soon led to the mass production of Mazda lamps in Japan.

Two years later a similar association was concluded between General Electric and Shibaura Engineering. Some of Mitsui's captains opposed "selling out" to foreigners, but Masuda answered: "It doesn't matter who does it. All we want is to transplant Western industry to Japanese soil."[3] Taking this cue, Mitsubishi and Sumitomo made similar arrangements with Westinghouse and International Telephone & Telegraph, respectively. Under American tutelage Japan's electrical industry was the first in the world to be fully modernized and became a spectacular success.

The wisdom of Masuda's stewardship was demonstrated further in the major reorganization of Mitsui in 1909. During the "partnership period" inaugurated in 1893, Mitsui Bank had been the central organ of the house, and its business had undergone tremendous expansion. The forward leap was most conspicuous during and immediately after the Russo-Japanese War, when the Bank's profits quintupled in three years. And yet, with so many new and growing companies under its wing, the Bank continually had to seek new sources of capital, since the Mitsui concern's liquid assets were far from sufficient to satisfy its demands. Therefore, in 1909 Bank was reorganized as a joint-stock company with a paid-up capital of twenty million yen divided into 200,000 shares, of which 38,000 were taken up by Mitsui family heads. The remaining shares were purchased by other Mitsuis or their trusted associates. To increase income from outside sources, the Bank began underwriting stocks and bonds and handling various securities transactions.

Mitsui Takayasu, a tenth-generation descendant of founder Hachirobei, retained the presidency of Bank, a position he had held since 1891. (In 1916 he, too, was made a baron, the second Mitsui to be so honored.) Chief managing director was Hayakawa Senkichiro, a high official in the finance ministry until Inoue Kaoru brought him in to replace the dying Nakamigawa. A former comptroller in the Bank of Japan, Hayakawa was noted for having successfully floated several huge bond issues during the Russo-Japanese War and for untangling the financial complications afterward. He became the first of several banto from Mitsui to attain the coveted position of president of the South Manchurian Railway.

As a joint-stock company, Mitsui Bank could no longer offer the degree of absolute control over assets that had been so jealously guarded through the centuries. Therefore, in 1909 Masuda organized a holding company, called Mitsui Gomei Kaisha, to supplant the outdated partnership as supreme headquarters of the business empire. Gomei, in turn, was nominally subject to the will of Dozokukai, the clan council that had supplanted Motokata in 1900. The initial capital of Gomei Kaisha was fifty million yen, all of it invested by the eleven Mitsui houses, whose heads remained its sole owners. Baron Mitsui Hachiroemon Takamine was president of Gomei Kaisha but, as usual, business affairs were managed by a general staff among whom Masuda, Dan Takuma, and Ikeda Seihin, another Harvard graduate, were the most powerful.

Mitsui's harmonious collaboration with leading banks and industrial concerns in the United States and Great Britain had given promise of better things to come; yet even as the modernized Mitsui Gomei made its debut there were discordant notes. The Japanese had assumed that the Americans assented to their preemption of Manchuria, but Washington showed clear signs of vexation at having been all but excluded. Relations were further embittered by anti-Japanese discrimination in the United States, especially in California. American nationalists, exploiting the economic grievances of workers and farmers, were successfully disseminating propaganda about the "yellow peril," and their Japanese counterparts responded with warnings against a "white peril" threatening Asia. Only two years after the love feast occasioned by the Russo-Japanese War real fear of an impending war between Japan and the United States developed on both sides. Nervous Japanese businessmen persuaded their government to conclude a gentlemen's agreement with the United States, reducing Japanese immigration to a token number; but in California discrimination continued to be so severe that Japanese (as well as other Orientals) were prohibited from buying land and had to send their children to segregated schools.

These developments, which provided fuel for Japan's nationalist incendiaries, were distressing in the extreme to Mitsui's American-educated executives, who had worked unremittingly to maintain cordial ties with their American counterparts. The United States was the principal market for raw silk and textiles, which at the time constituted the bulk of Japan's exports, and Bussan was the biggest supplier. With such considerations in mind, Masuda and Dan groomed Baron Mitsui Hachiroemon Takamine for a grand tour of the world, beginning with the United States. The term "public relations" was not a familiar one in 1909, but its concepts and techniques were fully understood by

Count Kaneko Kentaro, who supervised preparations for the Mitsuis' journey.

Knowing the weakness of rich Americans for titles of nobility, the planners included in the party Baron Mitsui's daughter, Marchioness Nakamikado, whose husband was a descendant of an eighteenth-century emperor, and Viscount Iwakura Tomoaki, grandson of the famous Prince Iwakura Tomomi and brother-in-law of Baroness Mitsui. The baroness, a daughter of one of Japan's wealthiest daimyo, was every inch a noblewoman, modest and retiring, but with the dignity and poise of her lineage. The baron himself, having undergone lifelong training for his role, knew how to be convivial with his peers and quite at ease with the mighty. Baron Mitsui's English had deteriorated since his sojourn in New Jersey and Massachusetts during the 1870s, but this scarcely inconvenienced him, because Dan Takuma (who had been educated at MIT) was always at his side and knew the right questions and answers much better than did his boss. Also in the party were an English-speaking director of Bussan, several secretaries, and at least ten servants. The party occupied nearly a whole floor of the Plaza Hotel, their headquarters in New York.

While the baroness and the marchioness saw the sights of Manhattan in the company of a number of patrician matrons, the baron made the rounds of banks and corporation offices to conduct some high-level negotiations with such nabobs as John Pierpont Morgan, his partner Thomas Lamont, John D. Rockefeller and his sons, E. H. Harriman, George Eastman, and steel tycoons Andrew Carnegie and Elbert Gary. It was during this visit that Baron Mitsui formalized the agreement through which General Electric bought into Shibaura Engineering Works. At that time, too, Thomas Edison gave Baron Hachiroemon a talking machine, equipped with a diamond stylus, and a selection of shellac cylinders upon which the voices of several famous singers had been recorded.

In his own country the baron held himself haughtily aloof from the public and the press; but in New York he relaxed somewhat and even allowed himself to be interviewed by reporters. When asked about the possibility of a war between the United States and Japan, he replied, "Impossible," and had nothing but praise for his host country. "Americans," he said, "are the most tactful, accurate, and reliable businessmen in the world. I prefer to deal with them above all others." Whether or not this feeling was reciprocated by his American associates, the baron's party was treated with such courtesy and cordiality that reports of anti-Japanese feeling on the part of Americans must have struck them as being wildly exaggerated.

For posterity's sake, the baron conscientiously kept a diary of his junket to the world's major capitals, during which he exchanged views with innumerable members of royal families, statesmen, and business tycoons—Battenbergs, Hapsburgs, Hohenzollerns, Romanovs, Rothschdils, Schroeders, Schneiders, Krupps, Putilovs, and such. Judging from his character, the diary might well have been bland, dignified and well larded with platitudes about international good will and the responsibility of prosperous nations to cooperate in the economic and cultural development of Asia. Unfortunately for historians, however, and perhaps for history, the diary was lost when his home in Tokyo and its contents, including the gifts from Thomas Edison, were destroyed by American firebombs in 1945.

15 · A Foothold on the Mainland

THE JAPANESE SECRET SOCIETIES were amazingly ubiquitous and versatile. With organizations extending into every town and village in Japan and its colonies, they also had well-established units in all the seaports of East Asia and operated no less effectively in the backlands of Tibet, China, and Mongolia. Their more scholarly members, funded by men of substance, established institutes for the study of languages, history, geography, and politics, along with nationalist indoctrination and martial arts. From those centers dedicated agents—popularly called "continental ronin"—fanned out to places of strategic or economic interest, posing as students, teachers, shopkeepers, salesmen, and even as coolies or vagabonds. Their tasks were to gather information, make maps, recruit informants or political allies, smuggle gold or opium, bribe warlords, sabotage railways, assassinate opponents, or foment rebellions in furtherance of various conspiracies.

Such adventurers worked tenaciously and discreetly, scoring brilliantly at times; yet even when exposed and tortured, they kept silent so that their principals—the army, government bureaus, politicians, or businessmen—could plead ignorance of what was happening. In order to succeed they had to be utterly merciless in their methods, but often they were idealistic in their aims. Patterning their outlook and way of life after loyalist samurai of the bakumatsu period, they called themselves *shishi*—men of high purpose—and even used the old slogan of sonno joi. Serving the emperor as of yore, now they would expel the barbarians from China, enabling their brother Asians to enjoy the blessings and benefits of Japanese rule.

In addition to the Black Ocean Society and Kokuryukai, the Black Dragon Society, there were hundreds of clandestine groups—even thousands if the smallest ones were included. Some of the leaders were men of means, and others financed their activities through gambling, prostitution, protection rackets, strikebreaking, blackmail, or small business monopolies such as labor recruiting, entertainment, and street vending. Most of them seemed to be motivated by a fierce individualism, often differed in their theories, and were split among rival

175

camps; but as the expansionist movement gained speed at the turn of the century they submitted to firmer guidance from more or less presentable leaders such as Toyama Mitsuru, Uchida Ryohei, and rightwing politicians whose contacts with the business world enabled them to finance operations on a considerable scale.

Major terrorist societies were linked informally with more acceptable organizations, whose members included representatives of the aristocracy, politicians, and important businessmen. Toa Dobun-kai, or East Asia Common Culture Society, founded by Prince Konoe Atsumaro, speaker of the House of Peers, was such a dignified front. Its ostensible purpose was to promote solidarity between Japan and China through student-exchange programs. However, a good many so-called "students" from the Japanese Dobun colleges actually were spies who made hazardous trips into remote parts of Asia to gather strategic information. Not uncommonly the continental ronin were assisted by local managers of the colonization companies, or SMR, or trading firms when operating in regions where there was no government representation, or when they needed a convincing "cover." Bussan's men helped them as a matter of course, either from sympathy, or patriotism, or fear of displeasing the agents' highly placed sponsors, some of whom were among Mitsui's leading executives.

The best-organized and most effective of the terrorist groups was the Black Dragon Society, supported by industrialists of northern Kyushu and staffed mostly with men from that region. The society, in addition to maintaining order and discipline among workers, served mining companies by procuring underground mineral rights from reluctant landowners and settling disputes over damage caused by mining operations. Since the establishment of the Yawata Iron Works in Kyushu, Black Dragon Society leaders had been active in getting or maintaining control over Chinese coal and iron deposits for their benefactors, but their deeper purpose was to establish Japanese hegemony over all of China and Manchuria.

Their confidence in being able to accomplish this immense task was based upon a simple concept, evolved by Toyama and Uchida. This was, in essence, to overthrow the decaying Manchu empire by supporting pro-Japanese revolutionaries in China. In the resulting confusion China's sovereignty over Manchuria would be open to question, and the Russians would undoubtedly move in to fill the power vacuum. But the Japanese, having formed an alliance with a reformed China, could then roll the Russians back to the Amur River, gaining control of all Manchuria and of eastern Siberia as well. "Thus love of country and chivalry went hand in hand in the Japanese help of the Chinese revolution,"[1] as the Black Dragon Society's official historians wrote.

Although thousands of ronin operated on the continent, some of their most effective work was done among the overseas Chinese, particularly in Tokyo and Yokohama. After the antiforeign Boxer uprising had nearly toppled the Manchu dynasty, the Chinese government decided belatedly to modernize. Following the example of the "Meiji enlightenment," they sent abroad large numbers of students to acquire knowledge from the modern world. Those studying in Japan numbered about five hundred in 1902 and increased to thirteen thousand by the end of the Russo-Japanese War three years later.

Those youths were supposed to be the future leaders of China, so the Japanese nationalist societies spared no effort or expense to influence their thinking, cultivate their friendship, and help them organize anti-Manchu conspiracies. Because Japan was the only Asian nation to have modernized itself and had proved its ability by trouncing the Russians, many Chinese students learned to admire the "island dwarves" they had been taught to despise. They hoped to imitate Japan's fine example and responded enthusiastically to the nationalists' pan-Asian program.

The Chinese leader most favored by the Black Dragon Society and related groups was Sun Yat-sen, a physician, scholar, and crusader for a free and democratic China. After a series of abortive revolts, he had taken refuge in Japan, where he posed as a language teacher under the solicitous sponsorship of Toyama Mitsuru, Uchida Ryohei, and several politicians who were interested in Chinese problems.

Sun's ability as an organizer and propagandist had won him a worldwide following. To the Chinese students he was a hero, even a messiah, while the Japanese nationalists regarded him as a pliable and promising instrument for separating Manchuria from China. Japanese politicians, business tycoons, and military leaders, whose opinions about China were molded by clever ultranationalist thinkers, believed that if an upheaval occurred in China as predicted, revolutionaries who were controlled by the secret societies would be most able to advance Japanese financial and strategic interests on the continent. Therefore, Sun and his colleagues were treated most hospitably, even by leaders of divergent views, who nonetheless continued to supply funds liberally. The governor-general of Taiwan, for example, had given Sun a military base from which to launch attacks upon the mainland of China. Okuma Shigenobu lobbied actively to win support from Japan's oligarchs; and the secret societies always seemed able to get contributions from Kyushu's coal magnates. Mitsui's old newspaper adversary Akiyama Teisuke, also a member of the Black Dragon Society, was an ardent backer of Sun, and when the publisher went too deeply into debt he used his talents of persuasion or extortion to collect more money from the zaibatsu. Among them Mitsui and Okura, a similar industrial and trading concern, were the most generous.

With China in ferment, investments there were unsafe, so Japan's businessmen preferred to work jointly in collaboration with the "China watchers" of the secret societies. A typical consortium was the Nisshin Kogyo Chosa-kai (Japan-China Enterprise Investigation Association), organized by barons Masuda Takashi and Shibusawa Eiichi before the Russo-Japanese War and reactivated in 1909. Other leading figures in the organization were Baron Kondo Rempei (president of the N.Y.K. Line) and Baron Okura Kihachiro (head of the Okura combine), but the thinking and planning were left to continental ronin working closely with Toyama, Uchida, and Sun Yat-sen. As a result of investigations and clandestine arrangements with Chinese politicians, an all-Japanese company called Toa Kogyo Kaisha (East Asia Industrial Company) was formed in 1909 by thirty zaibatsu leaders meeting at the Mitsui Club. This company, it is said, eventually channeled investments of about sixty million yen into China.

"The object for all this was nothing but to help develop China, to promote a better understanding between the two countries, and mutually to enjoy the happy outcome of coexistence and prosperity,"[2] wrote Shibusawa's biographer, Obata Kyugoro. Hypocritical as this may sound two world wars later, many Chinese and all but the most cynical Japanese took it seriously. Behind their idealism was a belief that if the loyalist ronin of the Meiji era, starting from the very beginning, had been able to industrialize Japan in fifty years, the new generation of Japanese could do the same for China and in much less time. With vastly greater experience than their fathers had possessed, and the inexhaustible resources of China to support them, they felt quite capable of forging a united, autonomous Asia as the heartland of the world.

Mitsui had an old and abiding interest in the China trade, with which the House had become familiar through its centuries-old branch in Nagasaki. In 1877 Masuda Takashi and Shibusawa Eiichi had visited Shanghai together to negotiate a loan for China and to ask permission for establishing a branch of Dai-Ichi Ginko. When the Yawata Iron Works was established in 1896, Bussan contracted for ore from the Ta-yeh mines, near Hankow, which later became part of the Han-Yeh-P'ing Coal and Iron Company, China's principal industrial complex. By 1911 Bussan had extended loans totaling eighteen million yen for the development of those mines, a main source of ore for Japan's blast furnaces. This, of course, was only a fraction of Mitsui's growing investment in China.

With such stakes at hazard, Mitsui and other zaibatsu were drawn into dozens of Lilliput-like schemes to tie down the sleeping giant. Their agents were in close touch with most Chinese leaders of any stature or promise, and the ronin in China were reporting voluminously about the smoldering political situation. Their energy seems to have exceeded their accuracy, for despite all this surveillance the Japanese schemers and even Sun Yat-sen himself were caught off guard. When the first revolution scorched central China in October 1911, Sun Yat-sen was in New York soliciting funds for his cause. It was scarcely a coincidence that his friend Mori Kaku, Bussan's keenest expert on China, was there at the same time.

Mori embarked immediately for Tokyo and upon his arrival learned that the insurgents had seized control of the Yangtze valley, where Japanese investments were heavily concentrated. The operations of the Han-Yeh-P'ing mines had been disrupted and Bussan's ore supplies to the Yawata works cut off. It was apparent that the revolution had got beyond Japanese control. But because the unpredictable Dr. Sun had stopped off in London to do some lobbying, the insurgents had no leader capable of unifying them and the zaibatsu were without a Chinese protector.

Sun arrived in Hong Kong about Christmas time, accompanied by a motley entourage of foreign advisers, sycophants, soldiers of fortune, and munitions salesmen rushing to fish in China's troubled waters. Among the Japanese waiting for him were numerous continental ronin, zaibatsu agents, army officers, bureaucrats, and lawyers, not to mention the doctors, nurses, smugglers, police spies, and ruffians who trailed along. With so many surrounding him, the great man was not easily approachable for private conversation. But Mori Kaku, anticipating this confusion, had dispatched as his agent one Yamada Junsaburo, who was an old friend of Sun's. During the trip by train from Hong Kong to Shanghai, Yamada seized the first opportunity to talk business and found Sun more than receptive.

It is perhaps the shortest conference in the annals of Japanese commerce. According to Yamada, Sun went right to the point: "You're in with the Mitsui moneybags. Get me some money."

"About how much?" Yamada inquired.

"The more the better—one or two million yen would do."

From such encounters Japanese leaders got the impression that the Chinese revolution was for sale to the highest bidder, and they did not quibble over the price. When Sun was elected provisional president of the newly formed Republic of China, Mori immediately got him 150,000 yen from Mitsui for buying arms, and larger loans were arranged for the Han-Yeh-P'ing Coal and Iron Company. In compensation, plans were made to give a majority interest in the Chinese company to Mitsui, Yawata Iron Works, and other Japanese investors.

Upon the outbreak of hostilities Japanese commercial adventurers and gunrunners had swarmed into China seeking quick profits, selling arms indiscriminately to Sun's rebel government in Nanking or to the Manchu government in Peking. This angered Sun's nationalist supporters in Japan, and Toyama Mitsuru went personally to Shanghai with a squad of burly "enforcers" to root out the opportunists. The small-time brokers fled in terror, but Toyama learned that Mitsui, too, was playing both sides of the street. At his behest, Sun Yat-sen cabled the friendly genro Katsura Taro and Inoue Kaoru, indicating the displeasure of his republican government. Mitsui was duly informed and got squarely behind Sun with a new loan of three million yen.

Such handouts, smacking of bribery, naturally caused indignation in Peking, since Tokyo still maintained diplomatic relations with the Manchu regime. The avarice of the Japanese, and their suspected intention of absorbing China rather than of liberating it, also weakened the position of the pro-Japanese elements in the republican government. Sun, who had no divisions under his control, was losing influence; his supporters were disunited and their armies demoralized. Opposing them were the well-equipped and disciplined forces of General Yuan Shih-k'ai, the strong man of Peking, who had been ordered to put down the revolution. Instead of doing so, he conserved his strength and angled for a deal with Sun while waiting for the rebel forces to deteriorate. Meanwhile, he engineered the abdication of the child-emperor Henry Pu-Yi, last of the Manchu dynasty, whose guardians conferred full authority on Yuan himself. Sun, whose own position had become untenable, came to terms with Yuan early in 1912 and handed over the provisional presidency to him.

Sun's capitulation was an unmitigated disaster for Japan's nationalists and zaibatsu, who had worked hard for so many years to secure an exclusive position in China. Yuan was strongly anti-Japanese and also was supported by the United States and other foreign powers who had been alarmed by Sun's favoritism toward Japan. These powers had formed a new consortium for channeling funds to China and now offered Yuan a large "reorganization" loan to win his adherence to the Open Door policy. Japan, being a member of the consortium, had no alternative but to participate in the loan, which bolstered the power of Yuan's hostile regime.

Sun, still a personage to be reckoned with, was given charge of China's railway development program. In that capacity he visited Japan early in the spring of 1913, no longer a furtive exile but a leading statesman, welcomed as a hero by his old friends, especially the zaibatsu. These gentlemen found the ex-president more responsive than ever to their blandishments. Having been shunted aside by Yuan, he was further disgruntled by the latter's arrogance. Once in control, Yuan had used the foulest means to crush the republican revolution and to achieve his ambition of restoring the monarchy with himself as emperor. Sun, a Western-educated Christian, had been ill-prepared for the scabrous realities of Oriental politics. But after having experienced them he seemed to shed his idealism and become as calculating as the Japanese schemers wooing him. In Tokyo he attended frequent conferences at the Mitsui Club and at Bussan's headquarters. The most conspicuous result was the formation of the Chugoku Kogyo Kabushiki Kaisha (China Industrial Company), for which the Mitsui, Mitsubishi, Okura, and Yasuda zaibatsu provided the capital. Perhaps as a sop to Sun's pride the directors elected him president. Shibusawa Eiichi, the copresident, later recalled that the company "became an important medium to promote industrial enterprises in both countries. Bankers and businessmen vied with each other to make investments in China, and an enormous amount of money was put up for China by that company."[3]

A potent stimulus for Mitsui's enthusiasm may have been an alleged secret agreement between Prime Minister Katsura Taro and Sun Yatsen that the latter was prepared to part with Manchuria—for a price. If such an agreement existed, Katsura would presumably have confided it to his kinsman and confidant, Count Inoue Kaoru, Mitsui's senior adviser. Whether or not Inoue was the source, Mitsui did get the information that Manchuria was on the block, and worked out an audacious scheme for buying it.

It is doubtful that obanto Masuda Takashi would have originated such a plan. Mitsui's foreign operations were based upon international good will and bank credit, particularly with Great Britain and the United States. An underhanded deal for Manchuria, to which Japan had promised them equal access, would have provoked damaging antagonism. A more likely hypothesis is that the idea germinated in the receptive brain of Yamamoto Jotaro, the dynamic chief of Bussan, whose ambition to dominate Asia's resources was of Alexandrian proportions.

Yamamoto's consuming urge to succeed was partly due to an affront suffered in his youth, according to an anecdote told by his biographers. Yamamoto came from a shabby-genteel family but had a wealthy uncle named Yoshida Kenzo, an executive of the British trading firm of Jardine, Matheson and Company. Yoshida's adopted son, Shigeru, was rather spoiled. One day when Kenzo and his family were out for a ride in their carriage, they overtook young Yamamoto on the road. "Shigeru, here is your cousin Jotaro," his mother said as Kenzo stopped the horses. "Get down and say hello to him." But Shigeru looked down upon the poorly dressed youth and cut him cold. At that moment Yamamoto Jotaro made up his mind to become rich and powerful.

He joined Bussan in 1882, and after thirty years of intense effort he had worked his way up to the highest position open in the trading field. He also had the satisfaction of knowing that the snobbish Shigeru was only a second secretary in the Japanese Embassy in Washington, D.C. Still, Shigeru had made an excellent marriage: his wife was the daughter of Count Makino Nobuaki, son of the renowned Meiji leader Okubo Toshimichi and a member of the privy council. With such connections, cousin Shigeru, despite his plodding course in the foreign service, might amount to something after all, and Yamamoto was determined to keep ahead of him. For such a man the purchase of Manchuria would have a special appeal.

Count Inoue, nearing the age of eighty, had less incentive for the adventure but perhaps was agreeable to carving out a secure place for Mitsui's future expansion on the continent as his parting contribution to the clan. Of course the purchase of Manchuria would create some delicate problems for the foreign minister. A comparable situation would have been an attempt by the House of Rothschild to buy America's Pacific Northwest by bribing Confederate President Jefferson Davis. But the current foreign minister, Kato Takaaki, happened to be supremely indifferent to the world's opinion; moreover he was a son-in-law of the founder of the Mitsubishi zaibatsu and, since his family's concern would be no less favored than Mitsui, he was willing to take the risk.

The man chosen to complete the grand design was Yamamoto's lieutenant Mori Kaku, who was, if possible, more ambitious than his boss. After helping Yamamoto trap Russia's Baltic Fleet, Mori had married the daughter of an admiral and been promoted to manager of Bussan's Tientsin branch. There he had proved himself an astute politician with a remarkable knack for handling assignments in the murky borderland between business and crime. As part of his concurrent job as an executive of the China Industrial Company he was in charge of funneling money into Sun's personal treasury, and otherwise assisting in attempts to liquidate the Yuan regime. One of his more sinister projects was to set up a laboratory in Peking for a Japanese pharmacist recruited through the Black Ocean Society, whose sole mission was to poison China's president, Yuan Shih-k'ai.

That crafty warlord was not such an easy prey, however. Evading the innumerable Japanese ronin and Chinese nationalists who were stalking him, he disposed of his own enemies with terrifying competence. In fact, his atrocities and corrupt relations with the Western powers generated such wrath that several opposing factions united to overthrow him. When the second Chinese revolution broke out in the summer of 1913, Sun Yat-sen (again taken by surprise) rushed back to China from Japan. With a barrage of oratory, in which he alluded pointedly to the friendship and generosity of the Japanese, he exhorted the newly formed Kuomintang and other rebel forces to destroy Yuan and seize power.

When the rebels started to advance on Peking, Mori, being fully conversant with the state of their exchequer, sent a coded cable to the Bussan office in Nanking with instructions to make Sun a firm offer for Manchuria. His emissaries were Bussan's Yamada Junsaburo, once again, and Sun's dear friend Miyazaki Torazo (the Black Ocean Society patriot who had recruited the pharmacist-poisoner for Mori). Those gentlemen had no difficulty in calling upon Sun and presenting Mitsui's terms: twenty million yen in cash and enough arms to equip two divisions. Sun asked for half an hour to think it over, and after a private discussion with his military commander, he agreed to accept Mitsui's offer, urging that the details be settled as quickly as possible.

Such a sensitive matter, however, called for a personal conference between Sun and his Japanese backers, especially Katsura and Inoue, so the imperial navy was asked to send a warship for his transportation to Japan. Unfortunately, Prime Minister Katsura had been forced to resign (for the third and last time) and his sanguine foreign minister, Kato, was replaced by the ultracautious Count Makino Nobuaki, a strong opponent of the scheme. Educated at an American university (he had accompanied Kaneko and Dan on the Iwakura mission in 1871), Makino was both an internationalist and a professional diplomat. Heedful of Japan's reputation abroad, he vetoed Mori's project. It was just as well, because Yuan Shih-k'ai, sustained by the "reorganization" loan to which Japan had regretfully contributed, bought off some of the strongest rebel leaders and the revolt collapsed.

Once again Sun fled to Japan, where he was given shelter by Toyama while he pleaded for renewed support. But now his zaibatsu benefactors were exceedingly cool. Mitsui alone had paid out several million yen and had little to show for it. The firm of which Sun had been copresident froze him out when it became the Chunichi Jitsugyo (China–Japan Industrial) with Yuan Shih-k'ai as copresident. Mori persisted with his plot, but although his hired poisoner was still on the job in Peking—presumably at Mitsui's expense—Yuan survived to die a natural death three years later, after having been recognized by the consortium powers as the first president of the Republic of China.

It would appear that Mitsui had some hope of reaching an accommodation with Yuan. His legal assistant, Ariga Nagao, a noted Japanese scholar who helped him write China's constitution, was the elder brother of Ariga Nagabumi, an executive with Mitsui Gomei. Since the younger Ariga himself was deeply involved in ultranationalist intrigues on behalf of Mitsui, it is probable that the position of his brother Nagao would have been used to advantage had Yuan remained in power.

Japan's shortsighted and transparently devious policy had been a dismal failure, however. In China it generated hatred and contempt for the Japanese; internationally Tokyo's motives and methods were condemned; and domestically there was more rioting, nationalistic agitation, murder, and political uncertainty. Four cabinets had collapsed within three years, as the nation clamored for a more satisfactory solution to the "China problem." Statesmen generally agreed that a unified, consistent policy had to be formulated and acted upon firmly. Instead, those concerned with the problem brought forth not one unified policy but several incompatible ones that were applied (as usual) at the wrong time, clumsily, and with counterproductive results.

16 · The Two Faces of Mitsui

ALTHOUGH JAPAN'S FAMILY-DOMINATED HOLDING COMPANIES passed into limbo a quarter of a century ago, the term zaibatsu still evokes memories or images of wealth, power, exploitation, militarism, and aggression. In contrast, the name Mitsui produces subjective overtones no more discordant than, let us say, do those of Rockefeller, Morgan, Rothschild, or Krupp. Since Mitsui was the prototype and most prominent example of the financial clique, why should the specific name of Mitsui call forth a different set of reactions from that elicited by the word zaibatsu? Perhaps the answer lies in the fact that Mitsui was not a monolithic institution, but rather a confederation of cliques whose motives and methods often were in conflict. As a commercial and financial concern Mitsui was respected internationally for its probity and relative progressiveness; but as a zaibatsu in Japan its name was necessarily identified with all the darker manifestations of a society still groping its way out of feudalism. Like Japan itself, Mitsui turned one face hopefully toward the Western world, while the other contemplated stubborn anachronisms from which it could not escape.

One of the brighter facets of Mitsui's modern side was Masuda Takashi (who, on the recommendation of his old business partner Inoue, was awarded the title of baron in his later years). Equipped with a native shrewdness sharpened by long experience with Westerners, Masuda knew how to cut through the circumlocutions of Japanese protocol and get to the heart of the matter—which for him was the arithmetic of profit and loss. Thus he had unusual ability to communicate with the business barons of other countries. But while learning willingly from the West, he had not become Westernized to the point of losing the qualities that made him Japanese.

Nakamigawa had divorced sentiment from business and, with his team of Fukuzawa-trained rationalists from Keio Gijuku, tried to lift Mitsui out of feudalism almost overnight. Applying logic and the example of foreign monopolists, he had organized the Mitsui concern as a pyramid of enterprises, with Bank at its apex. To Masuda, however, intuition meant more than logic, and people more than organization.

With the full approval of Baron Mitsui, he fostered talented men (including Nakamigawa's brain trust) and gave them as much leeway as possible to use their gifts creatively. In contrast to Nakamigawa, Masuda emphasized trade over finance, and left his decisive imprint upon the concern by keeping it primarily commercial. Avoiding long-term commitments to heavy industry, he operated flexibly, maintaining high liquidity of assets so that no commercial opportunity need be lost for lack of operating capital.

Mitsui Gomei Kaisha, the holding company organized by Masuda in 1909, was an admirable structure. Capitalized at fifty million yen, it comprised fifteen major companies, four wholly owned and eleven under tight control, with many more under its strong influence. The concern still stood solidly on its tripod of banking, mining, and commerce, to which the manufacturing enterprises were kept subordinate. Government-related business was no longer a decisive factor: the concern had now become capable of sustained and flexible growth with self-generated capital. It was then, if ever, that this eminently respectable organization could have reasserted its independence and become a private enterprise in the international sense.

Yet while Mitsui's businessmen had been trying to create a structure that could stand alone, Inoue Kaoru and his fellow oligarchs, still regarding Mitsui as an instrument of national policy, had been tightening the cords of gold and silk that bound it to the state. During the course of two wars within one decade the Mitsuis had had no choice but to fulfill their responsibilities to the emperor and his growing empire, but the fact that the interdependent relationship was so immensely profitable made a disengagement less enticing when the wars had ended. With victory, Japanese leaders dreamed of spectacular expansion rather than of sober, plodding development. With opportunity beckoning in China, they wanted, above all, to develop the means of making war. Thus in 1907, at the behest of the government, Mitsui entered the munitions industry by establishing Nippon Seiko, or Japan Steel Works, a joint venture with Britain's two largest makers of arms, Vickers and Armstrong (which later merged).* Japan Steel Works, in

---

* The international armaments industry was already organized into cartels, of which the Nobel Dynamite Trust and the Harvey United Steel Company were most powerful. The latter, organized to protect patents for case-hardening armor plate, included the major armaments makers, notably Vickers, Armstrong, Krupp, Schneider, and Bethlehem Steel. By forming Japan Steel Works with the two British firms, Mitsui became associated with the Harvey cartel, headed by Albert Vickers, and gained access to European and American munitions-making technology. Schneider-Creusot of France later invested in Japan Steel and other heavy industries of the Mitsui group.

which Mitsui Gomei Kaisha held the major interest, adopted British technology to make military and naval ordnance as well as huge castings, forgings, armor plate, battleship turrets, and the like. The firm also made industrial machinery, but it was essentially a government-subsidized arsenal with a monopoly in its field. At the stock exchange in Tokyo it was known as *aamu* (the Japanese-style contraction of Armstrong). Whether by choice or by force, Mitsui was slipping back into its old role as official purveyor to the military. And it was in this relationship, against which the founder had warned his heirs, that the Mitsui zaibatsu showed its darker face.

With China becoming a tinderbox, production of military equipment became increasingly important in Japan as well as in Europe, and there was strong competition among munitions makers for shares in the Chinese market. By joining with Mitsui, Armstrong and Vickers had gained some advantage over such competitors as Europe's Krupp and Schneider; and Mitsui, because of that association, could entertain hopes of catching up with Mitsubishi and Kawasaki, who led the way in Japan's heavy industries.

Japan's military chieftains, uncertain about how the situation in China would develop, hoped to avoid a disorderly scramble by Japanese manufacturers for munitions sales there. Wanting to harness the arms business to national policy, they decided to form a cartel. In 1908, well before hostilities began in China, war minister Terauchi Hisaichi summoned representatives of Mitsui Bussan, Okura-gumi, and a Mitsubishi affiliate, and instructed them to establish a joint organization for overseas arms transactions. Thus the Taihei Kumiai (Pacific Union), better known as the Taiping Company, was established. The three parent organizations were guaranteed a profit of five percent on their sales.

What happened to the remaining profit is obscure, since the firm's dealings were not open to public scrutiny. It is probable, however, that some of the proceeds were used for secret political and military purposes—perhaps lobbying for higher appropriations for munitions and subsidizing agents of the secret societies and their activities on the continent. The Taiping Company also enabled traders to engage in the machinations necessary for closing international munitions deals (in competition with such unscrupulous "merchants of death" as Basil Zaharoff of Vickers) without sullying the reputations of their respective houses. More than likely a good part of its profits would have been spent upon such arrangements. Understandably, its operations were shrouded in secrecy at first, but in time newspapermen referred to it as "the treasure house of the army."

While the Taiping Company channeled munitions to Japan's Chinese allies during the revolutions in 1911 and 1913, private firms and adventurers were able to make far higher profits from direct sales to competing Chinese cliques. Gunrunning became an immensely lucrative business, and since it required the connivance of government officials, army and navy men, trading companies, and secret societies, bribery and other illicit transactions were commonplace.

To the true Mitsui Bussan man the scent of profit was like a whiff of gunpowder to a war horse. With its long experience as a supplier to the military, Bussan did not balk at a bit of gunrunning slipped in with its more legitimate business through the Taiping Company. But Bussan's chief manager, Yamamoto Jotaro, had learned from his teacher Masuda to think in big terms. Once he became engrossed in the munitions game (Bussan was the exclusive agent for Japan Steel Works and for Vickers, as well as the middleman for suppliers of small arms and other military equipment), his ambition overcame his judgment, and he charged headlong into disaster.

The so-called *Kongo* affair began in 1910, when Bussan's intelligence network picked up a tip that the navy was about to order a new cruiser. Mitsubishi was capable of building it, but Yamamoto knew that if he could swing the order to Vickers, Bussan would get a fine commission. With commendable foresight Yamamoto had hired as "technical adviser" a reserve officer whose close friend was a vice-admiral in charge of naval stores. The adviser, knowing that a large sum of money would have to be passed under the table, consulted a Mitsui director, who in turn queried Vickers concerning the arrangement. Vickers agreed to increase Bussan's commission by five percent, to a total of 1,500,000 yen, thus enabling Mitsui to offer 400,000 yen as a gratuity. That amount was duly deposited in two of the vice-admiral's confidential bank accounts, and the details were properly, if imprudently, entered in Bussan's books.

By 1913 the great battleship *Kongo* was nearing completion at Vickers' yards and there had been no hint of trouble. But early that year a Tokyo police agent named Wada Yagoro, working on the "dangerous thoughts" detail, noticed a warehouseman who was spending more money than he could have earned honestly. Held for questioning, the suspect confessed to having embezzled, but in his defense alleged that financial irregularities were quite common in his office, a branch of Siemens-Schuckert Werke. Soon afterward, the Japanese manager of the German firm, which was installing wireless equipment for the navy, visited Wada's home to thank him for arresting the embezzler and gave him an expensive gift. Wada received no further orders concerning the case, but he was suspicious and kept his ears open. A few months later he happened to hear that one Karl Richter, a Siemens employee, was blackmailing the manager, and Wada decided to investigate.

The manager, confronted with the story, readily admitted that Richter was threatening him and asked Wada to assist him in getting the German expelled from Japan. The conscientious Wada refused and submitted a complete report on the affair, but to his surprise there was still no response from headquarters. Instead, he received a telephone call from the manager, who told him that Richter had returned to Germany. "The matter is settled" he said soothingly. "Please don't worry about it any more." Wada was still dissatisfied; but he could get no more information from the manager, and his supervisor told him pointedly to drop the case.

It is recorded that on November 17, 1913, a series of secret meetings involving the prime minister, the navy and justice ministers, the German consul, and a Siemens representative took place in Tokyo. Certain instructions were passed down to the public procurator's office and the police board. The trouble, whatever it was, seemed to have been suppressed. But two months later the *Jiji Shimpo* carried a startling cable from London under the headline "Siemens Company Bribery Case Disclosed." It was reported that Karl Richter, after his return to Germany, had been sentenced to prison for stealing documents from the Siemens office in Tokyo. During his trial he had testified that the company was using bribery to win contracts. From his testimony it appeared that certain officials in Japan's Ministry of the Navy were on the Siemens payroll, and that even commodore-class officers were being bribed.

Wada had taken the trouble to shadow Richter before his departure and had discovered that he worked with a British accomplice. Somehow this information was conveyed to a member of the Diet, who thereupon accused the navy minister of complicity in hushing up the case. Wada was placed under surveillance and told to keep his mouth shut. Another dietman offered to buy his report for 25,000 yen, and on more than one occasion he was assaulted by hired thugs.

There were good reasons for the government's anxiety to silence such meddlers. First, Prime Minister Yamamoto Gombei himself was an admiral, and some of his best friends were involved in the scandalous situation. Second, the Diet was then considering an expanded budget for a six-year naval buildup, and the national security was at stake. And third, some of Japan's leading businessmen stood in danger of being disgraced. But now, with *Jiji Shimpo*'s muckraking article on the streets, the case was in the open. The police had to arrest the Englishman, and apparently he talked to save his skin. Polemics in the lower house of the

Diet shifted from German wireless equipment being installed in Tokyo to a Japanese warship being built in Great Britain, and sharp questions were asked about Japan Steel Works' connections with the navy.

To Mitsui's discomfort the *Kongo* troubles broke just as public attention was being focused on the naval budget. The bribery issue was taken up stridently in the press and, as in the wake of the Portsmouth Treaty, there were riotous demonstrations in Hibiya Park. Other insiders began talking, and someone revealed that Bussan's panicky executives had altered the company's books to conceal their dishonesty. Yamamoto Jotaro and two others of Mitsui's ranking banto were arrested. What had been called until then the Siemens Scandal was now dubbed the *Kongo* or Mitsui Bussan Scandal, to the uncontained delight of Mitsui's competitors and the political rivals of Seiyukai, the party in power. Rioting against corruption spread from Tokyo to Kobe and Osaka, and troops had to be called out to quell the mobs. Overzealous police injured two newspapermen with their swords and the press went mad. Some heads had to roll, and Prime Minister Admiral Yamamoto's was the first. After the Diet slashed the naval budget, his cabinet collapsed. Two of his miscreant vice-admirals and other officers were tried with unprecedented celerity, found guilty, and convicted, along with Bussan's Yamamoto Jotaro, two of the firm's directors, and its "technical adviser" from the naval reserve.

Observing the Japanese custom of assuming his company's disgrace, Yamamoto Jotaro resigned, and shortly thereafter Baron Masuda found it expedient to retire from Mitsui Gomei after forty years of service with the House. As further atonement Bussan contributed its commission on the *Kongo* contract (less the amount that had been used for the admiral's bribe) to a fund for the rehabilitation of convicts. This was singularly appropriate, considering that Yamamoto and his accomplices at Bussan were in danger of going to prison. However, Mitsui's political influence had not waned perceptibly, and the culprits were released on probation after the hubbub subsided.

Although the Mitsuis themselves were not implicated, the ugly tarnish upon their name was not to be eradicated by resignations, apologies, or the rather clumsy public relations campaign conducted on their behalf in New York and London. "The whole incident was felt to be a public disgrace," wrote A. Morgan Young in the *Kobe Chronicle,* soon after the affair, "since directors of Japan's greatest mercantile firm and high officers of the navy, Japan's special pride, were involved. Commercial morality, it was generally recognized, was at a very low stage, but that the navy should be thus venal was a great shock to national confidence."[1]

That reference to "national confidence" seems to have been a bit of journalistic exaggeration, since the incidents just described were only the most conspicuous symptoms of a disease that afflicted the entire body politic—a serious condition in which the several organs functioned independently (and exuberantly) without regard for the well-being of the body as a whole.

What was happening to Japan, a nation that once had seemed to be well on the way toward greatness? The simplest explanation is that the government, which had been designed as a constitutional monarchy, had fallen into anarchy as several different power groups fought for supremacy. At the vortex of the struggle was the emperor, the unquestioned (but unquestioning) fountainhead of authority, and surrounding him were the genro—the same small band of samurai who had seized the imperial court in 1868 and had never relinquished their physical custody and intellectual influence over the sovereign. By the end of the nineteenth century the demands of the several power groups had become more strident, their resources more formidable, and their methods more crafty. Meanwhile, the genro moderators had become older and fewer. The exigencies of the Russo-Japanese War had enabled them to maintain a temporary unity among the rival groups, but by 1912, when Emperor Meiji died after a reign of forty-five years, the political situation was confused and malignant.

After the death of Katsura Taro in 1913 the only surviving Sat-Cho genro were Yamagata and Inoue of Choshu and Matsukata and Oyama of Satsuma. Those four patriarchs and Prince Saionji (soon to become a genro) controlled access to the new emperor, an ill-favored and mentally unstable youth whose reign was to be called Taisho, or Great Righteousness. By virtue of their position as "elder statesmen" they could procure imperial rescripts when necessary, and decide among themselves whom His Majesty should appoint as prime minister. But the increasingly rigorous conditions affecting the survival of the cabinet had seriously diluted the potency of these personal remedies. The politicians of their choice could not form a cabinet if the military disapproved of them, because the ministers of war and of the navy had to be officers on active duty and hence subject to orders from their superiors. Or, having formed a cabinet, the prime minister was at the mercy of the lower house, whose rejection of a budget could force his resignation. Since the political parties controlling the lower house were sustained by money from the zaibatsu, the prime minister had to be no less responsive to the wishes of big business.

At the other end of the political spectrum were the masses. Although they lacked formal representation, their frustrations could be easily exploited by the press or by agitators of the secret societies, whose services were available to the power elite. To cope with disorders, spontaneous or contrived, the government had the police and the military at its disposal, but the conspicuous use of force exposed the cabinet to new and often disastrous attacks of oratory. This dispersion of power had a paralyzing effect, and the official system of government, as prescribed by the constitution, had become utterly incompatible with political realities. In moments of desperation the genro could still invoke the imperial will; but ambitious men, while paying public homage to the god-emperor, privately worshiped almighty gold, the new talisman of power for those who were excluded from the palace coterie. As their power waxed and that of the genro declined, the conduct of national affairs degenerated. Outwardly, the government functioned as usual, but decisions of real public significance were made in private, and clandestine "teahouse politics" generated corruption, demagoguery, and, inevitably, terrorism when tempers turned ugly.

Inoue, now a marquis, was nearly eighty years old. Three successive blows in as many years—the death of his friend the emperor Meiji, the failure of his projects in China and Manchuria, and the besmirching of Mitsui Bussan and the imperial navy by the *Kongo* affair—had taken their toll of his health. Yet apparently the fortunes of the House of Mitsui were much on his mind, being essential, in his view, to the success of the empire. No one understood Japanese political processes better than the marquis, who had helped so much in designing them. Therefore, he marshaled his remaining energy to create a government that could rise above political bickering and impose enough unity so that a vigorous and consistent policy of expansion overseas could be set in motion.

The premier-designate chosen by the three other genro proved to be unable to form a cabinet, so Inoue intervened to propose a surprise candidate, Count Okuma Shigenobu. Perhaps because he had been politically inactive for so long, Okuma was still regarded as a liberal and a stout advocate of constitutional government. Known as "the Sage of Waseda," he had become famous as an educator and had innumerable friends and admirers both in Japan and overseas. He enjoyed a respect almost equal to that of the genro, yet was untainted by the misrule of the Sat-Cho oligarchs. Thus he was welcomed by a public that had become surfeited with Choshu's virtual monopoly of power during the preceding fifteen years. Such was the popular optimism that Okuma was expected to inaugurate a "Taisho Restoration," which would cleanse the national image of its accumulated grime.

It seems strange that Marquis Inoue, the patron of Mitsui, should have backed a man so closely connected with Mitsubishi, as Okuma was, and even stranger that he accepted Kato Takaaki, a Mitsubishi retainer, as foreign minister. However, Inoue knew full well that China was too big for Mitsui to handle alone and that expansion of Japan's interests on the continent required the cooperation of all the zaibatsu. There was also the redeeming fact that Kato's daughter was married to a kinsman of a Mitsui heir, and thus bore some responsibility toward the clan. Furthermore, in his three previous terms as foreign minister, Kato had shown himself capable of standing up under pressure from the military and their clamorous superpatriots.

At first things worked out as Inoue had expected: Okuma was supported by a majority in the lower house, and the opposition Seiyukai Party was unusually quiet. The Siemens-Vickers scandal still reverberated a bit, but the pro-Mitsubishi people, with their team unexpectedly in power, now had little incentive for belaboring Mitsui. Okuma proved to be tractable, the last flicker of his liberalism having guttered out, and once again, the ultraconservative genro were really running the government as Kato struggled to formulate a viable China policy.

The time of quiet lasted exactly two months. Then, on June 28, 1914, another act of terrorism changed the course of world history. Acting for the ultranationalist Black Hand (a Balkan equivalent of the Kokuryukai), a young Serbian terrorist assassinated Archduke Francis Ferdinand of Austria at Sarajevo, precipitating chaos in Europe. No country was more remote than Japan from the battlefields of the Great War, and the issues over which the Western world went suddenly mad were of only marginal concern to the Japanese. But the government was still bound by the Anglo-Japanese alliance, and when Great Britain declared war on Germany on August 4 Japan was requested to assist its ally by attacking German vessels, which already were harrassing British shipping.

The genro, although not unfriendly toward Germany, had decided that the Allies were more likely to win the war and hoped to sit among the victors at the peace table. They also recognized the white men's distant war as a providential opportunity for a Japanese thrust into China. Delaying only long enough to negotiate the most favorable terms for its intervention, Japan declared war on Germany on August 23 and thereby became the military ally of Great Britain, France, and Russia, ranged against the Central Powers.

While those countries were mobilizing for the titanic struggle in Europe, Japan swiftly invaded the Shantung Peninsula in China for an attack on Tsingtao, the main German outpost in Asia. By November 7, 1914, the army and navy had captured that important city and all other German concessions in Shantung Province. Meanwhile, the Japanese navy had occupied the Marshall Islands, the Marianas, and the Carolines. At a very modest cost and without risk, Japan had commandeered all of Germany's Pacific possessions north of the equator; and in exchange for promises of further military assistance, it extracted from the Allies secret agreements that these far-flung territories would remain in Japanese hands after the war.

At a single stroke national confidence and a degree of political unity had been restored, the navy had recovered its prestige, and Japan was clearly aligned with the more favored side in the world's most awesome conflict. But still there were bothersome doubts and unsatisfied ambitions. What would happen to Japan when its allies were free to turn their attention toward China again? With abundant capital and superior military power, would they not find ways to roll Japan back to its former place and status? There seemed to be little likelihood that Japan would have another such opportunity to break the imperialist grip on China, which was left unprotected and all but ignored. In Tokyo the decision makers, not content with the spoils that had fallen so easily into Japan's hands, agreed that the nation should press its advantage to the utmost. To do less would be to ignore the lessons in history that they had learned from the imperialist powers themselves.

Uchida Ryohei, perhaps the most influential civilian authority on continental problems, believed that in exchange for Japanese assistance the Chinese would now accede to the measures needed for strengthening Japan's economic position on the continent. Shortly after the fall of Tsingtao to the Japanese he completed a memorandum to this effect, specifying the demands to be made, and submitted it to Prime Minister Okuma and Foreign Minister Kato. The latter seems to have followed Uchida's advice in formulating the government's demands, which were presented to China's President Yuan in January 1915. The so-called Twenty-one Demands were essentially a compendium of the prizes and privileges long sought by the zaibatsu, and the special interests of Mitsui and Mitsubishi were unmistakably represented. The demands were arranged in five groups, the first four of which included the following rights or concessions:

Extension of the leases on Port Arthur, Dairen, and the South Manchurian Railway zone for ninety-nine years.

Control over the Kirin-Changchun Railway, also for ninety-nine years.

The right of Japanese to conduct business, hold land, and exploit minerals in Manchuria and Inner Mongolia.

Exclusive rights to build railways or lend money for this purpose in the two regions.

Assurance that China would not sell or lease, except to Japan, any harbor or territory along the China coast.

Exclusive Sino-Japanese control of all mining in the Han-Yeh-P'ing area. To protect this business, which was of great importance to Mitsui

Bussan and Yawata Iron Works, it was further stipulated that the Han-Yeh-P'ing company be made a joint Sino-Japanese concern and that the company not be nationalized or financed by any nation except Japan.

Harsh as these demands were, the fifth group was even more oppressive: China was to employ influential Japanese advisers on financial, political, and military affairs; police departments in places important to Japanese interests were to be jointly administered and were to employ "numerous" Japanese; China was to buy at least half its munitions from Japan (presumably through the Taiping Company); and Japan would have the right to build three railways in south China. This group of demands would have made China a political as well as an economic colony of Japan.

Japan's terms were supposed to have been kept secret, but the Chinese, indignant at such arrogance, released them to the world on the eve of negotiations in order to win foreign support for rejecting them. The United States protested strongly, and the European powers, too, were further alienated by Japan's opportunism. In the face of Chinese and world opinion Kato agreed, on his own authority, to withdraw the fifth group of clauses. But his concession brought the government under blistering attack from the nationalists and the Mitsui-backed Seiyukai. In Peking the ineffable Mori Kaku converted the offices of the Chunichi Company into a psychological warfare headquarters from which his hired journalists attacked Kato for his spineless capitulation. In Japan there were demonstrations and riots. A bomb was thrown at the car of Prime Minister Okuma, who had lost a leg in an attempted assassination under very similar circumstances in the 1880s.

(Okuma's reaction to these two outrages sheds a revealing sidelight upon Japanese politics and attitudes. While still recovering from the loss of his leg, Okuma made a substantial gift to the family of his would-be assassin, who had killed himself. On the thirty-third anniversary of the first attempt to kill him, a celebration was held under the sponsorship of Toyama Mitsuru, whose henchmen had perpetrated both bombings. After the ceremonies Toyama paid a friendly visit to Okuma and thanked him for his generosity to the assassin's survivors.)

Fortunately for Japan's economic advance in China, Russia had been forced to suspend competitive activities in the Far East. Its armies were being mangled by the Central Powers on the European front, and simultaneously the czarist regime was menaced by revolution. Desperate for military supplies, the Russians kept Japanese arsenals and mills working around the clock to supply them with munitions and equipment. In return for this cooperation, Japan secured agreements by which Russia acknowledged Japan's strengthened position in Manchuria and Inner Mongolia and recognized that no third power hostile to either Russia or Japan should be permitted to dominate China.

Okuma's "Mitsubishi Cabinet" could not take credit for these favorable agreements, which were kept secret for a change. On the contrary, it was sharply attacked by the Seiyukai opposition, whose representatives complained that the still obscure Taiping Company had been allowed to monopolize private munitions sales abroad. From 1914 through 1917, as postwar reports showed, the value of its supplies to Russia amounted to nearly 150 million yen, or half of its total sales.

Compared with European and American munitions cartels, this was just a small business. During the same years, prior to the United States' involvement in the war, the export department of J. P. Morgan & Co. supplied three billion dollars' worth of war goods to the Allied powers, and acknowledged receiving commissions of thirty million. Morgan's cartel arrangement, also secret, was not revealed publicly until nearly twenty years later.

The Taiping "death merchants" were accused of profiteering and bribery, and Seiyukai politicians tried to build up a "Siemens case of the Army" until they realized that their benefactor, Mitsui, was the biggest profiteer of all.

Meanwhile, China, unable to enlist the active support of other countries, acceded to a revised version of the Twenty-one Demands and signed new treaties that gave Japan most of what it wanted. Nevertheless, the Okuma government, castigated for its "soft" China policy, was replaced by a tougher one headed by Terauchi Hisaichi, the general from Choshu who had carried out the forcible annexation of Korea.

Terauchi was no less eager than his predecessors to make China an appendage of the Japanese empire. But before taking any overt steps he sent a special emissary, Viscount Ishii Kikujiro, to Washington with instructions to reach an understanding. In exchange for Ishii's pious pledge to observe the Open Door policy, Secretary of State Robert Lansing officially recognized Japan's "special interests in China, particularly those in the part of which her possessions are contiguous."[2] Whatever Lansing may have had in mind, Japan interpreted this to mean South Manchuria and Shantung. The American concession was just what Terauchi needed, but it presented colossal problems for Lansing's successors, including his nephew John Foster Dulles.

New treaties concluded on the basis of the Twenty-one Demands greatly augmented Japan's "special interests" in China. Meanwhile, the war-embroiled Allies had suspended their consortium loans to the Chinese government. This encouraged Terauchi to advance with redoubled vigor, but to assuage international wrath stirred up by the demands he adopted a conciliatory policy of a type known today as "economic cooperation." The abundant amounts of foreign currency that were pouring into Japan as war profits made it possible for him to extend big loans to several Chinese warlords who seemed capable of forming a viable government. Wary of leaks, he bypassed the Japanese ministries and dispatched his personal secretary, Nishihara Kamezo, to find suitable loan clients in China. Nishihara, although obscure in banking circles, was well connected with the army and the nationalist societies. He also had an excellent contact in Peking, finance minister Ts'ao Ju-lin, who had handled negotiations over the Twenty-one Demands. Ts'ao, who had studied in Japan for several years and had a Japanese wife, was a strong figure in the profoundly corrupt An-fu clique then ascendant. At Nishihara's instigation, Ts'ao proceeded to bribe amenable warlords to turn over what was left of the Chinese economy to the zaibatsu of Japan. At the same time the individual zaibatsu too did quite a bit of "cooperating," with the result that during 1918 the Japanese extended to China loans amounting to as much as 295 million yen, of which 177 million were semiofficial. It has been estimated that Mitsui interests supplied roughly one-quarter of the private loans granted to China during and immediately after the war. An unofficial list cites the following loans: Mitsui Bussan Kaisha to the central government for Bureau of Printing and Engraving, 2,000,000 yen; Mitsui Bussan Kaisha to military governor of Chihli, 1,000,000 yen; Mitsui Bussan Kaisha to Chihli Province for flood relief there, 1,000,000 yen; and Taihei Kumiai (Mitsui-Mitsubishi-Okura joint firm) to central government for arms, 14,000,000 yen.

The loans were marked for a variety of legitimate purposes—participation in the war, government reorganization, munitions, forestry, flood-relief projects, railways, and communications. The purposes for which they were actually used, and even the total amount of money involved, are unknown; but probably most of that money lined the pockets of Chinese officials.

To put the matter in perspective, it should be said that those Japanese politico-financial deals with China were by no means unique. Earlier in the century an American engineer, Herbert Hoover, had applied the same methods to take over the very productive and well developed Kaiping mines in northern China for a British firm in which he held a big interest. Sun Yat-sen often referred to this steal as an example of foreign depredations that provoked the Chinese revolution. Using the tactics he had learned in China, Hoover secured large interests in oil, minerals, timber, and water power in Russia. If he had been allowed to keep them, he would have become one of the richest men in the world. Unfortunately for his plans, however, in 1912 there was a massacre of strikers by Cossacks at a gold mine of which he was part owner. That so-called Lena Goldfields atrocity sparked a nationwide wave of strikes and, according to Joseph Stalin, was more effective than any other incident in arousing the revolutionary spirit of the Russian masses.

In 1916, when Czar Nicholas II faced overwhelming resistance from Russia's liberals, socialists and communists alike, an American syndicate headed by First National Bank of New York and J. P. Morgan & Company floated two bond issues totaling $75 million for the czarist regime, partly to protect British-American oil and mining rights against a radical change in the government. In the following year, after the Bolshevik Revolution, the United States Congress appropriated $100 million for economic relief in central Europe, then racked by strife between socialists and conservatives. Hoover, heading the American Relief Administration, used the threat of starvation to bolster authoritarian regimes in several countries and—unsuccessfully—to support counterrevolution in Russia, where his investments were concentrated. The amounts involved in those imperialistic transactions far exceeded, of course, the total sum of Japan's politically inspired loans to China during the same period. (It was largely to prevent shaky European countries from defaulting on their loans from America that the United States had taken part in the Great War.) It could be said, indeed, that the loans arranged by the insignificant Nishihara Kamezo—about 88 million dollars in all—were only pale imitations of the "dollar diplomacy" then being applied worldwide by righteous Americans.

Most of the money dispensed by Nishihara seems to have come from Yokohama Specie Bank, Industrial Bank, Bank of Korea, and Bank of Taiwan, in which the zaibatsu held big investments and considerable authority. The loans were extended against flimsy collateral or none at all, and about ninety-five percent of the total amount was defaulted, leaving the "national policy" banks holding the very empty bag. But those institutions, in which the imperial household was the biggest private investor, could not be allowed to suffer: to their rescue came the Ministry of Finance's deposits bureau, which administered the postal savings system used by Japan's workers, farmers, and small businessmen. In the end more than 150 million yen of the people's savings was paid to the banks in order to avert the fiscal consequences of Terauchi's recklessness, and of course the burden of repayment was loaded upon the general public, not upon the beneficiaries of that rescue.

From the viewpoint of the big businesses, this series of adventures had been rather successful. During the eight years since the first Chinese revolution the zaibatsu had advanced significantly on the continent, at least in strengthening their grip on natural resources, transportation, industry, and commerce. Their greatest "victory" was the agreement, reached at the Versailles Peace Conference in 1919, confirming Japan's succession to German rights in Shantung and its mandate over the Pacific islands seized from Germany in 1914. But the political price of these awards was yet to be reckoned, and there were unmistakable signs that it would be exorbitant. At home, awareness of the unholy alliances among big business, politicians, and the military bred dissatisfaction and radicalism. In the capitals of the allied powers, Japan's opportunism and duplicity had caused such distrust that wartime allies were turning into enemies, and the possibility of a peaceful settlement of the China question had receded to the vanishing point.

In May 1919, a month before the Versailles Treaty was signed, Chinese indignation was at its height. Leaders of a newly organized student movement called for mass protests against "national humiliation," represented by the Twenty-one Demands, the Nishihara loans, and the Japanese acquisition of Shantung. On May 4 some three thousand students assembled in Peking for rallies and then marched toward the foreign legation quarter. Deflected by police, they stormed into the residence of Nishihara's friend Ts'ao Ju-lin, screaming for the blood of the traitor. The minister had escaped, but they set fire to his house and thereby started widespread riots, strikes, and anti-Japanese boycotts that in a matter of weeks forced the resignation of the pro-Japanese government. The "May Fourth Movement," once ablaze, was never really extinguished. Out of it was born China's first socialist club (one of whose members was a young librarian named Mao Tse-tung) and the brand of revolutionary anti-imperialism that culminated in the victory of the Chinese communists thirty years later.

 17 · Which Way
to Utopia?

THE WAR YEARS AND THE DECADE that followed were for Japan, as for
the Western world, an era of intellectual and social ferment in which
old values were cast aside and new ones adopted uncritically. As in the
time of the Rokumeikan, or the Hall of the Baying Stag, superficial
aspects of European and American life were imitated enthusiastically if
often grotesquely. But along with the trivial there came an intoxicating
assortment of liberal and radical ideas that permeated the better-
educated members of Japan's authoritarian society, and an awakening
of the masses that carried with it some hope of a democratic transformation.

Japan's plutocrats viewed such a prospect with undisguised loathing.
Any expression of the popular will that was unauthorized by the Meiji
constitution, they felt, not only was an offense against the national
essence but was contrary to common sense and the nation's economic
interests. They saw that for the first time Japan was in a position to become one of the world's first-rate powers in every sense. They were
determined that the road to the utopia they envisioned should not be
blocked by a rabble of misled intellectuals, socialists, communists,
syndicalists, or anarchists, regardless of their numbers or their zeal.

The zaibatsu, although concerned over the "unwholesome" trends
gaining ground among the people, felt quite confident of handling the
situation, for their economic strength—which they sensibly equated
with political power—had been greatly amplified since 1914. After
groping their way through the initial confusion caused by the disrup-
tion of world shipping and commerce, they had discovered fantastic
opportunities unfolding on every side, and had exploited them to the
full. There was an insatiable demand for munitions, and as European
manufacturing countries shifted to war production there were shortages
in civilian goods of every description. Overseas markets formerly dominated by the colonial powers opened magically for Japan, whose merchant marine—protected by a powerful navy—became indispensable to
the Allied cause.

From the start of the war through 1918 Japan's exports tripled, to reach more than a billion dollars a year, and Mitsui Bussan handled more than one-third of the transactions. Since imports were drastically curtailed by shortages elsewhere the nation's trade balance, so long unfavorable, registered a net surplus of 1.37 billion dollars—most of it in gold. As imported goods became unavailable, Japanese entrepreneurs were subsidized to enter unfamiliar fields, especially heavy industries. Textile makers enjoyed an unprecedented prosperity and invested their profits in expansion of their facilities. Industrial production as a whole quadrupled. During this bonanza period Mitsui's Kanegafuchi Spinning and Oji Paper companies became gigantic by international standards.

The demand for shipping brought an elevenfold increase in Japan's income from sea transportation and doubled the merchant marine to three million tons. Of this total Bussan controlled 1,280,000 tons, mostly by charter. Meanwhile Bussan set up its own shipyard at Tamano, in Okayama Prefecture. This yard, forerunner of the Mitsui Shipbuilding & Engineering Company, built three vessels for the United States merchant marine during and immediately after the war. As an offshoot of the shipping business, Mitsui established the Taisho Marine & Fire Insurance Company. Using Bussan's worldwide network of branches and agents, Taisho was soon competing fiercely with Mitsubishi's dominant Tokio Marine & Fire Insurance Company.

With Germany isolated, Japan's chemical industry developed or imported new technology to fill the gap. The gases from Mitsui Mining's coke ovens at Miike yielded the basic materials from which a great variety of industrial chemicals, explosives, fertilizers, dyestuffs, and pharmaceuticals could be made. Mitsui's chemists already knew how to synthesize complex organic compounds in the laboratory, and now they learned to produce some of them on an industrial scale. Their first big success was with synthetic dyestuffs (until then virtually monopolized by German chemical firms), which liberated Japan's textile-dyeing industry from foreign dependence. From Miike coke was born a whole complex of industries based upon chemicals. One of the new units was Denki Kagaku Kogyo (Electro Chemical Industrial), established in 1915 to make calcium cyanamide by fixing the nitrogen in air. This, Denki Kagaku's particular process, devised by a Mitsui chemist named Fujiyama Tsunekichi, gave Japan's artificial-fertilizer industry great impetus.

Until the end of the Meiji era the Japanese had relied upon French and English machinery for the textile industry. Japanese engineers knew everything there was to know about the use of such equipment, but for economic rather than technical reasons they could not build it competitively. A struggling inventor named Toyoda Sakichi had spent twenty-five years in perfecting an automatic loom of great promise but was unable to attract any commercial interest in it. Early in the war, however, when foreign machinery was unavailable and textile makers were screaming for more spindles and looms, domestic inventors were appreciated at last. With financial backing from Mitsui, Toyoda got his loom into production and it turned out to be incomparably efficient. Other Japanese engineers adapted the latest Manchester spinning machinery and multiplied the number of the nation's spindles into the millions. Researchers, meanwhile, had been experimenting to find a formula for mixing short-staple Indian cotton with the more costly long-staple American variety. They produced a strong, economical thread that became the envy and despair of the world's spinners, who were unable to imitate it. Having started at a disadvantage, compared with the Western countries, Japan's textile mills emerged in the 1920s with the most modern and efficient machinery—tended, in some mills, by girls gliding on roller skates from loom to loom in order to increase their productivity.

The growth of the spinning industry gave Japan a chance to take over sources of raw cotton formerly monopolized by other countries. Bussan was by far the biggest dealer, handling twenty-five to thirty percent of Japan's cotton imports and twenty percent of its cotton-goods exports. After the end of the war, when cotton trading became dangerously speculative, Bussan separated its cotton department to form Toyo Menka Kaisha, or Oriental Cotton Trading Company, which maintained branches in the United States, China, Manchuria, Korea, India, Indonesia, and other cotton-producing regions. Within a short time after its establishment "Tomen" was handling almost ten percent of Japan's total trade in cotton, compared with about thirty percent for the parent company.

In New York, Bussan's branch manager Tajima Shigeki used Mitsui's ships and sources of supply like pieces on a chessboard. Working from an office at 65 Broadway, in the heart of Manhattan's financial district, he conducted a tremendous business in "third country" trade, moving food, raw materials, merchandise, and munitions from their cheapest sources to the markets willing to pay the highest prices.

Expanding Mitsui's interests in the United States, Tajima secured ninety percent of the stock in the largest American cotton-purchasing firm and made other opportune investments that assured Bussan of reliable sources of commodities and technology. One such venture was the Standard Aircraft Corporation, in which Bussan had invested capital just before the United States entered the war. Immediately thereafter Standard's business increased spectacularly. Income during the next three years was estimated at fourteen million dollars (against an investment of two million). Since Bussan owned all the preferred stock, its profits must have been substantial—so substantial, in fact, that the United States government subsequently brought suit to collect 2.5 million dollars in overpayments it had made to Standard Aircraft. In addition to profit, Mitsui got invaluable experience in aircraft manufacture and trading, not to mention relevant technology, that enabled the concern to exert indirect control over the Japanese aircraft industry for many years thereafter.

While the zaibatsu prospered hugely from the war, the rise of the *narikin,** or nouveaux riches, was even more spectacular. Those upstart financiers were, by and large, more enterprising than their conservative colleagues and less reluctant to enter risky fields of business. They cropped up in nearly every sector of business, but among the most successful were traders and shipowners. Nomura was the biggest narikin in banking; and Kuhara Fusanosuke, starting in copper mining and machinery, established the Hitachi Works and Nissan (Japan Industry) combine that soared into the economic firmament, eventually to challenge Mitsui.

One of the flashiest of the narikin was Uchida Shin'ya, who had left Bussan just in time to get in on the shipping boom. As a subordinate of Mori Kaku in the Shanghai office during the Russo-Japanese War, he had developed a taste for salt water when he was one of Mori's "sea scouts" stalking the Baltic Fleet. A rich man at thirty, he was one of the few Japanese to own a private yacht, an asset that may have helped him in his later political career with the Seiyukai.

A narikin of a very different type was Kaneko Naokichi, the obanto of Suzuki Shoten, a trading house that was well established before the war and grew like Jack's beanstalk during the boom. Kaneko, widely known by his nickname, Nezumi (meaning rat or mouse, a mildly pejorative term connoting slyness or stealth), had no personal ambition, devoting his life and commercial genius to building the fortune of the widow Suzuki, nominally the head of the company. Under his harddriving leadership, Suzuki staked out a world empire and boosted its transactions to more than a billion yen a year. It is reported that at one time about ten percent of the ships passing through the Suez Canal were owned or chartered by Suzuki.

Starting with trading in Taiwan sugar and camphor under the protection of the island's civil administrator Goto Shimpei, Suzuki Shoten pushed its way into textiles, rubber, mining, nonferrous metals, steel, chemicals, fertilizer—in short, into almost every field that Mitsui and

* Literally, "one who turns into gold." In *shogi,* Japanese chess, a pawn turns into a narikin, equal in power to a "golden general," when it reaches enemy territory.

Mitsubishi cherished as their own. Such famous companies of the present as Teikoku Rayon (Teijin), Kobe Steel, Ishikawajima-Harima Heavy Industries, and Nissho-Iwai Trading, as well as the Bank of Kobe, are descended from fragments of the Suzuki zaibatsu—which eventually was smashed by Mitsui and Mitsubishi.

Not unexpectedly, the iridescent war bubble burst about a year after the armistice. Rising foreign competition ruined many an export industry in Japan, the balance of payments turned sharply unfavorable, prices plummeted to nearly half their peak level, and a serious economic crisis ensued. Most of the narikin were wiped out, unemployment was general, and wages were cut. Under such harsh conditions radicals and labor organizers found large and attentive audiences. The ground had been well prepared for them. Alliance with the democratic powers had made quite an impression upon a people who had not yet known political freedom. Since the Russo-Japanese War they had developed a sympathy for the Russian people's struggles to overthrow czarist tyranny, and the Bolshevik Revolution of 1917 had aroused feverish interest among Japan's intellectuals. As Marxists explained the mechanics of the class struggle, popular sentiment for labor unionism, which had been spreading steadily over the years, became epidemic.

The zaibatsu considered the demand for labor unions as frivolous and unfair, if not downright pigheaded. The employees of their commercial and financial establishments were well paid by Japanese standards and enjoyed not only extra benefits but the prestige and sense of power that come from belonging to a winning team. While acknowledging their responsibilities to manual workers, employers thought of them as children, who had to be taken care of somehow whether they deserved it or not. But although employers seemed to think of themselves as philanthropists rather than exploiters, living standards among the proletariat did not speak well for Japanese paternalism.

More than half the wage earners were women, most of whom were farmers' daughters working in textile mills. Living in dormitories under close supervision, they were available for work day and night, putting in eleven hours or more a day—seven days a week—for daily wages of twenty-five cents or so. There were no stipulations about the maximum number of hours for men, but women and children under sixteen were protected by the Factory Act of 1911 (not enforced until 1916), limiting hours of work to eleven per day and providing for two holidays a month. Application of the law was left to the discretion of employers, however. The larger mills, wanting to recruit the most competent girls, offered slightly better working conditions. It is said that Asabuki Eiji, the head banto of Kanegafuchi Spinning, inspected the various mills personally and even ate occasionally with the mill hands in the company dining hall. His successor Muto Sanji, a Christian liberal, also was solicitous about the workers' welfare, but was opposed to raising wages because most girls wanted to quit and get married when they had saved enough money to do so. Instead, he set up welfare funds with attractive benefits for long service. But at best the life of the factory girls was dreary and confining, and on the average it was hideous, since smaller operators (who constituted the vast majority) were themselves hard pressed by the zaibatsu and had no alternative but to squeeze their scanty profits out of the workers.

The Mitsuis were not oblivious to the plight of their workers and seemed to believe that conditions at the concern's establishments were better than the norm. At Omuta, Mitsui Mining's big coal town in Kyushu, they had set up a hospital and a technical school that gave free training to young recruits. The company operated a nonprofit commissary and provided rent-free housing. Executives took pride in the fact that, until 1924, there had never been a strike at Omuta's famous Miike mines. But it is doubtful that the miners' tractability resulted from contentment, for until the 1930s their life was little different from serfdom.

Unexpectedly honest descriptions of Omuta in the early 1920s were written by a young aristocrat, Ishimoto Shizue, whose husband was employed there as an engineer—at a salary of about twenty-five dollars a month less deductions. According to Baroness Ishimoto (now Kato Shizue, a Socialist member of the Diet), there were no holidays at all: the great chimneys poured out smoke even at the New Year and on the emperor's birthday. The only surcease from work came with disasters, machinery breakdowns, or illness, in which case the workers were likely to go hungry. The company houses were little better than stables, built of rough lumber and roofed with sheets of galvanized iron. "One barrack was usually divided so as to house five to seven families, separated from the adjoining booths by thin boards. The average size of one family was five or six members, and there was only one lavatory for a whole row of barracks. There was neither gas nor water service."[1]

In Omuta some fifty thousand people lived under such conditions, closely watched, economically unable to escape, bullied and threatened by thugs hired to keep them in line, beaten or murdered when they resisted.

Miners worked a nominal twelve-hour day but usually spent fourteen hours on the job, including time consumed in the round trip from the surface to the work area. Since a miner's wage was insufficient to support a family, wives and children worked too. Pregnant women remained on the job as long as possible and not infrequently gave birth to their babies underground. Because of the intense heat miners of both sexes worked nearly naked, the men digging coal in narrow tunnels that were sometimes no more than three feet high, as women and children wriggled in and out dragging baskets of coal to the collecting points. Safety standards were lax and inspectors were commonly bribed to overlook violations; cave-ins and explosions took a heavy toll of lives, sometimes in the hundreds. The reported fatality rate was triple that of England, and hardly a miner escaped a disabling injury.

For this exhausting, hazardous toil, male miners were paid an average wage of twenty dollars a month, women twelve dollars, and children much less. But even so, the free miners were aware of being better off than were the red-uniformed convicts who, chained at the waist, were led into the mines every day under heavy guard. And they also knew that in case of labor trouble the company would not be averse to replacing the dissidents with low-cost convicts, a good many of whom were in chains for having expressed their dissatisfaction too loudly when they were free men. Labor organizers did not thrive at Omuta.

The political status quo, which helped to make Japan's exports competitive despite retarded technology, was maintained by a series of "peace preservation" ordinances. The first of those was enacted in 1877 by General Yamagata Aritomo to crush the movement for popular representation then threatening the oligarchy. An amended version, passed in 1900, effectively outlawed labor unions, strikes, and collective bargaining. The law was supposed to prevent the use of force, but was invariably used as a pretext to obstruct the organization of laborers and was never invoked in cases of reactionary violence against the dissidents. Since the civil and military police were vigilant against "intellectual offenses," many socialists, communists, anarchists, and even Christian reformers spent a good deal of their time in jail, to the serious detriment of the renovationist movements.

Nevertheless, there were always a few courageous men and women willing to risk their lives and liberty, and there had been sporadic labor disturbances since the late nineteenth century. In 1911, when the leftists seemed to be getting out of hand, the police arrested a dozen socialists and accused them of plotting to bomb the emperor's train. For their alleged crime the accused men—falsely labeled "anarchists"—were hustled to the gallows after a trial so secret that the real story has not been told to this day. This object lesson for "reds" brought a short respite. But during the First World War, when even conservative leaders were paying lip service to democratic ideas, strikes became commonplace, and between 1915 and 1917 the number of labor disputes tripled.

The zaibatsu, deeply disturbed by manifestations they interpreted as mutinous, began fighting labor organization by organizing against it.

Employers of course were exempt from the laws against syndicalism; in fact, a statute providing for collective action by businessmen had been on the books for nearly thirty years, and a bankers' club had been in existence since 1910. (Around that time Ikeda Seihin, a director of Mitsui Bank, organized a successful protest against the low salaries being paid to Mitsui's executives without attracting the attention of the police or even jeopardizing his career.) In 1917 the most active members of the power elite formed the Nihon Kogyo Kurabu (Japan Industry Club), which became the headquarters of militant businessmen in their campaign against militant laborers. Funds for establishing the club, still in existence, were supplied by Mitsui and Mitsubishi in equal amounts.

The first president of the Industry Club was Dan Takuma, who had succeeded Masuda as obanto of Mitsui Gomei and had guided the concern through its greatest period of expansion. Now, as *doyen* of the industrial magnates and one of Japan's most respected internationalists, the MIT-trained engineer (who might well be called the Herbert Hoover of Japan) tackled the labor problem. His long experience in the rough, tough business of mining had not hardened him outwardly. On the contrary, his personality was quite gentle. Those who knew him remember him as a shy and even a wistful man. Although he was wealthy and owned a trove of art objects selected with exquisite taste, he was not considered greedy and despised unscrupulous acquisitiveness in others. His attitudes toward business and labor reflected an idealism based upon his belief in the value of virtuous businessmen to society and, as the necessary corollary, in the divinely ordained destiny of employees to be submissive to them. "If you are in an enterprise," he once wrote, "no matter what it is that you do, that is your Heaven-given function. If you are successful in this and make some contribution to the Nation and your fellow countrymen, the sense of having contributed is your compensation."[2]

Dan considered himself not a member of the capitalist class but a managerial employee who was responsible to the workers as well as to the owners and whose duty it was to mediate between them. This concept, although familiar in the West, in Japan seems actually to have been an extension of the old relationship between the effete, incompetent daimyo and their loyal, able samurai. The assumption of authority by the university-educated management class, inaugurated for Mitsui by Nakamigawa and perpetuated by Masuda and Dan (and followed to some extent by the other zaibatsu), appeared to be "modern" to foreign businessmen, but in fact it bore no trace of the liberal thinking then gaining currency among managers in Western countries. To Dan, Masuda, and their colleagues, such concepts as workers' rights, individualism, and equality of opportunity were utterly foreign and irrelevant to the Japanese situation. Dan spoke of strikes as an "infection," the evil result of granting rights that destroyed traditional relationships between capital and labor.

Sugar magnate Fujiyama Raita, president of the federated Japan Chamber of Commerce (the counterpart of the Japan Industry Club in the commercial and smaller industrial fields), insisted, typically, that Japan could not adopt Western labor practices because its society was fundamentally "different." It was the Japanese family system, based upon ancestor worship, that made the difference. Since the institution of paternalism in enterprise was an integral part of that system, Fujiyama maintained, it could not be sacrificed to the Western principle of workers' rights. Labor problems could be solved only within the context of the allegiance due the imperial family, "a line unbroken for ages eternal." In Japan's Confucian kind of hierarchy, sanctioned by custom and codified in civil law, the idea of horizontal equality that is implicit in collective bargaining was unthinkable. All interpersonal relationships were vertical, and each person, from the emperor down to the coal miner's youngest child, occupied a distinct rung on the social ladder. Since this stratification was part of the "national essence," any interference with it was regarded as treason; it followed that any action taken to defend the integrity of the system was, ipso facto, virtuous.

In the sweltering summer of 1918, as the war in Europe was coming to a climax, Japan was engulfed in a wave of radicalism and rioting. As usual, the police and military forces killed scores of demonstrators and thousands more were arrested. It was clear that the situation could not be brought under control forcibly without unleashing terror on a much larger scale. The ruling cliques were united in their condemnation of the rebellious forces, and the law was on their side. But for several reasons they hesitated to use their full strength.

For one thing, the government had not yet been able to assess the depth of public discontent. Earlier in the year, at the invitation of the Allies, Prime Minister Terauchi had launched a military expedition into Siberia with the clear intention of countering the Bolshevik Revolution and gaining any other advantages that might be inherent in that chaotic situation. The Japanese, who had sent not one soldier to the European fronts, dispatched more troops than did any other country to Siberia and kept them there for much longer a time.* This campaign of convenience merely added to the fears of the allied powers, whose attitude

* Japanese troops were not withdrawn from North Sakhalin Island until 1922. At that time Moscow granted to Japan oil-development rights later exploited by the North Sakhalin Oil Company, in which Mitsui held a large interest.

had been considerably hardened by the Japanese seizure of Shantung.

More ominous for Japan at home was the fact that for the first time an overseas military campaign had failed to spark enthusiasm among the Japanese people themselves. An excessively brutal crackdown on the radicals at that time would have antagonized foreign powers and aggravated the ugly mood of the Japanese workers.

When the inept Terauchi's government collapsed, the unenviable task of pacifying the country fell to Hara Kei (also called Hara Takashi), who as Prince Saionji's successor had headed the Seiyukai for several years. The effect of his choice was electrifying, for Hara was the first commoner to hold the position of premier since the establishment of the peerage, and his was the first true one-party cabinet in Japan's history. The embattled Japanese were given hope that at last the grip of the Sat-Cho oligarchy had been broken and that now the nation would move, with the rest of the world, toward a more liberal and egalitarian political system. Hara was critical of the military's arrogance and its costly campaign in Siberia. Public enthusiasm ran high when he boosted the electorate to three million by reducing the amount of property that qualified a taxpayer to vote and introduced into the Diet a controversial bill to allow universal manhood suffrage.

To observers familiar with Hara's background, however, his liberalism appeared to be something in the nature of a Trojan horse. A former newspaperman, he had risen to the editorship of the Osaka *Mainichi Shimbun,* which was in the Mitsui fold. (Upon resigning that position to help establish the Seiyukai in 1900, he had assured his readers that he would continue to represent business interests as usual.) He was a protégé of Prince Saionji Kimmochi, whose brother was Baron Sumitomo; he was an "adviser" to the Furukawa copper zaibatsu; and he had friendly ties with Mitsui Mining, also. Although he was called "the great commoner" because he preferred to remain untitled, he was of upper-samurai origin and had presumably elevated his social status by marrying a stepdaughter of Marquis Inoue Kaoru. This union brought him into the family circles of former prime ministers Katsura Taro and Ito Hirobumi, for the heirs of the latter two, both adopted, were sons of Inoue's elder brother; moreover, Katsura had married Inoue's adopted daughter. By birth Hara was a northerner but, like Prince Saionji, he was a Choshu oligarch by "adoption."

Other advance guards of the zaibatsu in the cabinet were foreign minister Uchida Yasuya, a Mitsui kinsman, and communications minister Noda Utaro, Baron Dan's protégé. A further indication of Hara's big-business leanings was his choice of a home minister, the man who would be responsible for the preservation of peace and order throughout Japan. This personage was Tokonami Tokujiro, a shirtsleeves politician and "labor expert" who operated a semiunderground machine called the "Tokonami Kingdom" in his native province of Kagoshima. The peers of Tokonami's shadowy realm were mainly contractors and foremen in the construction industry, whose "troops" were the labor crews under their control. The construction workers, who considered themselves superior to common laborers, were bound to their bosses—called *kyokaku,* or "men of chivalry"—by a feudal sort of loyalty and could be depended upon to handle strikers as roughly as an occasion required.

Tokonami's response to the challenge of organized labor and radicalism was to expand his "kingdom" into a nationwide federation of kyokaku. Elegantly dubbed Dainihon Kokusui-kai (Great Japan National Essence Society), the organization was headed by home minister Tokonami himself, with the durable Toyama Mitsuru as his chief adviser. The Kokusui-kai claimed a membership of a million at its peak; actually, it may have commanded as much as one-fifth that number if Toyama's private army of terrorists was included.

The Kokusui-kai, contemporary with and similar in function to Mussolini's blackshirts, was most effective as a strikebreaking gang, and in emergencies—such as the great Yawata strike of 1920, in which 28,000 men walked out—its members worked side by side with the police, military gendarmes, firemen, ex-servicemen, and bully boys of the ultranationalist societies. Tokonami's men were allowed to carry swords or clubs and had much more freedom than did law enforcement officials in using them, not only against strikers but also for dispersing gatherings of any complexion or purpose that Tokonami or his zaibatsu friends considered subversive. "The Great Commoner" not only countenanced Tokonami's private army but, reacting against the radicalism he loathed, withdrew support for the universal suffrage bill and killed it by dissolving the Diet.

Having earned the trust of the zaibatsu, Hara was amply funded as president of the Seiyukai. At the end of each year dietmen belonging to the party used to visit his home to pay their respects and receive envelopes stuffed with money. It was generally assumed that Mitsui provided a share of the party's funds; evidence of the fact became public in 1920. At that time Hara, whose popularity had sagged as a result of his expedient reversals of policy, faced a general election. To fill his war chest he enlisted the help of communications minister Noda, who in turn approached his old friend Dan Takuma. Noda was given a "large sum" of money by his former boss; somehow this transaction became known to the press and provoked public outcry. A Mitsui Gomei director, Ariga Nagabumi, explained blandly that it was merely a token of friendship between Dan and Noda. "In this context, the incident makes a fine anecdote," he said. "It's nothing like Mitsui's doing something in conspiracy with Seiyukai."³ But the newspapers thought otherwise, and one of them editorialized: "Statesmen can hardly do anything nowadays without allying themselves with monetary magnates . . . the connection between businessmen and statesmen is getting more intimate than ever. . . . The Mitsui Club, the Industrial Club and the like practically have the power to control the Foreign Office and the police."⁴

How Hara rewarded his zaibatsu donors was a matter of conjecture then, but certain manipulations of the period throw some light on the matter. One of Hara's closest friends was Uchida Shin'ya, the shipping narikin. In 1920, prior to the election, Uchida visited the prime minister, who confided that the scarcity of political donations foreshadowed a financial panic. Uchida, who had expanded his fleet recklessly during the war, promptly approached the vice-president of the South Manchurian Railway and offered for sale his biggest ship, by then a white elephant. The vice-president, a Seiyukai executive, cancelled an existing contract for a ship and bought Uchida's vessel instead, at a grossly inflated price. Uchida is said to have made nearly three million yen on the deal, and presumably rewarded his benefactors suitably.

At about the same time the SMR bought an unprofitable coal mine from Mori Kaku, who (like Uchida) had become one of Seiyukai's bigwigs, for almost a million yen more than its estimated value. A discontented executive of the company exposed both transactions in a newspaper article, and Mitsubishi's political party, then called Kenseito, instituted criminal proceedings against two SMR officials. Uchida was well prepared for this little matter. After the indictment was presented he produced copies of letters proving that Mitsubishi's political representative, Kato Takaaki, had been no less venal than the accused. One letter, from Kato to Uchida, read: ". . . today your elder brother Tetsuro came to visit me, and I received five rare objects with gratitude." The "rare objects," Uchida said, were 10,000-yen notes. After that Kato's Kenseito, suddenly on the defensive, pursued the railway case listlessly, and the defendants were found innocent. But of course these glimpses behind the scenes did nothing to mollify public distrust of party politics.

By 1921, when the postwar depression was at its worst, Hara was in deep trouble. Hated by the left, discredited in the eyes of the liberals, and resented by the military, he also came under attack from the ultranationalists and the "men of chivalry." They blamed the "liberal" Hara for his failure to launch a stronger Asian policy. The zaibatsu too were under attack, not only from the left but also from idealistic rightists who resented their corruption of the emperor's government and the impoverishment of his subjects. There had been demonstrations outside many zaibatsu homes and offices, and one of Suzuki Shoten's warehouses had been set afire.

Perhaps the least popular financier was Baron Yasuda Zenjiro, who was compared with John D. Rockefeller for his reputed stinginess as well as his fortune, which was believed to be nearly two billion yen. An obsessively active man, Yasuda found occasional relaxation at his seaside villa in Oiso, not far from Mitsui Hachiroemon's residence. One autumn day in 1921 an insistent youth blustered his way into Yasuda's presence, excitedly set forth his visionary scheme for a workers' hotel in Tokyo, and demanded a contribution for it. Yasuda apparently was not alarmed. Like many zaibatsu chieftains, he was a generous contributor to rightist organizations—notably the Black Dragon Society—and felt entitled to immunity. But the unbalanced youth, acting on his own initiative, thought nothing of baronial rights. Enraged by the rejection of his proposal, he stabbed Yasuda to death on the spot.

The tragedy was particularly distressing to the Mitsuis, since Yasuda was not only a member of their class but a kinsman. (Yasuda's daughter and grandson were connected by marriage to separate branches of the Mitsui clan.) With the death of the tycoon the lives of Mitsui family heads, always hedged about with protocol, became even less free. Guards were reinforced at their homes and villas, and the routes they took to and from their offices were planned carefully to avoid trouble spots. A daughter of Mitsui Morinosuke, president of Bussan in the 1920s, remembers occasions when rightists armed with swords came to their house and shouted menacingly. During a shipping strike, union demonstrators assembled around the house and Morinosuke could not go out. When executives of Bussan came to see him on business, they disguised themselves as servants and slipped in and out through a side entrance.

Prime Minister Hara was less cautious, both by temperament and because of his position. He trusted Tokonami to protect him from the radicals and thought he had served the rightists well enough to expect their gratitude. Nevertheless, his favoritism toward the zaibatsu and his complaisance about corruption were held against him. Also he had defied Toyama Mitsuru by opposing the betrothal of Crown Prince Hirohito to a noblewoman of Satsuma lineage, thereby exposing himself to accusations that he had committed the crime of lese majesty. With respect to his conduct of foreign affairs he was vulnerable to criticisms of nationalists, and his opposition to the domination of the army and navy had not mellowed.

The "invisible government" struck on November 4, 1921, soon after Crown Prince Hirohito's return from a visit to Europe and a few days before the opening of the Washington Conference on naval disarmament. As Hara was passing through Tokyo Station to board a train, a young railway employee rushed upon him and plunged a dagger between his shoulder blades, killing him. The assassin, a nationalist fanatic, made no resistance. After his arrest he explained earnestly that Hara had "defiled the constitution" by assuming the naval portfolio in the absence of the minister, who had gone to Washington. Police authorities accepted this naive story, as well as the killer's assurance that he had acted alone and unaided, and they conducted only a cursory investigation. After securing the assassin's conviction they consigned the case to oblivion.

Had they pursued their inquiry the results would have been most revealing. For instance, it was known in higher circles that Prince Konoe Fumimaro, a relative of the imperial family and a prominent member of the House of Peers, had been told in advance of the plot to kill Hara. His informant was Ioki Ryozo, a prominent publisher and an ultranationalist boss connected inconspicuously with Toyama and Uchida Ryohei. Shortly before the assassination Ioki had said that within the next day or two Hara would be attacked. Konoe had good reason to believe Ioki, his adviser and confidant. Why, then, had he not intervened? Consider the fact that Konoe was a sponsor of the Dobunkai, which advocated aggressive expansion in Asia and conducted extensive operations, both open and secret, on the continent. Hara, in trying to silence the uproar caused by Japan's hard-boiled policy toward China, had assumed a gentler tone toward Peking and was also opposed to continuing the Siberian intervention, one aim of which was to protect Manchuria from Russian communism. Hara was prepared to accept at the Washington Conference a relative downgrading of the Japanese navy. But a powerful naval force was vital to the expansionist ambitions harbored by Konoe and his cohorts. The prince, therefore, had reason enough to wish the premier's removal. There is no evidence to show that he was active in the plot, but his silence would have been interpreted as tacit consent to the deed. The author of the scheme, whoever he was, would then have felt free to issue a discreetly phrased order that, passing down the ultranationalist network, would reach some patriotic simpleton trained to kill for the sake of the "national essence."

The publicity surrounding this and other political killings was damaging to Japan's international reputation. But, in fairness, it should be remembered that "government by assassination" was by no means a Japanese monopoly. In that era most of Europe was murderously split between forces demanding a new utopia and those clinging stubbornly to old privileges. It was the epoch of coups, pogroms, and *Putsche* perpetrated by secret societies whose names and causes were legion. With selfless (or selfish) zeal, patriots drew blood in the name of the Bourbons, Hapsburgs, or Romanovs. With equal gusto they slew for pan-Slavism, greater Islam, a revival of the Turkic race, Ukraine for the Ukrainians, or Rumania for Standard Oil. In the early postwar years there were literally thousands of political murders in Europe (more than three hundred in Germany during 1920 and 1921 alone), not to mention socialist revolutions and counterrevolutionary blood-lettings on an appalling scale.

By comparison the Japanese nationalists were quite restrained in seeking their utopia, which they called, poetically, "Eight Corners of the World under One Roof." For example, Hara's killer, although hailed as a patriot, was sentenced to twelve years in prison and served his entire term. When the prison doors closed behind him men of the opposite persuasion were still on the streets staging their demonstrations and strikes, yet there were no atrocities by Japanese Bolsheviks, nor retaliatory massacres by Cossacks, Blackshirts, or Brownshirts, as in Europe. Despite the harassment, imprisonment, and occasional murder of socialists and labor leaders, organization of workers continued and the number of unionists swelled into the hundreds of thousands. Radicals were persecuted but not ostracized, mass discharges of strikers were avoided, and Japan's coolheaded leaders saw to it that the nation was not irrevocably split between left and right.

Yet, while tolerating the dissidents and even granting a few significant concessions, the zaibatsu drew closer to the bureaucracy, the military, and the ultranationalists, their differences being bridged by the common fear of proletarian collectivism. They entertained no thought of a compromise with socialism, or even with social democracy, which was the antithesis of the emperor system. Avoiding provocations whenever possible, the combined forces of conservatism bided their time with patience.

Two weeks after Hara's death Hirohito became Prince Regent, taking over the imperial duties of his mentally deranged father. But the new regime was to leave the national policy intact: despite the changes that had taken place in the world, and the broadening effect of foreign travel upon his personal outlook, Hirohito introduced no political innovations. Japan's real masters still clung to the old Meiji dream—now tantalizingly close to realization—and subordinated all else to the task of strengthening and expanding the empire.

18 · The Clan in All Its Glory

THE GRANDEUR THAT WAS MITSUI reached its apogee in the 1920s, which brought a series of dizzying successes that seemed to assure the House of immortality. The Mitsui name and blazon were known around the world wherever business was done, through Bussan's branches in fifteen cities of the United States, France, Germany, England, and Australia and some thirty-five commercial centers of the Far East. When Japanese of prominence traveled abroad, they were customarily taken in tow by Bussan's branch managers or by executives of such prestigious subsidiaries as Société Anonyme Française Bussan in Lyons, Deutsche Bussan Aktiengesellschaft in Berlin, or Mitsui Bussan South Africa (Proprietary) Limited in Cape Town. The men of Mitsui were much better prepared than Japanese consuls, or even ambassadors, to provide the most suitable accommodations, introductions, and entertainment because they knew the country and its people thoroughly, had ample funds, and commanded deferential treatment in high places.

It was estimated by qualified observers, and not denied by company executives, that the House of Mitsui held assets in excess of one billion yen, a magic figure transcending any racial or national prejudice that might lurk in the minds of foreign hosts. An experience recounted by a Mitsui Mining executive, who was sent on an overseas mission by obanto Dan Takuma, seems to have been typical of the reception given Mitsui men traveling abroad: "Everywhere in the U. S. and England, I found that the business card of Mr. Dan was a powerful passport. By simply producing his card, introducing me to whomever I visited, I was warmly received and accorded hospitality. At factories, I could inspect everything and, while traveling, I encountered no inconvenience. I was impressed once again by the reputation that our Mitsui had."[1]

For the same reason, most foreign notables visiting Japan were recipients of the ministrations of Mitsui, which commanded social resources and skills far excelling those of the Ministry of Foreign Affairs. The palatial mansion of Baron Mitsui Hachiroemon and Mitsui Gomei's imposing Tsunamachi Club in Tokyo served the same purpose as had the old Rokumeikan in demonstrating to outlanders that Japan was indeed a modern nation well versed in the ways of the West. There were luxurious Mitsui clubs in other Japanese cities also, and comfortable ones even in remote areas where Mitsui mines and industrial plants were operating, so that guests could be treated to an extensive tour of the country without the need to make any independent arrangements—or the possibility of seeing anything disadvantageous to the concern's image.

The Tsunamachi Club, built in 1913 in the Mita district of Tokyo, adjacent to Keio University, was designed by the British architect Josiah Conder (1852–1920), creator of the Rokumeikan and many other Japanese public buildings. The structure, which appears to be a Renaissance palazzo mated back-to-back with a Victorian mansion, is still used by the Mitsui group of companies for stylish entertaining.

Mitsui and other zaibatsu houses maintained such facilities, staffed by foreign-trained stewards, hostesses, and interpreters, mainly for business purposes; but some of their most lavish hospitality was offered in the interests of diplomacy. For decades a small band of internationally-minded businessmen had been working hard to improve Japan's relations with Western countries by arranging high-level, person-to-person contacts. Among those most active in cultivating friendships in the English-speaking countries were Count Kaneko Kentaro, his brother-in-law Baron Dan, Baron Masuda, Viscount Shibusawa Eiichi, Mitsui Bank's Ikeda Seihin, Kushida Manzo of Mitsubishi, and the heads of the Asano, Furukawa, and Okura zaibatsu families. These men made frequent trips abroad, and they repaid the bounty of their foreign hosts munificently when the latter and their families visited Japan.

Such diplomatic entertaining became more necessary and consequently more sumptuous as the tempo of Japan's commercial rivalry and continental expansion accelerated, arousing fear and resentment among competitor nations in the West. In 1920, after Japan had infuriated Washington by some especially arrogant violations of the Open Door Policy in China, the anti-Oriental lobby in California was pressing for the enactment of several laws excluding new Japanese immigrants and severely limiting the rights of those already residing in the state. In an effort to defeat such discriminatory legislation the Japanese-American Relations Committee, comprising the gentlemen-associates of Mitsui mentioned above, sponsored two conferences with American colleagues. In one delegation invited to Tokyo were a number of California's political leaders who were concerned over the anti-Japanese legislation pending in their state; the other consisted of industrialists, bankers, and educators from the eastern United States. Among the latter men of good will were several university presidents, top executives of such organizations as Westinghouse Electric, Eastman Kodak, New York Life Insurance, American International Corporation, and the New York Stock Exchange. Also attending were a former secretary of the treasury and President Taft's brother. The Japanese welcoming committee, headed by Prince Tokugawa Yoshihisa and Viscount Shibusawa, represented the top layer of Japan's plutocracy.

On the evening of their arrival the second contingent of delegates and their wives were given an elaborate reception at the Peers' Club, where among other diversions a Noh play was presented for their edification. The days thereafter brought a round of dinners, luncheons, and garden parties given by Prime Minister Hara, Foreign Minister Uchida Yasuya, and Baron Mitsui Hachiroemon Takamine (whose granddaughter was betrothed to Count Uchida's son). When all pending problems had been discussed and resolutions agreed upon, the Americans and their ladies (all clad in kimono made up by the Mitsukoshi Department Store and presented by the Japanese committee) attended a farewell party at the Imperial Hotel. "It was a grand success in creating a cordial spirit between the hosts and guests," a chronicler reported. "These functions . . . contributed as much toward understanding and amity of feeling as the conference itself."[2]

The scene of Tokyo's most exclusive garden and dinner parties— except for those of the imperial family—was the mansion and thirty-acre estate of Baron Mitsui Hachiroemon Takamine, titular head of the clan and its arbiter in matters of taste and international protocol. As host to innumerable visitors, individually or in delegations, he invited his guests personally; but it was the whole clan, indeed the whole Japanese establishment, that gave the parties. The presence of such opulence in Imai-cho, an otherwise undistinguished neighborhood, would never have been suspected by the casual observer. The high-walled estate could be reached only through narrow, winding streets flanked on either side with the small shops or drab frame dwellings of the lower middle class. At the top of a steep grade one was confronted by unmarked steel gates guarded by sentries.

When those portals swung open to admit the limousines of invited guests, a very different scene was revealed, of overarching trees, extensive lawns, and winding hedges behind which one glimpsed enticing gardens, both in the English manner and in the Japanese. Nestled in groves of tall pines and cedars, or of supple lacy bamboos, were stone lanterns and pagodas, quaint little shrines, and a rustic teahouse beside a brook burbling among curiously shaped rocks that had been brought from afar but looked as if they had been lying there always. The stream originated in a miniature waterfall copied from the sacred cascade of Otowa below Kiyomizu Temple in Kyoto and flowed into a lotus-fringed pond abounding with golden and varicolored carp.

The mansion itself, like the original Mitsui-gumi building, had been designed by an amateur—in this case Hachiroemon himself—and built by the Shimizu company soon after the Russo-Japanese War. Rambling among the parklike groves and copses of the estate, the mansion was too big to be seen or photographed as a whole, which may have been just as well. Like most homes of the wealthy built during that first quarter of the twentieth century, it was a blend of Japanese and Western elements, with the austere but graceful native architecture in uneasy juxtaposition with European ornateness.

For Japanese guests there were some traditional-style rooms with tatami floors, sliding paper doors, and ceilings of richly grained woods. Such rooms had no furniture except one low table, square silken cushions, and an occasional screen painted by some noted artist of old. This simplicity dramatized the tokonoma, a stagelike alcove, in which there would be a priceless hanging scroll, changed with the cycle of the seasons, a superbly simple flower arrangement, and perhaps a piece of pottery or a bronze with a long history of its own.

Traditional Japanese living, however, has some conspicuous drawbacks. The rooms are unheated in winter and infested with mosquitoes in summer. People accustomed to the comfort of chairs and beds find it an ordeal to sit cross-legged on the floor and to sleep on thin mats. The Mitsuis had long since abandoned these practices and lived in a style that while retaining some of the esthetic features of old Japan afforded all the comforts and conveniences of the Western world. Baron Hachiroemon had not worn kimono since his world tour in 1909, and his sons also dressed in European clothes exclusively. The ladies wore kimono or Western dress as occasion required, but all the members of the family slept in soft beds, dined at table, and even wore their shoes in some parts of the house.

From the outside the mansion at Imai-cho was not particularly impressive, but the rooms used for entertaining would have done justice to any European millionaire or royal personage. The keynote was a tasteful but unashamed lavishness that included coffered ceilings in baroque style, prismatic crystal chandeliers, parquet floors, oriental rugs, oak-paneled walls, Gobelin tapestries, hand-carved period furniture, and gilt-framed oil paintings, the splendor of the ensemble multiplied by many mirrors. If there was a difference between this decor and that displayed by Hachiroemon's European colleagues, it was that nearly everything to be seen—including the tapestries, oil paintings, and chandeliers—had been made in Japan.

At dinner *chez* Mitsui they not infrequently seated thirty or forty guests in the spacious dining salon, yet somehow Baron Mitsui and his experienced lady gave every gathering a feeling of cordiality. This was no mean feat, considering that on an average occasion one might meet guests of half a dozen nationalities and of widely disparate social and professional backgrounds, usually including a few Japanese peers or even a relative or two of the imperial family. Presiding over the splendid table bedecked with flowers, crystal, and heirloom silver, the baron was at the peak of his form. As one visiting foreigner described him, "His face was long and keen, resembling those of warriors in the old Japanese prints, and the single gleaming decoration suspended on a ribbon almost covering his shirt front was a final touch to the picture."[3] If he had been portrayed in a cinema, no one could have resembled him more than a contemporary of his, the Hollywood actor Adolphe Menjou, waxed moustache and all.

The baron always sat stiffly erect, perhaps to compensate for his average Japanese height, but there the stiffness ended. He gave the impression of being on friendly terms with each of his guests, fixing his gaze upon one or the other successively as if conveying some personal message, raising his wineglass to a distant lady or motioning a servant to fill the glass of some foreigner who seemed ill at ease. At the other end of the table, the baroness took care not to distract attention from her husband or to outshine any of her guests. Her silks and jewels were of the finest quality, but unobtrusive. She made no attempt to be vivacious, yet without changing the expression of her rather long, patrician face she managed by graceful gestures to set her company at ease. This performance (for such it must have been, and a strenuous one at that) was achieved with scarcely a word of English spoken, or of any other foreign language, because the Mitsuis, despite their frequent travels abroad, were poor linguists and usually preferred to be silent rather than risk ridicule by speaking.

Whatever those princely repasts lacked in conversation was made up in other ways, however. After a visit to Japan in the early 1920s an American writer, Isaac Marcosson, wrote in the *Saturday Evening Post:* "At every Japanese dinner the guest gets a souvenir of some kind. . . . At Baron Mitsui's dinners these favors are magnificent. On one occasion he asked each one of the diners to indicate the bit of landscape in Japan that he liked best. When all the choices had been recorded they were given to one of the most eminent of Japanese artists. Two years later each guest received his picture handsomely framed."[4]

Although the setting for the baron's dinners was purely European, with no hint of Japan except in the features of the native guests and servants, the visitor was not likely to forget where he was. Wherever one looked one was likely to see the adopted Sasaki crest—four black squares with white centers—which was embossed upon the silverware, woven into the linen and formal kimono, painted upon the motor cars, printed upon the stationery, and worked into personal ornaments. In addition to the "four eyes" of Sasaki, the Mitsuis used a *kiri* crest—three leaves and the fruit of the paulownia tree, in white upon a black background—similar to one used by the imperial family.

Many foreign visitors recorded their observations of the Mitsuis and their environment, but it is very difficult to find any information about the clan in domestic sources. Members of the Mitsui families, like the Rothschilds and the Krupps, were extremely reticent about publicity and were much more successful in defending their privacy, partly because they were influential in the publishing business. For example, through the Oji Paper Company they controlled the Osaka *Mainichi Shimbun,* one of the most powerful dailies, and they owned the *Chugai Shogyo,* Japan's leading economic journal. The latter, founded by Masuda Takashi in 1876 as an outgrowth of Mitsui's private bulletin of market quotations, later became the authoritative *Nihon Keizai Shimbun.*

The Japanese press, with notable (and sporadic) exceptions, observed a taboo concerning the Mitsuis that was almost as strict as that applied to the imperial household. Published material about the Mitsui business concern seldom made any references to the Mitsuis themselves except those released by official sources. One frustrated biographer, Yamada Taketaro, although an authority on the history of the House, found himself at a loss even to describe any living member of it. "An interesting feature of Mitsui is its galaxy of able men," he wrote referring to its employees, and named a few of the most prominent. "Besides these banto, there must have been talented men among the family. But such persons are 'enshrined above the clouds' so that we are unable to learn their whereabouts."[5]

Apologizing for devoting so much space to the banto and so little to the Mitsuis themselves, he explained that he could find only the scantiest information about them, even in magazines about finance and business. Obviously, the idea of a mere Japanese journalist approaching such godlike figures personally was unthinkable.

Such awe was deliberately inculcated by the elders of Mitsui Gomei as a business principle, in recognition of the fact that the concern was in effect an empire and should be operated as such. Thus the head of the Mitsui clan was treated as an emperor, commanding reverence from his "shogun," the obanto, who did the actual governing and exacted almost equal reverence from his "ministers" on the board of directors and his "daimyo" heading the individual companies. Lesser executives and employees were expected not only to respect this hierarchy—just as they respected that of the larger empire—but also to be sincerely thankful for the benevolence of their rulers.

Baron Mitsui's subjects were kindly treated, indeed, and made to feel that they belonged to his "family." If the pay was low, there was no anxiety over losing one's job. As in a family, the individuality of each member was taken into consideration and employees were not pushed to the breaking point in the interests of efficiency. However, in some ways they were treated as children. Love affairs within the companies were forbidden, and if male employees were caught meeting their female co-workers outside the office their superiors were reprimanded. Marriage between employees was forbidden, and younger ones were scolded about their language, grooming, and even their manner of bowing to superiors.

Baron Mitsui's insistence upon protocol was legendary. One present-day executive in the company, then a freshman clerk, recalls that outside Mitsui Hachiroemon's office there were three separate waiting rooms, one for managing directors, one for middle executives, and a third for the lowly rank and file. An employee visiting this office, even on such a simple errand as to get the impression of the baron's seal upon a document, would first inquire: "Is his gracious highness present?" If he was, the visitor would be ushered into one of the anterooms. While awaiting the sovereign's pleasure, he might be served tea and sweets, but these would be of different quality for each social level. None but the most distinguished personages ever went into the great man's office. Directors were not actually forbidden to enter, but customarily avoided doing so. When the ponderous door did open, such a visitor would approach only as far as the threshold and, after a profound obeisance, conduct his business through the doorway.

Another executive, then working at Mitsui Chemical Company, remembers that when board meetings were held it was his duty to escort one of the Mitsuis, a director, from his car to the board room. Although that Mitsui was only in his thirties, the chairman, president, and other directors of the chemical company had to stand up and bow deeply when he entered. Executives of lower status seldom saw any Mitsuis except at a distance and only then if they worked in one of the Tokyo offices. However, they knew how His Highness Hachiroemon XV looked, for on New Year's Day they were duly assembled to hear his congratulatory message read aloud and to bow deeply before his photograph, just as schoolchildren bowed to a picture of the emperor.

Mitsui's high-ranking officers in Tokyo, however, were permitted to meet Baron Hachiroemon in person. Each New Year's Day they congregated at the Tsunamachi Club, or sometimes at the great mansion in

Imai-cho, to be presented to all eleven of the Mitsui family heads and their wives. On those occasions the clan constitution was read to them (or rather those parts of it that were not secret), just as the Imperial Precepts to Soldiers and Sailors were read periodically to servicemen. When this ceremony was over the executives would form a line (one would guess that they stood in the order of the capitalization of their respective companies) and advance one at a time, bowing to each member of the clan. This ritual completed, the guests were regaled with tiny cups of cold sakè and bits of dried squid. Such refreshments, so very different from the juicy beefsteaks, lobsters thermidor, and pheasants under glass served to foreign guests in the same setting, obviously were a matter of tradition rather than frugality, but presumably left the partakers with a renewed awareness that the Japanese people were still a long way from affluence.

More dreaded than those annual ordeals were the weekly high-level meetings held at the head office. Each Thursday afternoon managing directors of the main companies and major affiliates were assembled, together with the directors of Mitsui Gomei, to review the concern's activities. Under the chairmanship of Baron Dan, and usually in the presence of Baron Hachiroemon and two other family heads, the unfortunate executives faced the prospect of being called upon to explain (in the formal language appropriate for the ears of those celestial beings) the results of their humble efforts to promote the welfare of the Mitsuis' terrestrial empire.

Very different was the atmosphere during meetings of the *rijikai,* or board of directors of Gomei, the general staff of the Mitsui empire. In the tradition of the House, Baron Hachiroemon Takamine made every effort to pick completely trustworthy men as his obanto and directors; then, having made that choice, he left everything up to them and showed no favoritism thereafter. Occasionally there was bickering, and disgruntled executives complained to the baron about their colleagues. At such a time he was heard to say: "I have entrusted the job to him; don't bother me with trivial matters." Although he had his personal likes and dislikes, he treated members of his rijikai as if they were full-fledged members of the clan, or even of his immediate family.

Of those five men three, including chairman Dan, had close ties with the United States. Sakai Tokutaro was graduated from Harvard in 1897 and was ordained an Episcopal minister before entering the business world in Japan. Serving as president of the Tokyo Harvard Club, he was in close touch with the foreign business community and specialized in making arrangements for receiving, entertaining, and shepherding overseas visitors to Japan. Fukui Kikusaburo, a man of extraordinary business talent, had managed Mitsui's New York office for many years and had an intimate knowledge of American business and a wide acquaintance among its leaders. A less conspicuous asset was his family connection with Aikawa Gisuke, another of Japan's fast-rising industrialists, and with Aikawa's brother-in-law, Kimura Kusuyata, chief managing director of the Mitsubishi concern in the 1920s.

The most intriguing figure on the board of Mitsui Gomei was Ariga Nagabumi who, most unusually, had not entered Mitsui's employ until twelve years after his graduation from Tokyo Imperial University. Brought in by Inoue Kaoru in 1902, he had risen swiftly to a directorship in Gomei and the presidency of Mitsui Bank, perhaps by virtue of his experience in Seiyukai party politics and his connections with the military and Japan's "invisible government." As has been mentioned, his lawyer brother Nagao had been a legal adviser to the Japanese army and also to the Yuan Shih-k'ai government in the new Republic of China. The fifth member, Oshima Masataro, left little trace of his presence except a record of more than thirty years of unblemished service with Mitsui Bank.

What these five men discussed with Baron Hachiroemon in the innermost keep of Mitsui's headquarters would not have been recorded, but the subjects must have ranged far beyond the daily problems of individual companies and probably dealt with global strategy rather than domestic tactics. An American industrialist who met all of them in 1923 was puzzled by their seeming unconcern with matters of dollars and yen. "You couldn't see where any one of them was a businessman, as we understand it," he marveled. "They didn't convey the impression of business at all, and yet they're mixed up in every damn kind of business in the country."[6]

That general staff was typical of Mitsui Gomei's leadership during the first thirty-five years of the twentieth century. There was always a commander in chief, with an intimate, practical knowledge of the concern's domestic and international operations—financial, industrial, and commercial—to coordinate strategies. And he had his assistants, specialists in various aspects of business and privy to intricate details vital to the concern but of so confidential a nature that they could be imparted only in talk.

Although those men made collective decisions affecting the whole nation and its future, few of the individuals are remembered today. There were always one or two who were given star billing as front men for the reticent Mitsuis, but the rest were expected to be quiet and unobtrusive. However indispensable they might have seemed to be at a given time, always there were understudies waiting in the wings to play the same roles whenever the occasion arose. Collectively they were the brains of the House, but individually they were not significant in the grand hierarchy of Japan's power elite; and when they passed from the stage they were forgotten unless they happened to achieve success independently or to attract the unwelcome attention of the press inadvertently.

To be a permanent member of the ruling elite one needed more than brains, education, position, or wealth. A man with all these qualifications was still an outsider unless he was affiliated by blood or marriage with a family of high status. At the top, of course, was the imperial family and its collateral branches, followed by the families of former court nobles, shoguns, daimyo, high-ranking ministers of the shogunate or daimiates, the hereditary priesthood, and the samurai. Membership in the samurai caste was the minimum qualification for belonging to the aristocracy, but former ranking within the samurai hierarchy was less important than the contribution one's ancestor had made to the success of the Meiji revolution.

Such were the criteria for membership in the peerage, established early in the Meiji era and continued with occasional additions until 1945. The peerage, virtually synonymous with the ruling class, consisted of about one thousand family heads, of whom at least nine hundred were viscounts or barons. And nearly all the heads of zaibatsu and other merchant families who had attained the peerage were members of the lowest rank. It is quite understandable, therefore, that they should have been concerned almost obsessively with improving their *iegara*, or house status, by marrying their sons and daughters advantageously into houses of higher rank. This determined effort, encouraged by more exalted but less monied aristocrats with marriageable offspring, led to the formation of financial *keibatsu*, or family cliques, which gradually had wrested control of the economy from the landed aristocracy.

The Mitsui clan was the oldest and most successful of the merchant keibatsu; and when the Meiji revolution liberated the chonin caste from feudal restrictions, the Mitsuis were able to climb the social ladder rapidly by astute deployment of their numerous progeny. In order to contract an advantageous alliance, however, an aspiring father required the services of a matchmaker who was at least the equal, socially, of the family being approached. It was the good fortune of the Mitsuis to have at their disposal the services of Marquis Inoue Kaoru, one of the architects of Japan's peerage and perhaps its most indefatigable matchmaker.

Baron Mitsui Hachiroemon Takamine, who became head of the senior Kita-ke family in the 1890s, made brilliant use of his matrimonial resources to forge one of the strongest and most prestigious keibatsu in the nation. Takamine's father made a good start by marrying him to a daughter of Count Maeda Toshiaki of Toyama, head of a junior branch of the former "Million-koku Maedas," once the richest daimyo family in Japan. (Prince Konoe Fumimaro's mother was from another branch of the Maeda family.) Mitsui Takamine's eldest son and heir, Takakimi (the present Hachiroemon), married a daughter of a court noble, Count Matsudaira Yasukiyo. The Count's son Yasumasa (Takakimi's brother-in-law) was chief secretary of the imperial household and subsequently the secretary of Lord Privy Seal Kido Koichi, in which position he conducted the most delicate liaison between the government and the emperor's staff. (After the Pacific War Kido was convicted by the Tokyo war crimes tribunal and sentenced to life imprisonment, but Matsudaira, whose role in the war conspiracy was said to have been no less important than Kido's, was not tried.) Takakimi in turn married his youngest daughter to a scion of the Asano family, richest of the lesser zaibatsu.

Baron Takamine's eldest daughter was married to Marquis Nakamikado Keikyo, son of a court noble descended from the Fujiwaras of the Heian period; and their daughter married a son of Count Uchida Yasuya, who served as foreign minister in several cabinets and as interim prime minister twice, just after the assassination of Hara in 1921 and again at the death of Kato in 1926. Three other daughters from this union married viscounts.

An indirect relationship between the Mitsuis and the imperial family was established by uniting another of Takamine's daughters with a younger son of Prince Takatsukasa, a court noble, whose grandson married Emperor Hirohito's daughter Kazuko. Another of Takatsukasa's sons, chief priest of the Meiji Shrine in Tokyo (headquarters of modern Shinto), was wedded to a daughter of Prince Tokugawa Iesato, heir of Japan's last shogun, who served as president of the House of Peers for thirty years until 1933. Thus the House of Mitsui effected a kind of neo–kobu gattai union of court, shogunate, and zaibatsu. To make the union between the nobility and the merchant class even more binding, one granddaughter of Prince Takatsukasa and of Baron Mitsui Takamine married "Beer King" Magoshi Kyohei, who once had been the lowest paid clerk at Bussan but became enormously wealthy through his control of Japan's brewing monopoly.

The essence of Mitsui's matrimonial policy was the conviction that next to marrying above one's rank and station the best possible choice was to marry another Mitsui. Thus Baron Takakimi's daughter Koko married Mitsui Takanaga, head of the Isarago branch of the clan. Younger brother Takasumi married Hideko, daughter of Mitsui Morinosuke, head of the Nagasakacho branch and president of Mitsui Bussan. Morinosuke's heir Takaatsu married Takamine's daughter Reiko; and Shizuko—another daughter of Morinosuke—broke tradition and policy by marrying a grandson of Mitsui Gomei's obanto Masuda Takashi. This intricate series of alliances is significant, since all three siblings—Takaatsu, Hideko, and Shizuko—were first cousins of Baron Sumitomo Kichizaemon II, whose uncle was Prince Saionji Kimmochi. The Mitsui-Sumitomo alliance helped to eliminate competition between the two zaibatsu and strengthened both houses in their rivalry against Mitsubishi.

The Mitsuis' keibatsu citadel was fortified with bastions manned by subfamilies only indirectly related to the clan by blood or marriage but bound by mutual loyalties. One such clique, which included two former prime ministers, was based on a common Choshu heritage. Prince Ito Hirobumi's son married the daughter of General Katsura Taro, and Ito's daughter married a nephew of Marquis Inoue, Mitsui's protector in the political world. Ito's eldest daughter married his protégé Viscount Suematsu Kencho, his home minister and a member of the privy council. A grandson of Ito and Katsura married a daughter of Baron Shirane Matsusuke, a vice-minister of the imperial household whose sole function was to manage the emperor's investments. Shirane's tie to Mitsui was made through his father-in-law, auditor of Mitsui Bank.

A granddaughter of Ito and Katsura married Shirane's nephew, and Shirane's son married the daughter of Mitsui Takasumi (whose wife, Hideko, is a niece of Sumitomo Kichizaemon I). To complete the Choshu keibatsu ring, Sumitomo's niece (a daughter of Saionji Kimmochi) had married the son of Mori Motonori, former daimyo of Choshu. Inoue Kaoru had been the matchmaker for this Saionji-Mori union, and Inoue's adopted son performed the same service for Mitsui Takasumi and Hideko, Saionji's kinswoman. One could venture a guess that this most refined keibatsu served the purpose of uniting the money of Mitsui, Sumitomo, and the imperial household with the political influence of the Choshu clique in the Seiyukai Party, founded by Ito, Inoue, and Saionji and maintained with funds from those wealthy families.

A potent managerial keibatsu associated with Mitsui was established around the family of Nakamigawa Hikojiro, Mitsui's great obanto of the 1890s. Nakamigawa, it will be remembered, was a nephew of Fukuzawa Yukichi, the founder of Keio University and the leading teacher of businessmen in the Meiji era. Nakamigawa's sister married Mitsui Gomei's director Asabuki Eiji, and his sister-in-law married Fujiyama Raita, a former Mitsui mastermind who made a huge fortune in sugar. (Fujiyama's son Aiichiro is one of Japan's leading statesmen today.) Nakamigawa's son married a daughter of Muto Sanji, the great builder of Kanegafuchi Spinning. One of Nakamigawa's daughters married

Iwase Eiichiro, president of Mitsukoshi Department Store; another married Yamao Tadaji, later president of Mitsui Real Estate; and a third married Mitsui's future obanto Ikeda Seihin.

And here another network begins. Ikeda had two sisters. One of them married Usami Katsuo, governor of Tokyo, and their two sons became, respectively, director of the Imperial Household Agency, and president of Mitsubishi Bank and governor of the Bank of Japan. The other married Kato Takeo, former chairman of Mitsubishi Bank and a leading figure in the concern. Kato's sister married the auditor of Mitsukoshi, again crossing zaibatsu lines. To carry the Mitsui-Mitsubishi rapprochement one step further, Ikeda's daughter married a grandson of Baron Iwasaki Hisaya, head of his family and of the Mitsubishi concern.

One of the strongest satellite families was that of Baron Masuda Takashi, who after his premature retirement from the Mitsui concern in 1914 served as confidant and adviser of the Mitsui clan for more than twenty years. His son Taro, taking charge of the Masuda family's interests in Taiwan Sugar (Taito), Chiyoda Fire & Marine Insurance, and Morinaga Confections, married a granddaughter of Lord Itakura Katsukiyo, a high official in the shogunate, and later distinguished himself as a dramatist under the pen name "Taro-kaja." As has been mentioned, one of Masuda Taro's sons bested clan customs by marrying a daughter of Mitsui Morinosuke. Taro's son Katsunobu, a graduate of the University of Pennsylvania, became vice-president of Taito, which remained closely allied with Bussan. In the extensive Masuda family tree one finds, in addition to those named, many high executives of Mitsui-related enterprises, a supreme court justice, several members of the House of Peers, an army general, a prefectural governor, and officers of numerous enterprises not connected with Mitsui.

Another Mitsui-related keibatsu with interesting ramifications was founded by Viscount Yamao Yozo, one of the Choshu valiants who had plotted with Ito and Inoue to burn the British Legation in 1862 and who later went with them secretly to England. Yamao Yozo became Minister of Technology and Speaker of the House of Peers, and his younger brother Fukuzo played a creditable part in the industrialization of Japan. Yozo's son married a daughter of the Meiji leader Kido Koin, and his granddaughter was the first wife of the late prime minister Ikeda Hayato. One of brother Fukuzo's sons was president of Mitsui Real Estate, as mentioned; and another, who served as a director of Bussan and other Mitsui firms, married into one of the Mitsui branch families.

The importance of the Yamaos lay in their marriage connections with the families of a broad range of illustrious Meiji political leaders (Kido,

Prince Matsukata Masayoshi, and Marquis Okuma Shigenobu); court nobles (Prince Sanjo Sanetomi, whose descendants held high positions in the imperial household); financiers (Mishima Yataro, president of Yokohama Specie Bank and Governor of the Bank of Japan); and such business leaders as Nakamigawa Hikojiro, Muto Sanji, Iwase Eiichiro of Mitsukoshi, and Yasukawa Daigoro of Yasukawa Electric. The Yamao keibatsu was a strong buttress of the House of Mitsui from the Meiji era onward.

Such alliances, which must have cost the Mitsuis an enormous amount of thought, research, and negotiations of the most sensitive kind, served to entwine the clan with the most powerful and prestigious families in the empire—the imperial household, the court nobility, the former Tokugawa shogunate, the Shinto hierarchy, the *kambatsu* (bureaucratic clique), and important zaibatsu, as well as independent industrialists of the first magnitude. One glaring omission, however, was the absence of the *gumbatsu,* the military clique, and professional politicians from the clan's roster of eligible marriages, and perhaps this was a cause for regret in later years.

The ten Mitsui branch or collateral families also did their part in solidifying the clan as a keibatsu, allying themselves with numerous noble or aristocratic families, as well as with other zaibatsu. Baron Mitsui Takayasu, president of Mitsui Bank during the First World War, married one of his daughters to Prince Tokudaiji's son. Baron Mitsui Gen'emon, president of Bussan, married a son to the prince's granddaughter. Gen'emon's sister married Baron Fujita Tokujiro, a son of industrialist Fujita Denzaburo. Having strengthened the social and economic foundations of his house, Gen'emon made it more cohesive by marrying his heir, Takanaru, to Gen'emon's niece. Takanaru, in turn, consolidated clan ties by marrying two of his daughters into the senior Mitsui house, the Kita-ke.

Baron Mitsui Takaharu, heir of the Minami-ke, had boosted its prestige by marrying a daughter of Prince Ichijo Sanetaka, whose family was one of the *Gosekke*—the five noble houses from among which empresses were always chosen. Takaharu himself, educated in Germany, is one Japan's leading philatelists, an authority on the history of Japanese railways, and recipient of numerous decorations from European governments for his contributions to cultural exchange.

Mitsui Benzo, whose business career was gained mainly with Bussan, was the second heir of the newly established Mitsui Hommuracho-ke. His father, Yonosuke, was one of the five young Mitsuis who had gone to America for study in 1871. His wife, one of Japan's best women golfers, was a daughter of Viscount Okabe Nagakage, director of the International Association for the Advancement of Culture and education minister in the Tojo cabinet. (Okabe belonged to a select group of aristocrats who, because of their personal ties with Crown Prince Hirohito, exerted strong influence at court after he became emperor.) A daughter of Benzo married chemical tycoon Kosaka Tokusaburo, whose elder brother Zentaro became foreign minister in the early 1960s. Other big business houses with which Mitsui branch families allied themselves were the Sumitomo, Yasuda, and Konoike zaibatsu, the Toyodas (textile machinery and motors), and the Murayamas (who control the newspaper *Asahi Shimbun*).

Such unions served to raise the social status and, indirectly, the power of the clan. But while practicing this highly selective exogamy, the Mitsuis were extremely careful to avoid dispersion; they gave highest priority to concentrating their wealth and married their offspring to outsiders only when the advantages were manifest. It is probably no coincidence that the Mitsuis, Rothschilds, Du Ponts, and Mellons, all of whom married within the extended family group and managed their empires as clans (or "cousinhoods," as financial historian Ferdinand Lundberg puts it), owned concerns that are among the richest and most enduring in the world.

Frederic Morton wrote, in *The Rothschilds,* of fifty-eight marriages contracted by the descendants of the founder, Meyer Amschel Rothschild, exactly half took place between first cousins.[7] Blood relationships among the Mitsuis were more remote, since the House was nearly two centuries older; but even in the twentieth century, when the clan expanded its social horizons, Mitsuis have married other Mitsuis more often than outsiders. Through such intermarriages, and allegiance to a common house law, they remained capable of mobilizing the assets and influence of the eleven families, and of dozens of affiliated families, with devastating effect.

From the time of matriarch Shuho the Mitsuis had subordinated individual happiness or fulfillment to the prosperity of the House and the needs of the state. It is natural to assume that unhappiness and frustration should have been common among them, especially for those who had been thrust into uncongenial occupations or loveless marriages. From the modern point of view such an existence, further burdened with social responsibilities and taboos, would seem insupportable. But from what one can gather, life "above the clouds" at Baron Hachiroemon Takamine's Imai-cho estate was quite pleasant.

At home Takamine dropped his imperious public manner and was known as an affectionate husband, an indulgent father, and a kind and generous master. Although his marriage with Motoko had been arranged, the couple had been acquainted previously, and as the years passed their affection deepened. Takamine was at heart a family man and disliked visiting teahouses or restaurants. A rarity among Japanese men of his class, he was monogamous and did not disport himself with geisha, even innocently. His behavior toward women was distinctly un-Japanese: he was not at all domineering, but rather deferential, in public as well as private. Ordinarily a Japanese woman walked several paces behind her husband, but Motoko walked by Takamine's side. The females in the family were given the sunniest, most attractive suites in the house, and contrary to custom, they joined the males at table.

Motoko, being descended from a daimyo family, was not without education and accomplishments. As a girl she had learned to play the koto, or Japanese harp, and was considered adept at composing poetry. As a matter of course she was well versed in the essential arts of flower arrangement and tea ceremony. She often traveled with her husband in Japan and abroad and kept a diary faithfully. As for skill in domestic tasks, such training would have been utterly superfluous, surrounded as she was with experts in every aspect of housekeeping.

The Imai-cho mansion had at least eighty rooms and an even larger number of retainers. The magnitude of the establishment can be judged from the fact that one servant was assigned exclusively to the task of opening and closing the sliding wooden shutters that protected the mansion's windows. Members of the family said that by the time he'd got them all open in the morning, it was time to begin closing them again. As in a daimyo's castle, the servants were ranked according to their type of service, the highest being those who attended the master and mistress personally. Each of the seven children was assigned an otsuki, or nurse, and the five girls had governesses as well. In addition to the stewards, cooks, seamstresses, laundresses, and chambermaids working in the house, there were literally scores of gardeners, craftsmen, guards, and cleanup men. Most of those retainers came from families that had served the Mitsuis for generations. One family of cooks, who operate a Japanese-style restaurant in Tokyo and still cater for Mitsui weddings and other large parties, followed the clan from Matsusaka to Edo more than a century ago.

To manage the huge household staff there was a separate personnel department, one of whose tasks was to investigate the background of new employees. Such investigations ordinarily took six months. The turnover of female servants was rather high, because many of them went into domestic service in order to prepare themselves for marriage. The Mitsuis understood this and tried conscientiously to foster gentility among the maids. Sometimes Motoko would scold her daughters for breaches of etiquette, such as sitting upon the tatami with their legs sideways (instead of directly beneath them), because such unseemly behavior would set a bad example for the maids.

Takamine actually was more of an artist than a businessman, being talented in the family's traditional medium of silk collage, and in *sumi-e* ink painting and calligraphy as well. One of his favorite avocations was chanoyu, the tea ceremony, a form of spiritual communion which he practiced only with his closest friends. When he visited Kyoto he often went to visit the Kennin-ji, an old temple at which Urakusai, a younger brother of the warrior Oda Nobunaga, had taken refuge in 1615—the very year that the Mitsuis' ancestor Sokubei opened his sakè brewery in Matsusaka. During his sojourn at the temple Urakusai, a disciple of the renowned tea master Rikyu, founded his own Uraku school of chanoyu and designed an especially graceful teahouse, which he called Jo-an. Early in the twentieth century the abbot of Kennin-ji found himself in financial difficulties and sold the teahouse to Mitsui Takamine, whom he trusted to give it proper care. Takamine moved it to his Tokyo estate, where it became a gathering place for wealthy devotees of chanoyu.

Takamine's greatest enthusiasm was the Noh drama, for which he had built a special stage designed according to ancient specifications, within one of the larger rooms of his mansion. He himself, together with family members and friends, performed some of the roles and was quite skilled in the stylized dances, which require considerable muscular control. The children sometimes saw him with his Noh instructor, stripped almost naked so that his body's movements could be better observed and corrected. For entertaining his guests, however, he brought in a distinguished professional troupe that he supported financially. On the third day of each January he would engage the outstanding actors of the Kanze school of Noh to stage and celebrate the new year's first performance.

The children were not permitted to attend Noh performances when they were small, but listened from the hallway to the archaic music of the drums and flutes and the chanting of the chorus, sometimes glimpsing the masked actors. When the theater was empty they enjoyed stealing in and imitating the performers, stamping on the boards with their bare feet to evoke echoes from a huge urn placed beneath the stage for that purpose. Noh was one of the few tastes over which Takamine and Motoko differed. She preferred Kabuki, which he considered plebeian and inferior to Noh, the preserve of noblemen for centuries. He continually found excuses for not taking her to the Kabuki theater. Being a proper Japanese wife, Motoko suppressed her own wishes and endured this minor deprivation (perhaps her only one) in silence.

The boys occupied rooms widely separated from those of the girls, but the whole family dined together. The menus were arranged by Motoko, and emphasized the Kyoto style of cookery preferred by her husband. One might expect that the family heard from Takamine astonishing tales of big deals or decisions of international significance, but business and politics were never discussed at table. The father was far more interested in what his wife and children had to say and listened with flattering interest. Mealtime was also educational. Like their ancestors, the children were taught the virtue of frugality and were scolded if they wasted food. "You must learn to eat anything that can be eaten by human beings," he would say. And if anyone left so much as a few grains of rice in his bowl he would be given a lecture on the hardships of the farmers. Frequently, and especially on Sundays, the family ate *yoshoku*—Western-style food—which everyone liked. Those meals also were educational, for at such times the children were taught the table manners they would need when mingling with foreigners.

Although the children were not allowed to attend dinner parties, they were fascinated by the preparations for them. Takasumi says: "Father personally directed every detail of the dinners, the rooms, the decorations. I remember in my childhood peeking into the banquet hall, then going into the kitchen to sample all the good food." And Reiko adds: "As I grew older, I would meet the guests . . . who might include an ambassador or a king, a Japanese cabinet minister or an American industrialist. Father was host to Admiral Togo, who defeated the Russian navy in 1905. The present emperor, when he was Crown Prince, used to come often to our home."

Relations between Takamine's family and the imperial house seem to have been cordial. The emperor Taisho, being incapacitated, never visited the Imai-cho mansion, but the empress came frequently to take tea with the baroness Mitsui and her friends, among whom one of the closest was Nakamigawa Hikojiro's daughter Aki. The emancipated Aki, who became a member of the Diet after the Pacific War, had married an opera singer, Fujiwara Yoshie, from whom she was later divorced. But Baron Takamine and his son helped him establish and maintain his famous Fujiwara Opera Company, which is still in existence and still assisted by Mitsui Takakimi. Crown Prince Hirohito was often a guest at the Mitsuis' villa in the Hakone mountains, where he played tennis with the boys (who remember him as being hopelessly clumsy at all sports). The Mitsuis were also on rather close terms with a number of imperial princes and princesses, some of whom were their classmates, and dined, golfed, or played tennis with them when staying at their villas at Hayama, Oiso, Karuizawa, Hakone, and other playgrounds of the elite.

When Takamine and his family vacationed at their Oiso villa, they were not far from Baron Masuda and old Prince Yamagata, who had adjoining estates at Odawara. Yamagata was a kind of shirttail relative of the Mitsuis, since his adopted son, like Takamine, had married a girl from the Maeda family. Yamagata's twenty-acre garden, which he himself had laid out on the site of an old castle, was considered his masterpiece and was one of the few that Takamine had cause to envy. Both Yamagata and Masuda were widowers, but not lonely ones, for they were close friends and often together. In their later years both had taken mistresses, former geisha, and the arrangement was all the more agreeable because the ladies were sisters. They also had many distinguished visitors, for until his death in 1922 Yamagata was consulted on state affairs, and Masuda served as a genro of big business for many years thereafter. The elder Mitsuis of today also remember that as small boys they were taken by their tutor to visit Marquis Inoue Kaoru, who, like Prince Saionji, had established his residence in Okitsu, a fishing village on Suruga Bay. He was interested in the lads' development and asked them questions, but the youngsters were so overawed by the old genro's prestige and dignity that they were tongue-tied, much to the mortification of their teacher.

In his later years Marquis Inoue had shown deep concern over the character and education of the Mitsui boys, who were neither diligent nor very apt pupils. At his request Takamine had established a kindergarten for children of the eleven families—it was called Wakaba-kai, or young leaf society—and at the end of the Meiji era a dormitory for Mitsui boys of primary school age was set up nearby. Its purpose was to encourage study and to inculcate manliness and a sense of family solidarity. This establishment, which had some of the austerity of a samurai school in Tokugawa days, was supervised by Professor Naruse Ryuzo, who had trained many of Japan's future executives at the Tokyo Commercial Higher School. Naruse, chief secretary of the Mitsui family council, was a stern taskmaster, and his own sons were exceptional students. One became chief secretary of the House of Peers and president of the Nippon Life Insurance Company; another served as director of several Mitsui firms; and a third, after a career with Bussan, succeeded his brother at Nippon Life Insurance.

Under Naruse's discipline, enforced by carefully selected tutors who were veteran Mitsui employees rather than pedants, the unruly lads were licked into shape for enrollment in the Gakushu-in, or Peers' School, where they mingled as equals with scions of Japan's proudest families, including the imperial house. In that exclusive atmosphere they developed an easy familiarity with one another and the unconscious acceptance of their high status as a natural right. Years after his graduation from the Gakushu-in, Mitsui Takasumi was asked by an English theologian, perhaps chidingly: "Do you regard the emperor as God?" As a would-be Christian, yet still a loyal Japanese, Takasumi had to answer the question obliquely. "I was at school with the emperor," he said, and left it at that.

The girls' primary and secondary education was similar to that of the boys—Wakaba-kai kindergarten, private primary schools, and Gakushu-in girls' department—but less academic, because they were expected to be marriageable after completing their secondary education. Besides receiving the ordinary schooling, they were tutored in French and English and in Western etiquette by their governesses and took special training in chanoyu, ikebana, music, and art. Within this limited scope the Mitsui girls seem to have been more conscientious pupils than their brothers. Most of the Mitsui boys were rather indifferent to education, since material success was assured, and whatever they needed to know about business would have to be learned from the banto anyway. A few of them passed the highly competitive entrance examinations for Tokyo or Kyoto Imperial University, and others studied at foreign institutions—Dartmouth College, Birmingham University, the London School of Economics—but for most of them a few years of prep school or commercial college were considered adequate. A university degree was regarded as an ornament rather than a requirement; and only one Mitsui of that generation, Takanaru, a zoologist, attained much prestige as a scholar. Their financial contributions to education were more significant. In the 1920s, when the East Asia Institute was established at Columbia University, Mitsui and Mitsubishi donated thousands of books. The Mitsuis, two of whose heirs had studied at Birmingham University, endowed a professorship there.

Takamine was especially indulgent toward his sons and gave them whatever they wanted in the way of toys, excursions, and later, clothes and automobiles—always the best to be had. Whenever he could, he took them abroad, and when they were old enough he encouraged them to travel alone. Takasumi says: "He was always interested in other countries and their people and products. When I began to travel during school vacations he had me write books about the countries I visited—Indonesia, Malaya, New Zealand, Australia, the United States, Philippines, Indochina, Korea, China—and read them with interest."

These trips were made not merely for pleasure or cultural development, for on the way the young travelers would meet the most important of Japan's diplomats and Bussan's overseas managers, who showed them how the concern's business was actually conducted. As Takamine admonished his sons: "Seeing once is better than hearing a hundred times." When his heir Takakimi was married, he built for the couple a French-chateau-style house on his estate at Imai-cho and connected it with the main mansion by a covered corridor so that the families could visit comfortably in any weather. Takasumi and Hideko received as a wedding present an English-style half-timbered residence in one of Tokyo's most exclusive neighborhoods. It may be that the boys were overly pampered, but although they were perhaps too easygoing by Japanese standards, they were reasonably serious and dutiful toward their parents, whose tastes and values they shared to a gratifying degree. If they had one serious flaw, it was that they were too gentlemanly for the business and political world in which eventually they would have to struggle for survival.

By the time the girls reached maturity husbands had been chosen for them, not by their parents alone but upon the recommendation of the family council, which kept dossiers on all eligible bachelors. This was not so harsh an arrangement as it might seem, inasmuch as the arbiters took into consideration the tastes, personality traits, and horoscopes of each male candidate, as well as the wealth and social position of his family. The intent of both families was to arrange a stable, harmonious marriage that would produce healthy, untainted offspring; and although they sometimes made mistakes, their judgment was considerably more reliable than that of inexperienced adolescents, who are too often blinded by infatuation. Furthermore, the young maiden was not forced to accept the first male suggested to her. Usually she was given a choice among several possibilities and was allowed to meet the ones who seemed most suitable.

Among younger members of the aristocracy the circumstances were not very formidable, since most of those ready for marriage already knew each other or had mutual friends. Even after having made a tentative choice the girl was not trapped. Before a betrothal was concluded the couple had a *miai,* or formal meeting, in the presence of their parents or other relatives and the matchmaker. After the miai the prospective bride could veto the union without grossly insulting the suitor's family, and he could do the same.

Takamine's first three children had married extremely well, and the fourth, Takasumi, was engaged to Hideko, a daughter of Mitsui Morinosuke, president of Bussan. This union was not only agreeable to the principals but drew the Mitsui senior house closer to Morinosuke's brother-in-law, Sumitomo Kichizaemon II. It also provided a closer tie with the latter's uncles, princes Saionji and Tokudaiji Saneatsu, and hence to the imperial court.

Next in line among Takamine's children came Reiko, who was more independent in character than her older sisters. "In my childhood, I accepted circumstances as they were and played in the garden," she says. "After I entered girls' school, we were not permitted to go out so often, and although the house and garden were so big, I felt as if I were suffocating. I wanted freedom." The restless girl had been offered a husband, another Mitsui, when she was only sixteen, but had refused. The next offer was from Hideko's brother Takaatsu, who worked for Bussan and was in a position to take her abroad. Since he was already an old friend and at the same time opened new horizons to her, she accepted him with her father's blessing. About that time, too, Morinosuke's youngest daughter fell in love with Masuda Takashi's grandson Tomonobu, plunging the family council into an unprecedented crisis because of the House's taboo against intermarriage with banto families. But times were changing fast in the 1920s, and after almost a year of deliberation the betrothal (actually a most desirable one from the keibatsu standpoint) was approved.

The Mitsuis' "marriages of convenience" generally were successful and some turned out to be ideal love matches. The rare divorces resulted from barrenness, which the family-conscious Mitsuis considered impermissible. If there were some unhappy marriages, as there must have been, nothing was said about them, nor were there any apparent signs of emotional frustration such as alcoholism, promiscuity, neurosis, or suicide. The custom of arranged marriage suited the families so well, in fact, that even after the clan constitution was abolished and members were free to marry as they chose most of them continued to consult matchmakers and to marry other Mitsuis by preference.

The high point of the Mitsuis' social life was the visit of the Prince of Wales to Japan in 1922. The foreign ministry, planning for the great occasion, requested Takamine to assist in entertaining Prince Edward, who was due to arrive within a month. Takamine was overwhelmed by the honor but accepted it without hesitation. Since his hilltop palace had no hall large enough for seating the hundred or more diners who were expected, he ordered the Shimizu Construction Company to solve the problem. The firm, headed by a grandson of the builder who had designed the first Mitsui Gumi House in the 1870s, drew up plans and built a huge, English-style banqueting wing, finishing it within a few days of the prince's arrival.

There was great excitement at Imai-cho as the Mitsuis ordered new clothes for the occasion and tried to brush up their English. Reiko, who was just eighteen years old then, and something of a tomboy, was admonished to improve her etiquette. Since she and her younger sister had not yet been included in parties for foreigners, they practiced shaking hands and curtsying to each other, hoping that they would be able to suppress their giggling when the great moment arrived.

The managing director of Mitsukoshi took personal charge of providing suitable furniture, carpeting, linens, silverware, and crystal, while a team of cooks and waiters was mobilized from the best hotels and the imperial household. The most difficult part, however, was the guest list. In addition to Prince Edward and his entourage and Crown Prince Hirohito and his imperial relatives, the members of the cabinet, the foreign diplomatic corps, and the upper peerage, comprising some threescore ordinary princes, marquises, and counts, had to be given consideration. This left little room for mere viscounts and barons, except for a few financial leaders and renowned internationalists.

While the protocol experts of the foreign ministry were fretting over the selection, a young member of the Black Dragon Society blew himself to pieces with a bomb in front of the Imperial Palace, presumably in protest against the god-emperor's demeaning himself by mingling with barbarians—a scandalous situation about which Toyama Mitsuru delivered a few pointed remarks. But anxiety and bruised feelings aside, the royal visit, the greatest social event of the decade in Japan, went off smoothly, and the proud Mitsuis were briefly at the center of it. It made a deep impression upon them, especially the young ladies who had a chance to shake Prince Edward's hand. As for the guest of honor himself, one of his fondest memories of the state visit, he said, was of a fragrant Japanese cypress bathtub built especially for him in the imperial family's detached palace at Nikko.

The summer of 1923 was a happy one for the baron and baroness Mitsui Takamine. Their children were grown and well married or betrothed. The postwar economic crises were over, and the Mitsuis' assorted businesses had never been better on the whole. The advance of organized labor was being countered adequately by the police and their patriotic vigilantes, and the worrisome manhood suffrage bill had been voted down by the Diet. Japanese troops had been withdrawn at last from Siberia (under an agreement that left Mitsui with rights to exploit the oil and natural gas of North Sakhalin), and foreign hostility against Japan showed signs of abating. Socially speaking, the summer season had been the most pleasant in years, and at the end of August the young Mitsuis were still having a gay whirl at Hakone. Takamine was reluctant to forsake the bracing mountain air for the sweltering city, but the death of Prime Minister Kato Tomosaburo had elevated the baron's kinsman, Count Uchida, from foreign minister to premier for the second time; and the political situation, although unstable, was promising. On August 31 Mitsui Takamine and the baroness took their leave of family and friends and returned to Tokyo.

After midnight, when the revelers had departed from the pleasure quarters and the local trains stopped running, the usual silence fell, and the great city slept. But deep in the bedrock underlying eastern Honshu titanic forces were at work. Some people still believed that beneath Nippon's mountains and volcanoes lay a prodigious, somnolent catfish, harmless when asleep but terrible indeed when he awoke and began to move his great body. The mythical catfish had been drowsing fitfully since 1896, when his writhings had killed some 27,000 people. Since then he had been almost forgotten, but on the first day of September 1923, just at noon, he awoke again, in a terrible temper.

The great Kanto earthquake started gently, just as most Tokyo and Yokohama housewives were cooking rice for the noonday meal. As the temblors grew more frequent and more intense over a period of minutes, houses collapsed, charcoal braziers were overturned, and wisps of smoke began rising everywhere, as if the cities had been set afire by spontaneous combustion. The waters of Tokyo Bay and Sagami Bay heaved as though lashed by a gigantic typhoon, and as the waves gathered force, dreaded tsunami swept away whole villages along the coast. Within an hour vast areas of Yokohama and Tokyo were aflame. Millions of people, threatened by fiery blasts, fled in aimless terror through the streets.

At Gomei and Bussan headquarters the lunch hour had not yet begun, and almost everyone was on hand. Bussan's main office and that of the Yokohama branch were doomed to eventual destruction by fire, but the Gomei and Bank buildings stood up under the shocks and fires were prevented. Communications were kept open long enough to learn the dimensions of the catastrophe. When it became apparent that the conflagration would engulf the center of Tokyo, plans were made for orderly evacuation of employees, and instructions were issued for setting up alternate headquarters. Amid the chaos and horror that followed, Mitsui men, even before trying to ascertain the fate of their loved ones, salvaged company records, cash, securities, and portable property of high value or importance.

The salvaging was conducted with a cool professionalism born out of long experience with fires, of which the Mitsuis had suffered scores. In times of public catastrophe the House had always helped organize assistance for the victims, and as a matter of standing policy Gomei activated the Mitsui Relief Committee while the fires still burned. Transportation equipment, medicines, food, and other resources needed for the survivors were mobilized in outlying areas, as Bussan's branches in other cities rushed supplies by sea to the disaster zone. A number of Mitsui ships were at anchor offshore and, with the aid of lighters and small boats, vital rescue and supply operations were carried out. The Mitsuis jointly donated five million yen for erecting temporary barracks in Hibiya Park to shelter thousands of Tokyo's homeless people and to feed them. Much of the neighborhood around Imai-cho was burned out, but the mansion was spared, almost undamaged. To aid local refugees Baron Mitsui had barracks erected in his own garden and the baroness dispensed food to the needy. In a gesture of sympathy,

Prince and Princess Kuni Kunihiko with their daughter Nagako, who was betrothed to Prince Regent Hirohito, paid a visit to the homeless families encamped at Imai-cho.

Meanwhile, messages of condolence and pledges of material aid were dispatched from many countries of the world. The United States Pacific Fleet had been deployed immediately to ferry relief supplies from Asian ports, and the first ship arrived at Yokohama on September 3. On that same day a new prime minister took over from Count Uchida Yasuya, who was virtually prostrate from his tumultuous nine days in office. His successor was Yamamoto Gombei, the old admiral whose involvement in the navy scandal of 1914 apparently was overlooked in the interests of national unity. Although some unspeakable atrocities were committed against innocent Koreans and suspected radicals by police and terrorist gangs during the panic, the period that followed the Kanto catastrophe was one of conciliation. The heart of the world was with Japan in its time of affliction. At home, class and national rivalries were surmounted by mutual concern over human misfortune, and renewed manifestations of man's essential goodness breathed life into moribund ideals of tolerance and brotherhood. And the great catfish, appeased by such an immense and excruciating sacrifice, dozed off in another long slumber as the survivors began patiently to rebuild upon the still warm ashes of the ruined cities.

19 · Whom the Gods Would Destroy

SINCE THE TURN OF THE CENTURY almost everything touched by the Mitsui Midases had turned to gold. Even the insensate forces of nature dealt gently with them. Although for a time they were affected by the economic paralysis that followed the great earthquake of 1923, they eventually derived material benefits of unsuspected magnitude from the aftershocks that racked the Japanese economy.

The immediate effect of the quake was catastrophic. More than 100,000 people had been killed by the conflagrations, and millions more were homeless and destitute. Half a million families had lost their homes and nearly all their possessions. Total property damage was officially estimated at about 2.5 billion dollars, but considering the secretiveness of Japanese about their wealth, probably it was much larger. Insurance policies do not cover fire losses due to earthquakes. Perhaps that was just as well in 1923, because claims would have amounted to four or five times the combined assets of all the insurance companies in Japan. However, as an emergency relief measure, the government instructed the firms to pay up to ten percent of the face value of policies to holders of insurance and loaned them the money to do so. The Mitsuis' Taisho Marine & Fire Insurance Company, still in its infancy, was saddled with an enormous debt—which was not repaid in full until 1949, after the yen was drastically devalued.

Financial confusion was aggravated by the total or partial destruction of 121 head offices of banks—only seventeen were spared—in the Tokyo-Yokohama area. Two-thirds of the 310 bank branches in these cities were badly damaged or destroyed. An enormous amount of collateral was lost, and of course, most debtors were unable to meet their commitments. To stave off complete economic collapse, the government declared a one-month moratorium on all obligations contracted before the quake and payable during that period, and depositors were permitted to draw no more than one hundred yen a day from their accounts. In preparation for lifting the moratorium, the Bank of Japan was instructed to refinance debts to banks falling due in the interim and was to be guaranteed against losses resulting from these transactions, which were conducted by means of so-called earthquake bills. Such measures, and the relaxation of the central bank's loan policies to make more funds available, reassured the public; panic was averted, and the banks resumed more or less normal business.

From then on the government provided hundreds of millions of dollars for the rehabilitation of business and industry. Mitsui's head office in Tokyo and the Yokohama branch of Mitsui Bank were not seriously damaged, and fortunately their vaults were intact. Mitsui Gomei, Bank, and Bussan resumed operations within ten days; and with the help of branches and affiliated companies throughout Japan and in foreign countries, the concern was able to supply materials, commodities, equipment, and financing for restoring production and distribution in the devastated area.

Exhibiting once again their capacity for rebounding from disaster, the people began stoically the task of rebuilding Tokyo, which before the quake had been the world's third largest metropolis. Because of the need for importing large amounts of materials and machinery, the government relaxed its stiff attitude toward foreign investments, and bonds were floated in the United States and Great Britain. Within a short time many American companies—among them Western Electric, Westinghouse, General Electric, Libbey-Owens, Dollar Steamship Line, Standard Oil, Associated Oil, and Alcoa, for example—acquired or increased their shares in Japanese companies, bringing in new technology along with their capital. Big foreign loans were extended to the Japan Industrial Bank, the electric-power industry, and development companies such as Toyo Colonization. Many of those loans, which amounted to about 300 million dollars, were negotiated by Mitsui and other zaibatsu, who thus strengthened their ties with foreign counterparts. As a result Japanese industry began to expand and modernize.

Most of Tokyo was rebuilt according to the helter-skelter pattern that had persisted since the Edo period, with narrow zigzag streets and flimsy frame dwellings; but in the central part of the city, near the Imperial Palace, there rose a business center more imposing than any in the Far East. The rather scorched headquarters of Mitsui Gomei was replaced by a seven-story building ultramodern in construction but Greco-Roman in design. Obanto Dan Takuma had asked his architects from New York, Trowbridge and Livingston, for an edifice embodying "grandeur, dignity, and simplicity"; they gave him what appeared to be a replica of Pittsburgh's Mellon Bank, and it was opened in 1926 on the fiftieth anniversary of the founding of Mitsui Ginko. (It still accommodates the head offices of numerous Mitsui enterprises, as well as of the clan council and Mitsui family members, and if some of its grandeur has faded since then, at least it retains its dignity and utility.)

The established zaibatsu, whose efforts had assisted so substantially in the reconstruction campaign, participated in its benefits commensurately. Nevertheless, they were not carried away by the easy-money mood that prevailed, having experienced too many boom-and-bust periods in the past. A very large share of the government's earthquake-relief funds had been used for the artificial resuscitation of companies that had been overexpanded during the war, and in the midst of an inflationary boom there lurked the specter of overproduction. But while the older concerns bided their time, the more adventurous non-zaibatsu and new zaibatsu made the fullest use of their connections with the special banks through which most of the government's loans were channeled. Such entrepreneurs as Kuhara of Nissan, Mori of Showa Denko, and Noguchi of Nichitsu expanded rapidly into heavy industries and chemicals, while other parvenu tycoons continued their headlong advances into shipping, general trading, and manufacturing, regardless of demand.

The postwar collapse had either ruined or weakened many "war baby" enterprises, which in turn undermined the value of securities held by banks against debts outstanding. Then inflationary financing, followed by a deflationary reaction, caused severe distress among smaller or overextended firms. The banks held ample funds, but reliable applicants for loans were scarce. Excessive competition to make loans gave rise to unsound banking practices, and by the end of 1926 smaller or carelessly managed banks had a major share of their assets tied up in loans advanced against shaky collateral or none at all. On top of that about one-fifth of the "earthquake bills" discounted by the Bank of Japan were still outstanding.

About half the unsettled earthquake bills were held by the Bank of Taiwan, which had borrowed heavily from the Bank of Japan to save two politically favored companies from collapse. The companies concerned were the budding industrial empire of Kuhara Fusanosuke, called "the mining king" because of his wartime successes in copper, and Suzuki Shoten. Kuhara, a protégé of the late Inoue Kaoru, was feared because of his ruthlessness and his formidable connections with politicians, ultranationalists, and the military. The Suzuki combine had long been marked for destruction because, in its spectacular growth, it had already encroached dangerously on zaibatsu territory. The brilliant "Mouse" Kaneko had built it into a conglomerate of sixty-five large companies—including Teikoku Rayon (Teijin) and Kobe Steel—with a total capital of five hundred million yen (nominally larger than Mitsui's) and 25,000 employees. Suzuki's trading company alone had registered sales of 1.5 million yen a year, overtaking Mitsui Bussan. After the First World War, according to some authorities, Suzuki Yone, widow of the founder, who presided over the firm's head office in Kobe, was the wealthiest woman in the world.

But although "Mouse" Kaneko had secured a major interest in the 65th Bank in Kobe, finance was his fatal weakness. Like most of the narikin, he had been much oppressed by the zaibatsu banks. Because of his mania for keeping absolute control of their company in the hands of the Suzuki family, he had stubbornly resisted opening the concern's enterprises to public subscription, which would have invited invasion by the zaibatsu. Instead, he had relied for outside capital upon the 65th Bank and the Bank of Taiwan. The latter, still as badly managed as it had been at the time of the Nishihara loans, had advanced about ninety million yen to Suzuki and Kuhara after the Kanto earthquake and still was liable for one hundred million yen worth of earthquake bills whose due date had been extended and reextended by the Bank of Japan because of political favoritism. Obviously, the survival of the Bank of Taiwan hinged upon that of Suzuki and Kuhara, its principal borrowers, and upon its continued delay in paying those earthquake bills. The zaibatsu's banks knew, of course, how wobbly the Bank of Taiwan had become. Yet, curiously, Mitsui and Mitsubishi were providing it with large amounts of call money (short-term interbank loans), with which it kept their two rivals going as the recession deepened.

The unhealthy condition of the Bank of Taiwan had attracted so much public attention that early in 1927 the Diet passed legislation calling for early liquidation of the earthquake bills, with a proviso that the affairs of the Bank of Taiwan would be investigated. Heeding a warning from the government, the bank promptly cut off further credits to the Suzuki company, which in turn was forced to suspend business. As an immediate consequence, the 65th Bank (whose loans were heavily concentrated in the Suzuki complex) also closed its doors.

This sorry end, probably not unexpected, was the signal for Mitsui and Mitsubishi to call their short-term loans made to the Bank of Taiwan—which, having neglected to maintain its payment reserves, was also forced to suspend business. In the ensuing chain reaction hundreds of banks closed in quick succession, plunging Japan into the Great Panic of 1927.

The severest shock (though a salutary one for the zaibatsu) was the collapse of the Fifteenth Bank, one of the country's oldest and most respected financial institutions, which was headed by Prince Matsukata's eldest son. Called "the Peers' Bank," because it had been founded by former daimyo and court nobles early in the Meiji era, it catered to the nation's elite and handled much of the imperial household's banking business. The cabinet, personally appointed by the emperor himself, could not stand idle while the fortune of His Imperial Highness was in jeopardy. Emergency legislation to save the banks was introduced, and the Diet displayed extraordinary accord in passing it. Government funds amounting to seven hundred million yen were appropriated to stave off the Bank of Taiwan's private creditors (mainly Mitsui and Mitsubishi), and to indemnify the Bank of Japan against possible losses from the billions of yen it was advancing to succor tottering banks.[1]

While the panic still continued, the incumbent "Mitsubishi Cabinet" was replaced by a Seiyukai Party team with predominantly Mitsui coloring, although the finance minister was a Yasuda Bank man. A three-week moratorium was declared, and committees were appointed to dispose of the earthquake bills and to rehabilitate the Bank of Taiwan. Interestingly enough, Yamamoto Jotaro, the former chief of Mitsui Bussan who had been convicted in the *Kongo* bribery case, was appointed to both of those committees. Under these benign influences the banking laws were revised, very much in favor of the zaibatsu's institutions. The Bank of Taiwan was saved, but its capital was cut by two-thirds and its activities outside Taiwan were restricted. The emperor's deposits were preserved intact, but the Peers' Bank was whittled down to one-fifth its former size. Of the 1,445 banks still in existence by 1928, more than half were too small to qualify for franchises and had the choice of increasing their capital, merging with larger banks, or going out of existence. The "Big Five" naturally were aggrandized by this reform and found themselves in control of deposits almost double the prepanic amounts, comprising more than one-third the deposits of all Japan's private banks combined. Heading the list was Mitsui Bank, whose deposits had increased nearly twofold during the crisis and represented about fifteen percent of the nation's total.

Picking their way discerningly among the ruins, the zaibatsu also strengthened their industrial and commercial foundations by absorbing or taking control of broken rivals. Mitsui and Mitsubishi took over the most valuable fragments of the Suzuki empire. One of them was the Claude Nitrogen Industry, which Mitsui developed into the powerful Toyo Koatsu Industries (today called Mitsui Toatsu Chemicals), using modern technology through an association with the Du Pont Company of the United States. That acquisition gave Mitsui a leading position in producing chemical fertilizers just as heavy orders for this commodity began to flow in from Japan's overseas colonies and territories. Another Mitsui gain from Suzuki was the Harima Shipbuilding & Engineering Company, which developed into Ishikawajima-Harima Heavy Industries—now one of the world's largest builders of ships and heavy machinery. However, Suzuki's Kobe Steel, the 65th Bank in Kobe, and Teikoku Rayon came under control of an Osaka-based group of capitalists centered around the upstart Nomura Bank, which evaded the zaibatsu's stranglehold and became a major adversary. Nomura Bank later divided to become Daiwa Bank, which still is near the top, and Nomura Securities, Japan's largest firm in its field.

The Suzuki combine never gave Mitsui any more trouble. The widow lost her whole empire at one savage stroke, and her loyal obanto, despite (or because of) his commercial genius, was relegated to the shadows. In his dedication to securing the family's position, he had so neglected his own welfare that he ended destitute. (According to one of his old colleagues, he had to accept the charity of friends in order to send his children through school.) Such was the wrath of the zaibatsu when their supremacy was at stake.

The Kuhara combine proved to be far more resistant than Suzuki to the zaibatsu nutcracker. Its founder, Kuhara Fusanosuke, was a member of the Choshu clique in the Seiyukai Party and was related by marriage to Prince Saionji, Baron Sumitomo Kichizaemon, and Marquis Okuma. His brother-in-law, Aikawa Gisuke, not only was a shrewd businessman but was backed by one of Kyushu's wealthiest coal-mining families, whose heir had married his sister. After taking many a buffeting from the zaibatsu, for whom he formed an implacable hatred, Kuhara turned the management of the enterprise over to Aikawa and went into politics, becoming in time a cabinet minister and president of the Seiyukai. The two men built the maimed Kuhara firm into the fantastically successful Nippon Sangyo concern, or Nissan, which included the Hitachi and Nippon Mining companies among its hundreds of affiliates. Within a decade this "new zaibatsu," with the support of the military, became strong enough to challenge Mitsui, Mitsubishi, and the South Manchurian Railway—Japan's three largest business organizations—simultaneously and with devastating effect.

In the late 1920s, however, Mitsui seemed to be invincible, having widened its lead over all competitors. At the beginning of the First World War, Mitsui Gomei had been capitalized at fifty million yen and encompassed fifteen major companies. By 1928 capital had been increased to 500 million yen, and the companies under its control numbered at least 130, of which six were wholly owned. According to Gomei's own statement, the firms under its direct control were Bussan, Mining, Bank, Trust & Banking, Life Insurance, and Toshin Warehouse, and those in turn controlled more than forty subsidiaries.

Important companies partially owned and controlled by Mitsui Gomei were Oji Paper Mills, Kanegafuchi Cotton Spinning, Shibaura Engineering Works, Hokkaido Colliery & Steamship, and Taiwan Sugar, which in turn had at least thirty large subsidiaries. Other affiliates acknowledged by the Mitsui holding company were Electro Chemical Industrial, Onoda Cement, Mitsukoshi Department Store,

Toyo Rayon, Dai-Nippon Celluloid, and Japan Steel Works. This listing, published by Mitsui Gomei, is obviously an understatement, however. For example, it ignores Mitsui's very influential position in such outstanding firms as Toyoda Automatic Loom Works, Toyo Menka, Tokyo Electric, and Kyushu Electric Power, as well as its substantial holdings in such government-fostered enterprises as the South Manchurian Railway, Toyo Takushoku (or Oriental Colonization), Yawata Iron Works, and the national policy banks. Also ignored were numerous overseas mining, manufacturing, and transportation interests, some of which had been acquired under such peculiar circumstances that the management preferred not to bring them to public attention.

While Mitsui Gomei's capital was officially given as 500 million yen in 1928, an independent estimate for that time, which is considered to be authoritative, set Mitsui's total capital at 1.644 billion yen for 97 companies. Next in order among the zaibatsu, according to that same estimate, were Mitsubishi (65 companies, 712 million yen), Yasuda (66 companies, 308 million yen), and Sumitomo (30 companies, 244 million yen).[2]

Most Japanese intellectuals were familiar by then with the works of Marx and Lenin, and the relationship between monopoly and imperialism was being discussed in a scholarly way. The zaibatsu chiefs were mostly university graduates, and not a few were avid readers, especially in economics. They also made a practice of retaining professors as advisers. Thus they understood critical interpretations of Japan's position and its international implications. Although they avoided such pejorative terms, they must have been aware that they had achieved a mature form of monopoly capitalism, with its exploited and dangerously dissatisfied proletariat. Capital was highly concentrated in a market too poor and narrow to absorb the products of fast-growing industries or to provide adequate investment opportunities for surplus capital. In addition, there was the crippling disadvantage of not having unchallenged access to vital raw materials. These had to be imported at high cost, and the only way to make export manufactures competitive was to hold labor costs to a bare minimum.

Fujihara Ginjiro, whose Oji Paper combine was one of the Japanese empire's largest employers, made it all sound rather idyllic: "Our simple mode of living has an important bearing on the industrial development of Japan. The simple life is inexpensive, food not being costly among other things. The wages are low and the cost of living is consequently low."[3] He might have added that life expectancy was correspondingly low, being only three-fourths that of Americans, while

Japanese corporate profit rates and the diseases of poverty, especially tuberculosis, were much higher than those of the United States.[4]

True, the wide world offered vast untapped markets, unexploited natural resources, and untouched fields for investment. But most of the potentially valuable regions had been preempted by powers who had reached the stage of monopoly capitalism earlier and had responded to it by imperialistic expansion. Japan, the latecomer to their feast, had either to make deferential arrangements with the privileged powers or to continue striving, against all odds, to carve out an empire of its own in Asia.

Those Japanese who favored the course of conciliation were becoming fewer and less enthusiastic, and with good reason. At the Versailles Peace Conference in 1919 Japan had fought for a racial-equality clause in the League of Nations Covenant. This demand was opposed by six major powers, led by Australia and the United States (the country that had been so determined to "make the world safe for democracy"). Japan joined the League, despite its failure to reject racist discrimination; but the United States, partly because of Japan's greedy attitude toward China, changed its mind and refused to ratify the peace treaty or to join the League.

In this atmosphere of mutual distrust, anti-Japanese sentiment in the United States was being whipped up by the American Legion, the American Federation of Labor, the Asiatic Exclusion League, and many other local organizations, with the support of the Hearst newspapers and "yellow journalism" in general. In 1920 (after the American good-will mission to Tokyo) Californians voted by an overwhelming majority for a law that deprived "aliens ineligible for citizenship" (in another word, Asians) of the right to own or even to lease land. This law was aimed directly at Japanese farmers, whose hard-earned success had antagonized American farmers and evoked fear among workers who saw their jobs threatened by an influx of "coolie labor." Similar laws were passed by fifteen states in quick succession.

The federal government opposed such discriminatory legislation, but at the same time Washington, in furtherance of the Open Door policy in China, was making common cause with London against the Japanese advance on the continent. Great Britain and the United States, the world's leading naval powers, hoped to find a peaceful way of ending the naval arms race, in which Japan was rapidly catching up with them. Britain also wanted to end its alliance with Japan, which had become an embarrassment without compensating advantages. To solve these and other Far Eastern problems, the United States invited nine nations, including Britain, France, Italy, and Japan, to a conference in Washington.

Japan's internationalists were dismayed by signs of rising hostility and did their best to alleviate it. Late in 1921 Viscount Shibusawa, still believing that world peace could be preserved by closer relations between Japanese and Western businessmen, organized an economic mission to London, headed by Baron Dan. The mission was received with pointed coolness, and Dan and some of his fellow peacemakers proceeded to Washington with a sense of foreboding. It was just at that time, a week before the international parley began, that Prime Minister Hara was assassinated in Tokyo, perhaps as a warning to the delegates.

Representing Japan at the Washington Conference, held from November 12, 1921, until February 6, 1922, were Prince Tokugawa Iesato, heir of the last shogun; Admiral Kato Tomosaburo, the navy minister; and Shidehara Kijuro, son-in-law of Baron Iwasaki Yataro and at the time Ambassador to Washington. Attending as "people's representatives" (actually advisers) were numerous business leaders, including Shibusawa and Mitsui's men Dan, Fujihara Ginjiro of Oji Paper, and Muto Sanji of Kanegafuchi Spinning. One of the main items on the agenda was the conclusion of a naval treaty fixing the tonnage of capital ships allowed to each signatory power. The Japanese delegates had been instructed to strive for a ratio of 10:10:7 for Britain, the United States, and Japan respectively, but to settle for a 5:5:3 ratio at the very worst. Unfortunately for the delegates, the American Department of State had cracked the Japanese wireless code then being used, and the American and British negotiators found it easy to impose the lower ratio on Japan. In another setback the Anglo-Japanese alliance was replaced by a meaningless four-power Pacific treaty with Britain, the United States, and France, a pact that despite its face-saving phraseology was obviously aimed at isolating Japan. Swallowing this insult stoically, the Japanese delegation agreed further to vacate Shantung and return to the Chinese some of the most valuable concessions obtained by means of the Twenty-one Demands and the Nishihara loans. These agreements were made in addition to others that were included in a nine-power treaty acknowledging China's sovereignty, independence, and territorial integrity—while giving all the signatories equal rights to exploit its economy in competition with Japan.

The conference was successful in restoring a certain degree of mutual trust among participants, and the Western powers were satisfied with the results. But in Japan there were few congratulations: as at the time of the Portsmouth Treaty the acquiescence of the delegates was castigated as a shameful submission and brought loud protests from ultranationalists. And whatever international amity the conference had generated was dissipated in 1924 when Washington's "Gentlemen's Agreement" with Tokyo was abrogated by the passage of a law that limited immigration drastically and pointedly excluded all Japanese. This gratuitously insulting act (which decreed that even Japanese already residing in the United States and its territories were ineligible for citizenship) provoked such deep and widespread resentment in Japan that it brings back bitter memories even today.

Perhaps by coincidence, this act of Congress was signed by President Calvin Coolidge soon after the United States government filed suit in New York to recover 2.5 million dollars in wartime overpayments made to Mitsui's Standard Aircraft Corporation. Among sensational charges bandied about at the hearings was a Department of Justice report, released by a senator, alleging that Mitsui & Company was exerting an indirect but powerful influence in the United States, "which extends to Congress and departments of the government, and they have on their payrolls attorneys and politicians who are attempting to run roughshod over this country."[5]

The most damaging testimony in the case was not substantiated, and Baron Dan, who had just returned to Tokyo from New York, made light of the whole matter. Even after the exclusion act was passed he remained calm, assuring an American friend: "The leading men of my generation were educated in America at a period when the relations of the two countries were at their best. We refuse, on the ground of our experience then and since, to recognize discrimination as the true sentiment of the American people."[6]

Count Kaneko, with no business interests at stake, could be more forthright. Feeling betrayed, he resigned from the presidency of the America-Japan Society and issued a public statement protesting the exclusion law. He wrote later, in a foreword to Shibusawa's biography: "For sixty long years I have endeavored to promote better understanding and good will between our two countries, but the reward I received was 'a stone for bread and a scorpion for fish.' My patience was exhausted, and even now I cannot look upon America as I did in the days of President Theodore Roosevelt."[7]

At home in Japan the situation for the ordinary man was hardly more reassuring. The concentration of ownership in the hands of the zaibatsu had made their oppressive presence felt in every aspect of the economy; their political and financial maneuvers, which provoked nasty scandals and economic fluctuations that brought hardship to millions of people, had increased public distrust and hatred of big business and its corrupt political leaders. The spread of unionism threatened the national policy of cheap labor and cheap exports; socialists, anarchists, and the newly formed Communist Party continued to alienate workers, students, and intellectuals from their heaven-ordained leaders.

In addition, a new and alarming menace had arisen from the right wing. The rank-and-file ultranationalists, although devoted to the emperor and basically on the side of established power, were not indifferent to anticapitalist propaganda, a great deal of which was justified. Although remaining violently anticommunist, they were groping their way toward a kind of "class struggle" of their own, directed against the monopolists, their political henchmen, and as usual, the emperor's "evil advisers."

A leader in this school of radical nationalism was an original but undisciplined scholar named Kita Ikki, whose book *Nihon Kaizo Hoan Taiko* (An Outline of Principles for Reform of the State) had made a tremendous impact upon nationalists. Kita, a fanatical imperialist, believed that peace would come only when the Western powers had slaughtered each other and Japan had become "shogun" of the world. However, his domestic policy was humanitarian and, like those of Hitler and Mussolini, bore a superficial resemblance to socialism. A necessary step for achieving his aims was that of breaking the power of big capitalists and landowners by establishing an idealistic form of state capitalism. The middle and lower classes, however, were to retain their property as a sovereign right.

Kita's book, a vague and self-contradictory mixture of half-digested ideas, was terrifying not in itself but in its appeal to elements who, hitherto, had been considered allies of the elite—the ultranationalist societies, civil servants, and the military. Kita's idea of a rightist revolution was particularly welcome to younger officers whose vision of Japan—based upon idealized history and the imperial rescripts of the Meiji era—was so painfully at odds with sordid realities.

There was no immediate threat, however, since the "revolutionary radicals" were split among many factions and theories. The zaibatsu and government authorities felt reasonably confident of being able to handle leftists and unionists by time-tested means, but what would happen if the very forces of law and order should rebel? It was not forgotten that many rightists still active had opposed the government in Saigo's rebellion fifty years before and still kept his memory green.

The management of Mitsui Mining got an early warning of troubles in store for the country. In the mid-1920s, for the first time in history, there had been a strike at Omuta, and to cope with it, special police and strong-arm men had been recruited in unusually large numbers. Those tough and swaggering bullies had always been hard to handle. On one occasion some of them had attempted to assassinate Count Inoue Kaoru when he visited Omuta. In general, they had been loyal to management, but now they showed an unaccustomed defiance. Labor boss Tokonami, as home minister, had suppressed Kita's book; but he secretly admired it and even gave the author financial support. Perhaps as a result of this affinity the strikebreaking Kokusui-kai, the National Essence Society, had also taken on a radical tinge, and capitalists were receiving almost as much abuse—verbal, at least—as socialists.

Rightist radicals also agitated among local merchants, small landowners, and officials of the company town, whose grievances were many: landlords objected to the free housing provided by the management; merchants were offended by the company-store system, which deprived them of customers; fumes from metal-refining and chemical plants poisoned the air and killed crops; mine cave-ins caused the ground to collapse, damaging buildings; heavy rains triggered landslides around the workings; and in disputes over such matters the Mitsui-dominated local government seemed always to favor the company over ordinary folk.

A most disturbing symptom was the fact that among the agitators were some young army officers. Since Saigo's rebellion in 1877 military men had been expressly forbidden to engage in such activities. In Emperor Meiji's Precepts to Soldiers and Sailors, which officers knew almost by heart, servicemen were warned: "Neither be led astray by current opinions nor meddle in politics, but with single heart fulfill your essential duty of loyalty." Yet several officers had been collaborating with Kita Ikki in a secret society whose aim was to overthrow the government. The police knew, in fact, that a military coup d'état had been planned as early as 1927.

Against this background, as somber domestically as it was ominous internationally, a "Mitsui Cabinet" was formed during the Great Panic of 1927. Its composition and performance reflected the sense of emergency that gripped the power elite at that time. The prime minister then was Tanaka Giichi, another general from Choshu (although from a younger generation than those who plotted the Meiji revolution) and a Seiyukai politician known to be in sympathy with domestic reactionaries. He also favored a tough foreign policy, and to keep his hand on the reins he served as his own foreign minister. Holding the finance portfolio was Takahashi Korekiyo, a retainer of the Yasuda concern, whose mission was to settle the banking crisis in favor of the zaibatsu and prepare to finance projects in furtherance of their overseas investment programs. In charge of home affairs was Suzuki Kisaburo, a former justice minister and legal adviser to Mitsui. His position was particularly important because, with the passage of universal manhood suffrage in 1925, the electorate had been increased from three million to thirteen million. Inasmuch as no general election had been held since then, the mood of the new voters was uncertain, and the threat of a political upheaval could not be ruled out. Suzuki, an ultranationalist ally of Toyama Mitsuru and a director of Tokonami's National Essence Society, was ideally suited for the job. The communications minister was Kuhara Fusanosuke, whose ambition to stake out a personal empire in Manchuria had brought him into a symbiotic relationship with the Black Dragon and similar societies. And the railways minister, whose jurisdiction extended to the South Manchurian Railway, was secretary general of Prince Konoe's expansionist East Asia Common Culture League and a director of the South Seas Association, which had similar aims.

In Japan, however, the real locus of power is usually concealed, and the most potent men in that imperialistic Seiyukai cabinet did not hold ministerial rank. One of them was Yamamoto Jotaro, who was given the key coordinating position of chief cabinet secretary. Working with him (or against him, rather, as it turned out) was his former Mitsui Bussan colleague Mori Kaku, who bore the innocuous title of parliamentary vice-minister of foreign affairs. Those two, the master spies of the Russo-Japanese War, were now Mitsui's political bosses in the Seiyukai and its most knowledgeable China watchers. Also rather important in this respect was Yamamoto's cousin, Yoshida Shigeru, a career diplomat who as vice-minister of foreign affairs did the real work for Prime Minister and Foreign Minister Tanaka. Yoshida, being a son-in-law of Count Makino, one of Emperor Hirohito's most trusted advisers, may also have served as a confidential pipeline to the imperial court.

Tanaka's name, identified with the aggressive China policy adopted under his premiership, lives in infamy; but the policy itself was formulated behind the scenes primarily by Yamamoto and Mori, in collaboration with Yoshida. Tanaka, it appears, was little more than a figurehead erected by Mori, who was a much more powerful force in the Seiyukai. A few years earlier, when Mori had thrown his support to Tanaka as party president, he told the general: "Hereafter, we [Mori and another Seiyukai boss] want you to listen to whatever we have to say," and Tanaka humbly assented. Mori then turned to one of Tanaka's assistants and stated arrogantly: "You are Tanaka's subordinate, but I am no pliant servant of Tanaka. He is one who is going to take orders from me."[8] Mori's authority presumably derived from the fact that he had been the man who dispensed Mitsui's political largesse, and was now a henchman of Prince Konoe.

The Tanaka cabinet's first task was to exploit the possibilities of the Great Panic and to establish the zaibatsu more firmly in command of the economy. Next the ministers turned their attention to domestic unrest.

Under the terms of a strengthened Peace Preservation Ordinance passed in 1925, home minister Suzuki Kisaburo began a country-wide crackdown on the leftists. In preparation for the first dreaded election under universal manhood suffrage, his police secretly arrested about a thousand people suspected of entertaining subversive ideas. Such dissident organizations as the Farmer-Labor Party, Labor Union Council, and Young Proletarians League, as well as the Communist Party, were suppressed; and there were wholesale beatings and murders to dissuade the left-wing opposition from believing that the suffrage law was a prelude to democracy.

Meanwhile Mori was busy with his own favorite schemes. The first had been to gain control of the Seiyukai so that he could dominate its China policy. Having brought key members of the party as well as of the privy council firmly under his influence, he instructed Tanaka to dispatch a military expedition to Shantung, ostensibly to quell anti-Japanese disturbances in progress there. The government was opposed to this move, which was sure to aggravate the situation and incite protests from foreign powers. But Mori retorted: "If Tanaka will not assent to sending a military force, I'll make him resign." By such browbeating Mori brought the cabinet around, and the "strong policy" toward China, temporarily in abeyance, was resumed in earnest. In these maneuvers "he was in all his glory," Tanaka wrote to Yoshida in the summer of 1927.[9]

In order to coordinate this policy Tanaka, at Mori's urging, convened the Eastern Regions Conference, held in the summer of 1927. Among the participants were top-level cabinet members, staff officers, bureaucrats, political leaders, representatives of involved zaibatsu, and experts concerned with continental problems. Such a portentous conclave should have generated a rather voluminous report, but no official record of it was ever published by the Japanese. Instead, an intriguing document called "The Tanaka Memorial," purporting to be the prime minister's report to the emperor, was issued by the Chinese government in 1929. If it was a forgery, as the Japanese government alleged, it was a clever one, for it recounted accurately the known aims of the conference's participants and presented the general plan of the China program that the Japanese actually followed for the next decade. In essence it postulated the vital importance of rights in Manchuria and Mongolia to Japan's economic development and security; the necessity for conquering all of China to protect those rights; and the inevitability of eventual war with the United States and Great Britain in carrying out the alleged "Tanaka program."

Regardless of the authenticity of the document, it is known that matters of particular concern at the conference were the spread of communism from Soviet-held Manchuria in the north and the rising communist movement in China; nationalist resistance from China's Kuomintang and Manchurian rebels; and anti-Japanese boycotts or sabotage from any quarter. It was agreed that Japan, having assumed the task of developing the resources of the region, had the right to protect its interests by force if necessary. But there were serious differences of opinion about how much force should be used, and when.

The relationships among the protagonists were not so simple as they might seem at first glance. True, Prime Minister Tanaka, Yamamoto, and Mori all owed a certain allegiance to Mitsui, but the latter two had come to exercise independent power in the political and economic worlds. Yamamoto had used his position as obanto of Mitsui Bussan and a leading member of the Seiyukai to carve out an industrial subempire on the continent. As viceroy of this empire, which was based upon zaibatsu capital, he tended toward the conservatism of the business leaders with whom he associated and showed a preference for peaceful economic development. General Baron Tanaka was so close to Yamamoto that he called him "my other self," and may well have formulated his foreign policy accordingly. Mori was outwardly subservient to his former boss at Mitsui Bussan, but although he too was an avid industrial promoter, he was even more of a politician and also exerted an extraordinary influence over Tanaka. An inveterate conspirator of Prince Konoe's camp, he sought to augment his personal power by siding with more bellicose elements of the army's general staff and of the Kwantung Army stationed in Manchuria. Like many of the younger officers who were inspired by the writings of Kita Ikki, Mori believed that force should be used to seize Manchuria proper, regardless of the League of Nations Covenant, which Japan had signed. But as everyone could plainly see, in taking responsibility for maintaining peace in the region, Japan implicitly reserved the right to wage war. And although the Eastern Regions Conference apparently decided against conquest by military aggression, as urged by Mori, the "moderates" left a wide latitude for the extremists who had been chafing for so long under the "weak" policy of economic penetration by political intrigue.

The "moderates" seemed to have prevailed, and at the end of the conference, early in July 1927, Yamamoto was appointed president of the South Manchurian Railway, becoming the most powerful Japanese official on the continent. SMR's new vice-president was Matsuoka Yosuke, a relative and henchman of Yamamoto, whose cousin Yoshida Shigeru was named consul-general in Manchuria.

Yamamoto left immediately for Manchuria, where he proceeded with plans to build five new railway lines. To this end he was conducting secret negotiations with a Manchurian warlord, Chang Tso-lin, who with Japanese help had seized control over large areas of Manchuria, which he pacified for the benefit of the SMR and zaibatsu investors. By 1927 Chang was so powerful that his armies routed those of other warlords in north China and enabled him to set up his own regime in Peking. Although the Kuomintang had established a rival government at Nanking in south China, Chang claimed hegemony over all of China and dubbed himself generalissimo of its armed forces. This presumption was convenient for Yamamoto, who was an old friend of Chang and had already obtained his consent to expand the SMR. Chang was all the more responsive to these overtures because of his indebtedness to General Tanaka, who had saved his life during the Russo-Japanese War. (On the other hand, Yoshida despised Chang and was engaged in a legalistic maneuver to thwart his ambitions; and Mori, the parliamentary vice-minister of foreign affairs, was bent upon liquidating him.)

In October, Yamamoto met the Generalissimo in Peking to settle the railway matter. The groundwork had been carefully laid by officials of the China-Japan Industrial Company, a zaibatsu consortium, and Yamamoto quickly concluded agreements concerning the new lines. That done, he made arrangements with Mitsui and other zaibatsu banks to float debentures—which totaled 120 million yen during his incumbency—for financing the expansion of SMR. Earlier he had negotiated with Thomas W. Lamont to borrow the money from J. P. Morgan & Company but had been turned down.

Yamamoto's vigorous performance in Manchuria was greatly applauded in Japan, and in the spring of 1928 he was invited to the Imperial Palace on two occasions to explain his "new economic plan" to Emperor Hirohito. This plan, centered upon the construction of railways and harbor works, involved the establishment of a new steelmaking complex in Korea, a major plant for converting coal from Fushun into fuel oil (which later became Mitsui Mining's largest investment in Manchuria), expansion of an agricultural and forestry development company in the region, and numerous mining, chemical, and shipping projects. The emperor, presumably, was already familiar with the political strategy behind the economic plan. A unified government was to be established in China under General Chiang Kai-shek and other conservative elements of the Kuomintang. Concurrently, Generalissimo Chang Tso-lin was to be supported as the military ruler of Manchuria, which would be made "independent" of China in order to facilitate Japanese control.

Chiang Kai-shek, a graduate of a Japanese military school, was (like his teacher, the late Sun Yat-sen) closely associated with leaders of Japan's secret societies. Late in 1927 he visited Tokyo to discuss strategy and terms. His aging but increasingly influential host was Toyama Mitsuru, and he conferred also with Uchida Ryohei and publisher Akiyama, among other ultranationalist friends. Tanaka personally pledged support to the Kuomintang in its campaign to crush the communist forces and secure dominion over China south of the Yangtze River. At the same time, according to official Japanese documents, Chiang Kai-shek assured Tanaka that Japan's interests would be respected in the event of a successful campaign. Warlord Chang Tso-lin, thanks to Yamamoto's efforts, also was prepared to carry out his part of the bargain—not knowing, of course, that his Japanese friends actually intended to drive him out of China.

This masterly scheme, which Metternich himself could scarcely have improved upon, had the advantage of being more or less legal by international standards and might well have been successfully accomplished. But as Tanaka and Yamamoto toiled in the vineyards of the zaibatsu, the military extremists (abetted by Mori) made every effort to prevent their fruits from ripening. Japan's Kwantung Army and civilian ultranationalists, if friendly toward Chiang Kai-shek, were irreconcilably opposed to Chang Tso-lin. For many years the Black Dragon Society and certain junior officers in Japan's army had been trying to assassinate him and at one time had about three thousand men deployed for the purpose, all to no avail. Now, with his well-equipped armies and the backing of the Japanese government, he was a greater menace than ever to their plans. The firm establishment of a Manchurian puppet regime would help, of course, to stabilize the political situation, which had become precarious. But this very stability, if achieved, would deprive the impatient militarists of excuses for taking decisive action.

In May of 1928 the government—as though responding to a self-destructive compulsion—played directly into the hands of the aggressive faction by dispatching an army division to China, obviously to thwart the Kuomintang's military movements. In Tsinan, the capital of Shantung province, the Japanese found themselves face to face with Chinese troops commanded by Chiang Kai-shek. Japanese officers, exceeding their authority, provoked a battle in which they expelled the Chinese soldiers and seized Tsinan. This arrogance infuriated Chiang, who felt that he had been betrayed. Logically, he interpreted the action as part of an attempt to strengthen Chang Tso-lin's Peking regime. He took this assault so seriously that the Kuomintang appealed to the League of Nations and the United States for redress. Getting no satisfaction from them, Chiang resumed his attack upon Peking with redoubled vigor and partially encircled the city. Chang Tso-lin, realizing that he was about to be trapped, ordered his troops to withdraw into Manchuria and abandoned Peking on June 2, 1927.

During the night of June 4, he and his cadres were aboard a special train speeding toward Mukden. By dawn many Japanese and other foreign dignitaries had assembled at Mukden Station to welcome the old soldier back home. The long journey almost over, Chang and his staff, in the eighth coach of a twenty-car train, were preparing for the arrival. The train started across a bridge. Shouting above the clatter of the wheels, an aide told Chang: "It's cold; you'd better put something on." Chang stood up and reached for his overcoat, but at that moment there was a shattering roar as the bridge blew up. The train was derailed and the eighth car was demolished. The generalissimo, last of China's powerful warlords, was terribly injured and died a few hours later.

The Kwantung Army immediately blamed Chinese saboteurs for the explosion and so informed the government in Tokyo. When Prime Minister Tanaka heard the news he said with a groan: "My luck has run out." As a seasoned politician he knew what he was talking about. The army's story about the atrocity was just too transparent for belief, and the opposition could be depended upon to use Tanaka's failure to control the army as an excuse to belabor the government. He anticipated, quite correctly, that the issue, added to other scandals then brewing, would bring down his cabinet in disgrace and that his elaborately contrived Manchurian program was doomed.

Yamamoto Jotaro, having been informed about the explosion, was waiting in the SMR's office when Chang's death was announced. According to an assistant, the usually wooden-faced empire builder made a bitter grimace. "What I have been planning ever since I came to Manchuria has turned into bubbles," he said gloomily. After a silence someone asked: "What shall we do?" Yamamoto's cryptic reply was: "Wait awhile." Whatever else he may have had in mind, he was still president of the SMR, and he had to coexist with the Kwantung Army.

Opportunities for conciliation were not wanting, since military radicals continually pestered the big capitalists for money to promote their schemes. In the previous year Yamamoto had been invited, as a representative of Mitsui, to a teahouse in Tokyo where a group of officers tendered their thanks (in advance, apparently) for contributions to support some adventurous operation in China. In acknowledgment Yamamoto said with wry humor: "I am panic-stricken at being summoned by dignitaries of the army." But apparently he complied with their demand because, after his appointment to the SMR presidency, one of the officers he had met at the teahouse began importuning him to donate a preposterous sum for the construction of a hostel and recreation center for veterans, which would be dedicated to heroes who had fallen in the Russo-Japanese War.

After the assassination of Chang the same officer, Colonel Tsujimura

Nanzo, paid Yamamoto another visit and became insistent in his demand for one million yen. Yamamoto's business instincts got the better of his judgment, and he protested that the SMR was, after all, a profit-making company. At this ill-considered remark, the colonel became furious. He pointed out correctly that the SMR was no ordinary business enterprise, but had been formed to promote the national interest. Its existence had been made possible by an enormous sacrifice of Japanese lives, he declared, and its security was dependent upon miserably underpaid railway guards—the soldiers of the Kwantung Army—who, for a cash wage of little more than one yen per month, not only defended the SMR's properties at the risk of their lives but often worked as common laborers to repair its tracks. "If they are only protecting your profits, I'll have them [the army] remove the guards along the railway!" the colonel threatened.

Yamamoto, well informed about the intransigence of younger officers (who, as he probably knew by now, had wrecked his plans by blowing up Chang's train), changed his tack. "Don't be so angry," he said. "I really can't understand the purpose of the building because the prospectus is so full of jargon. Please tell me frankly about your scheme."

"It's for getting rid of the reds," the colonel explained intensely. "Nowadays communism is rampant, and even the military has been infiltrated with such thinking. Isn't it a noble project to have three million veterans rise up and expel the reds?"

"That's interesting," Yamamoto replied soothingly. "Why didn't you tell me sooner?" By rechanneling funds intended for another project—a hall commemorating the twentieth anniversary of the SMR's founding—he was able to donate the million yen without cutting into the stockholders' profits.[10] Thus he appeased the army's extremists temporarily, but his surrender further hardened the pattern of military arrogance and blackmail that soon brought great misfortune to his party and to its patron, the House of Mitsui.

20 · Challenging the World

JAPAN'S ECONOMIC POSITION at the end of the 1920s was expressed in the slogan "Export or Die." The Wall Street crash was indeed ominous for countries dependent upon foreign trade for a livelihood, and none seemed to be more vulnerable than Japan to the worldwide depression that ensued. Overseas markets for Japan's goods became exceedingly inhospitable as purchasing power declined and foreign governments restricted imports or raised tariffs to protect their own industries. By 1931 Japan's exports had plunged to less than half their predepression value. Prices sagged, production had to be curtailed, and unemployment reached unprecedented levels as the deflationary spiral ran its course.

Japanese as individuals have a morbid proclivity for self-destruction, but collectively they are tenacious of life. For them, in the Great Depression, there was no thought of a Gandhian reversion to the agrarian self-sufficiency of the Tokugawa period—which would have meant political as well as economic suicide. Instead, the whole nation was mobilized for a counterattack.

The international challenge was countered by two strategies, both familiar to trading countries. Having been excluded from overseas markets, and having lost in consequence the foreign exchange needed for purchasing raw materials, Japan redoubled its efforts to consolidate and expand its empire on the continent. And while proceeding ruthlessly to secure that empire at the expense of China, the zaibatsu launched an export campaign that provoked far greater antagonism among the major economic powers of the West than did their interference on the continent.

Using the poverty of other peoples as an entering wedge, Japanese traders shipped goods to depressed markets at irresistibly low prices. Cutting costs to the minimum, Japan's manufacturers sent forth a torrent of merchandise that, while often shoddy, found purchasers who could afford nothing better. At the same time they devised ways of producing standard-quality goods at prices that astounded even the most experienced competitors. By replacing old weaving machinery with the latest Toyoda automatic looms—and by cutting the wages of their employees—Japanese mills compensated for their geographic disadvantages. In 1932 they overtook the British, to make Japan the world's biggest exporter of cotton goods, by shipping during that year more than one billion yards of cloth. This helped, of course, to boost Japan's trade balance, but it virtually wrecked the British weaving industry. Cheap Japanese textiles drove British products out of that nation's own colonies and found willing buyers in the very shadows of its domestic mills in Manchester and Liverpool. The United States' textile markets in the Americas were invaded in the same way and in some cases were almost monopolized by Japan's fabrics.

Even after importing logs from the western United States and Canada, Japanese plywood makers were able to sell their product at $56.50 per thousand board feet delivered to the East Coast, while the United States product cost $137.50 on the West Coast where it was made. When 150-power microscopes made in the United States were wholesaling at $7.50, comparable Japanese products could be bought at $1.95 retail, duty paid, in Boston. Japanese imitations of American toothbrushes selling at thirty-nine cents were selling for only ten cents at Woolworth's; and Japanese flashlights cost only two-thirds as much as did similar American products. In Latin American markets the Japanese offered an imitation English bicycle with flashy trimmings for eight dollars, half the price of the nearest foreign competitor. One writer encountered a Japanese trade ship calling with samples at West African ports, including automobiles at $275, typewriters at $12.50, bicycles at $5, and bicycle tires costing only seven cents each.

Some makers of Japanese goods were none too scrupulous. The tale is told that certain export goods were boldly marked "Made in USA"; when charged with deception, sellers explained innocently that the merchandise came from the town of Usa in Kyushu. There were socks that bore the Old-English lettering made famous by Interwoven, but upon careful reading one perceived that this Japanese trademark spelled "Interwomen." Competitors believed such stories, even though many of them were canards; and the small, scurrying salesmen of Japan with their sample cases, once regarded with tolerant amusement, became objects of contempt and chauvinistic hatred. But the Japanese, who no longer entertained any illusions about qualifying for social equality in the West, persisted doggedly, quite satisfied with the feeling of superiority conferred upon them by a steeply rising trade index.

Mitsui Bussan was in the vanguard of this commercial crusade, of course, handling almost half of Japan's foreign trade and an even larger share of commerce with its territories in Taiwan, Korea, and Manchuria. One of the keenest minds in the Mitsui organization was

Bussan's obanto Yasukawa Yunosuke, fittingly nicknamed "Razor." A sharp and calculating trader schooled by Masuda, Yamamoto, and Mori, he outwitted even the British and the Dutch in winning markets and sources of raw materials in Southeast Asia. Through his efforts Mitsui gained control of huge rubber plantations in Malaya and Sumatra, and for many years afterward Bussan dominated international rubber markets. As he moved aggressively into the East Indies, the Dutch resorted to imposing trade restrictions that aggravated anti-colonialist passions among the islanders and weakened the Nether-lands' grip on those valuable possessions.

Yasukawa also set up sugar mills in the Dutch East Indies, secured supplies of Southeast Asian bauxite for Japan's young aluminum in-dustry, and scouted Canada by airplane to find good sites for pulp mills. (His interest in pulp was related to his favorite project, the Toyo Rayon Company, a fast-growing subsidiary of which he was founder and managing director.) Bussan dominated Japan's trade in petroleum, foodstuffs, and fertilizer. Bussan handled half of Japan's coal exports, forty percent of its machinery, and twenty-five percent of its raw silk, while importing thirty-three percent of the grain and eighteen percent of the cotton. Bussan was the biggest dealer in Manchurian soybeans, exports of which amounted to more than two million tons a year around 1930, and was almost alone in importing phosphate rock for use in fertilizers. With its control of Nippon Flour Mills, then Japan's largest miller, Bussan was exporting flour to China, Manchuria, and other Asian markets. Bussan owned more than 100,000 acres of forest in northern Japan, operated sawmills in Hokkaido and Sakhalin, and cut and imported timber from Korea, Taiwan, and the Philippines.

The firm's machinery department supplied the means for Japan's breathtaking industrial development. Among the sixty large foreign companies for which Bussan served as sole agent were Bucyrus-Erie, Pratt & Whitney, Sperry Gyroscope, Wright Aeronautical, Babcock & Wilcox, Mosler Safe, Bristol Aeroplane, Burmeister & Wain, Interna-tional Nickel, American Smelting & Refining, and International General Electric. The Japanese company also had established industrial ventures in cooperation with General Electric (which in 1973 is still the largest stockholder in the Mitsui-affiliated Tokyo Shibaura Electric Company), Vickers-Armstrong, Standard Vacuum, Babcock & Wilcox, Otis Elevator, and Carrier Engineering, among others. By that time, too, Mitsui was represented in the world's major cities and operated "independent" trading affiliates in Germany, France, and South Africa.

The early 1930s brought a rapid expansion of Japan's merchant fleet, and the integration of shipping with trade was a very important factor in making possible Japan's competitiveness in the world's markets.

When the depression was at its worst and, in all maritime countries, some sixteen million tons of shipping were idle, Japan had only sixteen thousand tons laid up and about three million tons plying global trade routes, usually loaded to the scuppers with exports, imports, or commodities picked up along the way for delivery to other foreign ports.

A considerable proportion of export and import cargo was carried by the Mitsui fleet, which consisted of fifteen motorships and twenty steamships aggregating 220,000 tons. In the twelve years since it was founded in 1919, Bussan's Tama Shipyard in Okayama Prefecture had built seventy-one oceangoing vessels, aggregating 263,000 tons, to strengthen Japan's merchant marine.

The word *bussan* means "products," and it is hard to think of any that Yasukawa's Bussan didn't handle. It has been said that the firm traded in every commodity except human flesh, but even that reservation was incorrect, because Japanese emigrants were considered legitimate instruments for promoting trade. Mitsui backed a company that gave assistance to Japanese settling in Brazil, whose coffee planters needed energetic workers willing to labor for low wages. By 1934 there were 173,000 Japanese in Brazil. Meanwhile Bussan and Toyo Menka (which had begun as Bussan's cotton department), seeing a good market for textiles, offered to buy Brazil's entire cotton crop, the bulk of which was then going to England. Japanese colonists were encouraged to grow cotton and received aid from Mitsui for doing so. Within a few years the state of São Paulo doubled its cotton crop, some forty percent of which was grown by Japanese.

The same two firms led Japan's advance into India, buying raw cotton and flooding the country with textiles—645 million square yards in 1932 alone—at prices not only lower than Britain's but lower than those of Indian mills, which employed the world's cheapest labor! By the early 1930s Japan was buying about forty percent of its raw cotton from India and was by far the largest purchaser of American fiber.

Wherever there were natural resources—in China, Manchuria, Korea, Southeast Asia, North and South America, or Europe—Yasukawa's agents were present and active. Such diverse and widespread activity inspired Fujihara Ginjiro, the "grand old man" of Oji Paper, to write in one of his books, *The Spirit of Japanese Industry:* "Our enterprising traders of the present day find their way to the remotest corners of the world. No matter how trying the climate may be, these modern pioneers go wherever they can to sell Japanese goods."[1]

But much of Japan's exported merchandise earned only a slim margin of profit and at times was even sold at a loss simply to earn foreign exchange. Increasingly there were charges of "dumping" and cries for protectionist legislation, especially in the prime markets of Europe and North America. Far from earning praise for her "spirit of enterprise," Japan was feared as a competitor, castigated as an imitator, and condemned as an interloper. A very large share of Japan's production came from tiny workshops manned by miserably paid workers living at subsistence level, and in many foreign countries those "sweat shop conditions" in Japan were played up as a pretext for excluding Japanese goods.

Much of the foreign criticism was exaggerated or unjustified. In major products, such as cotton textiles, labor costs constituted a very small fraction of the selling price; the competitiveness of Japanese goods, other than toys and sundries, was attributable largely to efficiency, the principles of which Japan had learned from the West. As *Fortune* magazine wrote in 1936: "The Italian government, while its press screamed Yellow Peril and Social Dumping and Wake Up Europe, admitted that one reason why Japanese silks were selling in silk-making Italy might be that Japanese machinery and Japanese organization were better."[2] Furthermore, Japan's share of world trade in the mid-1930s was less than four percent (as compared with nearly eight percent in 1972) and was only a marginal factor in the economies of other industrial countries. But Japan, being the most conspicuous intruder in many markets, was made the scapegoat for inefficient producers everywhere.

Such hostility and sharpening retaliation from foreigners stiffened the posture of those Japanese who argued that imperialism was the only possible solution to Japan's economic problems. Expansionist-minded people at the same time advocated domestic dictatorship, which they regarded as necessary for eliminating parliamentary confusion, political corruption, "dangerous thoughts," and restive laborers. Thus the issue of how trade should be fostered was inseparably entangled with the whole question of social and political organization.

Actually, among Japanese, no one disputed the thought that Japan should increase its power on the Asian continent. But as usual, some leaders advocated gradual expansion by economic and political means, while others demanded forthright aggression as soon as possible. The two main political parties were constantly struggling over this issue. The Seiyukai took the harder line, perhaps because the party's main backer, Mitsui, had by far the largest stake in disputed Manchuria and was also most active in China proper. The Mitsubishi-supported Minseito favored a course that gave more heed to international law and opinion, although the foreign policies of the rival parties were not always distinct. Both were dedicated to establishing Japan as a world power of the first rank. And that was precisely the position the dominant powers of the West would not tolerate.

Japan's military leaders generally were in favor of using force and enjoyed full support from the civilian ultranationalists, who had indoctrinated many younger officers. Most radical in this respect was the army, in which the rural population was strongly represented. At that time the peasantry was particularly hard hit by the depression. The price of rice had declined by about forty percent; and that of raw silk fell by fifty percent, as American demand was cut almost in half during 1930. In 1931 the average net income from agriculture (excluding silk) per farming family was less than $20 for the year. Misery was most intense in northern Japan, where it was common practice for farmers to sell their daughters into prostitution—at $30 to $150 a girl—so that the rest of the family could survive. Young men from depressed areas became itinerant laborers, emigrated to Manchuria, or, if lucky, enlisted in the army. Junior officers, many of whom came of peasant stock, learned about such demoralizing poverty from their men and sympathized with them. Unable to accept solutions offered by spokesmen for the socialistic left, they were increasingly attracted to the doctrines of revolutionary rightists, who rallied under the banners of authoritarian nationalism and imperialism.

The zaibatsu, although concerned over the extremist threat, were friendly toward the military services, who were not only their best customers but also very necessary as protectors in Manchuria, a place that had become even more turbulent since the assassination of Generalissimo Chang Tso-lin and the successes of the increasingly anti-Japanese nationalists in China. Japan's investments in Manchuria had risen steadily to approximately $735 million by 1931; and although the SMR was the biggest investor, the zaibatsu were the main beneficiaries. Those investments and the great volume of business they engendered were precious to the zaibatsu. Fujihara Ginjiro, one of Mitsui's most eloquent spokesmen, was unabashed in his support of military imperialism: "Money spent on armaments is capital which promotes the advance of us businessmen. From the people's point of view it is a kind of investment. They invest and develop the nation's power. Using this power, producers advance steadily in the world."

In the same vein, Fujihara wrote: "I am far from recommending the use of armed forces for economic expansion in an aggressive way, but I rely on the army and navy for the protection of our foreign trade needs. . . . We have a splendid opportunity to expand abroad; it is the manifest destiny of the Japanese nation."[3]

The key to Japan's control of Manchuria was the SMR, but that vast transportation and industrial complex, in the midst of a hostile people, could not function without the protection of the Kwantung Army. Under a treaty with China those forces served as guards of the railway zone and other leased installations. This role gave the Kwantung Army enormous power, which its officers had begun to use with scant regard for orders issued by the government in Tokyo. The rebelliousness of the officers, especially the younger ones, was largely a product of agitation by civilian nationalists, many of whom were employees of the SMR. The assassination of Chang Tso-lin (the details of which were concealed until after the Second World War) had been perpetrated by such elements in order to provoke hostilities and to use the occasion for a coup d'état to bring Manchuria completely under Japan's dominion.

The plot had failed because its ringleader, a colonel, had failed to obtain enough support from his superiors. Even so, Japan's army, and especially the Kwantung Army, was riddled with such conspiracies, the stated aim of which was a "Showa Restoration," similar to that of 1868, in which the latter-day "samurai" would create a "revolutionary empire." Participants were convinced that, if they could liberate the emperor from such pernicious influences as the zaibatsu and their political minions, they could build for His Imperial Majesty a wholesome, humanitarian dictatorship under which Japan would recover its ancient glory, assume a parental role in Asia, and eventually conquer the world. Kita Ikki called this crusade "a divine mission, an Asian Monroe Doctrine," by which the flag of the rising sun would "light the darkness of the whole world."[4]

The plot to kill Chang Tso-lin was indeed enlightening, but not in the way intended. It exposed the aggressiveness of the rightist radicals and helped to bring down Tanaka's essentially proarmy cabinet. It was supplanted by a generally hostile Minseito government headed by Hamaguchi Osachi. Members of his moderate cabinet were finance minister Inoue Junnosuke and foreign minister Shidehara Kijuro (who had married into Baron Iwasaki's family). Inoue was a "dove" whose aim was to hold down military expenditures; and Shidehara's long-range project was to build a bridge of friendship between Japan and China.

Even in more carefree days such "unpatriotic" activities were barely tolerated, but now, as the militarists began to flex their muscles, they became suicidal. This was vividly demonstrated by Prime Minister Hamaguchi, who lived up to his nickname "Lion" by refusing to kowtow to the brass hats. In 1930, at the London Naval Conference, Japan's delegates reluctantly agreed to continue the 5:5:3 ratio that subordinated their navy to those of Great Britain and the United States.

Their acquiescence outraged the navy's general staff, who urged the government to reconsider. Hamaguchi stood by his well-reasoned decision and advised the emperor that the naval treaty should be ratified. This action caused a country-wide furor, fanned by the ultranationalists and the opposition Seiyukai. Shidehara was attacked for his "weak-kneed" diplomacy, and Prime Minister Hamaguchi for having committed lese majesty. Hamaguchi's most violent detractors were civilian terrorists and junior army officers of a faction whose intellectual leader was Kita Ikki.

On November 14, 1930, as controversy over the naval treaty raged in Japan's press and in public meetings, Prime Minister Hamaguchi was passing through Tokyo Station. He was probably thinking about the late premier Hara, who had been assassinated at the same station, in the same month nine years before, and after the conclusion of an unpopular naval treaty. Hamaguchi should not have been too surprised when a pistol fired by a rightist patriot wounded him gravely. On that same day another young rightist happened to be visiting Uchida of the Black Dragon Society at his home. A student ran into the room, telling about the shooting at Tokyo Station, which had been perpetrated by a man they all knew well. The visitor, Kodama Yoshio, who today is Japan's leading ultranationalist gang boss, wrote in his memoirs: "I distinctly remember Uchida Ryohei turning toward me with bright sparks alighting in his dark eyes, saying, 'Japan has finally entered the tumultuous period. It's the march of time!'"[5]

In terms of *Realpolitik* there was good reason for the impatience of the expansionists. The Kuomintang government was gaining influence and military strength in north China, for which Japan had important plans. The Soviet Union, always regarded with suspicion by Japan's government and with hatred by its military, was building up its forces along the Manchurian frontier. And in Manchuria a violent anti-Japanese campaign had been launched. By assassinating Chang Tso-lin, the Kwantung Army had hardened the resistance of the Manchurians and especially of Chang Hsueh-liang, son of the murdered warlord and now commander-in-chief of the Chinese armies in the region. In fact, the Japanese militarists had driven him into the welcoming embrace of Chiang Kai-shek, who since his betrayal by Tanaka, wanted to reestablish Chinese control in Manchuria.

The Chinese had already begun to offer serious economic competition to the Japanese in Manchuria when "Young Marshal" Chang started a railroad-building program that threatened the dominance of the SMR. In addition, the Chinese government was determined to recover those of its territories that had been leased to foreigners, along with rights for railway operations and coastal trade. Following the example of Japan in the late nineteenth century, China was fighting for its economic independence; but the Japanese, now in the position of imperialists themselves, were indignant at such uncooperativeness. The SMR's profits were being undermined by the depression, and other Japanese firms doing business in China and Manchuria were also suffering. Under harassment by the mainland nationalists, the companies formed organizations clamoring for a sterner policy, and in this were abetted by the militarists, rightists, and the Seiyukai Party. From the Japanese nationalist point of view, the time for decisive action was long overdue.

Early in 1931 a group of army officers calling themselves the Sakurakai (Cherry Blossom Society) devised an elaborate conspiracy to bomb the offices of Japan's two main political parties and the prime minister's residence, as a prelude to seizing the Diet and installing a militaristic government that would take a tougher line. Although little was revealed publicly at the time, later it became known that this so-called March Incident was planned by Okawa Shumei, director of the SMR's East Asian Research Institute, and by Kita Ikki, who seems to have been a confidential adviser to Mori Kaku. Still functioning as Mitsui's kingmaker in the Seiyukai and its outpost in the extremist camp, Mori participated in the plot, which may have been an attempt to carry out his own plan of imposing a dictatorship upon Japan.

The conspiracy was revealed prematurely and therefore had to be abandoned. Under pressure from the military the Minseito government prudently hushed it up, just as the Tanaka government had quashed its inquiry into the death of Chang Tso-lin. So the conspirators went on with their plotting, observed but unhindered, to prepare the way for another attempt at a coup. In this they were assisted by such indefatigable underground organizers as Uchida Ryohei and Toyama Mitsuru, who despite their long and profitable association with the Mitsui interests, seem to have been no less dedicated than their militant associates to undermining the influence of the zaibatsu.

While maintaining close liaison with the Kwantung Army, Okawa and Kita unified the diverse elements of the rightist movement into a national federation called Nikkyo (Nippon Aikokusha Kyodo Toso Kyogikai, the All-Japan Patriots Joint Struggle Society), which worked cooperatively with like-minded societies, such as the Black Dragon. Those groups, in various combinations and amply funded by wealthy sympathizers, had long been able to sway public opinion, intimidate statesmen, and even overthrow cabinets. Soon, in secret alliance with military leaders, they were to overthrow what remained of constitutional government in Japan.

The hard-core nationalists had placed members or fellow travelers in all departments of the government. Baron Hiranuma Kiichiro, an ardent national socialist, was vice-president of the privy council (and later would be the council's president and a prime minister). His close associate in the Seiyukai, Mori Kaku, was an intimate of Toyama Mitsuru and had been implicated in earlier terrorist plots, including the attempt on Prime Minister Hamaguchi. The latter's Minister of Home Affairs was Adachi Kenzo, a Machiavellian politician who complemented his police duties with membership in the Black Dragon. (He had first gained notoriety by participating in the assassination of the queen of Korea three decades earlier.) A fiery spokesman for the hardliners was Dietman Matsuoka Yosuke, a former SMR vice-president under Yamamoto Jotaro, now a power in Seiyukai politics. An adviser, together with Baron Hiranuma, to a secret society for agitating army reservists, Matsuoka was one of the most eloquent civilian champions of expansionism. Early in 1931 he declared in the Diet: "We feel suffocated as we observe the internal and external situations. What we are seeking is that which is minimal for living beings. . . . We are seeking room that will let us breathe."[6]

Soon afterward, on the day when the dying Prime Minister Hamaguchi appeared in the Diet for the first time since the attempt on his life, members of Nikkyo marched through the streets of Tokyo shouting "Down with the Privileged Class!" and "Revolution under the Emperor's Banner!" Among the chanted slogans the names of Mitsui and Mitsubishi were heard with disturbing frequency.

Such demonstrations, unimpeded by the authorities (who no doubt were too busy suppressing "dangerous thoughts" among the leftists), had been only a prelude to the March Incident. That was followed by the dynamiting of finance minister Inoue Junnosuke's residence. Then, late in the summer, foreign minister Shidehara became aware that the Kwantung Army was preparing for "direct action" against Marshal Chang Hsueh-liang in Manchuria. He and Prime Minister Wakatsuki (who had formed another Minseito cabinet after the death of Hamaguchi) protested to war minister Minami. The latter, a violent critic of Shidehara's conciliatory policy, was uninterested in their protest, but after a personal warning from the emperor to prevent unauthorized actions in Manchuria, he wrote a letter to the commander of the Kwantung Army in Mukden, instructing him to cancel any aggressive plans.

Minami entrusted that extremely important message, stamped "Urgent and Confidential," to Major General Tatekawa Yoshitsugu. He, instead of flying to Port Arthur, took first a boat across the Sea of Japan and then a slow train through Korea, arriving at last in Mukden on September 18. He was met by a colonel from general staff headquarters and had a long conversation with him, but neglected to mention the letter he carried, although he knew its contents. Later he was taken to a geisha party by a major of the general staff, but still kept silent about his errand. After amusing himself with the girls and calming their fears when heavy artillery fire broke out late in the evening, he slept soundly until morning. His peculiar behavior was caused not by absentmindedness but by the fact that he was an important member of the Cherry Blossom Society, whose members had been leading participants in the March Incident, and a confederate of the Kwantung Army plotters, one of whom was the colonel who had met him the previous night.

He learned in the morning, with feigned surprise, that fighting had already broken out between Japanese and Chinese troops. According to the Kwantung Army, Chinese saboteurs had bombed a train near Mukden (a story recalling the Chang Tso-lin affair), and the army had been forced to open fire with heavy artillery, which curiously enough had been emplaced secretly a week before. During the confusion in Mukden as the Japanese forces prepared for action, the considerate General Tatekawa seems to have kept out of their way. At any rate he did not reappear officially until around midnight of September 19, by which time Mukden and Changchun had been occupied and the Japanese cabinet in Tokyo had been presented with a *fait accompli*. Only then did the dilatory envoy, after consulting with the general staff, remember to deliver the urgent letter from Minister of War Minami forbidding any such warlike action.

In the name of "self-defense" the Kwantung Army, defying its civil government at home, then set about conquering Manchuria. That proved to be easier than had been expected because Chiang Kai-shek, reserving his strength to fight internal rivals, ordered Marshal Chang Hsueh-liang "resolutely to maintain the principle of nonresistance."

The Kwantung Army's insolent coup, which definitely was not provoked by the Chinese but, rather, was prepared and executed by the imperial army with the full knowledge of its highest leaders, was almost universally hailed by the Japanese people. Rich and poor alike believed that the conquest of Manchuria would bring economic blessings and greater glory to Dai Nippon. Naturally, they were told nothing of the circumstances that had preceded the conquest. The government kept its own counsel and tacitly accepted the army's story. Major newspapers, including the previously antimilitary *Asahi Shimbun,* approved the invasion and followed the official line in reporting it. The foreign ministry made efforts, partially successful, to overcome the skepticism of foreign governments, while Mitsui Bussan carried on a private campaign to mollify its overseas clients. A letter from a director of Bussan to the president of a leading American corporation, with which

Mitsui had licensing agreements, was couched in these soothing phrases: "Your attention has of late been drawn to the Manchurian affair, the unfortunate collision of the Japanese military forces with the Chinese troops. . . .

"According to dispatches from Washington, the State Department is said to have been a little skeptical of Japanese aims at first, but has since modified its views. . . .

"Realizing, however, that there usually are all sorts of propaganda literature circulated, and given credence in some quarters, at times like the present, I venture to send you herewith a brief outline of the Manchurian question as it appeared in the *Asahi Shimbun,* the most impartial and influential newspaper in Japan."[7]

The enclosure from *Asahi* was, of course, the totally misleading version based upon the Kwantung Army's report. Why the central government and the zaibatsu accepted the coup so readily is puzzling, because it dealt a strong blow to the nation's technically legal expansion policy. Thereafter, in order to defend this clear act of aggression, the government would have to center its whole foreign policy around a position that was morally and legally indefensible. Undoubtedly, the zaibatsu hoped to gain abundant rewards from the army's secure control over Manchuria, but ominous signs to the contrary were not long in appearing. Very soon after the Mukden affair a trio of Kwantung Army officers celebrated the event with much sakè and were reported to have gloated over it in these terms: "We have succeeded! When we return to the homeland we shall carry out a coup d'état and do away with the party system, establishing National Socialism with the Emperor as the center. We shall abolish capitalists like Mitsui and Mitsubishi and carry out an even distribution of wealth."[8]

One of the gloaters was General Ishihara Kanji, the most brilliant political strategist of the Kwantung Army, who especially wanted to keep the zaibatsu out of Manchuria and even spoke of "severing relations with Japan in case the Manchurian expedition fails."[9]

Only a few weeks after the coup the government stopped a conspiracy, headed by Okawa Shumei and Lt. Col. Hashimoto Kingoro (a ringleader in the March Incident and the Mukden affair), which intended to establish a military junta after annihilating the whole cabinet by bombardment from the air. This "October Incident," too, was hidden from the public and again the plotters escaped unpunished. But Prime Minister Wakatsuki, remembering the fate of "Lion" Hamaguchi, lost all heart for his job and resigned quietly in December.

He was succeeded by the elderly Inukai Tsuyoshi, a maverick leader of the Seiyukai who had long fought for representative government and for closer ties between Japan and China. As one of Sun Yat-sen's dearest friends in Japan, he had taken part in many revolutionary schemes in China, and while supporting Japanese expansion, he opposed any action that would obstruct good relations between the two governments. For that reason he deplored the provocative actions of the Kwantung Army and was considered to be "antimilitary." Apparently this attitude was pleasing to the emperor, who upon asking Inukai to form a cabinet, told him: "The army's interference in domestic and foreign politics, and its willfulness, is a state of affairs which, for the good of the nation, we must view with apprehension."[10]

It is said that when he was offered the position Inukai was warned by his old friend Toyama not to take it, but that he felt obliged to carry out the emperor's wishes. The prime minister was far from being a liberal; indeed, he belonged to Hiranuma's Kokuhonsha, or National Foundation Society, a chauvinistic club among whose members were many high-ranking military officers and business leaders, notably Ikeda Seihin, who headed the Mitsui Bank. Nevertheless, one of Inukai's first acts was to send a secret mission to his friend Chiang Kai-shek, seeking a political settlement with China. Also secretly, he discussed with the emperor the issuing of an imperial rescript commanding the Kwantung Army to suspend its operations in Manchuria. Unfortunately for Inukai he confided in his chief cabinet secretary and trusted associate, Mori Kaku, who not only was a militarist with terrorist connections but also was ambitious to succeed Inukai or to replace him with the fascistic Hiranuma. Mori's position enabled him to intercept and decode the premier's secret messages to and from China and to prepare countermeasures.

A problem hardly less vexing than Manchuria was the gold drain, which was bleeding the treasury and threatening to bring on another financial panic. Since the Great War Japan had maintained an embargo on gold shipments as a means of protecting the yen; but in 1930, with economic conditions becoming critical, Minister of Finance Inoue Junnosuke decided to lift the embargo, reasoning that the move would stabilize foreign exchange rates, boost foreign trade, and improve the balance of payments.

His hypothesis was dubious and his timing calamitous. Faced with extreme competition in world markets, Japan's exports continued to drop. Moreover, a debilitating outflow of gold followed his action. Shortly after the coup in Manchuria, England abandoned the gold standard, causing serious depreciation of Japan's foreign reserves, most of which were held in London. In Japan prices fell, the number of bankruptcies rose, and the census of jobless workers approached one million. Still the stubborn finance minister clung to the gold standard.

The Seiyukai had long been demanding reimposition of the gold embargo. In anticipation of this inevitable change, which would cause a devaluation of the yen, financiers, traders, and speculators stepped up their purchases of dollars. From June 1930 to December 1931 the Yokohama Specie Bank alone sold 740 million yen worth of dollars. By far the biggest buyer was New York's National City Bank, but the zaibatsu also bought heavily. The Bank of Japan's gold reserve, which stood at one billion yen in 1929, had dropped to 470 million yen by December 1931, when the Inukai Cabinet assumed office.

The new finance minister, Takahashi Korekiyo, immediately reimposed the gold embargo and suspended the convertibility of Bank of Japan notes. Japan finally had abandoned the gold standard, and most businessmen were grateful. In his New Year's statement for 1932 Muto Sanji, head of Mitsui's Kanegafuchi Spinning Company, said: "We have fought for the replacement of the gold embargo for the past two and a half years, and our fight has resulted in victory. The nation must thank Adachi Kenzo."[11]

But shortly thereafter the charge was being made (without proof) that the egregious Adachi Kenzo, as home minister in the previous cabinet, had plotted with Mori the downfall of the Minseito government for the benefit of unnamed zaibatsu and had received almost one million dollars for his help. As expected, the value of the yen skidded dizzily. Takahashi, intent upon increasing exports, paid no attention to that domestic complication, and soaring prices were added to the nearly insupportable burdens of Japan's poor.

A campaign of vilification was launched against the "Dollar Buyers," who were accused of having sold out the national interest. Accusations of corruption and greed fanned hatred for the zaibatsu among workers, farmers, and small businessmen, still racked by the depression. The Mitsuis, who were said to have profited by some fifty million dollars overnight on their exchange deals, drew the severest criticism. Agitators distributed handbills saying "Death to the Dollar Buyers!" "Down with Mitsui!" "Down with Dan Takuma and Ikeda Seihin!" Postcards were sent anonymously to depositors, warning of a run upon Mitsui Bank. Soon after the gold embargo was restored, a gang of rightists made a noisy attack on the residence of Baron Mitsui Hachiroemon in Tokyo.

Mitsui Gomei's official explanation of these financial affairs was summed up by Ikeda, who wrote in his autobiography: "As soon as Britain abandoned the gold standard, the sterling bloc followed. The only countries maintaining the gold standard were Japan and the United States. Then Mitsui Bank's capital in London, amounting to 80 million yen, was frozen. In self-defense, Mitsui Bank immediately bought $21,350,000 from the [Yokohama] Specie Bank. That's all the Bank bought, but Mitsui Bussan also bought some dollars [about $20 million]. Compared with the National City Bank, who purchased 273 million yen worth of dollars, it's nothing."[12]

But even though finance minister Takahashi's economic policy was boosting foreign trade strongly, the people were not listening to the voice of reason. They knew that the profits of the "dollar buyers" came out of the taxpayers' pockets and that the zaibatsu were getting richer while the workers could barely survive. In 1932 farmers were so badly hit that they were mortgaging rice crops before they ripened, and in at least one prefecture half the people were reported to be starving.

Some time before these events agrarian rightists had formed a small group called the Ketsumeidan, or Blood Pledge Corps.* The leader was Inoue Nissho, a former army spy and China ronin who had become a Buddhist priest of the Nichiren sect. The Reverend Inoue, also a former follower of Toyama Mitsuru, told his blood brothers: "There is no construction without destruction. We shall sacrifice ourselves, each one killing one person of the ruling class."[13]

On their death list were sixteen leading politicians, statesmen, and financiers. Three, including Prime Minister Inukai and railway minister Tokonami, were from the Seiyukai, and three, including Inoue Junnosuke and Shidehara, were from the Minseito. Baron Dan Takuma and Ikeda Seihin represented the Mitsui zaibatsu. Three of Mitsubishi's leaders, notably Baron Iwasaki Koyata, were condemned, as were Prince Saionji, Count Makino (then lord keeper of the privy seal), and two other exalted peers.

This very mixed assortment of marked men indicated the ideological confusion of the hunters and an ignorance of the aims of their own nationalist movement, for some of the intended victims were themselves friends and supporters of leading terrorists. While the Minseito was not very friendly to the militarists, the Seiyukai had backed aggressive elements in the imperial forces, and Minister of Railways Tokonami had headed a rightist strong-arm society. Furthermore, recently both Mitsui and Mitsubishi had made large contributions to the army.

But confusion was no impediment to the Ketsumeidan's lust for blood. On a chilly evening in February 1932 former finance minister Inoue Junnosuke, soberly clad in black kimono and cloak, left his

* The blood pledge had been practiced by samurai since ancient times and the custom persisted in secret political societies and gangs after the abolition of the samurai caste. Disciples of Yoshida Shoin had signed oaths with their own blood, and it is not without significance that members of the Ketsumeidan and related societies favored the Yoshida Shoin Shrine in Tokyo as the setting for some of their most solemn ceremonies.

home to address a Minseito election rally. As the elderly statesman climbed out of his car, walking-stick in hand, a stony-faced youth fired three shots at him, point-blank. The assassin, a member of the Blood Pledge Corps, surrendered without defending himself. His duty—one man, one killing—was done.

The police knew much more than they admitted about the murder gang but somehow were unable to build a conspiracy case. After weeks of investigation, and few arrests, politicians and businessmen were uneasy. Agitation against Mitsui was particularly virulent, from labor and the left, as well as from ultranationalists. Baron Mitsui Hachiro-emon and his most conspicuous obanto, Dan and Ikeda, were given bulletproof vests and warned not to go anywhere without their body-guards.

The crescendo of anti-Mitsui feeling stemmed not only from the dollar scandal but also from a complex yet familiar situation that had developed in China. The secret mission dispatched to Peking by Prime Minister Inukai apparently had managed to reach an agreement according to which Chiang Kai-shek and the Kuomintang government, in exchange for Japanese help in defeating the Chinese 19th Route Army (whose leaders resisted Generalissimo Chiang's domination), would countenance the establishment of a Manchurian nation independent of both China and Japan. Early in January 1932, Japanese naval forces got themselves embroiled in a firefight with the 19th Route Army in Shanghai. Ignoring Chiang's order not to resist, the Chinese defended themselves so stoutly that several Japanese army divisions had to be called in to save the situation. During the battle imperial navy planes bombed densely populated areas in Shanghai. This barbarity, coming so soon after the Manchurian invasion, caused indignation in China and more misgivings in Western countries.

The Japanese people, of course, accepted their government's explanation of "self-defense" but were outraged at revelations that even while their brave lads were dying upon Shanghai's barricades the profit-minded Mitsui Bussan was selling barbed wire to the 19th Route Army. As it turned out, "Razor" Yasukawa was also supplying military goods to Marshal Chang, the chief gadfly of the Kwantung Army in Manchuria. Compounding Mitsui's "guilt" was the fact that Baron Dan, pleading poor business at Mitsui Bank (despite its profits from the dollar transactions), had been distinctly cool to the finance minister's request to purchase government bonds being floated to defray the costs of the engagement in Shanghai. The zaibatsu, having become alarmed at adverse foreign reactions to Japanese aggression, then decided as a bloc not to support the government's bond issue of twenty-two million yen. Whether or not Dan had inspired this unpatriotic decision, he was blamed for it by jingoists in the cabinet.

On February 18, 1932, while the fighting still continued in Shanghai, the Kwantung Army's Manchurian puppets proclaimed the "independent" state of Manchukuo, to be ruled by the last Manchu emperor of China, Henry Pu-Yi. The creation of Manchukuo was a transparent attempt to evade condemnation by the League of Nations, which, acting upon a complaint from China, had appointed a commission to investigate the aggression against Manchuria. As has been mentioned, the government of Japan and the zaibatsu had tried earnestly to convince foreign leaders that the Japanese coup in Manchuria had been a matter of self-defense. Soon after the establishment of Manchukuo the League's commission, headed by Lord Victor Alexander Lytton, arrived in Tokyo on their way to inspect the disputed region. Now it became the task of Japan's spokesmen to persuade the Lytton Commission that the Kwantung Army had not committed aggression, that Manchukuo was indeed independent, and that the government of Emperor Henry Pu-Yi represented the will of the Manchurians, not the ambition of its sponsors.

Japan's financial chieftains, for whom the new order in Manchuria represented unlimited opportunity, took the responsibility for indoctrinating the visitors. On March 4 the Industry Club gave a banquet for them; and Baron Dan, as president of the club, "prime minister" of Mitsui, and the most authoritative spokesmen for Japan's economic elite, had been delegated to explain Japan's position. While the others dined heartily Dan pondered over his speech, and made a few notes that ended with: "Any questions you may feel inclined to make we are pleased to answer frankly." Perhaps anticipating the queries such an invitation might elicit, he crossed out the last word before beginning his difficult task. Dan knew all the arguments by heart, and in his shy, unassuming way, presented them more convincingly than any nationalist firebrand could have done. The discussion over brandy and cigars was gentlemanly; and having done his duty, Dan retired, presumably in a mellow mood.

Breakfasting with the baroness the next morning, he glanced through the newspapers, laughing over a scurrilous cartoon in which he was labeled "dollar buyer." At about eleven o'clock a telephone call came from Mitsui Gomei, reminding him that he was to attend a board meeting. He departed without donning his bulletproof vest, although he was still high on the Reverend Inoue's death list. If Mitsui's security staff had been as alert as it was supposed to be, he might also have been warned that for the preceding week or more he had been under regular surveillance by a young member of the Blood Pledge Corps, who had gone so far as to get himself hired as a taxi driver so that he could follow the baron's car. Having become familiar with Dan's habits, the pursuer knew about when to expect him to go to his office. On that morning of March 5 the assassin had taken up a position in front of the Mitsukoshi Department Store, just across the street from Mitsui's headquarters, where he mingled with the crowd.

As expected, Baron Dan's car pulled up at the main entrance of Mitsui's building, the one that had been designed to suit his taste in architecture. At almost the same moment Baron Mitsui Hachiroemon, wearing his armored waistcoat, was entering a rear door of the same building. Dan had been warned to do the same, but complained that it was too far from his office. The waiting youth, who had been carefully drilled, edged up to the car, unobserved by the bodyguard. As Dan stepped down the assailant leaped forward, rammed a pistol against his chest, and fired twice—almost exactly as Inoue Junnosuke's assassin had done. Dan was rushed to a dispensary on the fifth floor of the Mitsukoshi store, and ten leading physicians were called to attend him. But his aorta had been pierced, and he was dead before any of them arrived. One man, one killing.

The assassin, a farm boy, explained to police interrogators that he had shot Dan to break up "the rotten political parties." According to his simple reasoning: "Behind the political parties are bosses of the zaibatsu. Mitsui is now in the limelight, and its central figure is Dan. So Dan had to be sacrificed."[14] There was some kind of warped logic in all that, especially since Dan had been denounced as the ringleader of the "dollar buyers." And yet the same gang had liquidated Inoue Junnosuke, chief opponent of the gold embargo and a critic of the profiteering that accompanied its imposition. Although the killer himself may have been quite guileless, there were deep-running currents of intrigue behind those assassinations that either escaped the notice of investigators or were deliberately ignored.

For one thing, Inoue Nissho was a disciple and confederate of Toyama Mitsuru, who—despite his long friendship with Dan Takuma —should have been immediately suspected of complicity in his murder. Just after Dan's death the Reverend Inoue, who had trained the assassin and provided him with the pistol and cartridges for his mission, took refuge in the quarters of a nationalist youth group—nicely named Tenkokai, the "Society for Heavenly Action"—adjacent to Toyama's residence and operated by the latter's son Hidezo. Ironically, Dan, who had been on friendly terms with the son as well as with the father, had contributed money (presumably Mitsui's) to support the society.

As though taking a warning from its ubiquitous enemies, Mitsui, nudged by the government, extended a loan of ten million dollars to Manchukuo even before it had been recognized by Japan, and Mitsubishi put up an equal amount. Their openhandedness was probably worth the risk, at least in terms of publicity, for now the "dollar buyers" enjoyed a bit of public commendation, typical of which was a piece in the *Jiji:* "The Mitsuis are to be admired for the loan to the Manchurian government. Their motive is not desire for profit but a desire to help the new state develop favorably. It is an international event worthy of praise."[15]

Complacency would have been premature, however. Although the Blood Pledge Corps was temporarily immobilized by the arrest of Inoue Nissho and several others of its members, the plotters of higher station, both civilian and military, were left free to commit fresh atrocities. The obvious reason for such leniency on the part of the police is that the chain of evidence led dangerously upward, through ascending levels of the power structure, to the highest echelons in business and government. For example, there were rumors that Mori Kaku had been supplying funds to the Blood Pledge Corps before the assassination of Inoue Junnosuke and Baron Dan. Mori was known to be greatly admired by Toyama and his son Hidezo and was their choice for prime minister in the event of a successful coup d'état. The only man having enough police authority to meddle with a friend of Toyama—still the invisible government—was home minister Suzuki Kisaburo, who was a close friend of both Toyama and Mori and also served as a consultant for terrorist societies. Bizarre as it may seem, Dr. Suzuki himself was included (along with his collaborator Tokonami) on the Blood Pledge Corps' list of men to be murdered, possibly because of his connection with Mitsui. So Mori, immune to any official restraint, continued plotting to form an ultrarightist Seiyukai cabinet and was not the type to balk at a few murders to pave the way.

Mori and Inukai, although close friends personally, had gravitated to opposite poles politically. Inukai, even though a fervid expansionist too, stood for the old party government system, friendly relations with the Kuomintang in China, a legal and independent government in Manchukuo, and strengthened civilian control over the South Manchurian Railway. Mori's extremist clique, which included many incumbent and former cabinet ministers, wanted to clamp an iron grip on Manchuria as a prelude to establishing Kita's "Asian Monroe Doctrine" on the continent by armed force. Japan's recognition of Manchukuo, Mori maintained, was a declaration that Japan had abandoned its servility and embarked upon an independent diplomacy. This would signal "the return of the Japanese spirit to Asia after sixty years of blindly imitating Western materialism."[16] Mori's group (opposed by

Yamamoto Jotaro and other Mitsui-Seiyukai moderates) supported the Kwantung Army's plan to develop Manchukuo along national socialist lines in preparation for imposing a similar regime upon Japan.

Such typically totalitarian thinking, which had gained wide currency in Japan since the Mukden coup, was revealed in an article that appeared on May 11, 1932 in the *Japan Times,* a mouthpiece for the foreign ministry. The writer, after denouncing doctrines of the left, asserted: "Fascism, on the other hand, safeguards the fundamental institutions of the country and at the same time puts a curb on capitalism, without eliminating private property. As for dictatorship . . . some elements might not be averse to exchanging the present economic thraldom, with its deceiving facade of freedom, for an out and out political subservience if it was accompanied by some surcease from the grinding heel of poverty."

Three days later another statement, addressed to "Like-Minded Peasants and Young Officers of the Army and Navy," was published in the *Hokkai Shimbun:* "Japan will die unless reforms are put into effect at once. People! Take arms. The only way to freedom is through 'direct action.' People! In the name of the Emperor destroy the evil officials of the Imperial Court, kill the rich. Annihilate the political parties which are the enemies of the people . . . wipe out the traitorous privileged class."

On the morning of May 15, 1932, a group of nine naval officers and army cadets, after having prayed at Yasukuni Shrine, set out for the prime minister's residence. Its leader was navy Lieutenant Koga Kiyoshi, a confederate of Inoue Nissho and a member of the fascistic Kokuhonsha, or National Foundation Society. Another old comrade of Inoue headed a second group, the Nomin Kesshitai, the "Death-Defying Farmers' Band," intent on sabotaging power stations. A third terror squad set out to bomb Mitsubishi Bank. Only Koga's group, with pistols presumably supplied by Okawa Shumei from army sources, succeeded in its mission. In broad daylight and in cold blood those uniformed members of the imperial army and navy murdered Prime Minister Inukai, in the presence of his horrified daughter and grandchild.

The May 15 plot failed in its main purpose, which was to install a militarist government, and several of the conspirators, including Okawa Shumei, Koga, and Toyama's secretary, were prosecuted. But although the nation was shocked at first, the people had been so well propagandized by the nationalists that in general they sympathized with the perpetrators rather than with the victims of those pitiless atrocities.

The crowning irony of the whole tragic affair came in the month following the assassination of Inukai, when the *Japan Times* published in

English a special supplement in homage to Toyama Mitsuru. This tribute appeared despite the fact that he, some of his close associates, and even his son, had been implicated in the murder of the nation's prime minister. It is inconceivable that the omniscient Toyama had been unaware of the plot to kill his friend Inukai. Yet one of the accolades in the *Japan Times* supplement (which was financed by Koku-honsha) had been written by the trusting Inukai himself.

The Toyama supplement, not published in Japanese-language newspapers, may have been intended to influence the Lytton Commission by presenting nationalist arguments for Japan's conquest of Manchuria. If so, the strategy was ineffective. In October 1932 the commission's report was presented, and as expected, it condemned Japanese aggression in China and Manchuria. In ensuing debates Matsuoka Yosuke, Japan's chief delegate to the League of Nations, argued that the move into Manchuria had been made to prevent the "bolshevization" of China, as well as of Manchuria and Inner Mongolia. According to the Japanese reasoning, if those two regions were to become communist, the peace and order of Korea would be disturbed immediately, and that, in turn, would affect the peace and order of Japan proper.

Such an argument, although widely accepted in 1950 (and since), seems to have been rather premature in 1933. However, President Herbert Hoover, before his defeat by Franklin Delano Roosevelt in 1932, had been reconciled to Japanese expansion in Manchuria. Although he disapproved of an aggressive Japan, he was much more fearful of Soviet or Chinese communism in Asia. Since intervention to stop Japan would mean war, and since war is a breeding ground for communism, he preferred to let the Kwantung Army establish "order" in Manchuria.

At about the time that the recognition of Manchukuo was an issue in the League of Nations, American corporation lawyer John Foster Dulles (whose uncle had signed the Lansing-Ishii agreement recognizing Japan's "special interests" in China) happened to be in Peking. At luncheon with Owen Lattimore, then a member of the United States foreign service, Dulles shared Mr. Hoover's opinion and fears: the United States should tolerate Manchukuo, said Mr. Dulles, because it was a barrier against communism in Asia. "Even at that early date," Lattimore wrote later, "he was clearly obsessed with the idea of monolithic world communism directed from the Kremlin, and particularly active and dangerous in Asia."[17]

The permissive attitude of such American conservatives was encouraging to Japanese expansionists, especially to the foreign minister, Uchida Yasuya. When he was serving as president of the South Manchurian Railway, Count Uchida (a favorite of Mori and a kinsman of

Mitsui Hachiroemon) at first had supported the milder diplomacy of Shidehara; but after the Kwantung Army had successfully indoctrinated him he became a fanatical advocate of its aggressive policy. When the question of recognizing Manchukuo was being argued in Japan, Uchida declared in the Diet that the people were "solidly determined not to concede a foot, even if the country turned into scorched earth."[18]

In September 1932, despite the adverse international reaction that was anticipated, Japan concluded an agreement under which Manchukuo became its protectorate. But only a fortnight later the Lytton Commission's unfavorable report on the Mukden incident was accepted by the League of Nations, which adopted the policy that Manchukuo should not be recognized and that Japan should desist from further military intervention there. It was very doubtful, however, that the League would apply any sanctions to enforce its policy, or that the United States would interfere with Japan's plans. Feeling confident of Japan's power to defy both international law and opinion, Uchida told the League in effect: "If you don't like what we're doing, try and stop us." So instructed, in May 1933 Matsuoka Yosuke led the Japanese delegation when it stalked out of the League of Nations.

Like Italy and Germany, who would learn from its successes, Japan chose to become an outlaw rather than accept limitations on its nationalistic ambitions. Mori had died in 1932, but his dreams were being realized. With the assassination of Inukai, party government had been crippled, and the new regime—dominated by army, navy, and civilian extremists—led the unresisting nation down the highroad of totalitarianism and aggression.

21 · The Honorable Men in Power

THE BLOODLETTINGS OF 1932, a symptom of the international and domestic disorders that afflicted the nation, brought grief and terror to the House of Mitsui. The bewildering political drama that was taking place made it imperative for Mitsui to propitiate the emerging power clique while adjusting to profound changes in the economic situation. But since the death of obanto Dan Takuma, in whom the clan had placed full confidence and responsibility, no one had been able to chart a safe and promising course for the concern.

For many years Mitsui Gomei Kaisha, the holding company, had been commanded by Dan, assisted by two old retainers, Ariga Naga-bumi and Fukui Kikusaburo, who were valued for their reliability rather than their organizing talent. Dan had made the big decisions, and without his guidance the concern drifted. In other business houses such a sudden loss of leadership could have been the occasion for a palace revolution, but the structure of Mitsui had been designed to prevent such an eventuality. Automatically, the clan council, although rusty from disuse, creaked into action. As the result of its deliberations, Mitsui Gomei's most trusted executives were called upon to join a six-man board. Its members, in addition to Ariga and Fukui, were Ikeda Seihin of Bank, Yoneyama Umekichi of Trust and Banking, Yasukawa Yunosuke of Bussan, and Makita Tamaki of Mining. All four of the new appointees were brilliant and very successful men. But as the Japanese say, "too many captains will sail the ship up a mountain." Each of them had been used to running things his own way, and it was obvious that one of them had to be given a free hand on the tiller that steered Mitsui Gomei.

Baron Hachiroemon's problem was much the same as the one his grandfather had faced in 1866, except that in 1932 he had no superman like Minomura Rizaemon at hand to help him. Within the firm many expected that Makita Tamaki (who also happened to be Dan's son-in-law) would succeed to his position as a matter of course. Makita had exhibited extraordinary talent at Mining, especially in building up the chemical and dyestuffs operations into an enterprise powerful enough to compete with Germany's I. G. Farben Industrie. With more than twenty years' experience in all of Mining's variegated activities and a decade in the head office with Dan, he was a logical candidate. On the other hand, he was a man of original ideas and independent character, accustomed to initiating action first and consulting his superiors as an afterthought. One quality demanded of all retainers by the Mitsui clan chiefs was subservience. Makita, for the lack of this quality, lost his chance to attain the top position.

Yoneyama possessed the necessary professional skills and personal traits and had distinguished himself as founder and board chairman of Mitsui Trust and Banking, which in its seven-year life had outstripped all other trust banks in Japan. He was a Harvard graduate and he had family connections with the Sumitomo zaibatsu. But unfortunately, he had begun his career with Japan National Railways; having entered Mitsui's fold rather late in life, he was considered to be something of an outsider and was passed over also.

Yasukawa was well liked by the clan because he produced more profit than anyone else, but his reputation with the public as a commercial buccaneer, and his favoritism toward men of his own stripe in the concern, were held against him. Thus the selection boiled down to Ikeda, who although somewhat colorless, had the fewest points marked against him.

Whether or not Ikeda was the wisest choice is a matter for conjecture, but his qualifications were indeed formidable. Like many of his colleagues, he was a graduate of Keio Gijuku and had worked for a while at *Jiji*. Unlike them, he had gone to America to earn a degree from Harvard College (Class of 1895) before entering Mitsui's employ. His marriage to a daughter of obanto Nakamigawa Hikojiro, his teacher in business, was another badge of worthiness. By 1909 he had become managing director of the newly reorganized Mitsui Bank, a position he held until 1933, when he accepted the clan council's invitation to become prime minister of the whole Mitsui empire.

Baron Mitsui reached the decision about Ikeda in consultation with Baron Masuda, who since his retirement from Gomei in 1914, had remained the closest confidant and adviser of the elder Hachiroemon. Masuda, born five years before the arrival of Commodore Perry's first expedition to Japan, died in 1938 at the age of ninety.

Having given his approval to this choice, Baron Hachiroemon Takamine resigned his position as head of the Mitsui clan, after more than forty years of service, in favor of his eldest son Takakimi. The new Baron Mitsui was then thirty-eight years old. After completing his secondary education at the Peers' School in Tokyo, he studied law and political science at Kyoto Imperial University. He took a job at the head office of the Bank of Japan and also gained some knowledge of the family business as his father's secretary. But by nature he was a bon vivant rather than a businessman and had been happiest when living abroad, remote from paternal supervision. While holding an undemanding post in the London office of the Bank of Japan, he had been able to forget the heavy responsibilities that lay ahead of him at home and to engage in such congenial pursuits as golfing, baseball, and driving powerful automobiles. After the death of Baron Dan he was ordered back to Tokyo, where he found escape from stifling protocol in motoring. Eventually his stable of cars included a Rolls Royce, a Bentley, a Mercedes Benz, a pair of Jaguars, two Bugatti racers, a Humber, and a Cadillac limousine, among others. Unlike most wealthy Japanese of the time, he took the wheel himself and spent most of his free time driving about the country—preferably at night when the roads were empty.

Despite his reputation as a playboy, he was reasonably discreet, quite personable, and well schooled in the social graces. His interest in the concern was tepid, at best, but in one sense this was an advantage to the business. Leaving important decisions to his banto, he performed his prescribed duties in a dignified but unobtrusive way that earned him the respect and gratitude of his subordinates.

This was not necessarily true of the heads and heirs of the ten collateral families, most of whom held positions as presidents or directors of Gomei, Bank, or the main companies. With few exceptions they were mere figureheads but enjoyed exercising power and demanded all the deference to which their positions entitled them. Most Mitsui family heads displayed their authority not only in their companies but among themselves, vying for positions, perquisites, and the adoption of their favorite policies. Their competitiveness was one of the most troublesome problems for Ikeda, who wrote in his memoirs: "I spent seventy or eighty percent of my energy mediating internal conflicts and the remainder was actually used for Gomei."[1] In addition, he had to bedevil politicians, whose influence was costly, to procure decorations and court ranks for the status-minded Mitsuis.

To eliminate interference in business matters, Ikeda decided very early that the Mitsuis should be removed from most of their executive positions, leaving only the president and a few directors of Gomei, who would make policy decisions in consultation with himself and Ariga. Otherwise the top posts in the several Mitsui companies were to be held by the actual working managers. The ostensible reason for this change was the fear that by making themselves conspicuous those bearing the family name would become targets of assassins. Some of them argued that in times of crisis the Mitsuis should advance courageously, shoulder to shoulder, to the front line, but Ikeda would not hear of such heroic sacrifices. In a meeting of the clan council that lasted for three days he was forced to be more blunt about his reasons. Citing examples from his experiences and studies of great business houses abroad, he argued: "In the actual practice of management by German financial councils there is no case in which, because of one's blood relationship, without talent or ability, a man is given a position in the field of active management. The less talented relatives usually devote their time and energy to public service and charity."[2]

Such directness touched some tender nerves, but the Mitsuis' urge to seek prominence in the business world had been dampened by the exposure of another assassination plot.

While Reverend Inoue Nissho of the Blood Pledge Corps was awaiting trial, his brother, a naval commander, attempted to revive the coup d'état that had cost the life of Prime Minister Inukai. His plan, known to Ikeda although it had not been revealed publicly, was to bombard the premier's residence from the air during a cabinet meeting, thus killing all the ministers of the government at one blow. Scheduled for private and individual extermination were the emperor's chief advisers, leaders of both main political parties, and business tycoons including Ikeda himself. Grotesque as it sounds, this conspiracy was no mere figment of a diseased imagination. It had solid financial backing from the proprietor of Matsuya, a major department store, and was to be effected by the Dai Nippon Seisanto (Great Japan Production Party), an offshoot of the Black Dragon Society—presumably with the knowledge, if not the approval, of Uchida and Toyama. Indeed, some of the arrangements were made from the residence of a relative of the emperor, Prince Higashikuni, who was to be installed as prime minister after the coup.

That so-called Heaven-Sent Soldiers' Incident was averted, but the Mitsuis were sufficiently intimidated by what they had heard about it to accept Ikeda's plan for transforming them into social benefactors and thereby creating a more attractive image for the concern. The new obanto was well prepared for this task, for soon after Dan's death he had been asked by director Ariga to formulate a policy for protecting the House against antizaibatsu forces. Ikeda's program was based upon his recognition of the fact that Mitsui was no ordinary business establishment but was, rather, a bulwark of the state and as such should strengthen its role in civil affairs. Ikeda would have been the last to admit that the men of the zaibatsu families were not fulfilling their responsibilities as citizens; but since the public failed to appreciate their beneficence, he advised that a more conspicuous display of their generosity was desirable.

The Mitsuis' ten million yen loan to Manchukuo, matched by Mitsu-

THE HONORABLE MEN IN POWER · 285

bishi, had been quite helpful in appeasing the press, and that effect was accentuated when the two houses let it be known that repayment was not expected. This was part of a campaign—later known as "the zaibatsu reformation"—in which the three leading houses coordinated their philanthropic activities. The plan was inaugurated by Ikeda, who prompted the Mitsuis to make a personal donation of three million yen for unemployment relief, simultaneously with an equal amount from the Iwasakis and one million from the Sumitomos.

For Ikeda, who thought big, these bequests, all made in 1932, were only an exercise to loosen the Mitsuis' purse strings. In the following year the full extent of his plan was revealed with the establishment of the Mitsui Ho-on Kai, or Repayment of Kindness Association, with a fund of no less than thirty million yen (8.4 million dollars) at its disposal. In nominal charge of this charitable foundation was Baron Hachiroemon Takakimi, who upon its inauguration issued a statement that henceforth he would devote his life to repaying the general public and the state for past kindnesses. He expressed it in phrases reminiscent of the original House constitution's admonition on the subject: "Those of our blood should never forget ho-on and gratitude toward the state."

Ikeda's program was inspired by those of American business tycoons, such as John D. Rockefeller, Andrew Carnegie, and Henry Ford, who earlier in the century had countered public opprobrium by establishing philanthropic foundations bearing their names. In 1913 Rockefeller, whose colossal Standard Oil had earned him a fortune estimated at a billion dollars, set up the Rockefeller Foundation with a gift of securities valued at a hundred million dollars. In explaining his action he told the American government: "The sole motive underlying the various foundations which I have established has been the desire to devote a portion of my fortune to the service of my fellow men."[3] The idea, however, seems to have originated with a press agent named Ivy Lee, who coined the euphemism "public relations counsel" for men of his calling. Ikeda Seihin, who studied his methods of humanizing corporations, has been called "the Ivy Lee of Japan."

The initial fund for Ho-on Kai was donated by the clan council, whose apparent purpose was to distribute it as fast as possible. Under the management of banker Yoneyama Umekichi of Mitsui Trust, the foundation gave money for typhoon victims, famine-stricken farmers, disabled veterans, and the jobless. There were scholarships for Manchurian students, pensions for retired war heroes, expenses for Japan's Olympic team, and subsidies for a Korean cultural museum and an aircraft research laboratory. To alleviate poverty in northern Japan, peasants were given sheep, on the theory that the animals would browse on untilled uplands and provide wool and meat. (They were distributed in pairs with the condition that the foundation would be repaid in lambs; but the Japanese showed little interest in sheep raising, and most of those "debts" are still carried on the Ho-on Kai's books.) Money was given to patriotic organizations, the Yasukuni Shrine, new religions, schools, and orphanages. Large grants went to a cancer research institute, tuberculosis hospitals, and a leprosarium. Inasmuch as these benefactions were attended by a good deal of publicity, fund raisers flocked to the Ho-on Kai with such enthusiasm that within three years more than sixty million yen had been disbursed.

Philanthropy was somewhat out of character for Ikeda, who was described by his contemporaries as shrewd, daring, and cold, "the very personification of capitalism."[4] If indeed his generosity was motivated by sympathy for the downtrodden, he had a rather unfortunate way of explaining the zaibatsu's position. In a magazine article published when the depression was at its worst, he wrote: "When you walk on the road, it is not your intention to crush ants. However, although you are not walking so as to especially crush ants, you do end up killing ants and other small insects. Our problem is just like that. Though we are walking down the road fairly and squarely, our bodies and our feet have become big and it naturally comes about that we trample down the small fellows."[5]

Although he was drawing one of the largest salaries paid to any Japanese executive, Ikeda was not an acquisitive person, and his cavalier attitude toward money was entirely consistent with his patrician background and exalted circumstances. His father, the highest official of a prosperous han, had increased his wealth after the Meiji restoration, and gave the young Ikeda every advantage. By marrying Nakamigawa's daughter, the ambitious aristocrat entrenched himself with the Mitsuis; and other marriages made him a brother-in-law of Kato Takeo, president of Mitsubishi Bank, and of Usami Katsuo, governor of Tokyo. Ikeda's relationship with the Mitsubishi zaibatsu was further strengthened by the marriage of his daughter to a son of Baron Iwasaki, head of the family and of Mitsubishi. And it was during Ikeda's term as Mitsui's obanto that the old rivalry between the two houses was tempered by cooperation, especially in formulating policies toward the government and the public.

In stark contrast to the gently bred Ikeda was "Razor" Yasukawa, whose hard-driving business style had made Bussan notorious for its ruthlessness and gained a nickname for himself. Abroad, he had brought upon the company accusations of cutthroat competition, dumping, and sharp financial practices that had inspired campaigns against "the Japanese trade menace." At home, Bussan was hated even more fiercely because of its oppressive policy toward small business-men. In 1932 nearly half of Japan's total production came out of small workshops, in which wages and labor standards were appallingly low. Although great zaibatsu enterprises were the most conspicuous features on the industrial landscape, companies employing fewer than five people accounted for two-thirds of the labor force. But these tiny enter-prises were in no sense independent. Most of them had been organized into cartels or associations under government supervision, and this situation was exploited by the zaibatsu trading companies, who sup-plied raw materials, specified the articles to be made, and monopolized the marketing of those products. Bussan was said to be the biggest patron of these "midget capitalists," who in most cases were no better off than their workers. In good times their profits were held to a mini-mum by high prices for materials and low selling prices; and in bad times their credit with Bussan was likely to be cut off, forcing them into bankruptcy.

In his campaign to make Mitsui more respectable, Ikeda singled out Bussan as a prime target. Since, in Ikeda's opinion, Yasukawa Yuno-suke had shown himself invulnerable to reform, the only solution was to remove him. But the Mitsuis were exceedingly reluctant to sack their most successful banto, so Ikeda had to await his opportunity. Whether by calculation or by chance, Yasukawa's weak point was ex-posed through Ikeda's policy of opening Mitsui companies' stocks to public subscription so that others could "share the wealth." For ex-ample, in 1933, when Oji Paper issued new stock, Bussan, the largest stockholder in the mammoth concern (which by then produced seventy-eight percent of Japan's paper), declined for reasons of social policy to take up its allotted shares and lost its predominance. By holding the exclusive contract to market Oji's output, Bussan maintained a large measure of control, but its voice at board meetings was somewhat weakened thereafter.

Yasukawa was obdurately opposed to such propitiation. Neverthe-less, when the capital outlay in his beloved Toyo Rayon was tripled to thirty million yen in 1933, the greater part of the new shares was al-located for sale on the public market. Having lost that battle, Yasukawa used his position in the company to channel to a newly formed syndi-cate a substantial block of shares at half their market value. He also saw to it that his supporters in Bussan got low-priced shares while his op-ponents were squeezed out. Whether or not he bought any shares for himself is not recorded; but since he had amassed a fortune estimated at twenty million yen during his reign at Bussan, he was obviously not the type to neglect his own interests in manipulating the sale.

Ikeda knew what was going on but said nothing until Yasukawa had overplayed his hand. Then he presented a fully documented case to the clan council, of which he and Ariga were codirectors. Yasukawa was found guilty of a breach of trust; and the council, in conformity with new regulations devised by Ikeda, perhaps for that very purpose, reluctantly asked him to retire. Yasukawa balked and had to be summarily discharged. Typically, Gomei's management saved his face by finding him a suitably prestigious job as president of a Mitsui affiliate; but Ikeda's victory was complete, and he immediately ordered a thorough housecleaning at Bussan.

Yasukawa's successor was the gentlemanly Nanjo Kaneo, who had spent many years in Bussan's London office and was acutely aware of the firm's declining reputation internationally. Although lacking Yasukawa's adventurousness and flair for speculation, he was thoroughly schooled in Bussan's financial operations, most of which were conducted through the great London banks. Low-interest credit was essential to the huge commercial transactions of Bussan, which was in turn a valued client of English bankers. The City men trusted Mitsui because the concern had always been punctilious about meeting its obligations. Nevertheless, they were unhappy to see their credits used by the Japanese firm to ruin British industries and trade, and after he became Bussan's president Nanjo did his best to appease them. Overseas employees chosen by Yasukawa for their aggressiveness were called home, and there was a big shakeup in the head office and in domestic branches as well. Headquarters executives were tutored in business ethics as preached, if not practiced, in the West; and they were urged to join the newly formed Rotary Club in Tokyo. Minor manufacturers and merchants were treated more humanely, and some less important lines of business were ceded to smaller operators for the sake of harmony.

While improving Bussan's reputation in commerce, Ikeda devoted more attention to conditions among the workers of Mitsui's companies, for Japan's low labor standards had also become an international issue. Although unionism had continued to spread in Japan in the early thirties, wages were shockingly low. Factories paid male laborers little more than ten dollars a month, and females received only half that much. Other kinds of manual laborers were paid even less than factory hands, and a very large sector of the labor force, consisting of the proprietors' family members, received no regular pay at all. Since the imposition of the gold embargo, wages had been cut by eleven percent and prices had risen at the same rate, causing a real loss of more than twenty percent in purchasing power. The low-wage situation was not due to low productivity or poor business conditions. In the period from 1931 to 1934 national production increased by thirty-five percent, although the increase in employment was only five percent; during the same time Japanese business profits expressed as a share of the national income were about double those of businesses in the United States.

Most of Mitsui's manual workers were employed by its mining and textile establishments, at which wages were about the same as those paid by competitors. It was not the concern's policy to raise wages unilaterally. Such matters were handled through national and regional economic organizations in which all major employers participated, and one of their main functions was to maintain a solid front against workers' demands. However, it was quite acceptable for employers to raise their workers' living standards in other ways, and under Ikeda's direction Mitsui Mining and Kanebo set the pace for paternalistic reform.

At Omuta, the center of Mitsui's coal-mining, smelting, chemical, and electric-power complexes in Kyushu, more than 100,000 of the inhabitants lived on the wages paid by Mitsui Mining; and as a result of reforms begun under Dan Takuma, they lived comparatively well. An American journalist, Oland Russell, was given a grand tour of the installations in 1938, and he found that considering the nature of the operations working conditions were modern and hygienic. At the pitheads were well-equipped bathhouses, locker rooms, and ultraviolet-ray equipment for sun-starved miners. Other facilities he observed were a cooperative store with ample stocks, an assembly hall where sound movies were shown, a YMCA, a nursery school, and a spacious club-house with a library, lounge, and game rooms. For recreation outdoors there were a large park, swimming pool, wading pool, and illuminated athletic field. Among other fringe benefits, the company provided cultural and practical courses for workers and their wives. Primary school education was free and compulsory, and for higher studies qualified young men attended the Mitsui technical school at a nominal tuition fee. The Mitsui hospital, with 132 beds, had a staff of forty-two doctors and nearly a hundred nurses; and there were clinics at each of the five mines. Workers' houses, although small, seemed to be adequate and rental was very inexpensive. The highest rate was less than one yen a month, and older houses were let without charge. In case of need workers could obtain low-interest loans from the cooperatives, and those reaching retirement age were awarded pensions sufficient for buying a house and lot. Although life in Omuta was far from being idyllic, brutish conditions of the past had been ameliorated considerably and no great hardships were evident.

The harbor and coal-loading facilities at Omuta, begun in 1902 and completed in 1928 at a cost of two million dollars, were the most modern in Japan and could accommodate the largest ships afloat. The harbor works employed nearly two thousand men; in addition, the crews of Mitsui Line ships were recruited in the Omuta district. Many of the crewmen could boast that their grandfathers too had worked for the Mitsuis. This tradition bred intense loyalty among the men, who were better paid than most sailors. Mitsui Line officials said their crews were punctual in returning to the ships, even when exposed to the temptations of foreign ports, and that none had ever deserted. For the convenience and enjoyment of visiting dignitaries, as well as well as ships' officers and executives of Mitsui's mines, smelters, and chemical works, the company maintained two posh clubs, one in central Omuta and the other adjacent to one of the pitheads. The latter, which the author visited recently, occupies a spacious old frame house surrounded by lawns and gardens and is appointed with antique European furniture, paintings, and art objects. (At that time, however, no one could recall that any Mitsui had ever visited Omuta.)

Model conditions were established also at the textile mills of Kanebo in Japan if not at its overseas branches. President Muto Sanji, who had been educated in the United States, was noted as an advocate of social reform. Because it was too soon to apply his democratic ideas to Japanese industry as a whole, he tried at least to improve conditions in his own mills. Although he kept wages down to less than twenty-five cents a day, he provided the mill hands, most of whom were young women, with comfortable dormitories and wholesome food costing only a pittance. During leisure hours the girls could change from company uniforms into their own kimono and were offered free instruction in sewing, the tea ceremony, flower arrangement, and home crafts.

Foreign visitors to Mitsui's modernized installations were numerous, and although some compared them with "Potemkin villages," most were favorably impressed. One of them, an Englishman, declared that Japanese mills like Kanebo's had made as much progress since the First World War as the "child-killing British factories" had made in a century.[6] What he may have overlooked was the fact that such improvements in Japan were made possible by Kanebo's merciless exploitation of Korean, Manchurian, and Chinese laborers, whose wages and working conditions were far worse than those of workers at home in Japan. With such an advantage Kanebo, which had become the world's largest exporter of cotton textiles, was also Japan's highest profit maker in the field, earning some forty percent on invested capital in the mid-1930s. In a similar fortunate condition were Mitsui's Bussan, Mining, Toyo Menka, Tropical Produce, and Taiwan Development, all of which were big employers of cheap labor in Japan's colonies, its puppet state of Manchukuo, and in China proper.

Mitsui's clerical workers, as beneficiaries of the concern's double-

The Many Faces
of Mitsui

25. *Yasukawa Yunosuke,*
a chief manager of Mitsui Bussan.

26. *Nanjo Kaneo, a chief manager*
of Mitsui Bussan and Mitsui Gomei.

27. *Fukui Kikusaburo,*
a director of Mitsui Gomei.

28. *Mitsui Morinosuke Takayasu (1875–1946),*
eighth heir of Nagasakacho-ke.

29. *Mitsui Gennosuke Takahiro (1868–1943),*
seventh heir of Isarago-ke.

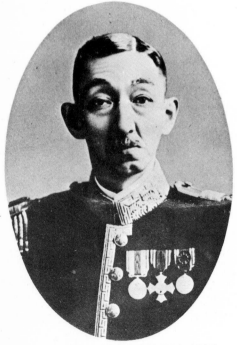

30. *Baron Mitsui Takanori (1874–1946),*
ninth heir of Minami-ke.

31. *Baron Mitsui Takaharu (1900–),*
heir of Mitsui Takanori.

32. *Yamamoto Jotaro (1866–1935), chief manager of Mitsui Bussan until 1914, became a potent president of the South Manchurian Railway and a promoter of industries in East Asia.*

33. *Ikeda Seihin (1867–1950), head of Mitsui Bank for many years, succeeded Baron Dan Takuma as chief director of Mitsui Gomei. He later served as minister of finance, governor of the Bank of Japan, and adviser to several prime ministers.*

Kyodo

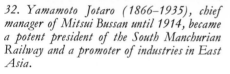

34. *Mori Kaku (1883–1932), Yamamoto's lieutenant in Mitsui Bussan and a vice-president of the South Manchurian Railway.*

35. Front row, left to right: *Matsuoka Yosuke (1880–1946), Yamamoto Jotaro, and Mori Kaku, during an inspection tour of China in 1931. Later, Matsuoka was a president of the South Manchurian Railway and minister of foreign affairs in the Konoe cabinet of 1940.*

36. *Baron Dan Takuma (1858–1932),*
a graduate of Massachusetts Institute of
Technology and the first head of Mitsui
Mining Company, was chief director of
the Mitsui empire when he was assas-
sinated.

37 *(below, left). Fujiyama Raita*
(1863–1938) started his business career
with Mitsui Bank and later became a sug-
ar tycoon in his own right.

38 *(below, right). Baron Go Seinosuke*
(1865–1942), a director of Oji Paper
Company and a chairman of Tokyo
Electric Light Company.

39. Baron Mitsui Hachiroemon Takamine (1857–1948), tenth heir of the
Kita-ke, was head of the House of
Mitsui and president of Mitsui Gomei
until his retirement in 1933.

40 (below, left). Mitsui Hachiroemon
Takakimi (1895–), eleventh heir of
the Kita-ke, was president of Mitsui
until 1945.

41 (below, right). Baroness Mitsui
Motoko, wife of Hachiroemon Takamine.

42. Fortune's *photograph shows the Yawata Iron and Steel Works contributing to Japan's progress.
The Yawata Works was a state-run monopoly expanded in the early 1930s by consolidating government
facilities with those of six zaibatsu concerns, including Mitsui's.*

Kyodo   Asahi Shimbun

43. *Carrying out orders from
Washington to dissolve the major
zaibatsu holding companies—foremost of which were Mitsui, Mitsubishi, Sumitomo, and Yasuda—
SCAP began the process by im-
pounding the firms' securities. On
October 8, 1945, a convoy of trucks,
complete with MP guards, hauled
away Mitsui's securities, valued at
more than two hundred million dollars. Stored in the Hypothec Bank
by the Holding Company Liquidation
Commission, the impounded securities
eventually were sold to the public.
The holding companies themselves
did not revive when the occupation
ended, but the respective groups of
companies have emerged stronger than
ever.*

44. On August 6, 1945 the first atomic bomb ever used in warfare demolished Hiroshima. At Mitsui Bank's Hiroshima branch, there were no survivors.

45. *As part of the postwar democratization program, the emperor was encouraged to meet his people. In 1949, when he visited the Miike mines at Omuta, Yamakawa Ryoichi, president of Mitsui Mining Company, led the inspection tour.*

47. Ishizaka Taizo, former president of To-kyo Shibaura Electric Company and of Keidan-ren. (1952)

48. Hirashima Toshiro, first chairman of reor-ganized Mitsui Bussan. (1959)

◁ *46. The Mitsui Minato Club at Omuta, near the entrance of the Mikawa mine, built in the early 1900s, was refurbished for the emperor's visit in 1949. Since that occasion, it has been used for entertaining executives and for meetings of the local Lions Club.*

49 (overleaf). The longest strike in Japan's history was staged by the Miike Coal Miners' Union at ▷ Omuta, in protest against the labor policy of Mitsui Mining Company. In July 1960, when the strike approached its climax, 100,000 workers, students, and other sympathizers rallied at the main pit-head, while financiers and politicians hammered out a solution in Tokyo. This photograph, showing a relatively small demonstration, was taken earlier in the strike.

50. *Niizeki Yasutaro, president of Daiichi Bussan, later chairman of Mitsui Bussan. (1950)*

51. *Mizukami Tatsuzo, organizer of Daiichi Bussan, later chairman of Mitsui Bussan. (1950)*

52. *Tashiro Shigeki, founder of Japan's nylon industry, former chairman of Toyo Rayon Company. (1973)*

53. *Kurata Okito, present chairman of Mitsui Mining Company. (1973)*

54. *Fujihara Ginjiro was the* doyen *of Japanese businessmen before his death in 1960.*

55. *Sato Kiichiro, retired chairman of Mitsui Bank. (1970)*

56. *Shirai Kuni, proprietress of the Yamaguchi teahouse. (1973)*

57. *Mukai Tadaharu, chief manager of the Mitsui concern in the 1940s. (1970)*

58. *Doko Toshiwo, President of Tokyo Shiba-ura Electric Company. (1972)*

59. *Edo Hideo, President of Mitsui Real Estate Company. (1972)*

60. *Wakasugi Sueyuki, late president of Mitsui Bussan. (1972)*

61. *Omoto Shimpei, President of Mitsui Mining and Smelting Company. (1972)*

62. Hashimoto Eiichi, Chairman of Mitsui Bussan. (1973)

63. Ikeda Yoshizo, President of Mitsui Bussan. (1973)

64. Mitsui Shipbuilding and Engineering Company's main products are huge tankers and containerships, but it also makes diesel engines, structural steel, industrial machinery, entire chemical plants, offshore drilling rigs, antipollution equipment, and prefabricated houses.

65. *Mitsui O.S.K. Lines, formed in 1965 by merging Mitsui Line and Osaka Mercantile Steamship Company, is Japan's second-largest shipping company. Its fleet of 300 vessels now aggregates about 7,000,000 deadweight tons.*

66. *Mitsui Bussan has invested in about 150 overseas joint ventures. A typical enterprise is Thiess Peabody Mitsui Coal Pty., Ltd., which operates the Moura open-cut coal mine in Queensland, Australia, with specially designed machines.*

67. *When SCAP dissolved the great zaibatsu holding companies, the eleven Mitsui families lost most of their wealth and all of their economic power. Today, they live much as ordinary citizens do. At left is Mitsui Hachiroemon Takakimi, former head of the clan and of the Mitsui empire, with his brother Takasumi, head of the Mitsui Foundation. Both are directors of their own private schools. This photograph was taken at Hachiroemon's Tokyo residence in 1971.*

standard labor policy, tended to overlook its negative consequences or to condone them as being inevitable. While enjoying elite status among salaried men and women, they were also grateful for the security and the many nonmonetary rewards offered by the companies. One of these was free membership in the San'yu Club, located on the top floor of the eight-story Sanshin Building, which had been built on the site of the old Mitsui Club after the earthquake of 1923. In spacious rooms overlooking Hibiya Park and the Imperial Palace grounds were billiard tables, a library, a European-style restaurant, and other facilities for the recreation of white-collar employees regardless of rank. To Mitsui men the generosity of the House of Mitsui was too well known to require comment. More than a thousand of them owed their success in life to an education in the Mitsui technical school. Many more of Mitsui's employees and their families had been patients at the Izumibashi Hospital in Tokyo, established in 1909 and endowed solely by the Mitsui clan. This institution, one of Japan's largest charity hospitals, had a capacity somewhat larger than the hospital in Omuta, and a staff of well-qualified physicians and surgeons.

Public recognition of the Mitsuis' past philanthropies was, however, disappointingly limited, and in announcing the establishment of Ho-on Kai in 1933 Ikeda explained to the press that it had been decided upon by the clan council "in the traditional spirit of the Mitsui family." Nearer the truth is the fact that it was planned by Ikeda as part of a subtle design worthy of old Inoue Kaoru himself. For in addition to the foundation's public benefactions, Gomei was spending perhaps an equal amount secretly or indirectly for the purpose of investigating the fast-changing political situation, appeasing or influencing the men who seemed to be emerging as dominant figures, and supporting or frustrating schemes likely to affect the interests of the House. In a way, this too was done "in the traditional spirit of the Mitsuis," whose fundamental tenet was to keep on the good side of the honorable men in power—and thus in touch with the times.

Understandably, there were many cynics who questioned Mitsui's motives. One of them was Wada Hidekichi, an editor of *Chugai Shogyo* (Domestic and Foreign Commerce), a newspaper owned (but obviously not tightly controlled) by the concern. His suspicion was aroused when he heard about the plans for the foundation from army radicals rather than from the firm itself, and he concluded that its establishment was an admission of guilt extracted under duress rather than a spontaneous act of charity. In an article entitled "How Big Capitalists Camouflage Themselves To Show Their Penitence," he wrote: "Mitsui controls a capitalist kingdom larger than any other and its business principle has been one of aggressive commercialism sweeping over all lucrative

fields. . . . These measures [such as the Ho-on Kai fund], though acclaimed as signs of penitence and exaggerated as sweeping reforms by
the press, are nothing more than an attempt to find shelter from unfavorable circumstances by sacrificing a small fraction of stupendous
earnings gained at the expense of the economic interests of the nation
at large."[7]

This hit pretty close to the mark, for the Mitsuis and not a few of
their executives were terrified. As they knew, at the time of Dan's assassination a member of the Blood Pledge Corps who was assigned to
kill Ikeda had rented a room near his residence and for weeks had been
trying to get a shot at him. When Ikeda stepped into Dan's position at
the head of Mitsui he was not too hopeful of surviving the honor, and
gossips said that he wore his bulletproof vest even when he slept. His
demeanor reflected the tension under which he lived: he seemed always
to be on the alert for hidden assailants, and the gravity of his expression
shocked those who saw him for the first time after Dan's murder. It
was while he lived under such strain, at the beginning of his service as
obanto, that he became deeply involved in another kind of "charity,"
about which Mitsui's public relations men never boasted.

Entrusted with initiating Ikeda into the deepest and darkest mysteries
of Mitsuidom was Ariga Nagabumi, whose influence in the concern
derived from the fact that he was privy to all the family and company
secrets. A poet's son and a graduate of Tokyo Imperial University, he
had been befriended by Count Kaneko, and through his influence had
become a secretary in the House of Peers and then in the Ministry of
Agriculture and Commerce. Later, while studying economics in London, he met Count Inoue, who recruited him as a managing director
of Mitsui Gomei. His rapid advancement was undoubtedly assisted by
his brother Nagao, a law graduate of the same university, who had
served with Kaneko as secretary in the privy council and then as legal
adviser to the army general staff. After the first Chinese revolution in
1911 Ariga Nagao was legal adviser to President Yuan Shih-k'ai, at the
time when Mori Kaku was trying to poison Yuan. It is probable that
there was a close liaison between Ariga and Mori, for by this time Nagabumi was already a confidential intermediary between Mitsui and the
Seiyukai (of which party both the Ariga brothers as well as Mori were
active members).

In the Mitsui combine all contributions of a political nature were
supposed to be handled by Gomei. Until his death Dan had been in
charge of this field of operations, assisted by Ariga, Fukui, and, of
course, Mori, who was entrusted with disbursements on the continent.
Apparently the payment of confidential funds was the main function of

THE HONORABLE MEN IN POWER · 293
...

Gomei's "general affairs" and "research" departments, which Ikeda now supervised personally.

Ikeda and Ariga, being members of the clan council and right-hand men of Baron Mitsui, had no difficulty in obtaining funds for secret projects, such as employing labor spies, strikebreakers, and undercover agents in the military and police forces. Special funds were set aside to provide "gifts" for government officials and "contributions" to terrorist groups, extortionists, blackmailers, and the like. In general, payments were made in cash and no records of them were kept, but police investigations conducted at a later time revealed that Gomei was spending nearly two million yen a year for intelligence operations alone.

It seems reasonable to assume that this money was used mainly to learn what the right-wing radicals were doing, so that the concern could adapt to the impending transition from party governments, which were controlled by the zaibatsu, to regimes that would be headed by militarists then hostile to the zaibatsu. Ikeda of course was well acquainted with such right-wing chieftains as Toyama and Uchida and with key men in the army and navy high command. But in view of the mutinous spirit then prevailing, he sought to broaden his contacts with the radical rightists, civilian as well as military. Through Ariga, who had numerous terrorists on his payroll, he met Kita Ikki, ideological godfather of the most fanatical military faction. From 1932 on, Kita, whose legitimate income had always been scanty, was to be seen riding in a chauffeured automobile. His domestic circumstances improved correspondingly, and his wife was assisted by three maids. Formerly he had been a grateful recipient of small handouts, but now he was able to give money to several disciples and henchmen, thanks to Gomei's "research" department.

Ikeda's interest in lower-echelon military fanatics seems to have dated from 1931, when he dined at the Peers' Club with Baron Hiranuma and Lieutenant Colonel Hashimoto Kingoro, a ringleader of the most radical group of younger officers and a participant in several terrorist conspiracies. Ikeda was most alarmed to hear the officer, then assigned to the Russian intelligence section of the general staff, launch into a violent denunciation of the zaibatsu and declare that he would disobey orders rather than defend their interests. Later that year, in a talk with Prince Saionji, last of the genro, Ikeda warned: "It is worthless to listen to the talk of marshals and generals. You should listen to what the young officers are saying."[8]

With Kita in his employ, Ikeda found it easy to single out some of the most militant hotheads and to meet them with a reasonable expectation of survival. His first recorded encounter with them took place at the residence of Marquis Hachisuka Mochiaki, an old family friend of the Ikedas and a supporting member of the Black Dragon Society. At this meeting, which lasted several hours, he met four army officers, the senior of whom was a colonel. Information about the discussions is fragmentary, but it is known that he made one friend, a finance officer, and one deadly enemy.

The latter, Lieutenant Colonel Mitsui Sakichi (no kin to the zaibatsu Mitsuis), was already well known to Ikeda by reputation. During his tour of duty with a regiment stationed in northern Kyushu, he had helped to stir up hatred against the Mitsui concern by making fiery speeches—while in uniform—to the people of Omuta.

At the conference with Ikeda, Colonel Mitsui started into a diatribe about a recent incident in the Miike coal fields. As an economy measure Mining had laid off half of Omuta's twenty thousand miners, causing severe hardship. The local people, stirred up by such agitators as the young colonel, had staged an angry demonstration. The Omuta authorities, at Mining's request, had called in six hundred policemen from other towns to quell disorders, and many of the demonstrators had been sent to prison. When Ikeda pleaded ignorance of the affair, the young colonel became incensed. "Mitsui is buying up Fukuoka!" he shouted. "The police, prefectural government and even the courts. But you don't say a word." Ikeda countered this blandly: "You say that Mitsui bought up the prefectural government; but it wasn't for Mitsui's sake. It was for social order." This bit of hypocrisy and other evasions further enraged the army man, whose hostility led to extremely serious consequences.[9]

Ikeda's subsequent contacts with military zealots seem to have been amicable, and large amounts of Gomei's special funds were distributed for a variety of projects—secret and otherwise—sponsored by army groups. This had the desired effect of placating elements that might otherwise have been a threat to Mitsui, while at the same time demonstrating the concern's patriotism. But even as Ikeda was conducting this appeasement campaign, the struggle between the militarists and party politicians brought another tragedy to the concern.

It began in the usual way, with a scandal. During the crisis of 1927, when the Suzuki combine collapsed, the Bank of Taiwan had turned over to the Bank of Japan a large block of foreclosed shares in the Teijin Company (Teikoku Rayon), formerly Suzuki's subsidiary. This was held as security against the Taiwan Bank's unpaid debt to the Bank of Japan. The stock was coveted by a group of businessmen—known as the Bancho-kai—led by Baron Go Seinosuke, a former Mitsui executive who had become a powerful capitalist in his own right. Through alleged bribery of certain officials at the Bank of Japan, bureaucrats, and politicians, the Bancho-kai had managed to buy the frozen stocks at a very favorable price and with them secured control of the Teijin Company. It so happened that some of the men involved in the business maneuver were leaders in a political movement to unite the Seiyukai and the Minseito parties in a solid front to oppose the military-fascist groups. But before their plans could be carried out rumors of the Teijin scandal began to spread and were fully exploited by opponents of party government.

One of the first to take up the case seriously was Muto Sanji, who had retired from the presidency of Kanebo to head the *Jiji* newspapers. Perhaps to expiate his past sins as a zaibatsu chieftain, the old liberal began a series of articles exposing the unsavory relations between big business and politicians. Perhaps he should have taken warning from recent attempts on the lives of two other leading newspaper editors, but he thought the story was just too important to suppress. He persisted in flaying the Bancho-kai and its collaborators with such vigor that two misbehaving cabinet ministers and a vice-minister felt compelled to resign. Before he could finish the series, however, Muto was murdered at Kamakura railway station, near Yokohama, by a person or persons unknown. There were rumors that agents of Bancho-kai had killed him, and some people said that Mitsui or Mitsubishi agents had intervened, either to protect business secrets or to defend their henchmen in the cabinet; but there was no evidence to sustain any of these suppositions, and the culprits were never found.

The Teijin case was not very remarkable in itself, and under ordinary circumstances it would have been settled quietly. It is widely believed that the famous trial that ensued had been instituted for the purpose of destroying the corrupt party system to make way for totalitarianism. If so, it was only the coup de grâce. The Seiyukai and Minseito had been thoroughly discredited not only with the public but with the financial cliques who supported the two parties. The zaibatsu lost interest not because the politicians were crooked—that was taken for granted—but, rather, because as the military interlopers and their accomplices strengthened their positions in the power structure, the political parties could no longer deliver the goods.

The "goods" at stake were orders for munitions, trade and development concessions in Manchukuo and China, and the good will of the government, without which the zaibatsu could not hope to preserve their empires. The military age was beginning in earnest, and it offered fabulous opportunities for business. Between 1931 and 1935 "national defense" expenditures had nearly doubled, and their share of the budget had risen from thirty-eight to fifty-two percent. Since the Mukden coup and the subsequent Japanese invasion of China south of the Great Wall, overseas investments had skyrocketed. Those in Manchukuo alone had risen from 1.6 billion yen to 2.35 billion, and most of that was zaibatsu money. But the concerns getting the choicest contracts, subsidies, and concessions were "new zaibatsu," such as Nissan and Showa Denko, whose leaders had long ago formed close ties with the Kwantung Army in Manchuria and antizaibatsu elements in the government at home. The new concerns were especially generous toward civilian ultranationalists and young officers under their intellectual guidance.

Ikeda, with his expensive intelligence system, was well aware of these developments and was no less generous than his competitors. But the matter wasn't to be resolved as simply as that, because the military and civilian radicals were divided into two opposing factions and many subfactions. In the mid-1930s the Kodo-ha, or Imperial Way Group, in the army was struggling against the less hotheaded but more calculating Tosei-ha, or Control Group. In simplest terms, those following the Imperial Way (whose civilian mentor was Kita Ikki) were the younger and more fanatical officers. They wanted to stage a coup d'état at home, establish some form of national socialism, and strike north to crush the Soviet Union in a holy war as a prelude to the conquest of Asia.

The Controllists, counselled by Kita's former comrade Okawa Shumei of the South Manchurian Railway, attracted somewhat older and more elite officers who, though no less fascistic, were willing to pursue their aims within the established economic and political framework. They believed that the wiser course was to strike southward and westward in China, while maintaining peaceful relations with the Soviets until Japan was strong enough for an irresistible advance to the north.

In 1935 the Imperial Way men were being outmaneuvered by the Controllists, who had succeeded in placing one of their leaders, General Nagata Tetsuzan, in a very strategic position in the Ministry of War. Nagata promptly forced the resignation of his strongest Imperial Way opponent in the high command. In August 1935, as the losers began plotting to regain their influence, a lieutenant colonel, imbued with the belief that he was acting in the name of the emperor, "the incarnation of God who reigns over the universe," strode unannounced into Nagata's office, whipped out his sword, and hacked and stabbed the general to death.

This mutinous deed was clearly intended to fix public attention on the schism in the army. The Imperial Way officers used the trial of the assassin as a rostrum from which to preach the nobility of their cause, the venality of the Controllists, and, as usual, the corruption of national institutions by the zaibatsu. Concurrently, the capitalists and their parties were being pilloried at the marathon Teijin trial and were getting a very bad press. To make matters worse, the assassin's special defense counsel turned out to be Ikeda's personal enemy, Lt. Col. Mitsui Sakichi. In presenting his case Colonel Mitsui offered to prove, among other things, that Ikeda had been paying off the late General Nagata and that the two had been plotting to suppress the Imperial Way faction—this despite the fact that Ikeda was also giving money to its master, Kita Ikki. There was also to be testimony, from the man who had introduced Ikeda to Nagata, that the latter had intended to impose by force a joint military-zaibatsu cabinet, with Ikeda as prime minister. To establish his case, Colonel Mitsui asked the court to summon several leading businessmen as witnesses, and Ikeda was scheduled to appear on February 27, 1936. The date is significant.

In such a feverish atmosphere a general election was held on February 20. The Seiyukai, conspicuously identified with corruption and now with militarism, took a severe drubbing at the hands of the more moderate Minseito; and the ostensibly left-wing Social Mass Party, Shakai Taishu-to, which proclaimed itself to be anticapitalist, anticommunist, and antifascist, more than doubled its representatation in the Diet.

This shake-up had two important effects. First, Ikeda, facing an extremely unpleasant ordeal at the hands of Colonel Mitsui, decided that the Seiyukai had outlived its usefulness and that further involvement with dirty politics could ruin the Mitsui concern. It was a delicate decision to make, considering the uncertainties within the militarist camp and the explosive nature of the Nagata assassination trial. Nevertheless, he broached the matter to Baron Mitsui Hachiroemon and got his approval for cutting off further financial support to the Seiyukai, regardless of the indignation that would surely ensue. The second effect was less direct: the election results served as an alarm to the Imperial Way men, who had thrown their support to the Seiyukai as the lesser of two evils—and lost the gamble. Already under severe counterattack from the Controllists, they would now have to contend with an inimical government as well.

As a measure for curbing rebellious elements, the army's high command had ordered the First Division, a hotbed of Imperial Way extremism, to be transferred from Tokyo to Manchukuo. If that happened, the Controllists would be in an invulnerable position. For the Imperial Way faction, time was running out. In Tokyo rumors were already rife that some kind of a *Putsch* was in preparation.

Throughout the night of February 25 a heavy snow fell upon the capital. Despite rumors, there was no unusual activity in the city and the streets were deserted. Then, in the small hours of February 26, a few Imperial Way activists trudged around to newspaper offices delivering a manifesto blaming Japan's economic difficulties on the zaibatsu and attacking the elder statesmen, bureaucrats, and party politicians. The document concluded, in the usual hackneyed language of fanatics: "The recent strained relations between Japan and other powers are due to our statesmen's failure to take appropriate measures. Japan now confronts a crisis. Therefore it is our duty to take proper steps to safeguard our fatherland by killing those responsible. . . . We think it our duty as subjects of His Majesty the Emperor. May heaven bless us and help us in our endeavor to save our fatherland from the worst."[10]

The nature of those pious endeavors became evident at about 5:00 A.M., when fourteen hundred infantrymen of the First Division marched through the deep snow and, without encountering any resistance, seized the Diet buildings, the Ministry of War, and Metropolitan Police headquarters. Simultaneously, execution squads sped to the homes of high government officials. One group crashed into the residence of finance minister Takahashi, who had offended by trying to curb the budgetary demands of the military. An armed officer entered his bedroom shouting: "Punishment of Heaven!" As the old man opened his eyes the executioner fired three shots from his revolver and an accomplice slashed the dying Takahashi with his sword.

Admiral Saito, the lord keeper of the privy seal and an opponent of the army extremists, was also slaughtered in bed as his wife tried to protect him by covering his body with her own. General Watanabe, leader of the Controllists, was shot to death in his home. Prime Minister Okada was marked for death on general principles, but the assassins made a mistake and killed his brother instead. Admiral Suzuki, the emperor's grand chamberlain, was seriously wounded; and Count Makino and Prince Saionji, the emperor's "evil advisers," narrowly escaped assassination.

It would seem that despite all his precautions Ikeda's intelligence apparatus failed him in this crisis. When news of the attempted coup came through he was at his seaside villa, far from Tokyo, presumably rehearsing his testimony for the Nagata assassination trial, at which he was supposed to appear on the following day. Thus the Mitsuis were not forewarned and took no immediate precautions. Hachiroemon's second son Takamitsu recalls that he went to school as usual that morning, but that soon after his arrival a servant came to take him home. The baron then bundled his wife, sons, and daughter into one of his less conspicuous cars and drove to a distant teahouse, where they were hidden in an unheated upstairs room and warned to keep very quiet.

Ikeda could be of no help to the family. He was not permitted to leave his villa, which was guarded by twenty policemen. When it was reported that a death squad was tracking him down, the police spirited him away to Yokohama, where he entered a private hospital incognito and stayed out of sight until the danger subsided. Later he learned that the report had been false. When the death list was being compiled and Ikeda's name was mentioned, Kita Ikki, one of the conspirators, had come to his rescue with the unflattering comment: "Why bother with him? He's only a banto."

The rebellion, known in Japan as the "Ni-ni-roku," or February Twenty-sixth, Incident, was a dismal failure. The plotters, having issued an ultimatum from their stronghold in a downtown hotel, waited for the government to capitulate. Instead, the government declared a state of martial law, and the rebels, receiving no support from other army units, were kept under siege until, on the fourth day, they obeyed an unequivocal order from the emperor to surrender and straggled back to their barracks.

Because of the general confusion occasioned by the incident, Ikeda was spared the ordeal of being grilled by Colonel Mitsui. But when Kita, under interrogation, revealed his financial connection with Ariga and Ikeda, even worse things seemed to be in store: the obanto, who had been accustomed to using the Kempeitai, or military police, for his own purposes, now found himself a subject of their investigation. The officers were polite about it, questioning him in his own home at night so as not to attract attention. But they were nonetheless inquisitive, especially concerning his foreknowledge of the coup. The investigating officers reached these rather charitable conclusions: "Ikeda Seihin gave Kita Ikki thousands of yen every month for living expenses. In exchange Kita supplied Ikeda with information about the military and the right wing. From this money Kita every month gave Nishida [his chief accomplice] several hundred yen. The money in excess of Kita's living expenses was used as political funds and to gain control of the young officers. At the beginning of February . . . Ikeda gave money to Kita. However, he asserts this was the usual money for information and was not given as funds for the uprising. It is not clear if around the time of the uprising Kita did or did not give a confidential report to Ikeda. Kita keeps his mouth shut and will say nothing, Ikeda himself strenuously denies it, and no material evidence has been obtained."[11]

That was an extremely serious matter, however. For once the government, and even the army, acted decisively against the less exalted conspirators, whose trial by court-martial was prompt and secret. Without any propaganda or histrionics, thirteen officers and four civilians, including Kita and Nishida, were sentenced to death and executed. Ikeda was not arrested, ostensibly because the Kempeitai were unable to elicit enough evidence that he took an active part in the conspiracy. Actually, the extent of his involvement with the Imperial Way was less than that of Kuhara Fusanosuke and Ishihara Koichiro, the heads of two "new zaibatsu" giving the strongest financial backing to the rebels. In addition, a number of high-ranking military officers and government figures were implicated, and the authorities probably thought it preferable to avoid a showdown that would elicit reprisals from above or aggravate public unrest.

Nevertheless, as the court-martial got under way and rumors spread, public hostility against Mitsui became as strong as it had been before the great "face-lifting" operation, and Ikeda decided (or was asked) to retire. Since there is still some difference of opinion over the reason for Ikeda's withdrawal less than three years after his appointment as obanto, in 1971 this writer asked Mr. Mitsui Hachiroemon Takakimi whether it was related to his connection with the rightists in the February rebellion. "No," the last Baron Mitsui answered firmly. "He himself set the retirement age, and he was just that age."

Biographical data indicate, however, that Ikeda, at sixty-nine, was actually well beyond the retirement age that he himself had established (sixty-five for a president or chairman and sixty for other executives). This discrepancy, and the fact that the retirement system had not been invoked regularly before the February Incident, led to speculation that the departure of Ikeda, like that of Yasukawa Yunosuke, had been effected for reasons of policy rather than senescence. Although Ikeda retired ceremoniously on the fortieth anniversary of his being employed by Mitsui, people were asking whether he might not have been pushed out of the concern. It would have been more pertinent to ask whether he really parted company with the Mitsuis at all, and many did ask that question. The obanto stepped down in the spring of 1936, but in September of that year *Fortune* reported cannily: "Under this [retirement] plan Mr. Ikeda moved out of the titular leadership of Mitsui Gomei Kaisha. It is generally suspected in Tokyo that he moved out of nothing else."

22 · The Wave of the Future

MESMERIZED BY THE PECULIARITIES of the Japanese way of life and the supposed inscrutability of the Orient in general, many foreign observers assumed that the turmoil culminating in the February Incident was a typically Japanese phenomenon. Japanese it was in its strategy and rhetoric; but when its exotic trappings were stripped away, it could be seen to be part of a cosmopolitan and highly fashionable trend known as fascism.

For every significant political event and movement in Japan during the 1930s there had been a European or American parallel, and the similarity was often striking. Prime Minister Inukai's assassination in 1932 had given Japanese politics a sinister reputation, yet soon afterward an assassin's bullet narrowly missed President Franklin D. Roosevelt and took the life of Chicago's mayor, Anton Cermak. In France in 1933 the Stavisky "pawnshop scandal" resembled the Teijin scandal of the same year in Japan, was exploited for precisely the same political purposes, and had equally profound repercussions. In 1934 the Imperial Way-Controllist schism in the Japanese army was foreshadowed in Germany by the split between Hitler's ultraradical Sturmabteilung SA Brownshirts and his more conservative Schutzstaffel, or SS Blackshirts, ending in the assassination of SA commander Ernst Roehm. The "Blood Purge" of that June in Germany, like the February Incident of 1936 in Japan, was used to suppress the anticapitalist zealots and to establish more disciplined fascists as the wielders of power. All over Europe, as in Japan, the rancors and frustrations of the "little men" against the power elite were channeled into superpatriotic or pseudo-revolutionary movements. In imitation of Mussolini's Blackshirts and Hitler's SA and SS men, uniformed paramilitary units—the Croix de Feu and Cagoulards in France, the Rexists in Belgium, the Iron Guard in Rumania, the Ustashi in Yugoslavia, the Falange in Spain, and the British Union of Fascists, to name a few—marched, sang nationalistic songs, chanted puerile slogans, and perpetrated bloody assaults on communists, socialists, Jews, labor unionists, and other "enemies" designated by their perspicacious leaders.

301

In every case the fascists' mass organizations, parading under the banners of patriotism, national honor, or racial destiny, supported militarism, aggression, and forcible suppression of dissenters. Behind the uniformed rabble were the terrorist societies, and behind the terrorists were the owners of wealth—latifundists, industrialists, bankers, merchants, and the clergy—who linked arms almost to a man against the one great menace, proletarian collectivism. Basically, it was a pitting of the economic power of the rich against the numerical power of the poor, of besieged capitalism against a seemingly irresistible upsurge of Marxian socialism, which contrary to all pundits' predictions, had been established in the Soviet Union, was sweeping through Europe, and threatened to engulf Asia, as well.

Japan was being criticized for its aggression in Manchuria, but not too sharply, for each of the leading nations had its own noisome Manchuria. The British, French, and Dutch empires were no less vulnerable to condemnation than was that of the Japanese. The economic empire of the United States, seized by force and held by threat of force, included most of Latin America and a string of Pacific possessions extending to the very shores of Asia. In 1928 President Herbert Hoover, in his inaugural address, said: "We have no desire for territorial expansion, for economic or other domination of other peoples." Yet troops of his government still occupied Nicaragua, Haiti, and the Philippines and were a menacing presence in many other regions of the globe, including China.

It was in such an international context that obanto Ikeda had employed the financial power of Mitsui, but not in support of any ideology, or of a special brand of militarism as such. Like any successful manager in any country, he was determined to keep his enterprise on the crest of the wave if possible and to prevent its being swamped at all costs. As the term "fascist" was applied in those years, Ikeda certainly was a fascist. Probably, the word had rather a pleasant ring to him because he recognized the fascistic system, otherwise known as the corporate state, as the key to the survival of his class in a world being torn asunder by the demanding masses. So impressed had he been with the achievements of Mussolini (then famous for the unbelievable feat of making Italy's trains run on time) that in 1929 he made a special trip to Rome, in order to study the effects of fascism on wealthy Italian families. Being satisfied that the system was tailor-made for the rich, he had no qualms about applying it to Japan for the benefit of the Mitsuis, to whom his life was dedicated.

Although later Ikeda was singled out as a war-crimes suspect by the Allies, his predilection for fascism and militarism was far from unusual among men of his class in Japan and elsewhere in the world. After all,

Mussolini had been brought to power by the financial elite of Italy, aided by a hundred-million-dollar loan from J. P. Morgan of New York. Hitler, following his example, won generous support and full cooperation from the steel and munitions trusts and rebuilt the German war machine with substantial help from such American industrial giants as General Motors, Du Pont, and Ford. In fact, the chief intermediary between German and American industrial finance during the Hitler years was the pious John Foster Dulles, a partner in the powerful Wall Street law firm of Sullivan & Cromwell, representing I. G. Farben and other large industrial and banking combines supporting Hitler. His brother Allen, also a partner in the corporation law firm, negotiated secretly with Nazi financiers in Switzerland during the Second World War, a few years before he took command of the Central Intelligence Agency under the administration of President Eisenhower.

In England avowed fascists were members of highest social circles, notably the "Cliveden set" assembled by the American-born Lady Astor. American businessmen traveling abroad caught the infection as easily as they did other tourist ailments. William S. Knudesen, president of General Motors, arriving home from Europe in the fall of 1933, told a *New York Times* reporter that Hitler's Germany was "the miracle of the twentieth century." Bruce Barton, a leading advertising tycoon, praised "the sense of national obligation which Mussolini has recreated in the soul of Italy." The patriotic but impulsive Charles Lindbergh, son-in-law of J. P. Morgan's partner Dwight Morrow, accepted a Nazi decoration (as did numerous American and British personages) and informed his countrymen that Nazism was "the Wave of the Future." The *Reader's Digest* of November 1939 carried an article by "Lindy," in which he warned his fellow Nordics: "Oriental guns are turning westward. Asia presses toward us on the Russian border, all foreign races stir restlessly. It is time to turn from our quarrels and build our white ramparts again. . . . We can have peace and security only so long as we band together to preserve that most priceless possession, our inheritance of European blood, only so long as we guard ourselves against attack by foreign armies and dilution by foreign blood."

Besides giving their moral support to and accepting honors from Hitler, Mussolini, and Franco, American men of wealth financed rightist organizations not dissimilar to those in Europe and Japan. One such group, preparing a coup d'état by means of a private army of American Legion veterans, offered the "presidency" to General Smedley Butler, who (like General Tojo Hideki) had proved his mettle by putting down insurrections in countries whose economies were dominated by his nation's investors. The conspirators' second choice was General Douglas MacArthur, former son-in-law of another Morgan partner, who had won his Wall Street spurs in 1932 by commanding a successful assault on thousands of hunger marchers encamped in Washington, D.C., when they petitioned for relief from the miseries of the Great Depression. Butler, rediscovering his conscience, exposed the plot. In subsequent testimony he explained why he had been chosen as the American *Führer:* "I was a high class racketeer for capitalism. . . . I helped purify Nicaragua for the international banking house of Brown Brothers in 1909–12. I brought light to the Dominican Republic for American sugar interests in 1916. In China in 1927 I helped see to it that Standard Oil went its way unmolested."[1]

The target of the conspirators was Roosevelt's New Deal, which they confused with communism. An investigation by a congressional committee implicated founders and leaders of the American Legion, the governor of Massachusetts, several wealthy Wall Street brokers, and high executives of Guaranty Trust, Anaconda Copper, Goodyear, Bethlehem Steel, Du Pont, and Remington Arms. But most Americans never learned the real story. Just as it happened in Japanese investigations of rightist plots in Japan, so did it happen in the United States: the most damaging testimony against America's fascists was suppressed, and some major newspaper chains refused to print even expurgated reports of the story.[2]

Among American businessmen there were many, among the Christians, at least, who were well disposed toward Nazism—Henry Ford, William Randolph Hearst, DeWitt Wallace, Charles Edison, and Harvey Firestone, to name only a few. These were some of the wealthy backers of a quasi-religious international organization called Moral Rearmament founded by Dr. Frank Buchman, also an American. When Buchman exclaimed, "I thank heaven for a man like Adolf Hitler," they were not estranged from the movement. Ford had been an early admirer of Hitler and was quite at ease in the anti-Semitic atmosphere of MRA —among whose German members were Gestapo chief Heinrich Himmler and the *Führer's* right-hand man Rudolf Hess. It is not at all surprising, then, that Buchmanism, the new religion of big business, was eventually introduced into Japan by the nation's biggest business family, Mitsui.

While fascism held out glittering inducements to the middle class, which had been financially stricken by postwar inflation and depression, and even seduced the proletariat with the promise of "national socialism," it was essentially the ideology of the monopolists. They had the most to gain from foreign expansion, preparations for war, and the suppression of domestic dissent. In Japan there wasn't really much of a middle class. In the mid-1930s less than one percent of Japanese families were even moderately wealthy; ninety-three percent of the households, which numbered about 13,500,000 in all, lived on an average income of $166 a year—and more than fifty percent of those families lived on cash incomes of about $110 a year. But there was a relatively prosperous segment of about 1.5 million families with annual incomes of $2,500 and up; and the breadwinners of those, together with other white-collar workers who hoped to attain such affluence, were easily indoctrinated to fear the loss of their prerogatives in a red revolution. As for the poorer folk, with no other hope of relief in sight, they were willing to give the government a chance to make good its claims that conquests overseas would eventually relieve their penury. With such arguments, the military fascists won enough support from the masses to be able to cope with their relatively few opponents.

Needing no persuasion were the one hundred families who dominated the Japanese economy and enjoyed an aggregate annual income of approximately 350 million yen, or nearly 100 million dollars (at a time when the yen was worth 28 cents). That amount represented sixteen percent of the nation's total profits from business (exclusive of capital gains, which by far exceeded their cash receipts). In terms of individual income, the top earner was the emperor, who received something like thirty million yen a year. Next was Baron Sumitomo Kichizaemon, reportedly earning about twenty million a year, as compared with about thirty million for all eleven of the Mitsui families. However, the Mitsuis' bookkeeping techniques were so intricate that no one, even the government, really knew what they owned. When Baron Mitsui Hachiroemon Takamine handed over his estate to his son Takakimi in 1933, a battalion of tax officials spent more than a year trying to assess its value, which they finally estimated at thirty-five million dollars for tax purposes. The tax levy was more than five million dollars, and since even the Mitsuis didn't keep that much money in liquid assets, the young baron was allowed to pay it in installments— which, calculated by the day, amounted to almost as much as the prime minister received in salary for the year. But this tax was not unbearable, considering the extent of Mitsui Takakimi's personal fortune: by one conservative estimate, it amounted to 130 million dollars, and heads of the eleven Mitsui families were worth a total of 450 million dollars. (For the sake of comparison, John D. Rockefeller's fortune reached as much as one billion dollars at its peak; and despite his huge gifts to foundations, his son, John D. Rockefeller, Jr., held oil stocks worth more than 250 million dollars in 1935. On the other hand, the great J. P. Morgan left only a meager 78 million dollars at his death in 1913.[3])

The power of the zaibatsu was attributable not only to the wealth they possessed but also to the assets they controlled indirectly. For example, Mitsui Gomei was capitalized at 312 million yen, of which the

Mitsuis held all but twelve million. Gomei had absolute control over six major companies and financial institutions and dominated a dozen more whose total capital was measured in terms of billions of yen. These in turn controlled hundreds of large companies, whose influence was strongly felt by thousands of smaller affiliates and client firms. The structure of each zaibatsu was more or less pyramidal and control was exercised in part through such devices as the appointment of executives by the holding company, interlocking directorates and stockholdings, selective credit, and, through the trading company, exclusive contracts for buying, selling, patents, technical licenses, and so on. In addition to these controls, there were moral ties based on feudal concepts of the mutual obligation between leaders and followers (the *oyabun-kobun* relationship), and "family" solidarity—enforced, in the case of executives, by signed loyalty oaths. By means of such a tightly meshed structure the Mitsui clan was in control of some fifteen percent of Japan's financial capital. Eight zaibatsu families together controlled as much as fifty percent of the country's financial capital in the mid-1930s, according to *Fortune's* independent estimate. By the same estimate, fifteen zaibatsu concerns controlled almost seventy-five percent of the nation's business.

Such monopolization of the economy had been achieved in the 1920s and was further solidified in 1931, when the Important Industries Control Law was enacted to combat the depression by organizing large producers into cartels. In 1934, as "preparedness" became the economic keynote, the government-controlled Yawata Iron and Steel Works merged with six private producers of ferrous metals to form Nippon Seitetsu, Japan Iron and Steel. Soon afterward this national-policy company was accounting for half of Japan's steel and four-fifths of its pig-iron output. The government's move, although superficially socialistic, was not opposed by the zaibatsu, because they had been worried about overproduction due to the depression and also got very favorable compensation for their equities. Furthermore, the government-controlled steel monopoly was still partially owned by the zaibatsu; of its 359 million yen capital, approximately seventy-five million was privately held, with Mitsui and Mitsubishi the largest private stockholders. In addition, the zaibatsu participated in management and, through their affiliated companies, supplied raw materials to Japan Iron and Steel and distributed its products, earning comfortable profits in both ways with negligible risk.

The same situation existed in the electric-power industry, which had been slow to recover from the depression. With the sharp decline in the exchange rate of the yen after imposition of the gold embargo, private companies found it difficult to service the huge loans that had been extended by American bankers. In 1936, to strengthen the industry and stabilize it in preparation for war, the government consolidated all the related facilities by forming Nippon Hassoden, the Japan Electric Power Generation and Transmission Company. Here, too, the zaibatsu retained ownership and management to a considerable degree and supplied the utility company with fuel and equipment to their own profit. The Kyushu Electric Power Company, supplying current to the factories, mills, and mines of that highly industrialized island, remained under Mitsui influence.

With every major sector of the economy except agriculture under their domination, the zaibatsu cooperated wholeheartedly with the government and the armed forces in suppressing any kind of activity, mental or otherwise, that seemed to represent a challenge to their power. As union membership rose to a peak of 420,000 in 1936, the ranks of the Kempeitai and of the special thought-control police swelled correspondingly. Schoolchildren were given increasingly strong doses of "moral education," consisting mainly of exhortations on Shinto mythology, emperor worship, and racist chauvinism. The newspapers were gradually harnessed to the war chariot, and the people were indoctrinated mercilessly. As early as 1934 they were expected to believe the war ministry's dictum that war is "the highest ideal of humanity, the father of culture and the mother of creation," and that "all ideas of individualism, internationalism and liberalism must be eliminated."[4]

For dissenters there were graduated stages of control, ranging from warnings by the police and threats by terrorists to arrest, torture, indefinite imprisonment, and execution, with or without trial. Between 1928 and 1937 some sixty thousand people had been arrested for "dangerous thoughts" on evidence so frivolous that less than ten percent of them could even be indicted legally. Among the prisoners at one time or another were practically all those identified as procommunists, radical socialists, anarchists, pacifists, or labor agitators. As in the Tokugawa period, scholars were punished for commenting favorably on certain foreign books or espousing liberal philosophies. Hundreds of schoolteachers were imprisoned for questioning the Shinto myths telling of Japan's creation and the origin of the imperial house. A bevy of chorus girls was locked up for making a collective complaint about the color of the paint in their dressing rooms; and a famous legal scholar (the father of Minobe Ryokichi, the present governor of Tokyo) was forced to resign from the House of Peers (and in addition was threatened with assassination) for the "crime" of having theorized, many years earlier, that the emperor is an "organ of the state" rather than the state itself.

Members of the Japanese left did not stand up very well under the literal as well as figurative bludgeoning dealt them by the thought-control police. Torture and brainwashing, long Oriental specialties, were so perfected that out of the tens of thousands of people arrested for radicalism all but a few score were "converted" to the satisfaction of the police and released—under close surveillance—to convert their comrades. A considerable number of Japanese prominent in the period after the Pacific War, notably the late newspaper and newsprint tycoon Mizuno Shigeo, were one-time communists "rehabilitated" by police brainwashing.

Such effective work by the forces of law and order had reassured the zaibatsu that the threat from the left was no longer serious, and the crushing defeat of the Imperial Way rebels in 1936 encouraged them to believe that the threat from the radical right was also receding. But many of the politicians and generals still working behind the scenes were known to be antizaibatsu, and the financial community watched anxiously as a new cabinet was being formed to replace the one brought down by the February revolt. It had been hoped that after the disgraceful excesses of that year, which had aggravated public distaste for the militarists of both factions, there would be a swing back toward moderation. The emperor had been emphatic about his desire to curb the extremists, and genro Saionji, whom he had delegated to select a new prime minister, was no friend of the extremists. Since the old prince had nearly fallen victim to them in the February madness, he was expected to pick someone with a level head to lead the nation back to normalcy. Instead, he called first upon Prince Konoe, an arch-imperialist in league with fanatics. When Konoe declined, Saionji picked Hirota Koki, who despite his long experience in diplomacy, was identified with the most rabid politicians. Hirota, a native of Fukuoka, not only was a member of the proto-fascist Black Dragon Society but also had been a disciple of Toyama Mitsuru since boyhood and was considered by some people to be an agent of that mastermind of Japanese terrorism. Obviously the emperor had been deceived. So had the United States Ambassador to Japan, Joseph C. Grew, who cabled Washington that although Hirota would play ball with the army to some extent he was "a strong, safe man."[5]

Some foreign observers believed that Hirota's mission was to harmonize the bureaucracy and the zaibatsu with the military "moderates." Surprisingly, he did try to appoint some less reactionary ministers, among them Yoshida Shigeru (much to the disapproval of Ambassador Grew, who considered him too liberal). But Hirota was thwarted by Minister of War General Terauchi Hisaichi, who had the power to topple the cabinet simply by resigning from it. After that the new prime minister all but grovelled before the army, which proceeded swiftly toward its goal of a "total defense" economy. In response, Minister of Finance Baba Eiichi, a nonzaibatsu banker close to the bureaucracy, presented the Diet with a national budget of unprecedented size, nearly half of it marked for military expenditures, along with a bill that imposed oppressive taxes to cover it.

Before the year was out the "strong, safe" Hirota and his cabinet had taken drastic and irreversible steps toward war. The most important of those steps was the reenactment, by devious means, of an old law specifying that the ministers of the army and of the navy must be generals or admirals on active duty. Because those two ministers had the implicit power to end the term of any cabinet by refusing to cooperate with their fellow ministers, and since they would be acting under direct orders from their respective superior officers, the triumph of military totalitarianism seemed to be at hand. A second step was the adoption of a five-year plan for Manchukuo, under which the new-zaibatsu firm of Nissan was enabled to take over all the major holdings of the South Manchurian Railway Company except the transportation network itself. Finally, at the end of 1936, the imperial army, acting outside normal diplomatic channels, arranged with Hitler's Germany an anticommunist pact, which tied Japan to the newly formed Rome-Berlin axis.

The army, in a further effort to weaken the Diet and the political parties, now maneuvered to replace Hirota with a general. The new prime minister, General Hayashi Senjuro, though lamentably deficient in statesmanship, could see that the grandiose plans formulated under Hirota could not be realized without sound finances and the cooperation of businessmen, who had been appalled by the Hirota government's fiscal recklessness. After consultation with military colleagues, the prime minister sent an envoy to Ikeda Seihin, Mitsui's genro in retirement, asking him to become finance minister.

Ikeda declined the honor, pleading ill health (he had been plagued with gallstones), but recommended his friend Yuki Toyotaro, managing director of Yasuda Bank and a director of companies controlled by both Mitsui and Mitsubishi. Besides representing three of the four largest zaibatsu, Yuki was also a member of the ultrarightist National Foundation Society, along with Ikeda and several top-ranking generals. Moreover, Yuki's daughter was engaged to Fujiyama Aiichiro, the heir of sugar magnate Fujiyama Raita, who like Ikeda, was related by marriage to Mitsui's late obanto Nakamigawa. Yuki accepted the ministership and persuaded Ikeda to become governor of the Bank of Japan.

This political comeback (preparations for which had been made long before by Ikeda through his financial support of the army Controllists) was considered to be a long stride toward a zaibatsu-military amalgamation, and so it was. For Ikeda and Yuki, prudent men, made no attempt to interfere with military plans, already well advanced, to begin an all-out assault on China. Instead, they devised realistic methods for fitting those plans into the nation's economic and financial structure. Ikeda's main contribution at this point was to evolve a scheme for selling government bonds without drawing too heavily on the funds of private banks, which were needed for industrial expansion. The trick was to have the Bank of Japan purchase government bonds, as well as sell them, thus increasing the money in circulation as if by magic. Financially, it was no more sound than printing extra banknotes; but since few people understood the inflationary scheme, Ikeda got away with it. Although their terms in office were brief, Ikeda and Yuki proved the usefulness of having shrewd capitalist brains behind military brawn, and from then on zaibatsu executives remained at the financial controls.

In March 1937, after a general election that again demonstrated popular dissatisfaction with military rule, a semblance of civilian government was restored with the appointment of Prince Konoe Fumimaro as prime minister. As president of the House of Peers, Konoe had shown his ability to get along with the various factions and was on good terms with most bureaucrats and financiers because he avoided taking sides in disputes. His political tutor was the moderate Prince Saionji, but Konoe was also very acceptable to the militarists because he was an enthusiastic supporter of the Great East Asia Association, whose aim was to unite at least the eastern part of that vast continent under Japanese hegemony. With friends in the highest civilian and military circles and a lofty position in the imperial court, Konoe was welcomed as a unifying influence.

At first representatives of the zaibatsu were excluded from Konoe's military-bureaucratic cabinet, but Ikeda remained as governor of the Bank of Japan until replaced by Yuki. As a token of reconciliation with the business community, the court trying the Teijin case found all the defendants not guilty (despite earlier confessions of embezzlement and the acceptance of bribes) and the government let the case drop. Soon afterward the ringleader of that stock deal, Baron Go Seinosuke, became one of Konoe's closest advisers.

The strongest card in the Kwantung Army's hand was Manchukuo, which the radical rightists hoped to develop into an economic empire even stronger than Japan. Ostensibly their purpose was to preserve Manchukuo's "sacred soil" as a new frontier for Japan's oppressed farmers, small businessmen, and surplus workers. It appears, however, that the radical rightists were no less interested in developing Manchukuo as a basis for political power that would enabled them to "liberate" Japan from the zaibatsu and strengthen it for an eventual showdown with the Russians.

The job of building a modern nation in the vast underpopulated reaches of Manchuria, without zaibatsu capital or strong financial support from the imperial government, fell to a group of men chosen for their extraordinary resourcefulness and ruthlessness. Most powerful of the civilian administrators was Hoshino Naoki, a former tax official who had managed the puppet empire's finances for several years and was appointed chief of its General Affairs Board in 1936. Heading Manchukuo's industrial bureau was Kishi Nobusuke, who was an ardent convert to Kita Ikki's brand of state capitalism and, as director of industrial affairs in the Ministry of Commerce and Industry in Tokyo, had made a name as an adversary of the zaibatsu. In close liaison with those civilian bosses was General Tojo Hideki, the Kwantung Army's chief of staff. After the adoption of the five-year plan for Manchukuo, Emperor Pu-Yi's Japanese administrators set up the Manchurian Heavy Industries Company as the prime agency of economic development. It would have been the height of folly for the army to try to run such an enterprise. Instead, Hoshino and Kishi carried out their ingenious plan of transplanting Kuhara's up-and-coming Nissan concern to Manchukuo and giving its managers control over Manchurian Heavy Industries. By that time the Nissan concern, most powerful of the "new zaibatsu," consisted of Hitachi, Ltd. (which produced heavy, electrical, and general machinery and ships), Nippon Mining (coal, nonferrous metals, etc.), Nippon Marine Products (fisheries), Nissan Motors (motor vehicles and engines), Nissan Chemical Industries, Manchurian Heavy Industries, and hundreds of subsidiaries, all controlled by the holding company officially called Nippon Sangyo, but known familiarly as "Nissan." According to Eleanor Hadley, in 1941, at the height of its power, Nissan accounted for three-fourths of all overseas investments held by the eight largest zaibatsu.[6]

While Kuhara managed political affairs in Tokyo, his brother-in-law Aikawa Gisuke applied his keen organizing talents to developing the new firm into a superzaibatsu, with the full support of the Kwantung Army. In pursuance of the five-year plan, Aikawa began immediately to take over the industrial properties of the SMR, much to the distress of its zaibatsu stockholders, whose industrial operations in Manchuria were closely integrated with the SMR enterprises. The takeover was also a blow to Matsuoka Yosuke, a political heir of the dying Yamamoto Jotaro, who in 1935 had assumed the prestigious governorship of SMR. The position had become more important than ever, since the company had taken over the management of all former Chinese railways in Manchukuo after the Mukden incident and also ran the old Chinese Eastern Railway, which had been sold to the Japanese by the Soviet Union in 1935. But Matsuoka's power was greatly reduced by Nissan's assumption of the affiliated enterprises, which produced more income than the railways themselves; therefore, Matsuoka at first opposed the plan.

Matsuoka was sympathetic in principle, however, and joined the Kwantung Army junta that was soon to exercise a veritable dictatorship over Manchukuo. The Japanese, who have a predilection for acronyms, called that group the "Ni-ki-san-suke" or the "two *ki,* three *suke*" clique, a name contrived by combining the last syllables of its members' personal names. In addition to the two "kis," Tojo Hideki and Hoshino Naoki, there were actually four "sukes": the bureaucrats Kishi Shinsuke (who later called himself Nobusuke) and Matsuoka Yosuke, and the industrialists Aikawa Gisuke and Kuhara Fusanosuke. It is worth noting that those "sukes," all Choshu men related by marriage, had started their careers under the protection of the Choshu oligarchs, whose political dominance they were destined to inherit—or to seize in the swashbuckling tradition of their clan.

The problem of getting capital for development was crucial. Upon taking office as the first president of Manchurian Heavy Industries, Aikawa stated: "It would be highly desirable to call upon the whole world to contribute all that is best in its institutions toward building up and starting this gigantic project of the newly founded empire. . . . I must frankly admit that almost my only hope rests with the capital which the world would be ready to marshal if the work is to be accomplished within the stipulated [five-year] period."[7]

Efforts were made to attract such investments from abroad. Whether from pragmatism or idealism, Henry Ford was keenly interested, and so was Herbert Hoover; but the United States government opposed aiding Japanese expansion, and British funding had ceased in 1933 after a loan of four million pounds to the SMR. Because the new zaibatsu had no strong banks of their own, they relied primarily upon quasi-governmental institutions, such as the Bank of Chosen (the fiscal agent of the Kwantung Army) and the Industrial Bank, which under the Ikeda-Yuki policy was drawing funds from the Bank of Japan to grant credits for shipping zaibatsu-made machinery to Manchukuo. But even then money was still so tight that the Industrial Bank found it expedient to augment its income through such sidelines as smuggling precious metals and opium into China.

Opium was an important source of revenue for the Manchukuo government, through the Opium Monopoly Bureau set up by Hoshino. Following the example of the British in another part of China about a hundred years before, the Kwantung Army used opiates to weaken public resistance, and deliberately fostered drug addiction in Manchukuo and occupied areas of China. One means of hooking new users was the distribution of medicines containing morphine and of special cigarettes bearing the popular Japanese trademark "Golden Bat" but with mouthpieces containing small doses of heroin. These various narcotics, supplied quite legally to the Opium Monopoly Bureau by Mitsui and other trading companies, induced euphoria not only in the unfortunate victims but also in the members of the "Ni-ki-san-suke" clique, because the traffic was racking up profits of twenty to thirty million yen a year for financing the industrial development of Manchukuo (according to testimony presented at the Tokyo war crimes trials in 1948). A witness testified further that Hoshino negotiated at least one large loan from Japanese banks against collateral in the form of a lien on the profits from Manchukuo's Opium Monopoly Bureau. Another authority stated that the annual revenue from the narcotization policy in China, including Manchukuo, was estimated by the Japanese military at 300 million dollars a year.

The old zaibatsu, alarmed by the Manchurian clique's rapid success in consolidating its position, worked cooperatively in China proper to monopolize trade, resources, and industrial investment, hoping thus to prevent encroachment by the Kwantung Army and its friends. Vehicles for the joint efforts of Mitsui, Mitsubishi, and Sumitomo were the Oriental Colonization Company (of which "Razor" Yasukawa from Mitsui Bussan had become president) and the newly formed North China Development Company, both government-sponsored. Among the strongest of Japan's private enterprises in China were Kanebo and Toyo Menka (both progeny of Mitsui) in textiles and cotton trading, respectively. Their executives, especially Tsuda Shingo, president of Kanebo, were very influential in formulating Japan's continental policies. Furthermore, under Ikeda's regime as obanto, Mitsui chiefs active in China had improved their relations with moderate elements in Japan's armed services, both to gain protection and to influence military policy.

Military extremists were understandably anxious to dislodge the zaibatsu from their increasingly secure positions in China and to accelerate the pace of aggression. What the antizaibatsu zealots needed was a national crisis that would serve as a pretext for the mobilization of resources and public opinion, further militarization of the government, and decisive moves that would enable them to assert themselves in China as they had done in Manchuria.

The opportunity came (or was fabricated) in the summer of 1937, when a unit of Japan's North China garrison got involved in an exchange of fire with Chinese troops at the Marco Polo Bridge on the outskirts of Peking.

Historians, and even participants in the incident, are still arguing about how it happened. Officers at the scene of action, Chinese as well as Japanese, seemed to believe that the clash, which occurred in the middle of the night, resulted from a misunderstanding. In retrospect, however, it seems more likely that the Marco Polo Bridge firefight and subsequent unexplained skirmishes were initiated on orders from the highest echelons in the Japanese army and the government. Ignoring truce efforts, foreign minister Hirota Koki in Tokyo issued a belligerent ultimatum to the Chinese. When it was rejected, Japanese units began to move aggressively against Chinese population centers and railheads.

Prime Minister Konoe had not planned, apparently, to start the war at that time. But under pressure from his minister of the army, a hot-blooded Controllist, he dispatched three divisions to China and started mobilization in Japan. By mid-August both Peking and Shanghai were in Japanese hands, and Konoe was assured by his deceitful generals that the quarrel would soon be settled. But the Chinese refused to capitulate, and the war continued to spread. In an attempt to appease foreign governments, Konoe declared: "In sending troops to North China, of course, the government has no other purpose than to preserve the peace of East Asia."[8] But whether or not he realized it, the militarists had drawn Japan into a second Sino-Japanese War that was to last eight years and would take a toll of more than ten million lives before it ended in Japan's first and only military defeat.

Showing their genius for euphemism, the Japanese called it the "China Incident." The European powers who might have taken collective action against Japanese aggression preferred to accept Japan's convenient fiction that it was only an emergency measure to protect Japanese lives and property. The United States was in a difficult position because of the Neutrality Act, which required the federal government to cut off military supplies to both belligerents if a state of war was recognized. Because such an action would have hurt China more than Japan, Washington went along with the Japanese pretense. President Roosevelt appealed eloquently to other nations to "quarantine the aggressors," without naming Japan; but his implied accusation served only to anger United States isolationists, pacifists, and conservative labor unions. It also displeased his complacent ambassador in Tokyo, who grumbled that Roosevelt was disrupting his peacemaking efforts.

Grew's tolerance of Japanese fascism may or may not have been connected with his being a cousin of J. P. Morgan, whose enterprises were the largest American investors in Japan and in Mitsui firms. (Interestingly, Grew's predecessor as ambassador, W. Cameron Forbes, was a director of Morgan-dominated American Telephone & Telegraph, the largest corporation in the United States. It can be surmised that these ambassadors to Tokyo were more interested in the imperial Japanese government's ability to protect American investments in East Asia than in the rightness of its cause.) The Japanese aggression in China did elicit mild criticism from the League of Nations; but as in the case of the Manchurian coup, no punitive measures were attempted, and the harbingers of Konoe's "peace in East Asia" penetrated ever deeper into China.

In December, with the monstrous "Rape of Nanking," the Japanese military fanatics managed to arouse world opinion to a realization that the China Incident was a real war. But the horrifying details were successfully concealed from the Japanese public. As at the outset of previous wars, enthusiasm ran high; the conquest of the Chinese capital was hailed by Japan's subservient press and duly acclaimed by the misinformed people. Nationalism reached new heights as the imperial forces marched from victory to victory, occupying most of eastern China.

But in the councils of state Japan's leaders realized soberly that the Chinese, with endless reaches of territory in which to retreat, were not going to surrender. This was a war for which Japan had not been prepared, and as it progressed the government had to plan for drastic changes in Japan's economy, which was suffering from a shortage of investment capital, inflation, declining exports, and a severe balance-of-payments deficit. The finance minister, Kaya Okinori, although experienced in military finances, was incapable of coping with the crisis. Konoe, after repeated pleas, finally persuaded Ikeda Seihin to reenter the cabinet as minister of finance and, concurrently, as minister of commerce and industry. At the same time foreign minister Hirota Koki was replaced by General Ugaki Kazushige (Issei), who although once associated with Colonel Hashimoto and Mori Kaku in a conspiracy, was esteemed by his friend Ikeda as a moderate and an internationalist. Ikeda and Ugaki were Prime Minister Konoe's confidential advisers, and the three worked together privately to maintain some measure of government control over the army. Ikeda's main problem, however, was to prevent total regimentation of the economy under a series of laws that the military had insisted on enacting. Most draconian was the General Mobilization Law of 1938, which empowered the government to establish compulsory industrywide cartels; to restrict foreign trade, production, and consumption; to regulate finance; to mobilize labor, materials, capital, and equipment; and to control prices.

Ikeda went along with most of the provisions of the law, but drew the line at allowing the government to limit dividends to stockholders and at forcing banks to make loans. To him this seemed to be the watershed between sound fascism and state socialism. The minister of home affairs, fearing that the mobilization of labor without enforcement of controls over finance would cause public resentment, demanded that the law be applied equally to business and to labor, but Ikeda retorted: "Do you really think a factory worker knows how much stockholders receive as dividends? Why do you say such a damned foolish thing?"[9]

The home minister, an admiral, was so angered that he threatened to resign unless Ikeda was sacked. But Konoe and other cabinet members considered Ikeda indispensable and retained him in office after a compromise that set a ceiling of ten percent on dividends and excused private banks from making forced loans. For this act of defiance, which took no little courage, Ikeda earned the gratitude and admiration of his former business colleagues, who could now hope to escape complete subjugation by the military and enjoy uninterrupted profits from the China war. As their obanto he had been called "Ikeda of Mitsui," but when his influence as a statesman increased he was referred to more often as "Ikeda of Japan."

Whatever private feelings the businessmen may have had about the way the war was being conducted, they voiced no misgivings publicly, possibly because they were destined—or so they believed—to fall heir to the choicest business and industrial opportunities as Chinese competitors were subdued and other foreign capitalists were squeezed out. The attitude of Japanese management was set forth by Fujihara of Oji Paper, whose continental ambitions were sanguine in the extreme. Two years before the China offensive had begun, he wrote prophetically: "A long war does not strike terror into the hearts of the Japanese people. . . . It is probable that before peace talks [with China] are started in real earnest Japan may have occupied Nanking and Shantung in addition to North China and Shanghai. Her military occupation may last from two to three years, even ten years if necessary, until China repents of her past stand and becomes disposed to listen to reason. . . . During this military occupation an army of robust and hustling Japanese business go-getters may invade these territories under the protecting wings of the army and navy, to double and treble Japanese exports."[10]

This prediction was amazingly accurate. Between 1936 and 1941 Japan's trade with China and Manchukuo more than doubled, and trade with the yen bloc—Japan's colonies, puppet Manchukuo, and occupied China—represented more than sixty percent of the empire's total trade. A very large share of it was in entrepôt trade between these regions and foreign countries, notably India, the Philippines, Australia, and the United States, as Japan encroached upon the commerce of Western countries with Asia. Mitsui was dominant in imports and exports, handling twice the volume of Mitsubishi Shoji, which held second place; and Mitsui accounted for almost sixty percent of Japan's transactions within the yen bloc.

During Ikeda's double tenure, as minister of finance and minister of commerce and industry, the Konoe government set up the Asia Development Board for coordinating political, cultural, and economic affairs in the regions occupied by Japan. Under its supervision were two national policy corporations, the North China and Central China Development companies, for guiding the economic exploitation of occupied areas—mostly by private enterprise. To finance their five-year plans, the estimated cost of which was nearly two billion yen, Ikeda boosted the Bank of Japan's loans to Industrial Bank, which under the forced loan policy increased its loan balance by 700 percent in five years. The Industrial Bank raised more capital by issuing government-guaranteed debentures and also floated all the bonds issued for financing the two China development companies and the many private firms that sprang up in Manchukuo and in China after the occupation of Shanghai and Nanking. For additional investment revenue the Japanese conquerors seized control of customs duties in occupied areas in China and imposed any number of local taxes and licence fees upon the populace. Abusing their control over customs, the Japanese smuggled in enormous amounts of commodities and thus were able to undersell competitors, who had to pay duties.

Of particular value to Japanese business was the great industrial city of Shanghai. As soon as the invaders had it under control, zaibatsu "carpetbaggers" began grabbing major industries, such as the public utilities, cotton mills, and silk filatures. By taking over the textile mills they were able to eliminate Chinese competition, which until then had been fierce. The damage to Shanghai's industrial and private property as a result of the invasion was approximately eight billion dollars, and most local businessmen were ruined. Those whose factories were operable could not reopen them without permission from the Japanese consulate; but a condition for receiving that approval was the acceptance of Japanese partners or "technical assistance," which amounted to surrendering control. It turned out that among eager Japanese only members of the Cotton Spinners' Association, dominated by Kanebo and Toyo Menka, were privileged to make such tie-ups with Chinese operators. Thus Mitsui interests were able to take over the biggest cotton-textile establishments in Shanghai and the other occupied cities. The same system of teamwork among the bureaucracy, national-policy companies, governmental banks, and the zaibatsu was applied in other industries and in each region as it fell to the advancing Japanese armies.

Within a few years after the outbreak of the China Incident, Bussan alone had established or bought its way into about thirty private companies having a paid-up capital of more than fifty million yen (many of them held jointly with other Mitsui companies), in addition to its large interests in eight semigovernmental "control companies" capitalized at one hundred million yen or so. Industrial fields ran the gamut from spinning, weaving, silk filature, and textile fibers, to foodstuffs, flour, oils, and fisheries. Among them were ironmaking, oil refining, chemicals, machinery, brewing, transportation, and warehousing. Mitsui Bank, Mining, Oji Paper, Kanebo, Toyo Menka, Toyo Rayon, and the others also had numerous Chinese subsidiaries in their own fields. The degree of dominance they exercised was indicated not so much by the percentage of their capital investment as by their political influence and the positions they commanded in the control companies that regulated the respective industries. It is safe to say that in the occupied areas of China Mitsui's sway over the economy was even stronger than it was in Japan, since the Chinese were powerless to resist and the Japanese ruled by force rather than under established law. Obviously, any Chinese trying to invoke due process against a representative of Mitsui would have found himself in serious trouble, not only with the cowed local government but also with the Kempeitai—the Japanese Gestapo.

Both Ikeda and Nanjo Kaneo, his successor as obanto of Mitsui Gomei, were aristocratic cosmopolitans. As such, if not as civilized human beings, they must have been repelled by the sadistic gangsterism of Japan's military bosses, even though it brought profit to the concern and advanced Japan's material fortunes. Soon after the Nanking horror Nanjo stepped down in favor of Mukai Tadaharu, a thick-skinned trader from Bussan; but Ikeda, despite recurrent illness, held on to his cabinet positions impassively. Perhaps he felt that if he resigned (as he was tempted to do after a military officer was put in charge of the Asia Development Board) his place would be taken by some flunky of the militarists. As it was, he saw at least the possibility of influencing the fanatics against following their more calamitous policies.

Believing that the China situation could be settled without a general war, he put up strong resistance against antagonizing the democratic powers by identifying Japan too clearly with the Rome-Berlin Axis. Through his long experience in financing Bussan's gargantuan trade operations, he knew that even in normal times Japan could scarcely maintain its commercial standing without both British money and American markets. As Arthur Tiedemann has said in his "Big Business and Politics in Prewar Japan," a very revealing essay: "It was inconceivable to Ikeda that the economic expansion planned for Japan could take place without access to Western machinery, Western raw materials, and Western short-term financing for the import of raw materials destined for export. Therefore in policy discussions his weight was always thrown on the side of maintaining friendly relations with England and America."[11] For such reasons he successfully opposed the appointment of the pro-Nazi Matsuoka as minister of foreign affairs.

However, the same "wave of the future" psychology that affected the people of the West was becoming epidemic in Japan as the forces of fascism advanced wherever they fought. Mussolini had conquered Ethiopia; General Francisco Franco, aided by Mussolini and Hitler, was crushing the Spanish Republic; Hitler had annexed Austria in March 1938; and in the fall Prime Minister Neville Chamberlain's capitulation to Hitler at Munich gave the Nazis control of Czechoslovakia and hegemony in central Europe. Concurrently, the Japanese forces drove southward to take Canton and Hankow in southern China. A puppet government like that of Manchukuo had been set up to rule occupied China, and in November Prime Minister Konoe made a flamboyant proposal to end hostilities in China by announcing his program for "a new order in East Asia"—actually an anticommunist bloc comprising Japan, Manchukuo, and occupied China. But although Konoe waived claims for indemnities, the Kuomintang and the Chinese Communists failed to appreciate his offer and stiffened their resistance.

Konoe, an introspective esthete, was disheartened by his failure to end the "incident" in China and weary of his struggle against the bellicose generals as well as their civilian allies in the government and the Diet. Ikeda, lacking support in his lonely campaign for a modicum of common sense in foreign policy, also found his spirits flagging, and at the end of 1938 he and Konoe decided to resign. Serious consideration was given to "Ikeda of Japan" as a possible prime minister, but his pro-Western stand had made him unpopular with the army. Konoe himself preferred the ultrarightist Hiranuma, whom Ikeda opposed at the time despite their long friendship. Ikeda was frozen out and never held another cabinet position, although he was accepted as a member of the privy council and continued to advise certain government leaders.

Under a series of short-lived cabinets headed successively by Hiranuma, a retired general, and a retired admiral, Japan was drawn into a military alliance with Germany and Italy, became more deeply mired in the China war, and was gradually reconciled to the inevitability of a war against the United States and Great Britain. In preparation, the mobilization laws were strengthened and economic activities, as well as education, labor, and political activity, were more tightly regimented.

This was no novelty to Japanese, of course. The Major Industries

Control Law of 1931, due to expire in 1936, had been renewed, and by the outbreak of the war in China there were more than a thousand industrial cartels—sponsored by the government but operated by the industrialists themselves—covering one-fourth of the nation's total production. In addition, there was the Central Union of Industrial Guilds, set up during the depression to relieve small businessmen and now used to integrate them with the zaibatsu war machine. The Union, with more than a thousand guilds enrolled, controlled distribution of materials and equipment. Under the leadership of Vice Admiral Godo Takuo, a Prussian-educated technologist (whose daughter had married the heir of the Asano zaibatsu family), the Union was hastily extending its dominion over most small industrial producers and eventually subjugated 52,000 guilds.

Such regimentation, dear to the military-bureaucratic mind, was accepted calmly by the zaibatsu, who had been called upon to make the cumbersome machinery work. After Ikeda's political "retirement," which again was only nominal, the economic ministries were usually filled by zaibatsu managers, notably Fujihara of Mitsui, relatives of the zaibatsu such as Godo, or their political henchmen. Far from being crushed by the military-bureaucratic bosses, the zaibatsu managed, on the whole, to dominate the economy to their advantage while seeming to act as the agents of those bosses. Indeed, the situation was comfortable for the big entrepreneurs: free at last from the gadflies of organized labor and party politics, they were able to organize the economic system to their own advantage, curb their overambitious competitors, coordinate the activities of smaller businesses with their own, and provide themselves with scarce raw materials, markets, loans, government subsidies, and whatever else they needed. The war, of course, was a nuisance and a nagging threat; yet without it they could not have hoped to enjoy such blessings.

But in the attempted regimentation of private business the interests of the zaibatsu had been served much better than those of the nation as a whole, and the various financial cliques still tended to compete rather than to cooperate. The economy, not yet prepared for the exigencies of war, staggered under the double burden of expanding munitions production in anticipation of a global conflict while continuing the enervating campaign in China. The government's reaction was to intensify its efforts to establish the "new economic order," or national socialist structure, that had been envisioned since the 1920s by antizaibatsu right wingers. As the movement gained strength, the most influential businessmen, realizing that they could not oppose the concept openly, made a convincing pretense of supporting it while scheming to emasculate it.

In the summer of 1940, after Hitler's blitzkrieg on Poland and his conquest of Denmark, Norway, the Low Countries, and France, Prince Konoe was called again to serve as prime minister and formed a cabinet that appeared capable, at first, of imposing a totalitarian economic system upon Japan. In vital positions were four strong men of the "Ni-ki-san-suke" clique from Manchuria: Tojo, minister of war; Matsuoka, minister of foreign affairs; Hoshino, state minister in charge of the National Planning Board; and Kishi, vice-minister of commerce and industry. But significantly, Kishi, the self-styled "creator" of the Manchurian heavy industrial complex that had buttressed the Kwantung Army's power, felt compelled to decline Konoe's offer of the top position in the ministry, presumably because he knew that he was not trusted by the old zaibatsu, whose cooperation was now more essential than ever. Instead, on the recommendation of Ikeda Seihin, the commerce and industry portfolio was given to Kobayashi Ichizo, a former Mitsui Bank director (related by marriage both to Ikeda and to Kato Takeo of Mitsubishi Bank). Also helping to relieve the antizaibatsu coloring of the Manchurian quartet were a Mitsubishi businessman-bureaucrat as finance minister and a high executive of Sumitomo as minister of railways and minister of agriculture and forestry, concurrently.

At the time, detailed plans for the "new economic order" were being rushed to completion by major business organizations, in liaison with the Ministry of Commerce and Industry and the National Planning Board, which were evolving their own. The zaibatsu master plan was being prepared under the guidance of Baron Go, head of the Japan Economic Federation, who worked smoothly with Ikeda Seihin, the Mitsui-oriented Governor Yuki of the Bank of Japan, Minister of Commerce and Industry Kobayashi, and his predecessor Fujihara, as well as their counterparts from other zaibatsu groups. According to the draft of their program, the wartime economy was to be run by a "Council of Key Industry Control Organizations," an organ for maintaining liaison among the cartels of major industries and also between the united cartels and the government. Its supreme council and eight subcouncils would regulate all production, distribution, and consumption in the empire. In addition, the businessmen's plan called for a restructuring of all private economic organizations into a similar monolith. This plan met most of the requirements prescribed by Planning Board chief Hoshino, who had instructed the businessmen: "Whether or not a state can display total power determines its rise or decline. Hitherto the government and the people [i.e., the capitalists] have been divided into two, controller and controlled. Such an idea should be corrected."[12]

The differences of opinion between the business fascists and the military-bureaucratic fascists had been boiled down to two main questions: who would be in control of the controllers, and how would the rights of private ownership be incorporated into the new structure? Minister of Commerce and Industry Kobayashi, a big capitalist in his own right, naturally stood for private enterprise and zaibatsu control over the totalitarian economy. He had recently returned from a trip to Italy and Germany, and although he expressed great admiration for Hitler's military strategy and even his diplomacy, he looked askance at the takeover of munitions industries by Nazi chieftains such as Hermann Goering. He was also somewhat worried about his own vice-minister, Kishi, who was rather too exuberant over the prospect of national socialism in Japan.

Baron Go's zaibatsu planners, getting the jump on their bureaucratic opponents, submitted their scheme to minister Kobayashi and waited for his opinion. But just then the latter, accompanied by Mitsui's new obanto Mukai Tadaharu, departed on a mission to the Dutch East Indies to negotiate for oil supplies vital to Japan's war policy. In his absence the Planning Board, with the collaboration of Kishi and Tojo, presented to the cabinet its own draft plan for industrial reorganization, which incorporated state-enforced controls rather than voluntary ones, government appointment of cartel directors, separation of capital from management, and other measures for establishing what was termed a "collective planned economy."

Kobayashi, although best remembered today as a backer of movie studios and of the Takarazuka all-girl light-opera troupe, was also a formidable fighter in the business arena. When he heard of the Planning Board's dastardly deed, he flew back to Tokyo (leaving Mukai to handle the oil negotiations) and mobilized the business world against the Hoshino-Kishi plan. "There is no country in the world but Russia," he said aggrievedly to a group of colleagues, "where the separation of capital from management could even be considered." The fiercely anticommunist Kishi took exception to the minister's inference that he was a "red," and after a violent quarrel Kishi was forced to resign. Then the Planning Board's draft was watered down with respect to enforced controls, encroachment on private ownership, and appointment of cartel directors.[13]

The press hailed this victory. One editorial, in the *Oriental Economist*, praised the businessmen for having "recovered their senses and . . . gotten up enough courage to criticize the government. If their courage is not short-lived and businessmen keep up their practice of communicating their views to the government, the trade and industry of Japan will be the chief beneficiaries."[14]

The editorialist's interpretation overlooked the fact that, under Ikeda's guidance, the zaibatsu had been quietly communicating their views to the government without interruption, and had spoken out more audibly only when it had become necessary to counterattack. Minister Kobayashi was forced to quit after a vengeful income-tax evasion charge was thrown at him; but Hoshino and Kishi were sacked too, and their successors were more friendly to big business. Although the Kwantung Army's fascists rode roughshod over Japan and crushed the last vestiges of other freedoms, they never quite established the economic dictatorship they hungered for. In the very darkest days that loomed ahead, servitors or friends of the zaibatsu appeared in every cabinet, holding positions that gave them enough of a voice in the affairs of state to bring the great financial houses through the Second World War not only intact but greatly aggrandized.

23 · Cracks in
the Foundation

THE HOUSE OF MITSUI, born in an era of peace, had nevertheless made its greatest leaps in times of revolution, rebellion, and international warfare, and its members had learned that the longer the war the greater the benefit to Mitsui. Within three years after the outbreak of the China Incident, war on the continent had become an institution, and a highly profitable one. The campaign had won for Japan a "second Manchukuo," greater in area than France, Germany, and Belgium combined, with a population larger than that of the United States. In China, Japan's armies had so disrupted the economy of occupied areas that some thirty million people were dependent upon governmental aid or private charity. Nevertheless, most of the cost of the occupation was borne by the Chinese themselves, and Japan's economy was invigorated by a sharply rising inflow of raw materials produced at lowest possible cost and obtained in exchange for relatively high-priced Japanese goods.

The cost in human life was exorbitant, but here again the Chinese bore the brunt of war. Approximately 800,000 Chinese servicemen had been killed (by Japanese estimate); and if civilian deaths from bombing, massacres, floods, and pestilences are included, the toll was around 2,500,000, according to British observers. This China Incident, through 1940, had cost Japan only about fifty thousand dead.

Even so, foreign experts believed that without a decisive victory soon Japan would bog down in the vast quagmire of China. But after the conquest of the southern provinces the Japanese armies curtailed their military operations; and Chiang Kai-shek, secure in the remoteness of his Chungking stronghold, sat tight, waiting for Japan to embroil itself with more powerful enemies—the United States and Great Britain. To those Japanese who feared that Japan was overextended, or that military investments had reached the point of diminishing returns, the newly appointed Minister of Commerce and Industry Kishi Nobusuke declared reassuringly: "It is a gross mistake to think that the economic strength of Japan has been weakened by the war today. It is true that the battle lines in China extend far and wide, but the total of materials being consumed in China today is only ten percent of the goods Japan is now producing [actually it was twenty-three percent of the gross national product]. It is just chicken feed to the Japanese empire of 1941."[1]

That was not just empty propaganda, for between 1936 and 1941 the national income had doubled, to about thirty-four billion yen. The paid-up capital of major industrial companies had also doubled; and the heavy industries, which had long since overtaken light industries in output, accounted for more than half of the total production. Most of the new capital had been put up by the zaibatsu banks either willingly or unwillingly; but added impetus for growth of production came from the control corporations set up under the National Mobilization Law. These were government sponsored, but were managed by leaders from private business who supervised production and distribution in each sector of industry. Since these corporations, dozens in all, were established by private as well as government investments, they actually produced profits for the concerns presumably under their control. One good example was the Industrial Equipment Management Control Association headed by Fujihara of Oji Paper, who at seventy-nine had become virtual czar of the industrial economy.

The control corporations, whose job was to eliminate bottlenecks in the economy, fostered the establishment of new companies wherever needed. Some of these were the "national project" companies that sprang up all over Japan and in its colonies and occupied areas. These also combined private and public investment, and of course the most attractive opportunities were preempted by the zaibatsu themselves.

Because capital was tight, and the zaibatsu were reluctant to overexpand, new companies were financed by the national policy banks, especially Industrial Bank of Japan, and by "temporary military funds" advanced to private firms. Between 1937 and the end of the war such funds amounted to approximately thirteen billion yen, of which more than sixty percent went to heavy industries. However, the next largest share, fourteen percent, was extended to trading companies, of whom Mitsui Bussan and its affiliates were the largest recipients.

This distribution is understandable, because Bussan played an essential role in securing huge stockpiles of raw materials, fuel, and other strategic goods needed for munitions production; also, through its entrepôt trade, Bussan provided a major share of the foreign exchange that was urgently needed as short-term loans from British and American banks dried up.

Less conspicuous was the Showa Overseas Trading Company (descended from the old Taihei Kumiai, or Taiping Company), a Bussan subsidiary that was supplying the largest share of materiel for the Japanese forces and their puppet armies, irregulars, and labor corps over-seas. According to Hadley's study, Showa Overseas Trading handled more than half the offshore contracts let by the Japanese army during the 1930s and remained its biggest supplier until the end of the Pacific War. Showa's sales were not confined to the Japanese army, however; the firm conducted a brisk business with other governments by means of its branches throughout the Far East and in the Near East, the Balkans, and Germany as well.

One of the more profitable items handled by Bussan was aircraft manufactured by the Nakajima company, Japan's largest producer by far. Since 1920 Bussan had enjoyed an exclusive contract to distribute Nakajima's products, and thus supplied the armed forces with most of their aircraft until the army and navy began buying directly in 1937 and 1940, respectively. Mitsui had no capital investment in Nakajima but made big profits from commissions on sales and on technical licenses obtained for Nakajima from Bendix, Chance-Vought, Douglas, Hamilton Standard Propellor, and Fokker, all of whom facilitated the rapid advance of Japanese aircraft technology until the eve of the Second World War. Also assisting directly in the Japanese military buildup was Sperry Gyroscope, whose ship-control systems and searchlights were being made in Japan under licenses obtained through Bussan.

There is a widespread belief, carefully encouraged by Mitsui executives after the war, that the concern played only a minor role in Japan's munitions industries. It is true that in the early 1930s Mitsui lagged behind Mitsubishi in heavy industries and was briefly overtaken by Nissan. Nevertheless, its contributions to the making of munitions were very impressive, except in shipbuilding, steel, motors, and a few other specialized fields. At the outset of the war in China, Mitsui was paramount in coal, some nonferrous metals, strategic chemicals, and ordnance, among other things, and thereafter moved forward rapidly into specifically military industries. Tokyo Shibaura (with General Electric still in the picture) was Japan's biggest producer of electrical machinery; and Japan Steel Works, sharing technology with Vickers, Krupp, and United Engineering of the United States, was the leading supplier of armor plate, ordnance, and equipment for the imperial navy's mammoth battleships, as well as of heavy artillery for the army. Equally important was Mitsui Chemical (separated from Mitsui Mining in 1941), which led the nation's makers of dyestuffs, and produced explosives, chemical- and bacteriological-warfare weapons, and synthetic oil from coal.

One of Japan's biggest problems was its lack of petroleum. Only eight percent of the nation's requirement was produced domestically, and most of the remainder was purchased through Rising Sun Oil (a subsidiary of Royal Dutch Shell), the Standard Oil group, and Associated Oil (later Tidewater). In 1934 Japan passed a law requiring the foreign oil companies to maintain a stock equal to at least six months' normal supply, obviously so that it could be seized in an emergency. The foreign companies protested, and as a compromise Bussan built tanks adequate for three months' supply and the companies provided the remaining storage facilities. After the China war began, this reserve was deemed insufficient, so the government stepped up its synthetic oil program, begun by Yamamoto Jotaro in Manchuria. A pioneer in applying this process was the Miike Synthetic Oil Company in Omuta, operating under license from the Krupp concern, which supplied assorted technological information to other Mitsui companies as well.

Also under government sponsorship, Mitsui Mining established the Nan'yo (South Seas) Aluminum Company to mine bauxite on islands of the southwestern Pacific and to refine it at Omuta. Before long the refining subsidiary was merged with a chemical firm in Korea to form Toyo Light Metal, later called Mitsui Light Metal.

As in every other war during the preceding half century, Mitsui Mining produced most of the lead for the army's bullets and more than one-third of the nation's coal. Mitsui Chemical supplied a major share of the explosives, and Japan Steel Works about fifteen percent of the heavy weapons. In addition, by 1944 Mitsui affiliates were supplying eighty percent of Japan's paper, fifty-three percent of its dyestuffs and calcium cyanamide, twenty-five percent of its heavy electrical machinery, twenty percent of its portland cement and rayon, and sixteen percent of its nitric acid. The last-named commodity was used by Mitsui's Toyo Koatsu for making explosives under a patented nitric acid and ammonia process purchased by Mitsui Mining from Du Pont of the United States for almost a million dollars. At that time, and during the Second World War, Mitsui was part of an explosives cartel that included Du Pont, Imperial Chemical Industries of Britain, and I. G. Farben of Germany.

In 1937, when Bussan was forced to give up its lucrative position as middleman between Nakajima Aircraft and the army, Mitsui made a deal with the navy to establish its own company, Showa Aircraft, with an initial capital of thirty million yen. Through Bussan, Showa arranged to purchase semimanufactures from Douglas Aircraft and assemble them for the navy under supervision of Douglas engineers dispatched to Japan. Thus the company was able to go into production without delay. With Bussan as the majority shareholder, and the late Baron

Dan's son-in-law Makita in charge of production, Showa soon doubled its capital and established manufacturing operations at three major plants and two subsidiary factories in Japan and Korea.

Also in 1937 Bussan established Toyo (later Mitsui) Precision Machinery & Engineering to manufacture machine tools and rapidly increased its small initial capital to a peak of 100 million yen by the end of the war. Also in 1937 the Tama Shipyard of Bussan was separated to form a new organization (now called Mitsui Shipbuilding & Engineering), which expanded operations from its home base in Okayama Prefecture to Hiroshima and Osaka and took over "liberated" shipyards in Shanghai, Hongkong, and Nanking.

Despite such an impressive background in war-related heavy and chemical industries, however, Mitsui was not yet making the most of its opportunities as a "merchant of death." There were three reasons for this restraint: the concern's traditional emphasis upon banking, commerce, mining, and light industry; an extremely conservative financial policy; and the personal preferences of the clan and some of its most responsible retainers. The obanto of Mitsui Gomei at the time, Mukai Tadaharu, was a Bussan man who emphasized international trade and short-term credit rather than long-term investment in heavy industries. But as hostilities in China dragged on and foreign countries applied pressure, trade with the United States and Great Britain, which had accounted for half of Japan's exports in 1936, dwindled to one-fifth of the total by 1941; and the trade balance was so unfavorable that Japan, as in the early Meiji era, had to pay out large amounts of gold from its treasury reserves in lieu of foreign currency.

At home, too, capital was tight. Funds were available from government sources, but acceptance of such loans incurred obligations that would further hamper the concern's independence. And remembering the unfortunate consequences of the *Kongo* bribery affair and subsequent scandals, Mukai was not eager to become involved in the shady negotiations often necessary in dealing with bureaucrats and military authorities. Even more compelling was his belief (expressed recently to the author) that Japan was heading into a war it could not win.

Like most of the Mitsui family heads themselves, Mukai Tadaharu was an internationalist with many friends and clients in the democratic world, and he may have had personal reasons for his aloofness from the military. Another factor was a project, strongly backed by Bussan, to stage a world's fair in Tokyo. This would have been the first international exposition ever to be held in an Asian country, and Mitsui's elder statesman Fujihara Ginjiro headed its planning committee. The war with China had necessitated a postponement (until 1970, as it turned out), but some Mitsui people kept hoping for an early end to hostilities so that the exposition could be rescheduled.

Prime Minister Konoe's "new economic order," however, allowed no sentimentality about fairs or any halfheartedness in fighting a war. The military and the hard-driving Manchuria bureaucrats, armed with new laws, were putting relentless pressure on the zaibatsu to expand their war industries, regardless of the consequences. This put a severe financial strain on the owners of the great fortunes, who for several years had been paying out more than half of their reported incomes in taxes. In fiscal 1940 Japan's twenty-four richest subjects paid a total of fifty-seven million yen. Baron Mitsui Hachiroemon, who paid the largest tax that year, yielded to the government 4,450,000 from his income of 7,500,000 yen. In addition, there were inheritance taxes amounting to almost twenty percent of the value of an estate, and the Mitsui clan, having lost several family heads during the 1930s, owed approximately forty million yen in back taxes.

Mukai, faced with the double problem of expanding industries and keeping the Mitsuis solvent, temporized by selling stock in Gomei and other enterprises while continually juggling accounts to satisfy the government's insatiable demands. One auditor of Gomei, harassed beyond endurance, warned the directors: "Unless Gomei is reorganized, the Mitsui concern cannot survive." Whereupon, exhausted in body and mind, he killed himself.

Obviously a radical break with tradition was necessary, and a rather young section chief, Edo Hideo, was the one who dared to propose it. A very quiet man (perhaps because he spoke with a rural accent that was ridiculed by his colleagues from the better universities), Edo had been denied the advancement to which his mind entitled him, but he was stubborn. After he had thought things out thoroughly, he asked for a private conference with Mukai. Ordinarily, junior executives were stiff with fear when in the presence of the obanto, but Edo was not intimidated. He had already discounted the risk: when he stepped into the obanto's office he carried a retirement notice to be tendered in case his ideas were rejected. Mukai's thin face was impassive, his deep-set eyes motionless and cold. Edo, in his Ibaraki farmer's dialect, delivered his speech. Since the war will be a long one, he said in effect, Mitsui's emphasis should be on heavy industries. Why should the concern stick to finance and trade when the trend of the times is against it? Having survived thus far, he outlined his plan for mobilizing the full power of Mitsui behind the war effort.

This encounter took place in 1939, and in the following year the venerable house was transformed, structurally, almost beyond recognition. It had become imperative that Gomei, almost wholly owned by the eleven Mitsui family heads, be converted into a joint-stock company. But if the conversion had been direct, a huge tax would have been levied. Furthermore, the concern is believed to have held hidden assets of more than 1.2 billion yen, which would have been brought into the open and also heavily taxed. It seems to have been Edo's idea, approved by Mukai and adviser Ikeda, to take the extraordinary course of absorbing Gomei, the top holding company with a capital of 312 million yen, into Bussan, its subsidiary, whose capital was only 150 million yen. After complicated adjustments, the capital of the new Mitsui Bussan came out at 300 million yen. At the same time one-fourth of the new shares were sold to the general public. Mukai emerged as chairman, and Ishida Reisuke, obanto of the old Bussan, as managing director.

The new firm was a bewildering contrivance. Upon the trunk of Bussan, with its scores of commercial and industrial satellites, had been grafted Japan's largest bank, trust bank, and mining company. This pleased neither the subordinate companies nor the government, which found it most inappropriate for the financial institutions to be adjuncts of a trading company. For, although the Tokugawa-period prejudice against bankers had been overcome, commerce was still considered a somewhat degrading occupation. As a result of these dissatisfactions, another new organization, nominally the controlling organ of the whole concern, was formed to accommodate Bank, Trust, Life, Mining, and other subsidiaries. This body, Somotokata, or General Head-quarters—a name intentionally reminiscent of the ancient Omotokata—was headed by Baron Hachiroemon, with Mukai as chief manager and his predecessor Nanjo as adviser. Edo was appointed deputy general manager.

In assembling this two-headed monster, Mukai and his colleagues took great pains to protect the financial interests of the clan. For one thing, most of the stock in newly formed or reorganized companies, such as Shipbuilding and Mitsui Precision, was transferred to the family heads personally. As a most unusual measure, a new company called Mitsui Real Estate was created to administer urban properties formerly held by Gomei. According to Hadley, these properties, mainly office buildings, were bought from the top holding company at book value (less than one-quarter their market value of 125 million yen) by means of a loan from the holding company. All the shares were owned by members of the House, and thus the profits from renting these buildings and grounds, mostly to Mitsui companies, accrued to the clan directly.

If the Mitsuis themselves played a minor role in this reorganization, it was not because all of them were incompetent. A few of the family heads were businessmen of very respectable caliber. Mitsui Gennosuke had served well as president of Mining, and his son Takahisa (a Dartmouth College graduate) was an able director of Gomei, Bank, Mining, and Bussan during the 1930s and 1940s. Another family head, Baron Takanaga, a director of Mining and Bussan, became chairman of Mitsui Chemical when it was established separately in 1941, and president of Japan Synthetic Oil while serving as director of production in the same company. Baron Mitsui Takaharu, a cosmopolite, wrote a book on the history of Japanese transportation before assuming the positions of president of Gomei and a director of Bank, Trust, and Bussan. He also became chairman of the Japan-Germany Society.

In general, however, the Mitsuis were an average lot, and even at their best were hopelessly outclassed by their hired executives, carefully selected from among the most brilliant businessmen of the time. It is no cause for wonder, then, that as their enterprises became more complex and their wealth greater, their personal roles in the clan's multifarious enterprises should have diminished. Necessarily, the holding company and its subsidiaries, now beyond the control and even the comprehension of the owners, became increasingly independent as professional managers took full responsibility.

While Japan's real leaders struggled to resolve their differences and perfect the war machine, the Mitsui family heads who were still active in company matters had difficulty in reaching agreement on anything. Symptomatic of their disunity was the meteoric rise of a formerly obscure executive, Sasaki Shiro, to the presidency of Real Estate through the patronage of Baron Hachiroemon Takakimi, over whom he exercised an influence far out of proportion to his ability. Playing Iago to the baron's Othello, he traded shrewdly on suspicion and jealousy among the family heads and their favorites to advance his own fortunes.

Sasaki had developed his natural abilities as a schemer through his experience in Mitsui's "research department," which he had headed since the retirement of Ariga. In this position he managed the political affairs of the Mitsui combine, which had become more intricate since the concern had terminated its support of the Seiyukai and since the militarists had imposed their extraconstitutional government. Now it was Sasaki rather than Mitsui's political henchmen who handled the lobbying among cabinet ministers and dietmen, made confidential business arrangements with military officers and bureaucrats, procured or supplied intelligence in liaison with government agencies or undercover agents, and maintained contacts with the underworld. With the rapid decline of international trade and civilian production in Japan's wartime economy, the concern became more and more dependent upon government and military favor, and thus Sasaki's power was increasing as that of his superiors diminished. Since his own views matched those of the totalitarians and expansionists, he used his influence over Baron Hachiroemon to involve the Mitsuis ever more deeply in economic and political maneuverings that furthered Japanese aggression.

As in the past, payments from Sasaki's office (which was called the "Welfare Department") were made in cash, and usually went unrecorded. It is known, however, that Mitsui funds were used to support several organizations of a quasi-official nature, such as the Kokusaku Kenkyukai, or National Policy Investigation Society, established by zaibatsu leaders ostensibly to study urgent political problems and report their findings to the government. The actual manager of the society was Yatsugi Kazuo, an intimate friend of the late Kita Ikki and an irregular member of the research section of the Ministry of War. The society was supported by regular contributions from assorted ministries and the South Manchurian Railway, as well as from Mitsubishi, Nissan, and other zaibatsu. One of its numerous projects was the planning of the Greater East Asia Co-Prosperity Sphere, for which Mitsui and other zaibatsu made special contributions. Such offerings were not mere tokens of patriotism but, rather, were sound investments, because they gave the zaibatsu access to highly classified military secrets. Naturally, Mitsui's international intelligence operations were in turn a valuable source for research or espionage organizations connected with the imperial army and navy, so the relationship was symbiotic.

In September 1940—after the imperial army advanced into northern Indochina and the United States responded with an embargo on scrap-iron exports to Japan—the Konoe government, with General Tojo as war minister, set up the Total War Research Institute to "control basic study and research in connection with national total war." Members of the institute, at first headed by Hoshino Naoki, included high-ranking military men, bureaucrats, and staff members of large corporations such as the SMR, and, in addition, representatives from major banks and industrial corporations. Presumably it was Sasaki's job to provide funds and personnel from Mitsui's combine and to make profitable use for Mitsui's business of information gathered from participating in this top-secret agency. Sasaki's sinister Welfare Department also handled arrangements for Korean and Chinese conscript labor for the Miike mines and for the secret production of bacteriological weapons at Omuta for use in China and Manchuria.

The Welfare Department's most vital task, however, was to secure actual contracts and subsidies for Mitsui's companies, on the basis of information obtained through participation in secret agencies. Outright bribery, though still frequent, was probably too dangerous for a concern such as Mitsui, which was already a target of militarist vengeance. It was considered quite proper, however, to solicit favors from high-ranking officers by offering them sinecures in private corporations after retirement, and all the major concerns had constellations of admirals and generals on their payrolls. Employed by Japan Steel Works, for example, were General Yoshida Toyohiko, former chief of Army Technical Headquarters, a retired vice-admiral, and a colonel of artillery. And heading North Sakhalin Petroleum, a Mitsui affiliate, was Admiral Sakonji Masazo, a former chief of naval staff, who served concurrently as Minister of Commerce and Industry in the third Konoe cabinet.

By the end of the 1930s the military moguls, having silenced all opposition except that of the zaibatsu, had ushered in the ugliest and most disgraceful era in modern Japanese history. Every sector of society was organized for political regimentation and indoctrination. The labor unions were dissolved and their members absorbed into an all-embracing labor front patterned after Hitler's Arbeitsdienst. In announcing the change, the Minister of Welfare declared: "Our primary aim is to drive Communist ideas and dangerous social thoughts from the minds of the people by ordering the dissolution of the established labor unions, which have a tendency to sharpen class consciousness among workers, which hamper the development of industry, and disturb the peace and order of the country."[2]

The now toothless political parties were herded unprotesting into a federation called the Imperial Rule Assistance Association, or IRAA, headed by Prince Konoe and an advisory board of cabinet ministers, bureaucrats, military officers, politicians, and businessmen. This was the culmination of a movement begun in 1932 by General Araki Sadao (the most eloquent spokesman of the Imperial Way faction and a conspirator in the February rebellion and other incidents), with help from Mori Kaku, Yamamoto Jotaro, and other Seiyukai reactionaries.

Under the slogan "ichioku isshin," one hundred million people with one mind, coined by IRAA director Araki, the nation was rallied to win the "holy war," exterminate foreigners, purge the emperor's pure land of alien ideologies, and achieve a "Showa Restoration" in a reaffirmation of the Meiji renaissance begun in 1868. As education minister, Araki had already nationalized and overhauled the educational system, stressing patriotism, discipline, and physical training at the expense of academic learning. Meanwhile, his disciple Colonel Hashimoto, who longed to wage war on the West, formed a young men's association to propagate his venomous xenophobia and encourage emperor worship. In 1940 Araki merged the association, claiming five million members, with a nationwide youth federation professing the same noble aims. Through its good offices schoolboys from the remotest corners of

Japan were brought to Tokyo in large groups to prostrate themselves
before the Imperial Palace and to visit Yasukuni Shrine, which every
truly patriotic youth hoped to make his spirit's eternal abode. A popular feature of the shrine was a military hall, some of the funds for which
had been contributed by the Mitsuis as part of Ikeda's "face-lifting"
campaign. There the youths were indoctrinated with "a proper understanding of the meaning of national defense" and were allowed the
excitement of operating real guns and tanks electrically by pressing the
motivating buttons.[3]

To maintain the political purity of the state, laws against un-Japanese
activities were tightened steadily. In 1941 the Peace Preservation Ordinance was revised to prescribe penalties ranging from ten years in
prison to death by hanging for organizing or cooperating with any
association whose object was "disavowing the system of private ownership." This law did not apply, of course, to national socialists such as
Kishi and Hoshino, or to terrorists of antizaibatsu leanings, who were
treated with exceptional leniency. For example, Okawa Shumei, sentenced to fifteen years in prison for his role in the assassination of Prime
Minister Inukai, was released a few years later and resumed his position as director of the SMR's East Asian Research Institute. The Reverend Inoue Nissho, imprisoned for life after the murder of Baron
Dan in 1932, was released in a general amnesty in 1940 and was given
quarters in the home of Prime Minister Konoe.

Uchida Ryohei was dead, and Toyama Mitsuru, having put many of
his favorites into positions of power, seemed quiescent. Nevertheless,
their secret societies were still strenuously opposing the government's
more democratic policies, and terrorism was reviving. In 1939, when
pro-Nazis in the government were promoting a full military alliance
with Hitler and Mussolini, there was an upsurge of anti-British feeling
in Japan. Animosity was directed at statesmen and business leaders
considered dangerously pro-British, and some of Toyama's supporters
concocted a plot to assassinate several of them, including Ikeda Seihin
and Matsudaira Tsuneo, Minister of the Imperial Household. The
plotters were caught before they acted, but when the matter was investigated police learned that some leaders of the Kempeitai in Tokyo
were either involved in the conspiracy or sympathetic to it.

The political undercurrents at that time were confusing and have yet
to be clarified. It is apparent, however, that the various fascist groups,
though often working at cross purposes, had finally removed legal
obstacles to the establishment of a dictatorship. All that was necessary
after that was one man strong enough to seize supreme power. Early in
1940, as aspirants to that power maneuvered their forces, anxiety over
the likelihood of a coup d'état was so keen that Ikeda felt compelled to

warn the prime minister: "The army feel that their big blunder at the time of the February Incident was that they didn't win the emperor over to their side. This time there is said to be a plan of first winning the emperor over to their side [i.e., securing custody of his person] and then starting a disturbance. Does the navy have ideas on methods of protecting the emperor, either by getting him aboard a warship or by other means, in such an instance?"[4]

The prime minister, at that time an admiral, assured Ikeda that preparations for such a move—essentially, a preventive abduction of the sort so dear to the old loyalists of Choshu—had been made and told him not to worry. But in July the police uncovered a new plot—only a few hours before schedule—to assassinate the prime minister, the foreign minister, several imperial advisers and, once again, Ikeda and Matsudaira. A confiscated arsenal of firearms and grenades indicated that the plot, organized by a group closely identified with Prince Konoe's house guest Inoue Nissho, was backed by elements in the army and the national police bureau.

The Mitsuis, whom Ikeda had prudently removed from positions of prominence, seem not to have been endangered physically. Yet even in their walled and closely guarded eyrie within sight of the imperial Diet and national police headquarters they never felt secure, for if ever the fighting among power groups should take an unexpected turn the palatial home of Baron Hachiroemon could easily become a blood-soaked shambles.

The mental and emotional strains of those hectic times were taking their toll of the Mitsui clan, many of whose members were already disillusioned or demoralized by the bewildering course the nation was taking, and frustrated by their helplessness to do anything about it. As their House had grown to a greatness unimagined by their forebears, their personal roles in the nation's affairs had dwindled until, with few exceptions, their only contribution to its economy was the imprinting of ornate vermilion seals upon documents formalizing the endless—and now meaningless—accumulation of profits wrung from the victimized masses of Asia. Although instructed by their ancient charter to be in all things as brothers, the family heads no longer formed a close-knit group, and their infrequent gatherings (usually in necessary conclaves of the Somotokata, or corporate board meetings) were marred by polite but nonetheless spiteful wranglings.

The factors eroding clan solidarity were material and ideological as well as psychological, and after the mid-thirties the process of disintegration was distressingly apparent. In analyzing it some family members hark back to June 1938, soon after Ikeda had become finance minister. The summer rains had been long and heavy, saturating the soil of the baron's hilltop estate at Imai-cho in Tokyo. On the last day of the month, without warning, a massive slab of soggy earth broke away from his hill, engulfing the houses huddled below. Scores of residents were buried alive, and twenty-three perished. Baron Hachiroemon immediately acknowledged responsibility for the accident, and after emergency measures had been taken he sent five emissaries to the chairman of the *tonarigumi,* the neighborhood association, to offer condolences and arrange compensation. But as was usual in such cases, underworld agitators, expecting to be bought off, exploited the occasion to denounce the arrogant capitalists and stir up animosity among the neighbors. The baron was quite willing to make decent restitution, and eventually did so, but his agents refused to be blackmailed and the incident took an ugly turn. According to one member of the family an old woman, crazed by grief, called down the vengeance of the gods on the Mitsuis, and prophesied that their eldest sons would die young. Other Mitsuis deny any knowledge of this curse; but even without it the uproar over the owner's negligence, and the venting of popular hatred at the very doorstep of the main house, had a demoralizing effect upon the clan.

At the time of the landslide the baron's younger brother Takasumi was living in London with his wife and children while he studied at the London School of Economics and later at Magdalen College, Oxford. Like Hachiroemon Takakimi, he was an easygoing young man, who enjoyed the good things of life his father's fortune was so well able to provide. Having worked five years in the head office of Yokohama Specie Bank and written a book on the history of banking in Japan, he seemed content with the life of a scholarly socialite in the company of distinguished Britons and high-living Japanese businessmen and diplomats.

The China Incident, however, awakened Takasumi to the dangers of the course Japan had taken and the hostility it was arousing among the British, whom he admired. Through his Oxford dons, chief among whom was the Canon of Queen's College, he and his wife Hideko (a relative of Prince Saionji and Baron Sumitomo Kichizaemon) began serious studies of Christianity and were eventually baptized. At Oxford they were introduced to Frank Buchman, whose Oxford Group's brand of social evangelism had attracted the wealthy and powerful of many countries. At that time, just before Prime Minister Neville Chamberlain's capitulation to Hitler at Munich, Buchman had a strong following in Germany, especially among Nazi leaders with whose anti-liberal, anti-Semitic aims he was in sympathy. Apparently Buchman saw the unsuspecting Takasumi as an instrument for exporting his movement to Japan. It seems likely that Buchman also contemplated some kind of an Anglo-Japanese rapprochement that would induce Japan to settle the China affair and join a united front with Britain and the Axis powers for a crusade against Bolshevism, as envisioned by so many prominent men of his time.

In the spring of 1938 Takasumi and a group of his Christian friends drove down to Eastbourne in his custom-built Armstrong Siddley—called "the battleship" because of its color and size—to attend a weekend meeting of Buchman's Moral Rearmament movement. After the meeting Takasumi, having been carefully primed with tactful hints, decided to return to Japan, where he could spread the gospel of Buchmanism while "driving ahead boldly with our friends and business connections in Britain," as he put it. His resolve was fortified by Dr. Buchman himself, who told Hideko: "Sumi must become a peacemaker."[5]

He reached Japan in 1939, when anti-British agitation was so severe that hotelkeepers had posted signs announcing that no Britons would be accommodated. To make matters worse, Toyama Mitsuru, still unmellowed in his late eighties, had established a national federation to suppress Christianity, "a device of Jewish ideas which threatens to encroach upon the spirit of the Japanese race,"[6] as the federation stated it. Under such pressure the Government had forbidden the teaching of Christian doctrine, even in missionary schools.

Takasumi, undaunted, gave a series of lectures on "moral rearmament" before businessmen's clubs and to a captive audience of two hundred Mitsui executives. But his program for saving civilization hand in hand with Chamberlain and Hitler was called "dangerous talk" by some of his listeners and was regarded amiss by the thought-control police. And it undoubtedly stoked the hatred of the pro-Axis terrorists then plotting against pro-British elements in the imperial court and the government.

Perhaps because of his guilelessness, not to mention his connections with the power elite, Mitsui Takasumi escaped unpunished and was even allowed to open a school in Tokyo, near Hachiroemon's mansion, for the children of businessmen and diplomats forced by circumstances to return to Japan. He also became president of the Mitsui Ho-on Kai, a position that enabled him to satisfy his philanthropic impulses and escape involvement with the war-making activities of the Mitsui concern. But his inconvenient conversion to Christianity, with its implied criticism of the warmongers, did nothing to restore harmony within the clan.

Takasumi's deviation from the mainstream of zaibatsu thought was not unique in the family. His younger sister Reiko, married to the heir of one of the Mitsui branch families who worked for Bussan, had lived in New York for several years and had become something of a feminist and a liberal. She was friendly toward Americans and strongly opposed to a war. Furthermore, Takasumi's wife's cousin, Saionji Kinkazu, a grandson of the aged prince, had become involved with radicals in his student days; and his flirtation with Marxist thought attracted unwelcome attention from the Kempeitai. Young Saionji was, in fact, a close associate of Richard Sorge, a Russian spy who posed as a German journalist and enjoyed the full confidence of Hitler's ambassador to Tokyo. Information passed between Sorge and Saionji Kinkazu (who despite his political aberration was sometimes consulted by Prince Konoe and other statesmen) was helpful to some extent in dissuading the Japanese from attacking the Soviet Union and facilitated the conclusion of a nonaggression pact with Moscow in 1941. Sorge was exposed and hanged during the Pacific War; it is possible that Saionji escaped the noose only because of his exalted lineage.

Baron Hachiroemon himself was anything but a unifying influence for the family, having fallen, it seems, under the spell of the ambitious Sasaki Shiro. A consummate sycophant, Sasaki had wormed his way into the master's confidence to such an extent that to some members of the family he seemed to be running the concern. His methods were devious and subtle. For example, knowing that Hachiroemon and the baroness Mitsui were fond of performing Noh plays, Sasaki and his wife studied the art assiduously until they were skilled enough to take part in private performances at the Imai-cho mansion. Having penetrated the family circle, he enjoyed an intimacy with the chief that not even Dan or Ikeda had been able to attain.

Sasaki, an anti-Semite and an admirer of Hitler, seems to have weaned Hachiroemon away from his pro-British sentiments and inclined him toward chauvinistic attitudes. Because of his position as secret paymaster of spies, terrorists, and their organizations, Sasaki was deeply involved in and sympathetic with some of the most dastardly schemes afoot. Wisely, he did not burden his good-hearted master with details of Mitsui's role in Japan's dirty war. Like his forerunner Rasputin, he had only to create the mood of acceptance in the top echelon of the House to secure the necessary cooperation at lower levels.

The rambling Mitsui mansion, with its spacious salons, banqueting hall, and gardens, once the scene of festive international gatherings at which statesmen, industrialists, and men of learning mingled with Japanese and foreign aristocrats, was unusually quiet now. Despite severe rationing there was no serious shortage of food in the homes of the Mitsuis, who had their own farms, but displays of opulence were to be avoided when the rest of the nation went hungry. A large part of the family's heirloom silver, bearing the ancient "four-eyes" crest, had been donated for the relief of families of soldiers killed in China; but it was scarcely needed, for the baron's dinner guests were not numerous anymore. Hachiroemon was on cordial terms with the diplomats and business leaders of both the fascist and democratic camps, but they did not mix well, and even in carefully chosen company the guests tended to become contentious over certain topics. When Mukai, Ishida, or other top executives were invited, they and the family heads present were repelled by the toadying Sasaki, who, as they knew well, was maneuvering against them for his own advancement. Even dinners *en famille* were nerve-racking, because of ill-concealed disagreements over ideologies, business, and personalities.

The loosening of ties among the several families of the House seems not to have worried Hachiroemon, who was much more interested in his own immediate family than in the clan whose destiny he had been born to guide. He was happily married and devoted to his wife and children to such a degree that he seldom left his loved ones except on business. He attended geisha parties only under duress, and when drinking with his colleagues was inescapable, he did so with little pleasure. He was not really interested in business or politics or even social life; rather, it was the education and development of his four sons—and the marriages of his two daughters—that absorbed his attention.

Among the boys his eldest, Takao, seemed to be the most promising; and Hachiroemon had done everything possible to bring him up as an all-round man capable of assuming the responsibilities that he himself, the clan chief, had been unable to fulfill properly. But Takao, in his early twenties, was much like his father had been at the same age, being self-centered, pleasure-oriented, and indifferent to the stuffy traditions of the House. The prospect of succeeding to the title and cares of Baron Mitsui was not appealing to the insouciant youth, and the decorum required of an heir apparent was oppressive. Since currency restrictions prevented his being sent abroad, he gravitated toward the more relaxed life of his foreign friends, the sons and daughters of diplomats and businessmen, who managed to enjoy themselves despite the wars in China and Europe.

It is well that Takao savored life while he could, for he died in the summer of 1941, before he became of age. His death seems to have resulted from the kind of accident that could happen to any high-spirited and slightly reckless youth. But the circumstances were so well concealed that even the boy's close relatives do not know what really happened, or at least give conflicting stories about the affair—exactly as in the death of the Krupp heir in 1902, except that, unlike Fritz Krupp, Takao was not known to be involved in any scandal and presumably had no reason for committing suicide. Those whom the author has asked about the tragedy agree that Takao was visiting some German friends at Hayama, an exclusive seaside resort near Tokyo at which one of the emperor's villas was located, and that he died under "mysterious circumstances." There were rumors that he had fallen down a flight of stairs, or from an upstairs window, or had been beaten by juvenile delinquents. But Gomei's Welfare Department, which had handled the family's public relations so ineptly after the landslide, was more effective in covering up the details of this event; and if there was any police investigation at all not a word of it appeared in the press.

Hachiroemon's second son Takamitsu, who was then in his mid-teens, remembers that in his absence Takao was brought home and taken to an upstairs room. There had been an accident, he was told, but Takamitsu was not allowed to see the victim. For about three days many doctors came and went. On the last day he was called home from school and told that his brother was very ill. Actually, he was dead; but even this stark fact was kept secret temporarily, just as, by tradition, the death of an emperor or a shogun was concealed from the populace. Takamitsu was told that his brother had "some trouble with his stomach," but beyond that the matter seems not to have been discussed within the family, then or ever. But there was an awareness that the fabulous luck of the House had changed. During the next few years death was to strike several times at young Mitsuis, and especially at the eldest sons.

Grief over the death of his heir, still fresh in Hachiroemon's memory even today, was the most crushing that he was ever to experience. After the funeral and interment at the Shinnyo-do temple in Kyoto, Hachiroemon seemed not to be aware of this world. Always rather perfunctory in business, he now delegated all but his most essential duties to his lieutenants, some of whom must have rejoiced at the master's virtual abdication.

His lack of interest did not, of course, affect the concern: oblivious to personal misfortune, national tragedy, and global disaster, it moved with irresistible momentum toward its apogee—and its extinction.

24 · Not Necessarily to Japan's Advantage

THE LAST THING IN THE WORLD the zaibatsu wanted or needed was a war against the Western powers. American and British investors were equally unenthusiastic about a war with Japan, believing that their interests in Asia could be secured eventually by economic pressure. Yet the governments of the two camps persisted in taking steps that made war inevitable. Japan's fatal move in the summer of 1941 was to occupy strategic bases in southern Indochina, thereby threatening European and American footholds in Southeast Asia. Japan's reasoning was quite logical: in order to fight a prolonged war against China and to prepare for possible retaliation by the Western powers, it must secure access to the resources of the region. And in this conclusion the hard-pressed industrialists had to concur.

Japan assured the world that its expansion into southern Indochina was not a prelude to further aggression, but the government's statements inspired little confidence and the West had much to lose by accepting them. Some of the richest colonies of the European empires were in Southeast Asia, whose resources were vital to their industries. The United States, with a big stake in the Philippines and investments of some two hundred million dollars in China, was getting at least half of its imported raw materials, such as rubber, tungsten, tin, copra, silk, jute, and shellac, from Asia; and other industrial countries were even more dependent upon the region.

The United States had already begun to apply economic pressure, by denouncing its commercial treaty with Japan in 1939 and placing an embargo upon exports of scrap iron and aviation gasoline in 1940. The next step after Japan's new move southward was a joint embargo that the Japanese called the ABCD Encirclement (for the American, British, Chinese, and Dutch nations, which imposed it). This stopping of strategic fuels and raw materials was followed by the freezing of Japanese assets in the United States, a move that practically ended its trade with Japan. Japan was thus faced with a choice among three unhappy alternatives: economic strangulation, acceptance of foreign demands that were considered impossibly harsh, or war.

Prime Minister Konoe and most of his advisers, as well as officers responsible for naval operations, dreaded a war with the United States. In fact, Konoe made serious efforts to arrange a "summit meeting" with President Roosevelt, but his overtures were rejected by Washington because it was felt that even if the premier could be trusted he had too little control over Japan's military to make his decisions effective. Secretary of State Cordell Hull conducted long-drawn-out negotiations with Admiral Nomura Kichisaburo, the Japanese Ambassador to Washington. Economic leaders were pessimistic, however. In Tokyo, Mitsui Benzo, a family head who had served two tours of duty in the New York office of Bussan, confided his misgivings to a kinsman, saying that although Nomura would do his best to prevent a war the army was too powerful and would do as it pleased. He was right, for when Minister of War Tojo Hideki learned that Washington demanded Japan's immediate evacuation of Indochina and gradual withdrawal of its troops from China, he threw the weight of army opinion against compromises proposed by the premier and his moderate advisers. In September, at an imperial conference, top level statesmen and staff officers, with the emperor's acquiescence, agreed secretly that unless the Americans (who were negotiating for the British, as well) softened their terms by the middle of October Japan must go to war.

When the deadline passed and no compromise had been reached, Konoe found himself in an impossible position. In Washington, Nomura, now assisted by a professional diplomat, continued to negotiate with sincerity; but the Japanese navy had long since conducted maneuvers in preparation for attacks on Pearl Harbor and other naval bases. It was necessary, of course, to have contingency plans in case negotiations should fail; for it was well-known to Japanese intelligence that the Americans and British were quietly building up their own military strength in the Pacific in order to enforce the ABCD embargo. But Konoe no longer had any assurance that his military leaders could be curbed, even if Washington should make concessions acceptable to his government. Acknowledging defeat, he resigned and was replaced as prime minister by General Tojo.

This came as a shock to the zaibatsu, not only because of Tojo's known determination to go to war but also because he represented the danger of an economic dictatorship, which under the more pliable Konoe, they had managed to prevent. Such an intention was clear when Tojo took the home affairs and army portfolios for himself; anxiety increased when he brought back the reckless military spender Kaya Okinori as finance minister, and appointed leading members of the Manchukuo clique to other positions—Kishi Nobusuke as Minister of Commerce and Industry, Hoshino Naoki as Chief Cabinet Secretary, and their Manchukuo cohort, Aoki Kazuo, as Greater East Asia minister.

The zaibatsu leaders were by no means powerless and might have been able to obstruct Tojo's appointment or sabotage his cabinet by noncooperation, but apparently they made no immediate attempt to do so. One reason for their timidity was the fact that Tojo, as chief of the Kempeitai in Manchuria, had assembled voluminous dossiers about the unsavory collusion between business interests and military officers, which he used to blackmail both groups, not for money but as a means of forcing evildoers to tread the path of national righteousness. His attitude is understandable when one considers that even as a lieutenant general and chief of staff of the Kwantung Army his base pay had been only about $120 a month—scarcely enough to buy Baron Mitsui's cigars—and that he seems to have lived austerely. Through the years Tojo had seen the zaibatsu enriching themselves at the sacrifice of his men, most of whom came from impoverished rural families, and he felt no compunction about using his power to protect the emperor's fighting men against exploitation.

There is evidence that Tojo, like many other officers as they earned promotions, came to terms with the zaibatsu. After the war there were revelations that led T. A. Bisson to conclude in 1945: "Tojo, touted as the arch militarist, profited to the tune of millions in peculations with the zaibatsu."[1] Refuting this view is Courtney Browne, Tojo's biographer, who asserted twenty years later that this was "a calumny disproved by official inquiry after the war."[2]

Although the zaibatsu feared Tojo as a politician, they respected him as a soldier. And despite their wish to avoid armed conflict, most economic leaders had reconciled themselves to it as preferable to accepting American demands, which would have required them to give up almost everything they had gained on the mainland of Asia since the Russo-Japanese War. From their point of view, these demands were no more reasonable than asking the United States to abrogate the Monroe Doctrine or Great Britain to withdraw from India, Burma, and Malaya. Without occupation forces the Japanese could not hope to maintain their puppet regimes in China and Manchukuo, which would have been taken over by communist rebels in short order.

Tojo, they felt, would not tolerate this subversion of Japan's political interests, which they equated with their own economic interests. They also believed that Tojo, although dangerous in some ways, was the man most capable of controlling the army to prevent an accidental war; and that if war should come he was the man most likely to win it. With so much to lose by yielding to America, the possibility of an armed conflict offering even a slim chance of victory—or of a peace negotiated from a position of strength—was by no means an intolerable prospect.

Few knowledgeable Japanese were under any illusions about the imminence of war, and those working abroad for trading companies were especially conscious of it. Some years previously, a U. S. Department of Justice investigator had reported that "agents of the Japanese government are constantly collecting information of the most intimate character as to the industries, resources, harbors, and other information of a vital character concerning this country and that these agents work through Mitsui & Co."[3] In many larger foreign capitals Japanese diplomatic officials worked out of Bussan offices, and Bussan employees were attached to embassy or consular staffs for the sake of diplomatic immunity. As the international situation grew tense, some Bussan staff members were secretly commissioned as officers in the army or navy intelligence services but remained in their civilian positions so as to work undetected. Allied shipping was being watched closely in all foreign ports of any significance, especially in the Pacific. In Honolulu movements of the United States fleet in and out of Pearl Harbor were followed by Japanese and German spies and reported to the Japanese Consulate; some of this information was cabled to Tokyo by Bussan in a special code interspersed with the daily market reports.[4]

The Americans were not at all in the dark about such espionage, or its purpose. Quite a few of Japan's agents had been arrested or were under surveillance by the FBI. Cryptanalysts in the United States intelligence services had broken the Japanese diplomatic code in 1940 and were intercepting messages to and from Japanese embassies in many countries. These were often decoded and distributed to select foreign readers even before they were seen by the diplomats for whom they were intended. In Tokyo, Ambassador Grew also seemed to have good intelligence sources, for in January 1941 he had apprised Washington by cable of rumors that "the Japanese, in case of a break with the United States, are planning to go all out in a surprise attack on Pearl Harbor."[5]

The existence of such plans did not mean that Japan had decided irrevocably on war. At any time up to the morning of December 7, 1941 the imperial navy's secret plans could have been suspended—to the immeasurable benefit of both sides—if only Japanese and American leaders had communicated their real expectations frankly, clearly, and promptly. But given the pride and deviousness of the Japanese militarists, and the hypocritical idealism and bigoted complacency of the country-club types who were running the peacetime army and navy in the United States, such a sensible resolution of differences was too much to be hoped for. The incredible sequence of blunders that occurred in Washington, Pearl Harbor, and Tokyo early in that fateful December has been told so often that it need not be repeated here. Suffice it to say that everyone in a position of responsibility knew that war could break out at any minute, and that, although hardly anyone wanted war to come, no one made a vigorous and decisive effort to stop it until the opportunity for doing so had passed.

There was apparently not much secrecy among the Japanese concerning the impending hostilities. Niizeki Yasutaro, then manager of Bussan's branch in Bangkok (and postwar chairman of the firm) recalls that some days before the invasion of Thailand the association of Japanese residents there was told that the event would take place on December 8 (December 7 in the United States). On the night before the invasion he assembled Bussan employees, their families, and other Japanese at his residence. "We heard then that Japanese advance troops would land at the mouth of the Mae Nam River," he says. "So arrangements were made for members of the association to sprinkle lime on roads so that the advance troops could follow the marked roads into Bangkok. Five men from Mitsui Bussan participated in this task."[6]

Once the shooting started there was a feeling of relief in Japan, and the doubters were able to believe that Prime Minister Tojo had been right after all. As the Allies puzzled over the question of which target he would strike first, he amazed the world by striking them all. In masterfully executed operations, the Japanese launched their meticulously planned blitzkriegs on Pearl Harbor, Hong Kong, Malaya, and the Philippines almost simultaneously, crippling the U. S. Pacific Fleet and defeating the British on land, sea, and in the air. The vast regions of South Asia, Oceania, and the intervening archipelagoes were suddenly exposed to Japanese aggression.

Coming to them as "liberators," the Japanese encountered little resistance from peoples of British, European, and American colonies. Having prepared their way by decades of proselytizing and indoctrination, they found more allies than enemies in the conquered territories, and were thus in command of an inexhaustible labor force to assist them in garnering the freshly won resources—rubber, tin, bauxite, iron ore, cotton, timber, and, most precious of all, petroleum.

Oil was the life's blood of the naval and air arms in a war that was to be fought mainly at sea or on widely scattered islands. Although there was plenty of oil underground in the Dutch East Indies, Japan had on hand—a large portion of it in Bussan's storage tanks—only enough to last for two years, and since the ABCD embargo this hoard had been draining away at the rate of nearly thirty thousand gallons a day. Both military and economic leaders knew that the conquered oil fields would not be of immediate value and that the war would have to be won quickly or not at all. As Admiral Yamamoto Isoroku, commander of the combined imperial fleet, told Prime Minister Konoe in 1941: "I can raise havoc with [Britain and the United States] for one year, or at most eighteen months. After that I can give no guarantees."[7]

Scoffing at such warnings were stouter-hearted patriots, such as Toyama, who said in the same year: "There are some who are pessimistic because Japan is now short of materials. Materials are important, of course, but there is something more important, the spiritual forces."[8] Typical of those wishful thinkers was Baron Hiranuma, by now president of the privy council, who assured his countrymen that defeat was impossible because the divine imperial house, unlike dynasties created by men, was impervious to human power. It was generally accepted that the Japanese, favored by the gods and endowed with the spirit of bushido, the way of the warrior, were far superior to the foreigners as fighters and that the Americans were especially lacking in such spirit. The opinionated Colonel Mitsui Sakichi, who apparently had read something about the struggle between the Republicans and the Democrats over Roosevelt's reelection for a third term, stated confidently: "The United States is already divided into two great camps and is on the verge of revolution."[9]

Exhorted by such great thinkers, the Japanese imperial forces heaped victory upon victory, and close behind them, industrialists flocked to the Greater East Asia Co-Prosperity Sphere to exploit the resources won by their heroes. By the end of 1942 hundreds of industrial enterprises had been established or seized in the newly won satellite regions. In the zaibatsu vanguard was Mitsui, with more than fifty large-scale overseas subsidiaries and a labor force that soon surpassed a million people.

Responsible for the newly won additions to the empire was the Greater East Asia Ministry, which had relieved the Ministry of Foreign Affairs of its authority over China, Manchukuo, Korea, Taiwan, and South Sakhalin Island, as well as southern Asia and the islands in the Pacific. Control over this sprawling domain, through his deputy Aoki, brought Tojo to the height of his power and within tantalizing reach of the dictatorship to which he seemed to aspire.

The zaibatsu leaders had other ideas as to who would dictate to whom, but dislodging Tojo was not a task to be undertaken hastily. His reprisals against opponents were quick and ruthless. One way of controlling army men was to send them to some fighting front from which they were unlikely to return alive, and Tojo used it often. If the culprit was a civilian, he could be drafted and sent out to die for the emperor. One of the few critics still speaking out against Tojo was Ikeda Seihin, who had never ceased trying to organize a zaibatsu-led reversal of the Army's national socialist policies. Ikeda was about fifty years over the draft age; but his son, already thirty-five years old, was called to the colors and sent to China, where he died of malaria. This was considered to be one of Tojo's innumerable political "lynchings." It was quite unusual for the army to draft the sons of rich men, most of whom could reasonably claim to be performing essential economic tasks. Nevertheless, one of the younger Mitsui family heads—Takaosa, son of the pacifistic Benzo—was also hustled into uniform and sent to Manchuria. Like his ancestors, he lacked the attributes of a warrior, so he was put to work doctoring horses until the end of the war.

So great was the authority of Tojo, and so deep the confidence inspired by his successes, that otherwise sensible businessmen could half believe him when he trumpeted: "Japan is prepared to fight for a hundred years until victory is won and our enemies are crushed. We are confident that militarily and politically and economically we can bring this war to a successful conclusion."[10]

But despite the occupation of the Dutch East Indies early in 1942, Japan's oil was dwindling fast: there wasn't enough for a hundred weeks, let alone for a hundred years, and the hope of getting more became less tenable as the American Pacific Fleet, presumably annihilated at Pearl Harbor, was being resurrected. By a fatal omission the imperial navy had spared the enemy's submarines and modern aircraft carriers, which soon became active against Japanese shipping. In April 1942, sixteen American carrier-based B-25 bombers commanded by General James Doolittle jolted Japanese complacency by bombing Tokyo, ineffectively but ominously. In May, the Battle of the Coral Sea inflicted severe damage on the Japanese navy, which in the following month lost nearly half its strength in aircraft carriers at the decisive Battle of Midway. Thus by the middle of 1942 Japan's sensational victories had all been won, and rising American air and sea power was gnawing away at Japan's merchant marine. Ships loaded with troops and supplies for the overseas campaigns, or with essential war materiel gathered from the Co-Prosperity Sphere, were sunk with dismaying frequency. When a shortage of steel for new vessels developed, other materials, such as wood and concrete, had to be employed. Early in the war the Mitsui Wooden Shipbuilding Company was established to replenish the merchant fleet, but it didn't help much: for every ton of new shipping launched, ten tons were sunk, mostly by American submarines.

Japan had a strong undersea fleet at the beginning of the war, but its armed services had neglected to develop radar, and the imperial navy's "blind" submarines were ineffective against enemy vessels equipped with advanced electronic detection gear. As the lines of communication became overextended and surface shipping proved help-lessly vulnerable, Japanese submarines (many of them built at Mitsui's Tama Shipyard) were diverted from combat duty to ferry supplies to widely dispersed fighting units in an area of operations covering mil-lions of square miles.

Toward the end of 1942 Japan's "impregnable" fortress of Guadal-canal Island was overwhelmed, and the navy suffered crippling losses in the Battle of the Solomons. As more outposts fell and sea lanes were interdicted, the army and navy called frantically for more aircraft, submarines, fuel, food, and ammunition, and Japan's economic plan-ners strove to reorganize its industries to answer those calls. Between 1941 and 1943 there were nearly a thousand mergers of companies, as the zaibatsu amalgamated their enterprises and absorbed smaller firms in the name of efficiency. Unfortunately, most of this reshuffling was carried out by the industrial control associations, headed by zaibatsu leaders who were more interested in competing for scarce commodities than in boosting overall production, and their unscrupulous hoarding further disrupted the economy.

The army and navy, each with its own procurement system, also competed savagely for scarce materials needed by their suppliers of munitions. By this time most of Bussan's overseas business consisted of military procurement, and managers of branches in the Co-Pros-perity Sphere had to cope with a barrage of blandishments and threats from the rival services. In Djakarta the Japanese military governor of Sumatra told the local Bussan manager, Niizeki Yasutaro: "This is not a war between the United States and Japan, but between the Japa-nese army and navy."[11]

When they could not obtain necessary materials through channels, the respective services set up their own clandestine agencies, headed by terroristic "ronin" types, who combined their transactions in con-traband with the irregular gathering of intelligence for competing power groups in the military.

One of the most effective of these undercover agencies was the "Kodama Machine," whose mastermind, Kodama Yoshio, was a junior associate of Toyama Mitsuru and Uchida Ryohei in ultrapatriotic or-ganizations and thus had excellent contacts in China. Working mainly for naval aviation, his group served as a clearinghouse for industrial materials and personal valuables looted by Japanese soldiers or offered on the black market by Chinese. The Kodama Machine (which had its counterparts in Southeast Asia, the Middle East, and other regions) allegedly imported into China many contraband commodities, includ-ing luxury goods, liquor, medical supplies, and narcotics, and used the proceeds to pay for copper, nickel, cobalt, foodstuffs, and other strategic items, as well as precious metals, for its sponsors. The Kodama Machine used branch offices of private companies—Mitsui Bussan, Toyo Menka, and Oji Paper, for example—for cover in their illicit operations. Mitsui's men, of course, had no choice but to cooperate with such agencies. They did so without much reluctance because the influence of the secret agents with the military authorities was useful, even essential, for carrying on business in an otherwise lawless environment.

Political conditions in the Co-Prosperity Sphere were no better than those in the economic field. The ripple of insubordination that began among younger officers in the early 1930s swelled gradually to a tidal wave that threatened to engulf the overseas expeditionary forces. The Minister of War could not control his general staff officers, who in turn were so occupied in building up their personal power machines that they lost touch with commanders in the field. In occupied areas corruption permeated every level of command. Luxurious brothels, which had been established originally for the seduction or blackmail of local personages, eventually became hangouts for Japanese officers who, surrounded by bevies of "comfort girls" and geisha from the home country, spent their days and nights in drinking, gambling, lechery, and intrigue as the dream of a Greater East Asia dissolved into one long debauch.

While the government of Japan tried to win the cooperation of conquered peoples by organizing "patriotic associations" under such slogans as "national salvation through peace," the arrogance, brutality, and greed of the occupying soldiery bred hatred and contempt instead. On the continent, Chiang Kai-shek's Kuomintang resisted only passively, but the communists, winning the support of more and more anti-Japanese peasants, were counterattacking effectively even in areas occupied by the Japanese forces. Hundreds of thousands of imperial troops were pinned down to policing, pacification, and counter-insurgency duties, or to performing menial tasks for their officers. Drunkenness, drug abuse, and venereal disease became rampant, and the troops shared the demoralization of their officers. The imperial army had succumbed to the temptations of easy victory, and to the vices introduced for the undoing of the Chinese, while the intended victims seemed to gain strength from the adversities imposed by their tormentors.

The situation was similar in the Southeast Asian colonies, where the occupying forces strutted insolently in their newly won authority. Coming as "liberators," they soon revealed themselves as ruthless conquerors flaunting their racial, national, and cultural "superiority." Japanese in the East Indies occupied the imposing mansions and villas that had been abandoned by their Dutch owners—now rotting in concentration camps—and lorded over the local people like oriental satraps of old. According to Bussan's branch manager Niizeki, the social ranking in Djakarta descended from Japanese officers and soldiers through military civilians, military horses, military dogs, and military carrier pigeons, to the brown-skinned indigenous people, the lower orders of whom were beaten, abused, and humiliated by their lighter-hued masters as a matter of routine.

Such behavior was embarrassing to experienced employees of Japan's trading firms, who were trained in diplomacy as well as sound business practices and could anticipate the evil results of antagonizing the people of a host country. Still, they had a job to do, and they had to adapt to circumstances. Bussan's job in the Dutch East Indies was to mine gold, produce chemicals and sugar, and collect rubber, tin, timber, and coconut oil, as well as boats for the army. Japanese businessmen were despised by the military but tolerated because their services were necessary and because they had money. In such an atmosphere bribery was endemic, for without it nothing could be accomplished. As the war dragged on, men who had gone into the Co-Prosperity Sphere inspired by the high purpose of their endeavors became cynical. They also learned of the successive defeats of Japan's army and navy that were effectively concealed at home. As early as 1943 some of Mitsui's executives working overseas were being told, very confidentially, that the war was lost, and the general decline in morale was aggravated by a conviction that their work was futile.

Military corruption was not universal, however, as the Mitsuis learned to their mortification. In the spring of 1943 the Japanese high command in Shansi Province, northern China, took drastic measures against traitors who subordinated the national interest to profit. In the crackdown the manager of the local Bussan office was sentenced to ten years in prison on charges of black marketing. The harshness of the punishment seemed to have been due to the Kwantung Army's hatred of the zaibatsu rather than to the gravity of the offense, which involved the sale of beer and other products at prices higher than those decreed by the occupying authorities. Since nothing could be done in Tokyo about rescuing their man, Bussan's obanto Mukai went to Shansi personally, accompanied by his assistant Matsumoto Kisashi, in an effort to settle the matter discreetly.

The Mitsui men were not optimistic, because the commander in chief of the occupying forces, General Hanaya Tadashi, was known to be very intolerant of the plutocracy. As a major in Mukden he had helped to plan the Manchurian coup d'état in 1932, and boasted thereafter that the army would "abolish capitalists like Mitsui and Mitsubishi and carry out an even distribution of wealth." However, Mukai's preliminary inquiries showed that the problem was not entirely an ideological one, for there was a woman in the case: General Hanaya and Bussan's manager had been wooing the same girl, it was said, and the general had been defeated.

Mukai and Matsumoto were invited to dinner by Hanaya and his aide, Colonel Kawamoto Daisaku. The latter, a disciple of the terrorist Okawa Shumei, was the officer who had engineered the assassination of warlord Chang Tso-lin in 1928; and since then he had served as a director of the Manchurian Coal Company controlled by the Nissan combine, Mitsui's competitor. According to one story, the guests were given a hostile reception and were threatened with drawn swords. Mukai denies this, and says that he and Matsumoto were treated correctly and even pleasantly. But whatever the manner of their reception, the mission was a failure: not only did they fail to help their imprisoned manager, but Mukai was informed categorically that Mitsui was to withdraw completely from Chinese soil.

Since Mitsui was the largest Japanese investor in China and the largest supplier of both military and civilian imports, General Hanaya's order was obviously unenforceable, but Mukai couldn't say so then and there. Obediently, he closed the Shansi office and returned to Tokyo to wait for the storm to blow over. However, ultranationalist henchmen of the Kwantung Army made a big scandal of the affair and public criticism of Mitsui was incited again. Baron Hachiroemon was led to believe that the only way to avert disaster was to ask all the directors of Bussan to resign, thus taking responsibility for the Shansi incident. As a result Mukai and two other managing directors were sacked, causing great confusion and uncertainty in the management. When this occurred Tojo sent word to Hachiroemon that such a drastic shake-up was unnecessary, but the baron's answer was that "nothing could be done because the resignations had already been announced." At least one Mitsui suspects that the mass firing was done at the urging of "welfare" director Sasaki to clear the way for his own rise to power, but the facts of the case are still obscure.

Needless to say Bussan did not withdraw from China; after a nominal reorganization, in which the name was changed temporarily to "New Mitsui Bussan," the enterprise carried on as before. Mukai was succeeded by Ishida Reisuke, a trader reputed for his bold speculation, and Mitsui's interests in China continued to expand. Before long Ishida also incurred the displeasure of the military for his allegedly antiwar views (probably through the machinations of Sasaki) and was forced to resign too; but he bounced back conveniently as president of the newly formed Foreign Trade Management Corporation, whose ostensible function was to nationalize overseas commerce except that being conducted with the Co-Prosperity Sphere. The corporation effected the reorganization and concentration of all private trading firms, which then became its "agents," handling merchandise on a commission basis. But since most of the staff came from trading companies, mainly Bussan, the change made very little difference operationally, except that it increased the power of the Mitsui and Mitsubishi complexes.

The zaibatsu no longer found it necessary to kowtow before Tojo, who, like his predecessor Konoe, had been unable to make himself a dictator or anything resembling one. Although wielding extraordinary powers granted by the emperor, he had been pressured into appointing a seven-man Cabinet Advisory Council, comprising "magnates of financial and industrial circles" who were also heads of the industrial control associations. Among them were Admiral Toyoda Teijiro, son-in-law of a Mitsubishi director, president of the government-run Nippon Seitetsu, and head of the Iron and Steel Control Association; Fujihara Ginjiro, boss of Oji Paper and the Industrial Equipment Management Control Association; and Yuki Toyotaro, an old Yasuda-Mitsui ally heading the Bank of Japan and the Financial Control Association. Each of those men held a rank equivalent to that of a state minister and belonged to the Supreme Economic Council charged with "the execution of the important policies of the government."

Working in liaison with key economic leaders, such as Ikeda Seihin and Go Seinosuke, these advisers held the line against Tojo's national socialist encroachment upon private enterprise until the drain of war losses brought on a crisis and a showdown. The most drastic legislation presented was the Munitions Company Act drafted by Minister of Commerce and Industry Kishi. Going even further than the National Mobilization Law, it was intended to subjugate private business to the military government. The zaibatsu could not oppose it openly, since by then it was obvious that Japan's last chance for victory depended upon a thorough reorganization of the economy, so they applied their usual tactic of envelopment.

Thus, in the autumn of 1943, the cabinet structure underwent the most drastic changes in its history and vast powers were centered in a new Ministry of Munitions, of which General Tojo was nominally in charge. To make matters more ominous, Kishi was installed as vice-minister and presumably the real boss. But at the insistence of the zaibatsu representatives in the advisory council, Fujihara was appointed a state minister without portfolio, actually to supervise Kishi. In that way Mitsui's shrewdest industrialist, one of the few men in Japan with enough courage to talk back to Tojo, became an extremely powerful figure in the general's supposedly military government.

In reshuffling the cabinet to appease the resurgent zaibatsu, Tojo appointed Hatta Yoshiaki, head of the Mitsui-aligned Teikoku (Imperial) Oil Company, as minister of a new Ministry of Transportation and Communications set up to unify civilian land, sea, and air transportation facilities, as well as all forms of nonmilitary communication in Japan, Manchukuo, and China. The new Ministry of Agriculture and Commerce, controlling fabrics, retail commerce, and civilian prices, as well as farm, forest, and marine production, was the responsibility of a Bussan alumnus, the flamboyant shipping magnate Uchida Shin'ya. The Ministry of Education went to Viscount Okabe Nagakage, father-in-law of Mitsui Benzo. Ikeda Seihin, meanwhile, had been appointed, over army protests, to the privy council advising the emperor. Thus, under quiet but unrelenting pressure from the zaibatsu, the Tojo regime had been diverted from its national-socialist course and was moving back toward a moderate, big-business-oriented fascism resembling that of Italy rather than that of Germany.

A major challenge to the zaibatsu was meeting the government's demands for more capital investment. To solve the staggering problems of wartime finance, the authorities had been forcing mergers at a rate that, between 1936 and 1942, reduced the number of Japanese banks from more than 400 to 186. But in 1942 even more drastic unification was required. Fortunately, the president of the Financial Control Association, Yuki Toyotaro, was a zaibatsu capitalist to the core, and he arranged the mergers to the satisfaction of his colleagues. One result was the formation of Teikoku (Imperial) Bank by amalgamating Mitsui, Dai-Ichi, and the old Fifteenth (Peers') banks. Thus the finances of the Mitsui combine were wedded to those of the Shibusawa, Furukawa, and Kawasaki zaibatsu, with Mitsui dominant. The emperor, who had held shares in all three banks, was also a large shareholder in Teikoku Bank, so that the name "Imperial" was not merely ornamental. His Majesty did not attend board meetings personally. His deputy was Baron Shirane Matsusuke, a vice-minister of the Imperial Household, whose father-in-law was an auditor of Mitsui Bank and whose son married into the Mitsui's main family.

Under the same merger program Mitsubishi, Sumitomo, Yasuda, and Sanwa banks took others under their willing wings, thereby reducing the number of private banks to 88. However, the "big five" held more than half the deposits of all ordinary banks. Largest of all, until 1945, was Teikoku Bank, with Akashi Teruo (Shibusawa Eiichi's son-in-law) as chairman, and Bandai Junshiro, Mitsui Bank's former chief banto, as president.

With their financial problems smoothed over for a while, the Mitsui managers turned their attention to a reorganization plan for the whole concern, under discussion since the tax-dodging stratagem of 1940 had divided the holding company into two unequal and incompatible parts. Mitsui's ungainly structure was in sharp contrast to that of Mitsubishi, which was tightly organized and controlled personally by Baron Iwasaki Koyata, head of the family. During the war years it had made astonishing progress, especially in shipping, trade, and munitions. Receiving more government subsidies than Mitsui, the concern had moved aggressively into the Co-Prosperity Sphere, and its heavy industries—in Japan and overseas—had earned it the reputation of being "the Krupp of the Orient."

The Mitsuis, under pressure from the government, merged the stockholding division of Bussan with the ineffectual Somotokata, to form a new holding company called Mitsui Honsha (main company). Bussan's commercial activities were concentrated in a "new, new" Mitsui Bussan subordinate to Honsha, which thus became the supreme holding company, with ten "first-line" subsidiaries, thirteen "second-line" subsidiaries, and more than eighty listed sub-subsidiaries. In addition, there were such whole subempires as Oji Paper, Kanebo, Toyoda, Tokyo Shibaura, Onoda Cement, and so forth, in which Mitsui had substantial interests but wished to keep separate from the Honsha structure. The president of Honsha, one of whose functions was to reassert centralized control over the increasingly competitive and intransigent subsidiaries, was Baron Mitsui Hachiroemon Takakimi, and the chief managing director was Sumii Tatsuo, who until then had been heading Bussan.

In the meantime deliveries of raw materials from the more distant regions of the Co-Prosperity Sphere had shrunk to negligible amounts because of losses at sea, and production was concentrated in Korea, Manchukuo, and occupied China. But the new zaibatsu, who had been so pampered by the Kwantung Army, were unable to meet the government's expectations, and therefore the frustrated Tojo was forced to put more and more reliance on the old zaibatsu, who with their superior financial resources had already taken over numerous mining and industrial facilities from their younger competitors. Earlier, Baron Hachiroemon had been called on the carpet by economic czar Kishi and scolded like a schoolboy for not realizing the full potential of the concern. But as Nissan's Manchurian Heavy Industries and other new zaibatsu companies failed to meet their quotas, the baron and his adviser Mukai were summoned to another conference with Kishi, Minister of Finance Kaya, and Nissan chieftain Aikawa and were earnestly requested to take over the entire Nissan concern. "But the terms were harsh beyond description," Hachiroemon recalls, and Mitsui declined the offer.

However, Mitsui and Mitsubishi did join forces with their Nissan rivals and through that alignment were able to gain readmission to Manchukuo. Mitsui Chemical formed a joint venture with Manchurian Heavy Industries to make synthetic petroleum, while Bussan took over a tractor factory and an alcohol plant. Gasoline was in such short supply that every effort was being made to produce substitute fuels, and a huge agricultural project was planned to grow potatoes for alcohol production.

Concurrently, the army had developed a new rocket that gave promise of being effective against B-29 bombers; Mitsui and Mitsubishi were recruited to build, equip, and operate plants, also in Manchuria, to produce a mysterious fuel for those rockets. This they proceeded to do, with characteristic energy and dogged disregard for the fact that the war was lost and their conviction that not one enemy bomber would be downed by the army's secret weapon.

For at that time, in the spring of 1944, Tojo's last major offensive was being repulsed, and his campaign to take Bengal with the help of Indian rebels ended in the catastrophe of Imphal, with enormous losses in both men and materiel. As starving remnants of the imperial army straggled back to north Burma, enemy troops invaded the Marianas and landed on Saipan in June. Since Saipan was only 1300 miles from Tokyo and well within range of America's land-based bombers, it was apparent to clearheaded leaders that the loss of the little island could mean the defeat of Japan. Kishi, then largely responsible for munitions production, tried to convince Tojo of this fact: "Saipan is Japan's lifeline. If it is taken, surrender!"[12]

Tojo, stubborn as ever, shouted him down: "Don't poke your nose into the affairs of the high command!" Only a few days later B-29 superfortresses based on Saipan began to bomb Kyushu and soon were striking the major Japanese cities regularly. Kishi, his point having been proved, now suggested that the cabinet resign, but Tojo was unshaken.

Meanwhile, Fujiyama Aiichiro, president of the Tokyo Chamber of Commerce, was working on a scheme to force Tojo's resignation. Supporting the plan were his father-in-law Yuki, heading the Financial Control Association, and his close associate, Ikeda Seihin. Together they were able to enlist the support of Prince Konoe and Lord Privy Seal Kido Koichi, whose secretary and confidant was Mitsui Hachiro-emon's brother-in-law, Count Matsudaira Yasumasa. With such formidable influence, it was not difficult to persuade foreign minister Shigemitsu Mamoru, agriculture minister Uchida Shin'ya, and education minister Okabe to spearhead a mass resignation. Kishi, who seemed always to be keenly aware of the trend of the times, listened coldly to the tearful entreaties of Tojo, his old comrade and benefactor, and in the middle of 1944 the Tojo cabinet resigned.

It would be reasonable to suppose that the success of this coalition of statesmen, financiers, and bureaucrats against Tojo heralded some effort to end the war; but instead the post of prime minister was given to another general, who called not for peace but for more swords. In fact, he demanded that the whole economic machine be geared to maximum production of aircraft and fuel. A series of reverses during the previous year had almost eliminated Japan's navy, and the few warships that remained were being laid up for lack of oil. The last chance for victory—or even for a defeat with honor—seemed to lie in a naval air force capable of holding off an enemy assault on the homeland.

Navy planners had conceived the idea of recruiting volunteer pilots who, by crashing their bomb-laden planes into enemy vessels (and thereby ensuring their own heroic deaths), could multiply the striking effect of existing aircraft many times over and also save the fuel that otherwise would be consumed on return trips. The inhumanity of this arrangement caused certain qualms among even the most hardened militarists; but as someone pointed out with unassailable logic, by increasing the efficiency of the air force the loss of planes and pilots could be actually reduced. Inevitably efficiency (and need) took precedence over humanitarian considerations, and the kamikaze program was activated. Named for the "divine wind" that had been sent by the Sun Goddess to save Japan from Kublai Khan's armada over six hundred years before, kamikaze weapons became the core of naval strategy for the rest of the war. The program had the great virtue of requiring only readily available components: Zero fighters, of which there was a surplus because fuel was lacking; piloted flying bombs and manned torpedoes, which could be built from relatively cheap materials; and young men, most of whom were willing (or were constrained to appear willing) to die for their fatherland.

For the task of overhauling the economy in accordance with this new strategy the invariably successful Fujihara was recruited, at the age of seventy-five, to head the new Ministry of Munitions. Urged on personally by the emperor, he tackled the job with unabated vigor and imagination. It wasn't an easy one, for by then shortages of materials and labor made it almost impossible to build even a single reliable airplane. All too often factories and industrial plants, staffed mainly by housewives and high-school or middle-school children (most able-bodied university students having already been drafted), were put out of operation by enemy bombs, simply because, during safer times, no one had thought it necessary to decentralize production of armaments and munitions. The largest factories were located in or around Nagoya, which became the favorite target for American bombers. To make matters worse, on December 7, 1944, the Nagoya area was rocked by an earthquake more severe than the Tokyo temblor of 1923. Like any bad news, it was hushed up by the all-pervading censorship, but after the war people learned that losses of life and property were tremendous and damage to aircraft plants was crippling.

The largest producers of warplanes were Nakajima and Mitsubishi, but after Mukai had been installed as Mitsui's aircraft boss his interest in aviation overcame his initial reluctance, and the concern's output increased remarkably. Mitsui now operated at least four aircraft companies, the biggest of which was Showa. Its main products were airframes and a twin-engine navy transport, the L2D2, essentially an imitation of the Douglas DC-3. But Japanese planes, which had been superior to the enemy's at first, had become outmoded, and there was no time to retool for new designs. For lack of proper materials many substitutes were being used, and the finished planes were so defective that more airmen were being killed in training than in combat. Most fuselages were made of plywood. Only one plane in four had a radio, and radar was still almost entirely unavailable. As the Allies sent more and more flights of bombers from island bases that were only a few hundred miles from the Japanese homeland, losses of Japan's fighter planes were devastating, and output of replacements was disrupted.

Undeterred by these heartbreaking obstacles, Fujihara rapidly decentralized domestic factories, expanded manufacturing facilities in Korea and Manchuria, and despite a crescendo of strategic bombing by the Allies, succeeded in doubling production. The continued presence of a Mitsui man in such a powerful position naturally evoked some resentment from rival concerns, and it was pointed out that Mitsui had been favored with exceptionally large amounts of military funds during his tenure. Apparently under pressure from Mitsubishi and Sumitomo, Fujihara resigned at the end of 1944, for reasons of ill health. Before that time arrived, however, he had made an impressive effort to solve the chronic fuel shortage by consolidating all artificial petroleum facilities under two companies, the largest of which was the Mitsui-dominated Japan Synthetic Oil, with a capital of more than 250 million yen.

The chief raw material for synthetic oil was coal, perhaps the one essential item of which there was a sufficiency. Although the majority of Japanese miners had been called up for military service, there was no labor shortage because Kishi, as Minister of Commerce and Industry, had arranged in 1941 to bring in Korean and Chinese conscripts, who were used mainly as miners and construction workers. According to a recent report in Ushio magazine, about 750,000 Koreans and fifty thousand Chinese were conscripted forcibly or by deception and brought to Japan in labor gangs as a result of Kishi's decision, confirmed by fifteen other members of the Tojo Cabinet. In addition, a million Chinese and a somewhat larger number of Koreans were rounded up each year on the mainland by the Kwantung Army to serve as laborers in Korea and Manchukuo. The Koreans, being subjects of the Japanese empire, were given preferential handling: they were treated like slaves, while the Chinese, having no rights at all, were treated worse than draft animals.

Like the captive laborers at Nazi industrial plants, the Chinese were kept under armed guard in concentration camps surrounded with barbed wire (sometimes electrified), and they worked under extremely harsh and dangerous conditions. Figures supplied by the government and employers after the war show that among the 50,000 Chinese prisoners brought to Japan between 1941 and 1945 the death rate was 17.6 percent for the period, as compared with 1.63 percent for the Japanese population as a whole. Independent observers, however, believe that the death rate was much higher and that nearly all the prisoners would have died if the war had continued much longer.

The largest employer of conscript labor was Mitsui Mining, which had a total of 16,368 Chinese and a larger number of Koreans (as well as a few American POWs) digging coal and other minerals at ten sites in Japan during the Pacific War. A Japanese miner who worked at one of the Miike pits described their hardships: "In the pit where I was working, there were thirteen Japanese and thirty Chinese . . . [who] were engaged in heavy labor and died one after another. At the peak, there were nearly a thousand Chinese [at the mine] but the number declined to five or six hundred."[13] Some were boys in their early teens, he said. Another Japanese miner said that the slave laborers were watched constantly while working and were beaten with clubs if they showed signs of trying to escape. They were also clubbed when they failed to understand orders given in Japanese.

The mania of the managers to boost production at all costs was illustrated by an incident in 1944, reported by a technician at the Miike mines. A fire broke out in one of the pits, and carbon monoxide began to seep into an adjacent shaft through the joint ventilation system. After perfunctory efforts to rescue the miners still underground, the managers ordered the sealing of the entrance to the pit in which the fire had broken out, and fifty-seven miners were immolated. Most of them were Chinese, but thirteen Japanese were also sacrificed on the altar of production. Of course no compensation was paid to the families of conscript laborers who were killed in accidents or worked to death. Instead, the company was compensated—with cash payments amounting to a total of 22,880,983 yen—for the patriotic service of employing those unfortunates.

From the beginning of 1945, air raids were an everyday occurrence in Japan, and they became more savage after the Americans wrested Iwo Jima from its fanatical defenders. In March, Osaka was devastated and large areas of Tokyo were razed by incendiary bombs. In that air assault upon Tokyo, even more destructive than the Kanto earthquake of 1923, as many as 200,000 people were killed or badly injured, a million more were made homeless, and economic life in the capital was paralyzed.

On May 25, five hundred B-29s destroyed most of central Tokyo and adjacent residential areas with incendiary bombs. The main targets seemed to be the zaibatsu's offices, government buildings, and the homes of the wealthy, but in the consequent firestorms about sixteen square miles of the city were burned. Whether intentionally or otherwise, the Imperial Palace was set ablaze. Directing the air defense brigade was vice-minister Shirane, who says the palace was bombed. In the conflagration eighteen guards, who could not escape because they were not familiar with the maze of pathways among the buildings, were burned to death. Assuming responsibility for the loss of life, Baron Shirane felt compelled to resign his position as the emperor's financial adviser.

In that same raid the mansion of the main Mitsui family at Imai-cho —together with Baron Hachiroemon's collection of automobiles—was totally destroyed. All that survived of its past grandeur was the priceless Jo-an teahouse, built by Oda Nobunaga's brother in the seventeenth century, which the baron had prudently removed to his estate in Oiso. Most of the Mitsuis had been evacuated to safer locations, and there were no casualties among them. Takasumi and his wife were staying with the pupils of their Tokyo school in the exclusive resort town of Karuizawa, where most of the German residents of Tokyo also had taken refuge. On the day of the raid, however, Takasumi's son, Takayori, happened to be at the family's home in the fashionable Aoyama district, where Takasumi's school was also situated. When a large part of the district was suddenly enveloped in flames the fleeing residents, misguided by air-raid wardens, crowded into a street that became an inferno when the wind shifted. Takayori, instead of following the crowd, wisely headed for the nearby Aoyama Cemetery and survived.

When the conflagration had burned out, he returned to find both the school and the residence destroyed. He had not eaten for many hours, and felt terribly hungry. He remembered that just before the sirens started wailing he had seen some rice soaking in a pot of cold water.

Among the smoldering ruins he found the covered pot, still on the stove, with its contents perfectly cooked. That was about as close as any Mitsui came to experiencing the horrors of war. Their anecdotes about those unhappy months are more concerned with inconveniences, anxieties, and losses of property than with real hardship or suffering.

On April 1, as survivors were being evacuated from the stricken cities, enemy troops landed on Okinawa, and Japan's last big battle began. The general-turned-prime-minister, still talking of "a god-given opportunity for decisive battle," was replaced by the octogenarian Admiral Suzuki Kantaro, who formed a government backed by peace-minded conservatives from navy, court, and business circles. But apparently no one dared tell him to end the war. Instead, he declared grandly: "The enemy shall take Japan only over my dead body."

To bolster defenses and relocate defense plants in remote areas or underground, the Wartime Construction Corporation was set up under Kato Kyohei, former president of Mitsui's Taiwan Development Company. Fujihara was called back once more to increase iron and steel production, which had skidded from forty-five million tons in 1941 to what would be a mere 270,000 tons in 1945. Similar declines hit most other strategic materials. Output of synthetic oil had been disappointing, and petroleum was so lacking that almost all merchant and naval shipping had ceased to move. At small improvised plants all over Japan, farmers and woodsmen were trying to distill an ersatz "gasoline" from pine roots.

The war should have ended with the fall of Okinawa, for after that a massive invasion of the home islands was inevitable. But even that penultimate defeat failed to quench the militarists' hopes: the kamikaze heroes had scored many shattering hits on enemy warships, and the navy still had five thousand planes, mostly hidden in underground hangars. In addition there were thousands of man-guided flying bombs, torpedoes, and other suicide weapons, as well as midget submarines lurking in shallow coves to strike when the invasion fleets approached for amphibious landings. And in case even the kamikaze failed to disperse the enemy armada, there was the Civilian Volunteer Corps, which was mobilizing all able-bodied men, women, and children to defend the emperor's sacred soil inch by inch, with bamboo spears if all else failed.

The people had not been told, of course, that the emperor himself had been trying to stop the slaughter, with the support of close advisers such as Prince Konoe and Marquis Kido. The conservative statesmen were not carrying on the conflict solely for the sake of Japan's honor, or the emperor's, but rather for fear of domestic repercussions from the extreme right and the revolutionary left. In audience with His Majesty in February 1945, Konoe revealed this obsessive apprehension: "The more critical the war situation becomes, the louder we hear the cry of 'One hundred million die together!'

"Although the so-called right-wingers are the ones who shout the loudest, it is the Communists, in my opinion, who are the instigators of it all, for they hope to achieve their revolutionary aim by taking advantage of the confusion that will arise from defeat. . . .

"This may be slightly wishful thinking, but if the extremist group is purged, is it not possible that the character of the army will so change that the atmosphere in America, Britain and Chunking may improve somewhat?"[14]

Although army diehards and ultranationalists made life very dangerous for anyone speaking of a solution short of victory, Konoe was working quietly to put together a peace faction and to arrange an armistice. The Mitsuis, through their kinsmen in the imperial court, may have been aware of these developments; at any rate, they were known to be sympathetic to them. In April, Yoshida Shigeru, an old friend of the family, dropped in at Hachiroemon's villa in Oiso and had a confidential talk with Takasumi, requesting his cooperation in some undisclosed peacemaking scheme. (Secretly, Yoshida was collaborating with Konoe to end the war.)

"I myself have always been on the side of international culture," Yoshida said (according to Takasumi). "International-minded people should fight for the new Japan. So you must help, too." Takasumi, conscious of having been singled out as a peacemaker by Frank Buchman in the 1930s, was eager to participate in such an effort. But Yoshida would say no more at the time and failed to reappear for further conversations. Takasumi learned later that he had been arrested secretly, along with some four hundred fellow "defeatists," and was being held for trial by a court-martial.

The episodes surrounding the termination of the war were as agonizing and baffling as those of any time in the world's history. With the surrender of Germany, the Allies, including the Soviet Union, were free to mass all their power for a final assault on Japan. Recognizing the hopelessness of the situation, foreign minister Togo was then trying to arrange for a mission to Moscow, headed by Prince Konoe, to seek a negotiated peace with the Allies. Late in July, Stalin met Truman and Churchill in Potsdam and passed on this information—which was already known to Washington through decoded messages. One of them, from Togo to his ambassador in Moscow, dated July 12, read: "It is His Majesty's heart's desire to see the swift termination of the war . . . however, as long as America and England insist on unconditional surrender our country has no alternative but to see it through . . . for the survival and honor of the homeland."[15]

Instead of heeding the emperor's overtures through Konoe, the Allied statesmen issued a joint declaration calling for Japan's immediate and unconditional surrender, the alternative to which was "prompt and utter destruction." Unknown to the world, the United States had made two atomic bombs with which to back up the Allies' ultimatum.

Japan was clearly prepared to surrender if the emperor were allowed to keep his position. Washington knew this, and Secretary of War Stimson was preparing to grant such a condition. Yet, tragically, Japan was led to believe that the Potsdam Declaration really did call for unconditional surrender, and so felt compelled to reject it.

At the headquarters of Mitsui Honsha in Tokyo, scarcely damaged by the air raids, the mood among its banto was one of anxiety and impatience as they thought about the future. Few of the concern's productive facilities had been destroyed, and the defense industries were still functioning somehow but running far short of capacity because materials were scanty and transportation was disrupted. Peace could not be far away, but there would be a considerable interval between the armistice and the resumption of full-scale operations. Meanwhile, as responsible Japanese employers, they would have to keep all regular employees on the payroll and find jobs for those who would be returning from the armed services.

Matters could have been much worse, however; for the zaibatsu leaders who were advising the government—the very ones who had so stoutly resisted the encroachment of the government on private enterprise—had reversed their stand and forced the passage of a law "nationalizing" the munitions industries, which they foresaw would soon turn into white elephants. This shrewd move meant that the government would continue to guarantee their profits as long as the war lasted and then absorb their losses after it ended. Moreover, the "nationalization" wasn't intended to be permanent. Actual ownership remained in private hands, so that when the crisis was ended the zaibatsu would be able to resume control of the economy and make the most of the anticipated reconstruction boom.

For Mitsui, the first hint of a break in the deadlock between Japan and its enemies came on August 6, just before noon. Communications between the Tokyo headquarters and several Mitsui branches in Hiroshima had been suddenly cut off. Gradually it became apparent that some kind of catastrophe had occurred in Hiroshima. Two days later, as details of an extraordinary explosion were trickling through censorship, word came from Mukden that the Soviet Red Army was sweeping into Manchuria, where thousands of Mitsui men were stationed. This unexpected event caused more consternation than did the truth about Hiroshima. Mitsui's leaders were reconciled to defeat and seemed to believe that, since their company had been on good terms before the war with the Americans and the British through Bussan and Bank, they wouldn't be in for too much trouble when the war ended. Like such would-be peacemakers as Konoe and Yoshida, they were more concerned now with the prospect of postwar communism than with any punishment the Allies might inflict upon them. It was clear that Manchuria was lost. But if the Russians should occupy Japan, everything would be lost. August 8 was perhaps the gloomiest day in the whole war for Mitsui men.

On the following day, August 9, another unexplained disaster at Nagasaki led many Japanese to believe that a further delay in surrendering would lead to the total annihilation of Japan. At the Tokyo headquarters of Mitsui Chemical a young section chief, Narita Tomomi, was one of the very few Japanese civilians who understood the significance of the two explosions. Because he was responsible for his company's liaison with the military, he had gained some inside information and reported it to his president, Sohara Kazusaku. The latter, a leading authority in chemical engineering, listened skeptically and explained to his subordinate that such a weapon as the atomic bomb was "impossible from the scientific viewpoint."

When more extensive reports proved that Narita was right, he approached Sohara again. "Now Japan is defeated," he said. "Executives of Mitsui will be charged with responsibility for the war." He insisted that all the Mitsui family members in business positions, and all executives directly connected with them, should resign. His proposal, if it had been accepted, might have been construed later as an extenuating circumstance when the victors assessed the war guilt of the zaibatsu; but Sohara rejected it flatly. And Narita might well have become president of the company if he had been less impulsive; instead, he resigned in protest, took up a career as a left-wing politician, and eventually became chairman of the Japan Socialist Party.[16]

As the Red Army sped almost unresisted across the Manchurian plains toward the Sea of Japan, the nation remained in horrified suspense, expecting the "flash-bang" terror weapon to strike again—this time on Tokyo. Yet even in that time of dread the diehard patriots tried forcibly to prevent Japan's surrender. Not until August 15, and only after a revolt of the imperial guards, an abortive army coup, and a wave of assassinations and mass suicides, did the emperor dare to tell his people that the war had come to an end.

At noon on that day his subjects in the home islands and in the remaining overseas territories of the empire assembled submissively before radios or amplifiers to hear their sovereign's voice for the first time. The national anthem, "Kimigayo," was played by a military band, and when it ended on a descending, inconclusive note, there was a nerve-stretching silence before the Son of Heaven spoke. The recorded voice was high-pitched, quavering, and had a quality described as "unearthly." His message, delivered in the obscure circumlocutions of the court idiom, was not fully intelligible to the listening people, but something of its intent must have come through to them—if only a sense of relief—for observers in many places reported that survivors of the "holy war" sobbed uncontrollably.

After announcing acceptance of the Allied joint declaration, His Imperial Majesty then intoned: "We declared war on America and Britain out of our sincere desire to ensure Japan's self-preservation and the stabilization of Southeast Asia, it being far from our thought to infringe upon the sovereignty of other nations or to embark upon territorial aggrandizement.

"But now the war has lasted nearly four years. Despite the best that has been done by everyone—the gallant fighting of military and naval forces, the diligence and assiduity of our servants of the State, and the devoted service of our one hundred million people, the war situation has developed not necessarily to Japan's advantage . . . "

He did not distinctly say, however, that Japan had lost the war. Perhaps his delicacy on this point was due to his desire to soften the humiliation of his subjects. It is also possible that, like the more steadfast of the nation's leaders, he did not think of it as a surrender at all, but only as a truce in the unfinished war for international equality that had begun with the treaties forced upon his great-grandfather by Commodore Perry and Consul Harris some ninety years before.

25 · Ashes, Ashes, All Fall Down

THE VANQUISHED WAITED IN DREAD of vengeance, and the victors were alert for treachery, but two weeks passed with only sporadic incidents as diehard patriots were brought under control by the Japanese government. On August 23 three hundred rebellious kamikaze pilots at the Atsugi Air Base near Tokyo were disarmed; and on the thirtieth General Douglas MacArthur, Supreme Commander for the Allied Powers, descended from his personal aircraft *Bataan* at the same field, puffing on a corncob pipe. With his unfailing sense of showmanship he ordered his staff to leave their pistols behind, and his party proceeded unarmed to temporary headquarters in nearby Yokohama. (Inasmuch as he had landed only one division to face the whole Japanese army, a few pistols wouldn't have helped anyway if trouble for them had been in store.) Along the way the triumphant Americans noticed that the Japanese were not to be outdone in showmanship: lining the road at regular intervals stood soldiers with their backs turned to the convoy—guarding the general in a manner reserved for the emperor.

On September 2, 1945, foreign minister Shigemitsu Mamoru, representing Japan, signed the surrender documents aboard the U. S. S. *Missouri,* anchored in Tokyo Bay, and the supreme commander began immediately to carry out the policies set forth in his instructions from President Truman. Those policies were, briefly, to disarm and demilitarize the Japanese nation, return the overseas portions of its empire to their former owners, remove obstacles to the development of a democratic society, and foster a free economy adequate for peaceful existence.

The impediments to such a program were formidable. Approximately 3.8 million armed men had to be demobilized and a total of 6.5 million Japanese repatriated from all over East Asia. Although a caretaker government under Prince Higashikuni, the emperor's uncle, was nominally in charge, in fact the nation was still controlled by its military and police forces operating under oppressive wartime laws. Although 2.3 million uniformed men and more than half a million civilians had been killed, the population of the home islands actually increased as repatriates arrived and swelled the ranks of the unemployed. Foreign trade had ceased, and industry—more than eighty percent of which had been converted to military production—was almost at a standstill. Scarcities and rising inflation provoked hoarding, and without the black market half the population would have starved. Destruction of national wealth was estimated at some fifteen billion dollars, about five times the cost of the great Kanto earthquake. This represented ten years of economic effort, and in addition some ten billion dollars worth of ships and aircraft had been destroyed. Overseas assets valued at twenty billion dollars had to be written off the books, all colonies were lost, and the size of the nation's territory was reduced by nearly half.

The heaviest property losses were suffered by the common people, however, rather than by business and industry. Of the one hundred and sixty thousand tons of conventional bombs dropped, about one hundred thousand tons had been used for mass destruction. Some major cities were nearly leveled, three million houses had been destroyed, and eight and a half million people evacuated to the countryside. The remaining sixty thousand tons of bombs had been aimed at military or industrial targets, with varying degrees of success. Oil refineries and aircraft-engine plants were eighty-percent destroyed, but in steel, light metals, and chemicals the loss of capacity was only ten to twenty percent, and some less strategic industries were practically untouched.

Somehow, life went on. In Tokyo the trains were still running; the business centers of Marunouchi, Nihombashi, and Ginza—oases in a desert of cinders—were functioning after a fashion. Mitsui's headquarters buildings and Mitsukoshi Department Store were almost intact, as were most of the Tokyo properties of Mitsui Real Estate. As the administrative staff took stock of the situation they found that the concern's main industrial subsidiaries, such as Mining, Shipbuilding, Toyo Rayon, and Toyo Koatsu, had suffered remarkably little damage. Even the factories of Showa Aircraft had escaped unharmed, and the Tokyo plant was immediately requisitioned by the United States army as an automobile-repair facility. Losses of overseas assets were enormous, of course, and had to be written off. But with demand for reconstruction all but insatiable, Mitsui and the other zaibatsu houses were confident about their eventual recovery.

Such optimism was bolstered by the demeanor of the occupation forces, who although forbidden to fraternize at first, were not unfriendly. And as for their supreme commander, few complaints were heard. If Japanese leaders had been asked to write the specifications themselves, they would have asked for a boss very much like MacArthur. He was a professional soldier able to enforce discipline, uncompromisingly conservative yet not lacking in boldness and imagination. As the son of a former governor-general of the Philippines and the possessor of a large colonial fortune of his own, perhaps he would not be too censorious of Japan's motives in trying to annex Greater East Asia. In short, the general—whose name was pronounced "Makkaasaa" by the Japanese—appeared to be the kind of leader the zaibatsu could talk to, man to man.

It seems, however, that the American proconsul was dissatisfied with the political complexion of Prince Higashikuni's government, which was composed mainly of wartime figures, and made it clear that he did not intend to recognize that regime. When Japanese leaders learned that he planned to establish a military government they were terrified, and foreign minister Shigemitsu (himself a legacy from the old Tojo cabinet) was delegated to dissuade him. Whether or not Shigemitsu influenced him, MacArthur acceded to the request. Because Japan's governmental and economic system was so labyrinthine, and because so few of the occupation personnel knew the Japanese language, MacArthur and his staff decided that Japan should be allowed to retain its own government, which would be useful for routine administration and executing orders from SCAP (Supreme Commander for the Allied Powers).

By negotiating successfully with MacArthur, Shigemitsu had made a long stride toward realizing his ambition of being Japan's postwar strong man, but he was in too much of a hurry to capitalize on his presumed exploit. Soon after the encounter he called a press conference and broke the news that there would be no military government. This breach of protocol irked the general, who could not tolerate being upstaged, and he ordered Shigemitsu's dismissal. The beneficiary of this incident was Yoshida Shigeru, who was recommended for the post by state minister Prince Konoe Fumimaro. Since his release from prison Yoshida had remained in obscurity, "eating cold rice," as the Japanese say. After being summoned to Konoe's villa near Tokyo and invited to accept the foreign affairs portfolio, Yoshida became so elated that he got thoroughly drunk and, having missed the last train, had to sleep the night on the station platform.

On October 9, the Higashikuni cabinet was replaced by one more to the liking of SCAP and the worried zaibatsu, whose resourcefulness the replacement demonstrated. This government, entrusted with carrying out the most drastic reforms since the Meiji revolution, was dominated by ultraconservatives representing the oligopolies. The prime minister was Shidehara Kijuro, an old-line Minseito politician whose father-in-law was the late Baron Iwasaki Yataro, founder of Mitsubishi. Finance minister Shibusawa Keizo, grandson of the great Meiji industrialist, was an officer and big shareholder in numerous zaibatsu enterprises, including Teikoku Bank. Welfare minister Ashida Hitoshi was a relative of the Muto family, which presided over Mitsui's Kanebo.

The justice minister was an auditor of the Sumitomo and Mitsubishi banks, and the commerce and industry minister was a former Seiyukai politician connected with the national policy banks financing Greater East Asia. Among the ministers without portfolio were former directors of Mitsui Bussan and the South Manchurian Railway Company.

Continuing as foreign minister was Yoshida, who proved to be the strongest member of the cabinet and an ardent champion of the old zaibatsu. He was a son-in-law of the exalted Count Makino, formerly lord privy seal, and his daughter had married into the Aso coal-mining family whose wealth was a political asset. Earlier, as ambassador to Great Britain, he had formed friendships with many prominent Japanese, including imperial princes, zaibatsu family members, and such executives as Ikeda Seihin, Mukai Tadaharu, and Kato Takeo of Mitsubishi. The latter three, who often visited London, became his intimate associates.

The zaibatsu were quite encouraged now by the way matters were developing, and their plans for the future were being formulated bullishly. At the time of MacArthur's arrival, Minister of Commerce and Industry Nakajima Chikuhei, a co-owner of the mammoth Nakajima Aircraft combine, had told American newsmen that he hoped for the immediate opening of trade with the United States and for the supply of basic commodities in huge amounts—on credit, of course. Mitsui Honsha, in preparation for reconversion to peacetime industry, planned to establish a new firm called Mitsui Rehabilitation Projects Company, with an authorized capital equivalent to some five hundred million dollars. Part of its program (later vetoed by General Headquarters) was construction of two hundred thousand dwellings and production of five million bushels of rice and two hundred thousand tons of salt by mobilizing the idle facilities and personnel of affiliated companies. Other zaibatsu houses were going ahead with similar plans and were seeking the approval of the occupation authorities in charge.

Control of occupied Japan was nominally vested in the Far Eastern Commission, comprising representatives of all the victorious nations, but from the beginning the supreme commander left no doubt that the commission's role would be secondary to his own. Unfortunately, the zaibatsu were unable to discuss their meritorious plans with MacArthur, who, consciously following the example of emperors, remained "above the clouds." Instead, they had to talk to underlings whose backgrounds and ideologies were not necessarily congenial. Furthermore, SCAP (a term used synonymously with General Headquarters, or GHQ) still had to take orders from President Truman, who in turn was guided by the decisions of the State-War-Navy Coordinating Committee

(SWNCC), in which various conflicting tendencies were apparent from the start.

This setup was favorable to the Japanese establishment in that it minimized the influence of punitive-minded powers, such as the Soviet Union. But at the same time it conferred considerable authority on American civilian officials, many of whom were still imbued with the spirit of the Atlantic Charter and determined to destroy Japanese military fascism at its roots in order to give the oppressed Japanese people a kind of Rooseveltian New Deal. Thus on the heels of the occupation's fighting troops came battalions of civilians-in-uniform, many of them experts in their respective fields, prepared to demolish authoritarian institutions—except the emperor system—and to democratize every aspect of Japanese society. Such a program was supported by the Far Eastern Commission; the Allies were at odds on many policies, but they were in general agreement that the oligopolies of Japan and Germany had not only profited from the war but had helped to incite it. Therefore, it had been resolved that the only way to extirpate militarism in Japan was to break up the zaibatsu and prevent their revival.

One preliminary alarm was the arrival of an advance party from GHQ at the Mitsui Bunko, a private institute in which the clan's archives were preserved. The probers asked first to see the Mitsui Constitution but were told by the shocked custodian that the document was not available and was, furthermore, a family secret. He was informed brusquely that there were no secrets from GHQ and commanded to hand over a copy without delay. While investigators were making similar forays on the archives of other zaibatsu houses, their fate was being decided in Washington. Only three weeks after Japan's surrender President Truman ordered MacArthur to start democratizing its economy: "To this end, it shall be the policy of the Supreme Commander . . . to favor a program for the dissolution of the large industrial and banking combinations which have exercised control of a great part of Japan's trade and industry."[1]

News of this sweeping command, released publicly in Washington on September 22, came as a thunderbolt to the zaibatsu, who had assumed that they were to march in the vanguard of postwar Japan. And though they were incredulous at first, they were soon apprised that General MacArthur was going to obey his orders scrupulously. As evidence of this, SCAP ordered the Japanese government to set up an agency for dissolving the industrial combines, and each of the four largest— Mitsui, Mitsubishi, Sumitomo, and Yasuda—was instructed to draw up a plan for dismantling its own holding company.

Zaibatsu leaders, who had not been given a chance to cultivate influence with GHQ officialdom, turned instead to the foreign press. As if by prearrangement, they began with one voice to make statements to the effect that Japan's militarists and their henchmen alone were responsible for imperialism and war and that the respectable business houses had served them only under duress, without profit.

Like the German industrialists who supported Hitler, the Japanese munitions makers seemed to feel that they had done nothing reprehensible and that if they asserted their innocence often and loudly enough they would be believed. Their protestations were received skeptically by most newsmen and occupation officials; but foreign minister Yoshida, whose motives were less apparent, was able to plead their case more effectively. Addressing foreign correspondents on October 19, 1945, he tried to dispel the belief that Japan's financial leaders were "a bunch of war criminals," as he put it.

"Mitsui, Mitsubishi and other old Zaibatsu have constituted the fabric of Japan's economy and have brought about Japan's prosperity," he assured the doubting newsmen. "Through operating various subsidiaries these Zaibatsu themselves suffered losses during the war period. With the deteriorating situation the government obliged them to build ships and planes . . . ignoring their losses.

"Those who enjoyed great profit and worked hand in hand with the militarists were the new Zaibatsu. Concerning the question of whether or not the old Zaibatsu had their core in colonial undertakings, the answer is indicated by the fact that the militarists excluded the activity of the established Zaibatsu in Manchuria and other occupied areas, and encouraged the new Zaibatsu. The old Zaibatsu, having their interests in peacetime industries, rejoiced at the war's end."[2]

Whether this disingenuous interpretation originated with Yoshida or was handed to him by his big-business backers is not clear. However, it was the official line of the zaibatsu themselves, and still passes as legal tender. In an interview with the author in 1971, Mitsui Hachiroemon Takakimi stated with deep sincerity: "I was against the war, but if I had said even a word about it, the consequences would have been horrible. So I kept my mouth shut." Asked whether it might not have been better to speak, he replied: "If I had said anything against it at that time, Mitsui might have been suppressed by the military. Notwithstanding, Mitsui was regarded as a peacetime enterprise. We did not have military industries and were sharply attacked by the military for this."

"But Mitsui had Japan Steel," I objected.

"Yes, but that was about all—and shipbuilding in addition."

"How about Showa Aircraft?"

"Well, we couldn't help it. Pressure. Kishi Nobusuke was Minister of Munitions. I was summoned by him and scolded that Showa Aircraft was not adequate . . . "[3]

Apologetics of this tenor gained such currency that in time people who questioned them were likely to be accused of spitefulness and even subversion. Thus Walter Simmons of the *Chicago Tribune* wrote of his more cynical colleagues in these reproachful terms: "There is always good sport sinking harpoons into people who have more money than we do. It gratifies a normal virtuous, human desire, implanted in all of us by the Creator and heavily incrusted with piety, defined by H. L. Mencken once as 'the itch to get our thumb into the eye of our betters.'

"The fiction was being nurtured in the United States that Japanese industry was backing the army's warlike adventures so it could reap the benefits of expanded markets. This theory—that businessmen (especially the Zaibatsu) were the militarists—was assiduously propagated by . . . such Commy-line writers as Andrew ('Dilemma in Japan') Roth . . . T. A. Bisson, Mark Gayn and many others."[4]

Yoshida, no businessman himself, may have been guileless in saying that the zaibatsu had not profited from the war. The fact is, however, that during the war years from 1937 through 1945 the paid-up capital of the ten largest zaibatsu increased more than fourfold, as against 1.8 times for business as a whole. The ratio of the paid-up capital of the "Big Four" zaibatsu to the national total more than doubled, from ten percent to twenty-five percent. Until late in the war zaibatsu profits were fabulous, and when things began to look gloomy a reasonable profit rate for munitions industries was guaranteed and risks were assumed by the government.

As for the "new rich" having monopolized overseas investments, Yoshida surely knew better. While serving as vice-minister of foreign affairs in the Tanaka cabinet, he had helped to forge Japan's East Asia policy, which was largely concerned with the interests of major zaibatsu combines already well established in China. It is true that from the seizing of Manchuria in 1931 until Pearl Harbor ten years later, the newer houses had advanced swiftly on the continent and acquired the lion's share of new overseas investments. But during the Pacific War the tables were turned: by 1945 the Big Four, led by Mitsui, held four-fifths of the total, and the share of the new zaibatsu became insignificant.

Still cut off from their influential business associates in New York and London, who might have been helpful, the Mitsui chiefs did the best they could to wriggle out of their predicament. Through an English-speaking employee of Bussan, Mitsui Honsha made contact with Colonel Raymond C. Kramer, who headed SCAP's Economic and

Scientific Section in charge of the zaibatsu dissolution. Kramer, an American textile manufacturer and retail merchant, had done business with Bussan in the past, and was not unsympathetic to their plight. Giving him red-carpet treatment, the company heads invited him to the Mitsui club at Tsunamachi, which had been reserved for the most eminent visiting dignitaries.

Using familiar arguments, backed by selected statistics, Honsha's chief managing director Sumii Tatsuo, aided by Bussan's president Miyazaki Kiyoshi and his second-in-command, Matsumoto Kisashi, sought to soften the dissolution order, pleading that Mitsui family members be permitted to retain their positions and their shareholdings in affiliated companies. According to Edo Hideo, who was also present: "The latter three people were high-minded and sincere, and it seemed that they were able to correct Colonel Kramer's mistaken view of the zaibatsu, but could not change the U. S. Government's policy."[5]

When Yasuda and Sumitomo knuckled under, it became apparent that further resistance by Mitsui would be dangerous as well as useless. On October 27, 1945, an extraordinary meeting of Honsha directors and Mitsui family heads was held at the Tsunamachi Club to reach a decision on the fate of their concern—or, rather, to acquiesce in the one already made by Washington.

After a review of the situation and a discussion that merely underlined the futility of every alternative proposed, Sumii Tatsuo, last of the Mitsuis' obanto, addressed the meeting somberly: "Unless we dissolve [voluntarily], they intend to order us dissolved. The situation is so urgent that there is no room for procrastination. . . . I ask you, gentlemen, to determine your final attitude at this moment."[6]

The men around the ponderous mahogany table were still, for the moment, masters of a mighty domain built through almost three centuries of planning, toil, aggressive management, and subtle political maneuvering. Men of talent nurtured by the House had always, even in the deepest adversity, been able to find some shelter from the gathering storm. But now, as the great, solid edifice called Mitsui seemed about to be swept away, not one of them could come up with a practical suggestion to prevent that debacle. The Mitsuis and their banto had been advised by founder Hachirobei to respect the tenka-sama, the honorable men in power. Now those men were the Americans, and their emperor was MacArthur. Without further protest or discussion the Mitsuis and their loyal banto voted unanimously that Honsha should be dissolved.

Of the five zaibatsu first designated for oblivion, Mitsubishi was the most reluctant to capitulate. Baron Iwasaki Koyata, a man accustomed to having his own way, even with foreigners, fought like a cornered badger. "I want to see General MacArthur," he insisted. "He will understand if we talk the matter over." But his bluster was unavailing.

On October 8, two trucks under military-police escort stopped at Mitsui headquarters. Under the supervision of SCAP officials, Mitsui employees obediently lugged out forty-two wooden cases, roped and sealed, containing securities valued at 1,200,000,000 yen (about $281 million at the prewar exchange rate of $.2343 per yen) and loaded them on the trucks. The convoy then proceeded to Mitsubishi's headquarters to pick up another fifty million yen worth of certificates. The impounded securities were stored in the vaults of the nonzaibatsu Hypothec Bank, pending disposition. The great American crusade against monopoly had begun with a bang.

At that time there were at least twenty zaibatsu, the number depending upon the definition of the term. For in addition to the broadly diversified concerns, there also were huge companies with near-monopolistic positions in limited fields. In addition to the Big Four and Nakajima Aircraft, there were Furukawa (copper, electric power); Shibusawa (banking, industry); Okura (mining, trading, engineering); Kawasaki (shipbuilding, aircraft, rolling stock, steel); Asano (cement, steel); and such "new" zaibatsu as Nissan (heavy industries) and Showa Denko and Nichitsu (chemicals, fertilizer).

As of 1945 the ten largest zaibatsu accounted for about thirty-five percent of the nation's paid-up capital, fifty-five percent of its bank assets, seventy-one percent of its loans and advances (in ordinary banks), and sixty-seven percent of its trust bank deposits. They also controlled three-fourths of non-life- and thirty-six percent of life-insurance assets. Among the ten, with assets estimated at thirty billion dollars, the four largest stood out like mountain peaks among foothills. Their banks accounted for half the deposits and sixty-five percent of the outstanding loans of all private banks (Yasuda alone held ninety-nine percent of savings-bank deposits); they also held one-fourth of all corporate and partnership capital, and one-third of the capital in heavy industries.

Mitsui in 1945 was probably the world's largest private business organization. The visible fortune of the eleven branches of the Mitsui family amounted to some six hundred million yen, invested mainly in Honsha and its twenty-odd operating subsidiaries. Those in turn controlled sub-subsidiaries numbering more than three hundred. Bussan, a huge holding company in its own right, had one hundred and twenty-six subsidiaries and Mining had thirty-one. The total number of Mitsui-controlled companies was estimated at 336 by some authorities, although Mitsui listed only 272 in reporting to the government. The Holding Company Liquidation Commission settled for 294.

Leading American authorities have stated that in 1945 the Mitsui companies employed as many as 1.8 million people in Japan and another million overseas. Others say that these figures are too high, but they are not unreasonable considering that Mitsui controlled as much as fifteen percent of the nation's paid-up capital and at least thirty percent of its overseas investments. Eighty Mitsui companies had more than three billion yen (approximately seven hundred million dollars) in aggregate paid-up capital, but this understates the case badly. The companies' assets were worth far more than their capitalization (Bussan alone, for example, had assets on the order of a billion dollars), and the concern's strategically deployed investments, agencies, and trade agreements enabled it to control a corporate empire of much wider scope than was ever admitted by the Honsha management or even alleged by SCAP.

The formula for fragmenting those economic monoliths—or "private collectives," as one authority dubbed them—was based upon a plan submitted by the Yasuda zaibatsu late in October 1945. It stipulated that Yasuda Honsha, the family holding company, would be dissolved and that Yasuda Bank (today's Fuji Bank) would cease to exercise control over its subsidiaries. Shares in affiliates held by the family, the holding company, and the bank would be sold to a government control commission and the proceeds invested in ten-year government bonds of severely limited negotiability. Family members and executives appointed by them or Honsha were to resign from their positions in all Yasuda companies.

The Big Four, in consultation with finance minister Shibusawa Keizo, worked out a common plan incorporating the Yasuda formula. This was accepted on November 6 by SCAP, which then issued instructions to the "Imperial Japanese Government" to effectuate it. To prevent evasion, the government was directed to prohibit "the sale, gift, assignment or transfer of any movable or immovable property, including securities and other evidences of ownership, indebtedness or control" by the designated companies or members or agents of the families controlling them. The government was further directed to prepare plans for the dissolution of other monopolistic businesses and to enact laws for the prevention of monopolistic practices and the fostering of a democratic economy.

It may well be asked how the Japanese government came to be entrusted with such an incompatible responsibility, for under the big-business-oriented Shidehara cabinet the most important administrative positions had been filled by zaibatsu members or sympathizers. Chairman of the Foreign Exchange Control Board, and later of the Foreign Investment Council, was Kiuchi Nobutane, grandson of Mitsubishi's founder and brother-in-law of finance minister Shibusawa. The Board of Trade, set up to handle all export-import transactions, was headed by Mitsui's Mukai. And presiding over the Holding Company Liquidation Commission (HCLC) was Sasayama Tadao, an official of Yasuda and Industrial banks. Sasayama's lieutenant and chief of liaison with SCAP was Noda Iwajiro, a trading and textile executive long associated with Mitsui Bussan, who had spent several years in the United States.

In the early occupation period those Japanese who spoke English and understood foreign processes of thinking had a strong advantage in dealing with the authorities. Foreign minister Yoshida Shigeru was one of the best qualified in this respect. He gathered around him a group of men, notably those from his London circle, who had overseas experience with trading companies and banks; and he proceeded to develop channels of influence with the Americans. The most useful one was the War Termination Central Liaison Office (CLO) established under the foreign ministry for communicating with SCAP, and he set about making it as effective as possible.

The director of the CLO was Okazaki Katsuo, an inconspicuous diplomat appointed by Shigemitsu; but the man most frequently in contact with SCAP was Shirasu Jiro, a businessman who had been a member of Yoshida's London coterie and prided himself on his English. An equally important advantage was the influence of Shirasu's father-in-law, Count Kabayama Aisuke, a dominant figure in the Japan-America Society and in the prestigious International Cultural Association. President of the latter organization was Prince Konoe, and it was through this connection that Shirasu had prevailed upon Konoe to appoint Yoshida as foreign minister. Kabayama, Shirasu, and Yoshida, incidentally, were neighbors and close friends of the Mitsuis and Ikeda Seihin in the Oiso seaside colony, and Kabayama was board chairman of Mitsui Takasumi's exclusive academy. All of these men had friends and former associates in Wall Street, the State Department in Washington, London's City and Downing Street, and such connections undoubtedly gave Yoshida a boost in his climb to power.

It was Shirasu who revealed to Yoshida the weakest point in SCAP's armor—the rivalry between the New Dealers pressing for a liberal democracy and the conservatives who intended to build up Japan, with the help of the business community, as a bulwark against communism. Shirasu had at first made overtures to SCAP's Government Section (GS), headed by General Courtney Whitney, which was nominally in charge of the democratization programs, but was snubbed. Then he turned to General Charles A. Willoughby's G-2 Section (intelligence), which was more concerned with countering radicalism in Japan and strengthening the country against Soviet influence. It was partly through Shirasu and Kabayama that Yoshida, despite his key role in Japan's policy of aggression in China, developed close relations with SCAP and was able to advance the cause of his friends in the economic world.

The support given to the zaibatsu by early postwar cabinets was not merely moral and political, but was very conspicuously financial. When defeat in the war had seemed certain, the zaibatsu advisers to the cabinet pushed through legislation providing indemnities to munitions makers for wartime losses. Immediately after surrender, the Higashikuni cabinet agreed that these indemnities should be paid, and began immediately to disburse funds for that purpose. By November 1945, when SCAP found out how the "death merchants" were raiding the treasury, some eighteen billion yen had been paid out. Such payments had put so great a strain on the treasury that SCAP ordered the government to prohibit all payments of benefits to ex-servicemen (except meager disability pensions) and to stop payments on munitions makers' claims. However, on the pretext that the latter reimbursements were an economic necessity, payments were continued into "blocked" accounts until August 1946, when the total had reached a staggering fifty-four billion yen. This action was in part responsible for the subsequent inflation that badly hurt people of fixed income, but it enabled the government and some private businessmen to pay off their wartime debts with drastically devalued currency.

In October Yoshida, having won the confidence of big business and of SCAP's right wing, skyrocketed into the premiership. Since the Central Liaison Office had taken over the only important functions of the foreign ministry—namely, negotiations with the occupation authorities—Yoshida looked for a man "of greater stature than the foreign minister" to head it. He abolished the directorship to get rid of the incumbent Okazaki and proposed Mitsui's obanto emeritus Ikeda as president of the council. With his Harvard background, American connections, and dignified persuasiveness, Ikeda would have been an ideal choice, from the conservative viewpoint. But although SCAP was remarkably lenient about other legacies from wartime, SCAP's Government Section boggled at Ikeda's earlier involvement with military fascism. Yoshida then decided to take the position himself, together with the foreign affairs portfolio.

One of his first acts was to remove formerly pro-Axis elements from the ministry. But at the same time he adopted a very strong anticommunist posture in harmony with that of Willoughby's G-2 Section, and got rid of CLO officials who followed the more liberal line of Whitney's

Government Section, which was already losing influence in its assigned territory. As Shirasu pointed out to Yoshida, orders conveyed to the Japanese government through the "red" GS were not to be taken seriously. Yoshida apparently confirmed the validity of this judgment through his frequent contacts with General MacArthur, for he gravitated increasingly toward the G-2 line in carrying out (or ignoring) GHQ's policy directives. Such useful lore soon trickled down to Mitsui's executives, who admit that from an early date they bypassed GS whenever possible and flouted its orders rather contemptuously. Having learned to coexist with Japan's indigenous military masters, they adapted rather easily to the more lenient Americans, though life for businessmen was anything but easy.

General MacArthur was the darling of American ultraconservatives and certainly was unsympathetic personally to the more libertarian policies emanating from Washington. Nevertheless, he carried out orders to the letter, and if there was intrigue among his subordinates and Japanese lobbyists for special interests, he himself remained aloof from any such trafficking. As a consequence, the democratizers went about their work zealously, and the old establishment was kept in a state of anxiety. In September 1945 the Japanese government had been ordered by SCAP to suspend all laws restricting freedom of speech, press, and assembly. Thousands of political prisoners, many of whom had been incarcerated for ten years or more, were abruptly freed, and later that autumn military men and civilian officials suspected of war crimes were rounded up and held in prison. Opponents of the conservative government and of the zaibatsu used their new freedom eagerly to form labor unions, political parties, and publishing ventures to advance reformist ideas and programs ranging from the six-day week and woman suffrage to the abolition of capitalism.

Meanwhile, SCAP was beginning to institute reforms no less horrifying to Japan's economic rulers. The reparations program, as proposed by a United States government commission, would have "pushed Japan back to the Tokugawa period," as some enthusiasts exulted. The land reform, actually carried out, virtually expropriated farm landholdings of absentee landlords in excess of 2.5 acres and redistributed it to the tillers of the soil, thereby threatening the feudalistic power structure based upon political control over the rural population to offset the more volatile urban working class.

The reborn Communist and Socialist parties evoked a strong response from the hungry resentful masses who, having so little to lose, found their programs inviting and not unreasonable. The JCP, for example, proposed the abolition of the emperor system and establishment of a people's republic, strict adherence to the Potsdam Declaration, dissolution of antidemocratic parties, severe punishment of all war criminals (including the emperor and empress), and the drafting of a new democratic constitution. Curiously, this program coincided closely with the American policy, except for the abolition of the emperor system; but there was no guarantee that even this reservation would hold, since a Gallup poll showed that thirty-seven percent of Americans wanted to punish Hirohito as a war criminal, and thirty-three percent said he should be hanged.

The Japanese conservatives had taken some comfort in the fact that they had been able to put one over on MacArthur by reinstating the old guard in government and were of course gratified to find stout anticommunist allies in the G-2 Section. The latter, in fact, was organizing clandestine intelligence agencies, somewhat similar to the Black Dragon, by recruiting personnel from the defunct imperial army and terrorist bands to spy on left-wing activities.

Conservatives also noted with a certain grim satisfaction that the Americans, who had goaded Japan into war by insisting that Japanese troops be withdrawn from China, were now using those very troops to resist the communist advance against the Kuomintang government. Although the imperial forces were supposed to have been disbanded and repatriated without delay, those facing communist troops were instructed to hold their positions until they were able to surrender to Chiang's men, in order to prevent their weapons and equipment from falling into the hands of the Chinese Red Army. Thus, at the end of 1945, Japanese patriots concluded that the Americans—the "good kind," at least—had now begun to recognize the justice of Japan's crusade in Asia. Nevertheless, SCAP's punitive policy was not softened, and the Yoshida government was instructed to purge from public life militarists and ultranationalists suspected of being a menace to peace and democracy.

As GHQ's investigators began to find their way around in the remnants of Japan's wartime economy, they made shocking discoveries about corruption and collusion between the military and the zaibatsu. Working through the wartime control associations (which were still functioning), major industrial companies had hoarded huge amounts of scarce materials in anticipation of Japan's defeat and were now using them for their own production or releasing them into the black market. Valuable caches of steel, copper, aluminum, and other metals sidetracked from aircraft production were discovered, one after another. Some nine billion yen worth of commodities was found sequestered on the premises of Nakajima's factories, and the other zaibatsu companies were also implicated. For example, American military police unearthed on Mitsui property five tons of hidden silver, reminiscent of the "cellar silver" reserve prescribed by the old House regulations. In 1947 a Diet investigation committee estimated the value of Japanese military stockpiles already diverted into the black market at one hundred and fifty billion yen.

Such exposures prompted a new crackdown on the unregenerate capitalists and their executives, and in 1946 SCAP was ordered by Washington to eliminate from business positions "all persons who have been active exponents of militant nationalism and aggression." In the absence of disproof it was to be assumed that "any persons who have held key positions of high responsibility since 1937, in industry, finance, commerce, or agriculture," were to be purged. General MacArthur justified the latter ruling in no uncertain terms: "It was these very persons [the zaibatsu leaders], born and bred as feudalistic overlords, who held the lives and destiny of the majority of Japan's people in virtual slavery, and who, working in closest affiliation with its military, geared the country with both the tools and the will to make aggressive war."[7]

The purges swept out 220,000 leaders of the military, bureaucratic, political, and economic cliques who had been running Japan. Included were the great majority of Diet members, as well as diplomats, aristocrats, imperial advisers, newspaper publishers, and gang bosses. Japan's highest economic leaders, fifteen hundred in all, faced indefinite suspension from all business positions. Among the Mitsui brain trusters so banished were Ikeda, Fujihara, Mukai, Ishida, Sumii, Miyazaki of Bussan, and Bandai Junshiro and Sato Kiichiro of Teikoku Bank. Furthermore, as the marathon Tokyo War Crimes Tribunal got under way, there was no assurance that such business leaders, as well as the zaibatsu family heads, would not be indicted as war criminals, just as Prince Konoe and Marquis Kido had been.

The occupation authorities, at their wits' ends to unravel the tangled skein of Japanese society and to enforce regulations that were resisted, evaded, or ignored by uncooperative bureaucrats and businessmen, had neither the resources nor the will to save the Japanese from all the consequences of their greed and folly. At the end of 1947, after Yoshida and two successive prime ministers had failed miserably in attempts to revive the economy, the livelihood of the people still depended largely upon Japanese government subsidies and American handouts. Indemnities for war damage and financial losses were at last canceled, but inflation still raged out of control, bank credit was almost nonexistent, industry was plagued by labor strife, and corporate initiative was paralyzed by threats of dissolution and implementation of the reparations program.

A new constitution drafted by SCAP toppled the ancient hierarchy headed by the god-emperor and vested state power in "the will of the people," a force that the zaibatsu equated with a pack of rabid wolves. The new charter not only had a bill of rights making all men equal under the law, but also emancipated and enfranchised women, unleashing a fearsome and unpredictable force in a society traditionally dominated by males. Most upsetting to nationalist-minded Japanese was Article 9, forever renouncing war as a sovereign right of the nation and banning the maintenance of "land, sea and air forces, as well as other war potential," which had been the driving force of economic and political expansion ever since the early days of the Meiji era.

The zaibatsu daimyo reacted to the loss of their financial domains in various ways, depending upon their circumstances and personalities. Baron Iwasaki Koyata struggled too hard against the dissolution decree and died of a heart attack soon after Mitsubishi's surrender. His brother Hikoyata, although deprived of most of his equities and positions in Mitsubishi companies, seems to have started planning a comeback quite soon after SCAP's first blow. Sumitomo Kichizaemon was rather indifferent to it all, since a large part of his wealth was in forest areas, which were unaffected by the land reform or the dissolution of holding companies. Perhaps he was glad of the chance to spend more time classifying his collection of Chinese bronzes (which ranks with that of Avery Brundage as one of the world's finest), started before the 1911 revolution and amplified greatly during the eight-year China Incident. Mitsui Hachiroemon's attitude was one of resignation rather than disappointment. At one time he said that "the Mitsuis must start anew, beginning with apprenticeship," but he himself never got around to it. He seemed, in fact, to be relieved at having the responsibility for the clan lifted from his shoulders and made only the most desultory efforts to repair its fortunes.

During the first winter of the occupation, when things looked darkest to Hachiroemon, Edo Hideo paid him a visit and asked what he could do to help. To his surprise, the baron—who had always been rather aloof with his employees—replied that he wanted to get thoroughly drunk. Liquor was scarce and expensive at that time, but Edo, an enthusiastic tippler himself, had kept up his friendship with a former schoolmate who worked for Dai-Nippon Brewing, once controlled by Mitsui. That evening Edo, Hachiroemon, and an admiral's son went to one of the company's breweries in Tokyo and were treated to all the beer they could drink. "We discussed the past and future of defeated Japan," Edo recalls. "That was one of my unforgettable memories." Hachiroemon remembers only that "it was snowing and very cold, and the place looked like a cellar."[8]

His apathy toward the adventure of reconstruction is surprising, since the dissolution of the concern had not left the clan destitute by any means. Although the Mitsuis' shares in the doomed Honsha represented ninety percent of their financial assets, the securities impounded by the HCLC had not been confiscated and were expected to yield a huge sum in ten-year bonds, as well as accrued dividends. And in addition to personally-held securities, the families owned extensive real estate and many art treasures. Nevertheless, the Mitsuis had to share the hardships of a vanquished people, and SCAP made sure that they did not get off too easily. Early in 1946 all bank deposits were frozen, and withdrawals for living expenses were limited to one hundred yen per month per person. Each of the fifty-six designated members of ten zaibatsu families was required to submit a monthly budget and an accounting of expenditures during the previous month in order to get even such a paltry sum.

Hachiroemon owned villas in Karuizawa, Hakone, Oiso, and Hayama, and a big house in Kyoto, but he had to remain in Tokyo, where he and his family lived in a garage that had escaped the conflagration in 1945. From his motor fleet he had salvaged one 1937 Bentley, but the tires were worn and gasoline was unavailable, so he had to walk when he went out, or use frightfully overcrowded public conveyances. His spacious office at Honsha headquarters was occupied by General MacArthur's political adviser, and Hachiroemon was relegated to a small adjoining room. Since he was not allowed to conduct any but personal business, he didn't really need an office; but the daily routine helped to keep up his morale and diverted him from brooding over the steady erosion of his fortune by inflation, taxation, and the depredations of SCAP. As a "designated person," he was under surveillance to prevent his engaging in forbidden activities or conspiring to circumvent SCAP ordinances; but at Honsha headquarters, under the very noses of SCAP officers, he could at least speak to his old business associates without being suspected of conspiracy.

Behind the scenes Honsha's men were using every stratagem, legal or otherwise, to salvage part of the concern for their former employers. The best prospect was Mitsui Real Estate, which was wholly owned by the Mitsuis and would not be affected by the holding company's dissolution. However, SCAP had ordered that all but six percent of the real estate company's one million shares must be sold to the public, excluding Mitsui clan members or employees. There was a rumor that "third country nationals" (presumably Koreans) were buying up shares in Mitsui Real Estate in order to get control of its numerous office buildings, which had miraculously escaped destruction and were in great demand. To prevent such a takeover, Mitsui executives pooled their funds and secretly purchased three hundred thousand shares, which were entrusted to the president, Sasaki Shiro. Then the certificates were placed in the custody of Sasaki's relative, Hayashi Hikosaburo, president of the nominally independent Sanshin Building Company, which was closely affiliated with Real Estate. Hayashi took advantage of his position by using the shares as collateral for a bank loan to himself, and when Real Estate tried to recover them he refused to cooperate. With one-third of the stock in jeopardy, preserving control over Real Estate became very difficult; and since someone brought in hoodlums to intimidate them, Mitsui's executives were afraid to take legal action.

The man who came forward to negotiate the dispute was Edo Hideo, then a director and now chairman of the company. Before confronting Hayashi personally, he increased his life insurance by ten times, he says, and for fear of poisoning he would not drink beer unless the bottle was opened before his eyes. He survived, but it took many years and enormous expense to get the stock back. Such incidents were common at the time. In a similar raid a member of a gangster organization, the Matsubakai, bought up 250,000 shares of Mitsubishi Real Estate and nearly grabbed off the whole Marunouchi business district in central Tokyo.[9]

Individual companies were able to put up a stiff fight against the depredations of SCAP as well as of financial brigands, but efforts to salvage the Mitsui fortunes were largely doomed by the capital levy approved by the Diet in 1946. This steeply graduated tax on personal assets, which netted the government forty-one billion yen, took away most of the clan's wealth. Sato Kiichiro, retired chairman of Mitsui Bank, explained why the capital levy hit the Mitsuis harder than any other family: "It was because the Mitsuis as a whole had no indebtedness but only assets." While some other zaibatsu families had liabilities about equal to their assets, the Mitsuis owed little money except to the government. When the capital levy struck, those whose assets were exactly offset by liabilities would have paid nothing and according to Sato, the capital levy on some major houses was "almost insignificant." On the other hand, the Mitsuis, with small liabilities, were in the highest bracket in terms of net assets, and the ones who were richest lost the most. The tax imposed upon Hachiroemon came to a calamitous ninety-one percent of his assets.

The Mitsuis still believe that the capital levy was designed by the New Dealers expressly to wipe out the zaibatsu families, and Sato shares this view. Whether or not this is true, the levy was highly selective, since it had no effect on the postwar parvenus—those who fattened on speculation, black marketing, and gains through inflation.

Hachiroemon's sense of persecution was aggravated when he was summoned to his own office by its temporary occupant, SCAP's political adviser William J. Sebald, and was told to sell his most valuable property—the hill-top estate at Imai-cho—to the American government. The absurdly low price offered was about nine dollars per tsubo (3.95 square yards). This thirty-acre lot, nearly as large as Hibiya Park, is now the site of two large apartment buildings inhabited by members of the United States Embassy staff. In 1972 it was worth at least three thousand dollars per tsubo, or 333 times the selling price. Hachiroemon could not have been forced legally to sell it, of course, but the instruction was given in such a way that to him it sounded like an order. Paradoxically, Sebald, who became ambassador to Japan after the occupation, later called SCAP's economic policies "vindictive, destructive and futile."[10]

When Edo Hideo visited Colonel Kramer at the Economic and Scientific Section in an effort to get permission for the Mitsuis to retain an interest in some of the properties owned by Real Estate—including family graveyards—Kramer is reported to have said: "The Mitsui family shall not live better than those people," as he pointed out the window at the shabby passers-by in the war-scarred streets below. The uncompromising morality of his position must be questioned, however. For by some legerdemain, Gerli International, a company in which he was a partner, acquired 850,000 shares in Katakura Industries, a major silk-textile firm dominated by Mitsui Bussan. Whether he obtained this stock by legitimate means or as compensation for services rendered, some conflict of interest is evident.

Such acquisitions were not rare. Some occupation officials used their authority to extort securities, real estate, and works of art from Japanese owners reduced to desperation by the freeze on securities and bank accounts, or went into "partnership" with businessmen seeking privileges. Quite a few of those carpetbaggers, especially Japanese-speaking American lawyers, became landed gentry by such means and still live in Japan as millionaires—or as billionaires, if their wealth is counted in yen.

It seemed that everyone with "connections" was making money, legitimately or otherwise, or reestablishing financial foundations. It is puzzling, therefore, that Mitsui Hachiroemon, enjoying personal and business relationships with the biggest tycoons in Japan and the world's major capitals, made no attempt to use his influence and credit advantageously. It was not from humility that he bowed so passively to fate, for he reacted with quite normal bitterness to his persecutors. But despite his experience as a globetrotter and international host, he either could not or would not speak English, and he felt unable to deal with the occupation authorities effectively. Moreover, he was aloof by nature, and could not assume the cheerful, hat-in-hand, good-loser manner that less sensitive men used as means to ingratiate themselves with the victors.

It is perhaps significant that until Japan's defeat the seclusive Hachiroemon had scarcely seen or spoken to the younger executives who were to keep the Mitsui name alive and eventually bring it into new prominence. And never was he able to establish rapport with them. He also had an unhappy obsession about the menace of communism and international Jewry and an abhorrence for having any dealings with organized labor. Rather than grapple with such adversaries, real or imaginary, he remained above the battle, and despite urging from his clansmen who looked to him for leadership, he seems never to have entertained seriously the idea of restoring the House to its former high estate. As one member of his family puts it, in good clear English (if not in an access of charity): "Hachiroemon had no—*guts.*"

After the dissolution, when many of his colleagues were already sorting out the pieces of their shattered empires, Hachiroemon organized a social club called Nagusameru-kai, or Commiseration Society, in which members of the Mitsui, Iwasaki, Sumitomo, Okura, and other "ruined" zaibatsu families sought mutual consolation. After the virtual confiscation of his Imai-cho property he acquired, with permission from SCAP, a smaller but still spacious tract in a high-class residential neighborhood. For reasons of economy, he had his old Kyoto mansion dismantled and reconstructed on the Tokyo site, where he established a ménage of modest elegance. Nearby was the Wakaba-kai school established in the Meiji era for Mitsui children, and when his finances improved through the piecemeal sale of art objects, he had it refurbished as a kindergarten for the offspring of former aristocrats. He seems to have found his true vocation as an educator. Recently the author asked him: "You were once a king of the zaibatsu, and now you are the director of a kindergarten. Which do you find more satisfying?"

"The kindergarten," he replied without hesitation. "It's more carefree and less responsibility—especially since the war, when the labor movement has been so difficult." For Hachiroemon, the loss of fortune, title, and prestige seems to have been an irritation rather than a tragedy and has made his life pleasanter in the end. Reestablishing his home and school gave him a creative outlet; and once he got his old Bentley back on the road he enjoyed motoring and playing golf with similarly leisured friends who inhabited the patrician colonies of Oiso and Karuizawa.

With the loss of the Imai-cho mansion as a gathering place, the clan disintegrated rapidly; and the eleven family heads, with few common business interests, seldom saw each other. Even the traditional New Year gatherings were abandoned, since all the places suitable for such occasions—including the Tsunamachi Club—had been requisitioned for use by occupation personnel. The country's new constitution, which deprived the emperor of power over his subjects, also abolished the legal basis for the authority of a family head over his house. "With regard to choice of spouse, property rights, inheritance, choice of domicile, divorce and other matters pertaining to marriage and the family," stated Article 24, "laws shall be enacted from the standpoint of individual dignity and essential equality of the sexes." This effectively ended the system of primogeniture and the hereditary preservation of great fortunes. The Mitsui constitution thus became a dead letter; from then on inheritances were to be divided equally among sons and daughters, none of whom had any legal authority over the others. With the simultaneous abolition of the peerage, the zaibatsu heirs became ordinary citizens; and they and their brothers and sisters were technically free to travel, marry, or seek employment.

The young Mitsuis, freed from the restrictions imposed by the old family system, lived very much like others of their age group. Hachiroemon's heir Takamitsu and his cousin Takayori, not having any allowances from their fathers, had to earn their own spending money. Since they spoke English, they gravitated toward the Americans. Takamitsu got a job as translator for the *Chicago Tribune's* Tokyo bureau, and Takayori made a pretense of attending Tokyo University. In their spare time they used their GI contacts for small-scale black-market operations, which enabled them to share some of the fun and excitement enjoyed by the victors. For them the House of Mitsui and its stuffy traditions were as dead as Emperor Meiji.

Most lighthearted about the Mitsuis' comedown in the world was Reiko, younger sister of Hachiroemon. She had long felt misgivings about the justice of the zaibatsu system, and the war confirmed them. The postwar liberation also had an exhilarating effect upon her. "We women had always been under the same system, with no freedom," she says. "Now, something suppressing us was gone, and I felt a sort of release. Although we were short of living expenses, we could have hope for the future."

After her daughter married she could at last pursue freely her avocation of historical research. As the first female ever to set foot inside the Mitsui Bunko, she delved eagerly into the family archives and, in collaboration with Mitsui scholar Yamaguchi Eizo, began an exhaustive history of the House, the first two volumes of which appeared in 1971 and 1972. She was also able to participate openly in Marxist political activity, to the unmitigated horror of her kinsmen. But once socialism became an established feature in the political landscape, her elder brother Takasumi could bring himself to say, in bafflement, but not without a hint of pride: "My sister is a Communist."

Takasumi, as president of the nonprofit Mitsui Ho-on Kai, escaped the purge, but for him too life was hard for a while. All that was left of his home was a concrete *kura,* or storehouse, which he converted into a makeshift dwelling. He and his wife Hideko were philosophical about it, knowing as good Christians that God worked his wonders in strange ways. Their first reaction to the loss of their home and school had been, unexpectedly, one of liberation. Almost everything they owned had vanished, yet life had not lost its savor. Perhaps all those possessions had been meaningless after all, Takasumi thought. Later on, Hideko began to miss certain things. "I wonder what happened to our grand piano?" she suddenly asked one day, then realized how little such deprivations had meant to her.

More worrisome was the absence of their eldest son Takayori, night after night, without explanation. As this strange behavior continued, scarce necessities and a few luxuries began to appear in their rough dwelling. Like most parents in those days, Takasumi was hesitant to assert his authority. His generation had failed in its responsibilities, he conceded, and he had no right to judge the young. "When he told us about his black-market activities, it was shattering but freeing as well," Takasumi says. "I knew I had been partly to blame. We Japanese hated the Americans telling us how to behave, yet not always doing it them-selves. Why should Yori have loved and obeyed his dictator father?"

Takasumi resumed his career in education by reestablishing his Kei-mei Christian Academy on the outskirts of Tokyo, in a villa acquired from a former prince. Japanese were not allowed to correspond with people overseas, but in 1947, with the help of an American officer, he was able to make contact with Frank Buchman. He learned that Buchman had built an imposing Moral Rearmament center at Caux, Switzerland, overlooking Lake Geneva. With a slight shift in emphasis, Buchman's movement had been revamped into a counterforce against communism, fostering conservative leadership in government and labor unions and preaching Christian reconciliation as an alternative to the class struggle that was then assuming formidable proportions in Asia, as well as in Europe and Latin America.

It was through MRA (generously backed by American industrialists and encouraged by the State Department) that Takasumi and Hideko got permission to travel—a rare privilege in those occupation days. As Takasumi explained: "We had been invited by Frank, through U. S. officials and Japanese being groomed for government posts, to an in-ternational assembly in Riverside, California. General MacArthur told us later of the special orders he had signed approving our travel. Our passport numbers came between 50 and 60."

Takasumi and Hideko attended the California assembly in 1948, with a small group of MRA adherents, and were given the mission (which turned out to be a rather significant one) of morally rearming the post-war leaders of Japan—which in Dr. Buchman's prescient words was to be "the Lighthouse and Powerhouse of Asia."

26 · All the King's Men

THE END OF THE WAR caught Niizeki Yasutaro in Hsinking, Manchuria, where he had been supervising Bussan's still unfinished rocket-fuel plant. As the Red Army advanced he assembled his staff members and their families—about fifteen in all—at his house. "Anticipating the invasion of unseen Soviet forces, we were in terror," he writes in his memoirs. "After a consultation among ourselves, we put up a sign in Russian, saying: 'Welcome Soviet Forces! In this house there are a telecommunication engineer, construction engineer, and business-men.'"[1] Niizeki was not confident of the effect, however. He had written his will and given it to his wife, but as the red menace became more imminent he took it back, tore it up, and gave her a vial of cyanide instead.

"At last, the dreaded moment came," he continued in his narrative. On August 19 he heard the approaching troops and saw a Soviet tank breaking through the hedge behind the house. "At that moment, I felt as if my blood was freezing. About ten soldiers came into the house. The chief of the unit . . . spoke a little German. 'This house will be occupied by the Signal Corps,' he announced. 'We have no place to go. Please let us stay here,' Niizeki pleaded. 'All right, we'll leave you the upstairs bedroom and downstairs dining room. All other rooms must be evacuated for our troops.'"

Bussan's people were unmolested, but soon afterward they found larger quarters in an abandoned hospital, where the "household" grew to two dozen members. The next problem was economic, and the Bussan men solved it with customary ingenuity. The engineers who had been installing the rocket-fuel plant devised a method for making almost 200-proof alcohol by the distillation of Manchurian *kaoliang* wine. "We bought empty cans, and with all the family members assisting we hammered them out to make a distilling tower . . . about twenty feet high." This was erected in a stairwell of the hospital, and with heat supplied by an electric rice-cooker the still worked perfectly. The bootleg-alcohol business brought in enough money for buying black-market food, and the stranded Japanese, completely out of touch with the homeland, resigned themselves to a long, uneventful wait.

The Russians left, taking the rocket-fuel plant with them. Soon, a battle between Chinese Communist and Nationalist forces broke out in the city. The Japanese barricaded themselves in the hospital, but Communist soldiers broke down the doors with the butts of their rifles, swarmed in, and herded the terrified residents into a small room where they cowered, expecting to be liquidated. It turned out, however, that they had been imprisoned for their own protection from machine-gun fire that riddled the walls. When the battle was over the uninvited guests were anything but hostile. "The soldiers helped us heat the bath, and sang Chinese songs to the accompaniment of an organ played by my daughter. It was quite friendly, and in song we found the talisman of Japan-China Friendship," Niizeki wrote.

While experiencing some misadventures with the Nationalists, who supplanted the Communist troops and were trying to recruit Japanese soldiers to fight against the Reds, Niizeki finally got some news from home. The telecommunication engineer had pieced together a short-wave radio, and Niizeki listened secretly to broadcasts from Japan. It was then that he learned about the dissolution of the zaibatsu, and spread the news through an underground newspaper circulating among the Japanese. The Bussan bootleggers were in despair. Even if they were lucky enough to be repatriated there would be no jobs, and for a Japanese, even death is preferable to unemployment. "I believed that Japan was in chaos, but wished at least to die on Japanese soil," Niizeki said.

At the end of 1946 he and his family got transportation to Tokyo, where he found that Bussan was not in such bad shape as he expected. He was at first put in charge of the General Merchandise Department, but soon afterward the top management was purged and Niizeki, an exceptionally competent executive, suddenly found himself managing director of the huge enterprise, with some seven thousand employees and valid sales contracts that amounted to more than six billion yen.

Niizeki's main job at that time was to appease SCAP and try to prevent the breakup of the firm, which, like Mitsubishi Shoji, was on the list of holding companies to be dissolved. Many of his colleagues thought that Japanese big business was doomed, but Niizeki was optimistic. It was apparent that the democratizers in SCAP were becoming isolated. The upsurge of organized labor under leftist leaders was unabated, but General MacArthur had taken a firm position by outlawing a general strike early in 1947, and Prime Minister Yoshida denounced the strikers as "lawless elements." In April the first postwar election gave Social Democrats a plurality in the lower house, but the upper house was controlled by the right wing. Although Yoshida's government was forced out of office, the new coalition government headed by Katayama Tetsu, a moderate socialist, was not regarded as a menace to capitalism. SCAP's economists tried to press on with their economic reforms, but the HCLC dragged its feet and the program was bogging down in a morass of technicalities and administrative confusions. A United States government mission to Japan recommended that reparations payments in equipment be scaled down drastically. The best news for Bussan that spring was SCAP's announcement that private foreign trade of limited scope would soon be resumed.

Niizeki was elated, but he didn't expect Bussan to get off unscathed. In consultation with GHQ the management had already agreed that the company would be divided into ten parts. The main task of the executives was to reduce the number of fragments, and to this end they were negotiating aggressively with HCLC and GHQ.

On July 3, without any prior rumbling, the sky fell. "Just when we thought the situation was turning for the better," Niizeki says, "the order for our dissolution was issued by GHQ. Bussan, like Mitsubishi Shoji, was forced to liquidate, and of its huge staff only the accounting and general administrative departments would remain to wind up the company's affairs."

Bussan was carved into 170 companies, and Mitsubishi Shoji into 120. To prevent their rebirth, SCAP stipulated that no more than one hundred former employees could assemble in any one company. There were severe limitations on the scale of capital and transactions and even an order forbidding the use of the Mitsui and Mitsubishi tradenames, known throughout the world. SCAP's action was taken suddenly, apparently without consulting Washington, and yet it passed almost without criticism except from the victims themselves.

MacArthur's ultimatum has puzzled scholars, American as well as Japanese. Eleanor Hadley, who called the dissolution of the trading firms "clearly the most drastic action taken in the whole deconcentration program," still wonders how SCAP got away with it so easily. "Was the absence of criticism to be explained by ignorance of the event; endorsement of dissolution over reorganization; disapproval of trading companies; or the loyalty of Republican critics to a fellow Republican?" Rejecting the first three answers, she concluded: "Seemingly, the only explanation is that supporters of MacArthur did not wish to embarrass him in a situation where responsibility was clearly his alone."[2]

Sakaguchi Akira, a critic writing for the influential *Nihon Keizai Shimbun* (Japanese Economic Journal) was more cynical: "In Europe and America, general trading firms such as those in Japan do not exist, so the existence of such companies must have seemed weird. Furthermore, traders in Europe and America who were Japan's competitors in markets of third countries put pressure on the occupation policy, and urged dissolution of Bussan and Shoji who were their foremost enemies. Such a thing can be imagined."³

The most curious aspect of the ukase against the trading companies was that it came at a time when the trend of government and civilian opinion in the United States had already turned against the reformists. Washington's Asian policy had been predicated upon having Nationalist China as a strong ally to be played off against the increasingly intransigent Soviet Union, which had long since been singled out as the enemy in a possible Third World War. But, instead, the Chinese Communists were moving relentlessly toward victory, and the specter of a Sino-Soviet military coalition had become an alarming reality to those who hoped for American hegemony in East Asia. In the thinking of the Pentagon, shared by conservatives in the State Department and the Senate, Japan should be rehabilitated as an ally rather than suppressed as a former enemy, and rapid economic recovery by the most convenient means should take precedence over liberal reforms.

Backing the antireform forces were many American businessmen, who had never been in favor of trustbusting at home and tended to sympathize with the zaibatsu. They were receptive to arguments that until Japan became economically self-sufficient again it would be a heavy burden upon the American taxpayers. Furthermore, leading American banks and corporations had capital and business ties of long standing with Japanese firms. In 1941 American corporations had held three-fourths of all direct foreign investments in Japan, amounting to $110 million (the largest was GE's stake of forty-seven million yen in Tokyo Shibaura Electric), and Japanese public utilities firms had borrowed large sums from banks in the United States. American creditors and investors were naturally anxious to recover their investments, which together with accrued interest, dividends, and licensing fees, brought their total claims to some four hundred million dollars. These creditors were lobbying vigorously against the economic reform programs in Washington and also through the Japanese Foreign Investment Council, which comprised representatives of fourteen Japanese firms in which Americans held large interests. When American leaders began talking about Japan as "the Workshop of Asia" and a "bulwark against communism," no one applauded more loudly than international businessmen, who saw Japan as the most promising field for future investments if only the trustbusters could be curbed.

The first big barrage of criticism in the United States began in December 1947, when a new law for the deconcentration of monopolistic enterprises was pending before Japan's National Diet. On December 1 *Newsweek* featured an article attacking not only the economic democratization measures but also the social, political, and labor reforms as being "far to the left of anything now tolerated in America." The basis for part of the article was a report prepared by an American lawyer, James Lee Kauffman, for the Pentagon, which apparently leaked it to the magazine. The purge of the zaibatsu was called "a lethal weapon in the socialization of Japan." Kauffman, who had taught at Tokyo Imperial University before the war and was personally acquainted with some of the zaibatsu chiefs, called the purge "tragic," and further deplored the fact that "both the Japanese government and business have been stripped of older men of ability and experience." Warning that the entire Japanese economy was in danger of collapse, he added that "Japan is costing the American taxpayers millions of dollars a year." But the most important part of Kauffman's message was this: "Were economic conditions otherwise, I am convinced Japan would be a most attractive prospect for American capital."[4]

During the next two months a number of prominent American conservatives leaped into the fray, attacking the occupation's economic program as ill-advised, burdensome, unjust, and possibly communistic, to the embarrassment and anger of General MacArthur, a staunch Republican capitalist. In March 1948, Undersecretary of the Army William H. Draper was sent to Japan, presumably to underscore a change in United States policy not yet comprehended by the general public or even by most occupation officials.

Draper, a former (and future) vice-president of Dillon, Read & Company, a leading Wall Street investment banking house, had been head of the economic division of the American military government in Germany. There he had helped to reverse the occupation government's antimonopoly program, thus preparing the way for reviving the German trusts (with which Dillon, Read had financial ties) and for resuming American investment activity. His firm, which worked closely with the Rockefellers and other major groups in developing overseas resources and industries, was also a leading supplier of brain power to the Truman administration. Secretary of Defense James Forrestal and the State Department's policy planning chief Paul Nitze were among several Dillon men on loan to the government.

Draper may have been perfectly objective in his appraisal of the situation in Japan. Nevertheless, his firm was particularly interested in a prewar investment of two million dollars it had made in the Daido Power Company, which later had been absorbed into the government power monopoly. So, in a sense, he was killing two birds with one stone. Oddly enough, lawyer Kauffman, who had written the report that *Newsweek* had used to start the controversy, was the very man who had arranged the Daido Power deal with Dillon, Read in 1924.

Accompanying Draper was an "investigation" committee headed by Percy H. Johnston, chairman of Chemical Bank and Trust in New York City. Like Draper, he knew Japan well. His institution had close ties with Mitsui Bank, and Ikeda Seihin's son had worked under Johnston in New York. At the same time a Chemical Bank man, Seymour Dribben, had been brought to Japan by Ikeda and had worked in Mitsui Bank before taking charge of the Chemical Bank office in Tokyo. Johnston, too, may have been judging the antitrust program on its merits alone. But investments must have been at the back of his mind; for during that visit he set the stage (presumably in league with Ikeda) for a most fortunate connection between his bank and Japan's most promising commercial firm, then known as Daiichi Bussan. Likewise, Draper, in frequent conversations with HCLC chairman Sasayama Tadao, had opportunities to drop hints about a project—the future Alaska Pulp Company—that materialized a few years later under the aegis of Dillon, Read and was headed by Sasayama.[5]

Naturally, the Draper-Johnston mission was received with jubilation by Japanese big business. Especially applauded was Draper's assurance that Japan would soon be reestablished as a self-supporting entity. According to a dispatch from Tokyo in the *New York Times* on April 20, 1948: "Before the visit of the mission, most of the 325 companies designated for reorganization were resigned to cutting their enterprises into a number of companies. Mr. Draper's emphasis on industrial rehabilitation, however, gave them the hope that they would not be obliged to go to extremes."

The Draper-Johnston Committee, reporting to the War Department on April 26, called for sharp cuts in reparations deliveries (eventually they were cut by three-fourths) and for large dollar grants to provide "the initial imported materials required to augment production quickly." By the end of the year the United States had provided some four hundred million dollars in aid. Presumably as a result of the committee's recommendations, the HCLC ordered fifty concerns to be removed from SCAP's deconcentration list and notified 144 that they would not have to make structural changes.

General MacArthur, in an effort to justify his performance in executing the Truman administration's economic policies, asked for an investigation, and in response the so-called Deconcentration Review Board landed in Japan in May 1948. Unlike the previous mission, which had spent only three weeks in Japan, the DRB did its job thoroughly, and during its eight-month stint some spectacular changes were effected. The list of companies designated for "deconcentration" was whittled down further, and in July the HCLC announced that the zaibatsu banks would not be subject to deconcentration at all. In

September the DRB held an informal meeting with the HCLC, after which they announced a new set of principles which, according to the *New York Times,* "make any deconcentration exceedingly difficult."

The role of the five-man DRB, none of whose members was prominent, was obviously to whitewash what was left of the zaibatsu establishment (after the dissolution of twenty-six holding companies) and to sabotage any further action on the deconcentration program. Whose interests those men represented is another question, but it appears that one of them, at least, was a paid agent of the zaibatsu. Edo Hideo, in his book of essays, *Sushiya no Shomon,* wrote: "As for Mitsui, one member of the five-man commission, W. R. Hutchinson, the lawyer [former special assistant to the United States Attorney General] offered his services . . . to change the policy of the U. S. government by negotiations with those concerned, and lobbying among the U. S. government authorities. But the compensation was very large, and would have been a heavy burden on the individual Mitsui companies who had suffered from war damage."

The outcome of all this was that Mitsui, Sumitomo, and Mitsubishi formed a joint committee consisting of Hutchinson and two prominent Japanese legal experts representing Mitsubishi and Sumitomo. (One of the latter was Dr. Hosono Gunji, a close friend of Senator John F. Kennedy.) Whether Hutchinson actually did any lobbying or not, his committee performed to the satisfaction of its private clients. For the zaibatsu dissolution program, which opened with such an alarming bang in 1945, closed with a whimper in August 1949, when MacArthur announced that he had applied all his government's recommendations for the reorganization of Japanese big business, thus marking "the completion of another major phase of the occupation mission." Chairman Sasayama of the HCLC said later: "I have expected all along that experienced, sympathetic consideration would surely get us where we are today." And DRB's chairman, Joseph V. Robinson, in saying *sayonara* to his friends in Japan, asserted that "excessive concentration of economic power" had been completely broken and conditions for free economic competition established.[6]

Forty-two holding companies were dissolved, eventually; of the three hundred and twenty-five operating companies slated for deconcentration, only eleven were actually required to reorganize, while seven had to divest themselves of some plants and securities. The semigovernmental electric-power and steel monopolies were split up, and the components reverted to private control. But only a few of the deconcentrated firms—Mitsui Mining, Oji Paper, and Toshiba—were closely connected with Mitsui. Still intact were the largest ordinary banks: Teikoku (which later dissolved voluntarily into its original components, Mitsui and Dai-Ichi banks), Yasuda (which became Fuji), Mitsubishi, Sumitomo, and Sanwa (a lesser zaibatsu). Despite a certain amount of reorganization and name-changing required by SCAP, Fuji, Mitsubishi, Sumitomo, Sanwa, and Dai-Ichi banks remained as nuclei, in place of the defunct holding companies, for the reconstitution of financial and industrial groupings remarkably similar in scale and membership to those of the prewar zaibatsu. This development was foreseen and deplored by SCAP's economists, who recognized that the control of bank credit, as much as ownership of stocks, had been a key factor in the prewar expansion of the zaibatsu.

Nevertheless, the dissolution of holding companies necessitated a stock-selling operation of unprecedented magnitude. The impounded shares, numbering almost 180 million, had an estimated value of 18.4 billion yen, or forty-two percent of the paid-up value of all the securities in Japan at the end of 1946. These had to be sold even though the stock exchange was closed. Yet the job was accomplished in less than two years, indicating that many Japanese were eager to buy into the economy that had been so largely monopolized by the zaibatsu. For example, about one-fifth of the shares were bought by employees of the respective firms or residents of the areas in which they were located, and other individual purchasers were very numerous. But in spite of a certain dispersion of ownership, shareholdings were not spread as widely as anticipated because the collapse of the deconcentration program gave banks and corporations an overwhelming advantage in buying those tempting shares. It appears that even before the end of the occupation approximately ten percent of the stockholders owned seventy percent of the shares and were thus able to secure a tight grip on the economy, as had the zaibatsu before them.

Niizeki Yasutaro found himself elevated to the presidency of Bussan just in time to supervise its dismemberment. In the summer of 1947 there was a mass exodus of personnel, but Niizeki decided to remain with the sinking ship, mainly because of his *giri*—the peculiar sense of obligation that makes Japanese society so cohesive. "I was determined not to establish a new firm nor even think about my plans for the future until all employees of the firm had secured jobs," Niizeki told the author. This was a tough assignment, since there were still thousands of employees to be placed, most of them specialists. Bussan had had hundreds of branches in the colonies and the Co-Prosperity Sphere—fifty in China alone—and the returnees from those places had to be helped too. On the bright side, however, Niizeki's position entitled him to the daily use of a company automobile for the first time in his life, an amenity that boosted his prestige enormously in those days, when most people felt lucky to own solid shoe leather for trudging the broken pavements in search of employment or black-market food.

His disheartening task was interrupted one day by a visit from a Kobe merchant named Miki Takizo. Niizeki, as chief of Bussan's Rayon Department, had dealt with this textile trader many years ago. He had been in difficulties then, Niizeki recalled, but now he looked prosperous. After an exchange of wartime reminiscences, Miki asked: "What will you be doing now, Niizeki-san?"

Surprised by Miki's concern, the lame-duck president replied hesitantly. "Well, I'm in no hurry to decide what to do with myself."

"I see. But whatever you decide to do, you'll need funds, won't you?" Miki then recalled that in the old days Niizeki had helped him out of a tight spot and proposed to return the favor. "I'll finance you with ten million yen. How about forming about twenty companies capitalized at half a million yen each?"

Niizeki was deeply touched and not unaware of the advantages of such an arrangement. With all of Bussan's business up for grabs, and so many talented men available to take it over, the offer was tempting. But Miki's proposition involved a conflict of interest, so Niizeki replied: "Thank you very much, Miki-san. I may ask your help sometime in the future."

While Niizeki and his dwindling staff were engaged in the depressing details of liquidation, the more opportunistic of Bussan's former employees were setting up new enterprises. Within a few months scores of splinter companies were born from Bussan, and the number eventually increased to nearly two hundred. Many of them were formed by the managers of departments or branches of the dissolved firm, and employed the subordinates for whose welfare they assumed responsibility. For example, the Petroleum Department, using its connection with Esso Standard, became General Bussan. The Machinery Department began a new life as Nippon Kikai; and the Wool and Textile departments of the Osaka and Nagoya branches emerged as Taiyo, or Ocean Trading, headed by Wakasugi Sueyuki. Bussan's warehousing and real estate activities were taken over by a new firm called Nitto Soko Tatemono, which also assumed control of the assets and liabilities of the defunct Bussan and claimed the right to use the Mitsui name and trademark after SCAP's ban was lifted. Another notable segment was Muromachi Bussan, organized by Hirashima Toshiro, former manager of the Metals Department. But none of the new companies showed much promise of developing into *sogo shosha,* or general traders.

Watching the business trend, a group of men in the construction material section of the General Merchandise Department decided that their experience would be in demand and asked Mizukami Tatsuzo, manager of the department, to lead them in the formation of an independent firm.

Their offer was gratifying, but Mizukami was critical of their plan. Construction materials, though important, would not always be in such demand as they were then. Of greater significance for the future was foreign trade, which could not be conducted piecemeal, he told his men. Having studied the permutations of SCAP's dissolution policies, he sensed the early possibility of reconstituting an organization not unlike the old company and proposed making the attempt. Although he was only forty-three years of age and had no experience as a general manager, he inspired such confidence that his visionary scheme was accepted. Joining forces with the assistant manager of the Foodstuffs Department, he established Daiichi Bussan, or First Products, capitalized at 195,000 yen. This was just short of the 200,000 yen maximum imposed by SCAP for splinter companies formed by personnel of the Mitsui and Mitsubishi trading firms.

But even such a modest sum (equivalent to less than two thousand dollars at that stage of the inflation) was hard to raise. Teikoku Bank was still intact, but the would-be traders, who had been overseas for many years, had no personal contacts with the bank—which in any case was so heavily committed to surviving companies that it had nothing left over for financing new ones.

All the help they could expect from the government was a "rehabilitation loan" of one thousand yen, so the founding members contributed their own meager savings. To make up the remainder Mizukami had to borrow from his wife's parents. This was the hardest part for him: at the office he was authoritative but, as a poor boy who had married into a wealthy family, at home he was a henpecked husband, intimidated by his in-laws as well as his wife. He got the money from them, however, and this loan enabled the intrepid entrepreneurs to rent a small office—for seven thousand yen a month—at Odenmacho, not far from Mitsui Honsha's former headquarters. With borrowed furniture, a small warehouse, and some handcarts, Daiichi Bussan went into business within weeks after the dissolution order had been issued.

The effrontery of the twenty-two members in trying to rebuild a sogo shosha with only a few hundred dollars in the bank seemed to border on insanity. Yet those who knew Mizukami's flair for business gave him an even chance to succeed. A clear, independent thinker, he was able to absorb information and make sound decisions with extraordinary speed. Because of his sharp perception and swift action he was called *Hayabusa Tatsu*, or Tatsu the Falcon, a nickname that was not always applied affectionately. Like many men of his stamp, he tended to be impatient with people whose minds worked less quickly. And since he had never mastered the art of flattery, his bluntness often antagonized his seniors as well as his peers. This was perhaps one reason why he took the position of vice-president and left the top slot open for an older man able to operate more adroitly in Japan's protocol-conscious business world.

To meet Mizukami's standards the president had to be a Mitsui man, a skilled trader, and completely trustworthy. The prime candidate was Niizeki, whose experience in dismantling Bussan had acquainted him with the inner structure of the company. A genial man, Niizeki enjoyed drinking with his younger colleagues and talked to them as equals. He was also a friend and distant relative of Mizukami, and thus there was a special bond of giri between them that would help to smooth things over when differences of opinion arose.

Niizeki welcomed the offer, but unfortunately he had already accepted a position as president of another trading company run by his landlord and next-door neighbor, to whom he also owed giri. To straighten the matter out Mizukami visited the other employer, who proved to be accommodating. "Let's have him work for both of us and split his salary fifty-fifty," he proposed. Niizeki was earning five thousand yen a month, so each of the two men agreed to pay him half the sum, thereby economizing on overhead. Despite inflation, one could survive on such a salary because price controls were still being enforced. Other members worked for much less, and Mizukami himself drew no pay at all until the books showed a profit.

Employed with Niizeki at the other company was Tanabe Shunsuke, his college classmate and Mitsui colleague, who was fluent in English and handled liaison with SCAP and the army post-exchange system. He was also a part-timer at Daiichi. Before long, business became so brisk that the firm was able to pay the full salaries of Niizeki and his assistant.

When asked recently what his most critical problems were in those early years, Niizeki replied instantly: "Money, money, money!" And getting it was his first assignment, but he soon found that there was none to be had in Tokyo. It was then that he remembered the friendly textile merchant. On the chance that Miki was serious about lending him ten million yen, he took a train to Kobe. To his delight, Miki's giri held good and he gave Niizeki a promissory note for the full amount. Naturally, there was a celebration, and although Niizeki was noted as a "strong drinker," his libations aggravated the ulcer he had acquired from business worries. After his return to Tokyo, he was laid up in bed for several days. But Mizukami couldn't wait and sent an accountant to help the president get the cash. With money so tight such a large note was difficult to negotiate, and Niizeki was in no condition to make the rounds of the banks, so he begged off.

"Haven't you any friends who are bank executives?" the accountant persisted. One would have expected Niizeki to mention Sato Kiichiro, who had succeeded the purged Bandai Junshiro as president of Teikoku Bank. But apparently Niizeki felt that Sato couldn't accommodate him. Instead, he thought of a managing director of Mitsubishi Bank who was under personal obligation to him. The ailing Niizeki drafted a letter, apologizing for not appearing at the bank in person, and dispatched it with the accountant. As expected, the director gave his approval, and the note was discounted without delay at Mitsubishi's Odenmacho branch in the Nihombashi district, near Niizeki's office.

More than twenty years have passed since then, but Daiichi Bussan's successor company, known once again as Mitsui Bussan, still deals with that branch of Mitsubishi Bank, despite the inconvenience of its location and the rivalry between the Mitsui and Mitsubishi groups. Of course the investment of Miki, the Kobe textile dealer, paid off handsomely, and in addition his own business prospered greatly from the friendship of his grateful competitors. Today Miki's company, Sankyo Seiko, is capitalized at 1.6 billion yen, up one-hundredfold from the time when he made his offer to Niizeki. He seems to have borrowed a bit of his benefactors' prestige by adopting a trademark that can easily be misread as "Mitsui," but no one makes an issue of it. These incidents exemplify the power of giri, the rigid and perpetual observance of mutual obligations, that gives Japanese society its stability and that enabled the shattered Japanese economy to recover so rapidly after the war.

In its early days business conditions were discouraging for Daiichi Bussan. Two of the most promising lines, fuels and fertilizers, were government controlled and could not be handled profitably. Sister companies had taken up lumber, chemicals, iron, steel, machinery, foodstuffs, and other basics, and although there was some rivalry, a tacit code forbade encroachment upon the business lines of another "family" member. Many of the companies drifted into black-marketing, which was almost universal, and into speculation in scarce commodities; but Daiichi's policy was to steer clear of such snares, regardless of immediate profits. At first the company transported goods for the occupation forces, operated small coal mines, and supplied lumber and straw mats for building miners' houses. Gradually the firm got back into fertilizers, sugar, nonferrous metals, and raw cotton, and a trickle of export trade developed. During this incubation period the firm was occupying office space owned by a black-market dealer who made the rent reasonable because he had hopes of joining with a Mitsui-line enterprise. He could see that business was brisk and growing fast. But when he learned that the firm, like the old Bussan, was operating on commissions of two percent or less he was shocked. Accustomed to black-market profits ten or twenty times higher, he concluded that such penny-wise businessmen could never succeed, and abruptly ordered them to vacate the office.

It was time to move, anyway. With the money from Miki (which amounted to some thirty thousand dollars) the firm increased its staff from forty members to nearly one hundred by employing more Bussan men idled by the liquidation. Larger quarters were needed, and because no proper office could be found in the slowly recovering city, Niizeki bought an old frame dining hall and had it moved to a vacant lot in central Tokyo. This provided plenty of space, but under SCAP regulations the firm could not have more than one hundred employees and no more than two who had held positions as high as manager or section chief in Bussan. So Niizeki and Mizukami set up several new "companies" (actually departments) to accommodate the growing staff—despite warnings that they would be shipped out to Okinawa as laborers if they were caught violating SCAP regulations.

Daiichi was fortunate in having the informal counsel of Bussan's former chief, Miyazaki Kiyoshi, who despite his purged status was crackling with ambitious schemes for reconstructing Mitsui. It was also fortunate that Daiichi had formed useful contacts with the occupation authorities in charge of economic matters and was thus in a position to know where trading opportunities lay and how projects could be carried out. But Miyazaki's schemes—one of which was a huge wheat-import deal with the Bunge international cartel—were too big for the capital-starved Daiichi Bussan to handle. According to one ruling, the firm had to get special permission from SCAP for every transaction involving more than fifty thousand yen (or about one hundred and fifty dollars). The wily traders managed to get around that somehow, but it was clear to them that such a hand-to-mouth existence was stunting their growth, and that Daiichi would have to find new sources of capital.

Niizeki had been getting advice from four of Mitsui's retired banto, Ikeda, Fujihara, Mukai, and Ishida, none of whom was optimistic about the prospect of reviving Bussan. However, Ikeda was sympathetic to Niizeki's ideas and discussed with him a number of schemes, one of which was a development company specializing in public works construction, flood control, and forestry conservation. Ikeda said that GHQ had agreed with this idea and had promised to order the government to lend at least one billion yen for the purpose. The company was formed, with Niizeki as a director, but the loan was not forth-coming, and the project languished.

Ikeda Seihin, even in his eighties, was an active and resourceful promoter, not easily discouraged. Although purged and threatened with a war-crimes indictment, he managed to keep in touch with business and political leaders, who consulted him on the sly. Ikeda's most valuable contact was Prime Minister Yoshida, his neighbor at Oiso, whom he served as informal adviser on economic and political matters, even on cabinet and staff appointments. Through Ikeda, Niizeki established a friendly relationship with Yoshida, who knew more about SCAP's policies and plans than any other Japanese. "Mr. Yoshida took very good care of me," Niizeki says cryptically.

One day, during a discussion of Daiichi's financial problems, Ikeda said frankly: "Mr. Niizeki, I will ask Mitsui Bank to help your company. But it will not be possible to obtain funds in Japan today." As an alternative, he proposed trying to obtain foreign capital and said he would send a telegram to his friend Percy Johnston, board chairman of Chemical Bank. This was done, and Johnston dispatched a research-staff member of Bache & Company, one of Wall Street's biggest broker-age houses, to investigate. The researcher's findings were favorable, and as a result Bache agreed tentatively to help the trading company. When he received the good news, Niizeki went immediately to Oiso and informed Ikeda.

"I will go to the United States to negotiate with Bache," Niizeki said. "But it would be embarrassing if I returned empty-handed. Could you arrange it so that they will invest without fail?"

Ikeda, who had already discussed financing with Johnston during the latter's official visit to Japan, knew that the outlook was favorable. "Yes, I will," he said, and apparently did so. This assistance to Daiichi Bussan was his last service to the concern to which he had devoted his life. Niizeki left for New York in July 1950, and Ikeda died a short time afterward.

One can only imagine what went on in the mind of Harold Bache when the undersized Japanese (Niizeki is only about five feet tall) from a miniature company in a shrunken, shattered nation stepped brashly into his office. It must have taken great perceptiveness for the multi-millionaire to see in his unassuming petitioner the future chieftain of the world's largest trading firm. But whatever his mental processes may have been, he listened carefully as Niizeki, in his tortured English, marshaled the facts and figures to prove that Daiichi Bussan not only was a good investment but was the logical heir apparent to the once mighty Mitsui Bussan.

He made an equally favorable impression at Chemical Bank, and it was agreed that Daiichi Bussan should receive $140,000—an amount 250 times larger than the firm's original capital. To spread the risk, a new company called C. A. England (a fictitious name) was formed with investments from Bache, Chemical Bank, and Lehman Brothers. In lieu of collateral, C. A. England took over twenty-five percent of Daiichi Bussan's stock. This was not the first postwar instance of foreign investment in Japanese business: General Bussan, for example, had formed a joint refining company with Esso Standard, and American and British interests had acquired up to fifty percent of the shares in Japan's major oil companies. But it set a precedent in the commercial field and accelerated Japan's reemergence as a trading nation.

In the interim, Sato Kiichiro decided that the only way for his bank to give proper support to Mitsui-line companies was to split Teikoku Bank into its original components, Dai-Ichi and Mitsui. This was done in 1948, with the Mitsui element retaining the name Teikoku until 1954, when it reverted to its former name. As the financial situation eased, the reorganized Teikoku extended considerable credit to the companies of the group; and with additional help from Fuji Bank, Daiichi Bussan was able, within four years of its founding, to increase its capital from the original 195,000 yen to two hundred million.

During the first three years of the occupation, Japan had been going through an extreme inflation aggravated by the government's policy of deficit financing to revive industry. Early in 1949 Detroit banker Joseph M. Dodge was sent to Japan to end the inflation: he imposed a stern policy of stabilizing the currency, balancing the budget, and concentrating on exports at the expense of domestic consumption. This brought on severe austerity, drastic constriction of credit, and a rash of bankruptcies. The "Dodge Plan," though resisted strenuously by financial and business leaders, enabled the Japanese economy, floundering in the quicksands of mismanagement, to touch solid ground and begin the steep climb toward recovery. That climb was greatly accelerated by an event that startled the world—the outbreak of war in Korea, which, like Germany, had been divided into two parts pending an agreement between the Russians and their erstwhile allies.

It is difficult to imagine an event better calculated to stimulate Japan's recovery, strengthen the right-of-center political coalition then under severe attack from the left, and to establish Japan as the "Arsenal of the Free World" and the northeastern bastion of a military and naval chain of bases for the containment of China.

The immediate effect of the war was to revive Japanese industry and to establish a cooperative relationship between Japan and the United States, thus enlisting Japan's active support in the global anticommunist campaign. The United States market was reopened to Japanese exports, and American foods, raw materials, and fuel were supplied under generous loans and grants. With American financing the Japan Development Bank and the Japan Export-Import Bank were established. Using "counterpart funds" from the sale of American aid commodities, these banks supplied the bulk of the capital needed for industrial reconstruction and the expansion of trade without creating inflationary pressure. Needless to say, the disbursement of such funds —by businessmen and bureaucrats selected for their conservatism and support of Washington's new policy—conferred enormous power upon those in charge and worked to the advantage of their political allies in the Liberal and Democratic parties.

As the war raged down the Korean Peninsula and up again to the Yalu, bringing China into the conflict, a wave of reaction, propelled by the most rabid anticommunists and "China Lobby" spokesmen, swept over the United States. With the FBI and congressional committees aping the defunct Kempeitai and thought-control police of Japan, and the CIA taking its cue from the Black Dragon Society, liberals and moderates were hounded out of the American government, beginning with some of the most able East Asian experts in the State Department. People from many occupations, especially government service, the mass media, and education, were subjected to "loyalty oaths," the purpose of which was to purge not only communists but "fellow travelers," liberals, and pacifists. Those who refused to sign, claiming their constitutional guarantees as specified in the Bill of Rights, were removed from positions in which they might influence public opinion against America's version of Japan's "holy war."

Japanese leaders, discovering that the vaunted "democracy" the occupation had been trying to impose on them was only skin deep, reverted to type and, with SCAP's blessing, started a massive rollback of Japan's leftist opposition. As wartime bigwigs, including many war-crimes suspects, were being depurged or released from prison, it was the turn of the progressives to feel the lash. The "red purge" began with journalism and extended to government agencies and the labor organizations of major enterprises. To assure the fulfillment of munitions orders, the electrical, mining, and steel industries ousted militants of left-led unions en masse, and some five thousand suspected reds were fired by the end of 1950. Despite constitutional guarantees the Communist Party and its publications were suppressed. MacArthur, who had written the no-war, no-armaments clause in Japan's new constitution so unequivocally, now backtracked, speaking of Japan's "inherent right of self-defense" as a justification for rearmament.* The national police system, abolished as an instrument of oppression, was revived, and a 75,000-man "Police Reserve" (actually the nucleus of a new army) was formed at SCAP's request "to cope with domestic disorders."

Soon after the Korean War began President Truman sent W. Averell Harriman (a partner in Brown Brothers, Harriman, a leading investment banking house and reservoir of presidential advisers) to Tokyo to negotiate a peace treaty with Japan. The first draft, completed in 1947 before the purge of liberals in the State Department, had been based upon on the belief that Japanese militarism was the major menace in Asia, but by 1950 the hobgoblin of a Moscow-Peking alliance and a red-dominated Japan had taken its place.

In preparation for this turnabout SCAP was instructed to reorganize Japan for strength rather than for peace and democracy. Already rightist organizations under younger, less notorious leaders than those surviving from before the war had been fostered; in 1951 some 2,500 former imperial army and navy officers and ultranationalist bosses were abruptly depurged and many of them moved into positions of leadership in the rightist groups, about 270 of which were already registered with the government. Quite a few of them were prewar terrorist societies in disguise, and all were strenuously opposed to communism, socialism, and organized labor. Typically, they advocated rearmament and strong police powers, but despite their general xenophobia they pledged full cooperation with the United States in the "holy war." Some of the postwar rightist leaders went so far as to try to organize a private navy of Japanese volunteers to help Chiang Kai-shek reconquer the Chinese mainland.

Concurrently, former high-echelon zaibatsu managers were depurged because they knew best how to run a war economy. Laws and regulations for curbing monopolies were softened or rescinded, and the concerns that had formerly dominated Japan's military economy began immediately to regroup their scattered forces. The Mitsubishi combine, Japan's biggest munitions maker during the Second World War (as it is today), reemerged almost intact at that time.

* General MacArthur had phrased Article 9 in such a way that there could not be the slightest doubt of its meaning: the renunciation of war as a sovereign right and of possessing the means of waging it, forever. His effort to open a loophole is equally ingenious but much less forthright: "While by no sophistry of reasoning can it be interpreted as a complete negation of the inalienable right of self-defense against unprovoked attack, it is a ringing affirmation by a people laid prostrate by the sword, of faith in the ultimate triumph of international morality and justice without resort to the sword." (New Year's address, January 1, 1950.)

Early in 1951 John Foster Dulles was appointed by Truman to visit Tokyo and sound out Japanese business leaders concerning the terms for the peace treaty. Before leaving Washington he conferred at length with Senator John B. Connally, chairman of the Senate Foreign Relations Committee. They had a lot in common, for Dulles's law firm, Sullivan & Cromwell, represented Standard Oil of New Jersey and other Rockefeller-affiliated firms, while Connally was associated with big Texas oil interests under Standard Oil and Dillon, Read influence. The Dulles mission to Tokyo comprised several State Department and Pentagon officials, brass hats, and just one businessman—John D. Rockefeller III, one of five brothers indirectly controlling the mammoth Chase Manhattan Bank and Standard Oil empire that was emerging as the largest foreign investor in Japan. Rockefeller stated in Tokyo that his purpose was to develop "long-range cultural relations" between Japan and the United States, but his Japanese hosts may well have construed his presence as foreshadowing the American-Japanese zaibatsu partnership that actually materialized.

On the day of the Dulles mission's arrival, Japan's main economic and business organizations adopted a joint resolution expressing their views, which was duly presented to Dulles. The latter, meanwhile, had conferred privately with Prime Minister Yoshida in Mitsui Hachiro-emon's former office at the Mitsui Honsha building and at MacArthur's headquarters in the Dai-ichi Life Insurance Building. He also met and exchanged views with political, economic, and labor leaders of various ideologies, but those whose opinions carried the most weight were mainly the rehabilitated bosses of the prewar and wartime empire. Among them were Hatoyama Ichiro, a reactionary politician who as education minister in the early 1930s had savagely repressed student movements and imprisoned nonconformist professors; the equally reactionary Ishii Mitsujiro, leader of the pro–Chiang Kai-shek lobby in the Diet; Nomura Kichisaburo, ambassador to the United States at the time of Pearl Harbor; Takasaki Tatsunosuke, president of the defunct Manchurian Heavy Industries; Ishikawa Ichiro, former head of the Nissan chemical complex in Manchuria; industrialist Kobayashi Ichizo, commerce and industry minister in the Konoe Cabinet in 1941; Ishizaka Taizo of Toshiba; Adachi Tadashi, former president of the Oji Paper empire; Sato Kiichiro of Mitsui Bank; and a strange exception, the relatively liberal Ishibashi Tanzan, publisher of the *Oriental Economist*.

To establish a bargaining position, the Japanese economic leaders asked for the moon—or, more specifically, for ample supplies of foodstuffs, raw materials, fuel, and technology for catching up with the West. They requested the restoration of economic and political independence, membership in world organizations, and military protection at the expense of the United States. They would have been delighted to get half of what they asked for. To their amazement they got it all, and much more besides.

Within two months a draft treaty incorporating the wishes of both sides was prepared, and by autumn—after lengthy arguments and the conclusion of ancillary agreements with Great Britain, Australia, New Zealand, and the Republic of the Philippines, who feared a resurgence of Japanese militarism—the historic document was ready. The so-called peace conference (actually the ceremonial endorsement of a *Pax Americana,* as the *Economist* of London called it) was convened on September 4, 1951, at the San Francisco Opera House (where the UN was born); the treaty was signed four days later by forty-eight of the nations that had been at war with Japan. Russia's deputy foreign minister Andrei Gromyko refused to sign, accusing the United States of reviving Japanese militarism, and Poland and Czechoslovakia also abstained. India, Burma, and Yugoslavia refused to attend; and China (which had suffered more losses of life than all the signatory powers combined in the war against Japan) was not even invited. Thus, although coerced by Dulles into signing a treaty with the government on Taiwan in 1952, Japan remained in a technical state of war with China until twenty years later. As a consequence of this rift United States interests promptly took over China's very substantial share of the Japan market for iron ore, coking coal, fibers, hides, tallow, grain, soybeans, and other commodities that, in addition to petroleum, made Japan America's largest overseas market in the subsequent decades.

Prime Minister Yoshida graciously hailed the treaty as one of reconciliation, magnanimity, and trust—as it surely was, from the viewpoint of the Japanese establishment. Dulles, in an unusual burst of frankness, called it an act of "enlightened self-interest" rather than of mere generosity. What he wanted more than peace or the well-being of the Japanese was the continued American military presence in Japan and its early rearmament as an ally in the cold war—which was already getting uncomfortably hot, especially since the Russians had discovered the "secret" of the A-bomb. As partial repayment for the generous peace treaty he had already extracted, Yoshida assented to a military alliance that also was signed at the San Francisco conference. This so-called Security Treaty has created more strife in Japan, and between Japan and its neighbors, than any other postwar issue. Obviously aimed at the containment or destruction of China and the Soviet Union, it permitted the United States to maintain military forces and bases in Japan while denying the same privilege to other nations. And despite the no-war article in Japan's new constitution, the treaty required Japan to assist the United States in military actions in the Far East and to "increasingly assume responsibility for its own defense."

It was bewildering. In 1902 Japan was able to conclude the momentous Anglo-Japanese Alliance by virtue of having won a minor war; and now, just fifty years later, the nation had become an ally of the world's greatest economic and military power by virtue of having lost a major war. Never in the annals of warfare have the victors shown such tender concern for vanquished foes, nor has a loser ever enjoyed such immediate and phenomenal blessings.

By the time the treaties took effect in 1952 nearly all sectors of Japanese industry were engaged in military-related production. Plants once designated for reparations had been restored to their owners, and heavy industries, retooled for producing munitions, or for servicing American ordnance and other military equipment, were back in full swing. Most of these belonged to former Mitsubishi, Mitsui, Sumitomo, or other zaibatsu affiliates.

MacArthur had once accused the prewar and wartime leaders of these enterprises (many of whom were back on the job again) of having "geared the country with both the tools and the will to wage aggressive war." But when the Americans believed themselves destined to grapple with imperial Japan's former archenemies, the Russian and Chinese communists, the zaibatsu overlords were embraced gratefully. Having snatched away Japan's spoils (in alliance with other anti-Axis forces), the United States now undertook unilaterally to give the still unreformed nation a favored position in what was left of the old Co-Prosperity Sphere—and the resources to develop and defend it.

27 · New Wine in Old Bottles

By the time the Allied occupation ended in 1952, opportunity was knocking at the door of every Japanese entrepreneur, large or small, who had productive capacity and the will to put it to work. Companies that had been strong before 1945 were coming back into bloom like hardy perennials, and ambitious men were encouraged to assert their abilities. It was not unreasonable, therefore, to expect that the inner circle of the zaibatsu, who had reigned supreme over the economy for decades, would find some way of regaining a measure of control over their former empires.

But the men in charge of winding up the affairs of the zaibatsu holding companies, like the vanquished barons themselves, seem to have despaired; and the spirit of enterprise that had made the name Mitsui a legend was thoroughly quenched. In the early 1950s caretakers of the defunct concern reported gloomily: "With the ruinous diminution of the Mitsui families' wealth, the dissolution of Mitsui Honsha, Ltd., the complete democratization of the shareholding system of Mitsui companies and the retirement of Mitsui family members and former executives, the powerful organization of the Mitsui enterprises has been thoroughly dissolved as a business concern. . . . Spilt water cannot be returned to its original vessel. . . . The restoration of a zaibatsu concern of old days in its dimension and substance is out of the question."[1]

In retrospect, such pessimism is hard to understand. Like other zaibatsu families, the Mitsuis, though short on liquid assets, still held tidy fortunes that had survived the inflation. They were related by marriage or blood to a number of the leading financiers and businessmen who, although inconvenienced by the war, had escaped ruin. With an illustrious name and unblemished credit the Mitsuis should have been able to get backing for any reasonably sound project. But having become dependent upon managerial talent other than that produced within the clan, they were unable to find a place in the changed economic order and watched in bewilderment as their former underlings and associates hewed out new and larger niches for themselves.

The aged generalissimo Ikeda Seihin died in 1950, but he had lived long enough to help the future Mitsui Bussan get started. Fujihara Ginjiro was not too old to serve as a valued adviser to prime ministers before his death in 1960 at the age of ninety-one. His main achievement, Oji Paper, was broken up, it is true, but his disciples played leading roles in reorganizing the pulp and paper business and became presidents of the four largest paper companies to emerge after the war. His last contribution to Japanese business was a bequest to his alma mater, Keio University, which was used to establish an engineering department. Mukai Tadaharu, former obanto of Bussan, after serving as finance minister under Yoshida, was an active member of the three-man Supreme Economic Council advising the government on vital matters and helped to make General Bussan a major oil company (of which he is still an adviser). Another Bussan alumnus to attain cabinet rank under Yoshida was Uchida Shin'ya, who served as chairman of the Mitsui-affiliated Meiji Shipping Company until his death in 1971.

Ishida Reisuke, retired obanto of the old Bussan, rusticated for ten years after being purged; then, at the age of seventy-eight, he was appointed president of the Japan National Railways, Japan's largest enterprise, and served for several years. While he was resting up for this exhausting assignment, Ishida Taizo (no kin) became president of Toyoda Automatic Weaving Machine Company and then of Toyota Motor Company—in time to get in at the beginning of Japan's automobile boom. Miyazaki Kiyoshi, the ebullient president of Bussan at the time of its dissolution, took the purge in stride and became chairman of the Riccar Sewing Machine Company. Then, despite his advanced age, he took the same position with Nippon Univac, which he built into Japan's most successful joint venture in the manufacturing of computers before his death in 1970.

Bandai Junshiro, purged from the presidency of Teikoku Bank, cast his shrewd eye on a fledgling electronics company—capitalized at five hundred dollars—and helped its talented founders get some money from Mitsui. Under his chairmanship the unknown firm—which adopted the improbable name "Sony"—made the transistor radio famous as a symbol of Japanese ingenuity. Since then the firm has grown so prosperous that it has become a major shareholder in Mitsui Bank—which in turn owns a huge block of Sony's stock.

Adachi Tadashi, who had been president of the mammoth Oji Paper combine since 1942, resigned after the war and founded Radio Tokyo, Japan's first private broadcasting company, in 1951. He organized the company that built Tokyo Tower, pioneered in television broadcasting, and became an outstanding economic leader as president of the Tokyo Chamber of Commerce and Industry and of the Japan Chamber of Commerce, as well.

Serving before Adachi as president of the two chambers was Fujiyama Aiichiro, an old friend of the Mitsuis and a confidant of Ikeda.
Fujiyama, a wealthy industrialist who made his fortune from the Dai-
Nippon Sugar Company, befriended Kishi Nobusuke after his release
from prison, helped to make him prime minister, and served meri-
toriously as his foreign minister before embarking on his own course
as a liberal politician and gadfly of his party's rightist factions. Fujiyama deserves much of the credit for Japan's recent, spectacular rapprochement with China.

As befits a baronial house, the Mitsuis had maintained a large staff
of loyal retainers who prospered while in the concern's employ. A
notable example was Naruse Ryuzo, a schoolteacher who had long
supervised the education of the Mitsui children and became secretary
of Mitsui Dozokukai, the clan council. His third son, Yugo, entered
Mitsui Bank and eventually became a director of Dozokukai, as well as
of Honsha and several subordinate Mitsui companies. His elder brother
served as secretary of the House of Peers and became president of
Nippon Life Insurance, organized with the backing of Mitsui. After
the war and the plummeting of the Mitsui fortunes, Naruse Yugo
helped to liquidate Honsha and soon stepped into the presidency of
the new Daiichi Fire & Marine Insurance Company. His younger
brother, Hirose Gen, after long service with Bussan succeeded to the
presidency of Nippon Life in 1953 and still holds that position. These
insurance companies, in the hands of friends, did much to strengthen
enterprises of Mitsui affiliation and to stabilize their stockholdings in
the period of turmoil.

If it was possible for the Mitsui obanto and retainers to make fresh
starts and rise to top positions after the war, why did the Mitsuis, with
their eminent family, business, and social connections, remain in obscurity? Although former baron Hachiroemon Takakimi was appointed
adviser to Mitsui Real Estate in the 1950s, and other family heads have
held honorary posts in companies they used to own, none of them has
resumed any important position. Younger members of the family have
taken ordinary white-collar jobs (a few with Mitsui companies), apparently without receiving any special consideration or showing any
special abilities. One occasionally meets a Mitsui in other Japanese
business offices, but if they have any distinction it is as minor curiosities
of yesteryear rather than as men of tomorrow.

One might suppose that Japanese giri, or obligation to benefactors,
would have elicited more help for the fallen Caesars of commerce. But
there were several obstacles to the natural operation of this social force.
First, the favors that lay within the power of those under obligation to
the Mitsuis were too trifling in comparison with the losses that the

House had suffered. Among the Mitsui's managers there were many who, by ordinary standards, were wealthy; but in terms of the zaibatsu family's holdings they were distinctly third-rate. And although Mitsui Hachiroemon had lost most of his assets, he still owned personal property nominally assessed at $330,000 in 1952, and its value was to rise steeply as the long business boom got underway. There isn't much one can offer a rich man except sympathy, which the proud Mitsuis never solicited. Among the family heads there were men of some ability, but none was experienced in everyday management problems. As overlords they had acquired neither the qualifications nor the humility to accept positions under former subordinates.

Having the means to do as they pleased, the family heads lived much as they had done before, pursuing their avocations. Hachiroemon, now in his seventies but robust, personally operates the former family school, Wakaba-kai, as a kindergarten. He participates in charitable work, such as the Mitsui Memorial Hospital, plays golf, and takes pleasure in driving his own cars—including his 1937 Bentley. Today he plays less golf because, having been accustomed to owning his own private golf course, he finds even the more exclusive clubs "as overcrowded as public baths."

He can afford such luxuries without strain, since in 1970 he cropped up as thirteenth on the list of Japan's highest taxpayers. This fact had nothing to do with a "zaibatsu revival," but was the result of a real estate deal. The property involved was his villa at Oiso, with two hundred acres of land and the seventeenth-century Jo-an teahouse on the premises. By taking advantage of a revised taxation law, he sold the estate and teahouse (designated as "an important cultural property") for 820 million yen, upon which he cleared 786 million. At that time the custodian of the Mitsui family assets explained that Hachiroemon's usual income was around ten million yen ($28,000) a year. "Itemized, it consists of monthly payments as a consultant of Mitsui Real Estate, allowances from Mitsui affiliate companies shared with the other ten Mitsui families, and income from selling art objects." Although he has lost some fine old pieces, by fire during the war and by theft afterward, the national treasures still in his possession are estimated (by the Cultural Agency) to be worth no less than one billion yen, or approximately $2.7 million.

Hachiroemon's younger brother Takasumi still heads the Mitsui Ho-on Kai and also directs a private school, the Keimei Christian Academy, near Tokyo. Until recently he was active in Moral Rearmament, which has built an international conference center adjacent to his comfortable but less-than-palatial home, formerly the villa of Prince Kan'in, at Odawara. An abstemious but genial man, his main luxury is travel. He spends much of his time maintaining the family's relations with friends abroad, as proxy for the less sociable Hachiroemon, promoting civic projects and burnishing the family's image in an unassuming way.

Others among the older generation of the eleven families include the president of the Japan-Germany Society, a director of a woman's college, a professor of botany, a bureau chief in the Imperial Household Agency, an independent documentary film producer, a well-known sculptor, and among the women, a historian, a former golf champion, and a talented creator of silk collages. But insofar as business leadership is concerned, the last spark seems to have guttered out with the retirement of Baron Hachiroemon Takamine in the early 1930s, never to be rekindled.

Other zaibatsu families were not so completely eclipsed as the Mitsuis. Members of the Iwasaki clan held high positions in a few Mitsubishi companies (such as Mitsubishi Real Estate, Paper, Asahi Glass, and Tokio Marine & Fire Insurance). Sumitomo Kichizaemon, because of the nature of his assets, remained one of the richest men in Japan and chairman of Sumitomo Real Estate. Yasuda's heir, Hajime, became chairman of Yasuda Mutual Life Insurance after the purge was over and actively promoted other businesses. Members of the Asano, Shibusawa, and Okura families—some of the lesser zaibatsu—also made impressive comebacks. But their connections with the main enterprises of their respective concerns are tenuous, and it is generally assumed that the families will never again exert any significant influence over their former empires.

Spilt water can never be returned to its original vessel, the zaibatsu elders had solemnly declared after the trustbusters finished their work. But this was true only in the narrow sense of ownership. For, incredibly, the new wine of postwar economic liberation found its way into the same old bottles, filling them almost precisely to the brim. Despite the breakup of the zaibatsu holding companies, the corporate pattern of Japan remained very much as it had been in the past. Centered around the major city banks, which in most cases held the same relative positions as formerly, the big industrial enterprises preserved their hierarchy in terms of capital, income, and market shares. Of fifty-three important Mitsui-dominated companies in existence in 1945, more than a dozen (mostly those based overseas) became defunct; and of the remainder, a few of the major organizations (Mining, Oji Paper, and Toshiba) were split into smaller units. But the rest, almost without exception, held their former status in the economy or improved it. Most of the companies in the Mitsui fold continued their primary dependence upon

Mitsui Bank, but that is not to say that Bank supplanted the defunct Honsha. Instead, Mitsui-line companies and financial institutions consolidated their stockholdings in enterprises of the group to such an extent that by the mid-1950s they owned enough of each other's stock to exert mutual control in almost every case.

Despite the antimonopoly law, the concentration of industrial production was also pronounced. Even before the Korean War the five largest firms in their respective fields accounted for all of Japan's plate glass, photographic film, aluminum, beer, automobiles, and tires. Their share was ninety to ninety-nine percent in crude oil, galvanized iron pipe, electrolytic copper, and iron; eighty-two to eighty-nine percent in electric power, dairy products, synthetic dyestuffs, and sulfur; and from sixty-eight to seventy-four percent in wool spinning, paper, cement, and steel. At that time Mitsui Mining and Hokkaido Colliery together mined one-fourth of the coal and supplied nearly all the domestic coking coal. Mitsui Mining & Smelting accounted for half of Japan's zinc and a third of its lead, while Mitsui Chemical produced more than one-third of its dyestuffs. Mitsui's Toyo Koatsu produced more than four-fifths of the urea fertilizer and forty percent of other basic chemical products, while its Toyo Rayon made twenty percent of the rayon filament yarn and all of the nylon.

Since this striking restoration of the prewar order was clearly no accident, the most obvious explanation is that it was the result of plans laid in some unknown sanctum of Japan's power elite. A less dramatic hypothesis, supported by fact, is that the zaibatsu combines were never really broken up, and that after the American antitrust zealots departed all the social and economic forces at work in Japan favored a revival of the system that had proved so successful in the past.

In that system, the complexities of which have been suggested by incidents described in this book, unseen forces are usually more decisive than those open to observation. Among such forces are relationships by blood and marriage; former rank and status in the imperial court; social caste; membership in school and university cliques; *oyabun-kobun* (boss and follower) relationships; informal associations of men with common backgrounds, regional provenance, years of birth, interests, ideology, or places of employment; political factions, including their financial backers (and therefore string-pullers); the entrenched, quasi-hereditary bureaucracy with its sub-bureaucracies; politically influential underworld, ex-military, or ultranationalist groups; and affinities based upon the possession or management of wealth. These various forces are competitive and often mutually hostile. Yet somehow (perhaps united by the power of "Japanism" or by the singular cohesion of the Japanese people) their differences are always resolved into a consensus, which emerges as a common program, is further refined into plans, and usually produces results anticipated long in advance by the stronger individuals among the planners.

During the Allied occupation and long afterward the influence of the United States government was a decisive one. But fortunately for Japan's conservative leaders—even those who had been imprisoned or purged—the interests of the American government coincided with their own in most important respects. As has been mentioned, with the advent of the cold war, Washington wanted Japan to recover as swiftly as possible and that meant full utilization of the most viable economic elements, namely the surviving fragments of the monopolistic combines that once had been denounced as having fostered militarism. This reversal of emphasis was of course welcomed as providential by Japanese economic leaders, conservative politicians, and the bureaucracy. Despite vociferous opposition from the liberals, labor, and the left, the government was able to impose its basically reactionary policy upon the country because its supporters had not only the political expertise gained through prewar leadership but also ample funds with which to maintain control over the legislative process. For in spite of nominal democratization, a secure majority in the National Diet enabled predominantly right-wing governments to ride roughshod over their Socialist and Communist opponents.

The rebirth of oligopoly may be explained by the fact that under successive military regimes the zaibatsu and the bureaucracy of Japan had jointly perfected a true corporate state in which every aspect of economic life was regimented. Although after the war the military was suppressed and the zaibatsu leadership was dispersed, the bureaucracy was preserved to keep the society in operation, and the most influential politicians were former bureaucrats and businessmen accustomed to centralized controls. With the postwar breakdown of the financial system, the main sources of substantial investment capital were quasi-governmental banks, with the former zaibatsu banks in a supporting role. Such a concentration of funds in the hands of bureaucrats and monopoly-minded businessmen naturally favored the reconstruction of major companies and groups. The laws imposed by SCAP to prevent the rebirth of monopolies, being diametrically opposed to Japanese business tradition, never won much support and crumbled steadily under united pressure of the ministries, economic organizations, conservative governments, and American financiers.

In such an environment other internal factors conducive to business concentration on prewar patterns were given full play. One was the traditional willingness, even the insistence, of banks to provide funds for enterprises of the same zaibatsu affiliation. No less important, perhaps, was the peculiarly Japanese employment system, under which workers are recruited directly from school or university and normally spend their entire working lives with one company. Once accepted as a regular member of the organization, the employee is made to feel that he is a member of the "family," and for most Japanese white-collar workers this relationship is the most important one of all. If asked about his job, a "salaryman" will not specify his position or occupation but only the name of his company. For to be a "Mitsui man" or a "Mitsubishi man" is a mark of distinction more significant than one's individual achievement within the firm. The salaryman wears the lapel button of a well-known company with pride because it usually means that he has survived fierce competition to pass the entrance examination and is entitled to share the prestige of his employers. Each company has its own criteria for suitable candidates, and a true Mitsui man is selected for "fighting spirit," initiative, or prowess in sports. While Mitsubishi is noted for organization, discipline, and harmony, Mitsui emphasizes aggressiveness, independence, and intramural competitiveness, and the employees of both companies unconsciously tailor their own personalities to fit the image.

In each big company there are cliques based on educational background, shared experiences, and personal affinities. Men of ability rise within the concern by winning the loyalty of peers and subordinates while seeking favor with superiors. In fact, a Japanese company is a microcosm reflecting national life as a whole. But transcending inter-clique rivalry is pride in and loyalty to the company itself, which is not so much an economic entity as a personal, spiritual one, representing a fraternity of friends and colleagues bound together by common efforts and ambitions and symbolizing the obligations each member has incurred toward his fellows through the years.

Before the war the hierarchy in each company and combine was based upon the Japanese feudal system, with its ascending scale of fealty culminating in emperor worship. In some zaibatsu concerns loyalty was exacted by a signed oath of allegiance, in which an employee pledged obedience to superiors and company regulations, secrecy concerning business information, and the promise never to undertake any transaction on his own judgment alone. Employees were usually forbidden to resign to accept a better offer elsewhere and even waived legal rights guaranteed by the commercial code. Only by carrying out his pledge to the letter, with a convincing show of earnestness, could an executive hope to climb the ladder, and no display of brilliance was sufficient to appease the wrath of the overlords if one's obedience was in doubt.

The zaibatsu family leaders and their most trusted retainers considered this formalized loyalty essential to the most effective operation of the combines. Yet the abrupt removal of those august personages from their positions after the war did nothing to diminish the loyalty of employees toward their companies. On the contrary, lower-echelon managers, freed from enforced fealty to their overlords, devoted themselves more sincerely to the company's welfare, which they equated with their own. The constituent enterprises of the group were now able to negotiate more freely, seek funds advantageously, shop around for materials and property, and engage in healthy competition with each other while still enjoying the advantages of "togetherness."

A former director of the Sumitomo holding company explained the unshaken solidarity of liberated member companies thus: "Because one's parents are dead, one is not prevented from continuing as before with one's brothers and sisters. What could be more natural than the brothers and sisters of a family helping each other to keep going as a group?"[2]

One should not forget American big brothers, either. Once the war was over, it was equally natural for investors in the United States to help rebuild the Japanese enterprises in which they held stock or with which they had maintained cooperative relationships in the past. Thus International Standard Electric (a subsidiary of International Telephone & Telegraph) helped Sumitomo Electric and Nippon Electric, in both of which it was the largest shareholder; General Electric helped Mitsui's Tokyo Shibaura Electric, in which it was the largest shareholder; Westinghouse helped Mitsubishi Electric, in which it was the largest shareholder; Getty's Tidewater Oil helped Mitsubishi Oil, in which it was the largest shareholder; and other American and British oil, rubber, smelting, and machinery companies helped zaibatsu-descended partner companies in which they had invested. Continuous and rising investment, loans, technology, and marketing assistance from well-heeled Americans gave the zaibatsu "orphans" invaluable advantages over competitors without such connections.

Liberation from the firm zaibatsu embrace affected talented managers in two opposite ways. Some ambitious men, wresting control of their respective enterprises from more complacent colleagues, consolidated their personal power and kept aloof from close identification with any group. Others sought in every way to strengthen group ties for mutual advantage and restoration of the familiar pattern.

In the first category were those whose companies had been less closely connected with the Mitsui main company or had strong ties with foreign capital. A conspicuous example was Tokyo Shibaura Electric, already a huge combine before the war. Under the leadership of Ishizaka Taizo, the Toshiba management took the same course as

Nissan's gigantic Hitachi, to become a diversified semi-independent machinery complex with scores of subsidiaries and satellites.

Ishizaka, though less closely connected with Mitsui, was an economic statesman in the tradition of Dan, Ikeda, and Fujihara, serving as supreme decision-maker not only for his own concern but also for the business and industrial community as a whole. He took his degree in German law at Tokyo Imperial University in 1911 and made his debut in finance as a clerk in the postal savings department of the communications ministry at a salary of about forty dollars a month. His capacity for thinking big was revealed soon afterward when he bought a tailor-made suit that consumed most of his month's pay and aroused the wrath of his father, a banker.

This extravagance made a better impression on his boss, Shimomura Kainan, who found in the imaginative Taizo-san a receptive audience for his radical idea of setting up a life insurance monopoly administered by the post office. A vociferous opponent of Shimomura's idea was his friend Yano Tsuneta, founder of the Dai-ichi Life Insurance Company, and their endless polemics formed a significant part of Taizo's education. Some years later, when Yano offered Taizo a job in his struggling company, the latter was reluctant to give up his snug post as section chief and a secure career as a bureaucrat. He accepted only on the condition that he be permitted to study abroad at the company's expense. He spent the better part of a year studying at the Metropolitan Life Insurance Company and inspecting several other American firms, extending his expense-account journey to circumnavigate the world before starting to work in Tokyo.

From then on, under a series of titles—from manager in 1919 to president in 1938—he actually ran Dai-ichi Life for Yano, who having realized his dream of introducing the mutual life insurance system into Japan, was concerned thereafter with public rather than private affairs. In nurturing the firm's sales and assets, Ishizaka was no doubt assisted by his former boss and mentor Shimomura, who successively became governor of Taiwan, vice-president of *Asahi Shimbun,* president of the Japan Broadcasting Company, and state minister for propaganda in the wartime Suzuki cabinet. Also standing behind Taizo was his personal *gakubatsu,* or university clique—diplomat Shigemitsu Mamoru, manufacturer Kawai Yoshinari, and politicians Kimura Tokutaro and Ashida Hitoshi. Ashida ascended to the prime ministry and the others attained cabinet posts. Another classmate and close friend, Makino Ryozo (also a graduate in German law and a disciple of Shimomura), was elected to the lower house for ten terms and served as a vice-minister.

By consorting with such companions, Ishizaka had his finger on the pulse of national and international affairs at all times. Combining this advantage with his natural aggressiveness, he built Dai-ichi's business so effectively that the firm climbed from thirteenth to second place in Japan's life-insurance field, excelled only by Nippon Life. While operating the sluice gates for this huge reservoir of capital, Ishizaka of course became conversant with every aspect of Japanese industry, and most of the major enterprisers were beholden to him for financial support at one time or another.

Thus Ishizaka was already a powerful figure when the war ended, and although Dai-ichi was not considered a zaibatsu company he felt endangered by the purge. To avoid it he resigned from Dai-ichi after twenty-eight years of service and cultivated his garden. (In tune with the times, he raised potatoes, not flowers.) His prudence paid off, for in 1948, when Toshiba's top executives were under orders to be purged, he was invited by Sato Kiichiro of Mitsui Bank to take a high managerial position in Toshiba. Ishizaka was no stranger to the firm, having served it as a director for several years. He was also a Mitsui insider, since his niece had married the president of Mitsui Life. Enjoying the confidence of the management and of Mitsui Bank, the firm's leading stockholder, he was given sweeping powers to save the concern from what seemed to be its impending bankruptcy.

The situation looked hopeless. Under the deconcentration law the number of Toshiba's plants had been reduced by nearly two-thirds, and because of labor struggles productivity was low. The company was greatly overstaffed, but layoffs were made difficult by the militancy of the communist-led union. The management had been afraid to grapple with the situation and would not even permit face-to-face negotiations between the president and union representatives. Ishizaka put an end to temporizing. He developed a drastic reorganization plan under which six thousand workers, more than one-fifth of the labor force, were to be discharged. As expected, the announcement of this move brought on a strike. The stoppage was prolonged, but Ishizaka's undercover agents had made a careful study of factional rivalries within the company union, and he planned his campaign accordingly. When the strikers walked out, Ishizaka assumed the presidency of the company and broke precedent by negotiating with the leaders personally.

Ishizaka was by breeding a scholar and a class-conscious aristocrat. His daughter had married the scion of an imperial prince whose mother was high priestess of the Grand Shrines at Ise, at which even the emperor must make obeisance. But Ishizaka was burly in build and blunt-spoken enough to argue effectively with his proletarian adversaries. And in case words should prove inadequate, he had hired some of the toughest and most experienced union-busters in the business. The company was near the end of its tether, but Ishizaka knew that the unionists were equally desperate, and at the psychological moment he presented a compromise offer that they were able to accept without loss of face.

Having topped this hurdle, he set about reorganizing the ungainly group of companies, pruning off a lot of deadwood in the management and firing 4,500 unionists, starting with the radicals. Just then the Korean War presented opportunities that he was quick to appreciate, and with typical decisiveness he backed his hunches with investments of more than eight million dollars to modernize production facilities. He streamlined the company's operations and, taking advantage of the new boom in home electrical appliances, began to show consistent profits.

At the end of the war in Korea he challenged the recession by starting an all-out campaign to win overseas markets for Toshiba. While maintaining fraternal relations with his Mitsui friends, especially Sato of Mitsui Bank, whom he served as an adviser, he largely abandoned the traditional practice of selling through Mitsui Bussan and established a sales subsidiary—Toshiba Shoji—in order to keep the extra margin of profit in the company. Of course the financial tie-up with GE was invaluable for securing technology and capital, as well as marketing assistance, and Toshiba's trade-financing problems may have been eased by the installation of Ishizaka's younger brother Rokuro as director of the Export-Import Bank of Japan.

While remaining somewhere within the Mitsui orbit, Toshiba—with forty subsidiaries and some forty thousand employees—was on the road to becoming an international giant in its own right rather than a member of the Mitsui group. In the 1950s International General Electric was the largest stockholder, with three percent of the shares (later boosting its stake to twelve percent), while Mitsui Bank trailed in fourth place. Ishizaka was not able to realize his ambition of overtaking Hitachi but kept close on its heels and made Toshiba Japan's seventh largest company, with sales of more than four hundred million dollars a year by 1960.

As the chief executive of a top-flight corporate group, he was able to strengthen the old-zaibatsu position in the economic organizations previously dominated by new-zaibatsu representatives and was elected by an overwhelming majority to the presidency of the all-powerful Keidanren (Federation of Economic Organizations)—a post he held until 1968, when it passed to Uemura Kogoro.

During Ishizaka's incumbency as president of Keidanren big business tightened its control over the warring factions in the conservative parties and welded them into a stronger counterforce against the reformist opposition. Taking an irreconcilable position against industrial unionism and any rapprochement with Peking or Moscow, he won the trust of his American counterparts and their cooperation in bringing Japan into the second phase of its postwar development. That phase was characterized by unbridled industrial growth, technical moderniza- tion, and expansion of exports that brought Japan, quantitatively, into the first rank among economically advanced nations. Such rapid success caused alarm in the countries whose markets were being invaded or whose economies were falling too much under Japanese influence; but Ishizaka, through personal contacts with foreign businessmen and political leaders, was able to dispel some of the suspicion regarding Japan's motives and methods and to generate a rather convincing at- mosphere of international trust.

Unfortunately, so many extraneous activities diverted his attention from what was happening at Toshiba. When a mild recession hit Japanese industries in 1964 he was not prepared to cope with it, and the firm's profits sagged badly. Ishizaka resigned from Toshiba in 1965, but despite his age, seventy-nine, he went on to new adventures, becom- ing chairman of the Arabian Oil Company (Japan's most important overseas investment), head of the organizing committee for the 1970 world's fair in Osaka, and a member of the International Advisory Committee of Chase Manhattan Bank, among the scores of business and civic positions that he was easily persuaded to accept.

A patriot of the old school who prides himself on being a rightist and a supporter of nationalist groups, Ishizaka is an exponent of strong government, rearmament, and a revival of the Shinto religion as a pillar of public morality. In 1961 he told an international meeting of Rotarians that the Japanese had not been prepared or trained for de- mocracy, which they tended to interpret as "individual or collective license." Pointing out that until 1945 the official philosophy of morals and education was based upon faith and patriotism, he said nostal- gically: "To the Japanese people, emperor worship was the only pub- licly allowed form of belief. . . . I am not interested here in saying whether such a system of thought is right or wrong. What I want to say is that an official doctrine on what the people were to think existed, and that this helped more than is generally acknowledged in facilitat- ing the establishment of a modern economy in Japan. It helped because it forced each member of a society, hurrying to modernize its economy, to accept an official line of thought." Since the people believed what- ever they were taught, Ishizaka explained, "modern industrial training was accepted with such unquestioning obedience that the people learned to accept low wages and lay aside a sizable sum of their meager pay in the form of savings."[3] Although not all of Japan's economic leaders are as frank as Ishizaka was on that occasion, his statement seems to represent the basic social thinking of the older generation, who still speak with great authority in ruling circles.

Toshiba, while steering clear of entangling intimacies with the main Mitsui organizations, except Bank, did maintain cooperative ties with two other independent combines of Mitsui lineage, the Toyoda group and Ishikawajima-Harima Heavy Industries. The Toyota Motor Company was established as a division of the Toyoda Automatic Loom Works in 1933 and prospered during the war but had a hard time reconverting to peacetime production. In 1950 veteran executive Ishida Taizo, then president of Toyoda Automatic Loom, was prevailed upon to take leadership of Toyota Motor as well. He was quite pessimistic about the future of the automobile industry in Japan and says that when he accepted the position he was more worried than he had been at any time in his life. But almost immediately afterward war broke out in Korea and his company was flooded with orders for vehicles and machinery. Then the government began to foster production of automobiles as an economic stimulant, and the export boom followed. When Ishida retired twenty years later, in 1970, Toyota was the second largest private company in Japan and the third largest automobile-maker in the world.

This group of companies remained under the strong influence of the Toyoda family, and is now headed by the founder's nephew, Toyoda Eiji. However, ties with Mitsui are still apparent. Bank is the largest stockholder in Toyota, and the Mitsui clan's former retainer Naruse Yugo is auditor. And incidentally, senior managing director Toyoda Shoichiro, heir of the family, is married to the daughter of a Mitsui heir. Nevertheless, Toyota, like Toshiba, broke with zaibatsu tradition by establishing its own distribution channel, Toyota Motor Sales, thereby depriving Bussan of Japan's most profitable export product.

Ishikawajima-Harima Heavy Industries, which is a top producer of supertankers and took a leading role in building Japan's first atomic-powered ship, owed much of its success to Doko Toshiwo, its chairman. Doko, who is very important in Japanese business circles, rescued IHI after the war, when it was foundering. In 1965, when Toshiba got into trouble, he was brought in to replace Ishizaka as president and overhauled that sprawling combine with gratifying results. A modest man despite his aggressiveness in management, he explained his achievement in these terms: "All I have done at Toshiba is to make its organizational activities as a private manufacturing company suit its goal." And the ultimate goal of any private manufacturing company, as he sees it, "is to make profits through efficient production."

No newcomer to the Mitsui group, Doko was formerly president of the Ishikawajima-Shibaura Turbine Company, and his brother-in-law Ogura Yoshihiko was managing director of Toshiba. Financially, IHI is closer to the Dai-Ichi Bank group than to Mitsui. Nevertheless, its largest stockholder is Toshiba, and it participates in Mitsui group endeavors, such as nuclear power development. Other "secessionist" concerns loosely identified with Mitsui are General Sekiyu (formerly the Petroleum Department of Bussan), Toshoku (the Foodstuffs Department), Oji Paper, and Onoda Cement.

In contrast to the "secessionists," the organizations that had been most tightly controlled by Mitsui Honsha seemed to be drawn together by the centripetal attraction of sentiment as well as mutual advantage. Promoting the cohesiveness of an emerging "Mitsui Group" were the financial institutions, Bank, Trust, Mutual Life, and Taisho Marine & Fire; former "main" companies, such as Mining (divided after the Pacific War into Mining and Mining & Smelting), Chemical, and Shipbuilding & Engineering; very close affiliates, including Toyo Rayon and Toyo Koatsu; and Real Estate, which absorbed the remnants of Honsha.

Worthy of special mention in the revival of Mitsui was Toyo Rayon, which became the nation's number-one profit-earner (next to the Bank of Japan) under "Potsdam President" Tashiro Shigeki. Like Dan Takuma, Tashiro was from Kyushu, an engineer, an internationalist, and a self-made man. After graduating from a technical college in Kyushu, he entered Bussan and spent many years working for the firm in New York and London, where he mastered English and made business contacts that were to be invaluable in later years. But like so many Japanese who have worked abroad for long periods, he found upon his return in the mid-1930s that he was a stranger in the home office, with poor chances for advancement. At the time, Ishida Reisuke was a managing director of Bussan, in charge of several subsidiaries, including Toyo Rayon. "He had a big hatchet," Tashiro says. "He could cut directors." Tashiro was apparently expendable, so he was chopped off Bussan's staff and exiled to Toray, whether he liked it or not. He didn't, at first, but he did his job so conscientiously that he was made Toyo Rayon's managing director in 1942, and its president after the war when his boss was purged.

In this position his boldness, experience, and command of English enabled him to salvage the company, whose output and personnel had shrunk sadly after military production ceased. When the occupation's antizaibatsu campaign was in full swing, one of its plans called for shipping rayon-making equipment to China and Southeast Asia as part of Japan's reparations. The United States government sent a textile mission to Japan to survey the production facilities and select those

most suitable for transplanting. Since Tashiro was accustomed to dealing with Americans, he was appointed to negotiate with the head of the
research mission, a high executive of the American Viscose Corporation. Before the war, Japan had been the world's second-largest rayon
producer, having edged out the United States; and Toray had been one
of Viscose's most dangerous competitors, so Tashiro was not too
hopeful of saving his equipment. But after a tour of Japanese rayon
plants and long discussions with Tashiro, the Viscose man decided
that Japan should be allowed to reconstruct its rayon industry and
advised the War Department accordingly.

Tashiro knew, however, that the rayon industry was already senile
and that without nylon, which was still unknown in Japan, Toray
would not be able to compete in the world's textile markets. Toray's
chemists and engineers were mobilized to develop a similar product
they called "Nylon 6," which was experimentally successful; but mass
production was far off, and there was a possibility that the process
would infringe upon foreign patents. In 1951, when the United States
was encouraging American corporations to share technology with
Japan, Tashiro went to Delaware and negotiated directly with Du Pont
for the superior "Nylon 66" process. The American company set very
stringent terms: for use of the patents Toray needed, the initial price
was about three million dollars in advance royalties. Toray's board of
directors balked at taking such a risk, but Tashiro was stubborn and
signed the contract.

The immediate effect was a sharp decline in the price of Toray stock.
But once production of Du Pont's nylon began, sales of the material
soared. Tashiro also bought polyester fiber patents from Britain's
Imperial Chemical Industries while pursuing the development of original techniques. In time Toray became the world's third-largest producer
of synthetic fibers and a foundation stone for rebuilding the Mitsui
industrial complex.

Another coup by Tashiro launched Japan's postwar overseas investments. After the war the loss of Japan's forest resources in Sakhalin, Korea, and Manchuria had led to a great boom in domestic
production of pulp. In the lean years from 1945 to 1950, as a popular
saying went, the only ways of getting rich were the "three P's"—
pachinko (pinball), pan-pan (prostitution), and parupu (pulp). Some pulp
companies were paying dividends as high as forty percent, and demand for pulpwood was so insatiable that Japan's forests were being
laid waste. To stop such destruction, SCAP set up the Council for the
Conservation of Natural Resources, headed by Kobayashi Jun'ichiro,
a forestry expert who had risen to the vice-presidency of Oji Paper and
was an associate of HCLC president Sasayama Tadao. Kobayashi pro-

posed establishing a Japanese company to exploit the timber resources of Alaska for pulp and lumber. Since the obvious alternative was to make a similar deal to use Siberian forests, and since Washington was particularly anxious to prevent any rapprochement between Japan and the Soviet Union, SCAP's first response to Kobayashi's proposal was mildly encouraging. Kobayashi enlisted the assistance of Tashiro, at that time president of the Japan Chemical Fiber Association, who was then in the United States negotiating with Du Pont. When he had finished his talks about nylon in Wilmington he went on to Washington and conferred with the departments of State and the Interior, which gave tentative permission to establish such a company and to import forest products from Alaska.

Overcoming strong opposition from the domestic pulp industry, Kobayashi, Tashiro, and other industrialists established the Alaska Pulp Company in 1953, with capital of about one million dollars. But twenty million more was needed, so the promoters retained attorney James Lee Kauffman to make a deal with his friend William Draper, who was back at work with Dillon, Read. Draper agreed to lend half the sum if Alaska Pulp could raise the other half in Japan. This required the concerted support of paper, rayon, and lumber companies from several groups, with further assistance by the Export-Import Bank and the Long-Term Credit Bank; but eventually the funds were forthcoming, and then Dillon, Read floated bonds in New York to raise the balance.

Alaska Pulp, incorporated in the United States, was Japan's first big overseas investment since the war and represented a long step in Japan-U. S. economic cooperation—as well as among the zaibatsu. The firm, with fifty-year rights to lumber enormous tracts on Baranoff and adjacent islands, opened a sixty-six-million-dollar pulp mill in Sitka in the early 1960s. President of Alaska Pulp was Sasayama, who had worked behind the scenes to get American permission for establishing it. Tashiro, whose company was a big investor in Alaska Pulp, served on the board of directors and was chairman at the time of his retirement from business in 1968.

Mitsui solidarity seems to have remained strongest in Real Estate, which had been wholly owned by the Mitsui families until they were forced by SCAP to sell their stock. Postwar presidents or directors after the war were Sasaki Shiro (Baron Mitsui's favorite); Naruse Yugo, whose father had supervised the education of whole generations of Mitsuis; Inoue Itsuro, former manager of Mitsui Honsha's Financial Affairs Office; Yamao Tadaharu, a Mitsui relative; and another kinsman, Matsudaira Yasukuni. One director, Minomura Seiichiro, was a direct descendant of the eminent Minomura Rizaemon who guided the destinies of the House of Mitsui during and after the Meiji Restoration. In both directorships and stockholdings the company remained under unusually strong control by Mitsui family retainers and was regarded as a likely nucleus for regeneration of the Mitsui group of enterprises. This company—which had been in effect the real estate department of the whole concern by leasing land or buildings to hundreds of Mitsui enterprises, as well as to the general public—came out of the war in good shape. In the subsequent spiraling rise of land prices, the company increased its net worth from some five hundred million yen in 1950 to eighteen billion yen in 1970.

The postwar success of Real Estate centers around Edo Hideo, former deputy-manager of Mitsui Somotokata, who became president of Real Estate in 1958. Because of his rural background and countrified ways he was regarded as something of a "hick" when he entered Mitsui Gomei in 1927, although he stood first among the hundred and two applicants who took examinations for the job. He was also burdened with a social conscience. This had led him to dabble in Marxism and to make a deep study of land tenancy laws, which he hoped to reform in favor of working farmers victimized by absentee landlords.

He applied the same standards of justice to his capitalist employers, however, and during the dissolution period after the war he fought strenuously for what he believed to be their rights. He was particularly angered by the liberal reformers in General Whitney's Government Section of GHQ, among whom Eleanor Hadley was the most conspicuous. Having worked for the Office of Strategic Services, she was transferred to the International Business Practices Branch of the State Department to conduct research on the Japanese oligopolies and then joined the Government Section of GHQ in Tokyo with the determination to destroy them. "She was known as a beauty," Edo says, "but she brandished the thesis of the New Deal left wing . . . and terrified those concerned." He seemed to hold her personally responsible for an order issued in 1948, even after SCAP's attitude had begun to change for the better, that trademarks and trade names of the zaibatsu were not to be used for a period of eight years, beginning in July 1950.

Edo took up the matter with SCAP officials directly, arguing that United States policy had been changed basically and that the dissolution of the zaibatsu had been almost completed. "Why is it necessary to change names?" he asked. "Mitsui Real Estate is not owned by the Mitsuis but by the general public." He estimated that merely to change names Mitsui, Mitsubishi, and Sumitomo together would lose 1.5 billion yen in direct expenditures and ten times that much indirectly.

That would surely weaken the Japanese economy, he said. Failing to make his point, Edo at last appealed to Prime Minister Yoshida personally as the deadline approached.

"Why did you neglect [to tell me about] such an important matter?" Yoshida scolded. The order had to be issued, of course, but Yoshida promised to postpone its enforcement. Representatives of the three zaibatsu concerns, assisted by attorney W. R. Hutchinson and the prime minister himself, then lobbied with friends in the G-2 Section, and immediately after the peace treaty was signed in 1951 the ban was rescinded.

Edo was not a man to hold a grudge, however. Fifteen years later Dr. Hadley, then working with the U. S. Tariff Commission, returned to Japan to study the effect of the dissolution on the Japanese economy and asked to see Edo. "I met her at the Mitsui Tsunamachi Club," he recalls, "the historic place in which the fateful discussion between Mitsui Honsha executives and Colonel Kramer of GHQ occurred. She repeated prepared questions about the status of old zaibatsu families and affiliate companies and the Japanese economy. Her posture was quite low compared with that shown at the time of the conquerors.

"The zaibatsu dissolution took effect on the Japanese economy as GHQ intended, and the gigantic structure of the zaibatsu, with Japanese families and their holding companies on top, was destroyed. But the Japanese economy had been reaping a remarkable harvest. It seemed curious to her, who had worked amidst destitution and ruin to weaken the Japanese economy in the name of democratization.

"After the meeting we went out into the garden. Fresh foliage and flowers in full bloom—the vigorous life of nature. Did she realize that in this there was a clue for deciphering the answers to her questions?"

A clearer answer was to be found, however, in the ruthless drive of Edo himself, who is known as Japan's pioneer "developer." Under his hyperkinetic leadership, the company embarked on a program of land reclamation and the development of coastal industrial zones that have transformed eastern Honshu's once beautiful Pacific shoreline into a hideous but efficient machine for economic growth. Mitsui, Mitsubishi, and other real estate companies, in league with their respective financial groups and "planners" in the government and economic organizations, unwittingly created a congested, blighted, and horrendously polluted megalopolis that extends for 350 miles from Tokyo almost without interruption to beyond Osaka and Kobe and accommodates nearly half of Japan's population. Meanwhile, the country's small towns, villages, and farms fell into decrepitude because the young people migrated to the factories, mills, refineries, gasoline stations, banks, department stores, and bowling alleys of this sprawling, suffocating Babylon in which nothing had been planned but production and profit.

A fitting monument to Edo Hideo's efforts is Mitsui Real Estate's thirty-six-story Kasumigaseki Building, Japan's first skyscraper, in central Tokyo. At its top is an observation lounge from which, on clear days, one can sometimes catch a glimpse of Mount Fuji's distant glistening peak. But seldom indeed can one see much of Tokyo at one's feet, obscured as it is by a dirty, gray pall of smog from gas-belching industrial zones and the bumper-to-bumper traffic that clogs the streets below.

Yet Edo, although typical of the business men who have earned the unmerited epithet of "economic animals" for the all-too-human Japanese, is no monster. He is a rather sensitive, poetic man who tends his own garden fondly in the freshness of the dawn, reads good books, and writes amusing, perceptive essays. (Among his favorite subjects are the conservation of wild birds and the responsibility of businessmen for improving the environment.) He is genial, an excellent conversationalist, and the most frank of all the Mitsui executives this author has met. Though he has long since overcome his penchant for radical solutions to social problems, he is broad-minded; in fact, one of his good friends is Narita Tomomi, the former executive of Mitsui Chemical who became secretary-general of the Japan Socialist Party.

Narita is equally tolerant. When elections are approaching and he is short of funds, he drops into Edo's office in one of the old Mitsui Honsha buildings to arrange a loan. "To my surprise," Edo says, "among his collateral are his wife's stock certificates. I tell him I cannot receive any interest from my friend, but he pays it without fail."

It may seem incongruous, even scandalous, that a leftist militant should receive electioneering funds from a zaibatsu chieftain. Yet the leaders of the faintly left-wing Democratic Socialist Party are funded regularly by conservative Liberal Democrats, and even the Japan Communist Party accepts handouts from businessmen not necessarily in favor of its policies but motivated by personal obligations or the hope of favorable treatment in business dealings with communist countries. As in days gone by, major corporations maintain special sections for doling out political funds to friend and foe alike—from the radical left to the terrorist right, including gangsters—apparently working on the principle that "wherein thou judgest another, thou condemnest thyself."

A case in point is that of Saionji Kinkazu, a grandson of the last genro, Prince Saionji, and a kinsman of the Sumitomo and Mitsui families, who has spent most of the postwar years in China as a devotee of Mao Tse-tung. This "blue-blooded black sheep" was by no means ostracized by his capitalist friends and relatives in Japan and presumably worked effectively for the restoration of Sino-Japanese diplomatic relations, which were resumed in 1972.

With more than thirteen hundred years of recorded history behind them, the Japanese have seen governments, institutions, and ideologies ebb and flow like the eternal tides, and have little confidence in the permanance of "reforms," however helpful or cataclysmic they may seem to be at the moment. Their tradition of tolerance, especially in not permitting conflicts of doctrine to destroy personal or business relationships based upon generally accepted values, has a lot to do with the solidarity that has prevented disruptive changes in their social structure, even during the tumultuous changes of the past century. When you think you are seeing Japan careening blindly into the future, you can be sure that some of its leaders (like any good general securing his rear, even while advancing unopposed) have their eyes fixed upon the past—just in case it should become necessary for them to withdraw to a prepared position . . .

28 · The Rebirth of Mitsui Bussan

As THE STIMULANT OF WAR-DEMAND resuscitated the Japanese economy after 1950, the big industrial companies turned instinctively to the trading firms of their respective groups for assistance in purchasing, marketing, and planning. They had always done business that way, and it had always worked. During the occupation the traders were more necessary than ever; for, having established their private pipelines to SCAP and the top levels of the Japanese government, they could predict future demand for materials, interpret regulations, arrange suitable contacts, and submit bids in the right places at the right time. They were more than middlemen: they were matchmakers, counselors, arbitrators, and even organizers of new enterprises to meet anticipated needs. Such services were indispensable and, at a profit rate of two percent or so, they were irresistible to producers.

Daiichi Bussan, as the most prominent of the Mitsui-line traders, naturally got a substantial share of the group's industrial business, of which the biggest bonanza was United States military procurement, including construction, warehousing, transport, and repair of aircraft, ships, and vehicles. At the same time Japanese demand for raw materials and foodstuffs increased sharply, and Daiichi was able to import iron ore, coal, grain, and machinery by the shipload, while supplying domestic fuel and construction materials for industrial expansion.

But money was still tight, and traders were put under terrible pressure for funds to finance their deals, some of which were running into six figures. Daiichi had little to offer except new stock shares as collateral for loans, and bankers were cautious. They knew that of the hundreds of new trading companies spawned by the dissolution of the zaibatsu only a few could survive, and they regarded a loan as an act of faith rather than a business proposition.

Many trading houses went under in 1951 and 1952, at the peak of the Korean War, because of speculation. With the revival of spinning and weaving industries, demand for cotton was frantic, and Daiichi's managers, lapsing from their conservative policy, were drawn into a scheme for cornering the American cotton market. Niizeki, an experi-

enced textile man, went along with them. But while he was in Osaka
on a business trip he had a discussion with his friend Seki Keizo, board
chairman of Toyo Spinning (the direct descendant of Osaka Spinning,
established by Shibusawa Eiichi in 1882). Niizeki asked for Seki's
reaction to the cotton-speculation plan and he replied: "In my opinion,
the price will level off when raw cotton is produced in large quantities
in California."

Niizeki was startled. If the deal failed to work out, his firm could
be ruined. Then intuition told him that regardless of California cotton
an unexpected end to the Korean War would have the same effect.
"Therefore, I told the whole staff to stop rigging the cotton market.
I made long-term and short-term deals 'square,' to use merchants'
jargon," he wrote.[1]

Less cautious Mitsui splinter companies were driven to the wall by
speculation, bad decisions, or sheer lack of operating capital. But even
in distress those companies were valuable repositories of expertise,
trading connections, and order backlogs. Therefore, the prospering
Daiichi Bussan and other surviving sister firms took them over one
after another, deficits and all, and made new departments out of them.
Because of that, and despite the war boom, Bussan was usually short
of funds.

In 1951 it was again necessary to tap the Wall Street market, and
Bache & Company agreed to lend Daiichi $500,000. But for some
reason the money failed to come through, and when the situation turned
critical Niizeki sent his faithful Tanabe Shunsuke to New York to
get things moving. Harold Bache, a master of business psychology,
sensed his advantage and offered to advance part of the money immediately in exchange for the right to be the firm's New York agent.
Since Daiichi had not yet been able to open an East Coast branch, he
knew the proposal would have a certain appeal. He broached it to
Tanabe, who called Niizeki by telephone and relayed the offer. There
was a moment of painful silence, some muffled conversation at the
Tokyo end of the line, and Niizeki came on again: "It can't be helped.
Give him the agency for three years."

But Bache drove a hard bargain: five years, he demanded, or no
advance. In Tokyo the board of directors was convened to discuss the
advantages and disadvantages of the offer. Thanks to Bache and his
partners, Daiichi now had a proper board room in a presentable building, so there was a matter of giri involved. Furthermore, if they accepted the offer, they would immediately acquire an imposing office
and a prestigious address in Wall Street. But Bache's price, the firm's
most profitable overseas agency for five years, was exorbitant. Niizeki
called Tanabe by phone again and told him to hold out for the shorter

term. "But we've got to have the money right away," he added, and rang off.

As Tanabe haggled in New York the board members in Tokyo drank innumerable cups of green tea to keep awake through the small hours of the morning. Then the phone rang again. "There's no possibility of getting the money unless we give him five years," Tanabe reported wearily. There was too much to lose by further delay, so Bache got his contract.

It was a Pyrrhic victory. Although the head office sent a few young staffers, who operated out of Bache's offices, the trading talent that had characterized Mitsui since the Meiji era seemed to have withered. In Tokyo, and at Daiichi's San Francisco branch office, business was going like wildfire; in New York it merely smoldered. Bache had hoped to harness the well-trained thoroughbreds of Mitsui to his own financial chariot, but he soon learned, as so many other foreign investors have learned before and since, that Japanese business is not just a matter of contracts. No less important are personal relationships and motivations that are often baffling to outlanders. Within a couple of years he recognized the hopelessness of his position and gave up the agency. Thereafter, independent of foreign meddling, it took off like a skyrocket. Later incorporated as Mitsui & Company (USA), it became the most prosperous foreign trading operation in the United States.

But as the occupation of Japan was drawing to a close, such triumphs were only the dreams of visionaries. Although Daiichi Bussan had increased its capital more than a thousandfold to two hundred million yen ($555,000) in the four years since its founding, it was overwhelmingly outclassed by Mitsui-descended financial and industrial companies, even those that had been "deconcentrated." Still, in that fiercely competitive field, it had survived the preliminary heats and was already being eyed as a possible captain for the leaderless Mitsui team.

The genealogy of the Japanese trading companies competing for supremacy reads like the fifth chapter of Genesis, with all its begats, except that among the leading companies the generations were counted in months instead of centuries, and the families got smaller instead of bigger. By 1952 only a dozen or so trading firms remained serious contenders for leadership among the sogo shosha. Four or five of those were of zaibatsu descent and the rest were Osaka textile houses.

The most powerful of the latter were called the "Kansai Gomen," or Big Five Cotton Merchants of the Kansai region, and after various mergers became the firms known at present as Marubeni-Iida, C. Itoh, Nichimen, Toyo Menka, and Gosho. (Toyo Menka was established in 1919 from Mitsui Bussan's Cotton Department.) When the zaibatsu traders were crippled temporarily by SCAP's dissolution decree, the Kansai Gomen (untouched by the antimonopoly program) had popped up suddenly as sogo shosha and threatened to dominate their Tokyo-based competitors. With the help of Wall Street money Daiichi was holding its own, but it was hard pressed by Kowa Jitsugyo (which became Mitsubishi Shoji in 1952), its sister Fuji Shoji, and Marubeni, all backed by powerful Japanese banks and all growing phenomenally.

These sogo shosha were staffed by experienced, aggressive traders, but the trend of the times was an equally significant factor in their growth. In 1949, with the reversal of SCAP's policy, the Antimonopoly Law was amended to permit intercorporate stockholdings, mergers, and interlocking directorates. Also, international agreements on business and technology could again be concluded without obtaining permission from SCAP. The zaibatsu banks and other major lending institutions, which had escaped the dissolution program unscathed, strengthened their ties with enterprises of their groups, which in turn consolidated their positions by cross-holdings of stock and exchanges of management personnel. In the 1951–52 emergency the bankers prudently chose larger firms as the best loan-risks, and lesser ones went by the board or were forced to merge with the major companies. As this process continued, the ban against using the old company names and trademarks was revoked, and various exemptions from the Antimonopoly Law were condoned. The Export Transactions Law of 1952 made it possible for stricken industries to take joint action to curtail production and for export associations to regulate prices. In the following year the Antimonopoly Law was again revised to facilitate monopolistic mergers and the formation of outright cartels to promote modernization, maintain prices, and prevent dumping.

While the favored few emerged as giants, reliance upon loans drew them more closely into the orbits of their respective banks. Even in the mid-thirties the major traders had been conspicuously dependent upon loans. While industry as a whole had borrowed about thirty percent of its funds, the borrowings of traders amounted to seventy percent of total capital. After the war, the ratio of owned capital to loans fell markedly. In 1952 more than ninety-five percent of trading capital consisted of borrowings, and although the situation improved subsequently, the ratio of owned capital seldom rose above ten percent. Thus, as had been predicted by the frustrated American trustbusters, the zaibatsu banks served as instruments for reviving oligopoly.

In retrospect, the efforts of the occupation to introduce free competition into Japan was one of the most quixotic episodes in economic history. The Antimonopoly Law of 1947 contradicted all principles and practices by means of which Japan had modernized its prewar economy so rapidly and successfully. It was similar to the American antitrust laws and in some ways stricter. These had been designed for an economy with a laissez-faire tradition, and even so they had failed in their purpose. How, then, could such laws have succeeded in Japan, which had never experienced true capitalism at all? For in the development of modern Japan, private investment and foreign trade were mainly devices for bolstering the power of the state and had more in common with the mercantilism of Renaissance Europe than with capitalism as the West knows it.

Judging from the actions and the oblique statements of postwar economic leaders in Japan, one can easily conclude that they never had the slightest intention of adopting the alien concept of free enterprise: the main thrust of their policy during the occupation was always toward evading, eroding, or abolishing the antitrust laws and related ordinances. This attitude reflected the unified opinion of business, finance, the conservative political parties, and the government itself. (Even the communists had been dubious about the breakup of the zaibatsu, suspecting that it indicated an imperialist scheme to gain control of the Japanese economy.)

Against this solid phalanx stood a powerless, understaffed, inadequately financed body called the Fair Trade Commission. This Japanese government agency (wryly called "The Twilight Commission" as its prospects dimmed) put up many a noisy rear-guard action but never won an important campaign. Within a few years after its inauguration in 1947, the antimonopoly structure had been whittled away until virtually the only barrier against the revival of the zaibatsu was the law prohibiting the existence of holding companies.

While the financial power of the banks quickly rebounded, they were not able to function as holding companies like Mitsui Honsha because they were prohibited from owning more than ten percent of the stock in any one industrial or commercial company. Therefore, the task of regrouping the zaibatsu combines was assumed, to a large extent, by the trading companies, which were under no such limitation. As appendages of the banks the trading firms served as pipelines through which industrial funds were channeled to manufacturers. Quickly reestablishing their network of branches, they kept in close touch with overseas markets, sources of imports, and technological trends. By giving sound advice and keeping goods and commodities moving both ways quickly and profitably, they helped to assure the success of client companies and hence the soundness of bank loans.

This arrangement enabled each major bank to establish a base in many sectors of the nation's industry without holding a very large equity in any of the companies concerned. At the same time each of the major trading companies built up its stockholdings in hundreds of affiliated manufacturing enterprises. Also, trust banks and insurance companies of the respective financial groups purchased stocks selectively in cooperation with their affiliated commercial banks, so that the latter, though holding less than one-tenth of the shares in any single enterprise, could exert strong influence over several mammoth industrial firms.

Revival of the zaibatsu groups was discernible even before the occupation ended. The initial move was the inauguration of informal "presidents' meetings," at which leaders of formerly affiliated enterprises could discuss common problems and future plans. Mitsui had its Getsuyokai (Monday Meeting), Mitsubishi its Kin'yokai (Friday Meeting), and Sumitomo its Hakusuikai (White Water Meeting). There was a Toyotakai for executives of the Toyota group, whose affiliation with Mitsui had become rather nebulous, and a Nissankai for the Nissan-Hitachi people, and so on.

By 1952 Mitsubishi was already moving rapidly toward reintegration. The Kin'yokai had developed from an informal gathering into an effective liaison and soon was organizing intragroup undertakings aimed at restoring unity. Successful measures were taken to keep stockholdings within the group, real estate assets were consolidated, directorships were exchanged, and dependence on the group's financial institutions was promoted. The same was true of Sumitomo, whose Hakusuikai provided much of the guidance that had been lost when its holding company was dissolved.

The rapid progress of Mitsubishi and Sumitomo as groups was due in part to their character and structure. Both had been more tightly regimented than Mitsui, and the nature of their main enterprises made them more essential to postwar recovery and hence more generously financed by the government. Under direct Mitsubishi influence were six big heavy industrial companies, in addition to coal and metal mining, chemicals, petroleum, refining, glass, paper, synthetic textiles, and shipping. Sumitomo, though smaller, had an even greater preponderance of heavy and chemical industries. Mitsui remained strong in chemicals, metal mining, and light industry, but its heavy industrial companies were not of the first rank. One of its traditional mainstays, coal mining, was retreating before the advance of petroleum; and of course its most important line, trading, had been shattered.

Furthermore, Mitsubishi and Sumitomo were backed by their own top-notch banks, while Mitsui Bank was much weaker financially. After its separation from Dai-Ichi Bank it was relegated to fifth or sixth place, and was further hampered by a serious overloan position. Postwar problems caused by strikes, weaknesses in management, and transition to peacetime production had made tremendously expensive the salvaging of Toshiba, Mitsui Chemical, Mitsui Mining, and Japan Steel Works, so that other "family" enterprises found it necessary to seek funds elsewhere. Although Sumitomo was particularly weak in trading, Mitsubishi made a fast comeback in this field, and soon after the trademark ban was revoked in 1952 Mitsubishi Shoji reappeared almost intact as a nucleus for group revival. Both Mitsubishi and Sumitomo had reached a point at which they could make joint plans for pioneering in petrochemicals and atomic energy, then recognized as key industries of the future.

Mitsui, by comparison, remained in a state of anarchy. Because of Bank's relative weakness the reintegration of Bussan seemed essential to the formation of a Mitsui group, but efforts in this direction foundered repeatedly through lack of teamwork. Getsuyokai, inaugurated early in 1950, comprised the top executives of twenty-seven companies (or their fragments) formerly governed by Mitsui Honsha, but at first its meetings were more like class reunions than sessions of a business committee. There was a difference of opinion concerning the desirability of reuniting, and even among the integrationists clashes of strong personalities made it impossible to agree upon a method of doing so.

The urge to consolidate was fortified by the revocation in 1951 of SCAP's ban on using the Mitsui name and trademark. Soon afterward a committee of executives from the principal Mitsui splinter companies, formed under Mukai Tadaharu, decided that the name "Mitsui Bussan," being too valuable to be used indiscriminately, should be kept in reserve pending a decision as to which firm would inherit it. Meanwhile, through a private arrangement with Mitsui Hachiroemon Takakimi (acting for the clan), the right to use the honored name was put into the custody of Nitto Soko Tatemono (Nitto Warehouse and Real Estate), which had been formed to take over the assets and liabilities of the liquidated Mitsui Bussan.

There was intense rivalry for the trade name and symbol, recognized and trusted by businessmen the world over. In April 1952 the battle lines were drawn at a session, held at the old Mitsui Honsha offices, of leading executives from all the Bussan splinter firms (which by then had boiled down to about twenty-five). This was their first meeting since the dissolution; but if anyone there felt any nostalgia it was soon dissipated by an acrimonious debate over the succession to the title. Niizeki and Mizukami argued that Daiichi Bussan, then in truth the number one sogo shosha of Mitsui lineage, was the logical nucleus for a reintegrated Mitsui Bussan. However, this solution was not agreeable to the other "number one" firm, Daiichi Tsusho, which actually stood in seventh place nationally. Also opposed to the proposal were several other strong contenders, as well as the insignificant Nitto Soko Tatemono, which clung jealously to the treasure that had been entrusted to its care. That meeting, from which so much had been expected by other companies of the group, proved to be fruitless.

The movement for unity became further snarled in 1953 when Muromachi Bussan, the former Metals Department, merged with Nitto Soko Tatemono. Contrary to the gentlemen's agreement among the splinter companies, Hirashima Toshiro, president of the merged firm, registered it with the government as "Mitsui Bussan Kaisha," although it bore little resemblance to its namesake. According to one Mitsui leader, Hirashima "stole" the coveted name, thus gaining an advantage far out of proportion to the importance of his firm.

Because of this maneuver the only way to reconstitute Bussan in its former dimensions was to merge Hirashima's firm with the much larger Daiichi Bussan on an equal basis. But here a serious hitch arose. Hirashima, though Niizeki's senior in years, had risen only as high as department head, while Niizeki had been elevated to chief managing director. According to Japanese business protocol one simply does not work under a former subordinate. When such a situation arises the man who is overtaken usually retires to save face. But Hirashima, legally in possession of the Mitsui talisman, obviously wanted to be the boss, and Niizeki had no intention of retiring.

In the past there had always been a Mitsui statesman, such as Minomura, Nakamigawa, Masuda, Dan, or Ikeda, to resolve such problems. But upon this one the two surviving elders—Mukai and Ishida—couldn't agree. Mukai, who had boosted his prestige by serving as Prime Minister Yoshida's finance minister in 1952, was in favor of centering operations in Daiichi Bussan, while Ishida favored the other pretender and was cool toward a merger.

The driving forces in the rival companies were Mizukami and Hirashima, both dynamic and imaginative businessmen. But both were individualists with distinct styles that were hard to reconcile. Mizukami, the more adventurous of the two, built up as broad an organization as possible, and one that was heavily capitalized through the efforts of Niizeki. He also had a knack for attracting high-caliber talent and for delegating authority commensurately. In contrast, Hirashima developed his company for soundness and strength in a few main lines, emphasizing hardware, metals, and steelmaking materials. He was satisfied with slower growth and was reluctant to expand his capital unless profitability was assured. His was more of a one-man operation, with a staff that was thoroughly disciplined and capable of attaining its limited objectives without fail.

Mizukami's style, abetted by Niizeki's financial and political contacts, proved to be more in tune with the times. The economic reaction to the armistice in Korea was less serious than anticipated, and Daiichi Bussan surged ahead. In 1955 the firm, having absorbed the Mitsui Lumber Company,* merged with two other major segments of the old Bussan—Nippon Kikai, Japan's leading machinery trader, and Daiichi Tsusho, which was strong in foodstuffs, fuels, metals, and other lines of business. Daiichi Bussan further increased its lead over Hirashima's firm by absorbing Kokusai Bussan, the parent company's former Chemical Department. Thus in one spectacular year the number of Daiichi's employees doubled to about four thousand and its capital quadrupled to some seven million dollars. Soon thereafter the price of the stock reached triple its par value, and the $140,000 investment of "C. A. England" (alias Bache, Chemical Bank, and Lehman) was worth more than a million dollars, including the value of stock dividends.

Daiichi Bussan now comprised at least two-thirds of the old Bussan's former elements and had nearly forty domestic and fifty-five overseas offices, as well as scores of affiliated companies in Japan and abroad. It was the same old Bussan in everything but name, and despite that disadvantage it had maintained its lead over the Kansai Gomen, although it had been overtaken by Mitsubishi Shoji in the previous year. Most other Mitsui-line companies were also doing very well, Japan's industrial production having recovered to the prewar level by 1955, and they were extremely impatient to get started on new types of industrial development that could be achieved only through intragroup cooperation. It had already been decided that a completely reintegrated Mitsui Bussan—in name, as well as in substance—was to be the core of the group, and since the split between Daiichi and Hirashima's firm showed no signs of healing, the heads of fifteen representative Mitsui companies formed a special committee to force the issue. The Fifteen-Company Committee consisted of Mitsui Bank, Mutual Life, Steamship, Shipbuilding & Engineering, Mining, Mining & Smelting, Chemical, Warehouse, Real Estate, Taisho Marine & Fire, Sanki Engineering, Toyo Koatsu, and Toyo Rayon, as well as the two principals.

Hirashima was a hard man to deal with. Extracting every possible ounce of advantage from his possession of the Mitsui name, he insisted that the companies be merged on a fifty-fifty basis although his capital was about one-third less than Daiichi's. He also insisted on going over Niizeki's head to become chairman of the board. To complicate matters further, the biggest stockholder in his company was Daiwa Bank, closely identified with Osaka merchants and "new zaibatsu" groups

---

* This firm had been separated from Bussan before 1945, and therefore was allowed by SCAP to keep the Mitsui name.

considered to be hostile to Mitsui. Despite these problems the Fifteen-Company Committee arbitrated successfully and the merger was about to be effected.

Then, without consulting the other negotiators, Hirashima declared a stock dividend, thereby putting a larger amount of stock in the hands of outsiders. His ostensible reason for the move was that he considered Daiichi overcapitalized and that the smaller capital of his own firm did not represent its relative strength. But the delicate balance arranged by the committee was upset. The whole deal had to be renegotiated, and a top-caliber task force, including Sato Kiichiro of Mitsui Bank, Tashiro of Toray, and Sato Hisashi of Shipbuilding, was deployed to save the situation.

How they did it is a mystery, but on August 5, 1958—just seven years after the initial meeting of the splinter company presidents—the task force and members of the Fifteen-Company Committee assembled at Mitsui Honsha's offices to witness the conclusion of the grand merger that restored Mitsui Bussan Kaisha (Mitsui & Company, Ltd.) to its former glory as Japan's largest trading firm. Hirashima won the chairmanship, but Niizeki remained as president, and Mizukami, the great thinker of the concern, obligingly settled for the vice-presidency. When the shares were added up, Mitsui Bank turned out to be the largest stockholder, and Taisho Marine & Fire Insurance and the Bank of Tokyo, both under strong Bussan influence, were third and sixth respectively. The merger was not an unalloyed victory for the Mitsui men, for among the top six stockholders were three "interlopers," Daiwa Bank, Nomura Securities, and Fuji Bank (formerly Yasuda Bank). Nevertheless, Mitsui dominance was sufficiently strong to make Bussan a center for effective group action during the halcyon period of unprecedented economic growth that began in the year of the merger and made Japan's gross national product the world's third largest within a decade.

29 · Behind the Curtain

JAPAN'S "MIRACULOUS" EMERGENCE as a first-rate economic power in the 1960s has been described exhaustively by Japanese and foreign writers, and yet very little of the literature provides credible explanations of how it was done, or by whom. This hiatus is particularly noticeable when we attempt to analyze the process by which the defunct zaibatsu were transformed into "enterprise groups" with enormous economic power, or try to trace the ways in which such power was expressed politically. It seems, in fact, that there has been a "conspiracy of silence" concerning the actual methods by which Japan is governed.

The reasons for such reticence are the same as those prevailing in other periods of Japan's modern century. In the early Meiji era the nation was ruled by a secret cabal that made little pretense of explaining its operations. In the 1880s Japan adopted the Meiji constitution to appease domestic opponents of the Sat-Cho oligarchy and to impress foreigners with the empire's political modernization, but the basic political processes still took place outside the constitutional framework, fairly well concealed from all but anointed members of the ruling cliques.

After the First World War, as described earlier, alien ideologies inundated Japan and aroused a new militancy among intellectuals and urban commoners, whereupon the members of the peerage, the zaibatsu, and their political, bureaucratic, and military cohorts drew together to form a common front in defense of the old order. Even Japan's defeat in the Pacific War failed to dislodge the ruling minority. After the initial shock of surrender in 1945 and the social upheaval that followed, the former elect, in their usual deliberate and resolute manner, formed a solid phalanx that was quite adequate for confounding, dividing, and eventually emasculating many of the reformist organizations. Despite perfervid claims to the contrary, Japan never became "free" in the Western sense, and the electorate remained subject to the will of a tiny minority whose power was based upon wealth and its claim to legitimacy upon a mythos of democracy supplied by the conquerors, replacing belief in the divinity of the emperor.

In order to maintain the image of an open society becoming to a new member of the "Free World," and yet to elude democracy's restraints, members of the postwar establishment ordinarily conducted their internal affairs and resolved their differences with utmost discretion. One does run across frequent exposés of venality in high places, but, unfortunately, those most eager to tell the "inside story" are outsiders whose sources are limited to hearsay; and the insiders, of course, tailor the facts to fit their personal or class interests. Among the former insiders, very few have granted the general public more than a tantalizing glimpse of what went on behind the scenes at critical moments. The most knowledgeable Mitsui people, for example, are still secretive about past political maneuvers, perhaps because such revelations would shed too much light on the group's present methods of operating or its confidential relationships with persons still living.

It would be reasonable, in this sense, to call Japan's dominant postwar cliques a new bakufu. The term literally means "tent government"; but the ideograph for tent also means curtain, so that the free translation "behind-the-curtain government" seems as appropriate today as in the Tokugawa period. However, Japan's new democratic constitution has the inestimable advantage of protecting freedom of speech and of the press, and because legal punishment can no longer be meted out for lese majesty or "dangerous thought," quite a few conscientious journalists, scholars, and even renegade executives have provided materials from which foreign observers can piece together a relatively coherent, if incomplete, diagram of Japan's postwar power structure as it reached maturity and survived its severest trials at the end of the 1950s.

The essence of "behind-the-curtain" rule anywhere is mutual trust among the participants. In Japan personal loyalties—based upon a great variety of common experiences, interests, beliefs, or purely accidental contacts—are often as vital as money, lineage, position, or prestige in deciding the outcome of important negotiations. Among the culture media in which such affinities developed into power foci, before and after the war, were clubs whose ostensible purpose was social but whose function was often quasi governmental. Some had their own quarters, and others held meetings in teahouses, exclusive restaurants, or private dining rooms of hotels.

In the larger groupings members of the various cliques could meet on neutral ground. Such a center was the Industry Club, housed in an inconspicuous rust-colored brick building across the square from Tokyo Station in the Marunouchi financial district. During the occupation this club was one of the few places in which purged zaibatsu chieftains were permitted to meet informally with their colleagues, as well as with the active leaders of the enterprises they had once owned.

The director-general of this GHQ of big business was Miyajima Seijiro, chairman of the nonzaibatsu Nisshin Spinning Company and acknowledged *doyen* of the business world. Among the members of his inner circle were Mitsui's Mukai Tadaharu and Mitsubishi's Kato Takeo, who even in exile from their companies were dominant figures in their respective groups. These three, with Shirasu Jiro, had been premier Yoshida's earliest financial backers and advisers. Once a month these gentlemen, with a few dozen economic leaders, purged or otherwise, assembled at the Industry Club for luncheon and a discussion of of public affairs. The membership of the group, called Mikka-kai (Third-of-the-Month Club), included such heavyweights as former aircraft tycoon Nakajima Kumakichi; former finance minister Shibusawa Keizo of the Dai-Ichi Bank combine; Asano Ryozo, representing the Asano zaibatsu; Sumitomo's genro Okahashi Shigeru; Goko Kiyoshi, who was assiduously rebuilding the fragmented Mitsubishi Heavy Industries; ex-president Adachi Tadashi of Oji Paper; and Toshiba's Ishizaka Taizo, a future president of the Industry Club.

Having heard that this group had had a significant influence on Japan's postwar development, the author asked Mukai about it recently. The ensuing dialogue is reproduced here verbatim.

Mukai: "Mikka-kai was nothing much, just a meeting of people who were purged. There was no purpose to that meeting."

J.R.: "But when you get a group of important people together they naturally talk about important things."

Mukai: "No. Besides, we were rather old people and we were not in touch with important matters."

Nevertheless, several top leaders of the new Japan were drawn from this "purposeless" club, where various matters of the highest importance were indeed discussed, often to the point of consensus. Parenthetically, Mitsui Hachiroemon, who was a member of the Industry Club and would have been welcomed by Mikka-kai, never attended; and of the prewar Industry Club members young enough to take an active part in national affairs, he was one of the very few who failed to make a comeback.

Pressing the matter further, the author asked Mukai: "People see that Japan has taken a course very close to the prewar pattern. The [zaibatsu] groups are in about the same relative positions and of about the same relative sizes as before, and some people think there must have been some kind of a plan that was made up early in the occupation and carried out secretly. I can't find any evidence of that, but . . ."

"No, that isn't true."

"But how did it happen? Why did Japan come back into the same shape as before, even though many efforts were made to change it?"

"Very fortunate," Mukai replied. "I think it was the good sense of the men in power."

"Whom do you regard as the most effective, the most important leaders in postwar Japan?"

"Hmmm."

Most Mitsui leaders, like Mukai, were uncommunicative concerning the formation of the postwar power structure, but from other sources, including foreign Japanologists and Japanese scholars and journalists of liberal or antiestablishment tendencies, it is possible to sketch in some of the outlines. Such an investigation leads inevitably to other "social" clubs of a more or less intimate nature, the centers of so-called *machiai* (teahouse) politics indispensable to Japan's real governing process.

One such club was the Shigure-kai named after the posh Shigure teahouse at which meetings were held. It was organized by the Industry Club's chief, Miyajima, and Uemura Kogoro, wartime president of the Japan Economic Federation and now president of Keidanren (Federation of Economic Organizations), to promote liaison between active business leaders and those who had been purged. Among the former were company presidents Kobayashi Ataru (Ishizaka's successor as chairman of the Arabian Oil Company), Nagano Shigeo (chairman of Nippon Steel), Asao Shinsuke (erstwhile chairman of Mitsubishi's NYK Lines), and other top-level economic leaders. This obscure club was influential enough to get one of its members, Ichimada Naoto, installed as governor of the Bank of Japan, of which Miyajima was a policy-board member.

Miyajima's successor as chief of financial circles was Kobayashi Ataru, a protean entrepreneur who had been a disciple of Go Seinosuke (the central figure in the prewar Teijin scandal) and who had spent some years in prison because of his implication in that affair. Kobayashi, also a protégé of Mitsui's Fujihara Ginjiro, inherited the leadership of Go's Bancho-kai, described earlier, and perpetuated it in the Kayokai, or Tuesday Club (one of several with this name), whose members, all prominent businessmen, formed a kind of suprapolitical policy board handling decisions of greatest moment, both domestic and international. This "New Bancho-kai" is credited with having engineered the reappointment of Prime Minister Yoshida in 1952, the merger of the two conservative parties in 1955, the selection of Prime Minister Kishi Nobusuke in 1957, and of his successor Ikeda Hayato in 1960.

The rise of Kobayashi had been propelled by his fellow members in a club called Nikokukai, all of whom were born in the Year of the Wild Boar. (In Japan, as in most of the Orient, each year is designated by the name of an animal, in a twelve-year cycle; and those people who are born under the same sign are believed to have traits in common.) Among these "wild boars" were finance minister Ikeda Hayato and Shirasu Jiro, both of whom were particularly close to Prime Minister Yoshida. At one club meeting Shirasu buttonholed Ikeda and proposed Kobayashi for the extremely important presidency of the Japan Development Bank, which was then being established under the orders of SCAP. Ikeda transmitted the recommendation to Yoshida, who consulted Mukai Tadaharu.

"What is this Kobayashi?" Yoshida asked. He learned from Mukai that Kobayashi was a former banker, securities expert, and head of a fantastically profitable life insurance firm that had specialized in policies for men drafted into the imperial armed forces. Being of nonzaibatsu background and conspicuously pro-American, he was acceptable to the occupation authorities. Yoshida endorsed the appointment, and Kobayashi, as the shrewd and forceful president of Development Bank, became custodian of the U. S. Aid Counterpart Fund, which at its termination in 1953, had amassed more than $800 million from the sale of U. S. aid commodities. It was by means of this reservoir of industrial funds that he extended his influence into every sector of Japanese business.

Although closely connected with nonzaibatsu and new-zaibatsu elements, Kobayashi recognized the political necessity of joint action to restore the status quo ante, and did much to form a unified *zaikai,* or financial community, in which the old zaibatsu were fairly represented. One means of doing so was an association of business tycoons born in mountainous Yamanashi Prefecture, his birthplace. Though poor in natural resources, this region of central Honshu produced some of Japan's leading financiers, who joined forces to form what is known as the Koshubatsu, or Yamanashi clique. One of the smaller groupings of the Koshubatsu was the Sanshinkai, also known as the Yamazarukai, or Mountain Monkey Club. Among its score of members, all business potentates, were Kobayashi, Mizukami of Mitsui Bussan, vice-president Iwashita Fumio of Toshiba, and distinguished representatives of the Mitsubishi, Sumitomo, Yasuda (now Fuji Bank), and Showa Denko combines.

The nucleus of the Kobayashi clique, a group known as Shi Tenno, "The Four Heavenly Kings" of finance,* kept Yoshida in power by

* The other "kings" were Sakurada Takeshi, Nagano Shigeo, and Mizuno Shigeo. All of them, including Kobayashi, were nonzaibatsu corporation managers noted for their toughness in handling organized labor.

mobilizing funds for conservative-faction leaders supporting him and also served as one of his brain trusts. When it became clear that the premier had outlived his usefulness (after a national furor surrounding the so-called shipbuilding scandal involving the alleged bribery of several cabinet ministers, including Sato Eisaku), the same group of zaikai leaders forced Yoshida to resign and replaced him with Kishi Nobusuke, former economic czar of Manchukuo and architect of Japan's wartime economy. Nevertheless, Yoshida, because of his prestige and influence with American leaders, remained a power behind the scenes. Whenever Yoshida "came up to Tokyo" he was entertained by an association centered around his disciples Ikeda Hayato and Sato Eisaku, both of whom in time became prime ministers. Among the leading members of that nameless association were Kishi, Kobayashi Ataru, Ishizaka Taizo, Sato Kiichiro, and Niizeki Yasutaro. Obviously, Kishi had long since settled his differences with the zaibatsu whom he had once harrassed.

After the deaths of Yoshida and Ikeda in the 1960s the same club focused its attention on Prime Minister Sato. Also paying tribute to Sato was a group comprising the top executives of fourteen Mitsui companies, who even since his resignation in 1972 continue to meet with him socially, not merely as a matter of giri but because he is still a leader in the ruling Liberal-Democratic Party.

Through another informal club, Mitsui-group executives maintain close relations with former prime minister Kishi Nobusuke, Sato's blood brother, who is still a power in the Liberal-Democratic Party and is its most influential liaison with the strong men of Taiwan, South Korea, and Southeast Asian countries in which Mitsui's overseas investments are concentrated.

As a commentary on Japan's "web society," it is of some interest to note that Kishi and Sato (both Choshu men, by the way) were related to Yoshida by marriage, and that these three men headed ten out of twenty postwar cabinets that held power for eighteen of the twenty-six years between 1946 and 1972, when the Yoshida-Choshu machine was defeated by Tanaka Kakuei. The premiership went to Tanaka not because he was more popular than Sato but because his supporting clubs were able to raise more money for influencing the party's election. (In practice the president of the majority party in the Diet becomes prime minister automatically.) Seen in this context, the perpetuation of the zaikai clubs is obviously a necessity of business rather than a social pastime. Although the House of Mitsui's constitution is dead, its precept about placating the "honorable men in power" is as alive as ever for the business community.

The continuity of the zaibatsu tradition in Japanese business is strikingly illustrated in the choice of a locale for Mitsui's "machiai politics." High-ranking guests are often entertained at an inconspicuous teahouse, the Yamaguchi, near the Kabuki theater in the Shimbashi area of Tokyo. (The name has a certain significance, for the stamping-ground of the Choshu clan, so important to Mitsui's development, was called Yamaguchi Prefecture after the abolition of feudalism.) The proprietress, Shirai Kuni, has been in business for more than seventy years, and her teahouse has been the favorite haunt of Mitsui men since the days of Yamamoto Jotaro, an enthusiastic patron of geisha. Born in Kyoto in the ninth year of Meiji (1876), Kuni studied dancing and shamisen as a child. Though not trained as a geisha, she was a talented hostess, and after being widowed in her youth, she went to work at the Osaka teahouse Kagairo, which was frequented by such Choshu loyalist leaders as Ito Hirobumi, Inoue Kaoru, and Yamagata Aritomo. Later, she went up to Tokyo and worked at the Yamaguchi, patronized by the same clientele, and eventually became its owner.

Shirai-san, bright and spry at the age of ninety-six, still attends her guests personally and operates the business, now a corporation, besides. She has known the most distinguished statesmen and financial leaders of modern Japan, and not a few of them were her close friends and confidants. Among those she mentions as having disported themselves at geisha parties in the Yamaguchi are nearly all of Japan's prime ministers and several princes and admirals—but relatively few army leaders, Mitsubishi men, or Minseito politicians, who frequented other houses. Concerning this peculiarity of machiai protocol, Hadley wrote: "Tea houses and the social restaurants of Shimbashi, Yanagibashi and Akasaka areas in Tokyo were divided between Mitsui and Mitsubishi. Where Mitsui men went, Mitsubishi men would not go or invite their guests and customers. High class *geisha* could not be shared between Mitsui and Mitsubishi men."[1]

Having mingled so intimately with the great, Shirai-san should have some fascinating stories to tell. Perhaps she has, but people in her line of business are noted for their discretion. When the author asked about Prince Ito she replied: "Ito Hirobumi? He was a quiet man. The geisha liked him very well." And about his dearest friend: "Inoue often came here. He was very kind to geisha. Maruko, one year younger than I— she has died already—was his mistress. But there was no offspring between the two." Other regulars she remembers well were Masuda Takashi, Ikeda Seihin, Dan Takuma, and Mukai Tadaharu, all Mitsui obanto in their respective eras. Mitsui Hachiroemon Takamine attended parties only occasionally, and his heir Takakimi quite rarely.

"He has been here," Shirai says unenthusiastically, "but when it came to playing, he lacked something."

One of her closest friends was Yoshida Shigeru, who had patronized her establishment for half a century and was like a member of her family. "He called me *Baba* [auntie]," Shirai-san recalls. Yoshida's wife Yukiko, granddaughter of the Meiji statesman Okubo Toshimichi, was a devout Roman Catholic, and rather prudish. His former aides say that he went to the teahouse when he wanted to relax and "be himself." After he became a widower, in 1938, he had little home life and spent his free time at the Yamaguchi. "He knew many geisha," Shirai says, "but his desire was rather light. He was very angry when I sent indecent geisha to him." He had three favorites, all of them famous, but he eventually settled on a retired geisha called Korin (her real name is Sakamoto Kiyo), who was introduced to him by Shirai-san and became his common-law wife in his old age. "It was not that they were in love, but the circumstances of the time brought them together," she explained.

When Yoshida was arrested by the Kempeitai as a "peace conspirator" toward the end of the war, he was kept in prison for forty days. Upon his release, instead of returning to his cheerless home he visited Shirai. "He had on something like prisoner's clothes," she remembers. She thought he was a fugitive but took him in anyway, bathed him, and dressed him in her late father's kimono. "I let him try on father's *tabi* [Japanese split-toed socks] and they were just right for him." Later, as prime minister, he used to wear white tabi, which with his kimono and pince nez, became a kind of trademark.

What was discussed by the businessmen and their political cronies at the Yamaguchi and dozens of other exclusive teahouses in the Shimbashi and Akasaka pleasure quarters is not for outsiders to know. When the time came to talk seriously, the geisha were sent away in their rickshas (usually a few of them are lined up near the Yamaguchi even today), and the hostesses would not enter without announcing their presence discreetly. But it is known that in the late 1950s the subjects of greatest concern were the resurgent labor movement, rearmament, and the impending renewal of the ten-year Mutual Security Treaty with the United States that had been signed in 1951. These were the issues that led to Japan's severest postoccupation crisis, culminating in the strikes, terrorism, and massive street demonstrations at the beginning of the 1960s.

The most dramatic and violent episodes in the postwar labor movement swirled around enterprises connected with the reviving Mitsui group. Mitsui was the logical target of the unions because it was one of the most powerful concerns and symbolized the economic exploitation and political corruption of the prewar period. It was also one of the most paternalistic concerns, and when modernization of the industrial structure called for mass dismissals of workers the reaction was one of unprecedented resistance. Among the companies hardest hit were Toshiba, Mitsui Chemical, Oji Paper, and Japan Steel Works. But of all the labor struggles in Japanese history the lockout and strike at the Mitsui's Miike coal mines in 1960 was the most significant, politically as well as economically.

The origin of the postwar mining strikes lay in the competition between coal and petroleum. According to President Kurata Okito of Mitsui Mining, sporadic strikes in the industry, beginning under the occupation, and the dumping of petroleum in Japan by foreign producing and exporting companies, made liquid fuel cheaper than solid and accelerated the decline of coal mining. The government, however, had the responsibility of making the best use of coal, Japan's most plentiful natural resource. "In 1959, [the government] decided that within five years the unit price of coal should be reduced by 1,200 yen per ton compared with that of 1958. The entire coal-mining industry exerted efforts in this direction. But rationalization provoked more and more strikes. The most famous, that of our Miike Colliery in 1960–61, lasted nearly 300 days. This was the result of cutting down the number of workers and increasing efficiency to reduce the price. But [meanwhile] the price of oil declined further, so we were not able to catch up.

"After the war," Kurata continued, "the so-called labor unions were formed; furthermore, the mayor of Omuta City and the governor of Fukuoka Prefecture, where most of our facilities were located, were Socialists. Maybe somebody gave the union instructions that they should achieve their objectives by force, even by the use of violence. At the time, the governor and mayor were backing socialist ideas, and Professor Sakisaka Ichiro of Kyushu University, a typical Marxist, also became involved. Such people came to Miike to preach Marxism and trained the workers very strictly. Workers were told not to worry about strikes. Even if the company should go broke, the coal would still remain, they said. And as long as the coal existed, someone would operate the mines. Professor Sakisaka insisted that our capitalistic system would be abolished in a few years, and that the strike was a frontier battle before the real revolution."[2]

The workers of Mitsui Mining were receptive to such indoctrination and formed a strong union, which affiliated with the left-wing Tanro (Japan Coal Mine Workers Union) and took part in the nationwide campaign for higher wages and against dismissals. At the end of the

Korean war, a time of recession, Mining's management attempted to solve its problems by a mass layoff, provoking a strike that lasted 114 days and cost the company more than four billion yen. The miners won, and the company's president, Yamakawa Ryoichi, was forced to resign.

The conflict between miners and management was not confined to Omuta. The entire coal mining industry was affected by the government-subsidized rationalization plan. Industrial leaders had announced their intention of eventually dismissing more than 100,000 miners, and by the end of the 1950s unemployment in the coalfields was already widespread. This program was, of course, a radical departure from the lifetime employment system by which Japanese entrepreneurs justified low wages, and it aroused fear in other sectors of organized labor. "Rationalization" was taken up as a major issue by the communist-led workers, and by the moderately left-wing Sohyo (General Council of Trade Unions), whose 3,600,000 members formed the backbone of the Socialist Party.

At Miike, Mitsui Mining's new president, Kuriki Kan, had announced a retrenchment program calling for the "voluntary retirement" of 6,560 workers and offering certain benefits, but only 1,670 workers responded. In August 1959 Kuriki presented a second program for dismissing five thousand workers, with the warning that even if violence should erupt he was determined to carry out the plan to the end. The union was stubbornly opposed, holding that it was the company's responsibility to provide employment and that if it was unable to operate profitably the mines should be nationalized. They also pointed out that although productivity had already risen significantly since the war the benefits had accrued almost entirely to the employers. Wages, less than fifty dollars a month as compared with the national average of sixty-two dollars, had risen much more slowly than productivity, and management had appropriated the surplus so obtained to invest in equipment that was now eliminating jobs. Additional amounts needed for rationalization were provided by the government or special banks. Mitsui Mining, for example, obtained nearly $100 million in outright subsidies or low-interest, long-term loans from the Industrial Bank of Japan during the 1960s. Thus the heaviest burden of the "energy revolution" was to be borne by the miners.

Left-wing theoreticians argued that the rationalization plan had been forced on Japan by United States interests, who saw Japan as the most promising outlet for their surplus oil. The best customers for coal were the nine regional electric power companies that had been established after the breakup of the government's monopoly. It was in these companies that American bankers, including those dominating the petroleum industry, had concentrated their postwar loans; and it was believed that their strategy was to reduce the price of coal as a first step and then to influence the power companies gradually to substitute oil for coal, regardless of the effect this would have on Japanese miners.

Attempts at compromise failed, partly because the company was adhering to a policy reached at the highest levels of government, and because the Central Labor Relations Council arbitrating the dispute merely echoed proposals made by the government and management. The combative President Kuriki selected more than a thousand men to be discharged at once. The union curtly rejected the dismissal and the company retaliated with a lockout, starting on January 25, 1960, that caused severe hardship among the families of miners, many of whom had been part of the Mitsui "family" for generations. This action was a shocking deviation from the Mitsuis' traditional paternalism. On the other hand, it demonstrated political continuity of a sort, since Prime Minister Kishi's labor minister handling the Miike problem was Matsuno Raizo, grandson of Mitsui's famous "labor expert" and political representative Noda Utaro. (At the time Raizo's father, Matsuno Tsuruhei [Noda's son-in-law], was speaker of the upper house, of which Noda's son Shunsaku was also a member. And Shunsaku's younger brother Hidesuke was executive director of Mitsui Shipbuilding & Engineering.)

The lot of unemployed and striking miners at Omuta that winter was miserable beyond endurance. Most of them lived in company houses, squalid barracks that were said to be collapsing from neglect. In houses of nonworking miners, water and power supplies were cut off. Dwellers had to use muddy water from abandoned wells, and after dark they lived by candlelight. The union dole was pitifully inadequate, and most families could afford only one or two meals a day. Since rice was too expensive, they subsisted on coarse grains, flour, sweet potatoes, and pumpkins. Many children were suffering from malnutrition and dietary deficiency diseases. Mothers were unable to nurse their babies because of undernourishment. Destitute families stayed in bed during the day (often huddled under the one blanket that remained after everything else had been pawned) to conserve their strength. An *Asahi Shimbun* editorialist wrote: ". . . the men looked like walking shadows. . . . It is reported that if one goes into these miners' homes, where the sky can be seen through holes in the roof, one finds many certificates framed on the wall commending them for increased production."[3]

One reason for the intransigence of the miners was that the company was using "rationalization" as a pretext for discharging several hundred of the most militant union organizers. The policy of the company had always been extremely oppressive toward unionism and political radicalism and, as has been told, gangsters and bullies of the "patriotic" societies had been used to intimidate or remove antimanagement elements. After the war the company became even more vigilant, and established hiring criteria under which anyone even suspected of being left-of-center or of being involved in antigovernment or anticompany activity of any kind whatever was considered ineligible for digging coal.

Obviously, such idealistic personnel criteria were unworkable in the new Japan, where more than one-third of the voters were sympathetic toward socialism or communism. In Omuta, if one can believe the management, the union was infested with communists and fellow travelers who had slipped through the company's dragnet. Whether "red" or not, a large majority of the miners supported the union despite the hardships involved and remained adamant. Since the labor retrenchment policy was being grudgingly accepted by the workers at most of the nation's coal mines, the Miike struggle was regarded as the last stand of the holdouts defending the principle of industrywide unionism. Thus the strikers received both moral and financial support from Tanro, the coal miners' federation, and also from Sohyo, some independent unions, and the left-wing political parties. Management, likewise, was guaranteed by other Mitsui companies against losses and enjoyed tacit government approval as well as full backing by the foremost economic organizations led by Ishizaka, Adachi, and other Mitsui allies.

The standard strategy for handling leftist labor organizations was to form conservative "second unions" under company sponsorship, splitting off the promanagement elements and gradually recruiting waverers by persuasion or coercion. As labor expert Kurata put it: "Marxist groups are being formed, and we cannot fight them back by telling each one not to join [the leftist union]. We have to organize counter-Marxist groups. That is the meaning of the second union."[4]

Acting on the reliable "fight-fire-with-fire" theory, Kurata hired as his "counter-Marxists" a few old-time communists who had been thoroughly brainwashed in prewar prisons by the thought-control police and emerged as very effective anticommunist propagandists and manipulators of labor. One of them, the late Mitamura Shiro, was a very sharp theoretician and teacher. Before and during the war he had served ably in swinging organized workers behind the patriotic labor front and afterward founded Mitamura Gakko, a school for training rightist labor bosses. Such experts, hired by companies with personnel problems, then established promanagement groups called *shokuba boeitai,* or organizations to defend workshops.

Another professional anticommunist was Nabeyama Sadachika, a member of the JCP central committee in the 1920s, who recanted in prison and became a spy for Japan's military forces in China. After the war he cashed in on his outdated knowledge of the communist movement as an informer for the G-2 Section of SCAP and as a union-buster for corporations troubled with left-wing labor movements. Although active in organizing ultranationalists, he was equally alert for opportunities on the other side of the street and worked successfully with right-wing socialists to split the party. Like several of his fellow renegades, he was engaged in propaganda and organizational work in support of the Chiang regime on Taiwan.

A labor expert of similar background was Tanaka Seigen, who after renouncing communism in prison during the early 1930s, became a follower of the notorious Inoue Nissho, leader of the Ketsumeidan (Blood Pledge Corps), which had engineered the assassination of Mitsui chieftain Dan Takuma in 1932. After the war, Tanaka's specialty was recruiting and disciplining labor crews for construction companies.

For organizing the "second union" at Miike, however, a man of greater prestige and charisma was needed. The one who seemed best qualified was Sagoya Yoshiaki, who as a youth had won fame by shooting Prime Minister Hamaguchi in 1930. At the time, Sagoya had been a member of a patriotic society believed to be sponsored by Mitsui's mystery man, Mori Kaku. Perhaps because of the high connections of those who had instigated the crime, Sagoya's sojourn in prison was brief, and he lived comfortably on the bounty of his admirers. After the war and the SCAP purge he became chief of the Gokokudan (National Protection Corps), founded by the Reverend Inoue as a revival of the Blood Pledge Corps. The new organization was a melting pot of ultranationalist zealots, terrorists, labor bosses, and ordinary thugs. Among its most distinguished members were the assassin of finance minister Inoue Junnosuke, an accomplice in the assassination of Prime Minister Inukai Tsuyoshi, and the gunman who had once been assigned to kill Ikeda Seihin. Sagoya, who died in 1972 while being investigated for his role in an extortion plot, was a kind of living saint among the rightists, and served as chairman of a federation of nationalistic action groups during the coalfield strikes. Such groups were also effective in the subsequent rollback of the left-wing labor movement.

These patriots were not working on their own, however. Behind them was a cabal that has kept its movements even better concealed than those of the zaikai whose interests it served. The importance of men like Toyama Mitsuru and Uchida Ryohei to the prewar zaibatsu has been described at some length. Since the postwar structure remained so similar to that of prewar zaibatsu regime, it is reasonable to assume that the counterparts of those two bosses, if not their direct legatees, remained somewhere in the background to perform their familiar functions.

As a matter of fact, there are numerous organizations, still extant, descended directly from the Black Dragon Society. For example, Toyama's son Hidezo founded the Society for Heavenly Action, which gave refuge to the Reverend Inoue after his henchman killed Baron Dan. Hidezo was killed in an automobile crash in 1952, but his organization lived on as the National Martyr Youth Corps, which was active at Omuta during the miners' strike and also in the struggles over the security treaty.

Uchida himself founded the Great Japan Production Party, which made its postwar comeback as the Anti-Bolshevik Corps composed of antiunion terrorists. One of its members was arrested in an alleged assassination attempt on Prime Minister Yoshida, and the organization was also conspicuous in the 1960 labor disturbances. Nevertheless, the bosses of such gangs were by no means the top leaders of the ultra-rightist forces. They were comparable to field-grade officers and took their orders from a general staff that included the well-known Kodama Yoshio and the rather obscure, but perhaps more powerful, Miura Giichi. Like their preceptors Toyama and Uchida, these two men were never visible at scenes of disorder and violence, which to them were merely like pins on a strategist's map. Their role, not unfamiliar in other societies, was that of liaison men between the legitimate establishment and the underworld, which work together so harmoniously in "modern" Japan.

Kodama's clandestine activities in China on behalf of the navy, and his huge financial contribution to the Minseito political faction after the war, have been described. His postwar career was temporarily interrupted by his incarceration as a "Class A" war-crimes suspect, along with Kishi Nobusuke, Hoshino Naoki, and a few score other prewar civilian and military leaders. Such propinquity gave him a splendid opportunity to forge ties of friendship and loyalty with a number of prewar imperialists who reached the top rung of the political ladder after their release.

Allegedly the paymaster of the right wing and channel of unregistered funds from big business and the underworld to politicians, Kodama seemed to know nearly everyone of importance in Japan. Among his closest friends were Kishi and Hagiwara Kichitaro, a former Mitsui Honsha executive who became president of the concern's subsidiary, Hokkaido Colliery & Steamship Company. The firm, which was a big contributor to Kishi's faction in the Tory party, was remarkably free from labor strife, and unlike other collieries, racked up big profits in the 1950s. The extent to which this good fortune was attributable to Kodama's help is a matter of conjecture.[5]

Nevertheless, there is a body of opinion that the kingpin of the professional nationalists was the late Miura Giichi, who wielded considerable influence in financial circles and was particularly close to Ichimada Naoto, governor of the Bank of Japan, as well as to Sato Eisaku, Kishi, and key industrialists in the employers' organizations. In the 1930s Miura was connected with Uchida's Great Japan Production Party, but branched off to form the National Policy Association, which in turn became the Great East Institute. This last organization became famous at the time of Japan's surrender, when fourteen of its members committed suicide together near the Meiji Shrine in Tokyo. Miura, a scholar and poet of note, was especially admired by General Tojo Hideki for his devotion to the emperor and his limpid interpretation of national polity based upon the imperial system.

Perhaps by virtue of his wide acquaintance among rightists and his knowledge of leftist movements, he quickly ingratiated himself with General Willoughby of GHQ and somehow escaped the purge. This circumstance proved an invaluable asset, which he used on behalf of the electric-power monopoly, then slated for dissolution. Having developed a close relationship with Sasayama of the Holding Company Liquidation Commission, he was in a position to provide inside information about dissolution policies and to inform his "clients," among whom Mitsui companies were important. Although Kodama and Miura had supported opposing factions of the conservative party, they worked together for the reestablishment of the old order and served as advisers to many ultranationalist organizations—including those mentioned above—and unified the rightist movement to counter the antitreaty and left-wing labor forces.

Two months after the Miike strike began, a most prestigious ally of the conservative establishment appeared in the person of West Germany's Chancellor Konrad Adenauer, who had come to Japan as a state guest of Prime Minister Kishi. His advent, in the wake of visits by munitions czar Alfried Krupp von Bohlen and economic minister Ludwig Erhard, had been intended mainly to promote business relations between Japan and West Germany—the Krupp companies, for example, had technical tie-ups with Mitsui Shipbuilding & Engineering, Japan Steel Works, and Sumitomo Machinery, while Siemens-Schuckert was the biggest stockholder in Fuji Electric of the Dai-Ichi Bank group—but the political overtones of the event were immediately apparent. For among those welcoming Adenauer's party at the airport were members of a fourteen-nation "international force," including a contingent of nattily uniformed German miners, then on a good-will tour of Japan under the auspices of Moral Rearmament. Since both Adenauer and Kishi were ardent exponents of Buchmanism, and proclaimed it as the only route to national salvation, the timing of the occasion seems to. have had more than economic or diplomatic significance.

The chancellor, addressing a joint session of the upper and lower houses of the Diet, declared that Japan and Germany, both in the front line of an international battle against communism, should fight it with spiritual weapons. "It may take years and even decades for the spiritual battle by free nations to succeed, but it is a battle that must be carried out," he said.

One goal of Adenauer's Wagnerian struggle was indicated clearly by the Speaker of the Lower House, Kiyose Ichiro, in an address to the "international force" tracing the chancellor's close connections with MRA. In 1948 West Germany, like Japan, had been wracked with agonizing labor problems, he explained. It was then that Adenauer had invited the MRA movement to work in the Ruhr, the German equivalent of coal-rich Fukuoka Prefecture. Within four years, Kiyose said, the proportion of communist workers' councils had dropped from seventy-three percent to eight percent of the total. And now the MRA team had come to help Japan perform the same miracle. One of the means to this happy end was an anticommunist morality play called *Hoffnung,* or "Hope." The troupe of Ruhr miners, trained by MRA instructors, was then on a world tour with the international force, staging that homespun melodrama for the edification of fellow workers ensnared in the toils of radicalism.

The message of Buchmanism was that social strife and war must be abolished by entrusting man's destiny to a God-guided elite, who qualify for leadership by "absolute honesty, absolute purity, absolute unselfishness, and absolute love." It seemed to be taken for granted that capitalists and their allies were better equipped than anticapitalists for attaining these absolutes. Accordingly, Buchman, a former Lutheran preacher and YMCA secretary, had spent his later years cultivating the rich, whose way of life he reproduced in luxurious MRA centers at Caux, Mackinac Island, Berkeley Square, Westchester County, and Tokyo, to name a few. When questioned by other Christians about his penchant for opulence, he would answer with a question: "Isn't God a millionaire?"[6]

Through his personal magnetism and promises of simple, dramatic solutions to knotty world problems, he attracted the financial patronage of plutocrats, glowing testimonials from the powerful and famous, and eloquent (but suspiciously standardized) verbal support from "converted" communists, labor and student leaders, Mau Mau chiefs, play-boys, and war criminals. Among those advertised as star pupils of his Moral Rearmament crusade, a kind of ecumenical Sunday-school-cum-confessional, were—in addition to Kishi and Adenauer—French political leader Robert Schuman, Archbishop Makarios of Cyprus, Generalissimo Chiang Kai-shek of Taiwan, Premier U Nu of Burma, Kim Chong Pil of the South Korean CIA, and presidents Ramon Magsaysay of the Philippines and Ngo Dinh Diem of South Vietnam. (By a curious coincidence, the politicians with whom Buchman collaborated were, with few exceptions, those most favored by the United States Department of State, the Pentagon, and the Central Intelligence Agency.)

Deserving much of the credit for bringing the blessings of MRA to Japan was Buchman's devoted disciple Mitsui Takasumi, who through such activities had won recognition as an internationalist. Early in the Korean War he helped to organize an imposing around-the-world MRA mission of about eighty leaders from Japan's business, political, educational, labor, and youth circles (carefully screened by SCAP, of course), a number of whom attained high status after the end of the occupation. This junket was essentially the reintroduction of the Japanese into international society and also served to indoctrinate a broad-spectrum elite with the new spirit of Free Worldism then being propagated by the Big Brothers in Washington. It is doubtful that many of the participants—judging from their past and future behavior—had been motivated by piety, repentance, or moral fervor, but at that time the privilege of travel, especially at expense of others, was irresistibly appealing.[7]

In his old age Dr. Buchman (who had been a friend of the idealistic Viscount Shibusawa) visited Tokyo frequently, and at his stately residence he personally proselytized a considerable number of conservative leaders. Among them were four ex-premiers, a constellation of ministers from the Tojo cabinet onward, survivors of the Manchurian clique, a former Kwantung Army general heading the Japan Veterans League, and presidents of some leading banks and corporations. Buchman even recruited two prominent Socialists, former premier Katayama Tetsu and Diet-member Kato Shizue (the former Baroness Ishimoto), who had been so deeply shocked by her experiences at the Miike coal mines earlier in the century.

The attitude of MRA toward Japan was delineated in a message from the MRA conference in Caux to Prime Minister Kishi in the summer of 1959, when the miners' protests were approaching the boiling point. It read in part: "The whole world must choose between Moral Rearmament and Communism. Everybody knows that in Asia Communism seeks to tie the manpower resources of China with the industrial power of Japan in order to forge the weapon to destroy the liberty of Asia and the world."[8]

When the actor-miners from the Ruhr arrived in Japan (actually as an advance party for Dr. Adenauer, whose skill in public relations equaled that of Dr. Buchman himself), they were treated like state visitors. The president of Japan National Railways, one of Frank's disciples, put a private train at their disposal, and accompanied by distinguished sponsors, they toured Japan from end to end, staging their variety show in improvised theaters at mines, mills, and military installations for six weeks. It is said that they were received enthusiastically, even by the embattled miners at Omuta, who far from suspecting that their fighting spirit was being sapped by capitalist exploiters, insisted on contributing money to the MRA entertainers.

What practical effect the miners' theatricals had on Japanese workers is hard to judge, but when it was time for the Germans to say sayonara Prime Minister Kishi assured them: "You are giving moral backbone to the whole world. I wish to express my gratitude for the massive impact MRA has had on this nation during the past six weeks." A few months later, after the great upheaval of June 1960, he went much further: "But for Moral Re-Armament Japan would be under Communist control today," he stated, and later urged the necessity of making "the ideology of Moral Re-Armament the policy of the Japanese government and its people so that Japan could play its part in saving Asia from tyranny."

During the period of MRA's active existence in Japan, from the Korean War until the mid-1960s, some fifteen hundred Japanese students, elite workers, and intellectuals received training at Caux, mostly in what communists used to call "agitprop." Two musical plays were launched from Japan to make amends for the transgressions of the nation's radicals and were seen in many countries. Although the MRA movement languished a decade ago, after the deaths of Buchman and his understudy, Peter Howard, its spirit and some of its material assets live on in an international propaganda organization called "Up With People," sponsored by DeWitt Wallace of the *Reader's Digest,* the United States Travel Service, Pan American Airways, and assorted angels of international finance, including Mitsuis.

The Miike lockout of 15,000 miners began on January 25, 1960, but by the end of March the anti-Marxist "educators" and organizer Sagoya, assisted by the National Protection Corps and other right-wing terrorist groups, had recruited some 4,000 scabs who seceded from the existing Miike Coal Miners' Union (backed by Sohyo) and formed the

"Number Two Miike Coal Miners' Union," supported by the centrist Zenro federation. Because a head-on clash between the two Miike unions seemed imminent, the Central Labor Relations Council offered to mediate the dispute, but the Mitsui management still refused to consider any terms short of surrender by the strikers. Toward the end of March the company began smuggling nonstrikers into the mine compounds by various ruses in preparation for a showdown.

In an initial skirmish at dawn on March 28, fought with staves, clubs, iron pipes, and stones, strong-arm men in business suits smashed through picket lines, enabling hundreds of splinter unionists to force their way into the compounds. Some 1,500 police had been stationed in Omuta to "stand by for emergencies" but did not appear until the worst of the fighting was over and dozens of miners lay wounded. By noon, a management spokesman boasted, for psychological effect, that the company had enough men and supplies on hand to resume operations and would replenish them by helicopter if necessary. But as the lockout continued, only token amounts of coal were brought to the surface, and the Miike mines and plants remained besieged by more than ten thousand strikers and supporters. It was no longer a question of profits and wages only, but of the future of organized labor and perhaps even the nation's social structure.

A curious sidelight on management's divide-and-rule strategy was the fact that Sohyo, denounced by conservatives as procommunist, was itself a product of right-wing splitting. In the late 1940s, the dominant labor federation was the National Liaison Council of Japanese Trade Unions, affiliated with the Marxist-oriented World Federation of Trade Unions. In 1950, at the behest of General MacArthur, the Council was suppressed and its top executives were purged. In its place the anticommunist Sohyo was established under SCAP's supervision and soon swung over to the U. S.-sponsored International Confederation of Free Trade Unions. But as the "rationalization struggles" intensified, Sohyo's member unions moved leftward and forced their basically anticommunist leadership to do likewise.

Meanwhile, Japanese labor leaders were being wooed by their American counterparts. With American money provided by conservative unions, joint Japan-U. S. management organizations, corporation-funded institutes, and uplift groups such as MRA, hundreds of Japanese labor leaders had been airlifted to the United States, where with all expenses and even wages paid, they were intensively indoctrinated with the principles of nonpolitical unionism and labor-management cooperation. Predictably, when Sohyo remained intransigent, Japanese labor specialists (assisted by the AFL-CIO and the ICFTU) split off Sohyo's right wing and established the anticommunist Zenro (Japan

Trade Union Congress). It came as no surprise when, years later, both the AFL-CIO and ICFTU, as well as several other American labor organizations operating internationally, were exposed as having received millions of dollars from the CIA, or from foundations serving as conduits for CIA funds, specifically for the purpose of destroying militant unions.[9]

Such splitting was by no means confined to the labor movement. Since Sohyo was the bastion of the Socialist Party, the schism between Sohyo and Zenro was accompanied by a political split and the formation of the Democratic Socialist Party, comprising moderate or anti-Marxist factions. With the same end in view—that of strengthening the conservatives and weakening the radicals—funds from the great U. S. foundations were interwoven with those of government agencies, including the CIA, to form a close-meshed filter against the penetration of dangerous thought. Activities promoted directly or indirectly by such funding covered the whole range of political, economic, and social activities by Japanese of all classes and conditions. The United States Embassy, which had expanded from its commodious prewar quarters to occupy in addition the head office of the South Manchurian Railway Company and new apartment houses built on what was once the huge estate of Mitsui Hachiroemon, had to rent space in several other buildings to accommodate more than a thousand employees and attached personnel.

Benefiting from this tender concern for their ideological welfare were, in addition to labor unions, political parties and student associations, such organizations as women's clubs, language schools, Christian churches, publishers of books and periodicals, schools, universities, research institutes, cooperatives, and cultural groups. Converging on Japan in a steady stream were right-thinking scholars, teachers, evangelists, lecturers, advisers, organizers, investigators, linguists, industrialists, economists, journalists, actors, dancers, musicians, technicians, and physicians, selected both for their professional reputations and for the effect they might have on the political orientation of their Japanese counterparts. Most were probably sincere and innocent of ulterior motives, but seeded among them were ideological missionaries whose assignment was to identify left-wing radicalism and isolate it from the relatively unperturbed mainstream of Japanese life.

Supplementing this more or less overt activity were no less than ten United States intelligence agencies, military and civilian, operating in Japan. Since 1945 they had infiltrated virtually every organization of any possible political significance with their Japanese agents. Some of the latter, remaining at their posts over periods of many years, had become high officials of their respective groups, and few have been dislodged even to this day except by retirement or death. This curious and little-known phenomenon may account for some of the unpredictable, erratic, and idiotic if not suicidal policies adopted by Japanese left-wing organizations with depressing regularity.[10]

Taken as a whole, this joint operation to suppress the left wing was perhaps the most massive and certainly the most sophisticated machine for political sabotage ever set into motion, and whatever its net effect may have been, it was fervently welcomed by its beneficiaries—zaikai potentates and their right-wing political establishment. Nevertheless, the anticommunist splitting strategy failed in its intended effect on the student movement, in which right-wing sympathizers were vastly outnumbered by leftists. The dominant Zengakuren, the National Federation of Student Associations, remained under strong Marxist and anti-American influence and became a formidable if unpredictable political force. In the struggles that developed around the Miike mines, Zengakuren students swarmed to Omuta together with Sohyo men and women to confront right-wing extremists, organized gangsters, and promanagement workers brought in from other areas to support the second union. Massive demonstrations and rallies became almost daily events, and rioting was so common that the strike began to look like an incipient revolution. During the conflict Sohyo alone called in some 350,000 outside supporters, and the number of demonstrators may have exceeded a million if other unionists, students, and intellectuals are included. In response the besieged establishment mobilized 530,000 policemen in addition to local constabulary, company guards, and civilian strikebreakers, presumably equalling the opposition in numbers.*

Yet, awesome as it was, the Miike affair was overshadowed by developments on the national scene. The revision and renewal of Japan's military alliance with the United States was strongly opposed by labor, the leftist parties, and by a large segment of the general public preferring unarmed neutrality. Most Japanese were in favor of resuming diplomatic relations with China and opposed the Dulles "containment" policy pursued by Japan's Tories. The slogan of "peaceful coexistence" advocated by the Russians and Chinese was heard sympathetically, and the presence of hundreds of United States military bases and more than 100,000 troops in Japan, including Okinawa, was viewed as a nuisance as well as a deadly hazard in case Washington should get embroiled in a nuclear war with the Soviet Union. The fear of nuclear weapons, im-

---

* Both figures are taken from *JFEA News,* published by the Japan Federation of Employers Organizations, Tokyo, January 1961, page 2. These were obviously the cumulative totals of successive mobilizations, some of the participants having been mobilized repeatedly.

planted by the atomic bombings of Hiroshima and Nagasaki, had been amplified by the hydrogen-bomb tests at Bikini, which showered a number of Japanese fishermen with radioactive dust and aroused nationwide protests. The movement against nuclear-weapons production and testing attracted millions of otherwise nonpolitical participants, especially housewives, professional people, and religionists, and the "nuclear allergy" (as irritated businessmen called it) extended even to the atomic-power plants coveted by zaikai. Efforts of conservatives to revise the constitution, especially the no-war clause, and to pass repressive police laws, were also targets of mass protest by those who saw evidence that the well-preserved corpus of militarism was being resurrected.

Making political capital out of widespread pacifist sentiment, Sohyo had established the People's Council Against Revision of the U. S.-Japan Security Treaty, with the support of neutral unions, the Socialist Party, and the Communist Party. Blocking the extension of the treaty was made the main objective of the 1960 "spring labor struggle," a campaign staged annually by the federation to underline its wage demands. The formation of a united front on the left and the espousal of purely political causes in labor campaigns were especially alarming to big business.

In January 1960 Prime Minister Kishi had gone to Washington and signed the revised treaty, the ratification of which became the subject of a marathon debate in the lower house. The opposition's acrimonious attacks on the government's pro-American posture were aggravated by an announcement from Moscow that an American U-2 spy plane had been shot down over the Soviet Union, on the eve of a summit conference between President Eisenhower and Premier Khruschev. The opposition presented convincing evidence that U-2 planes based in Japan were also flying espionage missions over Chinese and Soviet territory and thereby intensified public anxiety over the menace of war. During his visit to Washington Kishi had invited President Eisenhower to visit Japan, and he was scheduled to arrive in June. But when Moscow withdrew its invitation to the American president there was widespread agitation, sponsored by the left wing and taken up by pacifists generally, to prevent his visit to Japan, as well.

These successive misfortunes put Kishi in a precarious situation. It was imperative to get the Security Treaty ratified before Eisenhower's visit on June 20. But under Japanese law, ratification would not become effective until thirty days after approval by the lower house. Facing opposition not only from the leftists but from adversaries in their own party as well, Kishi's team resorted to outrageous trickery and force to ram the treaty through the lower house on May 20.

Kishi's flouting of constitutional government and contempt for public opinion, which was turning ever more strongly against him and the treaty, unleashed national pandemonium and drew into the mass movement even middle-of-the-road civic and labor organizations with millions of members. Professors, artists, religious leaders, and even some prominent businessmen joined the crusade, which now called for the cancellation of Eisenhower's visit and for the overthrow of Kishi's regime, as well as nullification of the treaty. The national press, which usually maintained an antigovernment posture anyway, became extraordinarily sympathetic to the movement. Several unions of government employees, legally forbidden to strike, did so illegally. Spokesmen for the resistance were getting an amazing response from people all over Japan. On three separate occasions in June fifty industrial unions with some 800,000 members staged the biggest political strikes in Japanese history, and the rallies and demonstrations in Tokyo became the focus of worldwide attention. When no such event was scheduled in the capital or other big cities, student demonstrators (who were having the time of their lives) would go down to Omuta—in squads or by the hundreds—to scuffle with the police and strikebreakers as a demonstration of their solidarity with the Miike struggle, which had become a national symbol.

The Eisenhower visit was to be a milestone in Japan's postwar resurgence, and was anticipated longingly by Japanese businessmen who saw it as heralding a new era of cooperation, expanded trade, and foreign investment in Japan. Hanging in the balance were World Bank loans on the order of $100 million for the development of basic industry, transportation, and communications. The Washington Export-Import Bank was expected to grant a forty-million-dollar loan for the purchase of raw cotton, a major share of which would be handled by Mitsui and Toyo Menka. Japan's Arabian Oil Company (of which Ishizaka and Kobayashi Ataru were principal promoters) was seeking $100 million to develop its wells in Kuwait, and numerous industrial firms were dickering for loans or the floating of bonds with private institutions in Wall Street. Also pending was Japan's two-billion-dollar debt for postwar aid, and the United States was in a position either to demand repayment in full or to reduce the amount drastically.

Needed as desperately as capital was technology. All the zaibatsu groups were avid for patents, technics, and equipment for developing electronic computers, nuclear energy, and petrochemicals, to which the United States held the key. The American market was equally indispensable, for without it the steel, automobile, electrical machinery, and synthetic textile industries, which had been expanding their production facilities recklessly, would be plunged into a crisis of overproduction.

But with public disorders becoming uncontrollable American statesmen, bankers, and industrialists began to wonder whether the Kishi regime was worthy of their confidence. The prices of Japanese bonds dropped in the New York market, and pending issues had to be canceled. Loan negotiations faltered, and the prospects for getting advanced technology and direct investments dimmed. There were few overt threats from the American side, but it was perfectly clear to all concerned that if the Japanese government continued to blunder so badly the economic consequences could be severe and lasting.

As the crisis sharpened, the zaikai leaders, who had achieved such gratifying unity in the late 1950s, became uncertain, and rifts appeared. The tough-minded heads of the Federation of Employers Organizations were against a retreat of any kind, but Ishizaka of the Federation of Economic Organizations and Adachi Tadashi of the Chamber of Commerce and Industry were advising caution. For on June 2, fifteen hundred faculty members of sixty-six universities had formed the National Society of Scholars and Researchers for the Defense of Democracy to demand Kishi's immediate resignation. As the businessmen of the Mikka-kai met for lunch at the Industry Club the next day, seven hundred members of the Tokyo University faculty were petitioning for dissolution of the Diet, and a nationwide general strike was scheduled for the following day.

From then on the clamor for Kishi's resignation spread across the whole political spectrum, and the postponement of the presidential visit was advocated by many businessmen and conservative politicians. But Kishi, with all the obstinacy of his Choshu forebears, was determined to brazen it through. The president's visit was the last hope for his government's survival, and only punctual ratification could make it a success. Washington also feared cancellation of the visit, which would mean loss of face for Eisenhower as well as for Kishi and would also jeopardize the treaty, keystone of American Far East policy. Kishi, despite prophecies of catastrophe, assured the White House that everything would turn out all right, and Secretary of State Christian Herter had either to take his word for it or to permit the "communists" to bring down a friendly government.

Kishi's self-confidence was not mere bravado. Foreseeing this imbroglio over the treaty, he had started making preparations long before. In 1958, in consultation with the former chief of the thought control police and a former Metropolitan Police chief who had been home minister during the war, he established the New Japan Council in which right-wing businessmen and politicians concerned with law enforcement collaborated with behind-the-curtain bosses, such as

Miura and Kodama, to mobilize ultranationalist organizations of the nonviolent type for participation in mass actions.

Supplementing this "respectable" federation was assassin Sagoya's All-Japan Council of Patriotic Organizations, composed of terrorists and underworld elements of various shades. Members of the groups belonging to both councils had been trained for participation in a so-called Mass Mobilization for Greeting Ike, and an estimated 100,000 men stood ready to answer the call.

The extent of the "Mass Mobilization" was a matter of conjecture at the time, but its dimensions were later revealed by the boasting organizers themselves: Kodama Yoshio stated publicly that he had been asked by the government to cooperate in controlling the demonstrations and mobilized two thousand to three thousand of his followers. One of his colleagues, who bossed many gangs of gamblers, had submitted a similar plan to deploy ten thousand of his stalwarts, declaring: "We gamblers cannot walk in broad daylight. But if we unite and become a wall to stop communism, we can be of service to the nation."[11]

In reserve was Japan's largest nationalist group, the Nihon Goyu Renmei (Japan Veterans League), with an active membership of some 300,000. Organized in 1955 by former military officers to combat communism, it advocated rearmament, a new constitution, devotion to the emperor, and belief in his divinity. It was headed by the former commander in chief of the Japanese expeditionary forces in China and the former chief of staff of the combined fleet. Among its advisers were members of the Tojo and other wartime cabinets, the ubiquitous Kodama Yoshio, several leading figures in Moral Rearmament, and by its own boast, "most of the surviving ranking officers of the old army, navy, and air force."

The arrogance of the government, the resurgence of the violent rightists, fear of a remilitarized Japan, and almost daily exposure, through the mass media, of clashes between demonstrators and overzealous police—exploited by generally antitreaty newsmen—had turned public opinion dangerously against both Kishi and the treaty ratification. Despite all this the government and important sectors of big business insisted that Eisenhower's visit should take place as scheduled, because "Japan's reputation for courtesy was at stake." At the earnest requests of Prime Minister Kishi and of Ambassador Douglas MacArthur II (the general's nephew), publishers and broadcasters agreed to try and persuade the Japanese people to "display their traditional hospitality to a foreign guest." But on June 10, when Eisenhower's press secretary James Hagerty arrived at Tokyo International Airport to begin final preparations, he was met by several thousand milling demonstrators, who surrounded and jostled the car in which Hagerty and Ambassador MacArthur were riding. The two Americans were imprisoned and heckled for half an hour before the police could break through and assist in their rescue by helicopter.

On the morning of the fifteenth more than five million people staged workshop rallies or other forms of protest, according to labor sources. The coal miners' unions launched a twenty-four-hour strike and railway unions disrupted train schedules. In the afternoon, seemingly endless columns of organized citizens—a moving forest of streamers, placards, and undulating banners—converged upon the National Diet area, marching, singing, and chanting slogans against the treaty, against Kishi, against Ike's visit, against American military bases.

Although the number of participants was estimated at more than 135,000, the demonstration was orderly and there was no serious friction between the marchers and the twenty thousand police on hand to keep order. Then, without warning or provocation, a gang of about a hundred and fifty ruffians launched an attack with spiked clubs on a contingent of actors and actresses among the marchers. Students who witnessed the assault reacted wrathfully, inciting their cohorts to break down a gate of the Diet grounds and swarm inside as an act of defiance. Some five thousand police, many of whom were nerve-frazzled by their frequent encounters with recalcitrant crowds, seemed to go berserk. Attacking from behind, they clubbed the invaders mercilessly. University professors who tried to intercede on behalf of the students were severely beaten by the police, who attacked reporters, photographers, and bystanders indiscriminately. In the melee that followed, scores of students were wounded and one of them, a girl, was trampled to death.

At last Kishi got the message. On the following day his cabinet, asserting that the demonstrations were "inspired by international communism" (an opinion echoed by Eisenhower and Herter), announced indefinite postponement of the presidential visit. It was a fortunate decision for, had the event actually taken place, Japan's "traditional hospitality" to be experienced by the president on his triumphal procession from the airport would have featured (according to informed estimates) perhaps half a million protesting citizens locked in hand-to-hand struggle with some fifty thousand policemen and firemen and at least fifty thousand "civil guardians," most of whom were gamblers, racketeers, labor goons, and uniformed storm troopers (one contingent of which had been thoughtfully provided with swastika armbands).

Despite the loss of such a stupendous opportunity for public protest, opponents of Kishi rejoiced and prepared to redouble their onslaught against the treaty. Such optimism was premature, however. As disgruntled businessmen and politicians canceled their plans for banquets and receptions, the stock market plummeted, and with the outbreak of fresh demonstrations, the establishment grimly closed ranks. Gone was the mass media's tolerant attitude toward the antitreaty campaign. Advertisers, warned by the government that red revolution was at hand, voiced their anxieties to publishers, whose editors then declared in unison that the students had "gone to extremes" and warned the public that succumbing to anti-Americanism was "playing into the hands of the Communists." On June 17 seven major newspapers issued a joint statement appealing to the nation to reject violence and to defend parliamentary government. "The use of violence," one editorial intoned, "is impermissible in any political situation, however difficult it may be."[12]

The implication, determinedly propagated by American diplomats and newspapermen, was that violence of insurrectionary scale was being perpetrated by leftist "mobs" or "rioters" manipulated by communists. In fact, however, the demonstrators were generally orderly and law-abiding (to the point of picking up every scrap of their own litter before leaving the scene), and the role of the Communist Party, with a membership comprising about three-tenths of one percent of the electorate, was secondary. Most of the so-called rioting had resulted from police attempts, usually on unreasonable pretexts, to deny marchers access to streets, parks, or grounds of public buildings. But there was very little brutality on either side, and astonishingly, during the gigantic labor and political struggles in the first half of 1960, only two persons were killed—a Miike striker and a Tokyo student. The former was stabbed by Sagoya's gangsters employed by Mitsui Mining, and the latter died as an indirect result of a police-instigated assault by hired hoodlums.[13]

A conspicuous exception to the nonviolence of the Communist and Socialist parties was the belligerence of Trotskyist factions then dominant in the leadership of Zengakuren. At the time, such provocative behavior was attributed to ultraleftism, but long after the tumult had subsided a more cynical explanation was suggested. For some undisclosed reason, Tanaka Seigen, the red-turned-rightist, revealed to the press that during 1959 and 1960 he had paid millions of yen to ultraradical students, including the heads of Zengakuren's finance and joint-struggle committees. This fact was freely acknowledged by the recipients.[14] Tanaka explained that he had supported the students because he felt sympathy for them and had used his own money. But in consideration of his long history of collusion with the police, big corporations such as Toshiba, and United States intelligence agencies, it would seem more likely that he had acted as an agent provocateur.

It has been estimated, and generally accepted, that to ensure the ratification of the treaty Kishi's party spent at least fifty million yen, donated by big business, and that most of it was used to strengthen right-wing and gangster organizations. Compulsory reports submitted to the government by political groups revealed that many large corporations were also contributing individually to rightist and terrorist groups, just as the zaibatsu had done in the past.

But if Japan's organized right wing had become its old self again, the left had changed considerably, refusing to be intimidated by the terrorists or responsive to the chiding of the mass media. The Kishi government, equally unchastened, ignored a climatic demonstration by more than three hundred thousand people on June 18, and at midnight the treaty was automatically approved. Having been ratified almost unanimously by the U. S. Senate, the treaty was a *fait accompli,* but protest marches and rallies, which had been held daily since June 15, continued until June 23, when Kishi, after a nationwide strike of railway and industrial workers, announced his intention to resign. Naturally, there was furious infighting among the faction bosses who aspired to succeed him. Kishi, trying to retain his supremacy within the party, made more promises than he could keep, and on Bastille Day he was stabbed in the buttocks by an old-time rightist, in the midst of a reception for party leaders at his own official residence.

Incredibly, Kishi, who had done more than any other postwar leader to revive terrorism, now felt it necessary to seek protection from the terrorists. Through his brother Sato Eisaku and Miura Giichi (according to published reports) he obtained the intercession of the master assassin Inoue Nissho, head of the prewar Blood Pledge Corps, who had been receiving financial support from Sato. Kishi survived that unkindest cut and replaced Yoshida as the gray eminence behind the cabinet.

Kishi's successor, chosen well in advance by the zaikai, was former finance minister Ikeda Hayato, who (like his college classmate Sato Eisaku) was a protégé of Yoshida. Ikeda was more moderate than Kishi in his political outlook, but was on excellent terms with ultranationalists. His mentor, Yasuoka Masaatsu, had been a close associate of the terrorists Kita Ikki and Okawa Shumei; and in the postwar period, as *doyen* of the ultranationalist thinkers, he wielded impressive influence in financial circles. Ikeda's foreign minister was Kosaka Zentaro, son-in-law of the late Mitsui Benzo of Bussan. Perhaps as a counterweight to the comparatively liberal Kosaka, Ikeda appointed as chairman of the Tory party's foreign policy committee ex-admiral Nomura Kichisaburo, Japan's "Pearl Harbor ambassador" to Washington and a postwar promoter of militarism. Ikeda's Minister of International Trade and Industry was Ishii Mitsujiro, the Diet's most influential lobbyist for Chiang Kai-shek and a member (with Admiral Nomura and a clutch of former imperial army generals and Tojo cabinet survivors) of the Free Asia Defense League, set up to "cooperate with the United States and Taiwan against communism . . . [and] to eradicate communists from the fatherland," according to its prospectus. Heading the Autonomy (Home) Ministry, responsible for law and order, was Yamazaki Iwao, chief of the Metropolitan Police Bureau in the third Konoe cabinet and wartime vice-minister in charge of the thought-control police.

By reviving and aiding the violent rightists, Kishi and his successors created a monster that has not been brought under control even today. Once again capable of inspiring fear, the unchastened troglodytes became as arrogant as ever, bullying their enemies with familiar threats that were made good often enough to be credible. In June 1960, during an antitreaty demonstration, a veteran Socialist leader was knifed, and in October the chairman of the Socialist Party, Asanuma Inejiro, was fatally stabbed on the stage of an auditorium, in the presence of the prime minister, by a seventeen-year-old fanatic. (Asanuma's offense had been a denunciation of American imperialism in a joint communiqué issued from Peking.) The assassin, a worshiper of the sainted Choshu militarist Yoshida Shoin, belonged to a small political club occupying an office provided by a former thought-control policeman. Among the many well-known business organizations that had made small contributions to the club were three Mitsui firms, whose general affairs officers had supinely given a total of seven thousand yen (about twenty dollars) —not to subsidize murder but simply to avoid offending the importunate solicitors.

Later on, Tanaka Seigen (who like Kishi had done his bit to rehabilitate the "patriots") was shot and seriously wounded by a fellow rightist of the underworld. Prime Minister Ikeda had a personal reason to regret his permissiveness toward the rightists, for in 1963 he nearly lost his life to a dagger-brandishing critic of his "lukewarm" China policy. Ikeda was further discomfited in the following year, when Ambassador Edwin O. Reischauer, Washington's Japan-born supersalesman for a Japanese-American "equal partnership," was knifed by an apparently deranged youth who imagined himself to be the reincarnation of General Tojo Hideki.

During the past decade there have been hundreds of incidents in which politicians, businessmen, labor leaders, publishers, teachers, writers, and other public figures were harassed, beaten, kidnapped, stabbed, bombed, or subjected to arson. The offenses for which such punishment was meted out were familiar: leftist radicalism, pacifism, advocacy of friendship with communist countries, suspected irreverence toward the imperial family, or derogatory comments about the "patriots" who are His Imperial Majesty's self-appointed defenders. Since 1960 organized underworld gangsters have outnumbered the police force.[15] If gangsters are lumped together with the active ultranationalists, their ideological and tactical allies, the number would probably exceed the combined active membership of the Socialist and Communist parties.

The persistence of such cryptofascism causes little concern in Japan, however. The leftists regard the right-wing extremists only as an irritating anachronism, irrelevant to the future of the society. The middle-of-the-road citizen is rarely annoyed personally by either gangsters or rightists and ignores them. As for the big business community and its conservative party, the presence of these elements is as necessary as it ever was and also gives the reassurance that Japan, after its short experiment with *demokurashii*, has settled back to normal.

30 · Japan, Unlimited

IT MAY BE INFERRED from Kishi's fate that he was a failure, but such was not the case. In Japan a prime minister is selected for his presumed ability to perform the most pressing tasks at hand, and is instructed to resign when new tasks require a leader with different qualifications. Kishi was damned by the public, to be sure, but kept the respect of the elite because he fulfilled his assignments of strengthening the anti-communist alliance with Washington, Taipei, and Seoul, and of erecting barriers against the advance of the domestic socialist, pacifist, and labor forces. To do so he had to sacrifice his political career, but of course he had been well aware that politicians who volunteer as the advance guard of big business are expendable.

Kishi's successor, Ikeda Hayato, was given the task of healing the social wounds inflicted during Kishi's regime and of uniting the country for a renewed economic offensive. Among the contenders for the premiership there were several who had the requisite background, ability, and connections. Ikeda obtained the strongest financial backing presumably because he offered the economic program that seemed best suited to the zaikai's needs and aspirations at the moment.

Born into a prosperous family of sakè brewers in Hiroshima, Ikeda had attended the prestigious Fifth Higher School in Kumamoto, Kyushu, where one of his classmates was Sato Eisaku. This friendship ripened in later years, when Ikeda and Sato became the right-hand men of Yoshida Shigeru. Another link with the still powerful Choshu clique was Ikeda's marriage to a granddaughter of Count Yamao Yozo, the Meiji loyalist whose nephews and grandnephews remained close to the House of Mitsui. Ikeda's daughter was married to the son of a fabulously wealthy moneylender and stock-market speculator, who in turn was the son-in-law of the high priest of the Meiji Shrine.

In addition to these qualifications, Ikeda was close to the "Four Heavenly Kings" of finance—especially to Sakurada Takeshi, who was his fellow disciple of Miyajima Seijiro, and to Kobayashi Ataru, with whom Ikeda, as finance minister, had collaborated in establishing the Japan Development Bank. Ikeda had several individual backers in the major financial groups. Those associated with Mitsui were Ishida Taizo of Toyota Motor, Doko Toshiwo of Ishikawajima-Harima Heavy Industries, and the presidents of Mitsui Mining & Smelting and of Onoda Cement. In 1959 Ikeda's faction reported a larger income than that of any other in the Tory party, 231,700,000 yen, but this must have been an understatement, since the same faction spent as much as one billion yen in the 1960 party election alone, conservative commentators estimated. It was also estimated that the average amount paid at that time to each of the five hundred electors was about three million yen.[1]

Each faction leader had behind him several clubs organized to raise money and to apply it effectively for the furtherance of policies advocated by businessmen members. The most powerful of the clubs backing Ikeda was the Kayokai, or Tuesday Club, mentioned earlier. Its key members were the "Four Heavenly Kings." Others were the governor of the Bank of Japan and the presidents of Development Bank, Tokyo Electric Power, and Nomura Securities, as well as the politician Kaya Okinori, finance minister in the Tojo cabinet and minister of justice under Ikeda.

Other important groups of Ikeda backers were the Wild Boar Club and Suehiro-kai, the Unfolding Fan Club. Suehiro-kai (the name also connotes rising prosperity or limitless expansion) had three main subgroups composed of Mitsubishi, Sumitomo, and Mitsui men, who took "lessons" from financial expert Ikeda once a month at a fashionable teahouse well provided with geisha. Among the pupils in the Mitsui class were presidents Edo Hideo of Real Estate, Shindo Koji of Steamship, Mizukami Tatsuzo of Bussan, and Mori Hirosaburo of Toray.[2]

Ikeda's chief theorist was Shimomura Osamu, called "Professor" though he was actually a bureaucrat from the finance ministry serving as a director of Japan Development Bank. Shimomura headed a small economics study group, one of whose leading members was Hoshino Naoki, Tojo's chief cabinet secretary and wartime economic planner. This small group, working with Ikeda, blueprinted the famous "income doubling plan" in which the subsequent decade of breathtaking economic growth was forecast with uncanny accuracy. Although the Economic Planning Agency predicted an average growth rate of about seven percent in the gross national product over the next ten years, Shimomura said it would be eleven percent. Actually, it came out at 11.6 percent, after allowing for inflation. (The probability that consumer prices, as well as workers' incomes, would also more than double during the period was not announced but was taken for granted by businessmen.) The zaibatsu-descended concerns and other oligopolies supported Ikeda's program not merely for higher profits but for the help it would give them in growing large enough to compete with the major international corporations abroad and in retaining their shares of the Japanese market after the liberalization of trade then being urged upon Japan by the United States.

The most immediate obstacle to achieving the "income doubling plan" was labor's opposition to the government's "rationalization" program, as represented by the Miike strike. At Omuta truculence on both sides had exacerbated the conflict, and during the summer of 1960, when the antitreaty demonstrations had subsided, more than three hundred societies for the defense of the miners were enlisting sympathizers nationwide. On July 17, just as Ikeda was forming his cabinet, an estimated 100,000 people rallied under a blazing sun at Omuta to express solidarity with the embattled strikers. The government and the zaikai, fearing that the tensions at Omuta would explode into deadly warfare, concentrated their full attention on the problem. Since Mining's managers were split over the issue of mediation, the new labor minister urged Mitsui Bank's chairman, Sato Kiichiro, to persuade the stubborn president Kuriki Kan of Mitsui Mining to accept a mediation plan already approved in principle by the union. Kuriki remained unconvinced, so the minister, accompanied by Sato and Uemura Kogoro, vice-president of the Federation of Economic Organizations, went personally to work on Kuriki. The meeting was later joined by Nagano Shigeo, Sakurada Takeshi, and a few other top men in the employers' organizations (but none from Mitsui companies), who agreed in warning Kuriki that the Miike dispute had become a national emergency.

Meanwhile, a comprehensive settlement plan was being hammered out privately in meetings of the Asameshikai, or Breakfast Club, an authoritative group that met at the Palace Hotel, just across the moat from the emperor's palace. Among its members were the same men who had visited Kuriki, as well as Kobayashi and such zaibatsu chieftains as Ishizaka, Adachi, and Shibusawa Keizo. The members of Asameshikai (one of several clubs with the same name) were all wealthy financiers or industrialists. They were also the men most active in the collection of funds from zaikai for the Liberal-Democratic Party. As such, they were not only assisting the Ikeda government but actually dictating the policy it would adopt.

Since the Miike union and Tanro were close to exhaustion from the long strike, and Sohyo was anxious to reach a dignified settlement, the Breakfast Club and Ikeda's potent Tuesday Club—in consultation with Miura Giichi and other members of the "invisible government"—agreed upon terms that represented an unmistakable defeat for labor, but not a crushing one. At Miike, some twelve hundred Mitsui miners were to "resign"; and nationally, production per miner was to be almost doubled by labor-saving measures, and the number of miners was to be reduced by seventy-six thousand to a total of 175,000 within three years, as envisaged earlier. At the same time management promised to help surplus miners find new jobs (Mitsui was exploring the appealing possibility of shipping them off to South America or Germany), while the employers' organizations had agreed to promote measures to relieve unemployment and retrain workers displaced by changes in technology. These were some of the first faint stirrings of the "welfare state" idea that became a major government and business policy toward the end of the 1960s.

Nevertheless, the Miike strike, which had been touted as a confrontation of "total labor against total capital," was the swan song of the coal miners' unions. Tanro, which had 200,000 members when the strike was settled in September 1960, declined in ten years to little more than a quarter of that strength as labor productivity increased phenomenally and slackening demand for coal closed one mine after another. Sohyo, which had come under severe public attack for its role in the demonstrations and miners' strikes, became more cautious about united action with the Communists and tried to reach a *modus vivendi* with unions of the center and right wing, paying less attention to industry-wide organization and being more tolerant of the paternalistic "Japanese-type unionism" as increasing prosperity and complacency took the edge off labor's militancy.

Mitsui Mining, claiming to have suffered losses totaling $27.7 million from the strike, took advantage of labor's more humble posture to push "efficiency" to its utmost limits. Mechanization of operations was most strongly emphasized at the Mikawa mine, the Miike colliery's richest, where the staff was augmented while less productive mines were closed. To boost output, operations were conducted in three shifts for twenty-four hours a day, with no breaks in between for inspection and adjustment of machinery. Before the strike there had been four maintenance men to every six producing miners, but by 1963 the ratio was only two to eight. The number of safety personnel was cut from eighteen to six, although the number of miners nearly doubled. The company's labor-management safety committee functioned only as a formality, and instructions from the prefectural safety office were not passed down to the miners regularly. Despite frequent warnings from union spokesmen, safety equipment was neglected and disaster drills were abandoned. The number of accidental deaths per year in the Mikawa mine tripled to fifteen from the prestrike average, and serious injuries quintupled to 1,800 a year.

In mid-afternoon on November 9, 1963 the second shift was taking over. The first shift was still below ground, and there were twice as many men as usual in the Mikawa mine. At 3:15 a dull explosion was heard and felt all over Omuta. Housewives shopping in Mikawa-dori, some five hundred meters from the pithead, screamed and ran for shelter as rocks, boards, and fragments of concrete rained down on the busy street. Lights went out all over the area and a column of black smoke soared skyward. An hour later a superintendent telephoned the Omuta police to report an accident, estimating that some twenty miners had been injured. At 5:30 an advance party entered the gas-filled pit for reconnaissance, but it was not until 6:30—more than three hours after the explosion—that full-scale operations were begun to rescue the nearly one thousand miners who remained below ground.

It turned out to be one of the worst mine disasters in Japanese history, killing 458 workers and seriously injuring a larger number. However, only about twenty-five men were killed by the blast itself: the others died from suffocation or carbon-monoxide poisoning, most of which could have been prevented if the company had taken prompt action. Before rescue operations got underway the company doctors had been dismissed for the night, and precious time was lost in recalling them to organize emergency treatment.

President Kuriki, arriving in Omuta to "take charge of rescue operations" two days after the disaster, told reporters: "We never thought such an accident was possible in the Miike mines." He knew, of course, that the company had installed an elaborate water-spray system for the very purpose of damping down the coal dust, known to be a serious hazard at high concentrations. The prefectural official in charge of mine safety had inspected the Mikawa colliery that year and took the superintendents' word for it that the protective spray was being applied daily. But after the explosion, which apparently resulted from the ignition of coal dust by accidental sparks, he discovered that the spray system had not been in operation regularly and that its water-supply pipes were clogged with rust. Kuriki denied that safety had been sacrificed to production. Apparently with one eye still on the balance sheet, he expressed regret that the accident had occurred just as the mine was beginning to show a profit for the first time since 1960. His concern with profit at a time when the fate of scores of men trapped underground was still unknown could be ascribed to coldbloodedness, but it may have been due to the fact that Sohyo had declared its intention of suing him and three Miike managers for criminal negligence, that Tanro was planning a nationwide strike, and that a joint committee of both federations was demanding condolence payments of one million yen (then $2,800) for each bereaved household. The financial threat was not quite so grim as it sounded, however; two days after the strike, even before launching an inquiry into the cause of the catastrophe, the cabinet had decided that a governmental loan of one billion yen be extended to Mitsui Mining Company for compensating the victims or their families.[3]

Battered by successive misfortunes, Mitsui Mining showed a cumulative deficit of nearly forty million dollars by the end of 1963, but with the help of government subsidies, loans, and support from the Mitsui group the company survived and made an astonishing success of its rationalization program. At Miike, from 1960 to 1970, the number of miners dropped from ten thousand to five thousand, yet output increased from seven thousand tons to twenty thousand tons a day. Before the Miike strike the output of coal per miner was around fourteen tons per month, but by 1970 it had risen to eighty-one tons (as compared with a national productivity figure of sixty-one tons). In that year Mitsui Mining and its subsidiaries accounted for more than thirty percent of the 38.5 million tons of coal produced in Japan, and almost reached the break-even point.[4]

The man most responsible for this comeback was the flinty Kurata Okito, who had been put in charge of labor problems at the Tokyo head office during the big strike and replaced the luckless Kuriki after the 1963 disaster. The walls of Kurata's roomy office, in the old Mitsui Honsha building in Tokyo, are lined with bookshelves containing one of Japan's most comprehensive collections of labor literature. Like his late brother Chikara, the postwar builder of the mighty Hitachi manufacturing combine, Kurata is intensely serious, patriotic, and pro-American. When asked by the author in 1971 why he always displays miniatures of the Rising Sun flag and of the Stars and Stripes on his desk, he replied: "We were helped very much by the Americans during the occupation and even after the occupation. Our two countries must maintain very close relations because we are brothers. . . . We must rely on each other for mutual prosperity." This is a fairly standard comment for any big executive from a major company in Japan, but Kurata speaks with more conviction than is usual, perhaps because his company was saved by efficiency methods learned from American instructors, and because two of his grandsons are American citizens.

To Kurata and his staff anything interfering with productivity is inherently evil, and most evil of all is socialistic thought. By dint of constant surveillance and screening of applicants, they keep the employment of leftists to a minimum. Morale is said to be high among the Miike miners, who share Kurata's pride in their productivity, and some of the benefits. Today the miners work in small teams, whose pay depends in part on their "score" in coal tonnage. Before going into the pits each team congregates in an assembly hall to plan and discuss

the day's project. After singing the national anthem and bowing politely
to their foremen, the team members take a train for the underground
labyrinths where they labor intensely under uncomfortable and dangerous conditions for eight hours (plus unpaid travel time to and from
the coal face). For their efforts, and the risks they take, underground
workers are paid an average wage of 100,000 yen a month (about
$333 in 1972) and in addition receive a twice-yearly bonus averaging
120,000 yen, free or nearly free housing, and numerous fringe benefits,
including medical care and pensions.[5]

Remarkable as it was, Mining's achievement was by no means unique.
The steep rise in productivity, which continued to outstrip the increase
in wages year after year, was characteristic of big business in general,
along with the swing back to paternalism, company unionism, and the
separation of labor problems from politics. This combination of policies
enabled the major companies to accumulate huge undeclared profits,
which were reinvested or kept in special reserves that supplied the
banks with funds for industrial loans. There were warnings from abroad
that such frantic expansion would result in overproduction and an
eventual trade war or a deflationary spiral, but Ikeda, assured by
American friends that Japan had nothing to worry about so long as
it supported Washington's cold-war crusade, pursued his original expansion policy without a letup.

During the 1960s Japan's exports rose by about seventeen percent
a year. The most potent stimulant to exports, both visible and invisible,
was the Vietnam War, which provided Japan with extra income estimated at more than a billion dollars a year from 1966 through 1972.[6]
This annual sum was equal to more than ten percent of Japan's total
exports in 1966. With the escalation of the Indochina war in that year,
Japan's favorable balance of trade, which had averaged less than $400
million a year since 1960, leaped to an average of $2.725 billion a year
in the 1965–70 period, and to $7.787 billion in 1971. This surplus,
and the foreign-exchange reserves that were accumulated as a result,
changed Japan from a debtor to a creditor nation and one of world's
biggest international lenders and investors.

Much of the credit (or blame) for this startling metamorphosis must
be assumed by leaders of the Republican Party of the United States,
who recently have been most vociferous in criticizing Japan for aggravating the American balance-of-payments problem. In 1959 Thomas
E. Dewey, an unsuccessful Republican candidate for president a decade
before, was retained by JETRO, the Japan External Trade Organization, as its representative in the United States. Dewey's corporation-
law firm, which also represented the interests of Laurance Rockefeller
and American Telephone & Telegraph, was to receive fees and ex-

penses amounting to a reported $200,000 a year for being Japan's "watchdog" in the United States and for presenting Japan's case against any attempts to limit American imports of its goods. (Dewey was an experienced lobbyist: for several years he had been representing the government of Turkey, at a fee of $75,000 a year, and had been able to secure United States aid amounting to about four billion dollars for that country.)

In 1960 Dewey's political protégé, Richard M. Nixon, who had served as vice-president under Eisenhower, ran for the presidency and lost to John F. Kennedy. After his failure to make a comeback in his campaign for the governorship of California, he devoted most of his time to clients of his own law firm, such as Pepsico (Pepsi-Cola) and Mitsui & Company (USA), Inc.

In April 1964, just as the cherry blossoms were reaching their prime, Nixon arrived in Tokyo, having been invited by Mitsui Bussan. His best friend and ally in Japan was Kishi Nobusuke, with whom he had established rapport during the treaty disturbances in 1960—the year in which both men had been denied the highest office in their respective lands. After a long private conference with Kishi and a visit to Prime Minister Ikeda, Nixon flew to Hiroshima, where he placed a wreath on the memorial to the multitudes killed by the first atomic bomb and officiated at the opening of a million-dollar Pepsi-Cola plant, smiling and waving as two hundred employees cheered his every move. Back in Tokyo, he told Japan's leading businessmen assembled at the Industry Club that the war in Indochina must be won soon and could be won by attacking North Vietnam. Before his departure, two days afterward, he conferred with several high-powered businessmen and, foresightedly, with finance minister Tanaka Kakuei, later to become prime minister. That evening he attended a reception given by Mitsui Bussan, where he was photographed shaking hands with the firm's major executives and chatting with a bevy of pretty lasses clad in their most colorful kimono.

Nixon visited Tokyo again that year, for discussions with Mitsui affiliates in finance, chemicals, metals, electronics, and heavy machinery. Presumably, he wished to assess their capacities for providing goods and materials needed by the United States and its client regimes in Southeast Asia. He also felt it necessary to renew his acquaintance with Sato Eisaku, who had been made prime minister after Ikeda's resignation because of illness.

A bureaucrat of the transportation ministry, Sato had been brought to the attention of Yoshida Shigeru by Matsuno Tsuruhei, an ardent Taiwan lobbyist whose outlook Sato shared. As Yoshida's protégé, Sato had broad support from zaikai in general and especially from a powerful *keibatsu,* or group of interrelated wealthy families—the Anzais, Moris, Iwasas, and Shodas—with whom he was connected by marriage. Shoda Hidesaburo, heading his Nisshin Flour Mills, had had the good fortune of marrying his daughter Michiko to Crown Prince Akihito, thus boosting enormously the prestige of his relatives, including Sato, Kishi, and Iwasa Yoshizane, chairman of Fuji Bank and zaikai's chief of liaison with American finance and multinational business.

Sato was even more conservative than Ikeda, taking his cues on basic policy from a club known as Soshin-kai, the White Heart Society, led by wartime bureaucrats, former military officers, and ultranationalists. Among them were three veterans of the Tojo cabinet (Kishi, Kaya, and Aoki Kazuo), Sato Kiichiro of Mitsui Bank, and Chiba Saburo, a former executive of Kanegafuchi Spinning who became a politician and a militant foe of socialism in all its forms after being proselytized by Frank Buchman. Sato Eisaku had been chosen to finish the tasks begun by Ikeda: to continue the program of rapid economic growth; to make a reasonably convincing pretense of freeing imports and foreign-capital investment in response to Washington's urging; to support American policy in Asia and prepare for another ten-year extension of the military alliance; to rearm Japan as rapidly as public opinion permitted; and to prevent any relaxation of the government's stiff posture toward Peking. It was an unpopular policy, but diplomatically it was realistic, and in the economic realm it worked wonders.

Although Dewey gave the impression of neglecting his duties, Nixon promoted Japan-United States trade and business relations energetically, visiting Tokyo at least once a year until the more important duties of running again for the presidency interfered. When in the capital, he was entertained lavishly at fashionable night spots, usually at parties arranged by a committee under Mitsui Bussan's sponsorship and headed by Kishi. It is probably impossible to learn precisely what benefits JETRO derived from its employment of Dewey, or Mitsui from Nixon's services. However, it can be deduced that the fees they paid were not wasted. Dewey, Nixon's political godfather, was the third man in a Republican triumvirate with John Foster Dulles and Winthrop Aldrich, brother-in-law of John D. Rockefeller Jr. and chairman of the Chase Manhattan Bank. Dewey's early financial backer had been C. Douglas Dillon, who controlled most of the voting stock in Dillon, Read & Company. Dillon had become Secretary of the Treasury under Kennedy, and Dean Rusk (like Dulles before him) had stepped from the presidency of the Rockefeller Foundation into the top spot in the State Department. Thus both Dewey and Nixon seem to have been ensconced in the upper echelons of the American "zaibatsu" concerns most interested in the Japanese economy. Dillon, Read was at that time negotiating the flotation of at least $100 million in securities issues for Japanese companies. It is perhaps worth observing that Dillon's firm handled a great deal of investment-banking business for Texaco and Standard Oil of California, which together controlled Caltex, the major supplier of petroleum products in the Far East. Caltex, in turn, owned a half interest in Nippon Oil Refining, the production subsidiary of Nippon Oil. The latter firm, Japan's oldest and largest petroleum company, was founded by Mitsui, and among its major shareholders today are Mitsui, Sumitomo, and Dai-Ichi group financial institutions. Caltex's biggest customer was the United States Department of Defense, whose assistant secretary (later Secretary of the Navy) was Dillon, Read's vice-president Paul Nitze. Caltex, fueling the Pentagon's gargantuan war machine in Asia, profited richly from the war in Indochina. It may be only a coincidence that between 1965 and 1971, the escalation years, Nippon Oil more than doubled its proceeds and its profit rate.[7]

It has been asserted that the "complete democratization of the shareholding system" by SCAP eliminated all possibility that the zaibatsu could be revived. Yet in 1953, a year after the occupation ended, there was already concentration of ownership to a striking degree. In nineteen major Mitsui-group companies, the total number of stockholders was more than a million, but those with more than 100,000 shares numbered only twenty-three (individuals and corporations) per company, on the average. This tiny minority owned an average of 36.6 percent of the stock in the respective companies; and in the case of Mitsui Bank only five-tenths of one percent of the shareholders owned 49.4 percent of the stock.[8]

This process, by no means peculiar to Mitsui, was accelerated during and after the Korean War. The proportion of all stocks held by individuals shrank steadily, while corporations increased their share of the total to fifty-five percent by 1965, when nearly sixty percent of corporate stocks were held by four-tenths percent of the stockholders. The trend toward oligopoly has continued into the 1970s, and is being deliberately accelerated as Japan girds for competition with multinational corporations and banks.

Between 1960 and 1964, years of phenomenal economic growth and consolidation, the hundred largest Japanese corporations (about one-fourth of which were of zaibatsu descent) increased the number of their wholly- or partially-owned affiliates by forty percent, to more than four thousand in all. In 1964 the hundred largest firms other than banks and insurance companies held more than forty percent of the aggregate capital of all incorporated enterprises in Japan (a slightly larger share than in 1937, a "normal" prewar year). It is significant, too, that by 1972 the share of total stockholdings in Japanese corporations held by financial institutions, mostly by the fifteen city banks including Mitsui, amounted to more than thirty-four percent.

Have the zaibatsu been revived, then, or have they been supplanted by innocuous "enterprise groups," as the managers prefer to call them? Economically speaking, the prewar zaibatsu and today's "groups" are remarkably similar, but a few differences are worthy of consideration. First, control is no longer exercised from the top, but mutually; and second, the concentration of stockholdings in the hands of mainstream companies of each group is much smaller, so that power is more broadly distributed. These two changes have greatly increased the importance of other factors for cohesion, which have already been discussed in Chapter 27. A third difference is that, whereas the zaibatsu were quite distinct, competitive, and exclusive (until the later war years, when some were forced into joint activities), they now cooperate rather freely in forming enterprises involving greater risk or larger capital outlays than any single group is willing to assume, or they join forces because of the sheer logic of a given situation.

Nevertheless, each of the "enterprise groups" is still more or less cohesive, competitive, and exclusive. Mitsubishi and Sumitomo, being the most centralized, bear a very close resemblance to their zaibatsu ancestors, while Fuji, Sanwa, and Daiwa are more loosely organized. Mitsui stands somewhere in between. A group's hardest problem has been to find a hub around which the different companies, often competing jealously for capital, markets, or supremacy within the "family," can coordinate their activities.

The transition from rivalry to cooperation within the Mitsui Group was fostered by intramural organizations, the first of which was Getsuyokai, the Monday Club. At this weekly luncheon, inaugurated in 1950, high executives from twenty-seven of the most closely related companies (excluding such "secessionists" as Toshiba, Toyota, Oji Paper, and Onoda Cement) gathered for fraternization rather than business discussion. In the mid-1950s fifteen members of Getsuyokai formed the team for reestablishing Bussan. When they succeeded in effecting the grand merger, the fifteen-company group (centered around Bussan) took permanent form. It is called Itsukakai, or Fifth-of-the-Month Club, because it holds its dinner meetings on the anniversary of the conclusion of that merger agreement on February 5, 1959. It is now attended by the chairmen or presidents of sixteen companies. Meanwhile, Getsuyokai expanded its membership to thirty-four companies and still holds twice-monthly meetings for the promotion of solidarity.

A distinct but overlapping group of representatives from seventeen companies, calling itself Nimokukai, or Second Thursday Club, was established in 1960. Its membership now includes the presidents or chairmen of twenty-one companies formerly under direct control of the Mitsui families. (These officials are also members of the larger Getsuyokai.) Nimokukai meets once a month, early in the morning, at Getsuyokai headquarters on the thirty-fourth floor of Mitsui's Kasumigaseki Building. The huge earthquake-proof structure symbolizes the achievements of Mitsui Real Estate Development, whose chairman, Edo Hideo, is a guiding spirit of the club and of the group, along with Wakasugi Sueyuki (who retired from Bussan's presidency in 1973),[9] president Koyama Goro of Bank, chairman Doko Toshiwo of Toshiba, and a few senior advisers, among whom are the former chief executives Tashiro Shigeki of Toray, Mizukami Tatsuzo of Bussan, Ishida Taizo of Toyota, and Tanaka Fumio of Oji Paper. Among other sensitive tasks, Nimokukai coordinates the group's public relations and advertising activities and enforces conditions for using the Mitsui name under arrangements with the clan's heirs. The rule today is that no company may call itself "Mitsui" unless at least half its stock is owned by member companies of Nimokukai. One of the latest to be so authorized is the Mitsui Urban Development Company, of which Edo Hideo is president.

Another example of Nimokukai's role was its decision to establish the Mitsui Consultants Company for executing port and harbor projects in underdeveloped countries where group members were investing capital. As a result of the committee's deliberations the firm was established in 1965 with the cooperation of twenty members of the group. More recently, Nimokukai consolidated the group's tourism and sightseeing resources, including rural landholdings, to form the Mitsui Tourism Development Company under the aegis of Real Estate, Bussan, Bank, and Hokkaido Colliery.

The reconstitution of Mitsui as a group is due in large part to external pressures created by the changing world economy and by the measures necessary for modernization. Because of Japan's isolation before and during the Pacific War, and the necessity of concentrating its industrial resources on production, the nation's technology was neglected. Japan emerged from the postwar reconstruction period with virtually no knowledge of such modern industries as synthetic textiles, electronics, petrochemicals, plastics, and atomic energy. In the early 1950s the government, assisted by a special committee appointed by the leading enterprise groups, enacted a number of laws for the promotion of new industries, budgeted funds for their development, and used its influence to organize corporate units for research and the establishment of pilot plants.

The petrochemical industry is a classic example. Until the 1950s Japan had relied mainly upon coal, carbide, and fermentation processes as sources of materials for organic chemicals. Meanwhile, the manufacture of high-octane gasoline in the United States during the war had laid the basis for a petrochemical industry utilizing waste gases from the cracking process. To catch up with the United States in this important field, the Japanese government worked out a plan for importing technology, allocating foreign exchange, and offering loans, tax benefits, and tariff exemptions to industrialists. Under such favorable conditions (reminiscent of government promotion of industry in the Meiji era), four major groups were established and began to build naphtha-cracking centers in 1957. The first integrated plant to start operating was that of Mitsui Petrochemical, formed by Mitsui Chemical, Bank, Mining, Daiichi Bussan, Toyo Rayon, Toyo Koatsu, and several other Mitsui companies, together with Koa Oil, a binational company in which Caltex bought fifty percent of the stock.

Located at Iwakuni on Hiroshima Bay, the complex opened in 1958, with the supporting companies cooperating in production, distribution, and utilization of the petroleum derivatives. Koa Oil supplied naphtha, which was processed into ethylene, propylene, polyethylene, and a dozen other products for which Bussan served as exclusive distributor. Toray, the biggest producer of synthetic fibers, was the principal user of those petrochemical derivatives.

Expansion was so rapid that the petrochemical complex soon outgrew the site at Iwakuni. But meanwhile, Mitsui Real Estate had launched an ambitious program of reclaiming land. This was partly to compete with Mitsubishi Real Estate, which had larger landholdings than Mitsui, and partly to secure industrial sites for the fast growing Mitsui group. In 1957 Real Estate began to reclaim land from Tokyo Bay in Chiba Prefecture near Tokyo, inaugurating what Edo liked to call the "reclamation age." At Goi, across the bay from the capital, a huge tract was developed for the Kyoyo (Tokyo-Chiba) complex of Mitsui Petrochemical, and no less than thirty Mitsui-line companies took part in the integrated operations. (Other organizations setting up plants there were Maruzen Oil, Idemitsu Oil, Nippon Steel, Tokyo Electric Power, Kawasaki Steel, and Asahi Glass, an indication that barriers between financial groups are being broken down by the advantages of sharing industrial complexes.) Mitsui Construction and other engineering firms of the group handled site development, buildings, and installation of machinery, much of it made by Mitsui companies.

To assure a stable supply of raw materials, a new refining company, Kyokuto Oil, was formed by nine Mitsui companies with Mobil Oil, which owns half the stock. Bussan played an organizing role and installed one of its executives as Kyokuto's president. At the Goi complex every stage of petrochemical production is performed, from unloading crude oil from tankers to exporting finished synthetic fibers.

With the drastic shift from coal to petroleum as basic material for the chemical industry, Mitsui Chemical and Toyo Koatsu also entered the petrochemical field, to some extent in competition with the Iwakuni and Goi complexes they had helped to establish. They merged recently with Miike Gosei to form Mitsui Toatsu Chemicals (making urea fertilizer, industrial chemicals, and plastics), which in turn formed a joint petrochemical venture to produce styrene. To supply other products and intermediates derived from petrochemicals, new companies were formed jointly by Mitsui and foreign firms, including Celanese, Union Carbide, Monsanto, and Du Pont. Thus the petrochemical industry not only strengthened ties within the Mitsui Group but brought it into fruitful relationships with other domestic and overseas enterprises.

The genesis of Japan's nuclear-power industry was similar. It was apparent that Japan, with limited energy resources, would eventually need atomic reactors. But the cost of development was staggering, and the public was outspokenly hostile to anything dealing with atom splitting; even today many Japanese resist the establishment of atomic facilities. Proceeding with utmost circumspection, the government enacted laws relating to production and use of atomic energy and set up a nuclear-research institute as a "special corporation" with almost equal investment by the government and private industry (an arrangement that kept it out of politics). By 1956 five atomic industrial groups had been formed around the major banks. The Mitsui organization was called the Nippon Atomic Industry Group (NAIG) because president Ishizaka of Toshiba complained: "I don't belong to Mitsui!" It included forty-two companies centered on Toshiba, with Bussan in a coordinating role. Toshiba was in the salient position because of its advanced research facilities and its close connection with General Electric. One of NAIG's projects is the construction of an atomic-energy plant for Tokyo Electric Power, which is in the Mitsui Bank sphere of influence. Subsequently, in 1967, the Japan Nuclear Fuel Company was organized by Toshiba, Hitachi, and GE; this was the first private firm in the field, and is another example of the blurring of group boundaries. Like other major traders, Bussan has long-term contracts for importing uranium; and as a specialty, NAIG and Toshiba are concentrating on technology for enriching it by the promising centrifugal method. At present NAIG, Toshiba, Mining & Smelting,

Japan Steel, and other Mitsui companies are manufacturing equipment related to the production and use of atomic energy.

The way in which new companies are formed by the group reveals Mitsui's characteristic mode of operation. There is no brain trust handing down decisions from on high. Ideas usually originate from opportunities recognized or needs felt by executives of individual companies, who in frequent social contacts with colleagues in other Mitsui firms exchange their ideas. If a proposal appeals to fellow members of one of the executives' clubs, a committee will be set up to examine the possible contributions from or benefits to various companies of the group and to evolve a plan accordingly. In the case of the Mitsui Aluminum Company, established in 1969, the idea was based upon three considerations: Mitsui was weak in light metals, which were of increasing importance in the economy; huge new deposits of bauxite had become available from Australia; and the coal business was in the doldrums. Why not use surplus coal, then, to generate electric power for making aluminum?

Schematically, such a project is worked out somewhat as follows, using aluminum as an example. A committee decides where the power and ore can be brought together for reduction: this turns out to be Omuta, site of the Miike coal mines, which has good port facilities owned by Mitsui. A development plan is drawn up by Real Estate, land is reclaimed adjacent to the harbor by Construction, and meanwhile, Bussan is rounding up suitable technology and equipment through its foreign branches. In Australia a new company—Mitsui Alumina—is set up by Trading and other interested members, together with local partners, to mine bauxite and process it nearby to reduce the cost of shipping, aboard Mitsui O.S.K. Lines' special carriers. The alumina and aluminum plants and docks are built and equipped through combined efforts of Consultants, Shipbuilding & Engineering, Construction, Sanki Engineering, Toshiba, and Miike Machinery. Metallurgical experience is furnished by Mining & Smelting, while Mining supplies coal, carbon for electrodes, and housing for employees. Bank has coordinated the financing, assisted by Trust & Banking, Mutual Life, and Taisho Marine & Fire. Before the mill is completed, Bussan works out marketing plans, the toughest job because in Japan aluminum is already in oversupply due to imports and stiff competition from other groups. However, there is one stable, built-in market: the Mitsui Group itself. Having a big aluminum producer within the group offers certain advantages that help to compensate for losses anticipated by the new company during its first few years of operation. Also, much of the money spent by Aluminum accrues as income to other member companies, who in turn cooperate to make it profitable.[10]

Unlike Mitsubishi and Sumitomo, which have a clear-cut vertical structure and table of organization, Mitsui is multipolar—a "group of groups," whose center shifts according to circumstances and whose boundaries are often in dispute. Financially, Bank could be called the hub of the group. Although it is only the seventh largest of the city banks, its involvement with the Mitsui Group is extensive. Member companies get about thirty percent of their borrowings from it, and its loans to group enterprises account for an equal share of its total loans, according to a spokesman of Mitsui Bank. But among Bank's "member" clients are such firms as Toyo Menka, Toshoku, and General Oil, which are keen competitors of Bussan. Thus the latter's definition of the group is quite different from that of Bank, and also from that of Toshiba, Toray, or Toyota.

Bussan's organizing role in the Mitsui Group seems to be the greatest in scale and scope. Holding at least half the stock in some fifty other enterprises, Bussan has dispatched board members to these and more than a hundred other companies. In this way the firm serves as a training school for executive talent and even as an "employment agency." As for business relations, Bussan handles some twenty percent of total sales for thirty-one members of the group. Companies in or around the Mitsui Group account for about one-fifth of Bussan's total transactions, which, at more than fifteen billion dollars a year in fiscal 1972, are by far the largest of any member company. Bussan's subsidiary, Mitsui & Co. (USA), alone registered sales of more than one billion dollars in 1968, the first Japanese company overseas to reach this level. In 1969 Bussan was Japan's largest trading firm, handling about ten percent of the nation's exports and thirteen percent of its imports, which amounted to thirty-three billion dollars for the entire country. Mitsui's share in 1972 was slightly less than that of Mitsubishi Shoji, but was well above that of any other contender.

The mainstays of Bussan's trade, both foreign and domestic, had long been iron, steel, and steelmaking materials. This field of business was greatly strengthened in 1964 by Bussan's acquisition of Kinoshita Sansho, Japan's biggest specialized trader in ferrous metal and materials. For many years Kinoshita Shigeru, the head of the company, had maintained a close relationship with Kishi Nobusuke and Nagano Mamoru (Kishi's former transportation minister and brother of Nagano Shigeo, president of Fuji Steel Company). Presumably by supplying political funds to the Kishi faction, Kinoshita enjoyed a preferential status with the government that enabled him to obtain heavily padded contracts for transportation equipment and other goods being supplied to Southeast Asian countries under war reparations agreements. In these transactions, business ethics had degenerated to such a point that even major companies could not sell goods to Indonesia or the Philippines without paying bribes to foreign officials or kickbacks to Japanese insiders. One former executive of Kinoshita told the author, for example, that whenever President Sukarno came to Tokyo he was regaled at the expense of Kinoshita and provided with beautiful female companions. Members of his entourage were permitted to buy on credit whatever merchandise took their fancy in the posh Imperial Hotel's arcade, and Kinoshita Sansho paid the bills. When Sukarno's wife Dewi (a Japanese girl who had been introduced to him by the president of a small but well-connected trading company) visited Japan, directors of Kinoshita Sansho were ordered to play mah-jong with her for high stakes and always to lose—again at their company's expense.[11]

Also, Kinoshita Sansho had some special influence with the steel companies (one of the firm's high officials was reported to be a son-in-law of Nagano Mamoru) and favoritism made it difficult for legitimate firms to compete. On one occasion the agent of an Indonesian politician had the effrontery to solicit a bribe from Mitsui Bussan's president Mizukami, who jettisoned an important deal rather than comply.[12] Irregularities and scandals surrounding the reparations business were costing the legitimate trading companies heavily and giving them a bad name abroad. But after Kishi's downfall the carelessly managed Kinoshita Sansho got into financial difficulties and its main creditors asked Mitsui Bussan to take it over. The discredited company, with enormous liabilities, looked like a bad bargain and most Mitsui men wanted no part of it. But Mizukami urged acceptance of the offer as a means of bringing Bussan's business in line with the preponderance of heavy industry in the economy as a whole. There was stubborn opposition within the management, but Mizukami, well schooled by the late chairman Hirashima in the vital importance of steel, prevailed and absorbed Kinoshita with all its accumulated losses. The transaction looked very dubious in the next annual report, but in the long run Bussan came out much stronger and assumed Kinoshita's favored position with respect to the Yawata and Fuji Steel companies. Those two later merged to form the Nippon Steel Corporation, now the nation's largest enterprise and Bussan's most important customer. Such are the critical decisions that must be made by the captains of sogo shosha, men who can gamble coolly even when the stakes run into billions of dollars.[13]

Assuming responsibility for keeping the hyperkinetic Japanese economy operating at full speed, the sogo shosha pursued a policy of moving into every phase of the economy where opportunity or need was detected. That meant, in addition to buying and selling goods and commodities already in existence, assertive intervention at every stage of production, procurement, shipping, and marketing. It meant exploring for resources overseas, organizing and financing joint ventures in Japan and other countries, exporting machinery and management skills, developing transportation networks, and establishing complexes for storing, processing, and distributing imported commodities.

For these purposes it was necessary for Mitsui Bussan, like other sogo shosha, to keep abreast of technology in the advanced countries, to import that which was needed, establish new companies for employing it, and introduce foreign capital to sustain it when necessary. A useful concept was the develop-and-import formula under which technology, machinery, and trained personnel were mobilized to exploit latent primary resources abroad and to process them for the home market. In order to build up the economic infrastructure in underdeveloped countries, the sogo shosha fostered the export of capital and served as contractors for heavy engineering works such as harbors, dams, hydroelectric plants, railways, and highways. Such efforts were backed by the export of technology and the training of foreign personnel, often in Japan, to take over operations in their own countries.

Mitsui Bussan owns or participates in about one hundred and forty overseas ventures with an equity on the order of half a billion dollars, in agriculture, forestry, fishing, manufacturing, commerce, and other lines. Mitsui joint ventures fell lumber in Indonesia, process fish meal in Peru, and grow soybeans in the United States, cacao in Cameroun, and chickens in Korea. They assemble automobiles in Canada, weave nylon cloth in Kenya, and manufacture tires in Thailand, chemicals in Belgium, and plastics in Portugal. The most important Mitsui investments, however, are in the extraction of raw materials and fuel for Japan's insatiable mills and factories. In Australia, Bussan and other Mitsui-Group companies are digging coal (in the Moura mines), iron ore (at Mount Newman and Robe River), and bauxite (at Gove). They are mining copper in Peru while searching for oil and gas in the Middle East, Africa, and Indonesia. In mineral ventures, the Mitsui companies are cooperating with such international companies as American Metal Climax, Cleveland Cliffs Iron, Peabody Coal, Amoco, Imperial Chemical Industries, and Alcoa. In joint ventures with foreign partners in Japan, Mitsui affiliates have capital ties with other multinational giants— International Nickel, Unilever, Sperry Rand, Mobil Oil, California Packing (Del Monte), General Electric, Remington Rand, and Bucyrus Erie, among many others.

In carrying out overseas projects it is often necessary to work through international organizations such as World Bank, the International Development Association, Asian Development Bank, or Private Investment Company for Asia, as well as through national development banks and regional economic associations. These activities involve concomitant problems of language and of cultural and political differences that require sophistication and infinite tact. A low handicap in golf is also quite helpful, and Mitsui's internationalists conduct some of their most important business on the greensward.

Mitsui's international activities demand also the closest cooperation with appropriate ministries and government agencies, for in "Japan, Incorporated," enterprise is far from private or free. The government is particularly inquisitive and officious about overseas business. In many cases, circumstances require companies of competing groups to work together, and the adjustment of differences among them can be a formidable problem in itself. For example, loyal Mitsubishi men are said to drink only Kirin beer, brewed by one of their companies. Mitsui men, though less rigid about it, usually stick to the Sapporo brand distributed by Bussan, while Sumitomo men drink the Asahi beer made by their own cohort. At a gathering of executives from two or three groups for discussion of some joint effort, an error in selecting the drinks could cause a serious hitch in the proceedings.

As operations became more complex and responsibilities heavier, the trading companies had to scrutinize world economic and technical trends constantly in order to secure a timely foothold in newly opening fields. Thus in 1965 Bussan formed the Council for Mechanization of Business Administration, which set up the Computer Systems Service Company. In 1970, on the recommendation of the Knowledge Industry Study Team comprising sixteen Mitsui members, CSS became the nucleus of the Mitsui Knowledge Industry Corporation newly established by Bussan, Bank, and seventeen other companies. It provides an information network, data bank, services for developing systems technology, and software for the group, which is increasingly dependent upon the accumulation, processing, and dissemination of information. The scope of the task can be visualized by observing the communications room at Bussan's head office, where an average of ten thousand messages a day are transmitted or received through seven teletype systems connected with Bussan's more than 125 overseas offices and a dozen subsidiary trading corporations abroad. (The telephone bill amounts to more than $20,000 a day.) Through the years the luster of Bussan's famous intelligence work has actually brightened, sometimes to the dismay of foreign customers or competitors. As one government official of Singapore put it: "Mitsui is better at information gathering than the CIA. They send in twenty men to look at an investment. They read everything and they take down everything, even the jokes cracked at meetings."[14]

The same relentless organizational drive led fifteen members of the group to form the Mitsui Housing Problems Study Council to attack Japan's woeful shortage of residential space, uniting their abilities to create a "systems industry" for the acquisition of land, as well as for the design, construction, equipping, financing, and insuring of dwellings. To make undersea resources available, Bussan and Shipbuilding organized Mitsui Ocean Development & Engineering, whose fleet of special-purpose ships is exploring for petroleum in Southeast Asian waters. Similarly, the Mitsui Oil Exploration Company has secured offshore leases around Japan and will cooperate with Ocean Development and other members in probing them.

How the Mitsui Group, with financial institutions of secondary scale, manages to finance its huge undertakings is a point worthy of attention. Of course, the government provides subsidies for a variety of activites related to technology, modernization, export promotion, market regulation and so on. But these funds are only minor compared with the vast amounts needed, and much of the remainder has been supplied or gathered by Mitsui Bussan. President Wakasugi Sueyuki explained the situation in these terms: " The general trading firms have unchangeable, original functions . . . the promotion of international and domestic trade and the financing necessary for supporting the distribution of commodities. But the nature of these functions changes with the times, the growth and diversification of the national economy, and its internationalization. . . . In this situation, the firms are required to display their international credit and development power all the more."[15]

That power has been boosted enormously by Japan's economic successes in recent years. Only a decade ago Japan was a net debtor abroad, and industrialists were short of money for overseas ventures. But by 1972 Japan's net overseas assets ($13.5 billion) were ample, and foreign exchange reserves were close to $20 billion. Pleased over this bonanza, Ogino Sachiu, general manager of Bussan's finance department, told the author in 1972: "We are now facing a new era, a revolution in finance. Throughout the hundred years elapsed since the Meiji Restoration the Japanese, including Mitsui, had difficulty in raising money. But now we can borrow from either the domestic market or foreign markets." Ogino and his staff explained the role of his firm as a "merchant banker" and gave some examples. "Mitsui Bussan has about six hundred subsidiaries and affiliates all over the world, including Japan," he said. "Our guideline for finance is that each company must stand by itself and not rely upon the parent company." Short-term money is no problem for them, he said, because their credit is good in the host countries and they can also borrow in Europe or in the Asian dollar market that has grown up around Singapore. When long-term money is needed, Bussan is able to remit it from Japan.

As an example of joint-venture financing, Ogino cited the project at Mount Newman, in Australia, one of the world's largest deposits of iron ore. A major part of the $300 million capital necessary for the project, which went into partial operation in 1969, came from American, British, and Australian partners. The Japanese share, ten percent of the total, was supplied jointly by Mitsui and C. Itoh & Company. Next in Australia was the Robe River Development Project, with an initial capital of $245 million. An American company, Cleveland Cliffs Iron, and Mitsui each supplied thirty percent of the capital while Australians put up twenty-five percent. Bussan serves as general agent for major Japanese steel mills that will absorb most of the ore under a $1.25-billion, twenty-one year contract. To perform this financial feat, Bussan established a wholly-owned subsidiary, Mitsui Iron Ore Development Company. Bussan then granted that company a loan of $90 million, which was in turn invested in the Robe River project. The funds were raised through the Japan Export-Import Bank and a syndicate of ordinary banks. Now, however, Mitsui Iron Ore is able to raise its operating funds independently in Australia.

The overseas projects in which the Mitsui Group participates are getting bigger and bigger, and investments on the order of $100 million or more are becoming commonplace. In 1972 three Mitsui firms, Toatsu, Petrochemical, and Bussan, signed a contract with Iran to establish a petrochemical complex jointly with the National Petroleum Corporation of Iran and Imperial Chemical Industries. In another venture, Mitsui companies will invest jointly with Bridgestone of Japan, British Petroleum, and other interests to produce liquefied natural gas. One phase of the operation is a liquefaction plant requiring a loan of $150 million, which will be raised by Bussan from Japanese banks. Mitsui, the largest stockholder, will supply Tokyo Electric Power with three million tons of LPG from Abu Dhabi annually over a period of twenty years. Another project for developing natural gas in Sumatra is being planned by Bussan and Mobil Oil at a cost of $700 million, of which Bussan, a major stockholder, would raise $300 million. The most important fund sources for Bussan, other than Mitsui Bank, are Fuji Bank, Bank of Tokyo (formerly Yokohama Specie Bank), Industrial Bank, and Japan's Long-Term Credit and Export-Import banks.

The scale of Bussan's "banking" activities can be glimpsed in the balance sheet for September 30, 1972, which shows that the firm's lendings receivable amounted to the equivalent of more than $700 million. Nevertheless, Bussan is a big debtor, and its borrowings at the same time amounted to a staggering $3.196 billion—an amount equal to forty times its capital stock. The fact that such a grossly over-borrowed position is viewed with equanimity illustrates the relationship of mutual confidence that exists among Japanese businessmen and bankers. It also suggests the reason why they are extremely intolerant of any policies or social experiments that might interrupt or inhibit the steady and vigorous growth of the economy.

Spectacular as its progress has been, the Mitsui Group has not re-gained the dominant position once held by its zaibatsu ancestor. In terms of capitalization, sales, and profits it has fallen considerably behind Mitsubishi. Only a few Mitsui companies—Bussan, Real Estate, Mining, Mining & Smelting, Toshiba, Mitsui Sugar, Mitsui Toatsu, and Oji Paper—are among the largest in their respective fields. The market share of Mitsui companies in manufacturing is less than half that of Mitsubishi and is also smaller than that of Sumitomo. This change is attributed to Mitsui's traditional indifference to heavy industries, which are the bedrock of Mitsubishi and Sumitomo. There have been attempts to establish a Mitsui heavy industrial concern, which would amalgamate Mitsui Shipbuilding & Engineering, Japan Steel Works, Mitsui Miike Machinery, and Mitsui Seiki Kogyo with other engineering firms and makers of heavy machinery and machine tools. However, the dispersion of stockholdings in the companies and the individualism of their presidents—as well as the necessity for specialized manufacturers to expand their market by cultivating business with other groups—has blocked such attempts, and the vision seems to be fading. As President Koyama Goro of Mitsui Bank explained: "Originally, we wanted to form a heavy industrial enterprise. . . . In the course of time, however, the concept somehow turned into a mere hope of challenging Mitsubishi Heavy Industries. We have no intention at all to create a Mitsubishi Heavy Industries type enterprise."

In chemicals the merger of Mitsui Chemical and Toyo Koatsu to form Mitsui Toatsu was a step toward unity, but now the group has two petrochemical companies, with their affiliated oil refineries, that show no signs of merging. However, there are contrary signs, too. In 1970 Bussan effected a merger of three companies of the group to form Mitsui Sugar, the largest company in its category. Meanwhile, several companies that had remained outside the Mitsui fold since the breakup of the zaibatsu have returned to it—nominally, at least. Among them are Onoda Cement, Toyo Menka, Sapporo Breweries, Oji Paper, and

Honshu Paper. At the beginning of 1973 three other secessionist companies, Toshiba, Mitsui O.S.K. Lines, and Mitsukoshi, rejoined the group formally by accepting membership in Nimokukai. If Ishikawa-jima-Harima Heavy Industries and Toyota follow suit, as some commentators predict, the Mitsui empire will have taken another long step toward recapturing its preeminence. It is believed that the new cohesion reflects a desire on the part of individual companies to form a solid phalanx enabling them to compete or negotiate more confidently with such adversaries as the multinational corporations and the monolithic trade and industrial groupings of China and the Soviet Union, with all of whom Mitsui is broadening and deepening its relationships in the post-Vietnam era.

Rivalry among the groups for supremacy seems to be as keen as ever, but much of it is illusory because in fundamental matters they work together much more than they compete. Indeed, by mutual consent and through coordinated effort they have quietly supplanted the prewar zaibatsu as masters of the Japanese economy—and of Japan.

That economy, which is still expanding at the rate of at least twelve percent a year despite earnest assertions that it is being curbed, achieved a gross national product of $200 billion in fiscal 1971, and by 1980 the annual GNP will have exceeded $700 billion, in the opinion of economic futurologist Shimomura Osamu.

Motive power for such expansion is supplied largely by the city banks, whose size has increased remarkably but whose relative ranking has scarcely changed since the 1930s. In March 1971 the borrowings of all Japanese companies listed on Japan's three stock exchanges amounted to about $90 billion. Of this total, the eight largest of the fifteen city banks supplied more than twenty percent. It is significant, however, that nine banks descended from the Mitsui, Mitsubishi, Sumitomo, and Yasuda zaibatsu supplied thirty percent of the total. If the loans extended by the insurance companies related to the four groups were included, the "old zaibatsu" banks' share of all commercial and industrial loans would be much larger.

In the case of the trading companies the situation is similar. The sales of the ten biggest sogo shosha in 1971 amounted to more than $90 billion, which accounted for eleven percent of the sales of all industries, an amount equal to twenty-eight percent of the nominal GNP, and two hundred and thirty percent of the national budget! These ten firms, the four largest of which belong to the Mitsui, Mitsubishi, Sumitomo, and Fuji (Yasuda) groups, handled half of Japan's exports and sixty percent of its imports in the same year. The economic control exercised by the zaibatsu-descended enterprise groups, shared as before by the public utilities monopolies and the reconstituted steelmaking oligopoly, permeates every level of society and of course has a profound effect upon the country's political, social, and cultural life.

Ineluctably, the genro of big business, now in their eighties and nineties, are relinquishing leadership to younger men. Most powerful today are those representing Keizai Doyukai, the Economic Friends Society, known abroad as the Japan Committee for Economic Development because of its close affiliation with the CED, American headquarters of international business and economic diplomacy. In the 1950s these men, as vice-presidents or managing directors of their respective companies, advocated a "new capitalism" under which narrow nationalism would give way to international cooperation, and concern for the welfare of small business and the general public would supplant the single-minded pursuit of profit. Today, their supreme headquarters is the Industrial Problems Study Council, abbreviated to Sanken, which seems to have gained the allegiance of all other economic organizations. The CED chieftains, now the top executives of their own companies as well as of zaikai, speak well, and if they mean what they say they will exercise their enormous powers wisely and with moderation. One hopes that they will, for their decisions will affect not only the welfare of Japan but the course of events throughout the world.

Epilogue:
The Turning Wheels

"My idea is that big corporations have some social responsibility. They have to serve customers, they have to take care of their employees and shareholders; and their business as a whole should be for the good of the nation."[1]—Sato Kiichiro, senior adviser to Mitsui Bank

"The Omuta River, which flows through Omuta City, is called 'The River of Seven Colors.' Not because it is iridescent in the sun's rays but because it changes its color seven times a day according to the hour . . . dark brown, chocolate, ochre. . . . At Mitsui Toatsu Chemicals, where the sewer pipes jut out, the water is covered with foam, and the eyes sting from fumes."[2]—From *Muddy Water,* a periodical published in Omuta

WHAT ARE THE OBLIGATIONS of the men of zaikai, and how are they being fulfilled? Although some of them may feel that enterprise is a game played for its own sake, or as a means of attaining prestige or power, most businessmen would agree with Sato: the purpose of business, indeed of all economic activity, is to provide satisfactions for basic human needs and aspirations. Needs are both physical and psychological. Beyond food, shelter, and clothing, every person longs for a sense of security and personal dignity. These are provided by Japanese business to a creditable degree: in his lifelong employment, a man is given work consonant with his ability; he is made to feel that he has a significant role to play in society; and he gets recognition for his achievements. The present economic system offers him hope for the future by raising the standard of living steadily and enabling him to take pride in the nation's progress. Also, Japan's citizens are relatively secure physically: violent crimes are rare, and the government follows a foreign policy of peace and conciliation.

But human beings have other needs that are not being satisfied. From the beginning of time, people have enjoyed and loved clear skies, bright sunshine, pure air to breathe, pure water to drink, green forests, and wholesome food suited to their tastes. Yet in Japan, as well as in other industrial countries of the world, the "new capitalism," despite its fine words, is poisoning the air with fumes from factories and automobiles, casting a pall over the sky and polluting the rivers and seas. Fish and shellfish, the favorite food of the people, are disappearing rapidly from the waters around Japan, and of those surviving many are poisonous. So-called development has made a shambles of the countryside, laid mountains bare to the ravages of the elements, and disfigured the once-lovely coasts by reclamation projects—sites for more industries that aggravate the pollution of air and water. Development of industrial and residential sites has led to such frantic speculation in land that prices have outdistanced the earning power of would-be home owners. Aggravating the land-price spiral is the endless proliferation of expressways—with disastrous effects on the landscape—to accommodate the vast numbers of automobiles from Japanese factories.[3] As the national wealth is squandered on unnecessary highways and private cars, public means of transportation, upon which people with lower incomes rely, deteriorate alarmingly. In the cities and towns the narrow roads are choked with cars. Since sidewalks are a rarity there, pedestrians are in constant peril: in 1972 more than 16,000 persons were killed by automobiles and nearly a million injured.[4]

As the outpouring of industrial wastes and combustion fumes increased in volume, strange and nameless diseases began to appear among the people. In the cities great numbers of residents suffered from chronic respiratory disturbances caused by chemical vapors; and around the oil refineries and petrochemical plants on the shores of the once-lovely Inland Sea many were afflicted with "Yokkaichi Asthma," named after the city in which it was first identified. At Minamata on Kyushu, and in Niigata City on Honshu, citizens began many years ago to complain about an illness that was debilitating and led gradually to helplessness and death. Some scientists blamed the "Minamata disease" on organic mercury compounds, discharged from chemical plants, and eventually contaminating seafoods eaten by local people, but the operators of those plants hired other researchers to disprove the theory.

At about the same time, people living along the Jinzu River, downstream from the Mitsui Mining & Smelting Company's plants at Kamioka, were found to be suffering from a disease that affected the bones, twisting the body out of shape and causing such pain that sufferers are unable to suppress their cries of anguish. *"Itai, itai"* is the Japanese way of saying "it hurts," and that is how the itai-itai disease, afflicting hundreds and perhaps thousands of people, got its name. Scientists blamed the disabling and often quickly fatal disease on cadmium wastes discharged from the Kamioka smelting plant, but company officials denied it. While visiting the mines and smelters in

1971 the author inquired about the disease and was told that it was caused not by cadmium but by lack of vitamins. Why the people living downstream along the Jinzu got less vitamins than those living upstream was not explained.

At long last, the people, whom Ikeda Seihin once compared with ants in the road, grew impatient with being stepped on; and suddenly zaikai, despite its enormous economic power, was put on the defensive. Statistically, the Japanese have never had it so good, yet seldom have they expressed their dissatisfaction with "the honorable men in power" as vociferously as they are doing today. For the first time the consumers are talking back to the producers. Mass protests and boycotts are occurring with a frequency and intensity that terrifies big business. The Tanaka government, after a strong beginning that featured a grandiose plan to "Remodel the Japanese Archipelago" quickly lost its popularity as consumer prices soared as a result of planned inflation and rampant speculation by monopolists. Wages have never been higher, nor the diet so rich in variety, yet in the last general election the Communist Party nearly tripled the number of its seats in the lower house, while the conservatives failed to win even a majority of the popular vote. Big business is under the severest attack it has experienced since the "Dollar Buying Scandal" of 1931, and citizens' groups are bringing lawsuits, for the first time successfully, to make corporations pay damages for the havoc they wreak.

In 1971 the District Court in Toyama found for the plaintiffs in their claim that the itai-itai disease that had allegedly killed or disabled more than five hundred residents along the Jinzu River had been caused in some cases by a poisonous substance in the effluents from the Mitsui smelter. This historic ruling was the first in which an industry has been blamed for any environmental hazard, and the impact on the nation's management was profound. Concurrently the government, goaded into action by public outcries, had revealed that contamination by cadmium, mercury, and other toxic pollutants was a nationwide problem possibly affecting millions of people.

The management of Mitsui Mining & Smelting denied that there was any connection between cadmium and itai-itai disease and carried the litigation to higher courts. The defendants in the Minamata disease case did likewise. Hundreds of patients and members of bereaved families besieged the head offices of the defendant companies in Tokyo. When the management of one firm refused to hold discussions with them, the demonstrators invaded the company's offices. Finally, the afflicted people picketing the office buildings were dispersed roughly by strong-arm men hired by the companies.

The public image of zaikai had never been uglier. Month after month the press headlined stories about the suppression of evidence, bribery of inspectors, and other scandalous behavior. Finally, in 1972, Mitsui Mining & Smelting was declared liable and ordered by the Nagoya high court to pay compensation to the plaintiffs amounting to $7.7 million. Soon thereafter new lawsuits from other alleged victims were instituted. In order to meet the costs, amounting to the equivalent of a normal year's declared profits, the company had to sell off securities, suspend payment of dividends indefinitely, and make plans to reduce its labor force by more than ten percent. Subsequently, another major company was ordered by the court to pay compensation to Minamata-disease victims. Since the principle of corporate responsibility was firmly established by these rulings, the courts are flooded now with lawsuits that may run into the hundreds of millions of dollars eventually. And yet as late as 1970 the Federation of Economic Organizations, headed by men who are noted for their foresight and precision in economic planning, adopted at its general meeting a resolution stating that pollution of the environment and increase in public hazards had been "unforeseen until now."[5]

The deteriorating environment, however, is only one of many burdensome problems faced by Japan's zaikai as its economic power increases and its role in global affairs becomes more important. As economic growth continues unabated, Japanese exports are again flooding world markets, bringing charges of unfair competition. The nation that had been so recently praised for its astute planning and diligence and rising GNP was being castigated by the very country that had given it such a vigorous push down the highroad to success and threatened with partial exclusion from its most profitable markets. A shortage of workers, coupled with rising wages, is causing Japanese entrepreneurs to seek cheaper labor in other countries, and swollen foreign-exchange reserves have made it possible, even necessary, to step up overseas investments. These activities are regarded in some quarters as "economic imperialism," and anti-Japanese agitation has become an alarming phenomenon in what is sometimes called the "new Co-Prosperity Sphere" in Southeast Asia.

"Japan, Incorporated" is now talking, with one voice as usual, about a drastic revision of priorities. The economy of rapid growth, steeply rising production, and expanding exports will, they say, be reoriented to stress public works, social security, knowledge-intensive industries, an international division of labor, and an excess of imports over exports. This is what foreign countries, especially the United States, want to hear. Unfortunately, the attainment of these goals appears to be highly improbable. The author realized the difficulty of slowing down the economy during a discussion with Omoto Shimpei, the scholarly and articulate president of Mitsui Mining & Smelting.

After the separation of Mitsui Mining into two companies after the war, Mining & Smelting had the best of the bargain, making steady profits on nonferrous metals while coal mining remained in the doldrums. Nevertheless, like many another top executive, Omoto is beset by the same kind of dread that is felt by a motorist on a steep downgrade upon discovering that his brakes are burned out. The really terrifying truth, he seems to say, is that ceaseless, rapid economic growth is essential for the survival of Japanese capitalism. In most countries economic growth must be stimulated occasionally or constantly. In Japan it is a built-in factor, and it must not be interrupted except in case of dire necessity. (When the growth rate of the GNP drops below ten percent, they call it a "recession.")

President Omoto states the case with almost painful clarity. In the first place, the labor unions became very strong after the war and constantly demanded higher wages even if the company was not making a profit. "To cope with it, industry decided to enlarge the scale of production units. As a result, major manufacturers expanded their facilities, not because goods were saleable but because it was necessary to increase productivity to overcome the labor problem. Therefore, Japan's productivity increased tremendously, regardless of demand. In a sense, this accounts for our so-called high economic growth."

As an example, he said that at the old zinc smelter at Miike, 1,300 men can produce ten thousand tons a month; but at the new smelter at Hachinohe, in northern Honshu, only three hundred men are required to produce the same amount. "Therefore, if our Miike smelter wants to enhance its labor efficiency or productivity, it would have to boost production to thirty thousand tons. Otherwise, the labor force of Miike Smelting would have to be cut by two thirds. In the United States it would not be so difficult to lay off men not needed, but in Japan it is almost impossible to reduce the number of workers." (Although his company now finds it necessary to reduce the staff by a thousand men to meet the costs of compensation for the itai-itai victims, this will be done gradually, by not replacing employees who quit or retire.)

"This is not only because of opposition from labor unions," Omoto continued gravely. "Their grandfathers and fathers have been working for the same mill, and we must respect such personal relationships. It is a social reality that labor cannot be considered just as an element of cost, or a commodity. It is our fate to expand facilities to support the labor force, and thus the productivity of Japan has grown enormously. People of the world call us 'economic animals,' but still we must sell what we have produced. We cannot reduce the labor force, so we [must] increase per capita productivity."

The problem, he said, is not overproduction, for most of the human race still lives without even the most rudimentary amenities. "In the world today there are three billion three hundred thousand people. Out of this number, maybe one billion are living without electric lights; maybe another billion are living without adequate shelter. . . . If we were to provide one electric bulb for each household, or a sheet of galvanized iron for each family with a leaking roof, the amount of copper and zinc needed would be greater than that used in the Pacific War. Then there could be no such thing as overproduction. . . . There is such a latent demand among the people for materials and products, but if their needs are left unfulfilled, world peace will be disrupted. In one country we have to curtail production, while in another part of the world people are in need of that specific product. This sort of picture is the typical weak point of capitalism. And I think the communists are attacking that very point. Capitalism must correct this weakness, don't you think so?"

Here was a representative of Japan's "new capitalists," a man of sincerity with the welfare of his employees and of his country at heart. Yet inevitably, like the more successful of his colleagues, he will be cast in the role of an oppressor. In helping to make the transition from the zaibatsu economy to the more enlightened zaikai regime of today, these men abolished many old evils and added impressively to the material well-being of the people—at least in quantitative terms. But there remained one basic contradiction: the antagonism between human welfare, in the broader sense, and the economic necessities of a small, overpopulated, and poorly endowed country that is trying to hold up its head in the world.

Among the chieftains of the Mitsui empire many have been out-standing managers and some have had an aura of greatness. Yet few if any were loved by the people, and none is commemorated as a hero. The tragedy of Japan today is that it can have no heroes, at least in the political-economic sphere. For, so far at least, the nation's leaders have found no way to achieve material progress without imposing hardships upon their own people and arousing the fear or antagonism of other nations. In any country, power and happiness are incompatible. In Japan, they are mutually exclusive.

Appendix A: Mitsui Constitution of 1722

THE MITSUI CODE OF REGULATIONS is believed to have been embodied in the will of Hachirobei Takatoshi, founder of the House, who died in 1694. It was formally promulgated in 1722, on the hundredth anniversary of his birth, by his heir Hachiroemon Takahira, also in the form of a will. Thus the will of Takahira is ostensibly a revised version of the original Mitsui House code attributed to the founder.

This translation is adapted from one prepared for Dr. Eleanor Hadley by Watanabe Hanako from a text supplied by the Mitsuis. It differs substantially from the translation submitted by the Mitsuis to GHQ-SCAP in 1945 and from other translations published in older sources—notably, portions quoted in Chapter 3. Since some of the original terms are archaic or obscure, it should be considered an approximation rather than an exact rendering.

THE WILL OF SOCHIKU

1. Soju-koji* has lately [that is, some thirty years earlier] redrafted the House Rules and left them as his will. The descendants shall forever observe these rules without fail.

2. The members of the House shall promote the common welfare with one accord. Those in authority should be kind to subordinates, who in turn should respect those in authority. The House will be more prosperous when its rules are observed punctiliously. One may be friendly with outsiders, but if he thinks only of his own pride and does not consider other members of the House, there will be no peace at home, and disorder and chaos may result. If one lives in luxury and neglects his business, there will be no prosperity for the House.

3. Unless a merchant is diligent and attentive, his business will be taken over by others. One must be painstaking.

* Sochiku and Soju are posthumous Buddhist names of Hachiroemon Takahira and his father Hachirobei Takatoshi, respectively. *Koji* is an honorific used for Buddhist laymen.

4. Farsightedness is essential to the career of a merchant. In pursuing small interests close at hand, one may lose huge profits in the long run.

5. The head [of the senior main family] shall be regarded as the head of the House; those under him should serve him as faithfully as they would their real parents, heeding his wishes and obeying his instructions.

6. It is the will of Soju that the family of Hachiroemon shall remain at all times as the senior main family. Therefore, the son of Hachiroemon, if he is sufficiently capable, shall succeed his father and become the head of the House even though he may not be of age.

7. When there are no children to succeed as head of the senior family, a son may be adopted from among other members of the House. When there is no male issue, a female may succeed to the headship.

8. Among the members of the House, the distinction of main families and associate families* shall be as follows:

Six Main Families [*honke*]

Hachiroemon [*soryoke,* or senior main family]

Gennosuke

Saburosuke

Jiroemon

Hachirojiro

Sohachi

Three Associate Families [*renke*]

Sokuemon

Kichiroemon

Onoda Hachisuke†

The appointment of the above-mentioned three associate families is documented elsewhere. It shall not be necessary to designate any more associate families.

9. The shares [of House assets] held by member families shall be as follows:

62   for Hachiroemon

---

* In the original will Takahira used the business titles rather than the given names of the family heads. These titles indicated the position held by the bearer: thus Hachiroemon headed the entire Mitsui clan, while Saburosuke managed the Kyoto exchange house, Gennosuke the Osaka branch, and Jiroemon the Edo branch. However, in time the titles, even that of Hachiroemon, became nonhereditary and passed from one family to another as occasion required, so a different nomenclature of the families was adopted.

† The Onoda family eventually took the Mitsui surname. Two other families were also established in the Meiji era, bringing the total to eleven.

   30 for Gennosuke
   27 for Saburosuke
   25 for Jiroemon
   22.5 for Hachirojiro
   22.5 for Sohachi
    8 for Sokuemon
    6 for Kichiroemon
    7 for Hachisuke
   10 for a reserve from which to grant awards [for merit] to the
second and other children of the main and associate families.

10. I am now seventy years old. During the remainder of my life,
which might turn out to be not more than a year [actually he lived for
fifteen more years], I shall save as much as I can from the funds for my
living expenses, and such savings shall be deposited with the chief
accountant. The exact sum of such savings shall be submitted to me for
my perusal once a year. The amount deposited during the year shall be
handed to me at the earliest possible date after the third of January every
year. Thrift is the basis of prosperity: luxury ruins a man.

11. Should any member of the House be prevented by ill health
from attending to his business duties, his allotment for living expenses
shall be reduced by twenty percent. This amount shall be laid aside for
distribution as a bonus among other members of the House who
worked diligently meanwhile.

12. The second and other younger sons may be given in adoption
to other members of the House or be allowed to establish branch
families at about thirty years of age, if they have acquired sufficient
business experience and are capable. The sum of money to be given for
the benefit of the above-mentioned children shall be as follows:
   (a) For talented children, approximately 3,000 silver pieces [value
       unspecified]
   (b) For children of above-average ability, 70 to 80 *kan* [3.75 kg]
       of silver
   (c) For children of middling ability, 30 to 40 kan of silver

13. Should the second son or other younger sons establish branch
families, they shall be allowed to use the business name of Echigoya,
but the use of the surname Mitsui shall not be allowed without special
approval.

14. Female children attaining majority should be married to sons
of House members whenever possible. When these girls marry into
outside families, however, an adequate sum of money shall be provided
for the wedding ceremony.

15. In principle, the eldest son is to succeed his father as head of the
family; but if his conduct should cause harm to the family, he shall be

expelled, even if he is the only son, and sent into the priesthood. In such a case, a successor will be adopted from among the other members of the House. Those members who prove incapable of maintaining their families or who conduct themselves immorally shall also be sent into the priesthood.

16. A considerable amount of silver shall be set aside as a reserve fund for the benefit of elderly employees of the House who have lost their property, and also for the relief of those suffering from fire and other calamities.

17. Three mature and capable members of the House shall be appointed as chief directors of the House to look after the business activities of the branch shops. A monthly meeting shall be convened with the managers of all stores present for mutual consultation. The conditions of the Nagasaki trade, loans, and the exchange business shall also be carefully studied.

18. All kinds of speculation and new and unfamiliar business ventures shall be strictly forbidden.

19. Boys of the House shall be sent to our Kyoto shop at the age of twelve or thirteen for apprenticeship and then back to the Edo shop at the age of fifteen to start learning bookkeeping and trading. They shall master these subjects by the time they reach the age of about twenty-five. During this period they shall have a sojourn in Osaka and have an opportunity to learn the money-exchange business and especially the dry-goods business. On occasion they shall make tours to Joshu and Gunnai [sericulture regions in central Honshu], where they should be given an intimate knowledge of raw-silk purchasing. At about thirty years of age they should be accomplished merchants to whom the management of some of the shops can be entrusted.

20. Concerning business with the government, the members of the House shall conduct themselves modestly and pay due respect to government officials. Honesty and business morality shall be upheld under all circumstances.

21. Persons in public office are not, as a rule, prosperous. This is because they concentrate on discharging their public duties and neglect their own family affairs. Do not forget you are a merchant. You must regard dealings with the government always as a sideline of your business. It is therefore a great mistake to cast the family business aside and give precedence to government service. Those who find it necessary to deal with the government, however, shall consider public duty and family responsibility as equally important, like the two wheels of a cart.

22. It is each man's duty to believe in the gods and Buddha and to follow the teachings of Confucianism. Nevertheless, it is not good to go

to extremes. Those who are immoderate in religion will never be successful merchants. They are bound to neglect their own business and are likely to lead the House to ruin. Special care should be taken not to donate huge sums of money or treasures to temples or shrines.

23. The gods and Buddha lie within one's heart. Therefore, you should not offer gold and silver to them and expect some special grace in return. Instead of wasting gold and silver on the shrines and temples, you should make appropriate contributions to the poor and the suffering; the return will be ten thousand times as large, and your charitable deeds will be valued greatly. You should be thoroughly aware of this fact.

24. The essential role of the managers is to guard the business of the House. They should give appropriate advice if their masters' conduct is not good and correct blunders that may be made. Since people become slow and obtuse as they grow older, an age limit of around fifty-five should be considered proper for members of the Board.*

25. In order to select worthy managers, keep an eye on the young men and train promising candidates for that position. The number of managers shall be limited to six or seven and they shall be selected as follows:

2 persons from Edo
3 persons from Kyoto
1 person from Osaka

These arrangements must be adhered to and care must be exercised to prevent any oversights.

The above articles are the instructions which I leave as my will. These instructions are to be obeyed strictly and without fail.

In the seventh year of Kyoho [1722], the Year of Water and the Tiger, the eleventh month, first day

Sochiku
(Stamped with his seal)

* This is still the most common retirement age for Japanese white-collar employees.

Appendix B: Mitsui
Constitution of 1900

THE MITSUI HOUSE CODE OF 1722 remained unchanged until 1900, when a new version prepared under the supervision of Count Inoue Kaoru was adopted. By that time, however, it was no novelty. Professor Hozumi Nobushige, who compiled the house codes of the Mitsuis, Shibusawas, and other families, wrote in 1912: "In recent years, it has become very common for noble and rich families to establish house laws in order to regulate their household affairs, especially with regard to the family and property relations. The house laws of aristocratic or rich families . . . have a common feature which shows that their foundation is laid almost without exception on ancestor worship. The house law usually begins with a preamble, reciting that it is established in accordance with the instructions bequeathed by the ancestors, or that it is established to put the ancestral house on a firm basis."*

The present version, supplied by the Mitsuis to GHQ-SCAP in 1945, would appear to be incomplete, as certain important matters are omitted and some references suggest the existence of supplementary regulations. For example, the definitions of business property and joint property in articles XXIII and XXIV are incomplete and family property is not defined at all, nor is its disposition prescribed. Likewise, the distribution of individual family reserve funds is not specified. It is presumed that these and other matters relating to financial assets were spelled out in documents that remained secret even after 1945. The translation used here is based primarily on that prepared for Dr. Eleanor Hadley by Watanabe Hanako from the text of the rules supplied by the Mitsuis. Dr. Hadley and the author have made minor changes.

THE MITSUI HOUSEHOLD RULES
(Revised Version Adopted in 1900)

ARTICLE I: What is termed the House of Mitsui in the present

---

* Hozumi Nobushige, *Ancestor-Worship and Japanese Law* (Tokyo: Maruzen, 1912), pp. 123–24.

Household Rules is the collective name of the eleven Mitsui Families which are descended from the Ancestor, Mitsui Soju-koji [Hachirobei Takatoshi], or have been specifically ranked as members of the House in accordance with the Family Rules hitherto maintained by the Mitsui House. The eleven families are those of: Hachiroemon, Gennosuke, Gen'emon, Takayasu, Hachirojiro, Saburosuke, Fukutaro, Morinosuke, Takanosuke, Yonosuke, Tokuemon, and their respective direct successors.

ARTICLE II: Six Mitsui families, namely, those of Hachiroemon, Gennosuke, Gen'emon, Takayasu, Hachirojiro, and Saburosuke shall be designated as the Main Families of the House of Mitsui, and among these, the first mentioned, the family of Hachiroemon, shall be the Senior Main Family according to the instructions left by Sochiku-koji.

ARTICLE III: In case any member of the House of Mitsui desires to establish a separate family in the future, such a family shall be able to establish a new branch [of the family in question], but the new branch shall not be admitted to membership in the House.

ARTICLE IV: In conformity with the precepts of their ancestors, the members of the House should always associate with each other in close fraternity and should combine their efforts harmoniously further to promote the great achievements of their ancestors, and thereby perpetuate the solid foundation of their respective families.

ARTICLE V: To refrain from a life of luxury and to practice strict economy are fundamental principles of the House which were set by the ancestors. All members of the House are under obligation to adhere to these principles and to have their children observe the same.

ARTICLE VI: The members of the House are forbidden to do the following acts:
1. to join any political party or to associate themselves officially with any political activity;
2. to incur debts;
3. to guarantee others' debts.

ARTICLE VII: The members of the House are forbidden to do the following acts without the permission of the Household Council:
1. to engage in business on their own private account;
2. to be a shareholder or to invest in commerce or industry on their own private account;
3. to become officers or employees of companies or associations on their own private account;

4. to enter government service or to participate in public organizations;

5. to participate in other matters designated as requiring the permission of the Household Council.

ARTICLE VIII: In case a dispute should arise between members of the House, the same shall not be permitted initially to be taken into court. The case in dispute must first be presented to an arbitrator or arbitrators appointed by the Household Council. If the judgment of such an arbitrator or arbitrators is not acceptable, the case may be submitted to legal arbitration following the appropriate formalities called for by law. If cancellation of the legal arbitration is wanted after such a procedure has been taken, the case in question should be returned to the House arbitrator for final judgment.

ARTICLE IX: The members of the House are required to engage in the business of the Mitsui Holding Company and its affiliated companies in accordance with the regulations of the Mitsui Holding Company and with the decisions made at the General Shareholders Meetings.

ARTICLE X: The Household Council shall consist of the full-fledged members of the House. Retired members of the House as well as heirs-presumptive of major age may be observers. Women are not entitled to be observers.

ARTICLE XI: The chairman of the Household Council shall be the head of the Senior Main Family. In case he is prevented from taking the chair, one of the members of the other Main Families shall take his place.

In case the head of the Senior Main Family is not a person of competence, the oldest member of the other Main Families shall take his place.

ARTICLE XII: The Household Council shall be convened at least once a month.

ARTICLE XIII: Matters requiring decision by the Household Council shall in general be as follows:

1. succession, marriage, adoption, divorce, separation, retirement, establishment of separate families, incompetency, quasi incompetency, recognition, and such other matters which cause a significant change in personal position or blood relation of the members of the House.
2. a. allocation of the Mitsui Holding Company dividend among:
   i. the Common Reserve Fund of the House;
   ii. the Individual Reserve Fund of each member family;

iii. the annual expenditure of each member family.

b. payment from the Common Reserve Fund of the House and from the Individual Reserve Fund of each family.

3. the disposal of assets in the event of the liquidation of the Mitsui Holding Company and disposal of property held by the members of the House who retired or were expelled from the Mitsui Holding Company.

4. matters pertaining to the joint property of the House other than the Common Reserve Fund of the House.

ARTICLE XIV: The meeting of the Household Council shall not be convened unless more than half of the regular members are present. However, concerning the matters outlined below, the meeting of the Household Council shall not be convened unless three-fifths of the regular members are present and the quota of their shares exceeds half the total shares held by all the families:

1. determination of the Common Reserve Fund of the House;
2. expenditure of the above Fund;
3. disposal of property after the liquidation of the Mitsui Holding Company.

ARTICLE XV: The matters presented to the meeting of the Household Council shall be determined by a majority vote of the regular members present at the meeting unless specified to the contrary in these Household Rules.

ARTICLE XVI: The Chairman of the Household Council shall not be prevented from participating in the discussion or from casting his vote at the meeting.

ARTICLE XVII: The observers of the Household Council may express their opinions but are not entitled to vote.

ARTICLE XVIII: The legal proxies or other representatives of the regular members of the Household Council may participate in the discussion and vote at the meeting.

ARTICLE XIX: In case a member of the House is not of good morality or recklessly wastes his property, the Household Council can appoint a guardian for him and have such guardian supervise his conduct and control his property, even if the said member is not so defective as to be legally declared a quasi incompetent.

ARTICLE XX: In case a member of the House desires to retire from active business, he shall obtain the approval of the Household Council in advance.

ARTICLE XXI: In case a member of the House desires to appoint or remove his legal successor, he shall obtain the approval of the Household Council in advance.

ARTICLE XXII: The property of the House shall be divided into three categories: Business Property, Joint Property, and Family Property.

ARTICLE XXIII: Business Property is that which is invested in the Mitsui Holding Company in the form of shares.

ARTICLE XXIV: Joint Property is the reserve fund which is to be used for relief in case of calamities suffered by some member of the House and for items which are to be borne jointly by the members of the House. It is also to be used for making needed increases in the Business Property.

ARTICLE XXV: The Common Reserve Fund of the House stipulated in the foregoing Article shall be expended for the following purposes in accordance with rules fixed elsewhere:
1. in case any member of the House falls in great financial difficulties due to natural calamities or other inevitable causes, thus making it difficult for him to maintain the dignity of the House;
2. in case a supplementary contribution is to be made to the fund reserved for the second and other children of members of the House, on such occasions as marriage, adoption, or establishment of a separate family;
3. in case of joint expenditure necessitated by extraordinary and unavoidable causes.

ARTICLE XXVI: The members of the House are required to appropriate the following items out of the dividend of the Mitsui Holding Company. First, maintenance cost of the Mitsui Household office. After the above sum has been deducted, five percent of the remaining amount shall be allocated to the Common Reserve Fund of the House.

ARTICLE XXVII: The remainder of the dividend is to be divided among the members of the House after thirty percent of this sum has been set aside for individual family reserve funds.

ARTICLE XXVIII: Apart from Family Property [kasan] the allocation of House Property shall be in the following proportion, regardless of the size of the investment which each has made:
23 % for the Senior Main Family
11.5% for the other five Main Families
3.9% for the five Associate Families

ARTICLE XXIX: Family Property can be disposed of at the discretion of its holder, unless special limitation is made in the present Household Rules, the Rules of the member family, or in some other rules made in accordance with the present Rules.

ARTICLE XXX: If any member of the House violates the terms of the present Household Rules, or the Rules of member families, or other rules fixed in accordance with the present Household Rules, or if any member of the House conducts himself so as to be subject to reproach or damages the dignity of the House, the Household Council shall, in due consideration of and in proportion to his misdeeds, (1) suspend his membership in the House for a certain period, (2) expel him from the House, (3) confiscate his share of the Business Property and Joint Property.

ARTICLE XXXI: In case any Article of these Household Rules should in the future conflict with statutes owing to changes made in the National laws, such revision as is deemed necessary shall be effected at once.

ARTICLE XXXII: Should any matter arise which is not provided for by the present Rules, the same shall be settled in accordance with the traditions and customs of the House.

Appendix C:

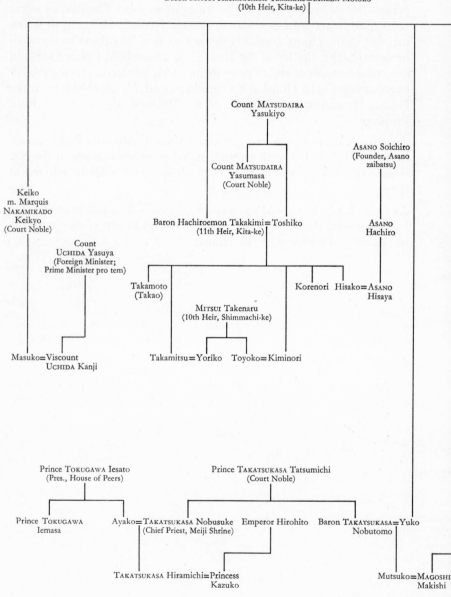

Baron MITSUI Hachiroemon Takamine=MAEDA Motoko
(10th Heir, Kita-ke)

Count MATSUDAIRA
Yasukiyo

ASANO Soichiro
(Founder, Asano
zaibatsu)

Keiko
m. Marquis
NAKAMIKADO
Keikyo
(Court Noble)

Count MATSUDAIRA
Yasumasa
(Court Noble)

Count
UCHIDA Yasuya
(Foreign Minister;
Prime Minister pro tem)

Baron Hachiroemon Takakimi=Toshiko
(11th Heir, Kita-ke)

ASANO
Hachiro

Takamoto
(Takao)

Korenori Hisako=ASANO
Hisaya

MITSUI Takenaru
(10th Heir, Shimmachi-ke)

Masuko=Viscount
UCHIDA Kanji

Takamitsu=Yoriko Toyoko=Kiminori

Prince TOKUGAWA Iesato
(Pres., House of Peers)

Prince TAKATSUKASA Tatsumichi
(Court Noble)

Prince TOKUGAWA
Iemasa

Ayako=TAKATSUKASA Nobusuke
(Chief Priest, Meiji Shrine)

Emperor Hirohito

Baron TAKATSUKASA=Yuko
Nobutomo

TAKATSUKASA Hiramichi=Princess
Kazuko

Mutsuko=MAGOSHI
Makishi

The Mitsui Main Family c. 1900-1945

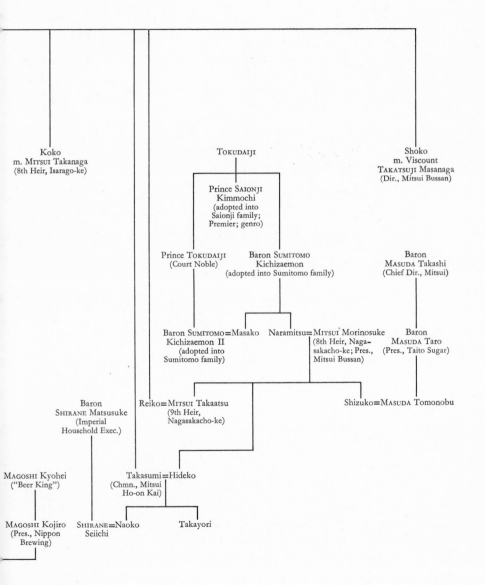

Koko
m. MITSUI Takanaga
(8th Heir, Isarago-ke)

TOKUDAIJI

Shoko
m. Viscount
TAKATSUJI Masanaga
(Dir., Mitsui Bussan)

Prince SAIONJI
Kimmochi
(adopted into
Saionji family;
Premier; genro)

Prince TOKUDAIJI
(Court Noble)

Baron SUMITOMO
Kichizaemon
(adopted into Sumitomo family)

Baron
MASUDA Takashi
(Chief Dir., Mitsui)

Baron SUMITOMO=Masako
Kichizaemon II
(adopted into
Sumitomo family)

Naramitsu=MITSUI Morinosuke
(8th Heir, Naga-
sakacho-ke; Pres.,
Mitsui Bussan)

Baron
MASUDA Taro
(Pres., Taito Sugar)

Baron
SHIRANE Matsusuke
(Imperial
Household Exec.)

Reiko=MITSUI Takaatsu
(9th Heir,
Nagasakacho-ke)

Shizuko=MASUDA Tomonobu

MAGOSHI Kyohei
("Beer King")

Takasumi=Hideko
(Chmn., Mitsui
Ho-on Kai)

MAGOSHI Kojiro
(Pres., Nippon
Brewing)

SHIRANE=Naoko
Seiichi

Takayori

Appendix D:

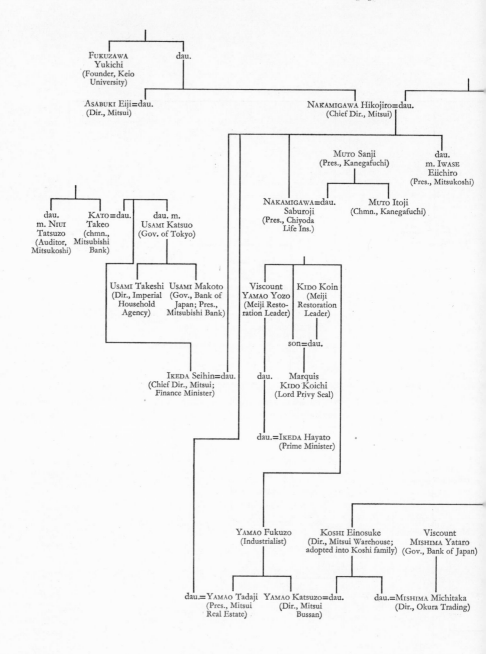

FUKUZAWA Yukichi (Founder, Keio University) — dau.

ASABUKI Eiji=dau. (Dir., Mitsui)

NAKAMIGAWA Hikojiro=dau. (Chief Dir., Mitsui)

MUTO Sanji (Pres., Kanegafuchi)

dau. m. IWASE Eiichiro (Pres., Mitsukoshi)

dau. m. NIUI Tatsuzo (Auditor, Mitsukoshi)

KATO=dau. Takeo (chmn., Mitsubishi Bank)

dau. m. USAMI Katsuo (Gov. of Tokyo)

NAKAMIGAWA=dau. Saburoji (Pres., Chiyoda Life Ins.)

MUTO Itoji (Chmn., Kanegafuchi)

USAMI Takeshi (Dir., Imperial Household Agency)

USAMI Makoto (Gov., Bank of Japan; Pres., Mitsubishi Bank)

Viscount YAMAO Yozo (Meiji Restoration Leader)

KIDO Koin (Meiji Restoration Leader)

son=dau.

IKEDA Seihin=dau. (Chief Dir., Mitsui; Finance Minister)

dau.

Marquis KIDO Koichi (Lord Privy Seal)

dau.=IKEDA Hayato (Prime Minister)

YAMAO Fukuzo (Industrialist)

KOSHI Einosuke (Dir., Mitsui Warehouse; adopted into Koshi family)

Viscount MISHIMA Yataro (Gov., Bank of Japan)

dau.=YAMAO Tadaji (Pres., Mitsui Real Estate)

YAMAO Katsuzo=dau. (Dir., Mitsui Bussan)

dau.=MISHIMA Michitaka (Dir., Okura Trading)

Some Family Ties in the Mitsui Concern

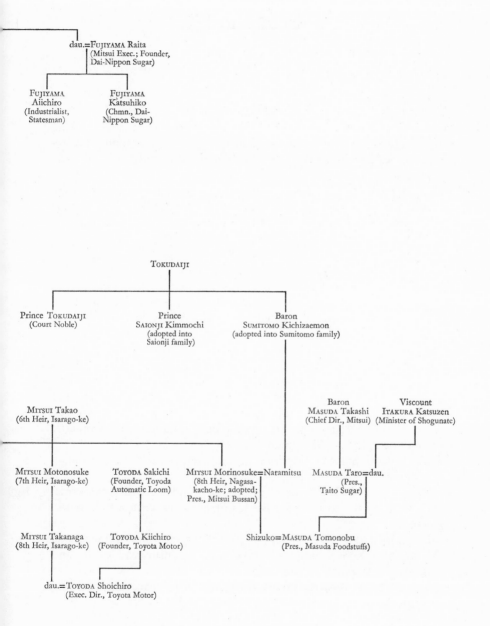

dau.=FUJIYAMA Raita
(Mitsui Exec.; Founder,
Dai-Nippon Sugar)

FUJIYAMA
Aiichiro
(Industrialist,
Statesman)

FUJIYAMA
Katsuhiko
(Chmn., Dai-
Nippon Sugar)

TOKUDAIJI

Prince TOKUDAIJI
(Court Noble)

Prince
SAIONJI Kimmochi
(adopted into
Saionji family)

Baron
SUMITOMO Kichizaemon
(adopted into Sumitomo family)

Baron
MASUDA Takashi
(Chief Dir., Mitsui)

Viscount
ITAKURA Katsuzen
(Minister of Shogunate)

MITSUI Takao
(6th Heir, Isarago-ke)

MITSUI Motonosuke
(7th Heir, Isarago-ke)

TOYODA Sakichi
(Founder, Toyoda
Automatic Loom)

MITSUI Morinosuke=Naramitsu
(8th Heir, Nagasa-
kacho-ke; adopted;
Pres., Mitsui Bussan)

MASUDA Taro=dau.
(Pres.,
Taito Sugar)

MITSUI Takanaga
(8th Heir, Isarago-ke)

TOYODA Kiichiro
(Founder, Toyota Motor)

Shizuko=MASUDA Tomonobu
(Pres., Masuda Foodstuffs)

dau.=TOYODA Shoichiro
(Exec. Dir., Toyota Motor)

Appendix E: The Mitsui Group in 1973

THIS UNOFFICIAL LIST WAS COMPILED from information in *The Mitsui Group,* a pamphlet published in 1971 by the Mainichi Newspapers; from *Mitsui Trade News,* published by Mitsui and Company; and from reports appearing in recent periodicals concerned with industry and business.

An asterisk (*) indicates a member of Nimokukai, the association coordinating the group's activities. A dagger (†) indicates a company that is not formally a member of the group.

FINANCE, COMMERCE, SERVICES

*MITSUI BANK—general banking and foreign exchange
*MITSUI TRUST & BANKING—banking, trusts, and related business
*MITSUI MUTUAL LIFE INSURANCE—life and accident insurance, annuities
*TAISHO MARINE & FIRE INSURANCE—non-life insurance
*MITSUI REAL ESTATE DEVELOPMENT—leasing, management, construction of buildings, reclamation of land, real-estate transactions
 MITSUI KANKO DEVELOPMENT—sightseeing and recreational facilities
*MITSUI & COMPANY—general trading business, foreign and domestic
 TOYO MENKA KAISHA—general trading business, foreign and domestic
*MITSUKOSHI LTD.—department stores
 MITSUI OIL SUPPLY—distribution and retail sales of petroleum products
*MITSUI LEASING & DEVELOPMENT—leasing of industrial machinery, etc.
*MITSUI WAREHOUSE—warehousing, port services, customs clearance, etc.
*MITSUI WHARF—warehousing, port services, customs clearance, etc.
 MITSUI AIR & SEA SERVICE—travel agents, insurance, cargo and customs clearance
 ASIA AIR SURVEY—aerial photography, mapping, surveying, planning of projects

*Mitsui O.S.K. Lines—marine transportation, ship agency, ship brokerage, warehousing, port and land transportation, etc.

Mitsui Knowledge Industry Corporation—information network, data bank, systems technology, software

Heavy Industries, Mining, Metals, Construction

*Mitsui Shipbuilding & Engineering—shipbuilding, heavy machinery, steel mills, etc.

*Japan Steel Works—castings, forgings, plates, welded structures, industrial machinery

*Sanki Engineering—construction equipment, chemical and mining machinery, etc.

*Mitsui Construction—engineering and construction of industrial plants

Ishikawajima-Harima Heavy Industries—ships, industrial plants, machinery, aircraft engines

†Ishikawajima Koehring—industrial plants, construction machinery, cranes

Showa Aircraft Industry—trucks, tank trucks, aircraft fuel tanks, containers, etc.

†Toyota Motor—cars, trucks, automotive parts

*Mitsui Mining—mining of coal, sale of coal, coke, cement, building materials

*Mitsui Mining & Smelting—zinc, lead, copper, precious metals, castings, etc.

Mitsui Kozan Coking—processing of coke

*Hokkaido Colliery & Steamship—coal and coke

Taiheiyo Industries—mining and sale of coal

Hokkaido Sulphur—sulphur and pyrites

Mitsui Miike Machinery—chemical plants, material conveyors, mining machinery

Toyo Engineering—chemical, oil-refining, and petrochemical plants

Mitsui Oil Exploration—petroleum leases, exploration, mining and sales

Mitsui Ocean Development & Engineering—development of ocean resources

Mitsui Aluminum—aluminum and other light metals and alloys

Mitsui Alumina—production of alumina

Fuji Sanki Pipe & Tube—steel pipes

Toyo Carrier Engineering—refrigerators and thermal regulators

Shin Nippon Air Conditioning—heating and cooling equipment

PRECISION MACHINERY

MITSUI SEIKI KOGYO—precision machinery, compressors, automotive parts

TOYO BEARING MANUFACTURING CO.—ball and roller bearings, conveyor rollers, etc.

ELECTRICAL MACHINERY AND EQUIPMENT

*TOKYO SHIBAURA ELECTRIC—electrical machinery, turbines, home appliances, computers, communication equipment, nuclear machinery

†NIPPON ATOMIC INDUSTRY GROUP—nuclear reactors, etc.

FUJIKURA CABLE WORKS—manufacture and sale of electric cables, etc.

SHOWA ELECTRIC WIRE & CABLE—manufacturing and sales of electric wire, cable, rods, relay lines, etc.

NISHI NIPPON ELECTRIC WIRE & CABLE—manufacturing of copper wire and cable of all types

CHEMICALS, PHARMACEUTICALS

*MITSUI TOATSU CHEMICALS—fertilizers, industrial chemicals, medicines, building materials

*MITSUI PETROCHEMICAL INDUSTRIES—ethylene, propylene, aromatics, etc.

DENKI KAGAKU KOGYO—plastics, synthetic rubber, chemical fertilizers, cement

TOAGOSEI CHEMICAL INDUSTRY—sodium hydroxide, chlorine, synthetic HCl, resins

TOYO SODA—cement, soda ash, ammonium chloride, vinyl monomerchloride, other chemicals

DAICEL—cellulose, synthetic resins, organic compounds, film acetate fibers, etc.

FUJI PHOTO FILM—photographic materials, optical apparatus, magnetic tapes, etc.

PFIZER TAITO—pharmaceuticals, medicines for livestock, etc.

TEXTILES AND FIBERS

*TORAY INDUSTRIES—synthetic fibers, plastics, textile products, manufacturing machinery

DAITO WOOLEN SPINNING & WEAVING—woolen tops, hosiery, yarns, fabrics, clothing

CERAMICS, CEMENT

CENTRAL GLASS—sheet glass, soda products, ammonium fertilizers
ONODA CEMENT—cement, wet concrete, limestone, etc.

FOODSTUFFS, BEVERAGES, FEEDS

*NIPPON FLOUR MILLS—wheat flour, bran, prepared mixes, pastes,
   protein, feeds
MITSUI AGRICULTURE & FORESTY—foodstuffs, tea plantations, ranch-
   ing, lumber, etc.
MITSUI SUGAR—manufacture of granulated, crystal, and cube sugar
SAPPORO BREWERIES—beer, soft drinks
NIPPON FORMULA FEED—feed for poultry, livestock, fish farming;
   veterinary medicines

PAPER, PULP, LUMBER

*OJI PAPER—roll newsprint, printing, tracing and writing paper,
   lumber
HONSHU PAPER—paper, pulp, byproducts, lumber, building materials,
   chemicals, packing machines
MITSUI LUMBER—general lumber, processed boards, prefabricated
   flooring

SOME OF MITSUI'S JOINT VENTURES IN JAPAN

NIPPON BRUNSWICK—bowling equipment; with Brunswick Corp.
NIPPON UNIVAC KAISHA—computer manufacturing and marketing;
   with Sperry Rand
TOKYO NICKEL—making nickel oxide sinter; with International Nickel,
   Shimura Kako
OJI CORN STARCH—with Oji Paper, National Starch & Chemical
ARBOR ACRES JAPAN—poultry products; with Arbor Acres (U.S.A.)
KYOKUTO PETROLEUM INDUSTRIES—oil refining; with Mobil Oil
NIPPON STRICK—marine containers and trailers; with several Japanese
   companies and Strick Corp.
NIPPON WAYNE—industrial sweepers; with Howa Machinery, Wayne
   (U.S.A.)
JAPAN AJAX MAGNETHERMIC (JAMCO)—electric induction furnaces;
   with Ajax (U.S.A.)

NIPPON HERR—continuous metal processing lines; with Herr Equipment (U.S.A.)

JAPAN CALPAK—canned foods; with California Packing Corp.

NIPPON PARKS—cleaning equipment for textile plants; with Parks Cramer (U.S.A. and U.K.)

KOMATSU-BUCYRUS—construction and mining machinery; with Komatsu, Bucyrus Erie

GENERAL AIRCON—air conditioners; with Japan Electric Heating, General Electric

NIPPON REMINGTON RAND—office machines and equipment; with Remington Rand

FENWAL CONTROLS OF JAPAN—controls and safety devices; with Fenwal Inc. (U.S.A.)

HOHNEN-LEVER—margarine, soap; with Hohnen, Unilever

GORDON JOHNSON JAPAN—poultry-processing equipment; with Gordon Johnson-Stephens (Holdings) Ltd. (U.K.)

MITSUI FULLER—paints and coatings; with W. P. Fuller (U.S.A.)

PERMELEC ELECTRODE—permanent electrodes for electrolytic machinery; with Chemnor of Panama, Oronzio de Nora Impianti Electrochemici (Italy)

NEW HOLLAND JAPAN—selling American agricultural machinery; with New Holland Division of Sperry Rand

FUJI XEROX—Fuji Photo Film and Rank Xerox (U.K.)

SOME OF MITSUI'S OVERSEAS VENTURES

CANADIAN MOTOR INDUSTRIES HOLDINGS—import, assembly, distribution of Toyota cars

ENGINEERING SERVICES (ASIA) PTE. LTD.—in Singapore; leasing of construction equipment; Mitsui and IHI Koehring

MITSUI IRON ORE DEVELOPMENT PTY.—holding company for Mitsui interests in Robe River Mining Project, Western Australia

KANEKA BELGIUM N.V.—chemicals; Mitsui and Kanegafuchi

AUSTRALIAN TUBE MILLS PTY.—pipes; Mitsui and local capital

MITSUI EXPORT CORP.—export marketing of U. S. products; Mitsui Bussan and Mitsui & Co. (U.S.A.)

MITSUI ALUMINA (AUSTRALIA)—alumina; Mitsui and Gove Alumina

SOCIÉTÉ MINIÈRE DE TENKE FUNGURUME—international oil consortium with Government of Zaire, Charter Consolidated, Amoco Minerals Co. (Standard Oil affiliate), Mitsui, etc.

HUANZALA MINE—copper mining in Peru; Mitsui Mining & Smelting

COMPANHIA INDUSTRIAL DE RESINAS SINTETICAS PORTUGAL—plastics; Mitsui, Shin'etsu, local investors

DEUTSCHE ROOSEVELT TRADING—West Germany; Mitsui and local capital

INOUE RUBBER THAILAND—tires, tubes, and rubber products; Mitsui, Inoue Rubber, local investors

KENYA TORAY MILLS—nylon cloth; Mitsui, Toray, Chori Co.

KOREA POLYESTER—polyester; Mitsui, Toray, Korean interests

GYEON BUG LIVESTOCK—poultry raising in Korea; Mitsui and Korean interests

PACIFIC GRAIN—Growing and exporting soybeans, grain, and feeds in U.S.A.; Mitsui and local investors

P. T. EMDECE MARINE DEVELOPMENT CORP.—fishing and importing shrimp, Indonesia; Mitsui, Taiyo Fishery, local investors

DURAKUT INTERNATIONAL—marketing drilling tools in U.S.A.; Mitsui and Kobe Steel

PARK AVENUE IMPORTS—marketing menswear in U.S.A.; Mitsui and Chicago interests

INDUSTRIAS SINTETICAS DE CENTRO AMERICA—manufacturing synthetic textiles in El Salvador; Toray, Chori, and Salvadorean interests

FERTILANZANTES MITSUI INDUSTRIA E COMERCIO—making fertilizers in Brazil; Mitsui and local interests

CIA. INDUSTRIAS QUIMICAS MITSUI IHARA—making chemicals in Brazil; Mitsui and local investors

ISEKI MITSUI MAQUINAS AGRICOLAS—manufacturing farm machinery in Brazil; Mitsui and local investors

CASAMAR—fisheries in Panama Canal Zone; Mitsui

MITSUI AGRO PECUARIA—growing, marketing, and processing pepper in Brazil; Mitsui and Brazilian interests

INDUSTRIAS MARITIMAS DE SUPE—making fish meal and fish oil in Peru; Mitsui

QUMICA SOL—making explosives in Peru; Mitsui and Asahi Chemical

TOYOTA DEL PERU—assembly of cars in Peru; Mitsui and Toyota

CEYLON ASSOCIATED RUBBER INDUSTRIES—tires and tubes; Mitsui, Inoue Rubber, local interests

CEYLON SYNTHETIC TEXTILE MILLS—synthetic fabrics; Mitsui, Toray, Sakai Textile Industry, local interests

UNITED INDUSTRIAL PAPER PRODUCTS—making paper in Singapore and Malaysia; Mitsui and local interests

SANGKASI THAI—making galvanized iron sheet; Mitsui, C. Itoh, Thai interests

MALAYAN SUGAR MFG.—sugar in Malaysia; Mitsui, Nissin, local interests

TOYO STEEL STRUCTURE—shell plates for oil tanks; Mitsui Bussan, Mitsui Shipbuilding & Engineering

SIAM ELECTRIC INDUSTRIES—copper wire in Thailand; Mitsui and Sumitomo Electric

JUJO WEYERHAUSER—newsprint in U.S.A.; Jujo Paper, Mitsui Bussan, Weyerhauser

MITSUI PETROCHEMICAL INDUSTRIES (U.S.A.)—sales of petrochemical products to U.S.A.

H-M PLASTICS—sales of plastics in U.S.A.; Mitsui and Hercules

THIESS PEABODY MITSUI COAL PTY. LTD.—coal mining in Australia; Mitsui, Thiess Holdings of Australia, Peabody Coal of U.S.A.

Notes

1 · FROM SWORD TO SOROBAN

1. Sokubei's speech is condensed slightly from the version given in Oland D. Russell, *The House of Mitsui* (Boston: Little, Brown & Co., 1939), pp. 67–68. In regard to its authenticity, Mitsui Reiko, the historian of the family, said that it is part of the House records and "may be authentic." However, it must be admitted that most of the Mitsui family history up to the 1620s is to some extent legendary.

The ancient history in the early chapters comes mainly from these books and articles (which are cited fully in the Bibliography): Yamada Taketaro's *Mitsui Monogatari* [The Mitsui Story]; Tsuchiya Takao's "Development of the Mitsui Zaibatsu"; Oland Russell's *The House of Mitsui;* Eleanor Hadley's doctoral thesis, "Concentrated Business Power in Japan"; *Mitsui, Mitsubishi, Sumitomo,* by Mitsubishi Economic Research Institute; *The House of Mitsui,* by Mitsui Gomei Kaisha; and interviews with Mitsui family members and with Yamaguchi Eizo, custodian of the family archives in the Mitsui Bunko.

2 · ECHIGOYA THE SHUNNED

1. Hachirobei's homily is taken from the manuscript *Shobai-ki,* written by Shuho's grandson Takaharu, cited by Miyamoto Mataji in *Gosho—Nihon no Chonin* [Great Merchants of Japan] (Tokyo: Nihon Keizai Shimbun-sha, 1970), p. 127.

2. Quoted in Tsuchiya Takao, "Mitsui Zaibatsu no Hatten" ["Development of the Mitsui Zaibatsu"], *Chuo Koron,* August 1946, p. 61.

3. Author's translation. An English translation of Ihara Saikaku's *Nihon Eitai-gura* [Japan's Eternal Treasure House] is cited in the Bibliography.

Other sources used for this chapter are the same as those for Chapter 1.

3 · THE SOURCE OF HAPPINESS IS PRUDENCE

1. The inventory of Yodoya's treasure is adapted from E. H. Norman, *Japan's Emergence as a Modern State* (New York: Institute of Pacific Relations, 1940), p. 107.

4 · "REMEMBER WE ARE MERCHANTS"

1. This and other sayings of Motoori are taken from Matsumoto Shigeru, *Motoori Norinaga, 1730–1801* (Cambridge: Harvard University Press, 1970), p. 144 ff.

The material concerning the House constitution is taken from several sources already cited and also from translations of the documents given by Eleanor Hadley in "Concentrated Business Power in Japan" (Ph. D. dissertation, Radcliffe College, Cambridge, Mass., 1949), and in Appendixes A and B of this book.

5 · LEGACY OF THE BARBARIANS

1. Norman, *Japan's Emergence,* p. 46.
2. Quoted in Foster Rhea Dulles, *Yankees and Samurai* (New York: Harper & Row, 1965), p. 29.

Some of the information about Oshio's revolt is from Najita Tetsuo, "Oshio Heihachiro," in Albert M. Craig and Donald H. Shively, eds., *Personality in Japanese History* (Berkeley and Los Angeles: University of California Press, 1970).

6 · TRADE OF BLOOD AND GUILE

1. *Washington Herald,* 1860; quoted in *Japan Times,* May 23, 1960.
2. Ernest Satow, *A Diplomat in Japan* (London: Seeley, Service & Co., Ltd., 1921), p. 46.

7 · THE MAN FROM NOWHERE

1. The letter from Kyoto, as well as most of the other information about the appointment of the new banto, is from Minomura Seiichiro, *Minomura Rizaemon Den* [A Biography of Minomura Rizaemon] (Tokyo: San'yu Shimbun-sha, 1969), p. 25 et passim.

8 · PICKING THE WINNER

1. Norman, *Japan's Emergence,* p. 28.
2. Ibid., p. 49.
3. Yamada Taketaro, *Mitsui Monogatari* [The Mitsui Story] (Tokyo: Bunsei-sha, 1934), p. 54.
4. Satow, *Diplomat in Japan,* p. 186.
5. Minomura Seiichiro, *Minomura Rizaemon,* p. 20.
6. Quoted in Albert M. Craig, *Choshu in the Meiji Restoration* (Cambridge: Harvard University Press, 1961), pp. 334–36.
7. Ibid.
8. Quoted in G. B. Sansom, *The Western World and Japan* (New York: Alfred A. Knopf, 1970), p. 306.
9. Quoted in Tsuchiya Takao, "Mitsui Zaibatsu no Hatten," p. 60.

9 · BY APPOINTMENT TO THE EMPEROR

1. Yamada Taketaro, *Mitsui Monogatari,* p. 70.
2. Ibid., p. 75.
3. Ibid., p. 69.
4. Ibid., p. 85.
5. Minomura Seiichiro, *Minomura Rizaemon,* p. 40.

6. John R. Black, *Young Japan: Yokohama and Yedo 1858–79* (Tokyo: Oxford University Press reprint, 1968), vol. 2, p. 258.

7. Minomura Seiichiro, *Minomura Rizaemon,* p. 106. The quotation about Mitsui and Ono being on bad terms is from Obata Kyugoro, *An Interpretation of the Life of Viscount Shibusawa* (Tokyo: Diamondo Jigyo Kabushiki Kaisha, 1937), pp. 89–90.

8. Minomura Seiichiro, *Minomura Rizaemon,* p. 114.

9. Ibid., p. 113.

10. Obata Kyugoro, *Viscount Shibusawa,* p. 107.

11. Minomura Seiichiro, *Minomura Rizaemon,* p. 136.

12. Grace Fox, *Britain and Japan, 1858–1883* (London: Oxford University Press, 1969), p. 396.

13. Minomura Seiichiro, *Minomura Rizaemon,* p. 136.

10 · FOUNDATIONS IN BANKING AND COMMERCE

1. Russell, *House of Mitsui,* p. 227.

2. *The Mitsui Bank—A Brief History* (Tokyo: The Mitsui Bank, Ltd., 1926), pp. 35–36.

3. Minomura Seiichiro, *Minomura Rizaemon,* p. 150.

4. Ibid., p. 154.

5. Okuma Shigenobu, *Fifty Years of New Japan* [Kaikoku Gojunen Shi], trans. and ed. Marcus B. Huish (New York: Kraus Reprint, 1970), p. 624.

6. Masuda Takashi, *Jijo Masuda Takashi Den* [The Autobiography of Masuda Takashi] (Tokyo: Uchida Rokaku Ho, 1939), pp. 163–67.

7. Russell, *House of Mitsui,* p. 186.

8. Minomura Seiichiro, *Minomura Rizaemon,* p. 168.

9. Tsuchiya Takao, "Mitsui Zaibatsu no Hatten," p. 166.

10. Minomura Seiichiro, *Minomura Rizaemon,* pp. 158–59.

11 · CAPITALISM, JAPANESE STYLE

1. Iwata Masakazu, *Okubo Toshimichi, The Bismarck of Japan* (Berkeley and Los Angeles: University of California Press, 1964), pp. 177 and 236.

2. Hoshino Yasunosuke, *Mitsui Hyakunen* [One Hundred Years of Mitsui] (Tokyo: Kajima Shuppan-kai, 1968), p. 82.

3. Obata Kyugoro, *Viscount Shibusawa,* pp. 123–24.

4. William Manchester, *The Arms of Krupp, 1587–1968* (Boston: Little, Brown & Co., 1968), p. 146.

5. Eleanor Hadley, *Antitrust in Japan* (Princeton: Princeton University Press, 1970), p. 37.

12 · THE ZAIBATSU BUILDERS

1. Quoted in Eleanor Hadley, "Concentrated Business Power in Japan," p. 144.

2. Quoted in Takahashi Kamekichi, *The Rise and Development of Japan's Modern Economy* (Tokyo: Jiji Press, Ltd., 1969), p. 242.

3. Shirayanagi Shuko, *Nakamigawa Hikojiro Den* [A Biography of Nakamigawa Hikojiro] (Tokyo: Iwanami Shoten, 1940), p. 213.

13 · Diplomacy by Other Means

1. Quoted in Joseph Pittau, *Political Thought in Early Meiji Japan, 1868–1889* (Cambridge: Harvard University Press, 1967), p. 39.
2. Quoted in Byron K. Marshall, *Capitalism and Nationalism in Prewar Japan* (Stanford, California: Stanford University Press, 1967), p. 45.
3. *Mainichi Daily News,* April 7, 1968.

14 · The Best Laid Plans . . .

1. Diary of John Hay, January 1, 1905; quoted in Yanaga Chitoshi, *Japan Since Perry* (New York: McGraw-Hill, 1949), p. 310.
2. J. J. Korostovetz, *Pre-War Diplomacy: The Russo-Japanese Problem* (London: British Periodicals, Ltd., 1920), pp. 86, 113.
3. "Japan and America" (part of a series), *Asahi Evening News,* April 21, 1971.

15 · A Foothold on the Mainland

1. Quoted in Marius Jansen, *The Japanese and Sun Yat-sen* (Cambridge: Harvard University Press, 1954), p. 111.
2. Obata Kyugoro, *Viscount Shibusawa,* p. 177.
3. Ibid., pp. 177–78.

16 · The Two Faces of Mitsui

1. Russell, *House of Mitsui,* p. 256.
2. O. Edmund Clubb, *Twentieth Century China* (New York: Columbia University Press, 1964), p. 79.
List of loans to China from A. Morgan Young, *Japan Under the Taisho Tenno* (New York: William Morrow and Co., Inc., 1929), pp. 99–100.

17 · Which Way to Utopia?

1. Ishimoto Shizue, *Facing Two Ways* (New York: Farrar & Reinhart, 1935), pp. 145–64.
2. Byron K. Marshall, *Capitalism and Nationalism in Prewar Japan,* p. 101.
3. Yamada Taketaro, *Mitsui Monogatari,* p. 111.
4. Quoted in Russell, *House of Mitsui,* p. 228.

18 · The Clan in All Its Glory

1. "Mitsui Group," *Mainichi Daily News,* April 3, 1970.
2. Obata Kyugoro, *Viscount Shibusawa,* p. 216.
3. Isaac F. Marcosson, "The Changing East," *Saturday Evening Post,* September 16, 1922.
4. Ibid., p. 137.
5. Yamada Taketaro, *Mitsui Monogatari,* p. 128.
6. George Marvin, "The Mitsui: Princes of World Trade," *Asia,* October–December 1924, p. 20.
7. Frederic Morton, *The Rothschilds* (New York: Atheneum, 1962), p. 58.

19 · Whom the Gods Would Destroy

1. *Banking in Modern Japan*, 2d ed. (Tokyo: Fuji Bank, Ltd., 1967), p. 88.
2. Estimate from a study by Takahashi Kamekichi quoted in Tsuchiya, "Mitsui Zaibatsu no Hatten," p. 26.
3. Quoted in Hadley, "Concentrated Business Power," p. 320.
4. Fujihara Ginjiro, *The Spirit of Japanese Industry* (Tokyo: Hokuseido Press, 1936), p. 84.

Life expectancy for men in Japan around 1935 was forty-four years; in the United States, it was sixty-two (*Fortune,* September 30, 1936). "It is probably safe to say that Japan has one active case of tuberculosis for every ten families, or thrice the American rate" (ibid.). In 1937 Japan's profit rate was 12.2 percent, compared with five percent in the United States (Hadley, "Concentrated Business Power," p. 315).

5. Quoted in Russell, *House of Mitsui,* p. 239.
6. Marvin, "The Mitsui," p. 20.
7. Obata Kyugoro, *Viscount Shibusawa,* p. xiv.
8. Yoshihashi Takehiko, *Conspiracy at Mukden: The Rise of the Japanese Military* (New Haven: Yale University Press, 1963), p. 20.
9. Eto Shinkichi, "The Proposed Interception of the South Manchurian Railway," *Acta Asiatica,* No. 14, 1968, p. 59.
10. *Yamamoto Jotaro Denki* [A Biography of Yamamoto Jotaro] (Tokyo: Hara Yasusaburo, 1942), pp. 729–33 et passim.

20 · Challenging the World

1. Quoted in Russell, *House of Mitsui,* p. 275.
2. *Fortune,* September 1936, p. 52.
3. Fujihara Ginjiro, *Spirit of Japanese Industry,* p. 201.
4. George M. Wilson, *Radical Nationalist in Japan: Kita Ikki, 1883–1937* (Cambridge: Harvard University Press, 1969), p. 81.
5. Kodama Yoshio, *I Was Defeated* (Tokyo: Radiopress, 1959), p. 24.
6. Sadako N. Ogata, *Defiance in Manchuria* (Berkeley and Los Angeles: University of California Press, 1964), p. 35.
7. Hadley, "Concentrated Business Power," p. 345.
8. Richard Storry, *The Double Patriots* (London: Chatto & Windus, 1957), p. 85.
9. Quoted in Ogata, *Defiance in Manchuria,* p. 94.
10. Richard Storry, *A History of Modern Japan* (London: Penguin reprint, 1967), p. 190.
11. Russell, *House of Mitsui,* p. 244.
12. Hoshino Yasunosuke, *Mitsui Hyakunen,* p. 274.
13. Ibid., p. 277.
14. Ibid., p. 280.
15. Russell, *House of Mitsui,* p. 296.
16. Wilson, *Radical Nationalist in Japan,* p. 85.
17. Reporter's interview with Owen Lattimore, in *Mainichi Daily News,* September 14, 1971.
18. Matsuoka was speaking for foreign minister Uchida Yasuya, but he did so with an air of pugnacious defiance that made him appear to be the originator of the policy. He may also have been speaking for Toyama

Mitsuru, of whom he once said: "I do nothing without finding out what Toyama's opinion is." (Marius Jansen, *The Japanese and Sun Yat-sen,* p. 38.)

21 · THE HONORABLE MEN IN POWER

1. Quoted from Ikeda Seihin, *Zaikai Kaiko* [Recollections of the Financial World], in Hoshino Yasunosuke, *Mitsui Hyakunen,* p. 282.

2. *Fortune,* September 1936, p. 166.

3. Gustavus Myers, *History of the Great American Fortunes* (1907; reprint ed., New York: Modern Library, 1936–37), pp. 702–3.

4. Yamada Taketaro, *Mitsui Monogatari,* p. 131.

5. Quoted in Arthur Tiedemann, "Big Business and Politics in Prewar Japan," an essay in *Dilemmas of Growth in Prewar Japan,* James W. Morley, ed. (Princeton: Princeton University Press, 1971), p. 286.

6. *Fortune,* September 1936, p. 83.

7. Quoted in Russell, *House of Mitsui,* pp. 306–7.

8. Quoted in Tiedemann, "Big Business and Politics," p. 286.

9. Quoted in Hoshino Yasunosuke, *Mitsui Hyakunen,* p. 289.

10. Quoted in Storry, *Double Patriots,* p. 187.

11. Quoted in Tiedemann, "Big Business and Politics," p. 301. For Kita's comment on Ikeda, see ibid., p. 300.

22 · THE WAVE OF THE FUTURE

1. George Seldes, *One Thousand Americans* (New York: Boni & Gaer, 1947), pp. 211–12.

2. George Seldes, *Facts and Fascism* (New York: In Fact, 1943), pp. 112–13; Buchman's statement, "I thank heaven for a man like Adolf Hitler," appeared in *Time,* August 18, 1962.

3. Wealth of Mitsuis, in Russell, *House of Mitsui,* p. 4; wealth of Rockefellers, in Myers, *History of the Great American Fortunes,* p. 704; wealth of J. P. Morgan, ibid., p. 636.

4. "The Meaning of Defense and a Call for its Strengthening," issued by the Ministry of War, October 1932; quoted in *Fortune,* September 1936.

5. Quoted in Leonard Mosley, *Hirohito, Emperor of Japan* (Englewood Cliffs, New Jersey: Prentice-Hall, Inc., 1966), p. 16.

6. Hadley, *Antitrust in Japan,* p. 41.

7. Hadley, "Concentrated Business Power," p. 164.

8. Quoted in Joseph C. Grew, *Report from Tokyo* (New York: Simon and Schuster, 1942), p. 82.

9. Tiedemann, "Big Business and Politics," p. 310.

10. Chuan-hua Lowe, *Japan's Economic Offensive in China* (London: George Allen & Unwin, 1939), pp. 125–26.

11. Tiedemann, "Big Business and Politics," p. 313.

12. T. A. Bisson, *Japan's War Economy* (New York: Institute of Pacific Relations, 1945), p. 42.

13. Ibid., p. 51.

14. *Oriental Economist,* January 1941, p. 6.

Information on Hoshino and the Opium Monopoly Bureau, from *Summation on Hoshino,* International Military Tribunal for the Far East, February

18, 1948 (mimeographed), pp. GG-16, 17. The figure of $300 million is from Robert J. C. Butow, *Tojo and the Coming of the War* (Princeton: Princeton University Press, 1969), p. 110. For narcotics traffic in China and Manchuria, see Roland Seth, *Secret Servants* (New York: Farrar, Straus & Cudahy, 1957), p. 127 et passim.

23 · CRACKS IN THE FOUNDATION

1. Bisson, *Japan's War Economy,* p. 6.
2. Quoted in Seldes, *Facts and Fascism,* p. 52.
3. Hillis Lory, *Japan's Military Masters* (New York: Viking, 1943), p. 211.
4. Storry, *Double Patriots,* p. 263.
5. From an unpublished autobiographical sketch by Mitsui Takasumi, 1952.
6. Lory, *Japan's Military Masters,* p. 213.

24 · NOT NECESSARILY TO JAPAN'S ADVANTAGE

1. Bisson, *Japan's War Economy,* pp. viii, 117.
2. Courtney Browne, *Tojo: The Last Banzai* (New York: Paperback Library, 1967), p. 211.
3. Russell, *House of Mitsui,* pp. 238–39.
4. Information from a former Mitsui employee who served concurrently as a military intelligence officer.
5. U. S. Department of State, *Papers Relating to the Foreign Relations of the United States: Japan, 1931–41* (Washington: U. S. Government Printing Office, 1943), vol. 2, p. 133.
6. Niizeki Yasutaro, *Watakushi no Rirekisho* [My Personal History] (Tokyo: Nihon Keizai Shimbun-sha, 1972), p. 83.
7. John Potter, *Yamamoto: The Man Who Menaced America* (New York: Paperback Library, 1967), p. 56.
8. "Toyama Mitsuru," *Asahi Shimbun,* August 30, 1941.
9. Otto Tolischus, *Through Japanese Eyes* (New York: Reynal & Hitchcock, 1945), p. 111.
10. Browne, *Tojo: The Last Banzai,* p. 153.
11. "Gendai-shi o Tsukuru Hitobito—Niizeki Yasutaro" ["Men Who Make Contemporary History—Niizeki Yasutaro"], *Ekonomisuto,* February 1, 1972.
12. "Kishi Nobusuke, Prime Minister of Japan," *Who's Who in Japan* (Tokyo: Rengo Press, No. 1 [Autumn 1958]), p. 84.
13. Fujishima Udai, "Kishi Nobusuke-shi ni Okeru 'Senso Hangai' no Kenkyu" ["Study on War Crimes: Kishi Nobusuke"] (part 1), *Ushio,* May 1972, pp. 201–10.
14. Condensed from reconstructed version in Robert J. C. Butow, *Japan's Decision to Surrender* (Stanford, California: Stanford University Press, 1967), pp. 47–49.
15. Quoted in Lester Brooks, *Behind Japan's Surrender,* (New York: McGraw-Hill, 1968), p. 15.
16. Edo Hideo and Narita Tomomi, "Mitsui Yameta no wa Wakage no Itari" ["He Quit Mitsui, Carried Away by Youthful Impulse"], *Zaikai,* March 15, 1971.

25 · ASHES, ASHES, ALL FALL DOWN

1. President's Directive of September 6, 1945, quoted in T. A. Bisson, *Zaibatsu Dissolution* (Berkeley: University of California Press, 1954), p. 239.

2. Quoted in Bisson, *Zaibatsu Dissolution,* p. 70, from *Asahi Shimbun* of October 21, 1945.

3. Author's interview with Mitsui Hachiroemon Takakimi, July 8, 1971, as interpreted by his niece, Mrs. Shirane Seiichi.

4. These calloused scribes seem to have survived Simmons' harpoon. Roth's book, suppressed by SCAP, was at last published in Japan in 1971 and attracted considerable interest. Bisson's *Japan's War Economy* and *Zaibatsu Dissolution,* quoted frequently here, are indispensable. Mark Gayn's *Japan Diary* (New York: William Sloane Associates, 1948) is an excellent antidote to the diplomatic eyewash obscuring that fascinating period from the younger generation.

5. Edo Hideo, *Sushiya no Shomon* [The Sushi Shop Pledge] (Tokyo: Asahi Shimbun-sha, 1966), pp. 162–63; and author's interview with Edo.

6. "Mitsui Group," (second article of a series) in *Mainichi Daily News,* February 20, 1970. The word "voluntarily" has been substituted for "spontaneously."

7. Quoted in Hadley, *Antitrust in Japan,* p. 98.

8. Kusayanagi Daizo, "Kunisukuri no Gotan Hyakusho Edo Hideo" ["Edo Hideo, A Poor Farmer Trying to Create Land"], *Bungei Shunju,* September 1970, p. 225.

9. Ibid., p. 226.

10. William J. Sebald and Russell Brines, *With MacArthur in Japan* (New York: Norton, 1965), p. 89.

26 · ALL THE KING'S MEN

1. Niizeki Yasutaro, *Watakushi no Rirekisho,* p. 153.

2. Hadley, *Antitrust in Japan,* p. 147.

3. Arita Kyosuke, *Sogo Shosha* [General Trading Companies] (Tokyo: Nihon Keizai Shimbun-sha, 1970), p. 53.

4. Quoted in Hadley, *Antitrust in Japan,* pp. 135–36.

5. Information about Alaska Pulp is from "Sengo Saidai no Kaigai Toshi" ["The Biggest Postwar Overseas Investment"], *Shukan Asahi,* October 11, 1959; and *Japan Times,* February 28, 1964.

6. Statement from Sasayama and Robinson quoted in Bisson, *Zaibatsu Dissolution,* p. 148.

27 · NEW WINE IN OLD BOTTLES

1. *Mitsui, Mitsubishi, Sumitomo* (Tokyo: Mistubishi Economic Research Institute, 1955), p. 30.

2. *Oriental Economist,* January 1959, p. 10.

3. *Asahi Evening News,* May 30, 1961.

Details about Edo and Hadley, from Edo, *Sushiya no Shomon,* pp. 33–34. Details about Edo and Narita from "Mitsui Yameta no wa Wakage no Itari," *Zaikai,* March 15, 1971, p. 50.

28 · THE REBIRTH OF MITSUI BUSSAN

1. "Gendai-shi o Tsukuru Hitobito—Niizeki Yasutaro," *Ekonomisuto,* February 1, 1972.

29 · BEHIND THE CURTAIN

1. Hadley, "Concentrated Business Power," p. 281
2. Author's interview with Kurata Okito, 1971.
3. "Vox Populi, Vox Dei" column in *Asahi Evening News,* November 25, 1959.
4. Author's interview with Kurata Okito, 1971.
5. Special factors were involved. For example, the company was producing very high profits, so it had less reason than Mitsui Mining to impose a harsh labor policy.
6. *Time,* August 8, 1962.
7. Told to the author by a member of the mission.
8. *Mainichi Daily News*, January 1, 1961.
9. The CIA's manipulation of the labor movement was exposed in 1967 when Thomas W. Braden, a former agent, wrote in the *Saturday Evening Post* that some two million dollars annually had been funneled from the CIA through American unions, including the AFL-CIO. One of the best known CIA fronts was the American Institute for Free Labor Development, "which has spent millions of dollars in Latin America, most of it from the CIA. . . ." (Drew Pearson, *Japan Times,* March 1, 1967). Victor Reuther, international affairs director of the UAW, admitted receiving $50,000 from Braden for buying off foreign labor unions (*I. F. Stone's Weekly,* May 22, 1967).
10. Since the author has learned from reliable sources that most left-wing organizations have been infiltrated by intelligence agencies, it is not unreasonable to suppose that political sabotage is involved.
11. Inakawa Hiroyoshi, quoted in *Mainichi Daily News,* July 19, 1964.
12. *Asahi Evening News,* June 17, 1960, and *Japan Press Weekly Bulletin,* June 18, 1960, p. 5.
13. The boss of the assailants' group (Restoration Action Corps) testified in a later trial that he maintained liaison with the police, with whom he discussed plans before the June 15 attack (*The Yomiuri*, January 18, 1961).
14. *Asahi Evening News,* March 20, 1963.
15. In 1964, police estimated that there were 5,200 criminal gangs with 184,000 members (92,000 in 1958). Police forces in 1963 totaled 137,277 men (*The Yomiuri,* October 21, 1958 and June 9, 1964).

30 · JAPAN UNLIMITED

1. "Seiji ni Kane o Dasuna" ["Don't Provide Money for Politics"], *Bungei Shunju,* November 1960, pp. 66–74.
2. Articles by staff writers on Ikeda Hayato, his business backers, and supporting clubs, *Shukan Asahi,* October 30, 1960.
3. Details of the mine disaster are from English-language newspapers in Japan, November 10–27, 1963. President's statement from *Japan Times,*

November 13, 1963. Details about the billion-yen loan, from *Yomiuri*, November 12, 1963.

4. Interviews with Kurata Okito and other executives of Mitsui Mining.

5. Author's interview with Kurata Okito, 1971.

6. *Kuristo Shimbun*, March 3, 1973, quoted in *Japan Times*, March 23, 1973, and supported by the government's figures.

7. Calculated by the author from figures in *Japan Company Directory* for corresponding years.

8. Calculated by author from data in *Mitsui, Mitsubishi, Sumitomo*, 1955.

9. Wakasugi died of cancer in May, 1973. His successor is Ikeda Yoshizo, who had been vice-president since 1971.

10. Interview with Kawaguchi Isao, Executive Vice-President, Mitsui Aluminum Company.

11. A magazine reported that Dewi was introduced to Sukarno by "Mr. K.," president of the "T" trading company. From a direct source the author learned that Kodama Yoshio and Hagiwara Kichitaro (one of the largest contributors to conservative party factions) were advisers to the "T" company. The "T" company, like Kinoshita Sansho, was said to be an instrument for extracting political funds from other companies by serving as an "influence peddler" for trade with Indonesia.

12. Robert Paul, "Mitsui's Merger," *Far Eastern Economic Review*, October 29, 1964, p. 263 (confirmed in author's interview with Mizukami).

13. It is not rare for Mitsui Bussan to sign contracts involving aggregate sales exceeding one billion dollars, as in the case of Australian iron ore.

14. *Japan Times*, February 24, 1970.

15. Author's interview with Wakasugi Sueyuki, 1972.

EPILOGUE: THE TURNING WHEELS

1. Author's interview with Sato Kiichiro, February 2, 1971.

2. Quoted in *Yomiuri Shimbun*, March 30, 1972.

3. There are already about twenty million automobiles in Japan, and the number per unit of land area is eight to ten times as great as that of the United States. Yet government planners anticipate an increase to nearly fifty million cars by 1985. Toyota Motor, the third largest automobile maker in the world, celebrated the completion of its ten-millionth vehicle in 1973.

4. Police statistics show that 15,918 persons were killed and 886,578 were injured by automobiles in the 658,742 accidents that occurred in 1972 (*Mainichi Daily News*, April 7, 1973). The deaths recorded, however, are those occurring instantly or immediately after an accident.

5. "Resolution adopted at the 31st Regular General Meeting of Keidanren [Federation of Economic Organizations]," released May 25, 1970.

Bibliography

English-language Publications

For general historical data on Japan and the Far East, the author consulted well-known works by G. B. Sansom, James Murdoch, John K. Fairbank, Albert M. Craig, Edwin O. Reischauer, Foster Rhea Dulles, Kenneth Scott Latourette, G. C. Allen, William W. Lockwood, O. Edmund Clubb, Richard Storry, Grace Fox, Chitoshi Yanaga, Saburo Ienaga, E. Papinot, William L. Langer, John R. Black, Ernest Satow, and many others. Contemporary works, such as those by Leonard Mosley, John Toland, David Bergamini, Lester Brooks, Herbert Feis, Robert C. Butow, and many other authors were scanned profitably for confirmation of details. However, for reasons of space this bibliography will cite only sources relating specifically to the subjects concerned, or to which the author is particularly indebted for material used in this book.

Periodicals from which materials were drawn regularly were the *Japan Times, Asahi Evening News, Daily Yomiuri, Mainichi Daily News,* and translations of articles from leading Japanese periodicals supplied by the U. S. Embassy Political Section. Of special value were those from the *Japan Economic Journal, Oriental Economist,* and *Journal of Social and Political Ideas in Japan.* Also used were newsletters, papers, and pamphlets issued by the Japan Federation of Employers Associations (Nikkeiren), the Japanese Federation of Economic Organizations (Keidanren), the General Council of Trade Unions (Sohyo), Japanese government agencies, the Japan Institute of Labor, and numerous private companies and banks. For current or historical data on companies and persons, useful sources were the *Japan Company Directory* published by the *Oriental Economist, Japan Business Directory* published by Diamond Lead Co., the third edition of the *Japan Biographical Encyclopedia and Who's Who* published by Rengo Press, and annual reports of companies mentioned.

Books

Adams, T. F. M. and Hoshii, Iwao. *A Financial History of the New Japan.* Tokyo, Kodansha, 1972

Banking in Modern Japan. 2d ed. Tokyo, Fuji Bank, Ltd., Research Division, 1967

Bisson, T. A. *Japan's War Economy.* New York, Institute of Pacific Relations, International Secretariat, 1945

————. *Zaibatsu Dissolution.* Berkeley, University of California Press, 1954

Black, John R. *Young Japan: Yokohama and Yedo, 1858–79.* Reprint with introduction by Grace Fox. 2 vols. Tokyo, Oxford University Press, 1968

Borton, Hugh. *Japan's Modern Century*. New York, Ronald Press, 1955

Brooks, Lester. *Behind Japan's Surrender*. New York, McGraw-Hill, 1968

Browne, Courtney. *Tojo: The Last Banzai*. New York, Paperback Library, 1967

Butow, Robert J. C. *Japan's Decision to Surrender*. Stanford, California, Stanford University Press, 1967

————. *Tojo and the Coming of the War*. Princeton, Princeton University Press, 1969

Byas, Hugh. *Government by Assassination*. New York, Alfred A. Knopf, 1942

Clubb, O. Edmund. *Twentieth Century China*. New York, Columbia University Press, 1964

Craig, Albert M. *Choshu in the Meiji Restoration*. Cambridge, Harvard University Press, 1961

————— and Shively, Donald H., eds. *Personality in Japanese History*. Berkeley and Los Angeles, University of California Press, 1971

Crowley, James E. *Japan's Quest for Autonomy: National Security and Foreign Policy 1930–1938*. Princeton, Princeton University Press, 1966

Dennett, Tyler. *Americans in East Asia*. 1922. Reprint. New York, Barnes & Noble, 1963

Dulles, Foster Rhea. *Yankees and Samurai*. New York, Harper & Row, 1965

Earl, David Magarey. *Emperor and Nation in Japan: Political Thinkers of the Tokugawa Era*. Seattle, University of Washington Press, 1964

Fox, Grace. *Britain and Japan, 1858–1883*. London, Oxford University Press, 1969

Fujihara, Ginjiro. *The Spirit of Japanese Industry*. Tokyo, Hokuseido Press, 1936, 1940

Grew, Joseph C. *Report from Tokyo*. New York, Simon & Schuster, Inc., 1942

Hackett, Roger E. "Political Modernization and the Meiji Genro." In *Political Development in Modern Japan,* ed. by Robert E. Ward. Princeton, Princeton University Press, 1969

Hadley, Eleanor M. *Antitrust in Japan*. Princeton, Princeton University Press, 1970

————. "Concentrated Business Power in Japan." Ph. D. dissertation, Radcliffe College, Cambridge, Massachusetts, 1949

Harootunian, H. D. *Toward Restoration, the Growth of Political Consciousness in Tokugawa Japan*. Berkeley and Los Angeles, University of California Press, 1970

Hirschmeier, Johannes. *The Origins of Entrepreneurship in Modern Japan*. Cambridge, Harvard University Press, 1964

Hozumi, Nobushige. *Ancestor-Worship and Japanese Law*. Tokyo, Maruzen Kabushiki Kaisha, 1912

Idditie, Junesay [Ichiji, Junsai]. *The Life of Marquis Shigenobu Okuma*. Tokyo, Hokuseido Press, 1956

Ihara, Saikaku. *Japan's Eternal Treasure House* [Nihon Eitai-gura]. Translated by Soji Mizuno. Tokyo, Hokuseido Press, 1955

Ike, Nobutaka. *Japanese Politics*. New York, Alfred A. Knopf, 1957

Ishimoto, Shizue. *Facing Two Ways*. New York, Farrar & Reinhart, 1935

Iwata, Masakazu. *Okubo Toshimichi, The Bismarck of Japan*. Berkeley and Los Angeles, University of California Press, 1964

Jansen, Marius B. *The Japanese and Sun Yat-sen.* Cambridge, Harvard University Press, 1954
———. *Sakamoto Ryoma and the Meiji Restoration.* Stanford, California, Stanford University Press, 1971
———, ed. *Changing Japanese Attitudes Toward Modernization.* Princeton, Princeton University Press, 1965
Japan and the Opium Menace. New York, Institute of Pacific Relations, 1942
Kodama, Yoshio. *I Was Defeated.* Translation and publication arranged by Taro Fukuda. Tokyo, Radiopress, 1959
———. *Sugamo Diary.* Translation and publication arranged by Taro Fukuda. Tokyo, Radiopress, 1960
Lockwood, William. *The Economic Development of Japan—Growth and Structural Change.* Princeton, Princeton University Press, 1954
———, ed. *The State and Economic Enterprise in Japan.* Princeton, Princeton University Press, 1965
Lory, Hillis. *Japan's Military Masters.* New York, Viking, 1943
Lowe, Chuan-hua. *Japan's Economic Offensive in China.* London, George Allen & Unwin, 1939
Lundberg, Ferdinand. *America's Sixty Families.* New York, Halcyon House, 1939
———. *The Rich and the Super-rich: A Study in the Power of Money Today.* New York, Lyle Stewart, 1968
Manchester, William. *The Arms of Krupp, 1587–1968.* Boston, Little, Brown & Co., 1968
Marshall, Byron K. *Capitalism and Nationalism in Prewar Japan: The Ideology of the Business Elite, 1868–1941.* Stanford, California, Stanford University Press, 1967
Maruyama, Masao. *Thought and Behaviour in Modern Japanese Politics.* Ivan Morris, ed. London, Oxford University Press, 1963
Matsumoto, Shigeru. *Motoori Norinaga, 1730–1801.* Cambridge, Harvard University Press, 1970
Mayer-Oakes, Thomas F., trans. and ed. *Fragile Victory: The Saionji-Harada Memoirs.* Detroit, Wayne State University Press, 1967
The Mitsui Bank—A Brief History. Tokyo, The Mitsui Bank, Ltd., 1926
Mitsui Gomei Kaisha. *The House of Mitsui.* Tokyo, privately published, 1933
Mitsui, Mitsubishi, Sumitomo. Tokyo, Mitsubishi Economic Research Institute, 1955
Morley, James W., ed. *Dilemmas of Growth in Prewar Japan.* Princeton, Princeton University Press, 1971
Morris, Ivan. *Nationalism and the Right Wing in Japan—A Study of Post-war Trends.* London, Oxford University Press, 1960
Morton, Frederic. *The Rothschilds.* New York, Atheneum, 1962
Mosley, Leonard. *Hirohito, Emperor of Japan.* Englewood Cliffs, New Jersey, Prentice-Hall, Inc., 1966
Murdoch, James. *A History of Japan.* London, Routledge and Keegan Paul, 1949
Myers, Gustavus. *History of the Great American Fortunes.* 1907. Reprint. New York, Modern Library, 1936–37
Norman, E. Herbert. *Japan's Emergence as a Modern State: Political and Economic*

Problems of the Meiji Period. New York, Institute of Pacific Relations, General Secretariat, 1940

Obata, Kyugoro. *An Interpretation of the Life of Viscount Shibusawa*. Tokyo, Diamondo Kigyo Kabushiki Kaisha, 1937

Ogata, Sakado N. *Defiance in Manchuria*. Berkeley and Los Angeles, University of California Press, 1964

Okamoto, Shumpei. *The Japanese Oligarchy and the Russo-Japanese War*. New York and London, Columbia University Press, 1970

Okuma, Shigenobu. *Fifty Years of New Japan* [Kaikoku Gojunen Shi]. Translated and edited by Marcus B. Huish. New York, Kraus Reprint, 1970

Perlo, Victor. *The Empire of High Finance*. New York, International Publishers, 1957

Pittau, Joseph. *Political Thought in Early Meiji Japan, 1868–1889*. Cambridge, Harvard University Press, 1967

Potter, John Deane. *Yamamoto: The Man Who Menaced America*. New York, Paperback Library, 1967

Russell, Oland D. *The House of Mitsui*. Boston, Little, Brown & Co., 1939

Sansom, George B. *The Western World and Japan*. New York, Alfred A. Knopf, 1970

Satow, Ernest. *A Diplomat in Japan*. London, Seeley, Service & Co., Ltd., 1921

Sebald, William J. and Brines, Russell. *With MacArthur in Japan*. New York, Norton, 1965

Seldes, George. *Facts and Fascism*. New York, In Fact, 1943

———. *One Thousand Americans*. New York, Boni & Gaer, 1947

Seth, Roland. *Secret Servants*. New York, Farrar, Straus & Cudahy, 1957

Sheldon, Charles David. *The Rise of the Merchant Class in Tokugawa Japan, 1600–1868: An Introductory Survey*. New York, J. J. Augustin, 1958

Storry, Richard. *The Double Patriots*. London, Chatto & Windus, 1957

———. *A History of Modern Japan*. London, Penguin reprint, 1967

Takahashi, Kamekichi. *The Rise and Development of Japan's Modern Economy*. Tokyo, Jiji Press, Ltd., 1969

Takahashi, Masao. *Modern Japanese Economy Since 1868*. Tokyo, Kokusai Bunka Shinkokai, 1967

Thayer, Nathaniel B. *How the Conservatives Rule Japan*. Princeton, Princeton University Press, 1969

Tobata, Seiichi. *The Modernization of Japan*. Vol. 1. Tokyo, Institute of Asian Economic Affairs, 1966

Tolischus, Otto. *Through Japanese Eyes*. New York, Reynal & Hitchcock, 1945

Toyoda, Takeshi. *A History of Pre-Meiji Commerce in Japan*. Tokyo, Kokusai Bunka Shinkokai, 1969

U. S., Department of State. *Papers Relating to the Foreign Relations of the United States: Japan, 1931–41*. 2 vols. Washington, D.C., U. S. Government Printing Office, 1943

Ward, Robert E., ed. *Political Development in Japan*. Princeton, Princeton University Press, 1968

Wilson, George M. *Radical Nationalist in Japan: Kita Ikki, 1883–1937*. Cambridge, Harvard University Press, 1969

Yanaga, Chitoshi. *Japan Since Perry*. New York, McGraw-Hill, 1949

————. *Big Business in Japanese Politics*. New Haven, Yale University Press, 1968

Yoshihashi, Takehiko. *Conspiracy at Mukden: The Rise of the Japanese Military*. New Haven, Yale University Press, 1963

Young, A. Morgan. *Japan Under the Taisho Tenno*. New York, William Morrow and Co., Inc., 1929

PERIODICALS AND PAMPHLETS

Eto, Shinkichi. "The Proposed Interception of the South Manchurian Railway." *Acta Asiatica*, No. 14 (1968)

Fortune. September 1936. (The entire issue is devoted to Japan.)

"Japan's Mammoth Trading Houses." *Asahi Evening News,* 21 articles, June 30, 1964–May 31, 1965

Marcosson, Isaac. "The Changing East: Japan's Financial Families." *Saturday Evening Post,* September 16, 1922

Marvin, George. "The Mitsui: Princes of World Trade." *Asia,* October–December 1924 (reprint)

Mitsui Group [pamphlet]. Tokyo, *Mainichi Daily News,* 1971

Mitsui Group [pamphlet]. Tokyo, Mitsui Group, c. 1970

Norman, E. Herbert. "The Genyosha: A Study in the Origins of Japanese Imperialism." *Pacific Affairs* XVII, No. 3 (1944): 266

The Russo-Japanese War Fully Illustrated. Nos. 1–9, April 1904–July 1905. Tokyo, Kinkodo

"The Story of Mitsui Bank, Limited." *Monthly Review,* articles, July 1958–June 1960. Mitsui Bank, Limited

This is Mitsui [pamphlet]. Tokyo, Trade Times, Limited, 1971

Who's Who in Japan. No. 1 (Autumn 1958), No. 2 (Winter 1958–59), No. 3 (Summer 1959). Tokyo, Rengo Press

Oriental Economist, 1949 through 1972

JAPANESE-LANGUAGE PUBLICATIONS

FOR GENERAL INFORMATION relating to Japanese history, economy, and social manifestations, both standard and specialized works were consulted, but only those used frequently are listed here. Periodicals scanned regularly for pertinent material include major daily newspapers, such as *Yomiuri* and *Nihon Keizai Shimbun;* such weeklies as *Asahi Journal, Shukan Asahi, Shukan Shincho, Shukan Gendai,* and *Shukan Bunshun*; and such monthlies as *Chuo Koron, Bungei Shunju, Seikai, Ushio,* and *Keizai Orai.*

BOOKS

Ando, Yoshio. *Nihon Shihon Chizu* [Map of Japanese Capitalism]. Tokyo, Shincho-sha, 1963

Arisawa, Hiromi, ed. *Nihon Sangyo Hyakunen-shi* [A One-Hundred-Year History of Japanese Industry]. Tokyo, Nihon Keizai Shimbun-sha, 1969

Arita, Kyosuke. *Sogo Shosha* [General Trading Companies]. Tokyo, Nihon Keizai Shimbun-sha, 1970

Danshaku Dan Takuma Denki Kokankai [Society for the Publication of the Biography of Baron Dan Takuma]. *Danshaku Dan o Kataru* [Talks About Baron Dan Takuma]. Tokyo, Asahi Shobo, 1932

Danshaku Dan Takuma Den [A Biography of Baron Dan Takuma]. Tokyo, Ko Dan Danshaku Denki Hensan Iinkai, 1938

Edo, Hideo. *Sushiya no Shomon* [The Sushi Shop Pledge]. Tokyo, Asahi Shimbun-sha, 1966

Fujishima, Taisuke. *Nihon no Joryu Shakai* [The Japanese Elite] Tokyo, Kobunsha, 1965

Hoshino, Yasunosuke. *Mitsui Hyakunen* [One Hundred Years of Mitsui]. Tokyo, Kajima Shuppan-kai, 1968

Ikeda, Seihin. *Watakushi no Ningenkan* [My View of Life]. Tokyo, Bungei Shunjusha, 1951

———. *Zaikai Kaiko* [Recollections of the Financial World]. Tokyo, Sekai no Nihonsha, 1949

Kubo, Akira. *Mitsui*. Tokyo, Chuo Koronsha, 1966

Kunimitsu, Shiro. *Mitsui Okoku* [The Mitsui Kingdom]. Tokyo, Shin Jinbutsu Orai-sha, 1972

Masuda, Takashi. *Jijo Masuda Takashi Den* [The Autobiography of Masuda Takashi]. Tokyo, Uchida Rokaku Ho, 1939

Masuo, Nobuyuki. *Mitsui Tokuhon* [Mitsui Reader]. Tokyo, Ajia Shobo, 1943

Matsushita, Denkichi. *Zaibatsu Mitsui no Shin Kenkyu* [A New Study of the Mitsui Zaibatsu]. Tokyo, Chugai Sangyo Chosa-kai, 1936

Minomura, Seiichiro. *Minomura Rizaemon Den* [A Biography of Minomura Rizaemon]. Tokyo, San'yu Shimbun-sha, 1969

Mitarai, Tatsuo. *Nihon Zaikai Nyumon* [A Guide to Japanese Financial Circles]. Tokyo, Gafuku-sha, 1956

Mitsui Ginko Hachiju-nen Shi [Eighty-Year History of the Mitsui Bank]. Tokyo, Kabushiki Kaisha Mitsui Ginko, 1957

Mitsui Jigyo-shi [Mitsui Enterprise History]. Tokyo, Mitsui Library, 1972

Miyamoto, Mataji. *Gosho—Nihon no Chonin* [Great Merchants of Japan]. Tokyo, Nihon Keizai Shimbun-sha, 1970

Murofushi, Tetsuro. *Oshoku no Susume* [Scandal Recommended]. Tokyo, Kobundo, 1963

Muto Sanji Zenshu Kankokai [Society for the Publication of the Complete Works of Muto Sanji]. *Muto Sanji Zenshu* [The Complete Works of Muto Sanji]. Vol. 1. Tokyo, Shingisha, 1963

Nakata, Sadanosuke. *Zoku Meiji no Shobai Orai* [The Ins and Outs of Meiji Business, Continued]. Tokyo, Seia Bo, 1970

Nakoura, Taro. *Nihon no Uyoku* [The Right Wing of Japan]. Tokyo, San-ichi Shobo, 1960

Niizeki, Yasutaro. *Watakushi no Rirekisho* [My Personal History]. Tokyo, Nihon Keizai Shimbun-sha, 1972

Nishihara, Yujiro, ed. *Fujiyama Raita Den* [A Biography of Fujiyama Raita]. Tokyo, Fujiyama Aiichiro, 1939

Noguchi, Tasaku. *Mitsui Kontsuerun* [The Mitsui Concern]. Tokyo, Shin Hyoron, 1968

Onishi, Rihei. *Asabuki Eiji Kun Den* [A Biography of Asabuki Eiji]. Tokyo, Asabuki Eiji Denki Hensankai, 1928

Otani, Kenjiro. *Rakujitsu no Josho—Showa Rikugun-shi* [Prelude to Sunset—A

History of the Army in the Showa Era]. Tokyo, Yagumo Shoten, 1959

Oya, Soichi. *Jitsuroku Tenno-ki* [Authentic Record of the Emperors]. Tokyo, Masu Shobo, 1952

Rekishi-gaku Kenkyu-kai [History Research Society]. *Nihon-shi Nempyo* [A Chronology of Japanese History]. Tokyo, Iwanami Shoten, 1966

Shibagaki, Kazuo. *Mitsui-Mitsubishi no Hyakunen* [One Hundred Years of Mitsui and Mitsubishi]. Tokyo, Chuo Koron-sha, 1968

Shimmyo, Takeo. *Showa Seiji Hishi—Chosaku Rin Bakusatsu Jiken o Chushin ni* [Hidden History of the Showa Era—Centered on the Assassination of Chang Tso-lin]. Tokyo, San-ichi Shobo, 1961

Shirayangi, Shuko. *Nakamigawa Hikojiro Den* [A Biography of Nakamigawa Hikojiro]. Tokyo, Iwanami Shoten, 1940

Shiroyama, Saburo. *Nezumi* [The Rat]. Tokyo, Bungei Shunju-sha, 1966

Soma, Masao. *Sengo Seiji-shi* [Postwar Political History]. Tokyo, San-ichi Shobo, 1963

Suchi, Masakazu. *Nihon no Kaken* [Japanese Family Precepts]. Tokyo, Nihon Bungei-sha, 1972

Suzuki, Yukio. *Seiji o Ugokasu Keieisha* [Businessmen Who Run Japanese Politics]. Tokyo, Nihon Keizai Shimbun-sha, 1968

Takahashi, Masae. *Ni-ni-roku Jiken* [The Two-Two-Six Incident]. Tokyo, Chuo Koron-sha, 1971

———. *Showa no Gumbatsu* [Military Cliques of the Showa Era]. Tokyo, Chuo Koron-sha, 1971

Takahashi, Toshitaro. *Mitsui Bussan no Omoide* [Memories of the Mitsui Trading Company]. Tokyo, Kyobunkan, 1937

Takayanagi, Mitsuhisa et al., eds. *Nihon-shi Jiten* [Encyclopedia of Japanese History]. Tokyo, Kadokawa Shoten, 1969

Tanaka, Akira. *Mikan no Meiji Ishin* [The Unfinished Meiji Restoration]. Tokyo, Sanseido, 1968

Tatamiya, Eitaro. *Showa no Seijikatachi: Nihon Shihaiso no Uchimaku* [Politicians of the Showa Era: The Inside Story About the Japanese Ruling Class]. Tokyo, Kobundo, 1963

Toyama, Shigeki et al. *Showa-shi* [A History of the Showa Era]. Tokyo, Iwanami Shoten, 1961

Wada, Hidekichi. *Mitsui Kontsuerun Tokuhon* [Mitsui Concern Reader]. Tokyo, Shunju-sha, 1937

Watanabe, Tsuneo. *Habatsu* [Political Factions]. Tokyo, Kobundo, 1964

Yamada, Taketaro. *Mitsui Monogatari* [The Mitsui Story]. Tokyo, Bunsei-sha, 1934

Yamamoto Jotaro-o Denki Henshukai [Society for Editing Yamamoto Jotaro's Biography]. *Yamamoto Jotaro Denki* [A Biography of Yamamoto Jotaro]. Tokyo, privately printed by Hara Yasusaburo, 1942

Yomiuri Shimbun-sha Staff. *Zaikai* [Financial Circles]. Tokyo, Yomiuri Shimbun-sha, 1972

Zaikai Kakizu [Lineage of Financial Families]. Tokyo, Jinji Koshinjo, 1957

PERIODICALS

Edo, Hideo and Narita, Tomomi. "Mitsui Yameta no wa Wakage no Itari" ["He Quit Mitsui, Carried Away by Youthful Impulse"]. (A dialogue.) *Zaikai,* March 15, 1971

"Gendai-shi o Tsukuru Hitobito—Niizeki Yasutaro" ["Men Who Make Contemporary History—Niizeki Yasutaro"]. (An interview in six installments.) *Ekonomisuto,* January 11 to February 15, 1972

Kusayanagi, Daizo. "Kunisukuri no Gotan Hyakusho Edo Hideo" ["Edo Hideo, A Poor Farmer Trying to Create Land"]. *Bungei Shunju,* September 1970

"Mitsukoshi." *San'yu Shimbun,* 1970

Tsuchiya, Takao. "Nihon Zaibatsu Shi-ron" ["A Historical Essay on the Zaibatsu, Introduction"]. *Chuo Koron,* August 1946

———. "Mitsui Zaibatsu no Hatten" ["Development of the Mitsui Zaibatsu"]. *Chuo Koron,* August through October 1946

Index

539

562 · INDEX

Toyo Rayon Co. (Toray): in 1920s, 246; in 1930s, 261, 287, 318; after World War II, 366; in 1950s, 413, 422–24, 437; in 1960s, 481, 484
Toyo Spinning Co., 430
Toyo Takushoku (Oriental Colonization Co.), 166, 169, 241, 246, 313
Toyobo, 124
Toyoda Automatic Loom Works, 246, 354, 421
Toyoda concern, 229
Toyoda Eiji, 421
Toyoda Sakichi, 201–2
Toyoda Shoichiro, 421
Toyoda Teijiro, 352
Toyota Motor Co., 409, 421, 470, 479, 484, 491
Toyota Motor Sales Co., 421
Toyotomi Hideyoshi, 9, 26, 31
tozama, 52–53
trademark ban, SCAP, 426, 435
trading companies, *see sogo shosha*
Trans-Siberian Railroad, 154, 158
treaties with foreign powers, discriminatory, 46, 96, 129–130, 144–46, 147
Treaty of Amity and Commerce (1858), 45, 48, 50
Treaty of Kanagawa (1854), 45
Treaty of Portsmouth (1905), 161–65
treaty with Great Britain (1894), 147
Triple Intervention, 148, 156, 162
Tropical Produce Co., 290
Truman, Harry S., 361, 365, 368, 369, 405
Ts'ao Ju-lin, 197, 199
Tsuda Shingo, 313
Tsujimura Nanzo, 257–58
Twenty-one Demands, 194–99, 248
Twenty-six News (Ni-roku-Shimpo), 150–53, 163

Uchida Ryohei: and Black Dragon Society, 163–64, 166; influence, 176, 194, 256, 266, 451
Uchida Shin'ya, 203, 211, 353, 355, 409
Uchida Yasuya: prime minister, 209, 217, 225, 237, 239, 279–80; marriage alliances, 225

Uemura Kogoro, 419, 442, 471
Ugaki Kazushige (Issei), 315
ultranationalist societies, 210, 212–14, 250–57, 264, 266–80; during occupation, 361, 404; revival of, 420–21, 450–52, 460–68; *see also* secret societies; right-wing organizations; military extremists; terrorists
Umanosuke Nobunari, 7
Unilever, 486
Union Carbide, 482
U. S. Aid Counterpart Fund, 443
U. S. Embassy (Tokyo), 458
U. S. Export-Import Bank, 461
U. S. Travel Service, 456
United Steel Co., 186
United Transportation Co. (Kyodo Un'yu Kaisha), 121–22
Usami Katsuo, 227

Versailles Peace Conference, 199, 247
Vickers, 186–88
Vickers-Armstrong, 261
Vietnam War, 475–80, 491

Wada Hidekichi, 291
Wada Toyoji, 142
Wada Yagoro, 188–89
wages, 204, 206, 288, 290; at Miike mines, 448, 497
Wakaba-kai, 233, 234, 411
Wakasugi Sueyuki, 396, 480, 488
Wakatsuki Reijiro, 268, 270
War Termination Central Liaison Office (CLO), 375, 376
Wartime Construction Corp., 360
Washington Conference (1921), 213, 247–48
"welfare state," 472
West Germany, 453, 454
Western Electric, 241
Westernization, 129–30, 144–46, 161
Westinghouse Electric, 217, 241, 416
Whitney, Courtney, 375, 376, 425
Willoughby, Charles A., 375–76, 453
Witte, Sergei, 161, 162
World Bank, 461, 487
World Federation of Trade Unions, 457

zaibatsu *(continued)*
389, 390–95, 404; revival, 404–7,
413–15, 428, 431–35; as "enterprise
groups," 439–68, 478–79, 490–92;
profits and incomes: from World
War I, 203; in 1930s, 273, 305–6;
from World War II, 370–71

zaikai, 443, 462; and Ikeda Hayato,
469–71; and Miike strike, 471; and
Sato Eisaku, 476; today, 492–98
Zengakuren (National Federation of
Student Associations), 459, 465
Zenro (Japan Trade Union Congress), 457–58

The "weathermark" identifies this book as having been designed and produced at the Tokyo offices of John Weatherhill, Inc. Book design and typography by Rebecca Davis. Layout of photographs by Dana Levy. Text composed and printed by Kenkyusha Printing Company, Tokyo. Photographs engraved and printed in offset by Kinmei Printing Company, Tokyo. Bound at the Makoto Binderies, Tokyo. The main text is set in 11-point Garamond, with hand-set Lydian for display.